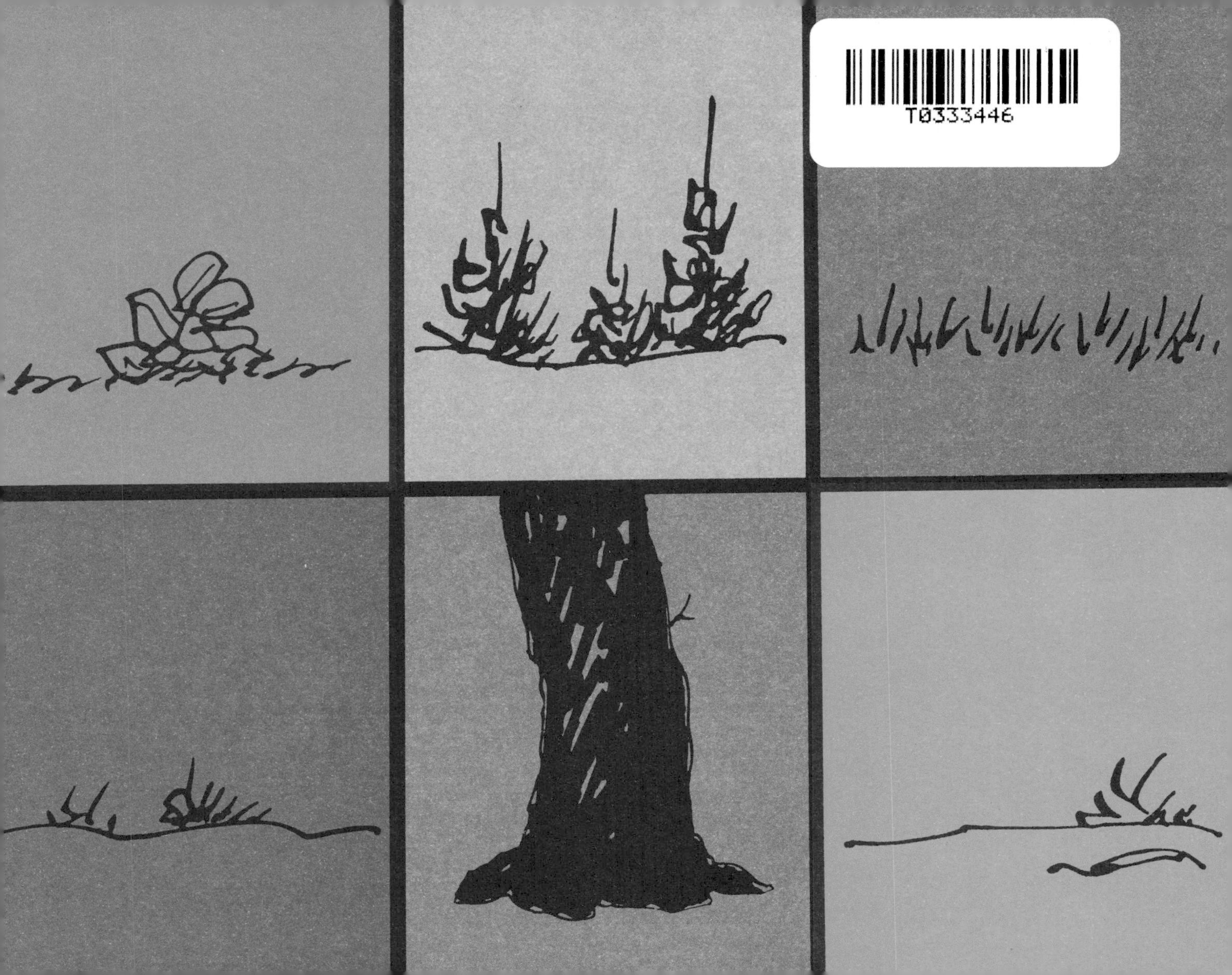

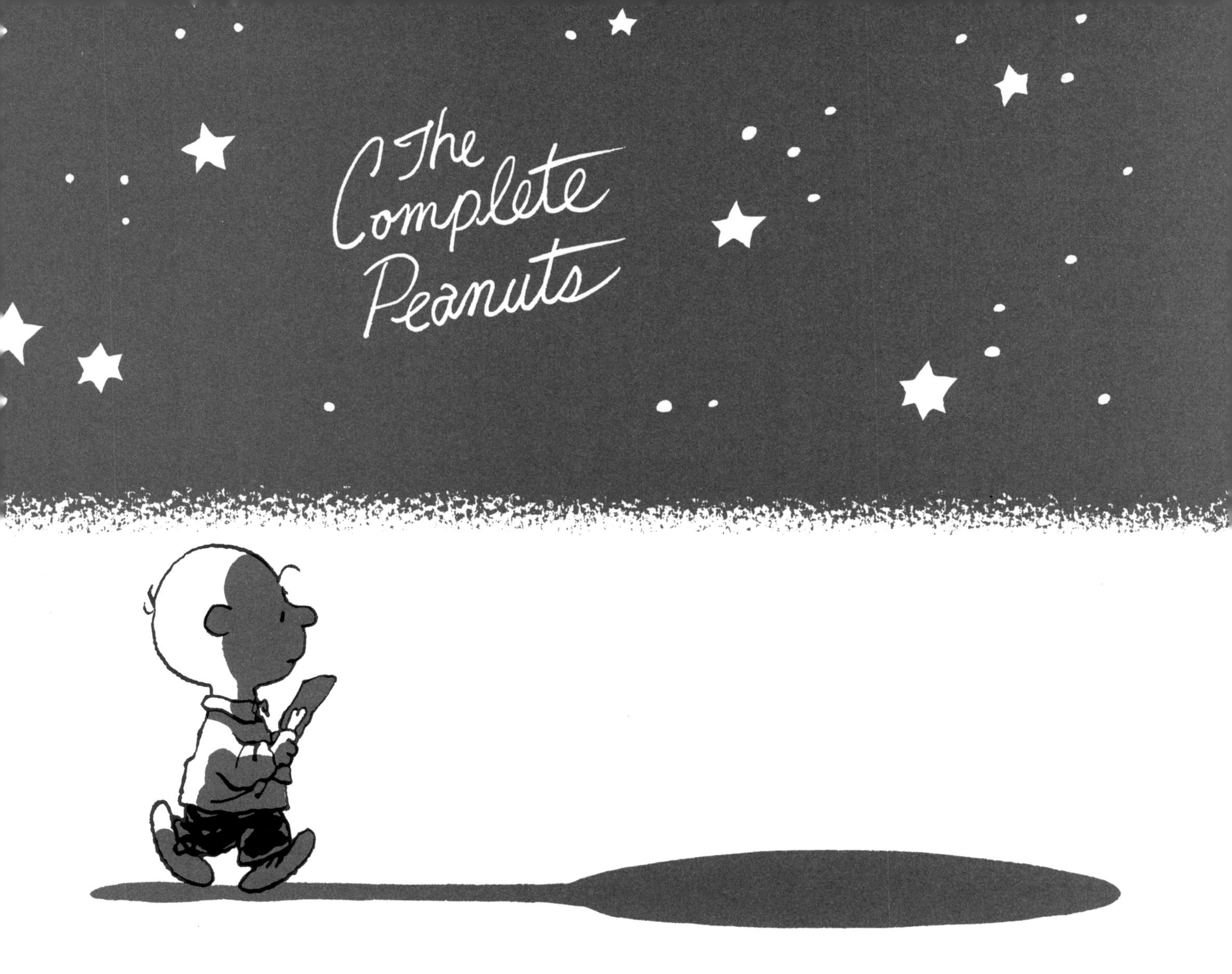
The Complete Peanuts

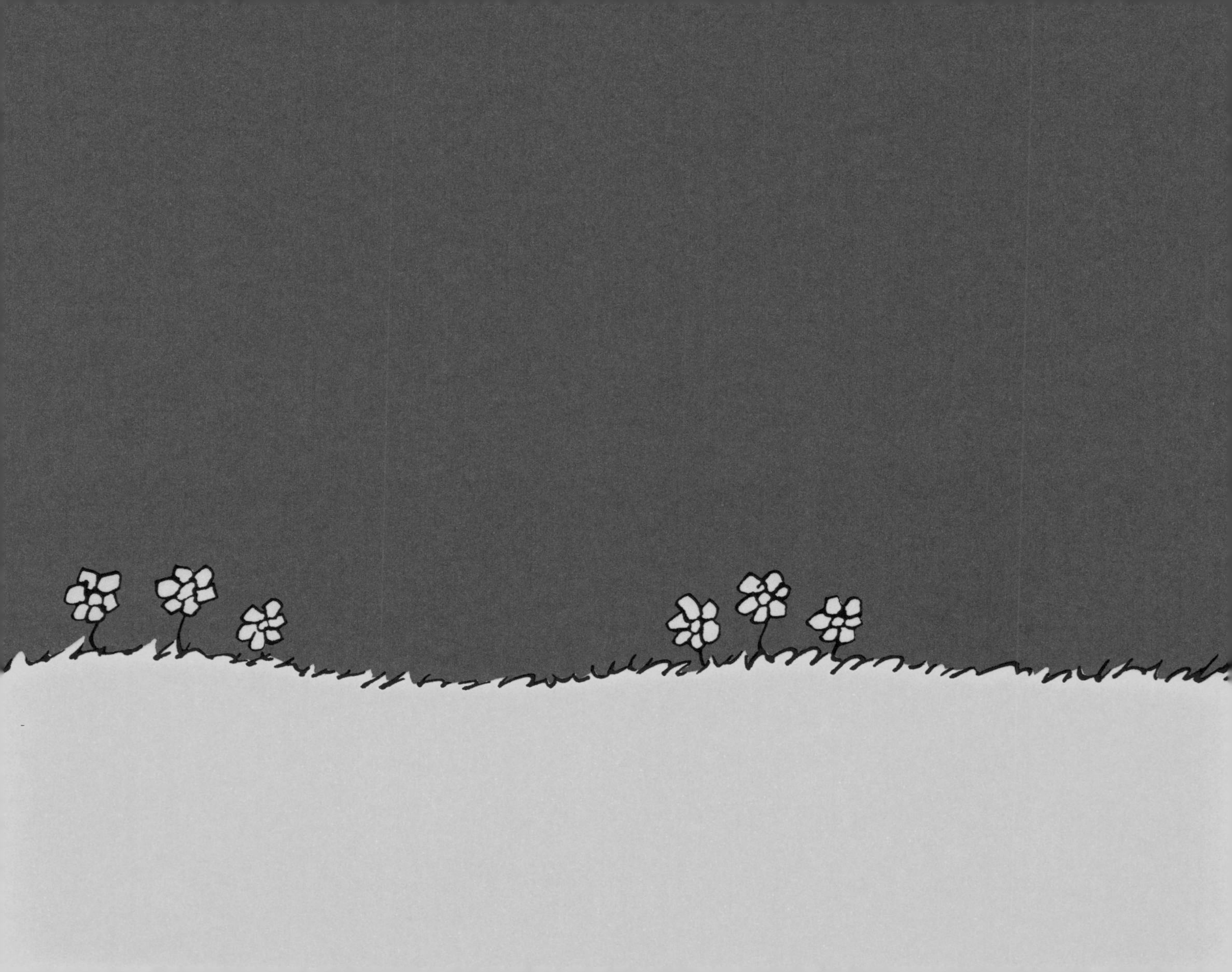

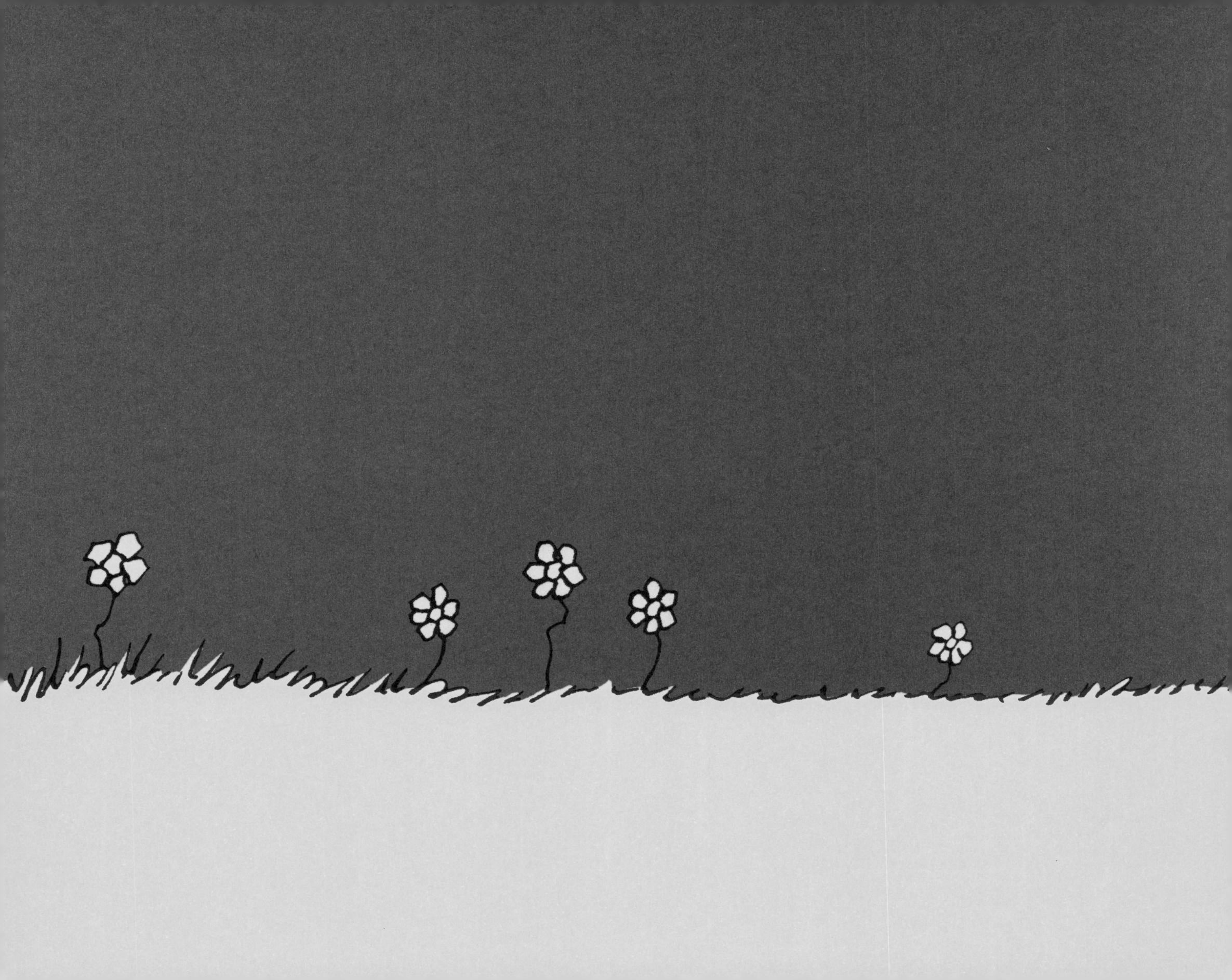

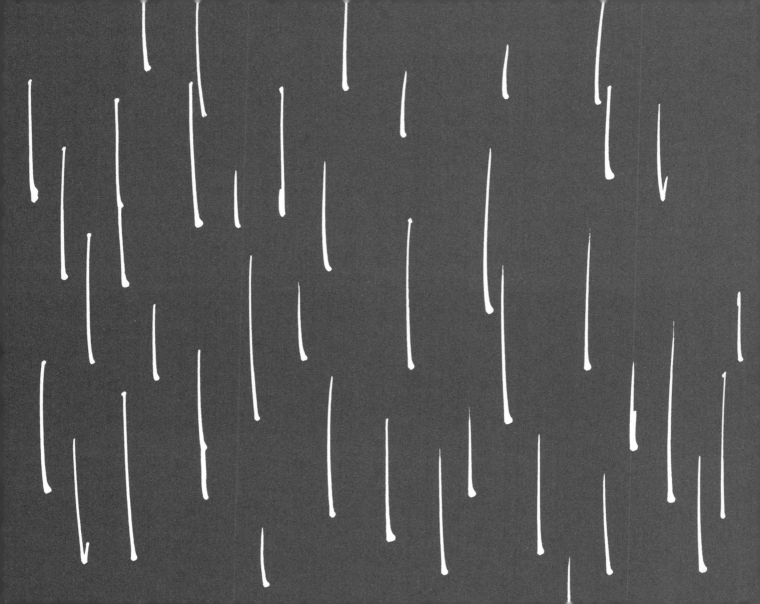

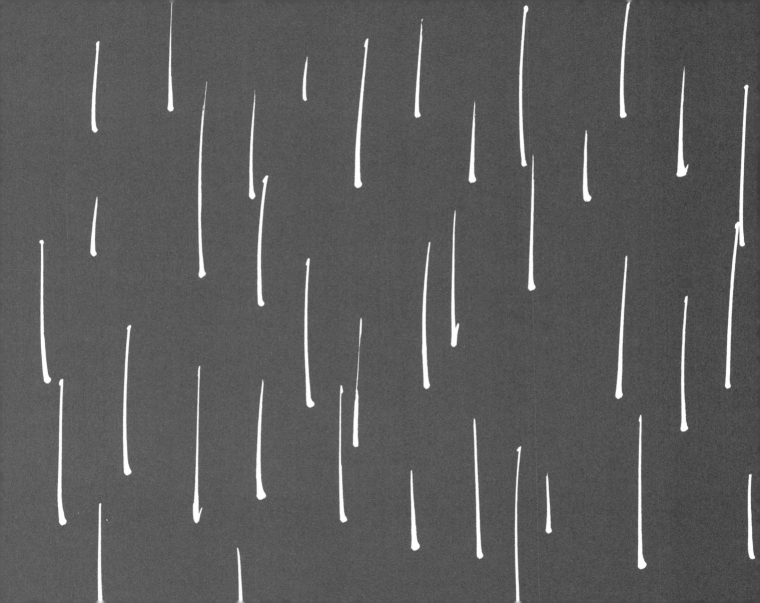

THE COMPLETE PEANUTS
by Charles M. Schulz

Editor: Gary Groth
Designer: Seth
Production, assembly, and restoration: Paul Baresh
Archival assistance: Marcie Lee
Index compiled by Daniel Germain, Ala Lee, and Kim Rost Bridges
Associate Publisher: Eric Reynolds
Publisher: Gary Groth

Special thanks to Jean Schulz, without whom this project would not have come to fruition.

First published in America in 2015 by Fantagraphics Books,
7563 Lake City Way, Seattle, WA, 98115, USA

First published in Great Britain in 2015 by Canongate Books Ltd,
14 High Street, Edinburgh, EH1 1TE

3

British Library Cataloguing-in-Publication Data
A catalogue record for this book is available on request from the British Library.

ISBN 978 1 78211 521 2

canongate.co.uk

Printed and bound in Malaysia for Imago

CHARLES M. SCHULZ

THE COMPLETE PEANUTS

1997 TO 1998

" A PERSON HAS TO
BE VERY CAREFUL
WITH VALENTINES.. "

CANONGATE BOOKS

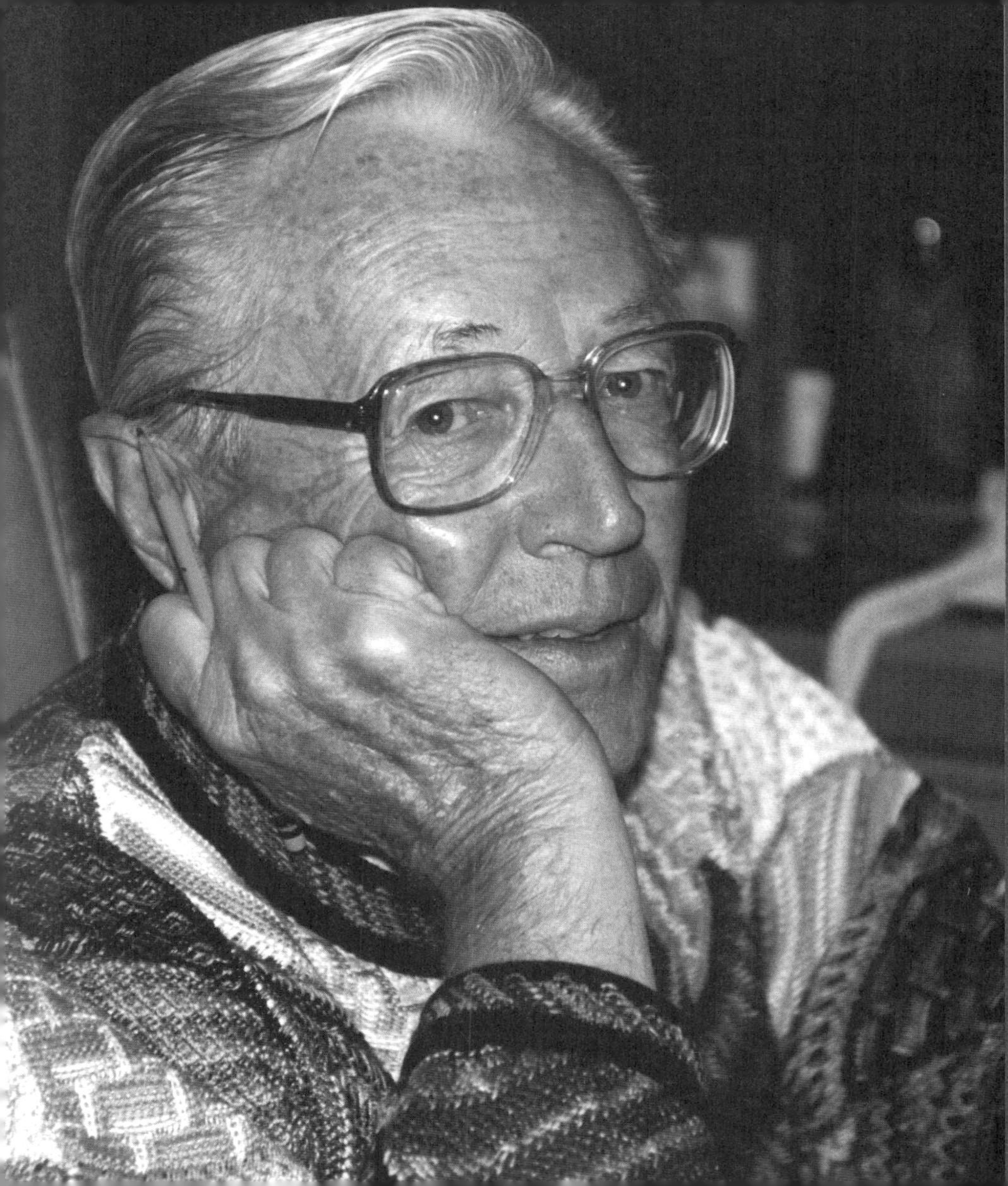

Charles M. Schulz in his home studio at the drawing board, Santa Rosa, California, mid-1990s: courtesy of the Charles M. Schulz Museum.

FOREWORD by PAUL FEIG

Charles Schulz made me the person I am today. I never met the man personally, but his influence is all over my childhood and all over my life. I grew up in a neighborhood very much like the one he drew. We lived in the suburbs — about twenty minutes outside of Detroit — and our houses and yards and streets looked like the ones that came out of his pen. We walked and talked and played and tormented each other the same way that the *Peanuts* gang did. We played sports poorly and hatched schemes and philosophized about what we thought the world and the people within it were

about and we had fun at each other's expense. And we always remained friends, no matter how tenuously, in the end.

Me? I was Charlie Brown. I was the optimist who faced every day as a clean slate, a chance to succeed, to prove my worth to the world. And every day I was slowly ground down by the realities of life. Things never worked out the way I thought they'd work out. People never reacted as enthusiastically as I hoped they would. The girls I loved never knew I loved them because I was too afraid to actually do something radical like go up and talk to them, hoping instead they would notice what a great guy I was and make the first move. And so I'd end most days a little down, a little depressed, but then go to bed and wake up the next day having hit the reset button. *TODAY* was going to be the day when it all went right, I'd say to myself. But it never was. And so back to bed, reset, and start fresh in the morning. And the cycle continued like this and still continues to this very day.

Unlike Charlie Brown, however, I was an only child. I was fortunate enough to live next to a wonderful family of eight kids who became my *Peanuts*-esque gang. But each night I'd return home from their house to my parents and my empty bedroom. Feeling lonely, I would pick up one of my many *Peanuts* paperback collections of daily newspaper strip and read them in bed. There was a good ten-year period of my childhood where I simply could not go to sleep without reading one of these books. I knew each strip by heart, and yet would get so excited when my favorites would appear as I turned the well-worn pages. I had a special fondness for the stories that continued through several pages of strips. Story arcs like Lucy stealing Linus's blanket and burying it to cure him of his habit, as well as Charlie Brown trying to be a baseball hero and convincing himself to steal home in the big championship game — these were but a few of my favorites. I learned how to talk like an adult through the *Peanuts* gang's dialogue. I'd never heard the word "sarcasm" before I saw Charlie Brown and Linus say it. I had no idea about World War I airplanes until Snoopy introduced me to the Sopwith Camel. I found myself getting a strangely diverse education as I was laughing along with Charlie Brown and friends.

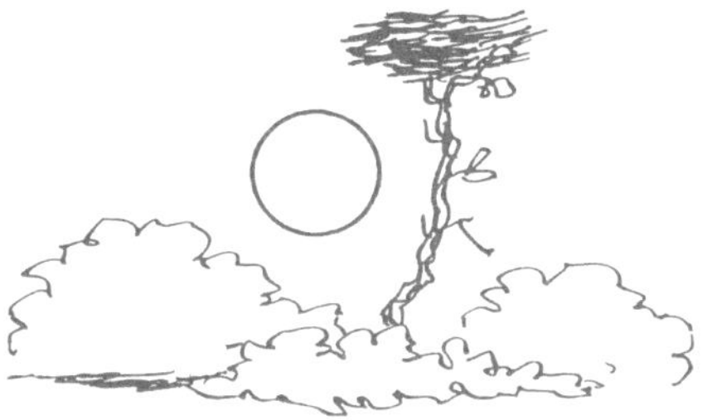

And, man, did I laugh. I still belly laugh every time I read the strips. When I came onboard *The Peanuts Movie* as a producer, the first thing I did was reread all the strips to refresh myself. I found myself once again laughing loudly and often, as if I were back in my bedroom in Michigan again. I remembered that *Peanuts* was funny but I had forgotten just how funny it was. And how masterfully done it was. Snoopy biting into Lucy's blow-up pool and deflating it as an act of revenge still makes me laugh to this day. Snoopy's look of sadness at being shooed away in the first panel; his angry "GROWFF!" as he bites into the inflatable pool as a shocked Lucy cowers away from the danger zone in the second panel; the sad "sssssssss" as the pool slowly deflates in the third panel; and then the final panel of an embarrassed Lucy sitting silently on her now-useless, former pool — this is as well constructed and executed as anything our greatest comedy film directors have done on the screen. Charles Schulz's pen and skill at making the complicated look simple and effortless has stuck with me throughout my comedy-directing career. His humor is never forced or far from pathos and emotionality. He hangs in wordless frames that allow us to take in a character's inner reaction to whatever has just happened to them. This is not a desperate attempt at getting laughs or trying to force jokes on us the readers. This is a confident, self-assured master letting us in on the human condition in its most honest, relatable, and funniest way. I strive to bring this level of artistry and respect for the intelligence of my audience to everything I've ever done and everything I'll ever do.

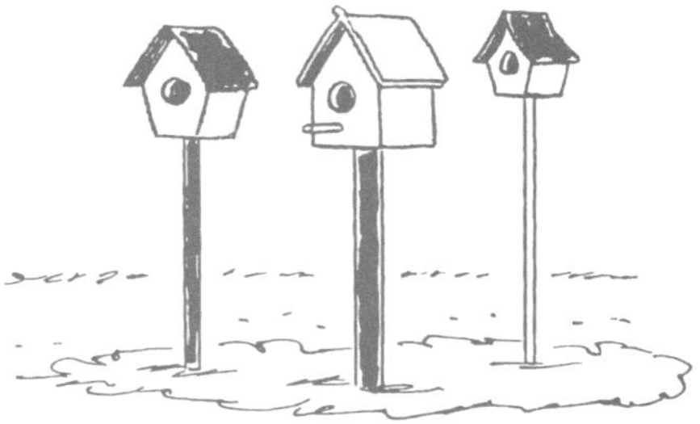

I can never thank Charles Schulz enough for all he has done for me. As a kid growing up in the very pre-Internet Midwest who he made feel not so odd and alone; as an adult who marvels at and is influenced by his wit and humanity; and as a member of the human race who simply appreciates his contributions to the never-ending quest of us all to find meaning and purpose in our time on Earth (contributions that continue to stand the harsh test of time); we all owe Charles Schulz an enormous debt of gratitude.

And many, many hearty, loud, embarrassing, awkward, and delighted laughs.

Thank you, Sparky.

—Paul Feig
May 3, 2015

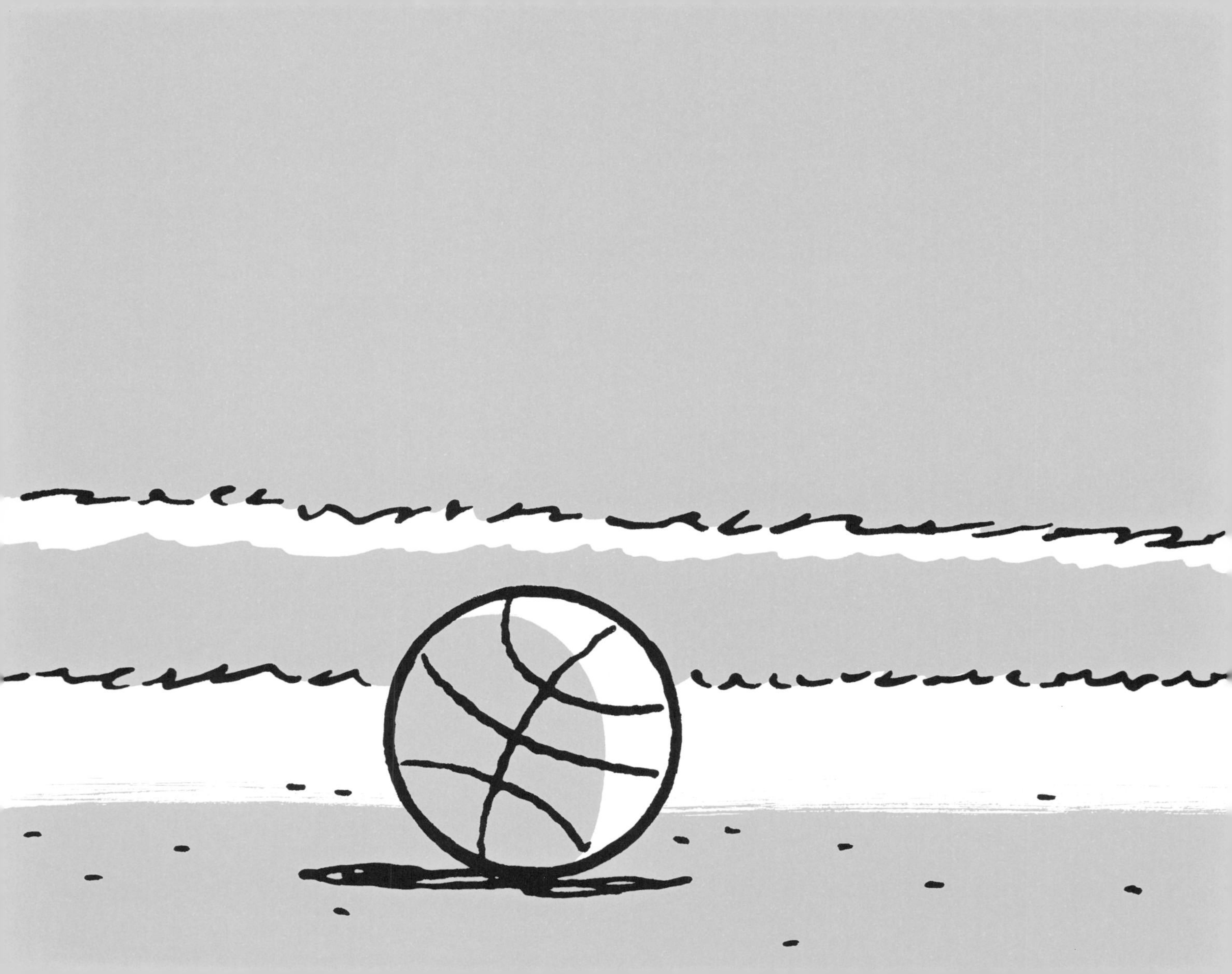

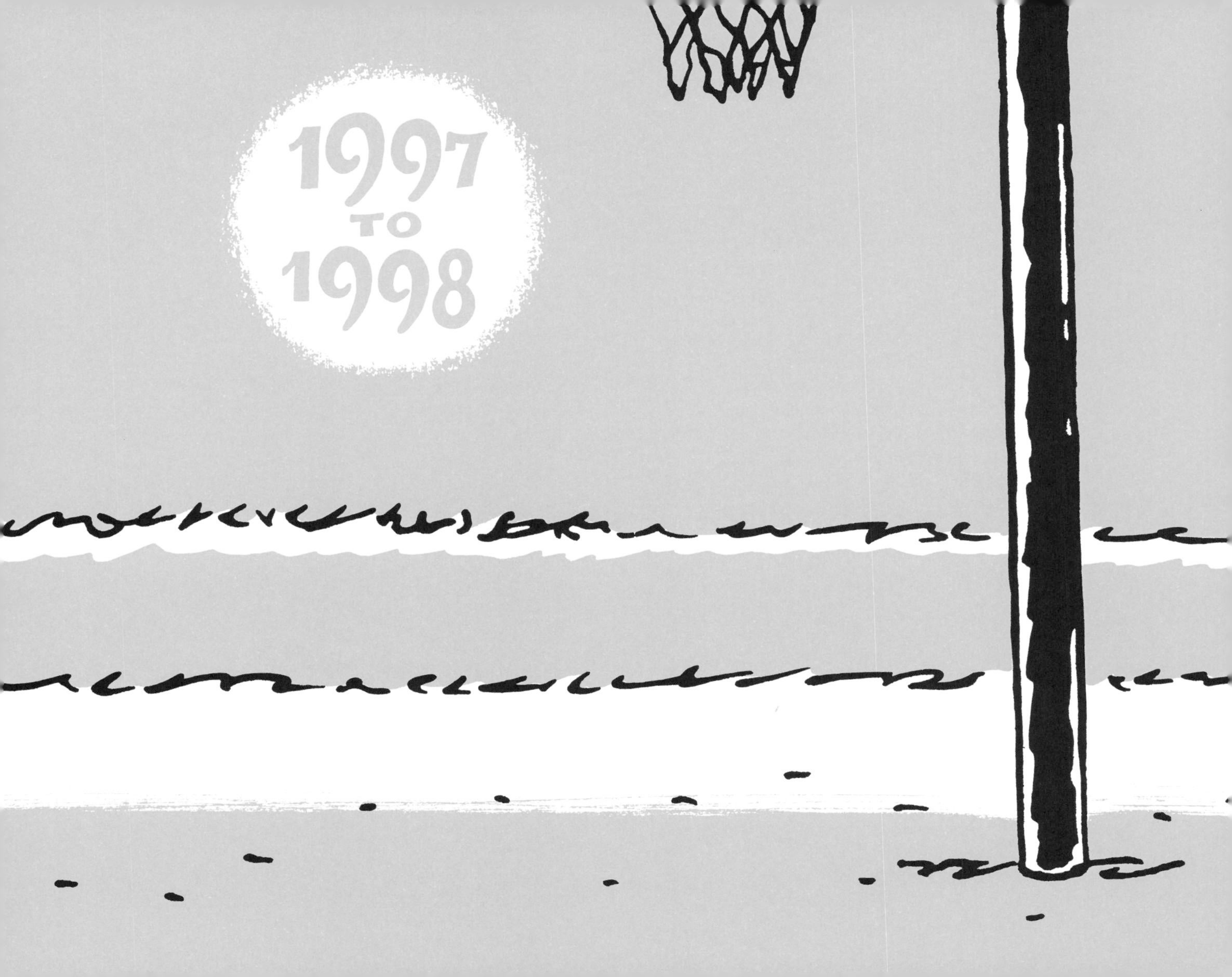
1997
TO
1998

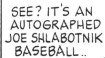
SEE? IT'S AN AUTOGRAPHED JOE SHLABOTNIK BASEBALL..

I DON'T THINK SO, CHARLIE BROWN..THIS ISN'T JOE'S SIGNATURE..

1-1-97

IT'S A FORGERY!

GOOD GRIEF!

THEY CHEATED A LITTLE KID! AN INNOCENT, TRUSTING, HERO WORSHIPPING LITTLE KID..

ME!

1997

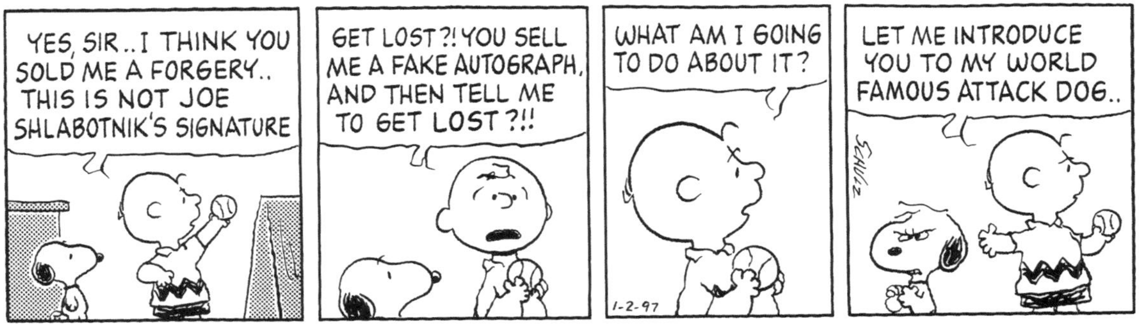
YES, SIR..I THINK YOU SOLD ME A FORGERY.. THIS IS NOT JOE SHLABOTNIK'S SIGNATURE
GET LOST?! YOU SELL ME A FAKE AUTOGRAPH, AND THEN TELL ME TO GET LOST?!!
WHAT AM I GOING TO DO ABOUT IT?
1-2-97
LET ME INTRODUCE YOU TO MY WORLD FAMOUS ATTACK DOG..

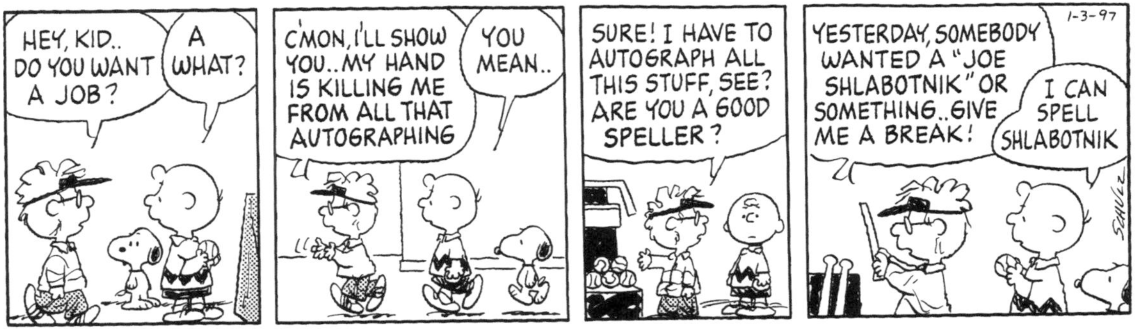
HEY, KID.. DO YOU WANT A JOB?
A WHAT?
C'MON, I'LL SHOW YOU..MY HAND IS KILLING ME FROM ALL THAT AUTOGRAPHING
YOU MEAN..
SURE! I HAVE TO AUTOGRAPH ALL THIS STUFF, SEE? ARE YOU A GOOD SPELLER?
1-3-97
YESTERDAY, SOMEBODY WANTED A "JOE SHLABOTNIK" OR SOMETHING..GIVE ME A BREAK!
I CAN SPELL SHLABOTNIK

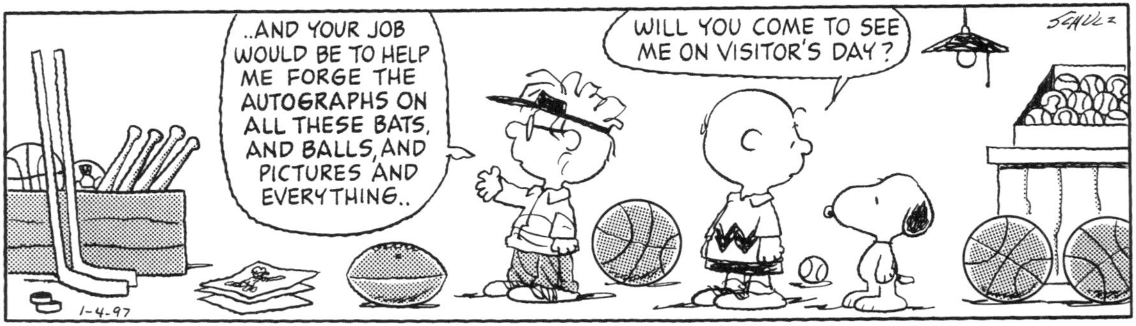
..AND YOUR JOB WOULD BE TO HELP ME FORGE THE AUTOGRAPHS ON ALL THESE BATS, AND BALLS, AND PICTURES AND EVERYTHING..
WILL YOU COME TO SEE ME ON VISITOR'S DAY?
1-4-97

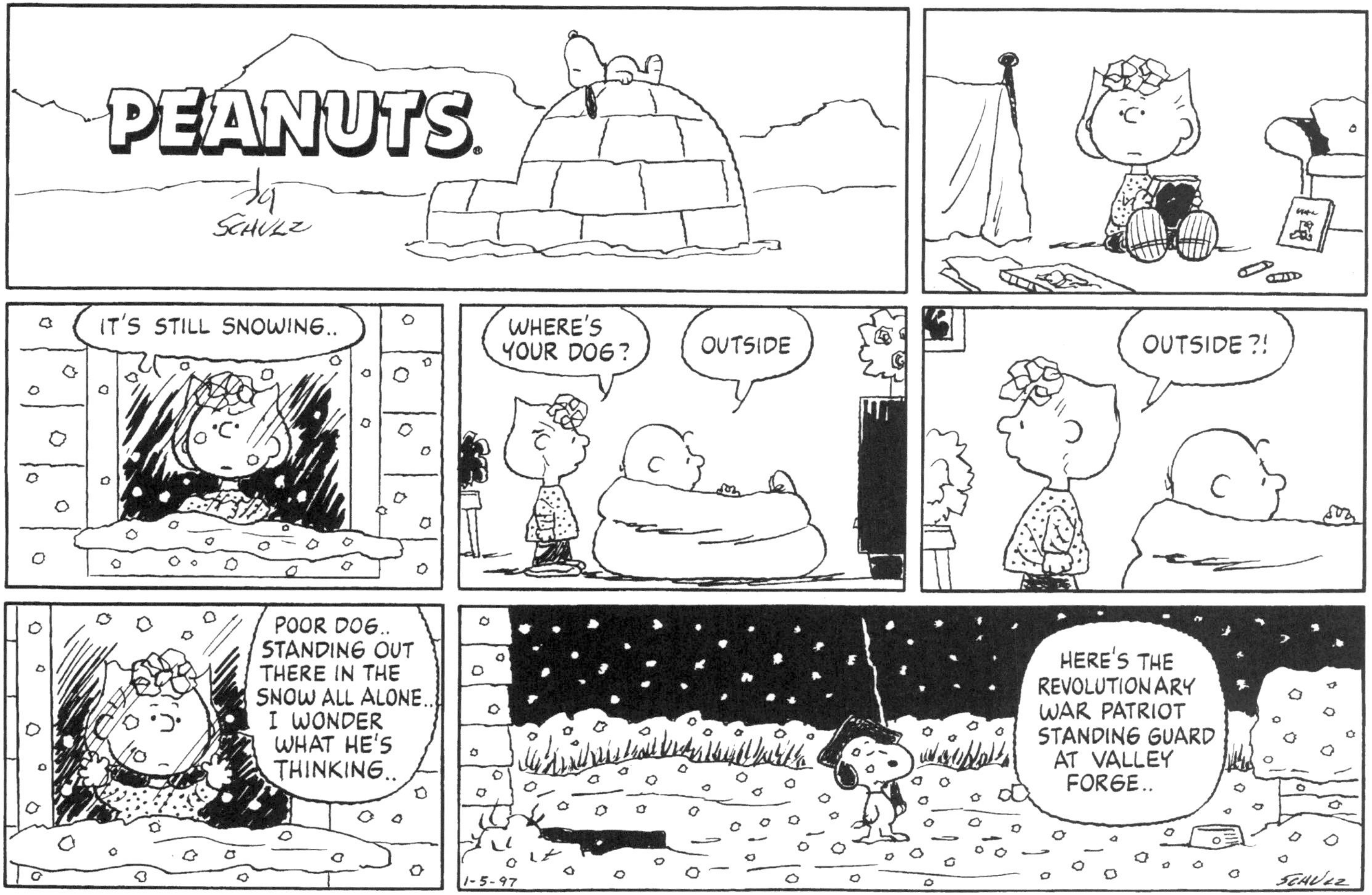
PEANUTS
SCHULZ
IT'S STILL SNOWING..
WHERE'S YOUR DOG?
OUTSIDE
OUTSIDE?!
POOR DOG.. STANDING OUT THERE IN THE SNOW ALL ALONE.. I WONDER WHAT HE'S THINKING..
HERE'S THE REVOLUTIONARY WAR PATRIOT STANDING GUARD AT VALLEY FORGE..
1-5-97
SCHULZ

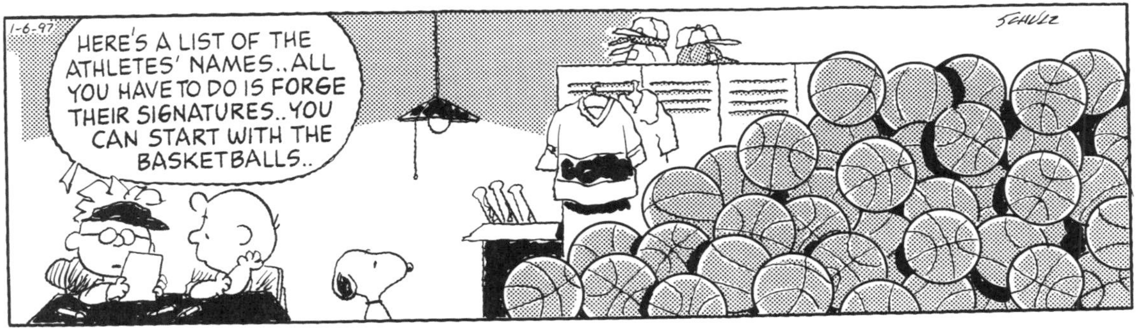
1-6-97
HERE'S A LIST OF THE ATHLETES' NAMES.. ALL YOU HAVE TO DO IS FORGE THEIR SIGNATURES.. YOU CAN START WITH THE BASKETBALLS..
SCHULZ

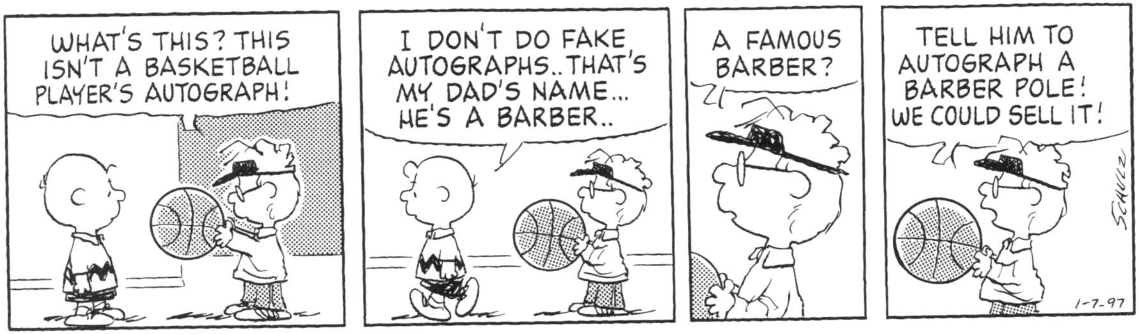
WHAT'S THIS? THIS ISN'T A BASKETBALL PLAYER'S AUTOGRAPH!
I DON'T DO FAKE AUTOGRAPHS.. THAT'S MY DAD'S NAME... HE'S A BARBER..
A FAMOUS BARBER?
TELL HIM TO AUTOGRAPH A BARBER POLE! WE COULD SELL IT!
SCHULZ
1-7-97

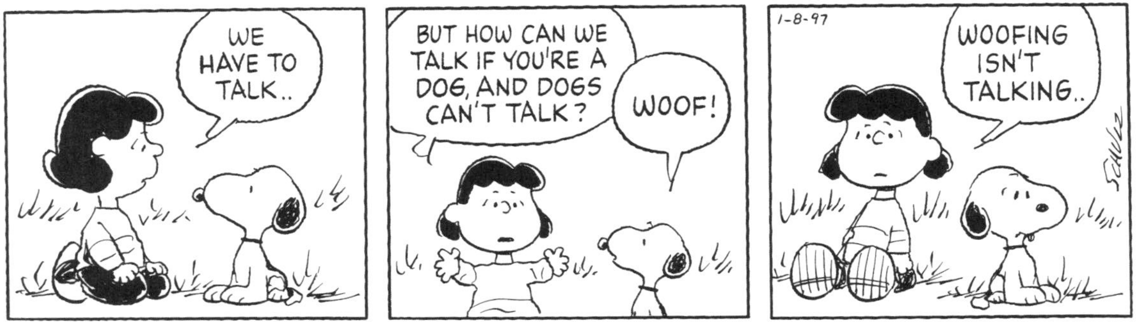
WE HAVE TO TALK..
BUT HOW CAN WE TALK IF YOU'RE A DOG, AND DOGS CAN'T TALK?
WOOF!
1-8-97
WOOFING ISN'T TALKING..
SCHULZ

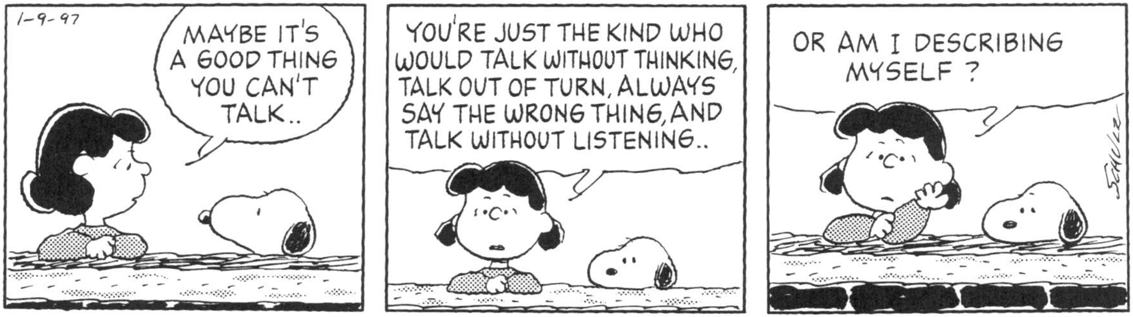
1-9-97
MAYBE IT'S A GOOD THING YOU CAN'T TALK..
YOU'RE JUST THE KIND WHO WOULD TALK WITHOUT THINKING, TALK OUT OF TURN, ALWAYS SAY THE WRONG THING, AND TALK WITHOUT LISTENING..
OR AM I DESCRIBING MYSELF ?
SCHULZ

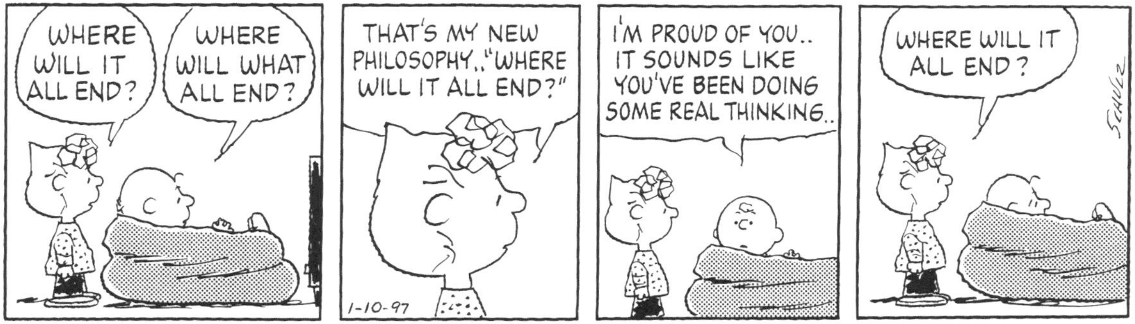
WHERE WILL IT ALL END?
WHERE WILL WHAT ALL END?
THAT'S MY NEW PHILOSOPHY.."WHERE WILL IT ALL END?"
1-10-97
I'M PROUD OF YOU.. IT SOUNDS LIKE YOU'VE BEEN DOING SOME REAL THINKING..
WHERE WILL IT ALL END?
SCHULZ

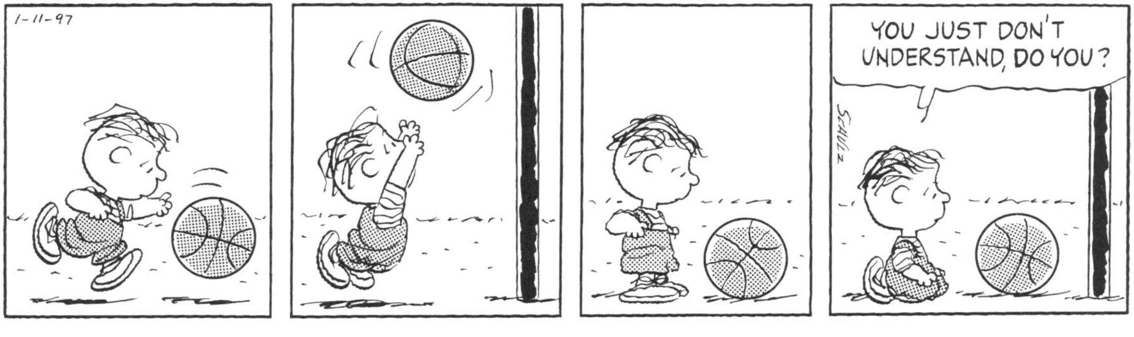
1-11-97
YOU JUST DON'T UNDERSTAND, DO YOU?
SCHULZ

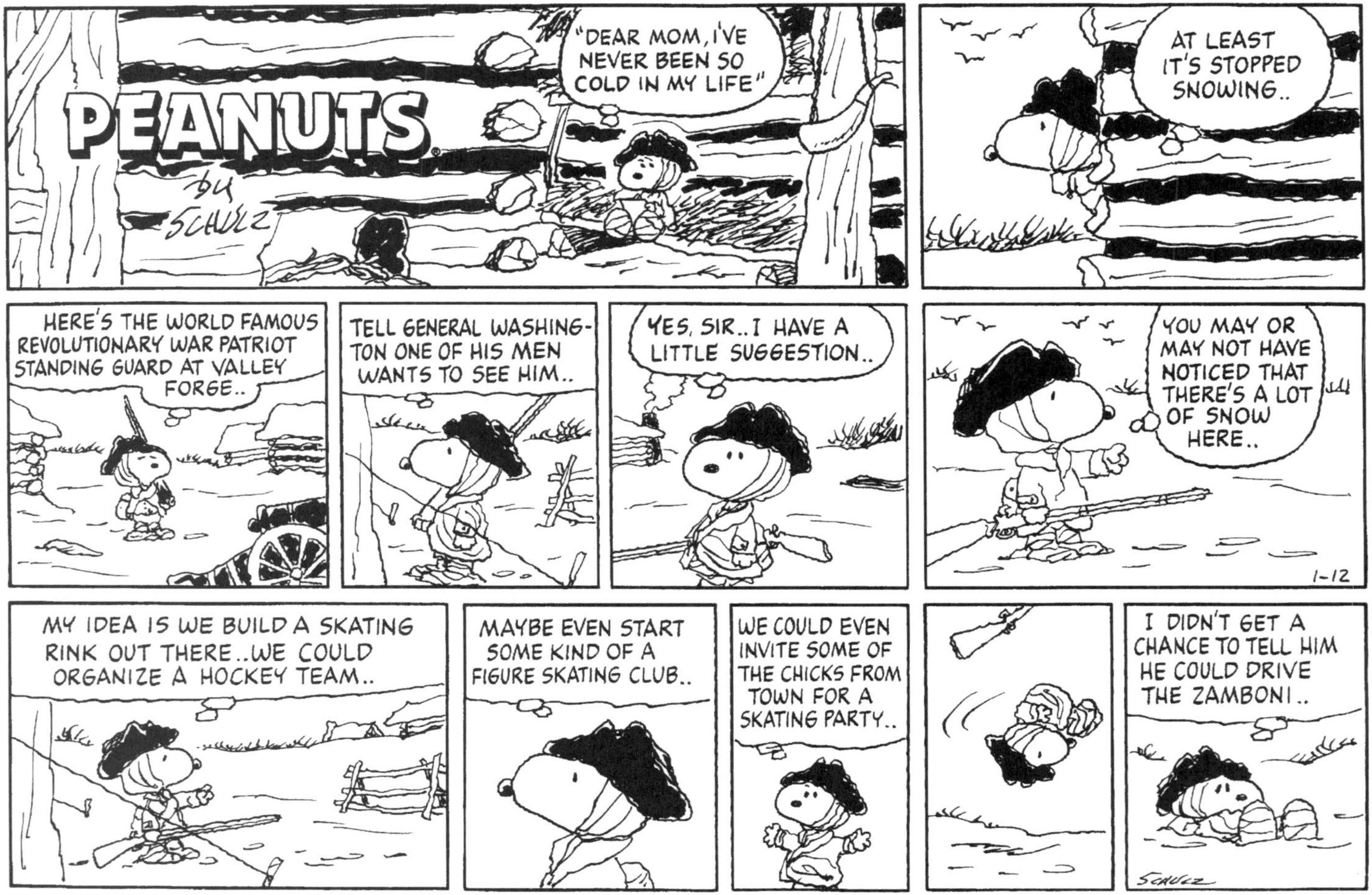
PEANUTS
by SCHULZ
"DEAR MOM, I'VE NEVER BEEN SO COLD IN MY LIFE"
AT LEAST IT'S STOPPED SNOWING..
HERE'S THE WORLD FAMOUS REVOLUTIONARY WAR PATRIOT STANDING GUARD AT VALLEY FORGE..
TELL GENERAL WASHINGTON ONE OF HIS MEN WANTS TO SEE HIM..
YES, SIR..I HAVE A LITTLE SUGGESTION..
YOU MAY OR MAY NOT HAVE NOTICED THAT THERE'S A LOT OF SNOW HERE..
1-12
MY IDEA IS WE BUILD A SKATING RINK OUT THERE..WE COULD ORGANIZE A HOCKEY TEAM..
MAYBE EVEN START SOME KIND OF A FIGURE SKATING CLUB..
WE COULD EVEN INVITE SOME OF THE CHICKS FROM TOWN FOR A SKATING PARTY..
I DIDN'T GET A CHANCE TO TELL HIM HE COULD DRIVE THE ZAMBONI..
SCHULZ

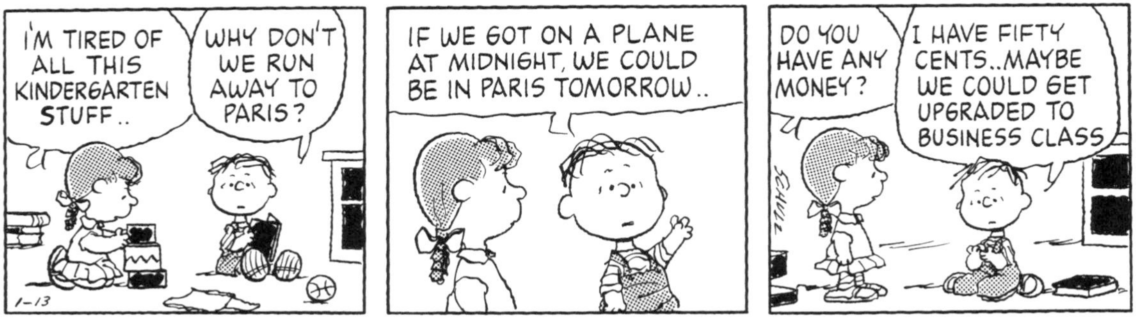
I'M TIRED OF ALL THIS KINDERGARTEN STUFF..
WHY DON'T WE RUN AWAY TO PARIS?
1-13
IF WE GOT ON A PLANE AT MIDNIGHT, WE COULD BE IN PARIS TOMORROW..
DO YOU HAVE ANY MONEY?
I HAVE FIFTY CENTS..MAYBE WE COULD GET UPGRADED TO BUSINESS CLASS
SCHULZ

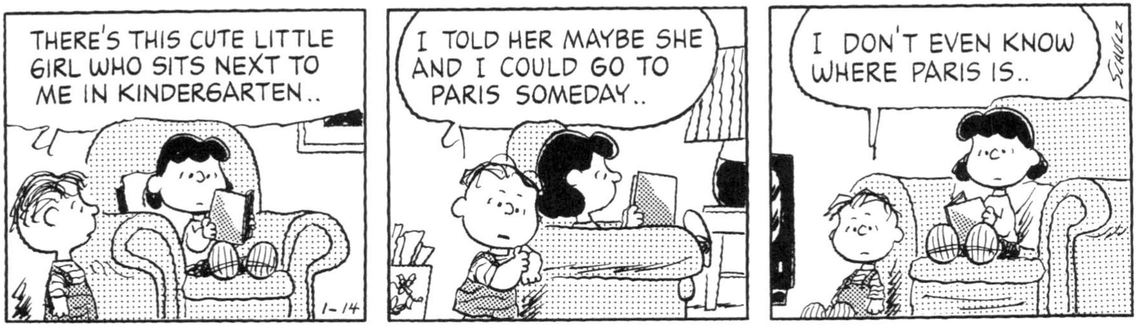
THERE'S THIS CUTE LITTLE GIRL WHO SITS NEXT TO ME IN KINDERGARTEN..
1-14
I TOLD HER MAYBE SHE AND I COULD GO TO PARIS SOMEDAY..
I DON'T EVEN KNOW WHERE PARIS IS..
SCHULZ

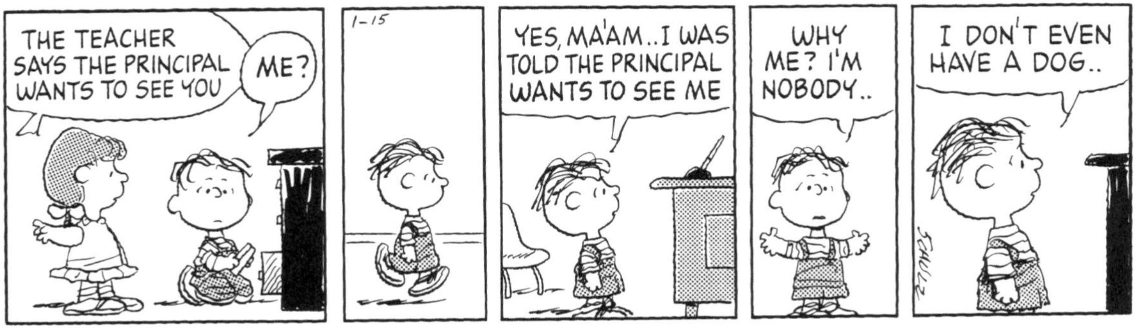
THE TEACHER SAYS THE PRINCIPAL WANTS TO SEE YOU
ME?
1-15
YES, MA'AM..I WAS TOLD THE PRINCIPAL WANTS TO SEE ME
WHY ME? I'M NOBODY..
I DON'T EVEN HAVE A DOG..
SCHULZ

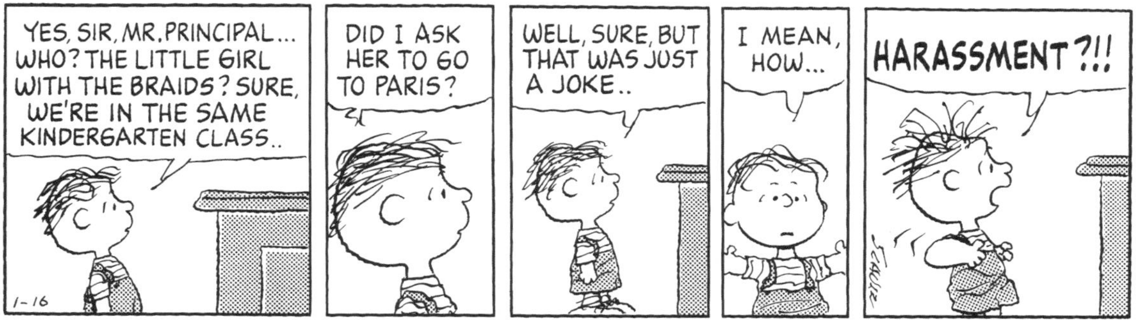
YES, SIR, MR. PRINCIPAL... WHO? THE LITTLE GIRL WITH THE BRAIDS? SURE, WE'RE IN THE SAME KINDERGARTEN CLASS..
DID I ASK HER TO GO TO PARIS?
WELL, SURE, BUT THAT WAS JUST A JOKE..
I MEAN, HOW...
HARASSMENT?!!

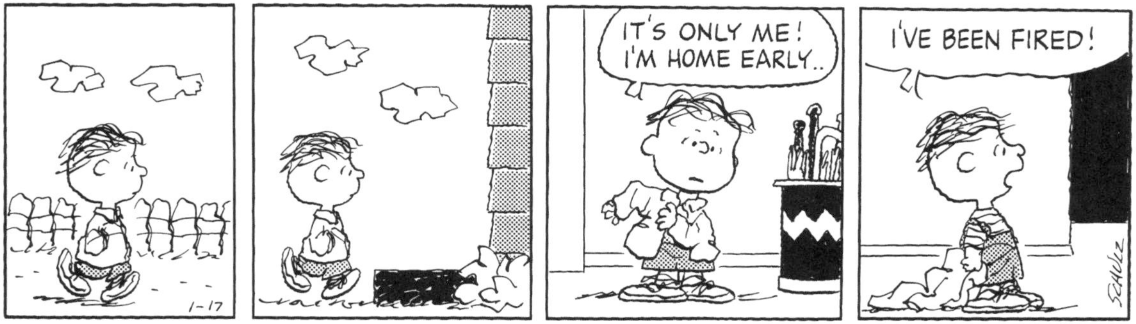
IT'S ONLY ME! I'M HOME EARLY..
I'VE BEEN FIRED!

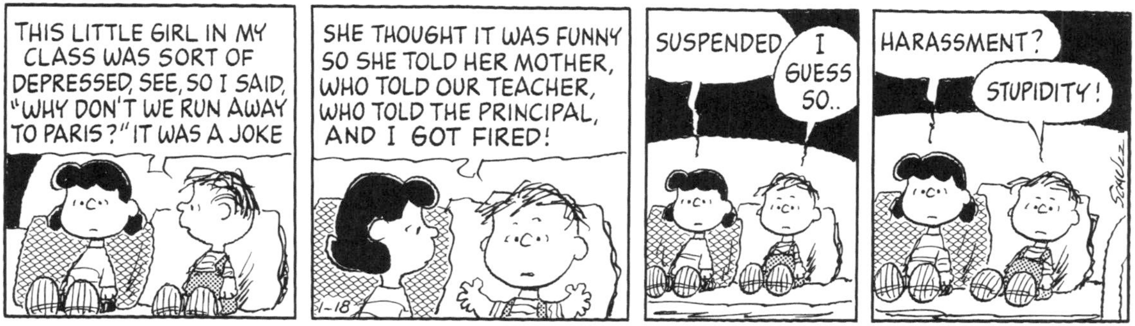
THIS LITTLE GIRL IN MY CLASS WAS SORT OF DEPRESSED, SEE, SO I SAID, "WHY DON'T WE RUN AWAY TO PARIS?" IT WAS A JOKE
SHE THOUGHT IT WAS FUNNY SO SHE TOLD HER MOTHER, WHO TOLD OUR TEACHER, WHO TOLD THE PRINCIPAL, AND I GOT FIRED!
SUSPENDED
I GUESS SO..
HARASSMENT?
STUPIDITY!

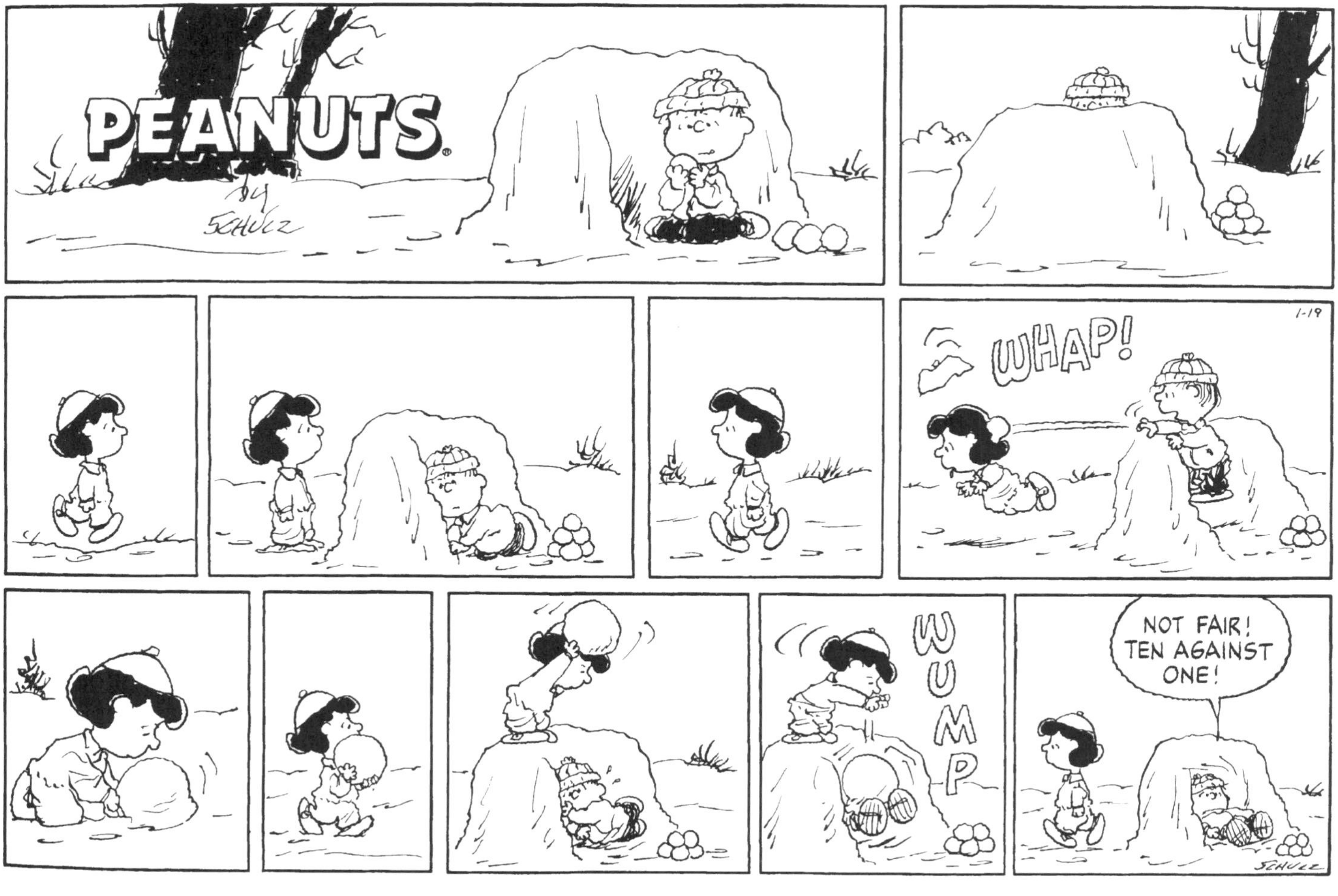
PEANUTS
by SCHULZ
1-19
WHAP!
WUMP
NOT FAIR! TEN AGAINST ONE!
SCHULZ

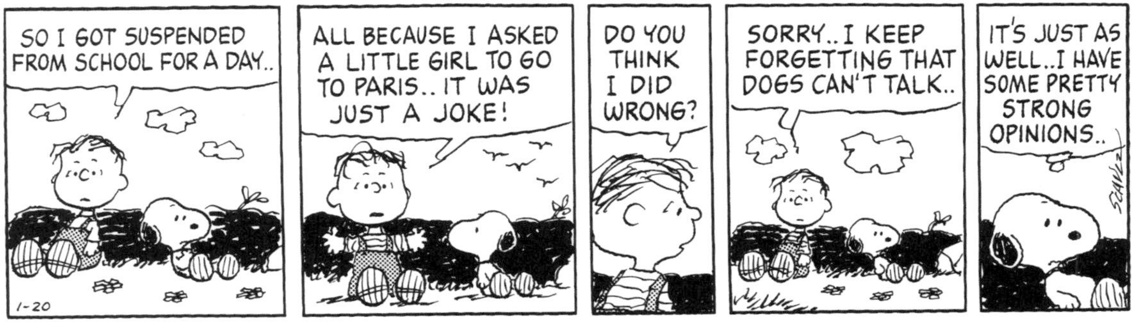
SO I GOT SUSPENDED FROM SCHOOL FOR A DAY..
ALL BECAUSE I ASKED A LITTLE GIRL TO GO TO PARIS.. IT WAS JUST A JOKE!
DO YOU THINK I DID WRONG?
SORRY.. I KEEP FORGETTING THAT DOGS CAN'T TALK..
IT'S JUST AS WELL..I HAVE SOME PRETTY STRONG OPINIONS..
1-20

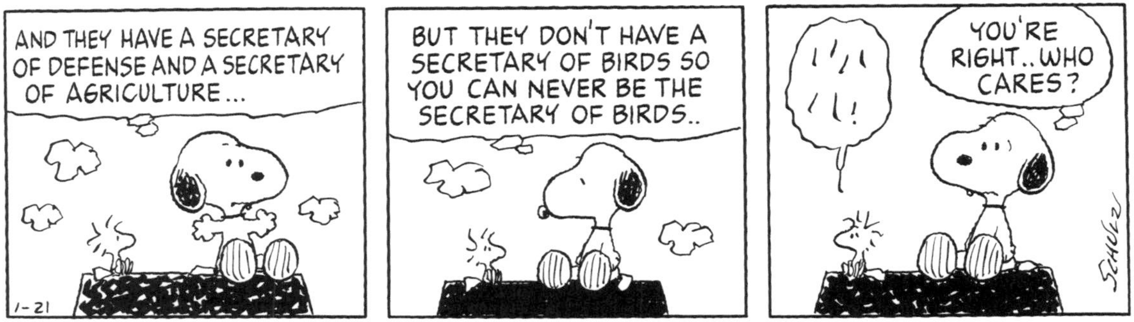
AND THEY HAVE A SECRETARY OF DEFENSE AND A SECRETARY OF AGRICULTURE...
BUT THEY DON'T HAVE A SECRETARY OF BIRDS SO YOU CAN NEVER BE THE SECRETARY OF BIRDS..
YOU'RE RIGHT.. WHO CARES?
1-21

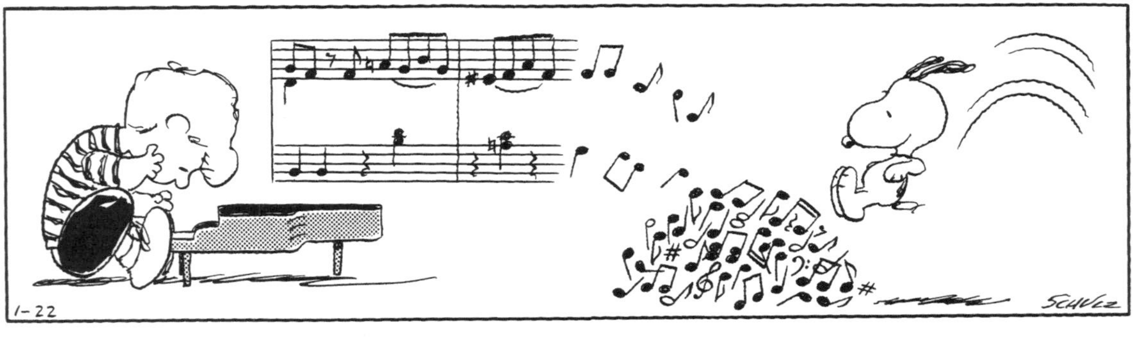
1-22

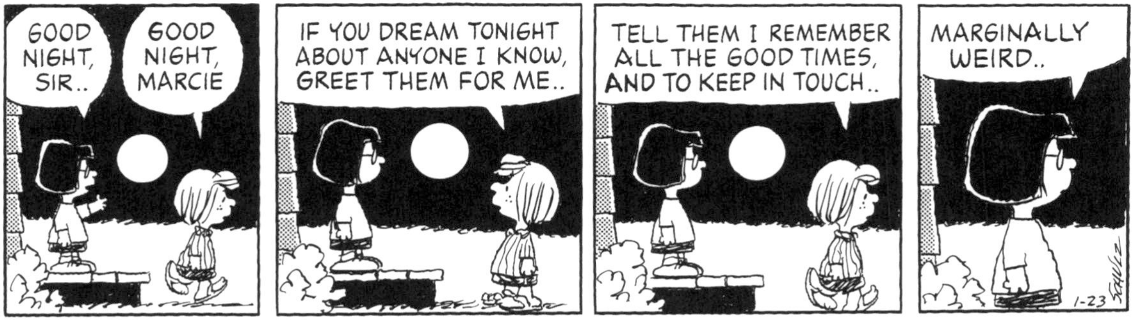
GOOD NIGHT, SIR..
GOOD NIGHT, MARCIE
IF YOU DREAM TONIGHT ABOUT ANYONE I KNOW, GREET THEM FOR ME..
TELL THEM I REMEMBER ALL THE GOOD TIMES, AND TO KEEP IN TOUCH..
MARGINALLY WEIRD..

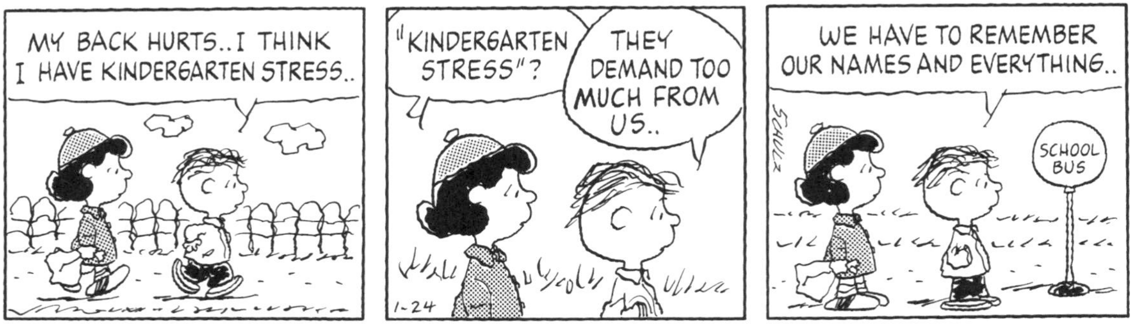
MY BACK HURTS..I THINK I HAVE KINDERGARTEN STRESS..
"KINDERGARTEN STRESS"?
THEY DEMAND TOO MUCH FROM US..
WE HAVE TO REMEMBER OUR NAMES AND EVERYTHING..
SCHOOL BUS

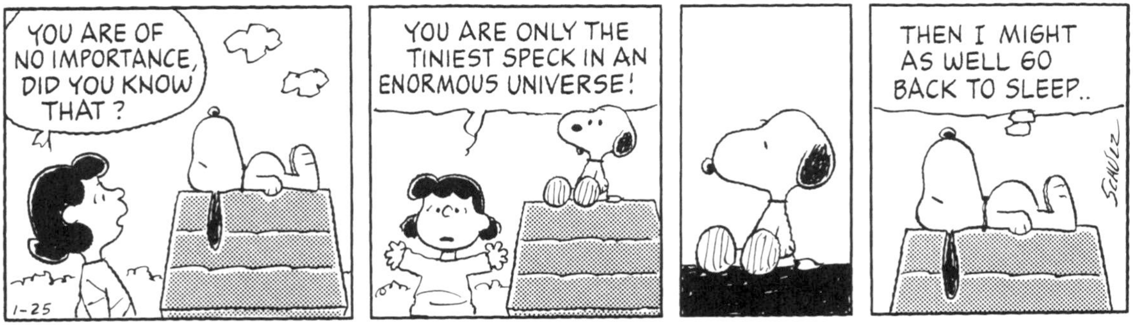
YOU ARE OF NO IMPORTANCE, DID YOU KNOW THAT ?
YOU ARE ONLY THE TINIEST SPECK IN AN ENORMOUS UNIVERSE!
THEN I MIGHT AS WELL GO BACK TO SLEEP..

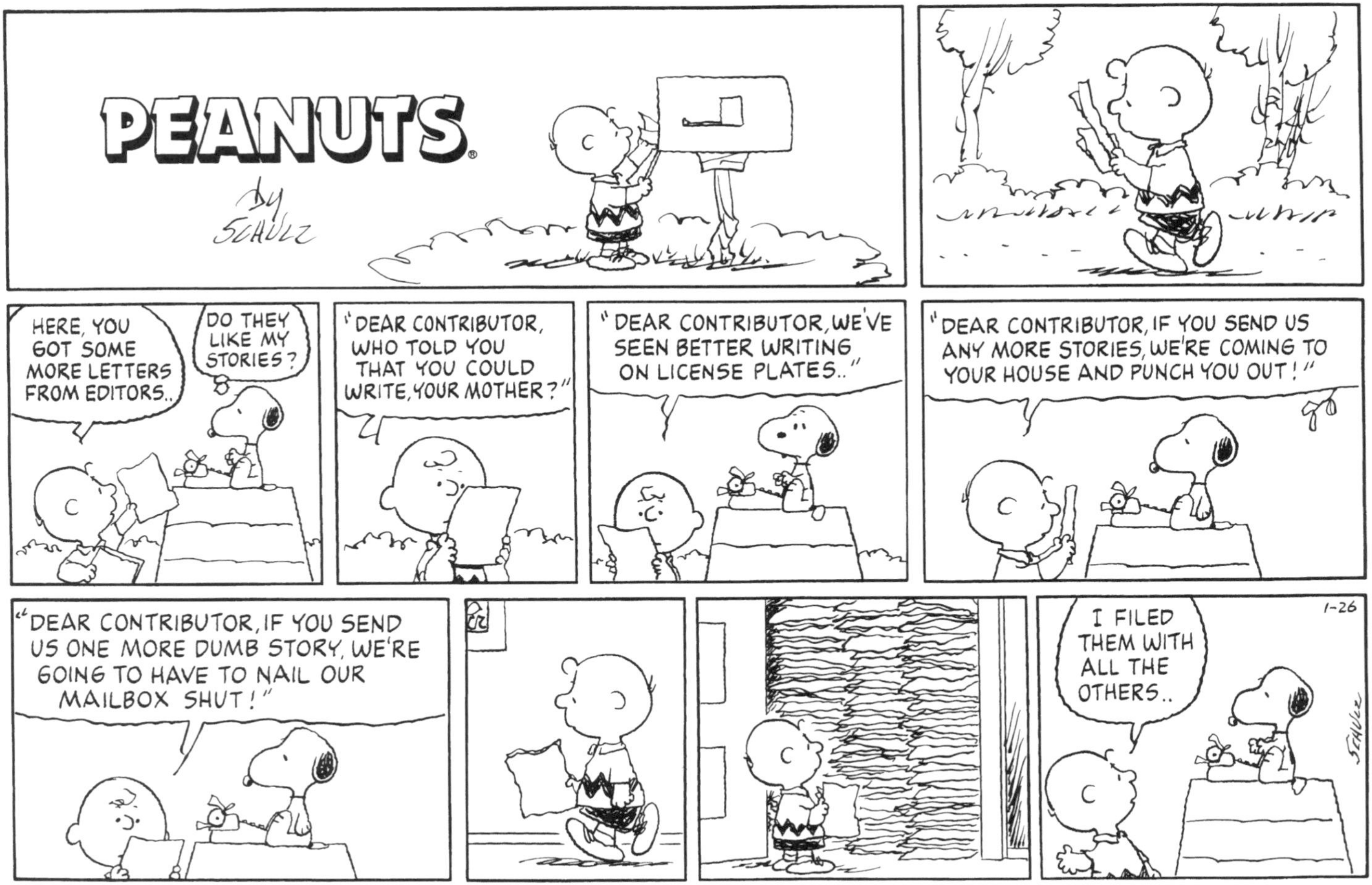
PEANUTS
by Schulz
HERE, YOU GOT SOME MORE LETTERS FROM EDITORS..
DO THEY LIKE MY STORIES?
"DEAR CONTRIBUTOR, WHO TOLD YOU THAT YOU COULD WRITE, YOUR MOTHER?"
"DEAR CONTRIBUTOR, WE'VE SEEN BETTER WRITING ON LICENSE PLATES.."
"DEAR CONTRIBUTOR, IF YOU SEND US ANY MORE STORIES, WE'RE COMING TO YOUR HOUSE AND PUNCH YOU OUT!"
"DEAR CONTRIBUTOR, IF YOU SEND US ONE MORE DUMB STORY, WE'RE GOING TO HAVE TO NAIL OUR MAILBOX SHUT!"
1-26
I FILED THEM WITH ALL THE OTHERS..
SCHULZ

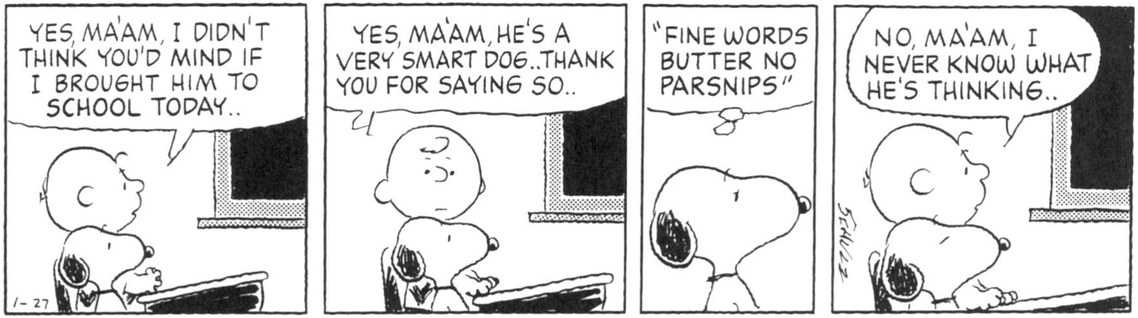
YES, MA'AM, I DIDN'T THINK YOU'D MIND IF I BROUGHT HIM TO SCHOOL TODAY..
1-27
YES, MA'AM, HE'S A VERY SMART DOG..THANK YOU FOR SAYING SO..
"FINE WORDS BUTTER NO PARSNIPS"
NO, MA'AM, I NEVER KNOW WHAT HE'S THINKING..
SCHULZ

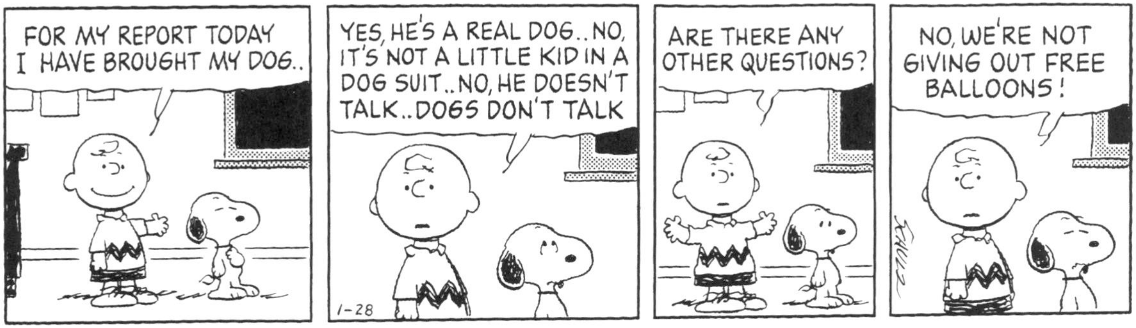
FOR MY REPORT TODAY I HAVE BROUGHT MY DOG..
YES, HE'S A REAL DOG..NO, IT'S NOT A LITTLE KID IN A DOG SUIT..NO, HE DOESN'T TALK..DOGS DON'T TALK
1-28
ARE THERE ANY OTHER QUESTIONS?
NO, WE'RE NOT GIVING OUT FREE BALLOONS!
SCHULZ

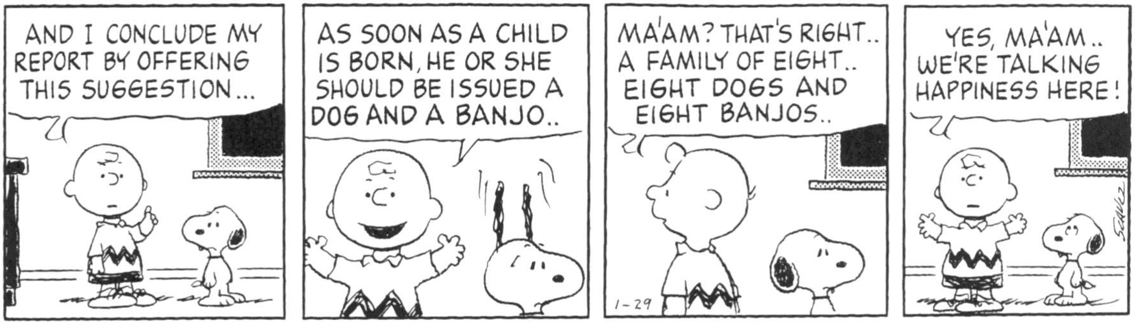
AND I CONCLUDE MY REPORT BY OFFERING THIS SUGGESTION...
AS SOON AS A CHILD IS BORN, HE OR SHE SHOULD BE ISSUED A DOG AND A BANJO..
MA'AM? THAT'S RIGHT.. A FAMILY OF EIGHT.. EIGHT DOGS AND EIGHT BANJOS..
1-29
YES, MA'AM.. WE'RE TALKING HAPPINESS HERE!
SCHULZ

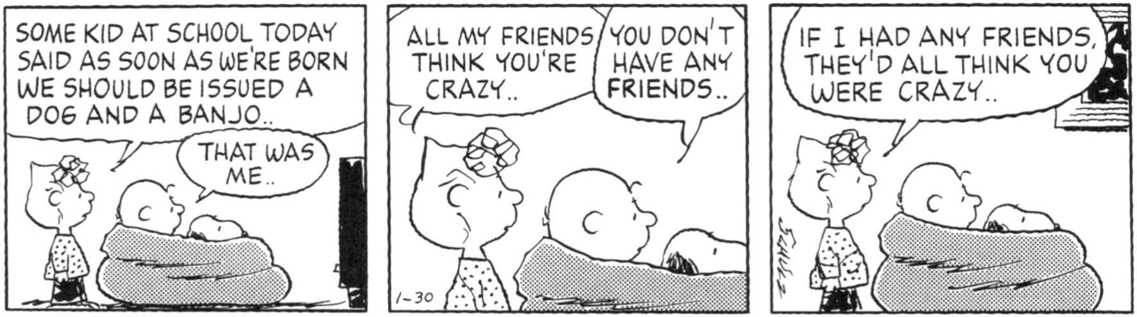
SOME KID AT SCHOOL TODAY SAID AS SOON AS WE'RE BORN WE SHOULD BE ISSUED A DOG AND A BANJO..
THAT WAS ME..
ALL MY FRIENDS THINK YOU'RE CRAZY..
YOU DON'T HAVE ANY FRIENDS..
IF I HAD ANY FRIENDS, THEY'D ALL THINK YOU WERE CRAZY..
1-30

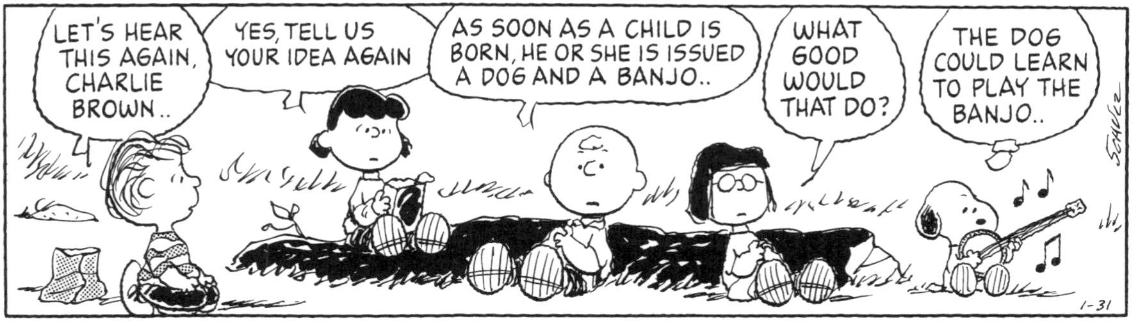
LET'S HEAR THIS AGAIN, CHARLIE BROWN..
YES, TELL US YOUR IDEA AGAIN
AS SOON AS A CHILD IS BORN, HE OR SHE IS ISSUED A DOG AND A BANJO..
WHAT GOOD WOULD THAT DO?
THE DOG COULD LEARN TO PLAY THE BANJO..
1-31

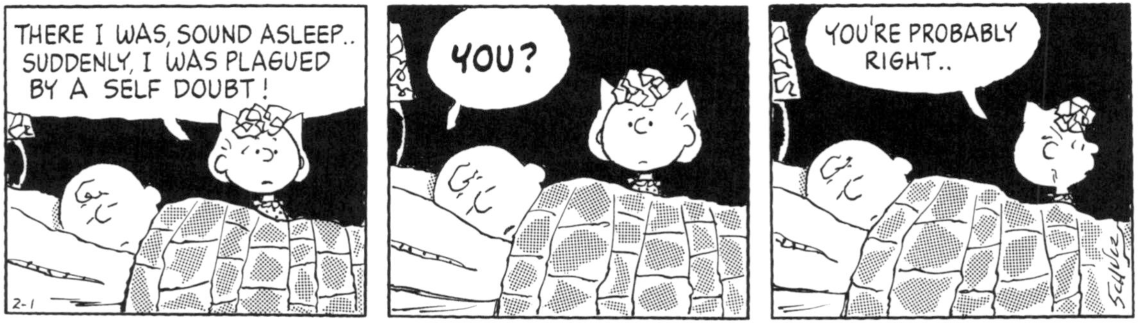
THERE I WAS, SOUND ASLEEP.. SUDDENLY, I WAS PLAGUED BY A SELF DOUBT!
YOU?
YOU'RE PROBABLY RIGHT..
2-1

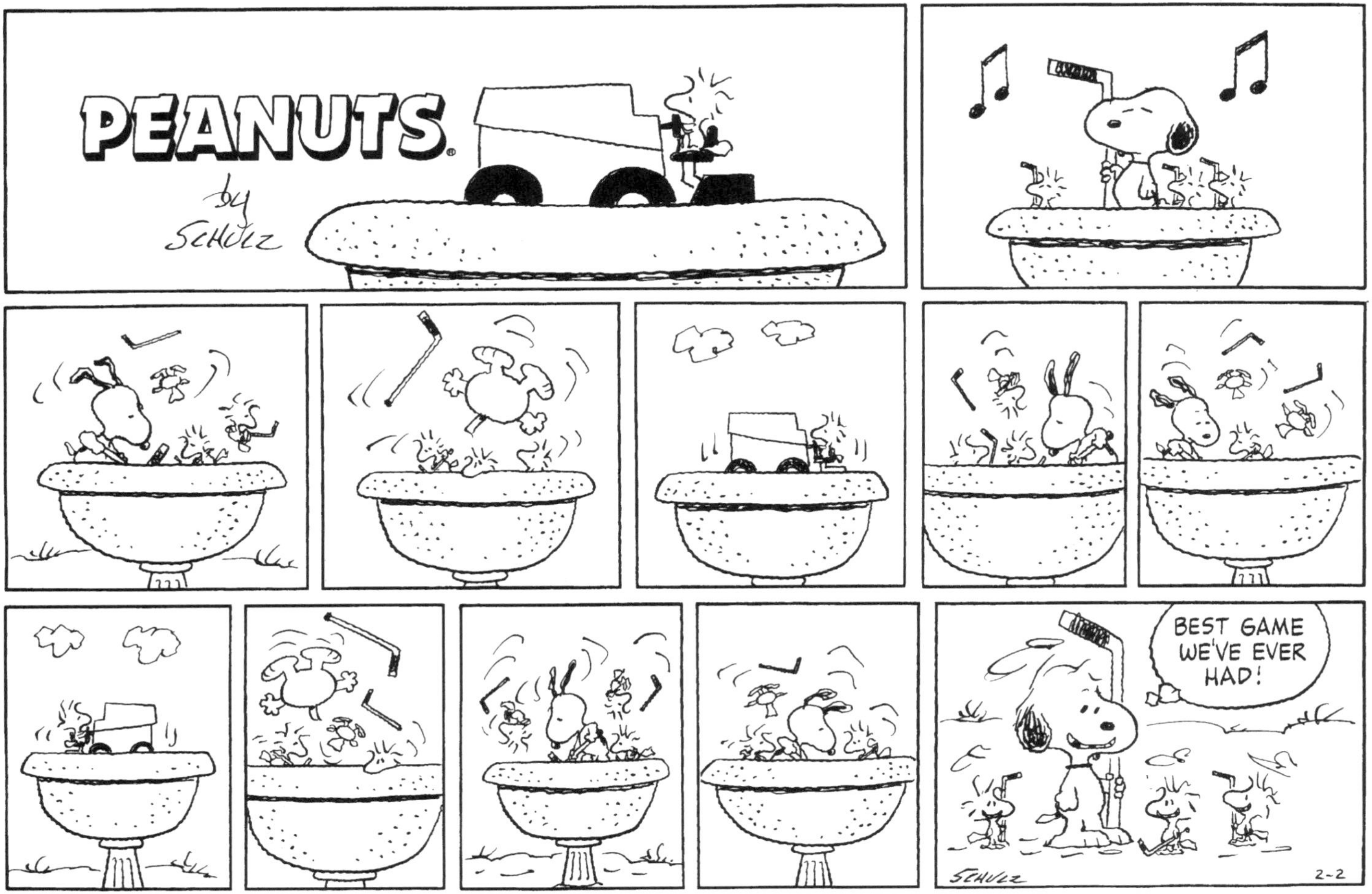
PEANUTS
by SCHULZ
BEST GAME WE'VE EVER HAD!
SCHULZ
2-2

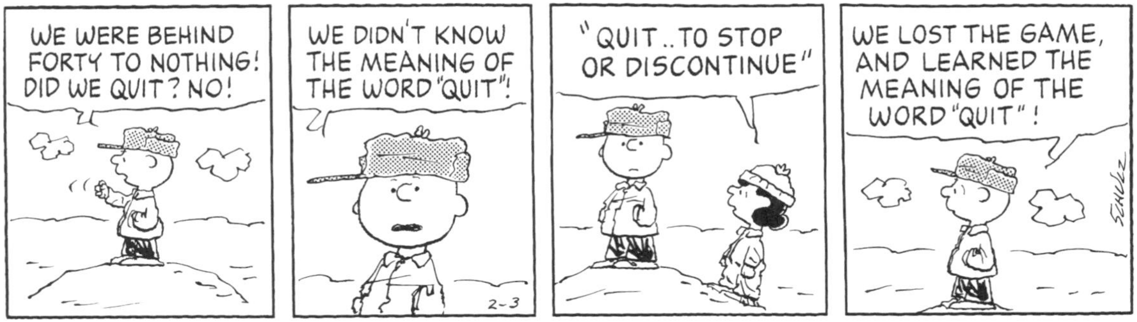
WE WERE BEHIND FORTY TO NOTHING! DID WE QUIT? NO!
WE DIDN'T KNOW THE MEANING OF THE WORD "QUIT"!
"QUIT..TO STOP OR DISCONTINUE"
WE LOST THE GAME, AND LEARNED THE MEANING OF THE WORD "QUIT"!

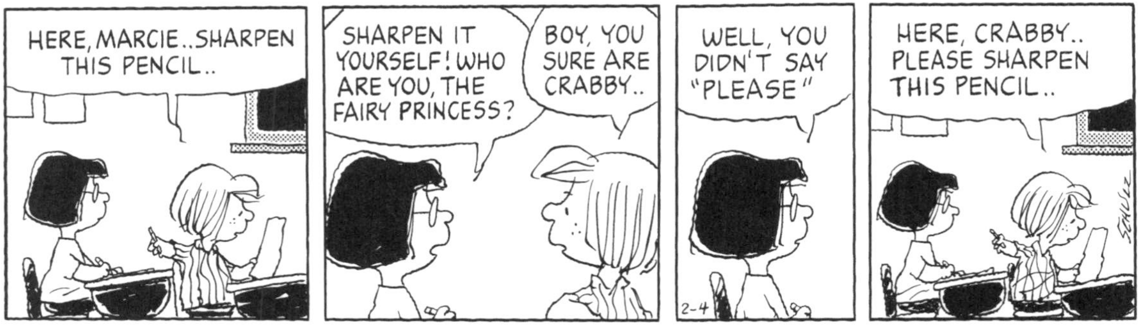
HERE, MARCIE..SHARPEN THIS PENCIL..
SHARPEN IT YOURSELF! WHO ARE YOU, THE FAIRY PRINCESS?
BOY, YOU SURE ARE CRABBY..
WELL, YOU DIDN'T SAY "PLEASE"
HERE, CRABBY.. PLEASE SHARPEN THIS PENCIL..

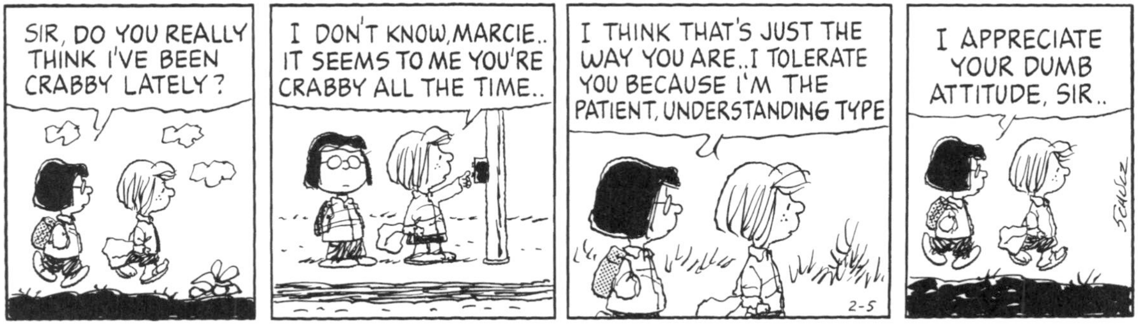
SIR, DO YOU REALLY THINK I'VE BEEN CRABBY LATELY?
I DON'T KNOW, MARCIE.. IT SEEMS TO ME YOU'RE CRABBY ALL THE TIME..
I THINK THAT'S JUST THE WAY YOU ARE..I TOLERATE YOU BECAUSE I'M THE PATIENT, UNDERSTANDING TYPE
I APPRECIATE YOUR DUMB ATTITUDE, SIR..

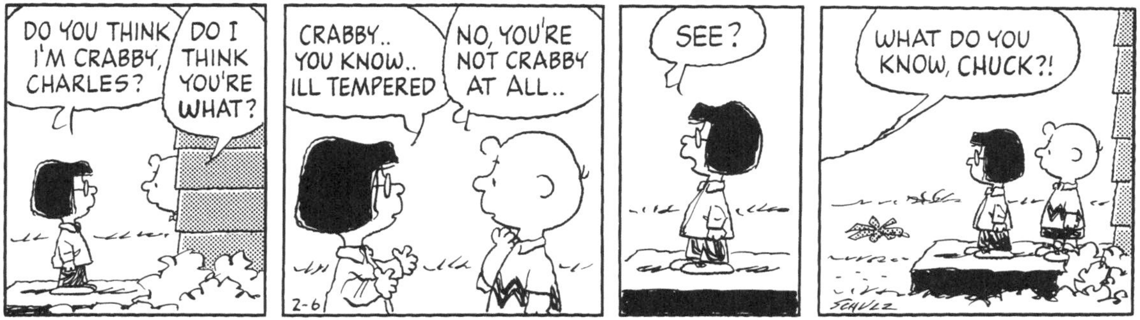
DO YOU THINK I'M CRABBY, CHARLES?
DO I THINK YOU'RE WHAT?
CRABBY.. YOU KNOW.. ILL TEMPERED
NO, YOU'RE NOT CRABBY AT ALL..
2-6
SEE?
WHAT DO YOU KNOW, CHUCK?!
SCHULZ

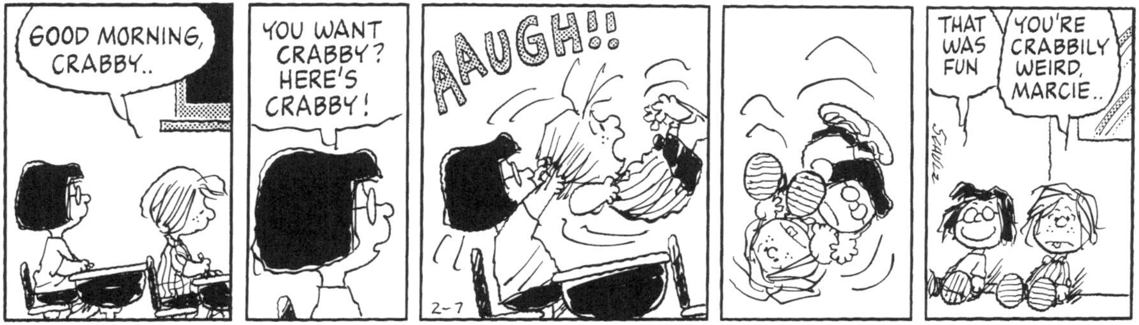
GOOD MORNING, CRABBY..
YOU WANT CRABBY? HERE'S CRABBY!
AAUGH!!
2-7
THAT WAS FUN
YOU'RE CRABBILY WEIRD, MARCIE..
SCHULZ

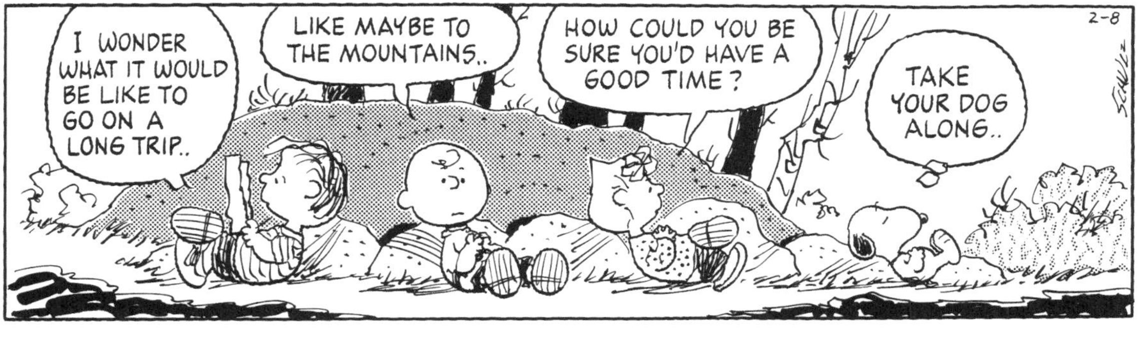
2-8
I WONDER WHAT IT WOULD BE LIKE TO GO ON A LONG TRIP..
LIKE MAYBE TO THE MOUNTAINS..
HOW COULD YOU BE SURE YOU'D HAVE A GOOD TIME?
TAKE YOUR DOG ALONG..
SCHULZ

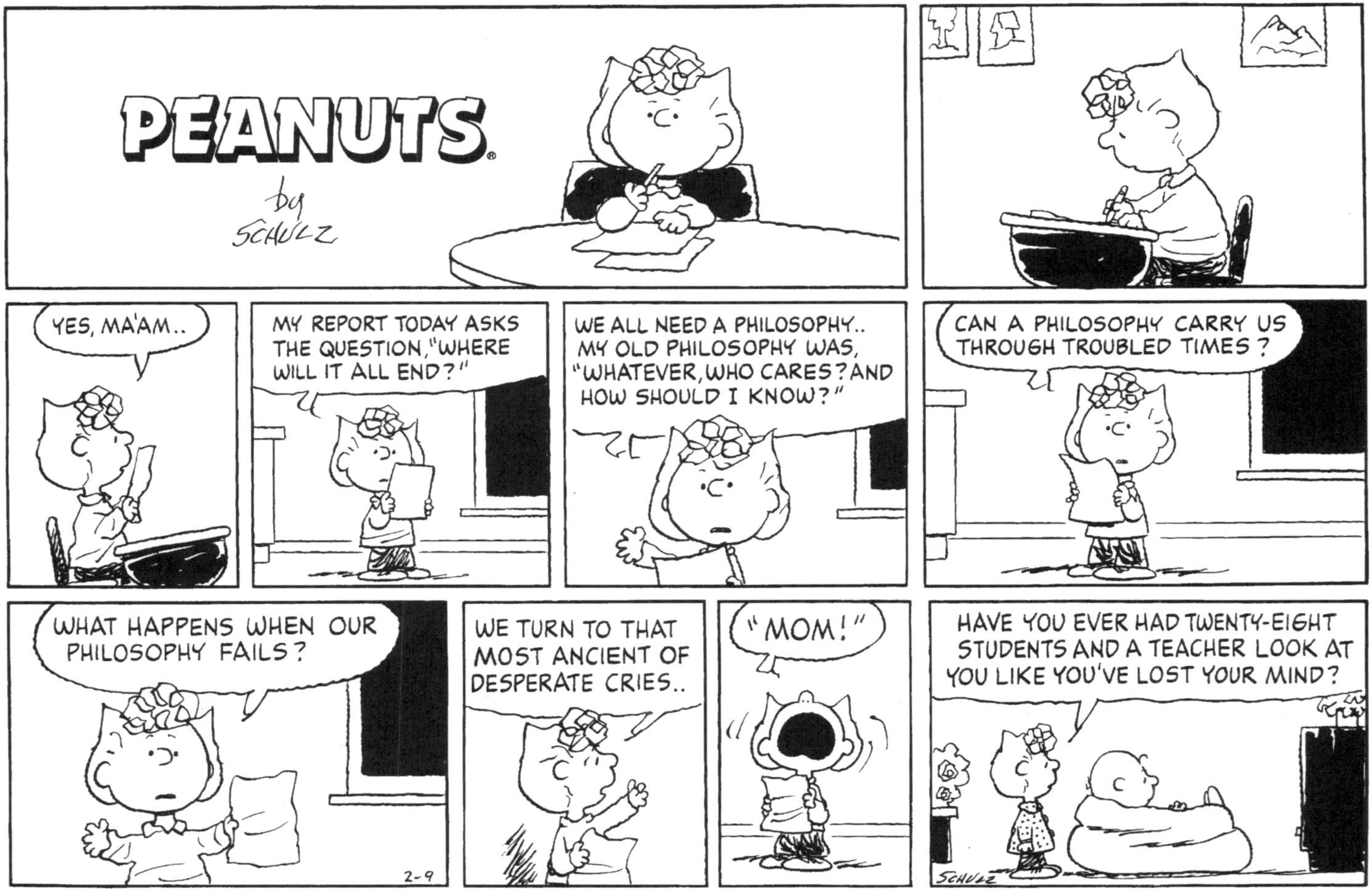
PEANUTS
by SCHULZ
YES, MA'AM..
MY REPORT TODAY ASKS THE QUESTION, "WHERE WILL IT ALL END?"
WE ALL NEED A PHILOSOPHY.. MY OLD PHILOSOPHY WAS, "WHATEVER, WHO CARES? AND HOW SHOULD I KNOW?"
CAN A PHILOSOPHY CARRY US THROUGH TROUBLED TIMES?
WHAT HAPPENS WHEN OUR PHILOSOPHY FAILS?
2-9
WE TURN TO THAT MOST ANCIENT OF DESPERATE CRIES..
"MOM!"
HAVE YOU EVER HAD TWENTY-EIGHT STUDENTS AND A TEACHER LOOK AT YOU LIKE YOU'VE LOST YOUR MIND?
SCHULZ

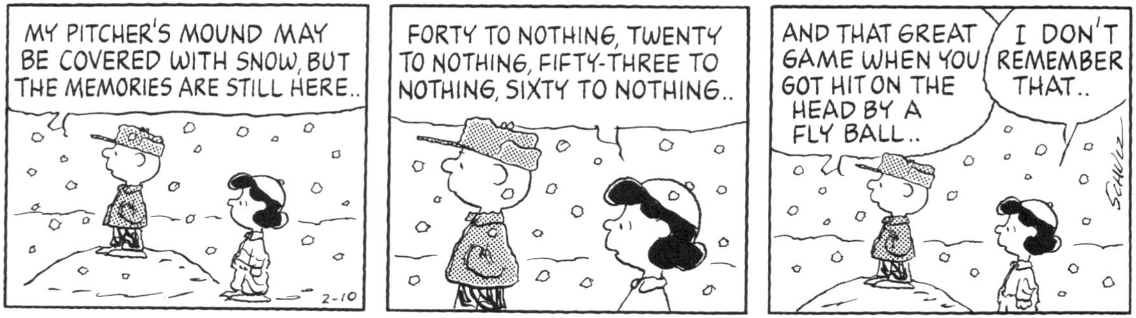
MY PITCHER'S MOUND MAY BE COVERED WITH SNOW, BUT THE MEMORIES ARE STILL HERE..
2-10
FORTY TO NOTHING, TWENTY TO NOTHING, FIFTY-THREE TO NOTHING, SIXTY TO NOTHING..
AND THAT GREAT GAME WHEN YOU GOT HIT ON THE HEAD BY A FLY BALL..
I DON'T REMEMBER THAT..
SCHULZ

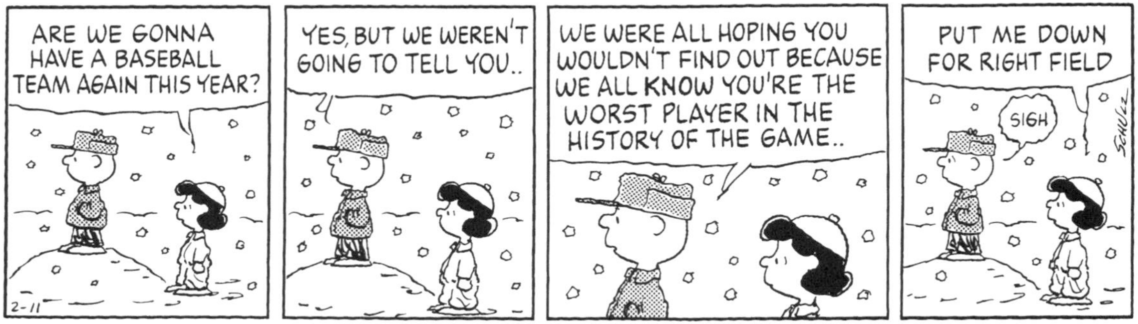
ARE WE GONNA HAVE A BASEBALL TEAM AGAIN THIS YEAR?
2-11
YES, BUT WE WEREN'T GOING TO TELL YOU..
WE WERE ALL HOPING YOU WOULDN'T FIND OUT BECAUSE WE ALL KNOW YOU'RE THE WORST PLAYER IN THE HISTORY OF THE GAME..
PUT ME DOWN FOR RIGHT FIELD
SIGH
SCHULZ

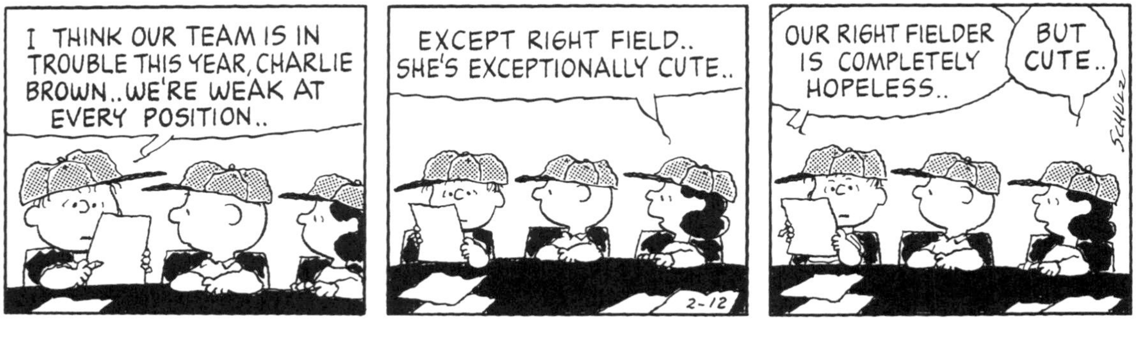
I THINK OUR TEAM IS IN TROUBLE THIS YEAR, CHARLIE BROWN.. WE'RE WEAK AT EVERY POSITION..
EXCEPT RIGHT FIELD.. SHE'S EXCEPTIONALLY CUTE..
2-12
OUR RIGHT FIELDER IS COMPLETELY HOPELESS..
BUT CUTE..
SCHULZ

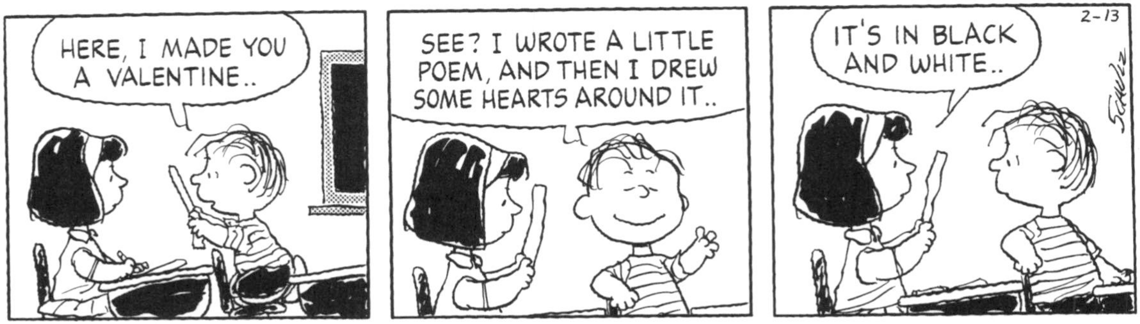
HERE, I MADE YOU A VALENTINE..
SEE? I WROTE A LITTLE POEM, AND THEN I DREW SOME HEARTS AROUND IT..
2-13
IT'S IN BLACK AND WHITE..

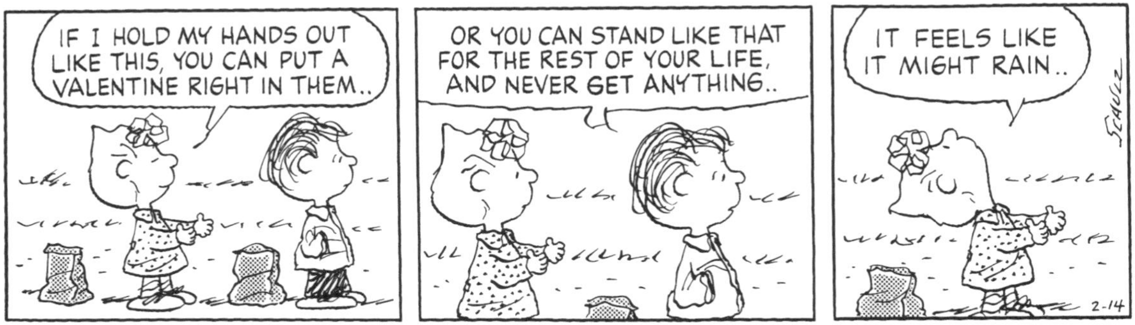
IF I HOLD MY HANDS OUT LIKE THIS, YOU CAN PUT A VALENTINE RIGHT IN THEM..
OR YOU CAN STAND LIKE THAT FOR THE REST OF YOUR LIFE, AND NEVER GET ANYTHING..
IT FEELS LIKE IT MIGHT RAIN..
2-14

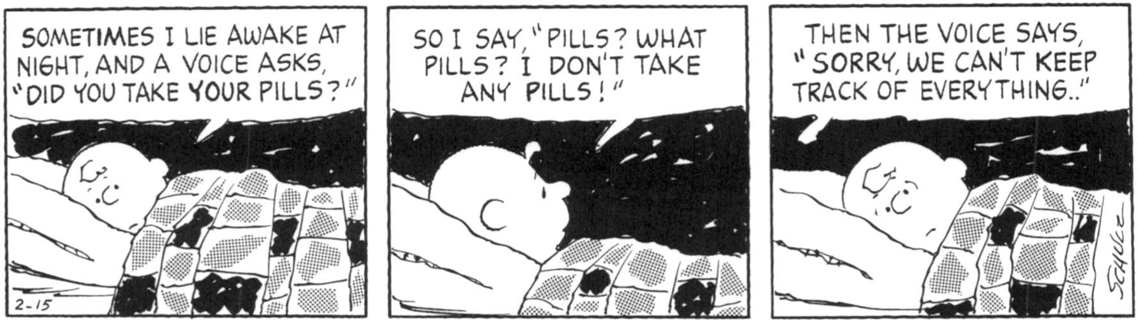
SOMETIMES I LIE AWAKE AT NIGHT, AND A VOICE ASKS, "DID YOU TAKE YOUR PILLS?"
2-15
SO I SAY, "PILLS? WHAT PILLS? I DON'T TAKE ANY PILLS!"
THEN THE VOICE SAYS, "SORRY, WE CAN'T KEEP TRACK OF EVERYTHING.."

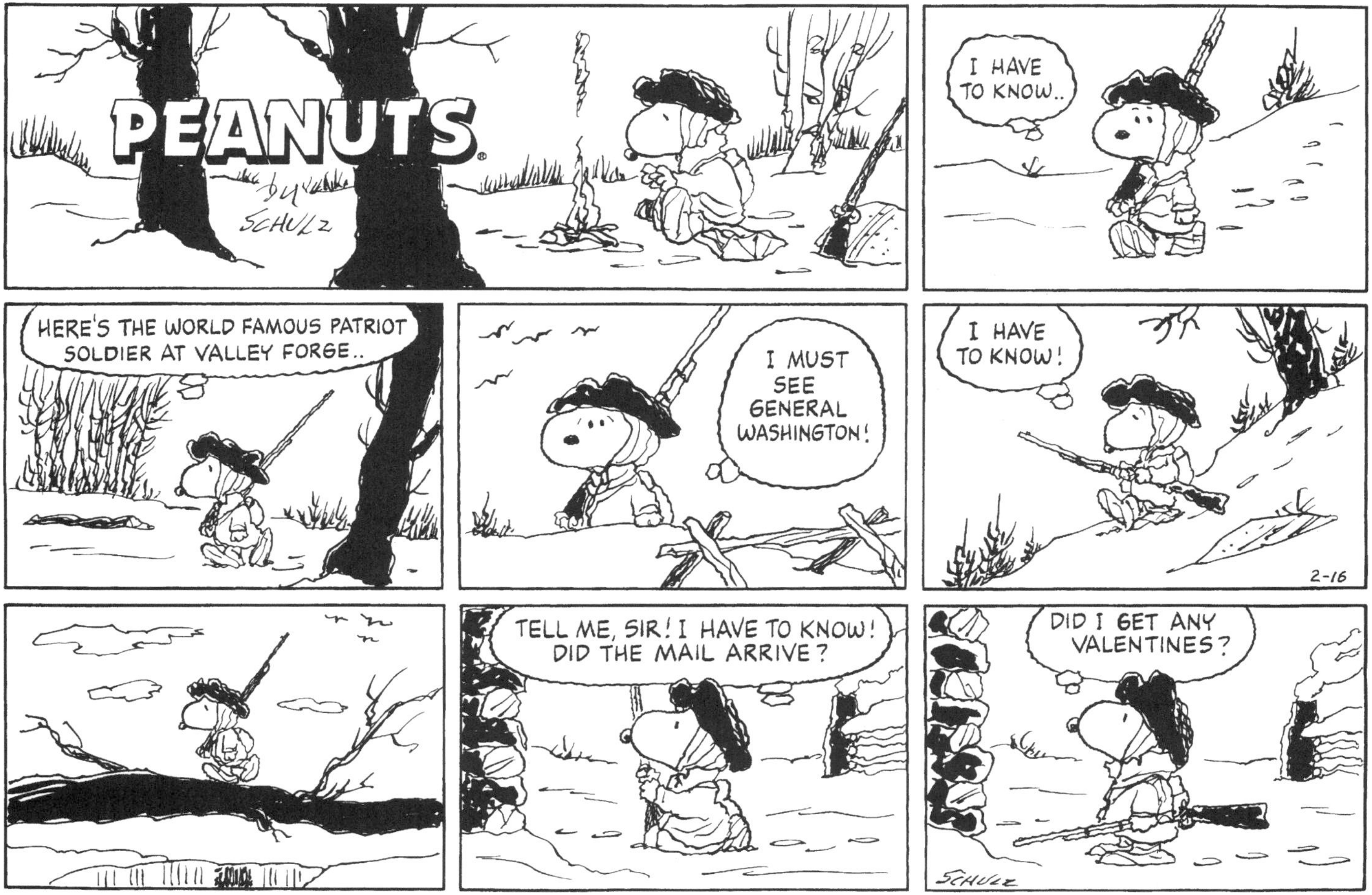
PEANUTS
by SCHULZ
I HAVE TO KNOW..
HERE'S THE WORLD FAMOUS PATRIOT SOLDIER AT VALLEY FORGE..
I MUST SEE GENERAL WASHINGTON!
I HAVE TO KNOW!
2-16
TELL ME, SIR! I HAVE TO KNOW! DID THE MAIL ARRIVE?
DID I GET ANY VALENTINES?
SCHULZ

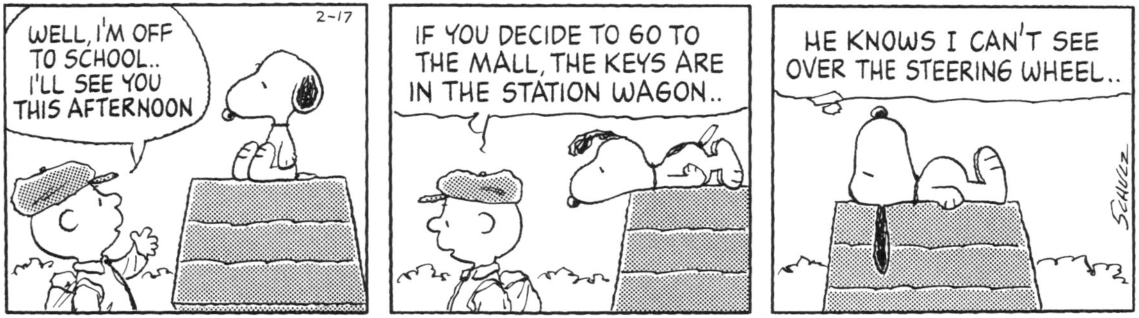
2-17
WELL, I'M OFF TO SCHOOL.. I'LL SEE YOU THIS AFTERNOON
IF YOU DECIDE TO GO TO THE MALL, THE KEYS ARE IN THE STATION WAGON..
HE KNOWS I CAN'T SEE OVER THE STEERING WHEEL..
SCHULZ

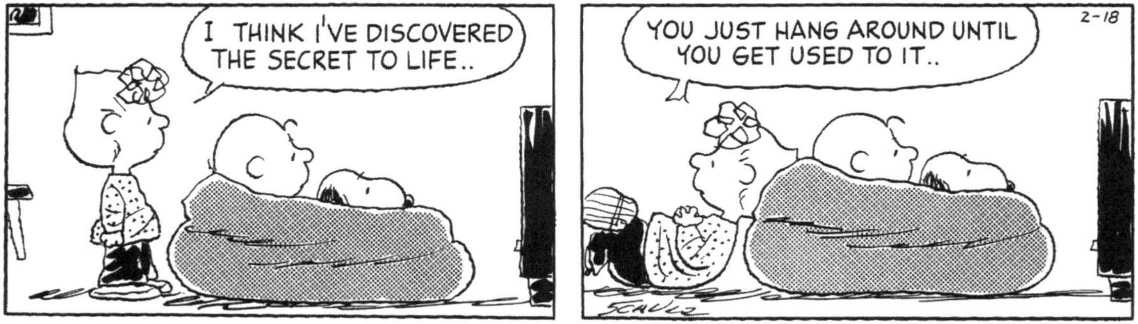
I THINK I'VE DISCOVERED THE SECRET TO LIFE..
2-18
YOU JUST HANG AROUND UNTIL YOU GET USED TO IT..
SCHULZ

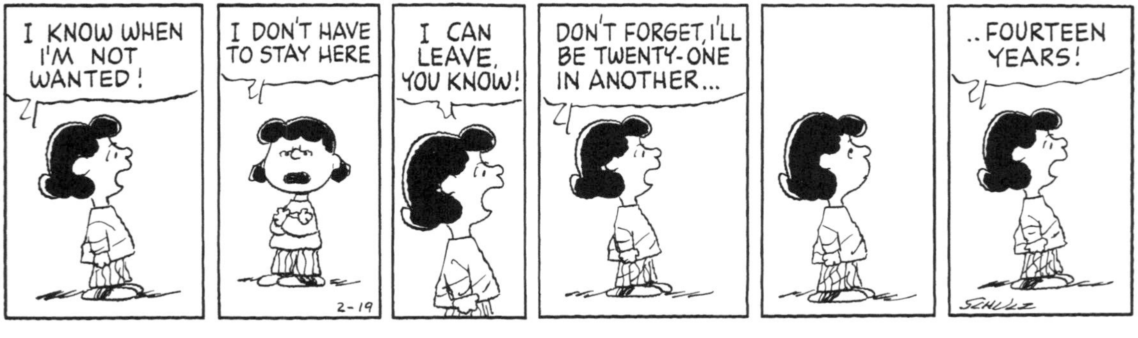
I KNOW WHEN I'M NOT WANTED!
I DON'T HAVE TO STAY HERE
2-19
I CAN LEAVE, YOU KNOW!
DON'T FORGET, I'LL BE TWENTY-ONE IN ANOTHER...
..FOURTEEN YEARS!
SCHULZ

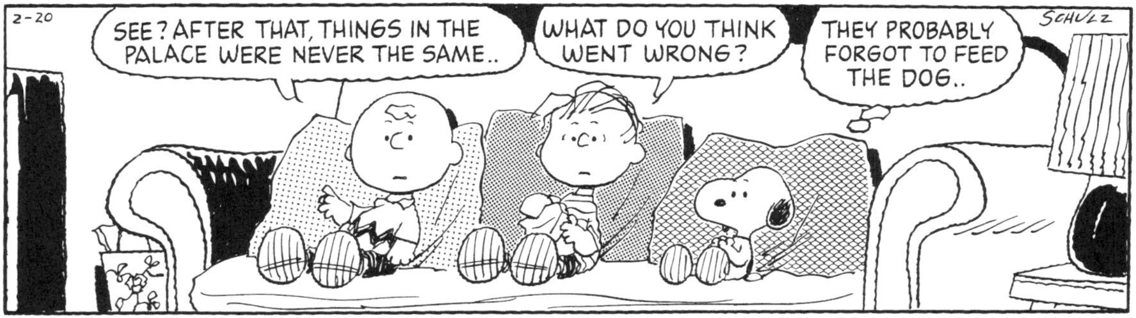
SEE? AFTER THAT, THINGS IN THE PALACE WERE NEVER THE SAME..
WHAT DO YOU THINK WENT WRONG?
THEY PROBABLY FORGOT TO FEED THE DOG..

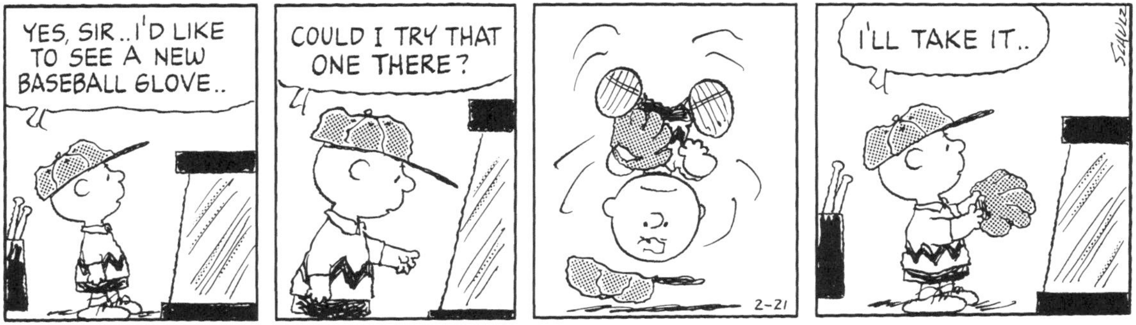
YES, SIR.. I'D LIKE TO SEE A NEW BASEBALL GLOVE..
COULD I TRY THAT ONE THERE?
I'LL TAKE IT..

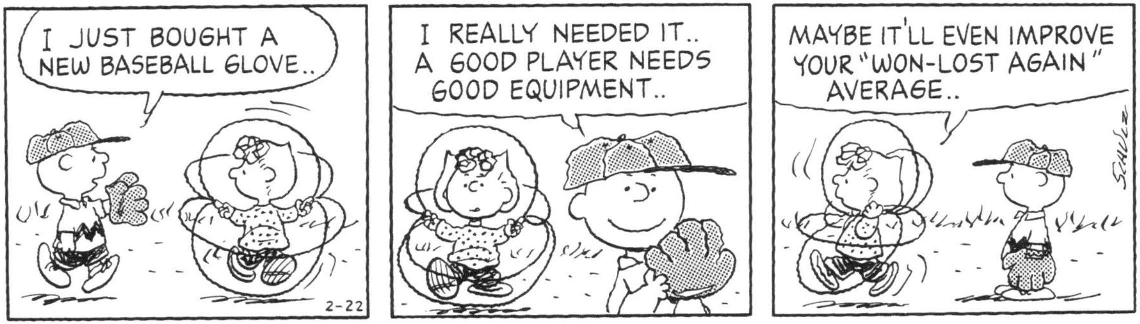
I JUST BOUGHT A NEW BASEBALL GLOVE..
I REALLY NEEDED IT.. A GOOD PLAYER NEEDS GOOD EQUIPMENT..
MAYBE IT'LL EVEN IMPROVE YOUR "WON-LOST AGAIN" AVERAGE..

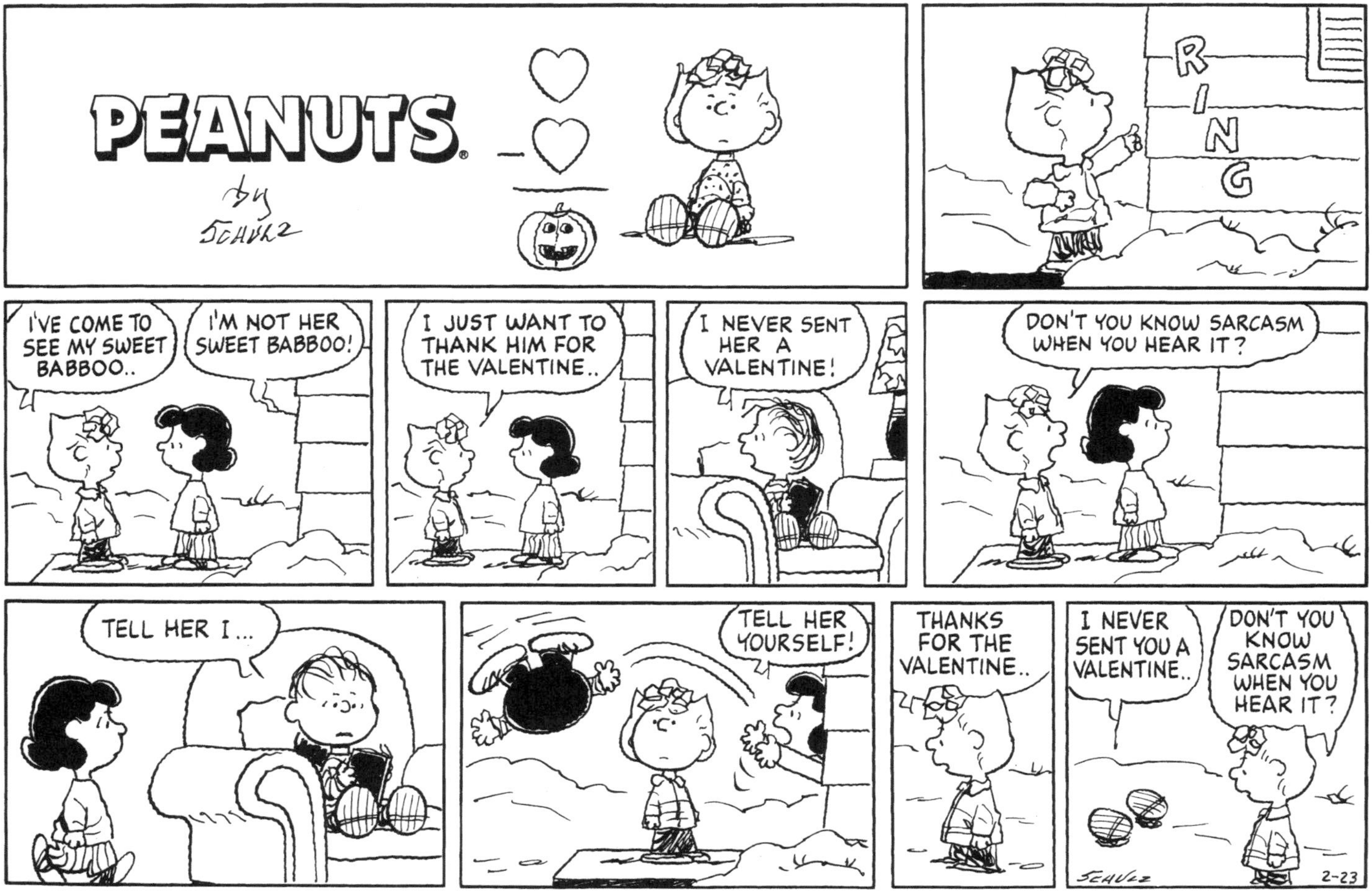
PEANUTS
by SCHULZ
RING
I'VE COME TO SEE MY SWEET BABBOO..
I'M NOT HER SWEET BABBOO!
I JUST WANT TO THANK HIM FOR THE VALENTINE..
I NEVER SENT HER A VALENTINE!
DON'T YOU KNOW SARCASM WHEN YOU HEAR IT?
TELL HER I...
TELL HER YOURSELF!
THANKS FOR THE VALENTINE..
I NEVER SENT YOU A VALENTINE..
DON'T YOU KNOW SARCASM WHEN YOU HEAR IT?
SCHULZ
2-23

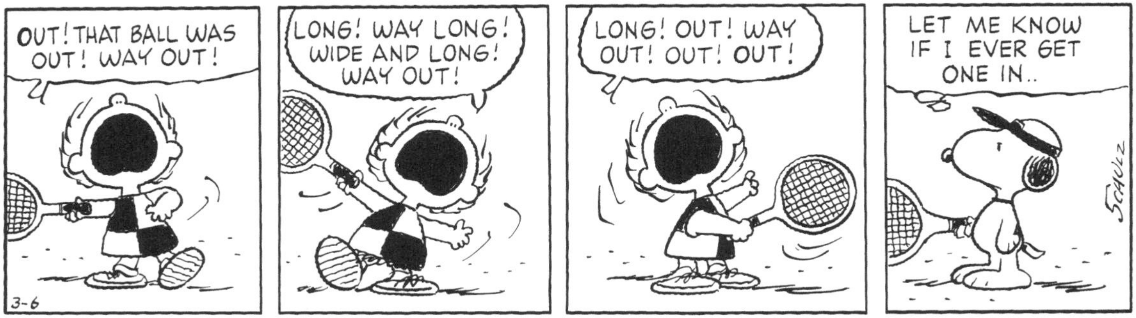

OUT! THAT BALL WAS OUT! WAY OUT!
LONG! WAY LONG! WIDE AND LONG! WAY OUT!
LONG! OUT! WAY OUT! OUT! OUT!
LET ME KNOW IF I EVER GET ONE IN..
3-6
SCHULZ

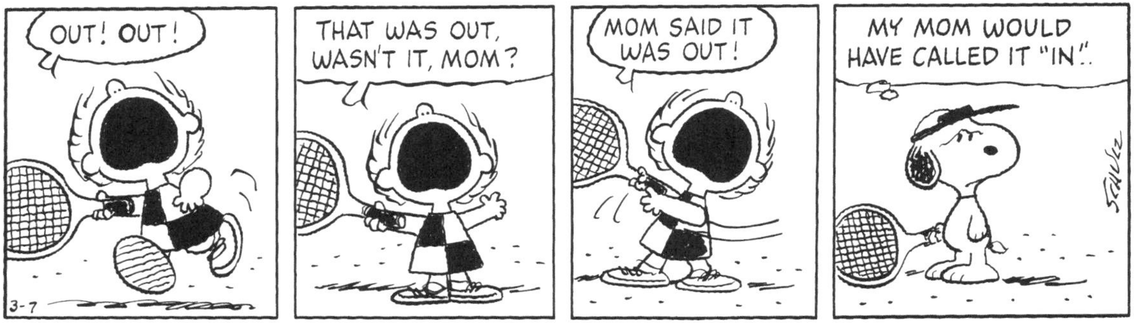

OUT! OUT!
THAT WAS OUT, WASN'T IT, MOM?
MOM SAID IT WAS OUT!
MY MOM WOULD HAVE CALLED IT "IN".
3-7
SCHULZ

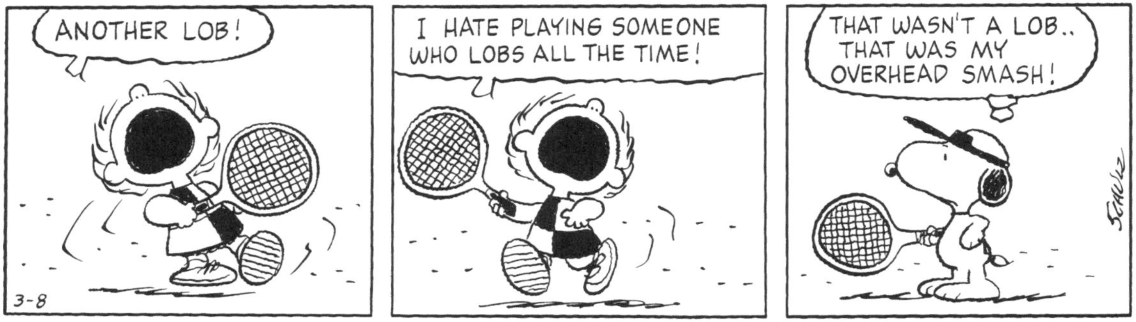

ANOTHER LOB!
I HATE PLAYING SOMEONE WHO LOBS ALL THE TIME!
THAT WASN'T A LOB.. THAT WAS MY OVERHEAD SMASH!
3-8
SCHULZ

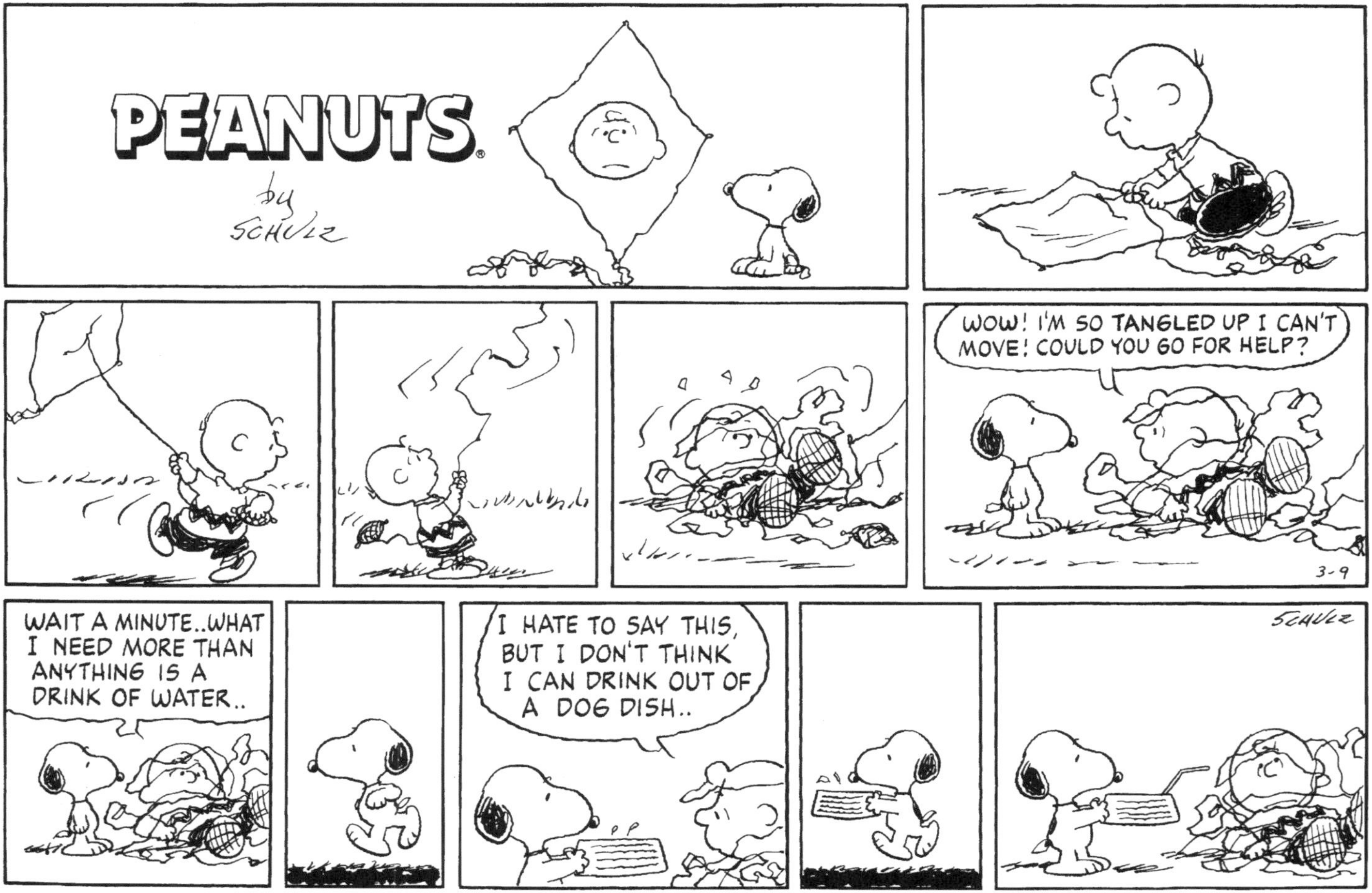
PEANUTS
by SCHULZ
WOW! I'M SO TANGLED UP I CAN'T MOVE! COULD YOU GO FOR HELP?
3-9
WAIT A MINUTE..WHAT I NEED MORE THAN ANYTHING IS A DRINK OF WATER..
I HATE TO SAY THIS, BUT I DON'T THINK I CAN DRINK OUT OF A DOG DISH..
SCHULZ

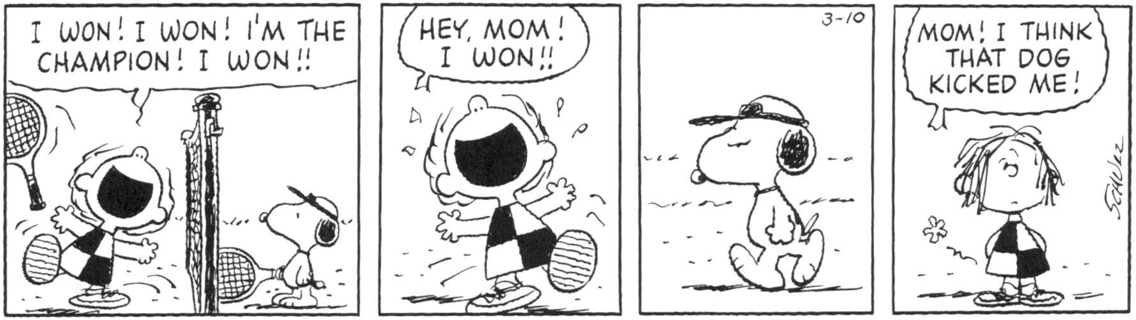
I WON! I WON! I'M THE CHAMPION! I WON!!
HEY, MOM! I WON!!
3-10
MOM! I THINK THAT DOG KICKED ME!
SCHULZ

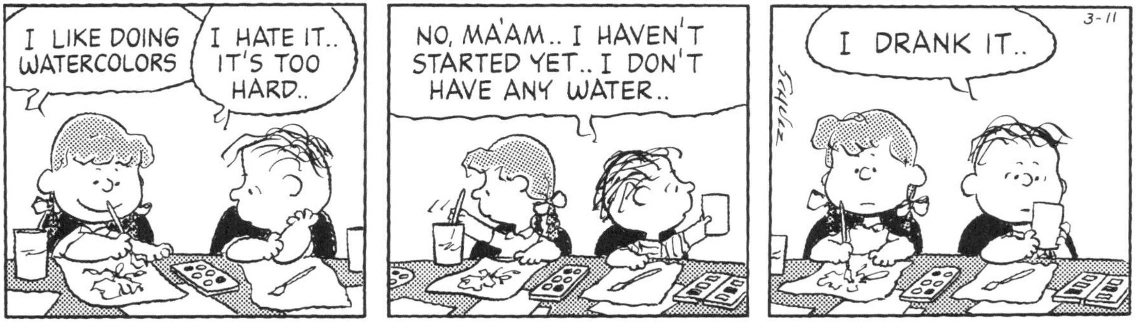
I LIKE DOING WATERCOLORS
I HATE IT.. IT'S TOO HARD..
NO, MA'AM.. I HAVEN'T STARTED YET.. I DON'T HAVE ANY WATER..
3-11
SCHULZ
I DRANK IT..

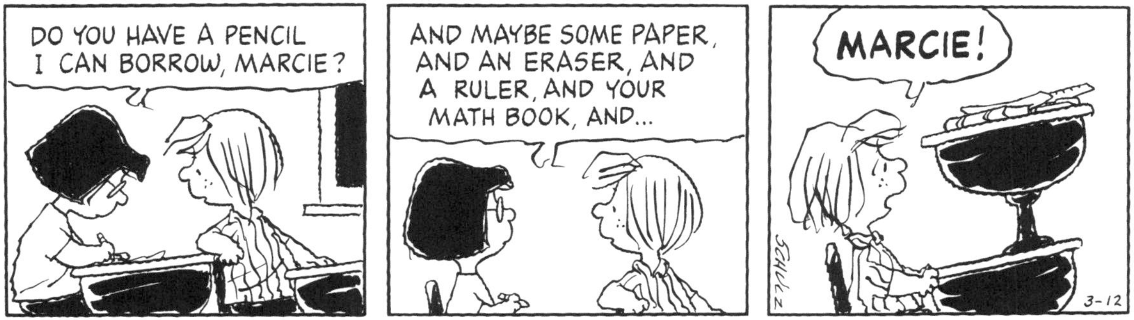
DO YOU HAVE A PENCIL I CAN BORROW, MARCIE?
AND MAYBE SOME PAPER, AND AN ERASER, AND A RULER, AND YOUR MATH BOOK, AND...
MARCIE!
SCHULZ
3-12

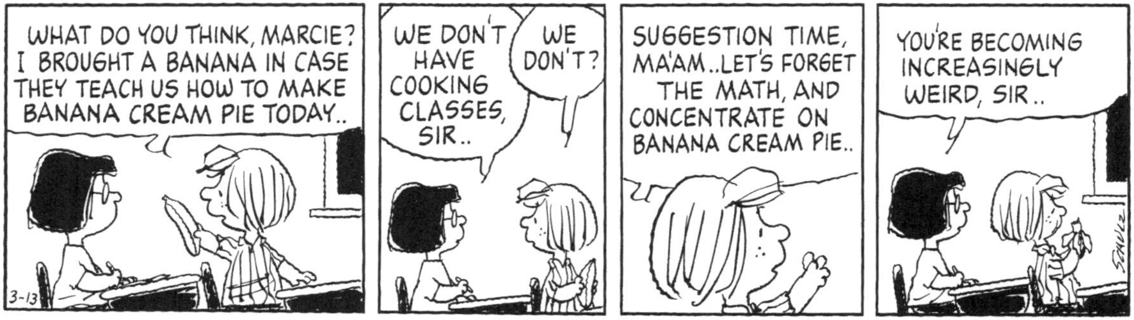
WHAT DO YOU THINK, MARCIE? I BROUGHT A BANANA IN CASE THEY TEACH US HOW TO MAKE BANANA CREAM PIE TODAY..
3-13
WE DON'T HAVE COOKING CLASSES, SIR..
WE DON'T?
SUGGESTION TIME, MA'AM..LET'S FORGET THE MATH, AND CONCENTRATE ON BANANA CREAM PIE..
YOU'RE BECOMING INCREASINGLY WEIRD, SIR..
SCHULZ

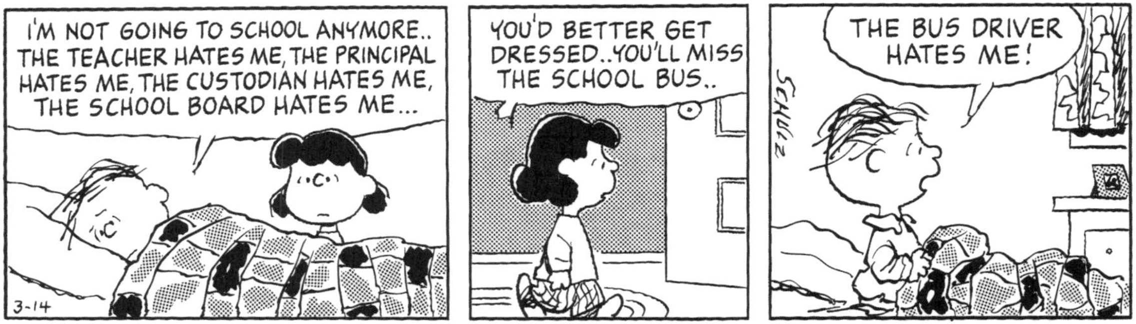
I'M NOT GOING TO SCHOOL ANYMORE.. THE TEACHER HATES ME, THE PRINCIPAL HATES ME, THE CUSTODIAN HATES ME, THE SCHOOL BOARD HATES ME...
3-14
YOU'D BETTER GET DRESSED..YOU'LL MISS THE SCHOOL BUS..
SCHULZ
THE BUS DRIVER HATES ME!

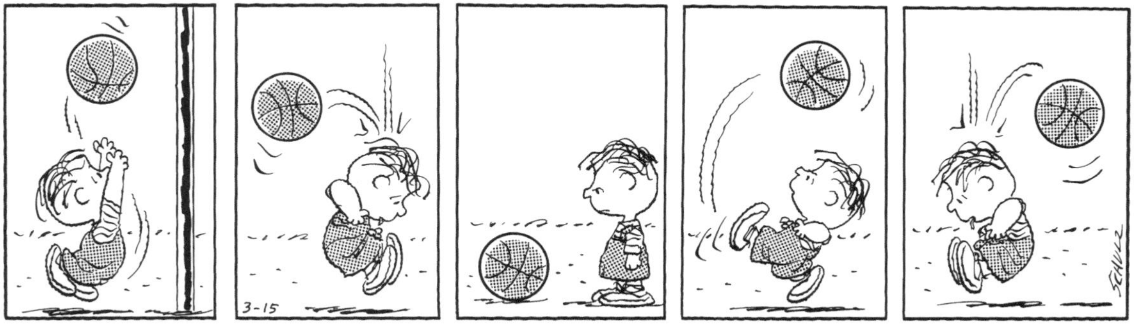
3-15
SCHULZ

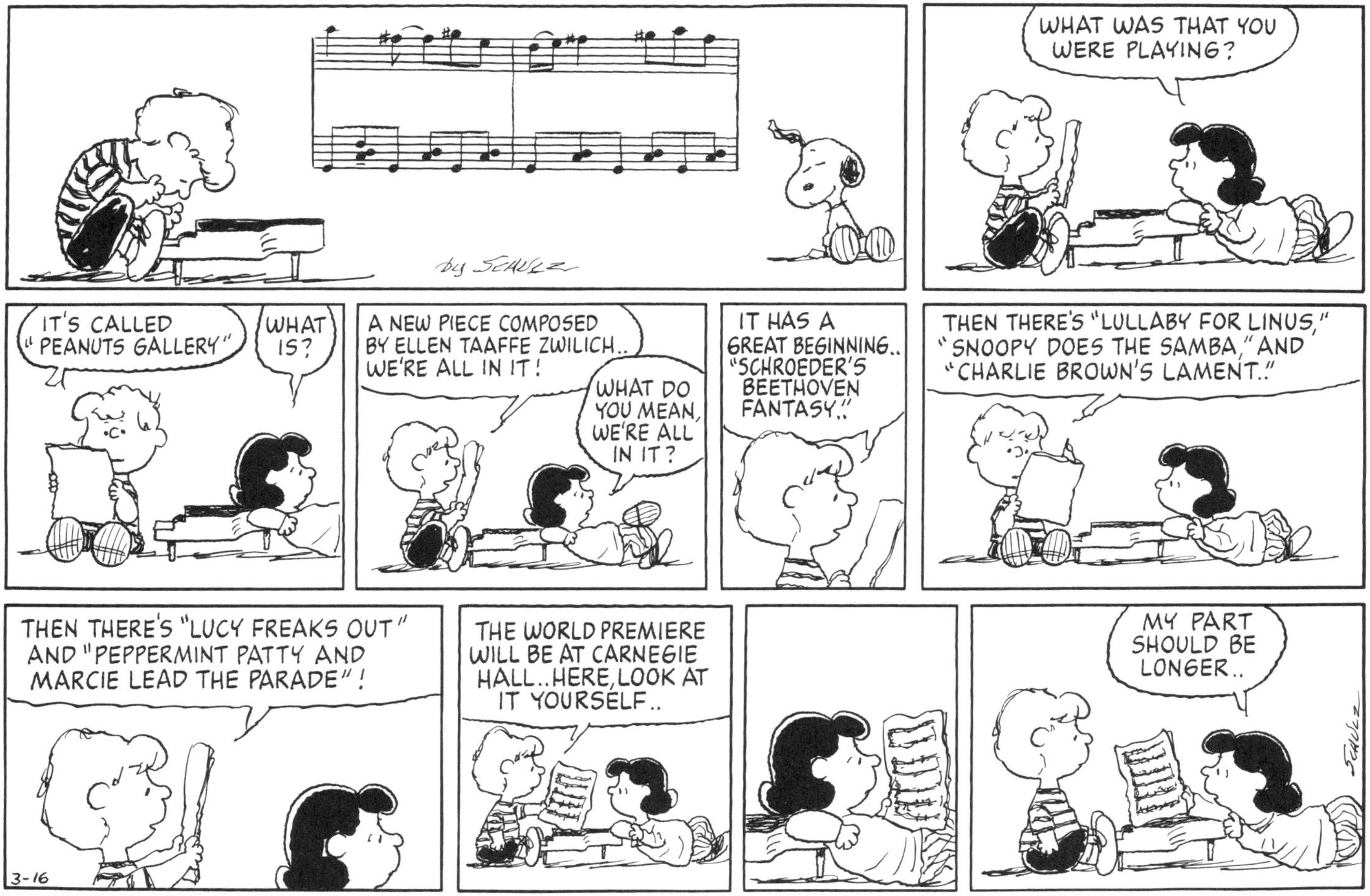
by SCHULZ
WHAT WAS THAT YOU WERE PLAYING?
IT'S CALLED "PEANUTS GALLERY"
WHAT IS?
A NEW PIECE COMPOSED BY ELLEN TAAFFE ZWILICH.. WE'RE ALL IN IT!
WHAT DO YOU MEAN, WE'RE ALL IN IT?
IT HAS A GREAT BEGINNING.. "SCHROEDER'S BEETHOVEN FANTASY.."
THEN THERE'S "LULLABY FOR LINUS," "SNOOPY DOES THE SAMBA," AND "CHARLIE BROWN'S LAMENT.."
THEN THERE'S "LUCY FREAKS OUT" AND "PEPPERMINT PATTY AND MARCIE LEAD THE PARADE"!
3-16
THE WORLD PREMIERE WILL BE AT CARNEGIE HALL..HERE, LOOK AT IT YOURSELF..
MY PART SHOULD BE LONGER..
SCHULZ

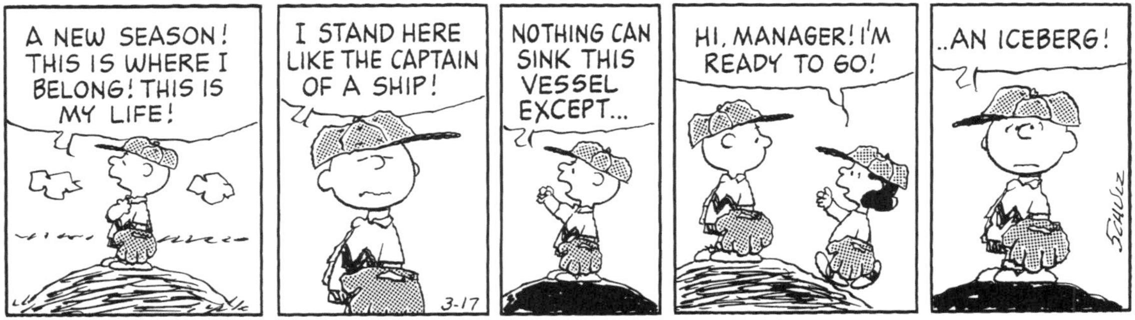
A NEW SEASON! THIS IS WHERE I BELONG! THIS IS MY LIFE!
I STAND HERE LIKE THE CAPTAIN OF A SHIP!
3-17
NOTHING CAN SINK THIS VESSEL EXCEPT...
HI, MANAGER! I'M READY TO GO!
..AN ICEBERG!
SCHULZ

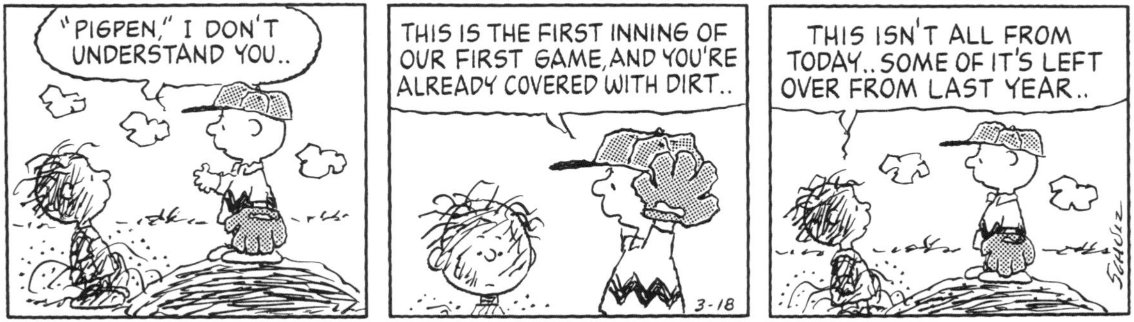
"PIGPEN," I DON'T UNDERSTAND YOU..
THIS IS THE FIRST INNING OF OUR FIRST GAME, AND YOU'RE ALREADY COVERED WITH DIRT..
3-18
THIS ISN'T ALL FROM TODAY.. SOME OF IT'S LEFT OVER FROM LAST YEAR..
SCHULZ

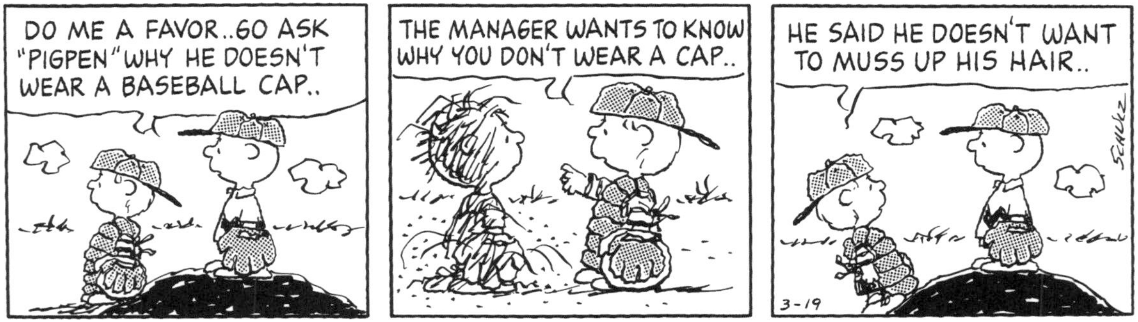
DO ME A FAVOR..GO ASK "PIGPEN" WHY HE DOESN'T WEAR A BASEBALL CAP..
THE MANAGER WANTS TO KNOW WHY YOU DON'T WEAR A CAP..
HE SAID HE DOESN'T WANT TO MUSS UP HIS HAIR..
SCHULZ
3-19

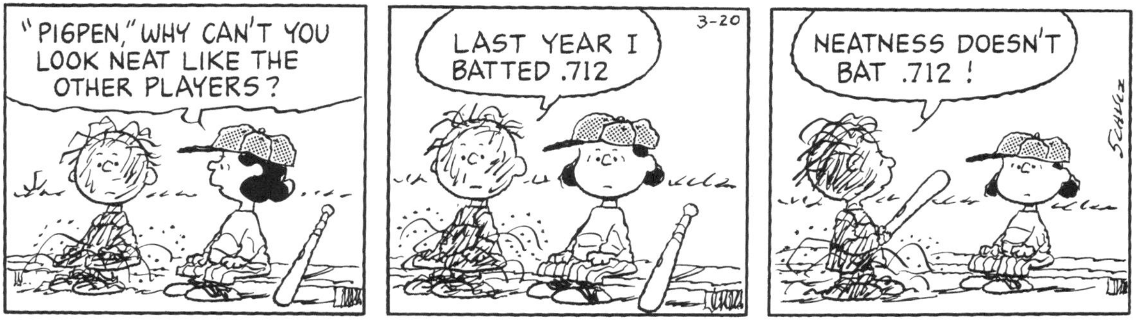

3-20
"PIGPEN," WHY CAN'T YOU LOOK NEAT LIKE THE OTHER PLAYERS?
LAST YEAR I BATTED .712
NEATNESS DOESN'T BAT .712 !
SCHULZ

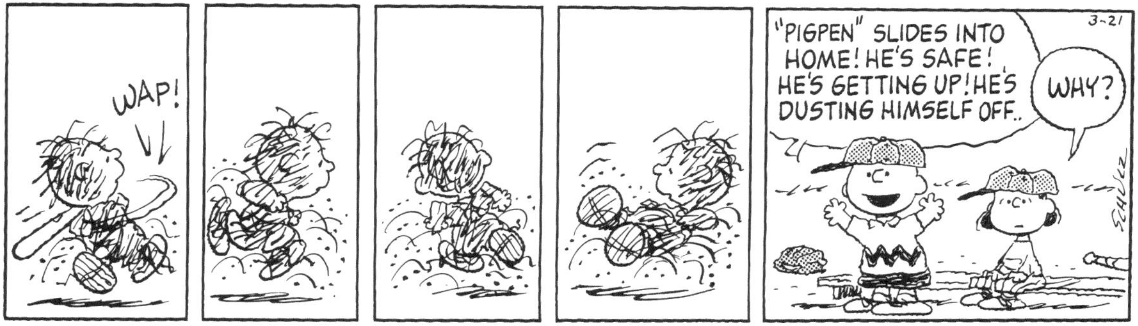

WAP!
3-21
"PIGPEN" SLIDES INTO HOME! HE'S SAFE! HE'S GETTING UP! HE'S DUSTING HIMSELF OFF..
WHY?
SCHULZ

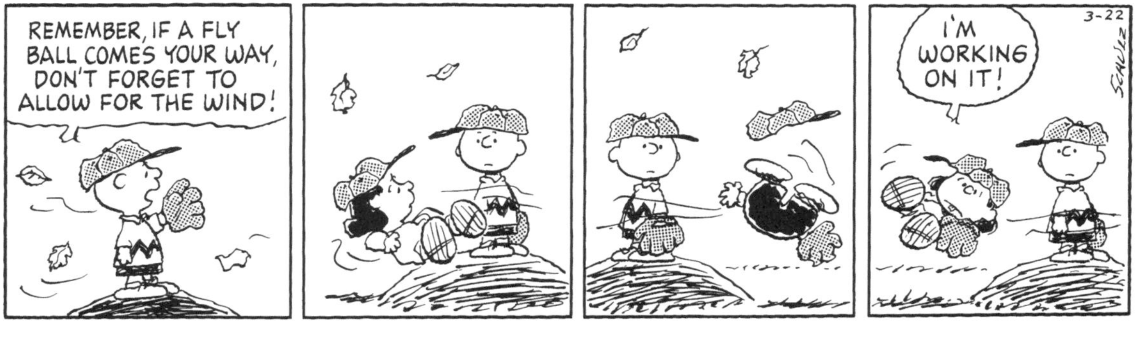

REMEMBER, IF A FLY BALL COMES YOUR WAY, DON'T FORGET TO ALLOW FOR THE WIND!
3-22
I'M WORKING ON IT!
SCHULZ

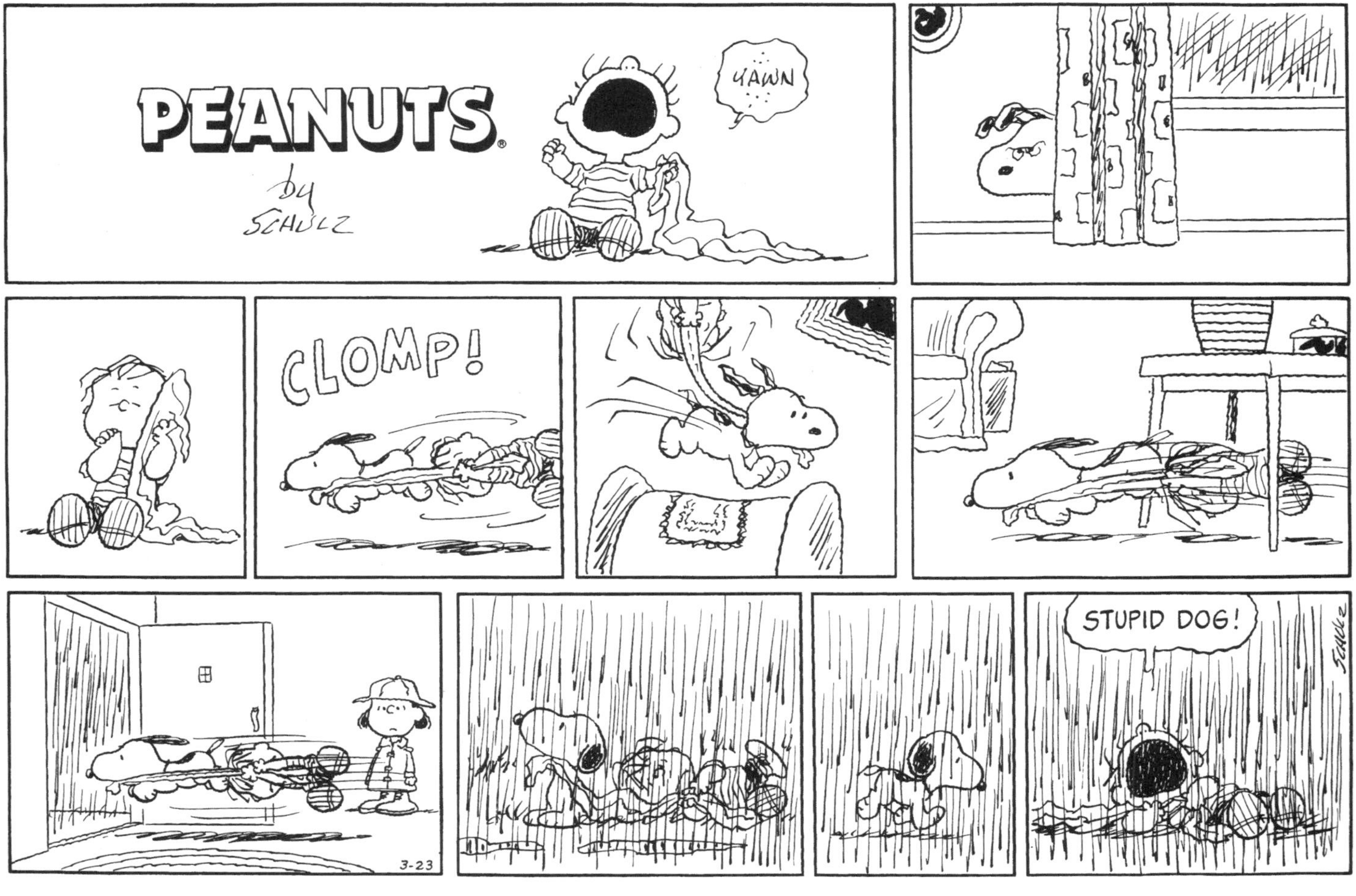
PEANUTS
by SCHULZ
YAWN
CLOMP!
3-23
STUPID DOG!
SCHULZ

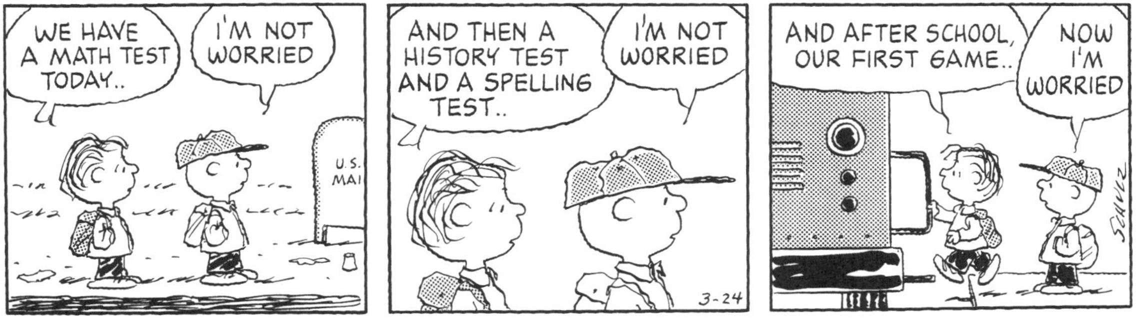
WE HAVE A MATH TEST TODAY..
I'M NOT WORRIED
U.S. MAI
AND THEN A HISTORY TEST AND A SPELLING TEST..
I'M NOT WORRIED
3-24
AND AFTER SCHOOL, OUR FIRST GAME..
NOW I'M WORRIED
SCHULZ

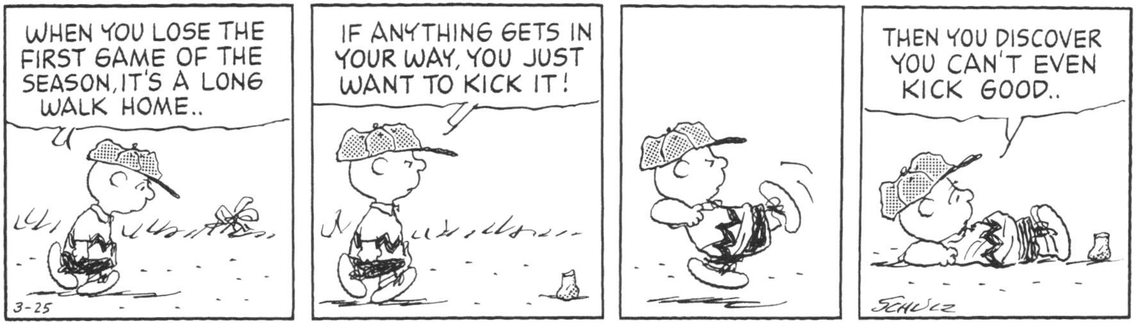
WHEN YOU LOSE THE FIRST GAME OF THE SEASON, IT'S A LONG WALK HOME..
3-25
IF ANYTHING GETS IN YOUR WAY, YOU JUST WANT TO KICK IT!
THEN YOU DISCOVER YOU CAN'T EVEN KICK GOOD..
SCHULZ

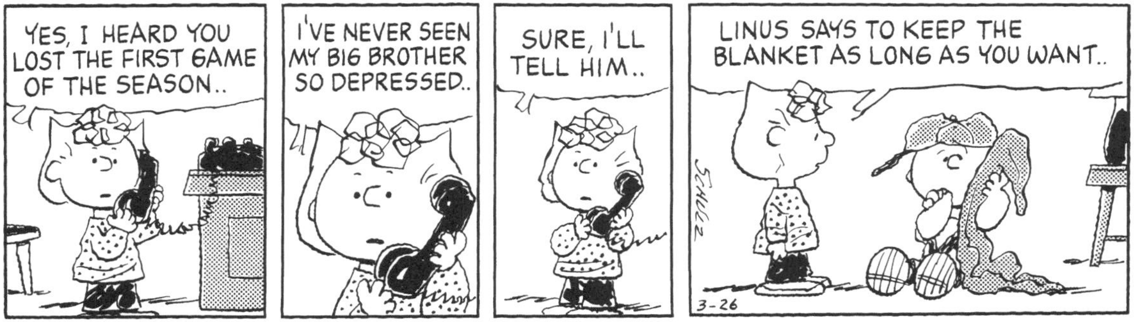
YES, I HEARD YOU LOST THE FIRST GAME OF THE SEASON..
I'VE NEVER SEEN MY BIG BROTHER SO DEPRESSED..
SURE, I'LL TELL HIM..
LINUS SAYS TO KEEP THE BLANKET AS LONG AS YOU WANT..
SCHULZ
3-26

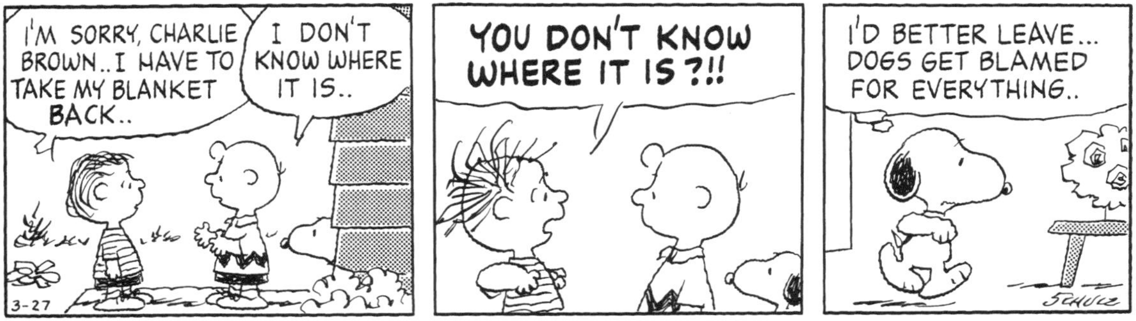
I'M SORRY, CHARLIE BROWN.. I HAVE TO TAKE MY BLANKET BACK..
I DON'T KNOW WHERE IT IS..
3-27
YOU DON'T KNOW WHERE IT IS?!!
I'D BETTER LEAVE... DOGS GET BLAMED FOR EVERYTHING..
SCHULZ

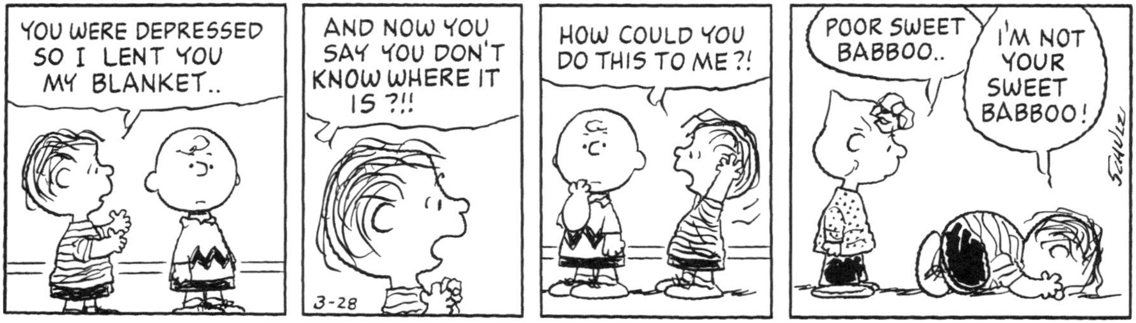
YOU WERE DEPRESSED SO I LENT YOU MY BLANKET..
AND NOW YOU SAY YOU DON'T KNOW WHERE IT IS?!!
3-28
HOW COULD YOU DO THIS TO ME?!
POOR SWEET BABBOO..
I'M NOT YOUR SWEET BABBOO!
SCHULZ

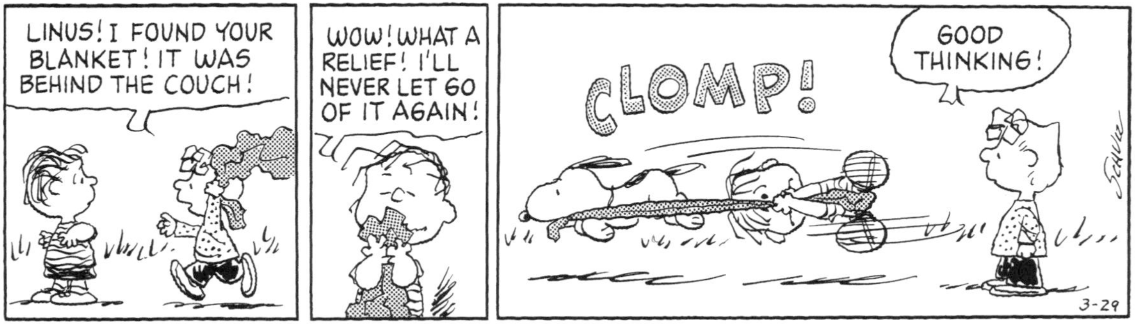
LINUS! I FOUND YOUR BLANKET! IT WAS BEHIND THE COUCH!
WOW! WHAT A RELIEF! I'LL NEVER LET GO OF IT AGAIN!
CLOMP!
GOOD THINKING!
SCHULZ
3-29

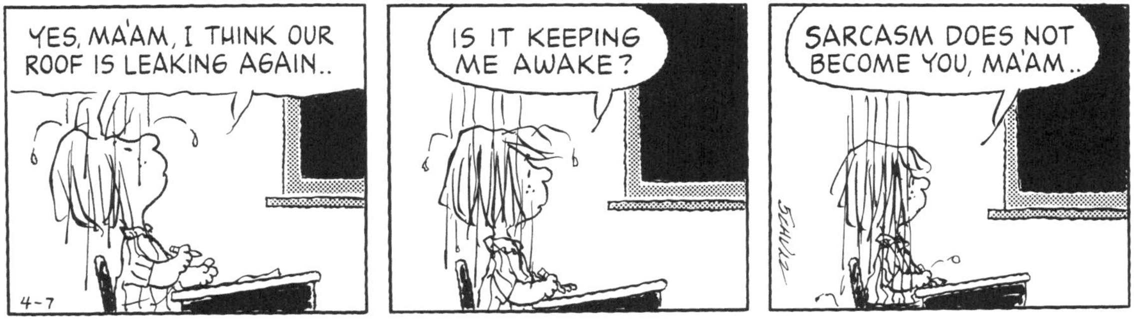
YES, MA'AM, I THINK OUR ROOF IS LEAKING AGAIN..
4-7
IS IT KEEPING ME AWAKE?
SARCASM DOES NOT BECOME YOU, MA'AM..
SCHULZ

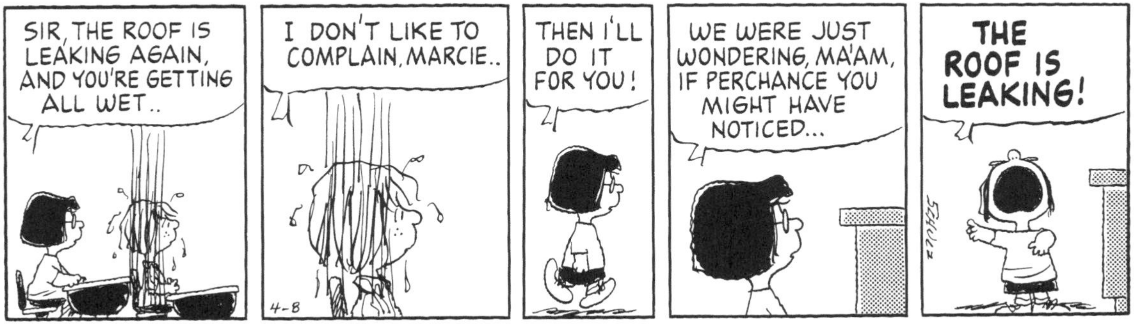
SIR, THE ROOF IS LEAKING AGAIN, AND YOU'RE GETTING ALL WET..
I DON'T LIKE TO COMPLAIN, MARCIE..
4-8
THEN I'LL DO IT FOR YOU!
WE WERE JUST WONDERING, MA'AM, IF PERCHANCE YOU MIGHT HAVE NOTICED...
THE ROOF IS LEAKING!
SCHULZ

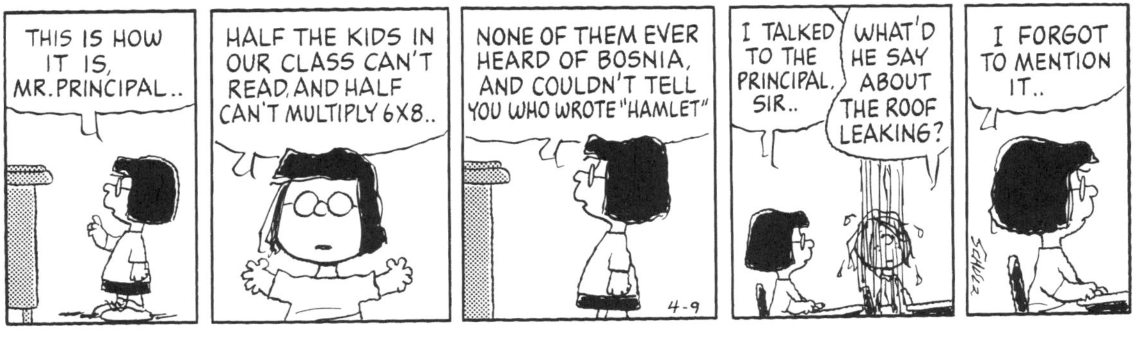
THIS IS HOW IT IS, MR. PRINCIPAL..
HALF THE KIDS IN OUR CLASS CAN'T READ, AND HALF CAN'T MULTIPLY 6X8..
NONE OF THEM EVER HEARD OF BOSNIA, AND COULDN'T TELL YOU WHO WROTE "HAMLET"
4-9
I TALKED TO THE PRINCIPAL, SIR..
WHAT'D HE SAY ABOUT THE ROOF LEAKING?
I FORGOT TO MENTION IT..
SCHULZ

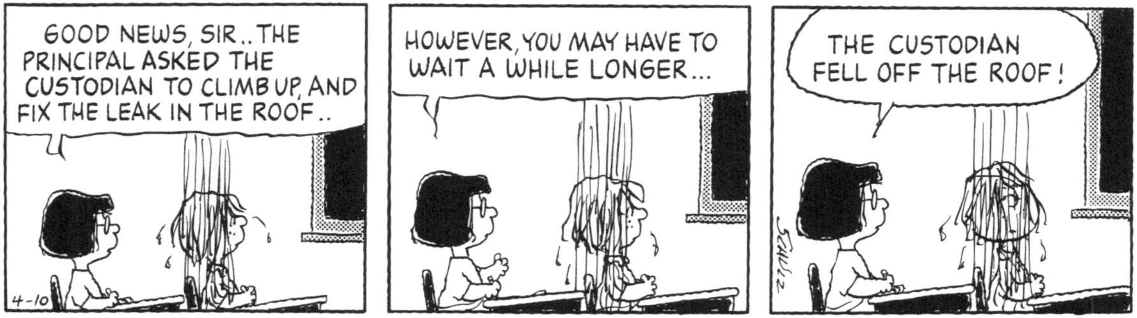
GOOD NEWS, SIR.. THE PRINCIPAL ASKED THE CUSTODIAN TO CLIMB UP, AND FIX THE LEAK IN THE ROOF..
4-10
HOWEVER, YOU MAY HAVE TO WAIT A WHILE LONGER...
THE CUSTODIAN FELL OFF THE ROOF!

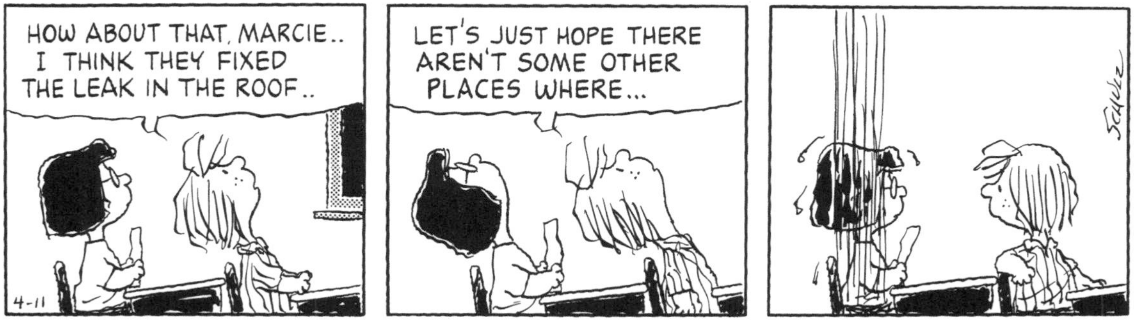
HOW ABOUT THAT, MARCIE.. I THINK THEY FIXED THE LEAK IN THE ROOF..
4-11
LET'S JUST HOPE THERE AREN'T SOME OTHER PLACES WHERE...

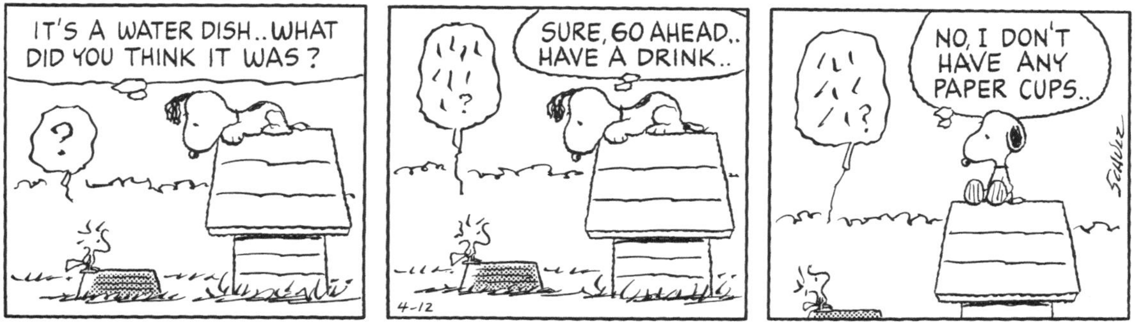
IT'S A WATER DISH.. WHAT DID YOU THINK IT WAS?
?
SURE, GO AHEAD.. HAVE A DRINK..
4-12
NO, I DON'T HAVE ANY PAPER CUPS..

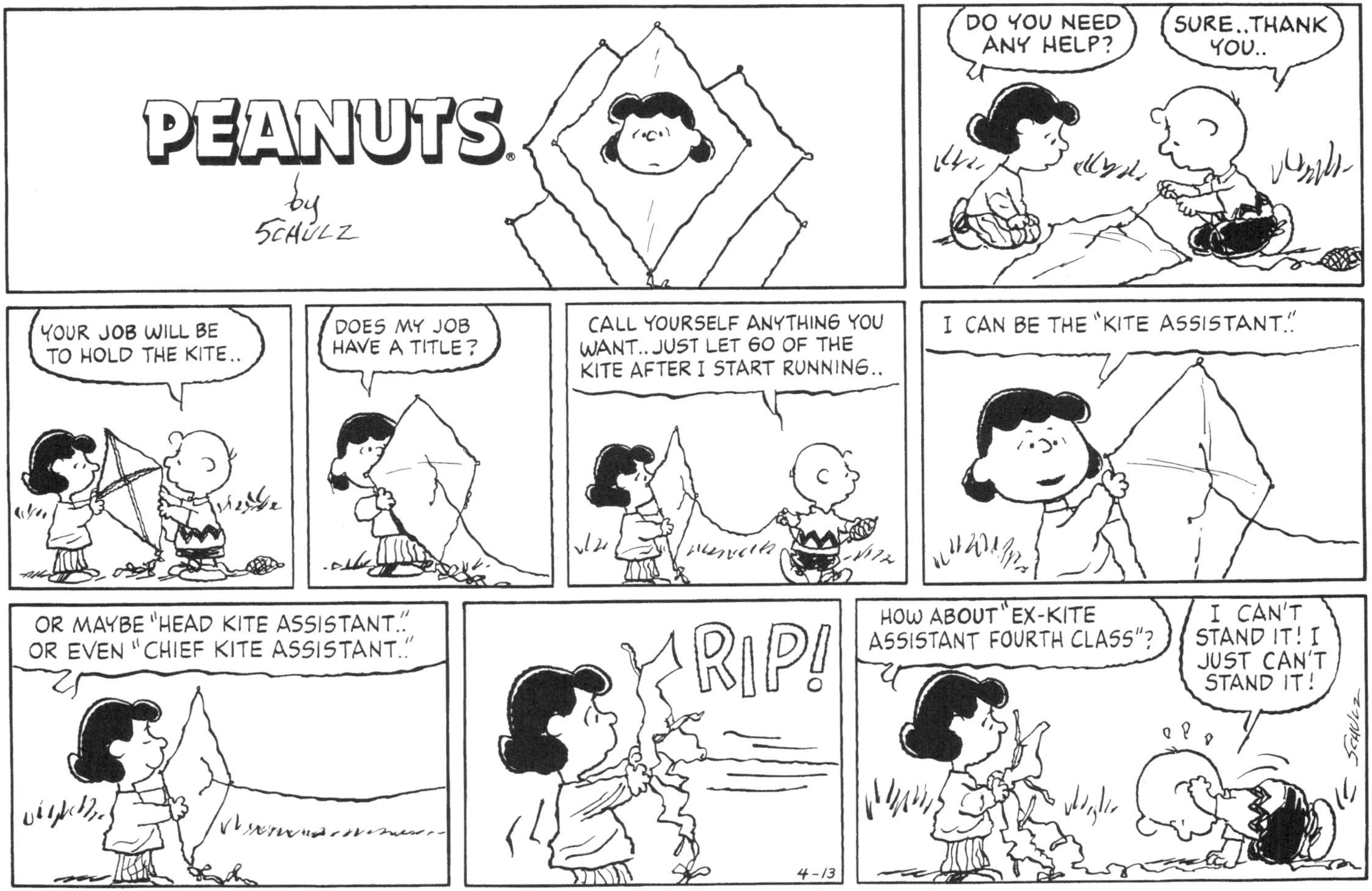
PEANUTS
by SCHULZ
DO YOU NEED ANY HELP?
SURE..THANK YOU..
YOUR JOB WILL BE TO HOLD THE KITE..
DOES MY JOB HAVE A TITLE?
CALL YOURSELF ANYTHING YOU WANT..JUST LET GO OF THE KITE AFTER I START RUNNING..
I CAN BE THE "KITE ASSISTANT."
OR MAYBE "HEAD KITE ASSISTANT." OR EVEN "CHIEF KITE ASSISTANT."
RIP!
4-13
HOW ABOUT "EX-KITE ASSISTANT FOURTH CLASS"?
I CAN'T STAND IT! I JUST CAN'T STAND IT!
SCHULZ

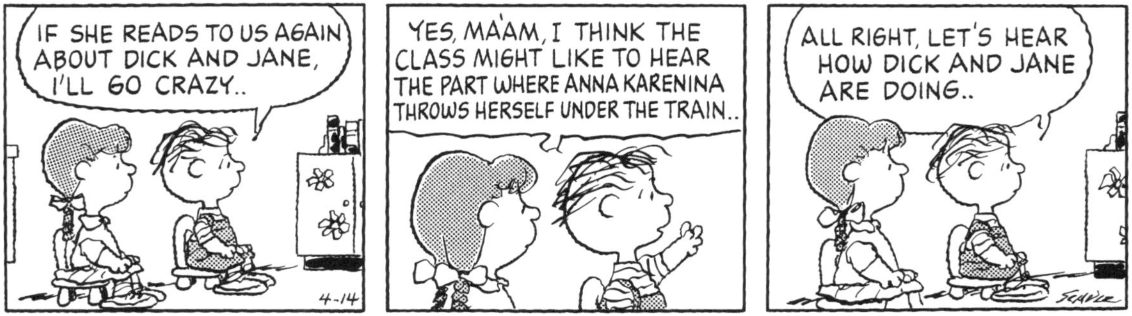
IF SHE READS TO US AGAIN ABOUT DICK AND JANE, I'LL GO CRAZY..
4-14
YES, MA'AM, I THINK THE CLASS MIGHT LIKE TO HEAR THE PART WHERE ANNA KARENINA THROWS HERSELF UNDER THE TRAIN..
ALL RIGHT, LET'S HEAR HOW DICK AND JANE ARE DOING..

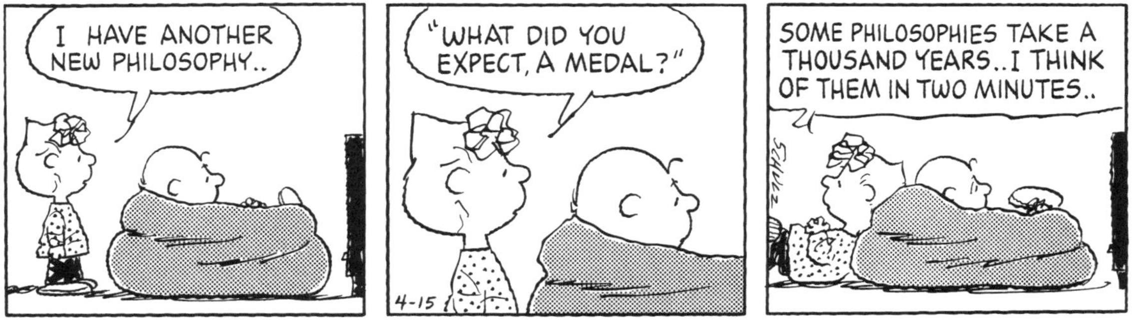
I HAVE ANOTHER NEW PHILOSOPHY..
"WHAT DID YOU EXPECT, A MEDAL?"
4-15
SOME PHILOSOPHIES TAKE A THOUSAND YEARS..I THINK OF THEM IN TWO MINUTES..

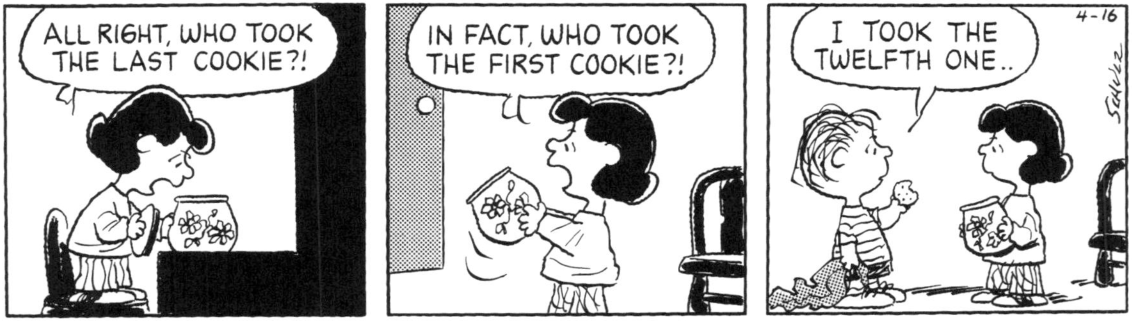
ALL RIGHT, WHO TOOK THE LAST COOKIE?!
IN FACT, WHO TOOK THE FIRST COOKIE?!
4-16
I TOOK THE TWELFTH ONE..

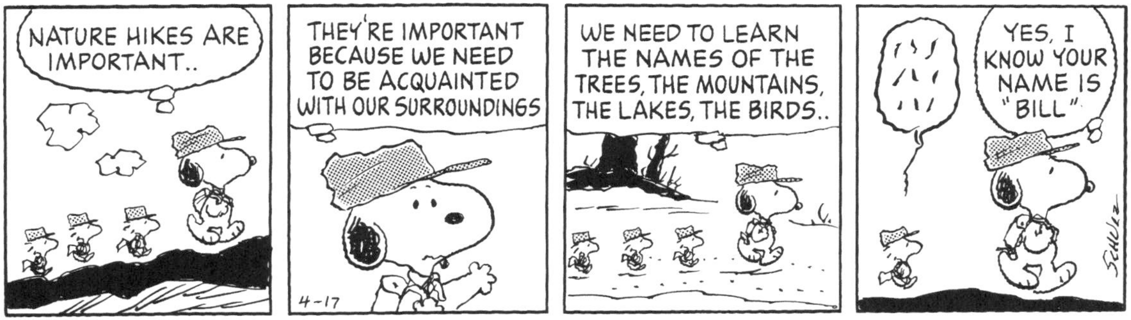
NATURE HIKES ARE IMPORTANT..
THEY'RE IMPORTANT BECAUSE WE NEED TO BE ACQUAINTED WITH OUR SURROUNDINGS
4-17
WE NEED TO LEARN THE NAMES OF THE TREES, THE MOUNTAINS, THE LAKES, THE BIRDS..
YES, I KNOW YOUR NAME IS "BILL"
SCHULZ

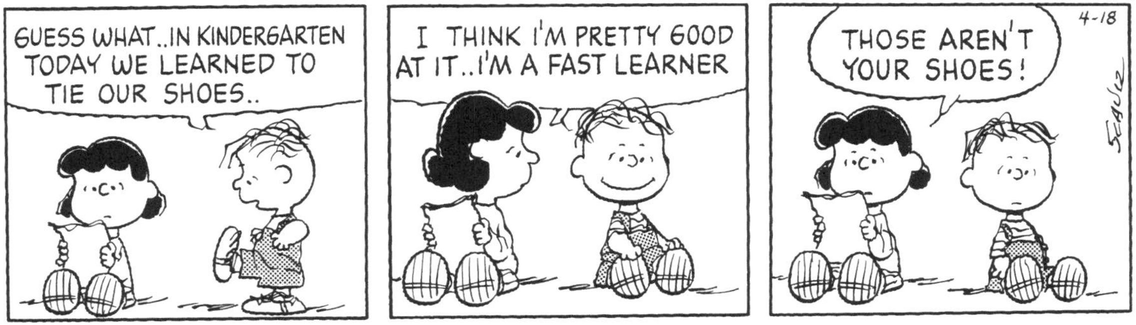
GUESS WHAT..IN KINDERGARTEN TODAY WE LEARNED TO TIE OUR SHOES..
I THINK I'M PRETTY GOOD AT IT..I'M A FAST LEARNER
THOSE AREN'T YOUR SHOES!
4-18
SCHULZ

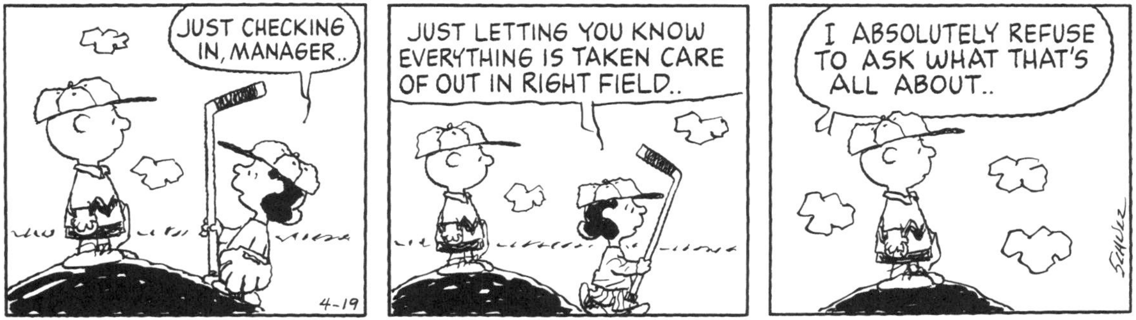
JUST CHECKING IN, MANAGER..
4-19
JUST LETTING YOU KNOW EVERYTHING IS TAKEN CARE OF OUT IN RIGHT FIELD..
I ABSOLUTELY REFUSE TO ASK WHAT THAT'S ALL ABOUT..
SCHULZ

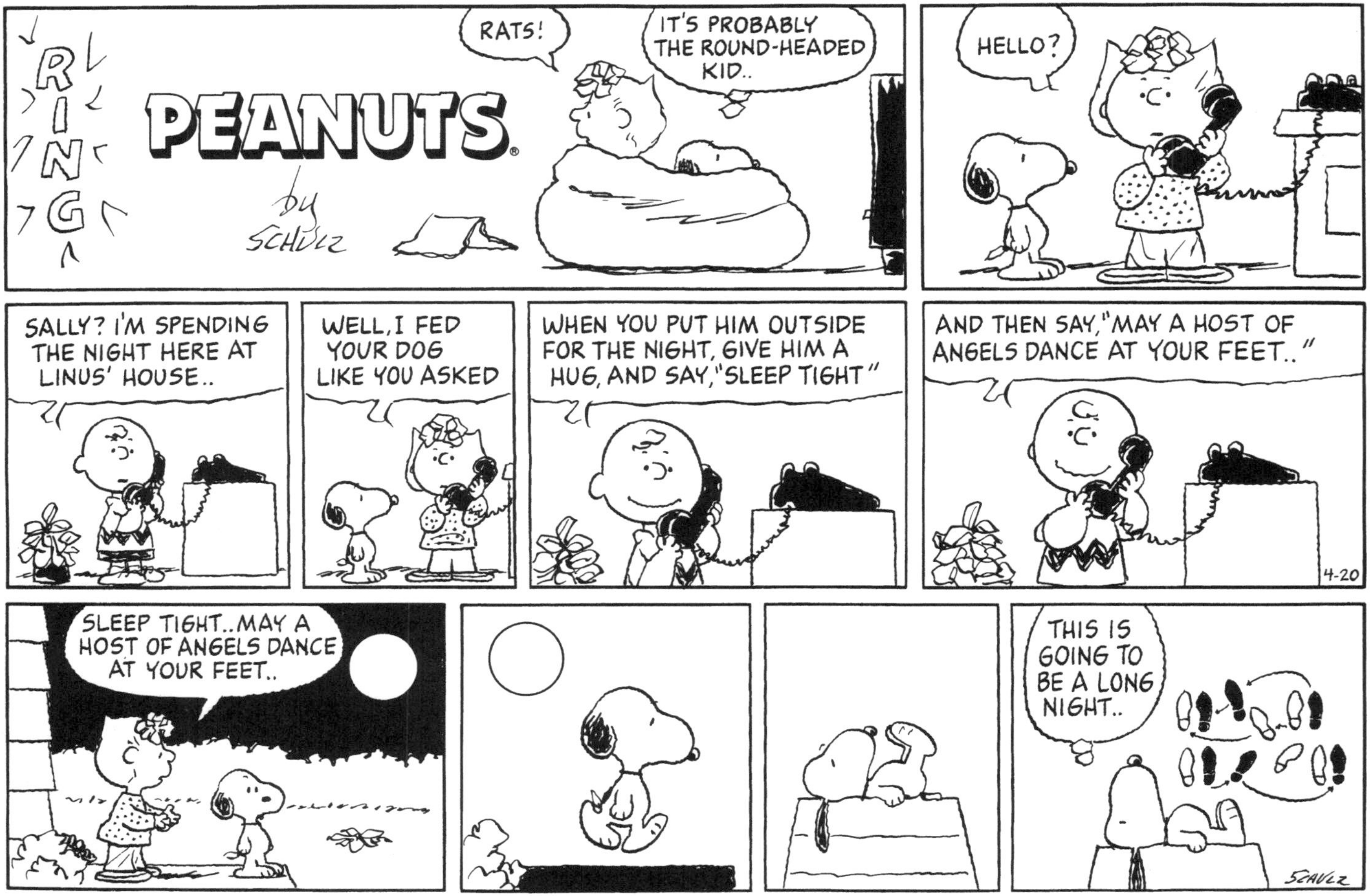
RING
PEANUTS
by SCHULZ
RATS!
IT'S PROBABLY THE ROUND-HEADED KID..
HELLO?
SALLY? I'M SPENDING THE NIGHT HERE AT LINUS' HOUSE..
WELL, I FED YOUR DOG LIKE YOU ASKED
WHEN YOU PUT HIM OUTSIDE FOR THE NIGHT, GIVE HIM A HUG, AND SAY, "SLEEP TIGHT"
AND THEN SAY, "MAY A HOST OF ANGELS DANCE AT YOUR FEET.."
4-20
SLEEP TIGHT..MAY A HOST OF ANGELS DANCE AT YOUR FEET..
THIS IS GOING TO BE A LONG NIGHT..
SCHULZ

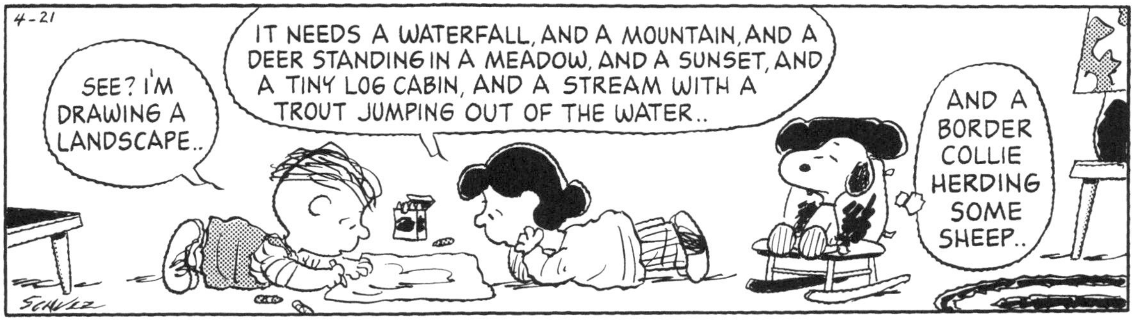
4-21
SEE? I'M DRAWING A LANDSCAPE..
IT NEEDS A WATERFALL, AND A MOUNTAIN, AND A DEER STANDING IN A MEADOW, AND A SUNSET, AND A TINY LOG CABIN, AND A STREAM WITH A TROUT JUMPING OUT OF THE WATER..
AND A BORDER COLLIE HERDING SOME SHEEP..

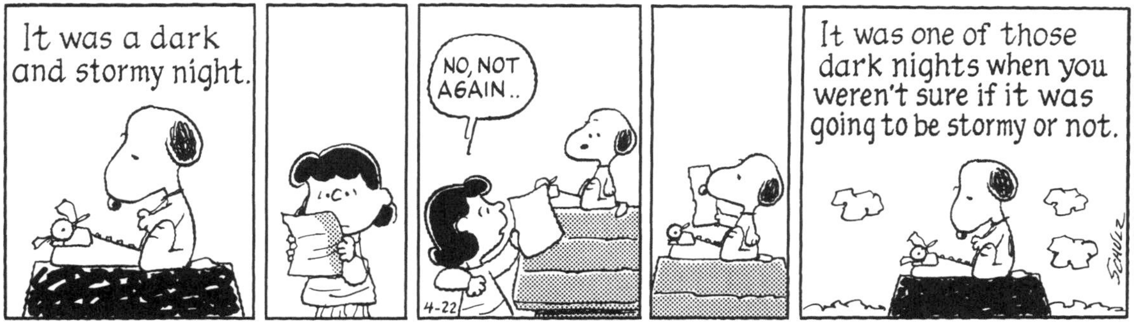
It was a dark and stormy night.
NO, NOT AGAIN..
4-22
It was one of those dark nights when you weren't sure if it was going to be stormy or not.

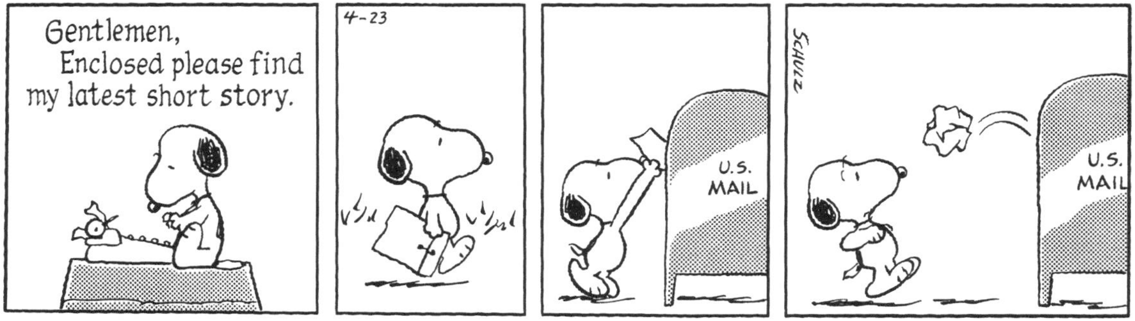
Gentlemen,
Enclosed please find my latest short story.
4-23
U.S. MAIL
U.S. MAIL

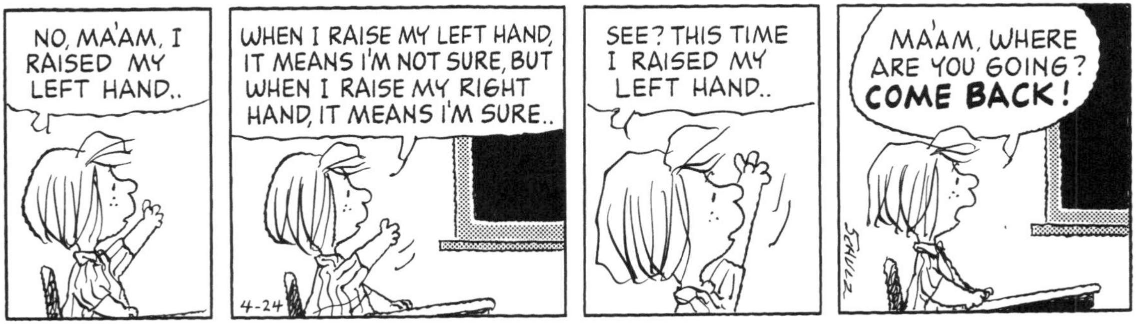
NO, MA'AM, I RAISED MY LEFT HAND..
WHEN I RAISE MY LEFT HAND, IT MEANS I'M NOT SURE, BUT WHEN I RAISE MY RIGHT HAND, IT MEANS I'M SURE..
4-24
SEE? THIS TIME I RAISED MY LEFT HAND..
MA'AM, WHERE ARE YOU GOING? COME BACK!

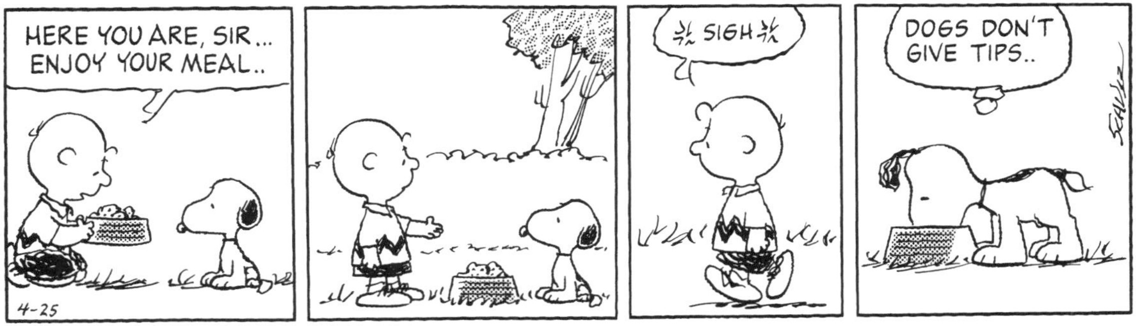
HERE YOU ARE, SIR... ENJOY YOUR MEAL..
4-25
SIGH
DOGS DON'T GIVE TIPS..

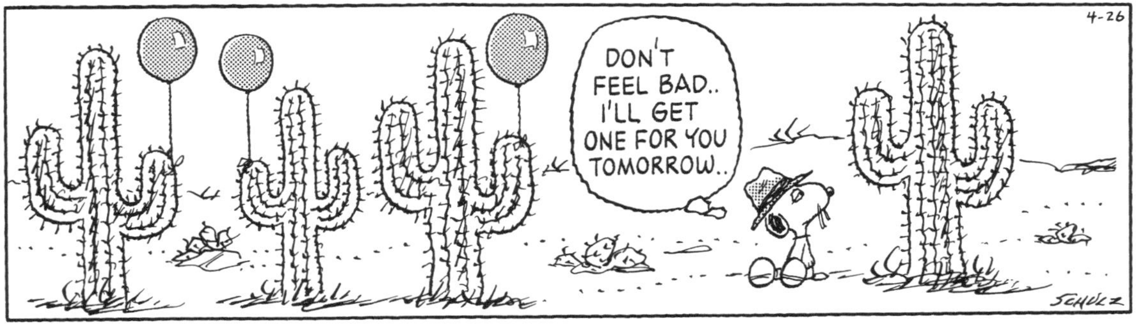
4-26
DON'T FEEL BAD.. I'LL GET ONE FOR YOU TOMORROW..

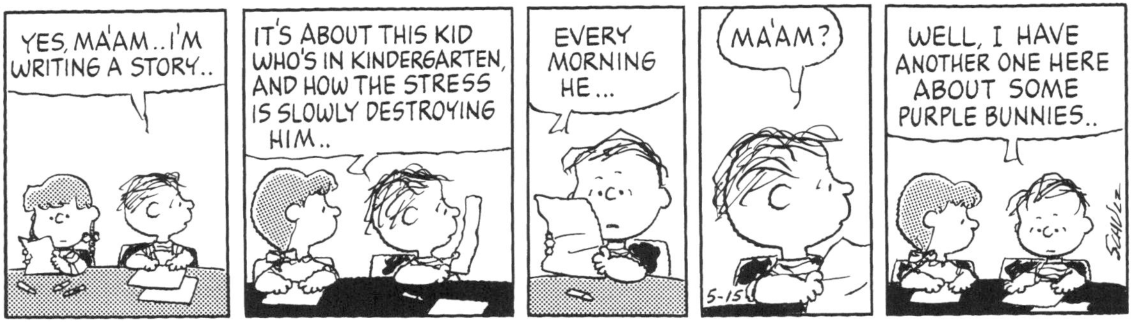
YES, MA'AM..I'M WRITING A STORY..
IT'S ABOUT THIS KID WHO'S IN KINDERGARTEN, AND HOW THE STRESS IS SLOWLY DESTROYING HIM..
EVERY MORNING HE...
MA'AM?
WELL, I HAVE ANOTHER ONE HERE ABOUT SOME PURPLE BUNNIES..

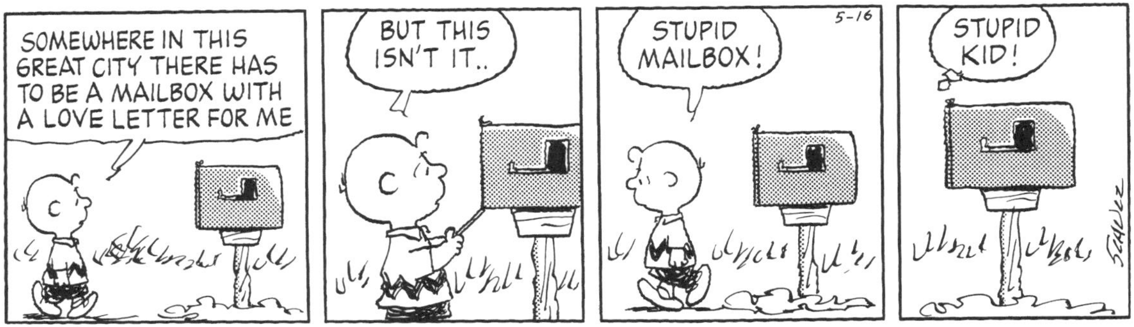
SOMEWHERE IN THIS GREAT CITY THERE HAS TO BE A MAILBOX WITH A LOVE LETTER FOR ME
BUT THIS ISN'T IT..
STUPID MAILBOX!
STUPID KID!

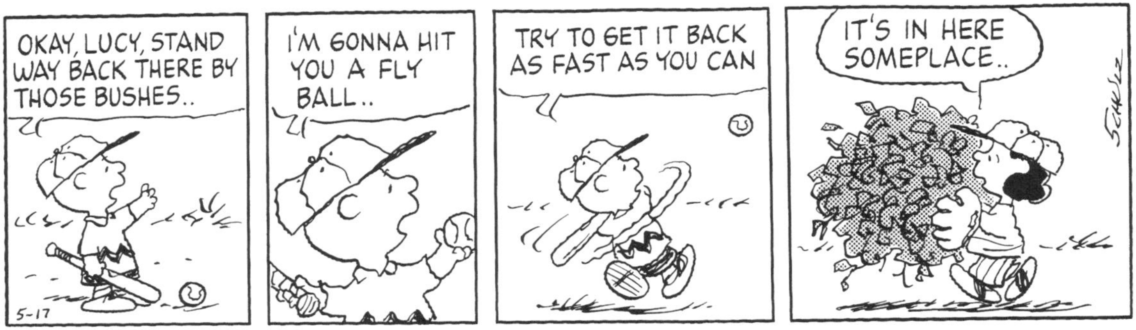
OKAY, LUCY, STAND WAY BACK THERE BY THOSE BUSHES..
I'M GONNA HIT YOU A FLY BALL..
TRY TO GET IT BACK AS FAST AS YOU CAN
IT'S IN HERE SOMEPLACE..

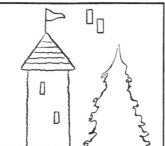

LIKE I'VE SAID BEFORE, NEVER TAKE A SHORTCUT THROUGH A MINIATURE GOLF COURSE..

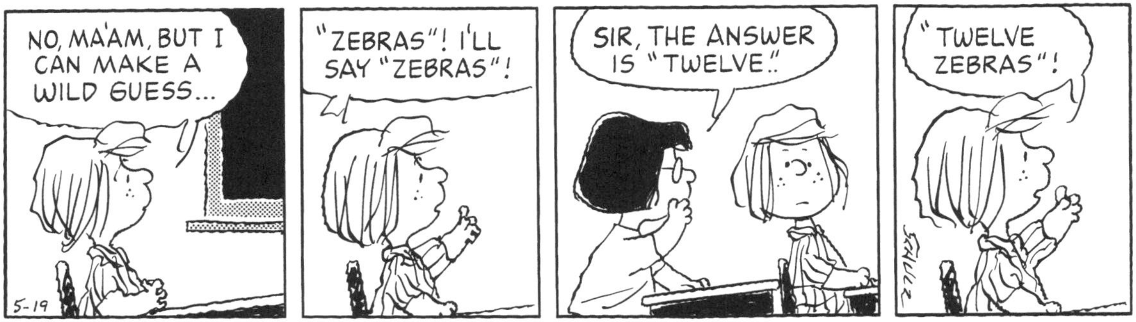
NO, MA'AM, BUT I CAN MAKE A WILD GUESS...
"ZEBRAS"! I'LL SAY "ZEBRAS"!
SIR, THE ANSWER IS "TWELVE."
"TWELVE ZEBRAS"!
5-19
SCHULZ

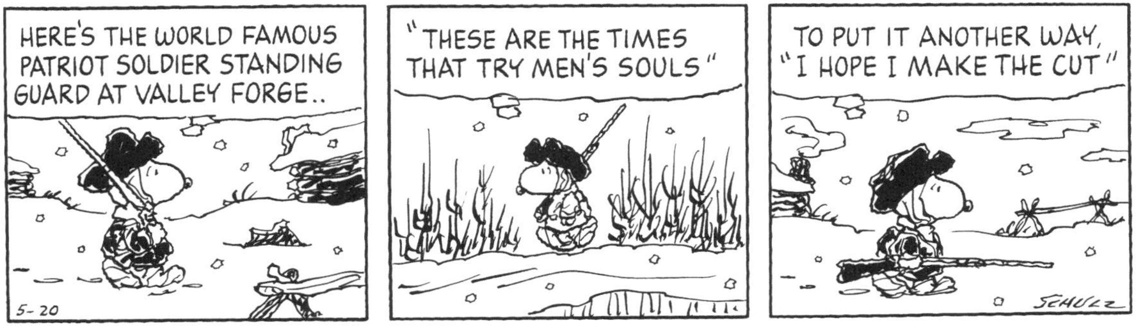
HERE'S THE WORLD FAMOUS PATRIOT SOLDIER STANDING GUARD AT VALLEY FORGE..
"THESE ARE THE TIMES THAT TRY MEN'S SOULS"
TO PUT IT ANOTHER WAY, "I HOPE I MAKE THE CUT"
5-20
SCHULZ

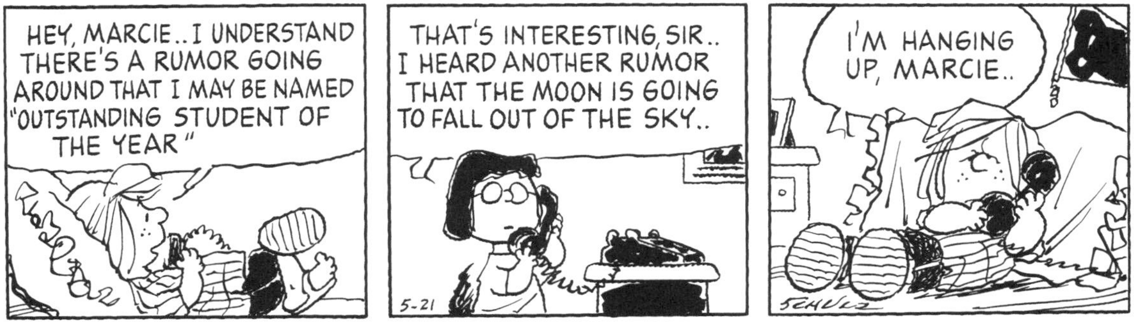
HEY, MARCIE..I UNDERSTAND THERE'S A RUMOR GOING AROUND THAT I MAY BE NAMED "OUTSTANDING STUDENT OF THE YEAR"
THAT'S INTERESTING, SIR.. I HEARD ANOTHER RUMOR THAT THE MOON IS GOING TO FALL OUT OF THE SKY..
I'M HANGING UP, MARCIE..
5-21
SCHULZ

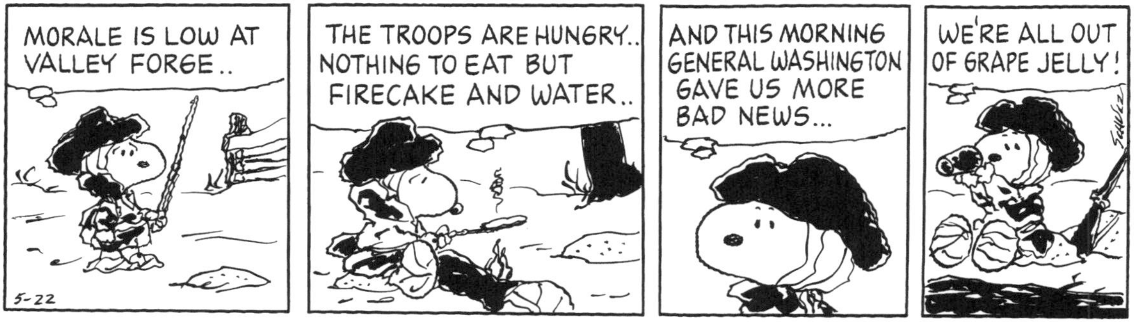
MORALE IS LOW AT VALLEY FORGE..
5-22
THE TROOPS ARE HUNGRY.. NOTHING TO EAT BUT FIRECAKE AND WATER..
AND THIS MORNING GENERAL WASHINGTON GAVE US MORE BAD NEWS...
WE'RE ALL OUT OF GRAPE JELLY!

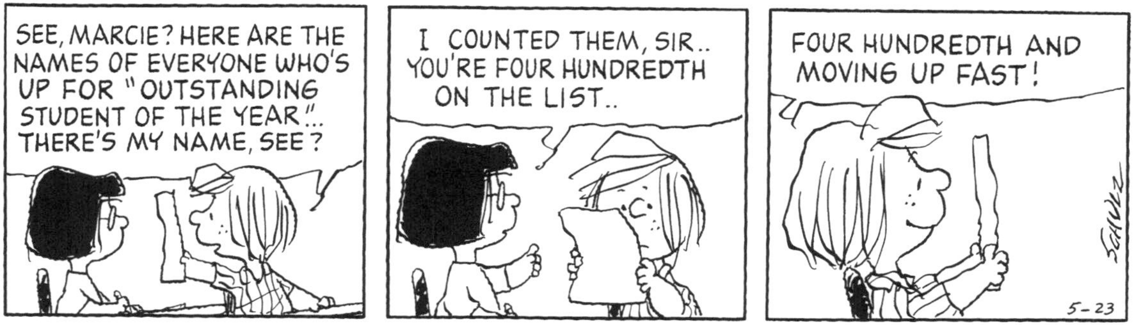
SEE, MARCIE? HERE ARE THE NAMES OF EVERYONE WHO'S UP FOR "OUTSTANDING STUDENT OF THE YEAR"... THERE'S MY NAME, SEE?
I COUNTED THEM, SIR.. YOU'RE FOUR HUNDREDTH ON THE LIST..
FOUR HUNDREDTH AND MOVING UP FAST!
5-23

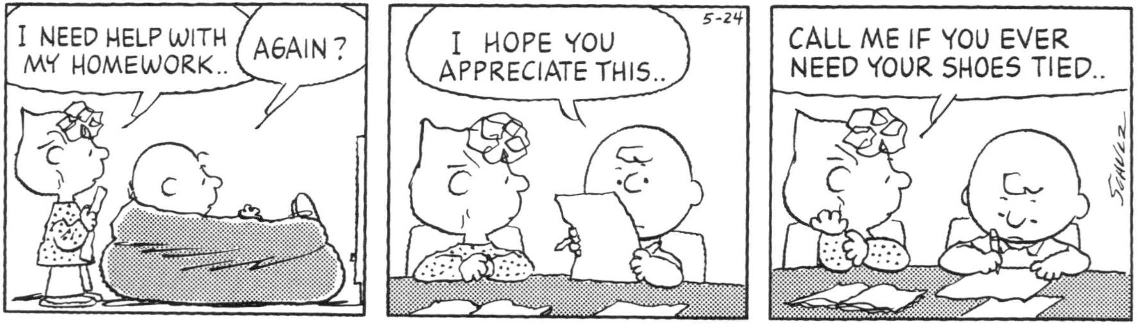
I NEED HELP WITH MY HOMEWORK..
AGAIN?
5-24
I HOPE YOU APPRECIATE THIS..
CALL ME IF YOU EVER NEED YOUR SHOES TIED..

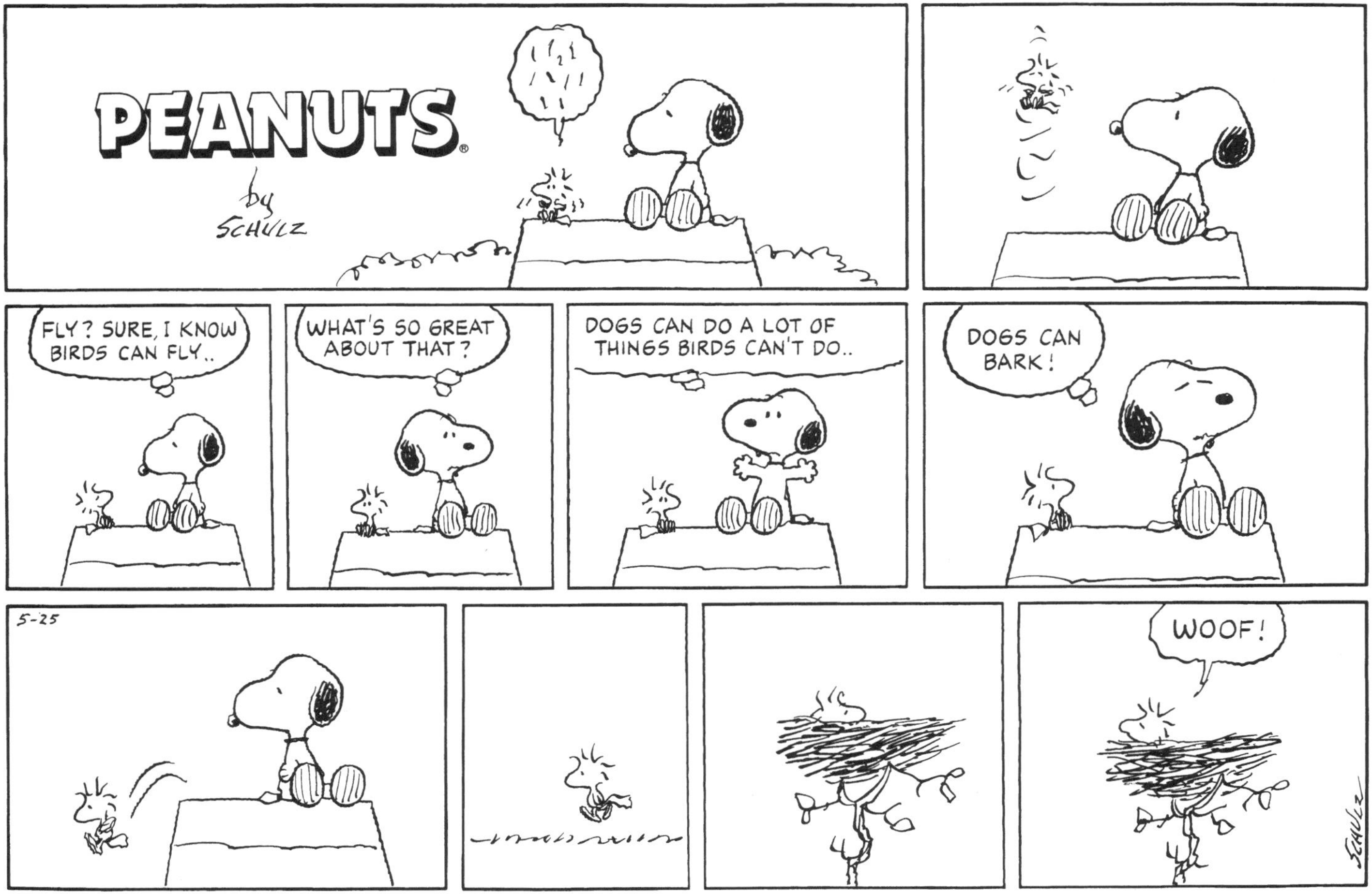
PEANUTS
by SCHULZ
FLY? SURE, I KNOW BIRDS CAN FLY..
WHAT'S SO GREAT ABOUT THAT?
DOGS CAN DO A LOT OF THINGS BIRDS CAN'T DO..
DOGS CAN BARK!
5-25
WOOF!
SCHULZ

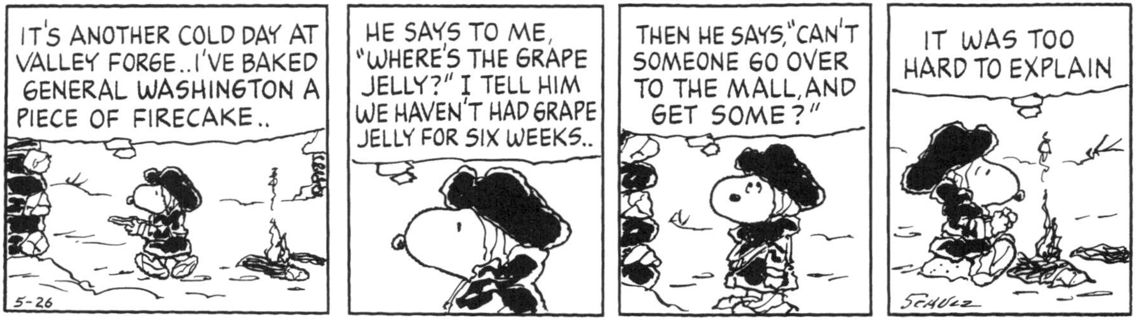
IT'S ANOTHER COLD DAY AT VALLEY FORGE..I'VE BAKED GENERAL WASHINGTON A PIECE OF FIRECAKE..
5-26
HE SAYS TO ME, "WHERE'S THE GRAPE JELLY?" I TELL HIM WE HAVEN'T HAD GRAPE JELLY FOR SIX WEEKS..
THEN HE SAYS, "CAN'T SOMEONE GO OVER TO THE MALL, AND GET SOME?"
IT WAS TOO HARD TO EXPLAIN
SCHULZ

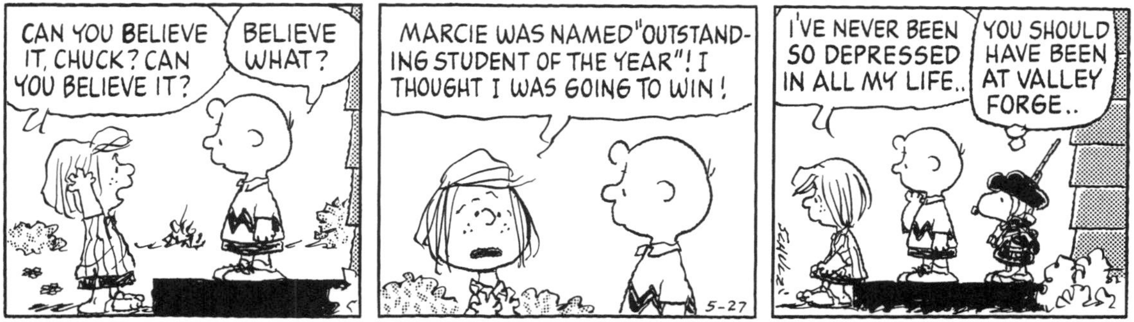
CAN YOU BELIEVE IT, CHUCK? CAN YOU BELIEVE IT?
BELIEVE WHAT?
MARCIE WAS NAMED "OUTSTANDING STUDENT OF THE YEAR"! I THOUGHT I WAS GOING TO WIN!
5-27
I'VE NEVER BEEN SO DEPRESSED IN ALL MY LIFE..
YOU SHOULD HAVE BEEN AT VALLEY FORGE..
SCHULZ

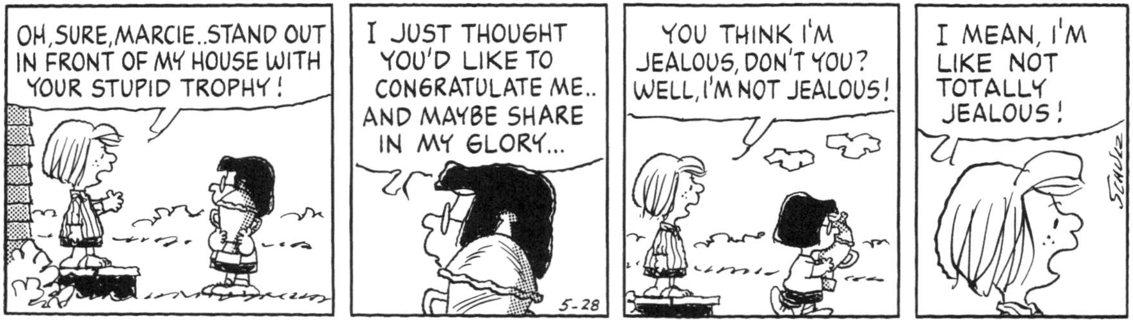
OH, SURE, MARCIE..STAND OUT IN FRONT OF MY HOUSE WITH YOUR STUPID TROPHY!
I JUST THOUGHT YOU'D LIKE TO CONGRATULATE ME.. AND MAYBE SHARE IN MY GLORY...
5-28
YOU THINK I'M JEALOUS, DON'T YOU? WELL, I'M NOT JEALOUS!
I MEAN, I'M LIKE NOT TOTALLY JEALOUS!
SCHULZ

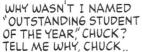

WHY WASN'T I NAMED "OUTSTANDING STUDENT OF THE YEAR", CHUCK? TELL ME WHY, CHUCK..

5-29

MAYBE BECAUSE YOU FALL ASLEEP IN CLASS EVERY DAY..

YOU DON'T LIKE ME, DO YOU, CHUCK?

I'M JUST TRYING TO EXPLAIN WHY YOU PROBABLY...

Z

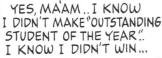

YES, MA'AM.. I KNOW I DIDN'T MAKE "OUTSTANDING STUDENT OF THE YEAR".. I KNOW I DIDN'T WIN...

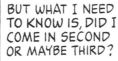

BUT WHAT I NEED TO KNOW IS, DID I COME IN SECOND OR MAYBE THIRD?

5-30

FOUR HUNDREDTH?!

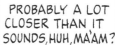

PROBABLY A LOT CLOSER THAN IT SOUNDS, HUH, MA'AM?

I SUPPOSE HAVING A DOG HELPS TO MAKE YOU FEEL BETTER WHEN YOU'RE DEPRESSED, HUH, CHUCK?

I WOULDN'T KNOW..

SAY "GOODBYE" TO VALLEY FORGE, MEN.. WE'RE MOVING OUT!

5-31

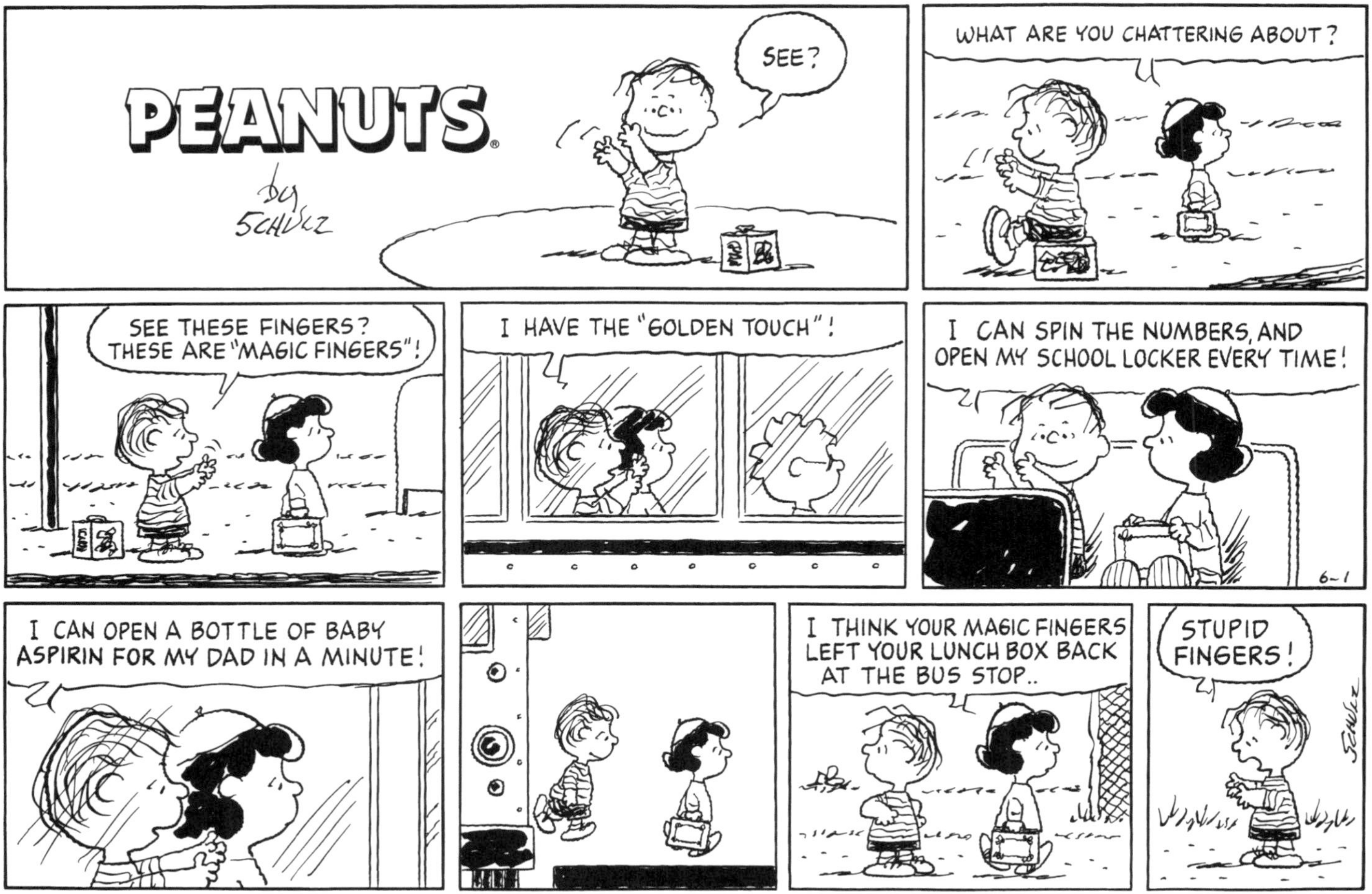
PEANUTS
by SCHULZ
SEE?
WHAT ARE YOU CHATTERING ABOUT?
SEE THESE FINGERS? THESE ARE "MAGIC FINGERS"!
I HAVE THE "GOLDEN TOUCH"!
I CAN SPIN THE NUMBERS, AND OPEN MY SCHOOL LOCKER EVERY TIME!
6-1
I CAN OPEN A BOTTLE OF BABY ASPIRIN FOR MY DAD IN A MINUTE!
I THINK YOUR MAGIC FINGERS LEFT YOUR LUNCH BOX BACK AT THE BUS STOP..
STUPID FINGERS!
SCHULZ

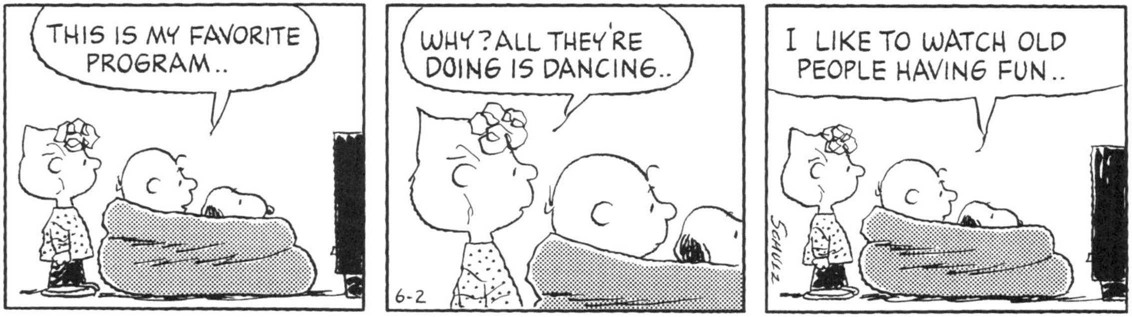
THIS IS MY FAVORITE PROGRAM..
WHY? ALL THEY'RE DOING IS DANCING..
I LIKE TO WATCH OLD PEOPLE HAVING FUN..

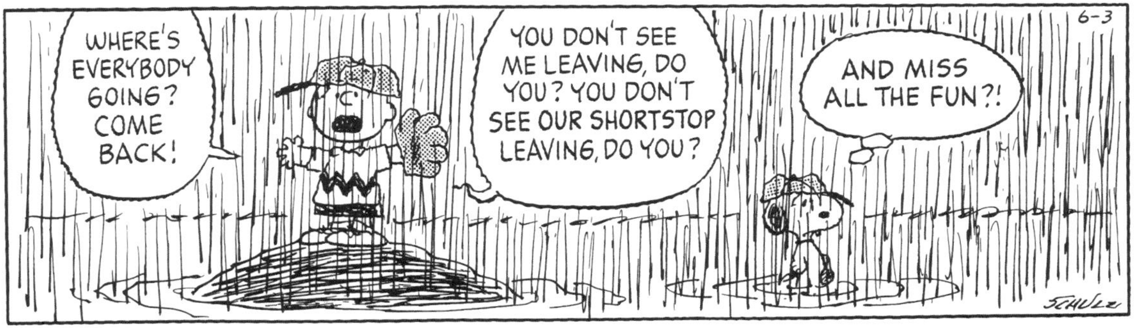
WHERE'S EVERYBODY GOING? COME BACK!
YOU DON'T SEE ME LEAVING, DO YOU? YOU DON'T SEE OUR SHORTSTOP LEAVING, DO YOU?
AND MISS ALL THE FUN?!

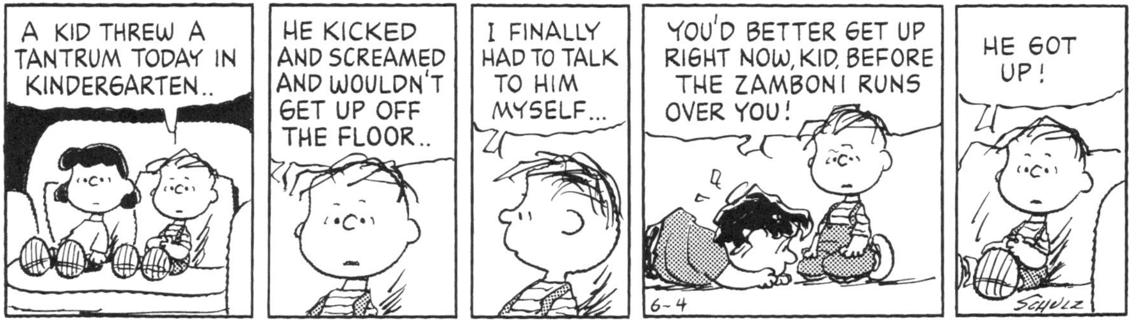
A KID THREW A TANTRUM TODAY IN KINDERGARTEN..
HE KICKED AND SCREAMED AND WOULDN'T GET UP OFF THE FLOOR..
I FINALLY HAD TO TALK TO HIM MYSELF...
YOU'D BETTER GET UP RIGHT NOW, KID, BEFORE THE ZAMBONI RUNS OVER YOU!
HE GOT UP!

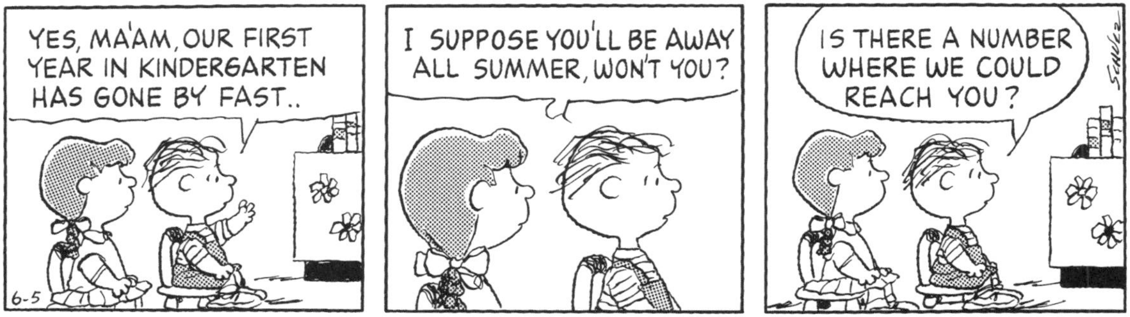
YES, MA'AM, OUR FIRST YEAR IN KINDERGARTEN HAS GONE BY FAST..
I SUPPOSE YOU'LL BE AWAY ALL SUMMER, WON'T YOU?
IS THERE A NUMBER WHERE WE COULD REACH YOU?

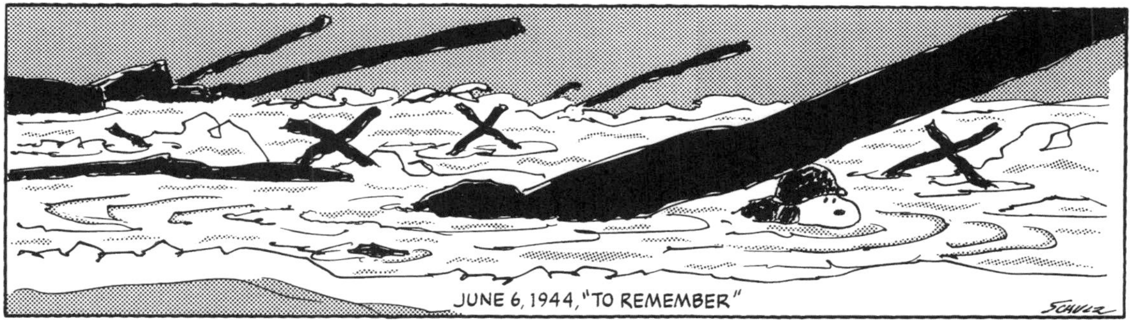
JUNE 6, 1944, "TO REMEMBER"

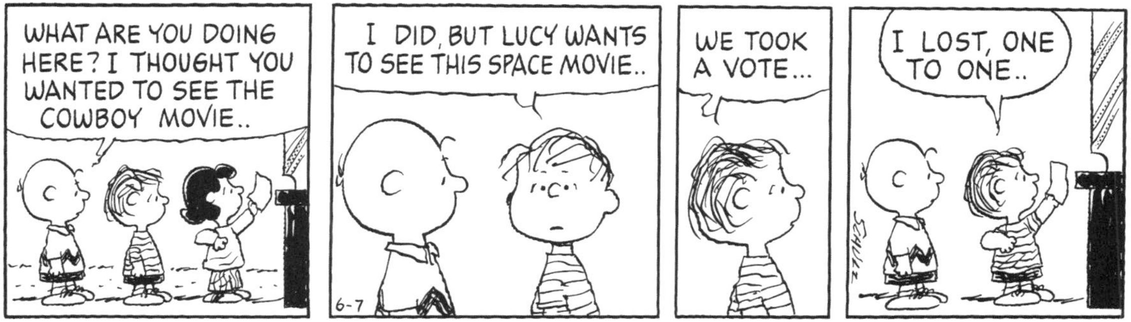
WHAT ARE YOU DOING HERE? I THOUGHT YOU WANTED TO SEE THE COWBOY MOVIE..
I DID, BUT LUCY WANTS TO SEE THIS SPACE MOVIE..
WE TOOK A VOTE...
I LOST, ONE TO ONE..

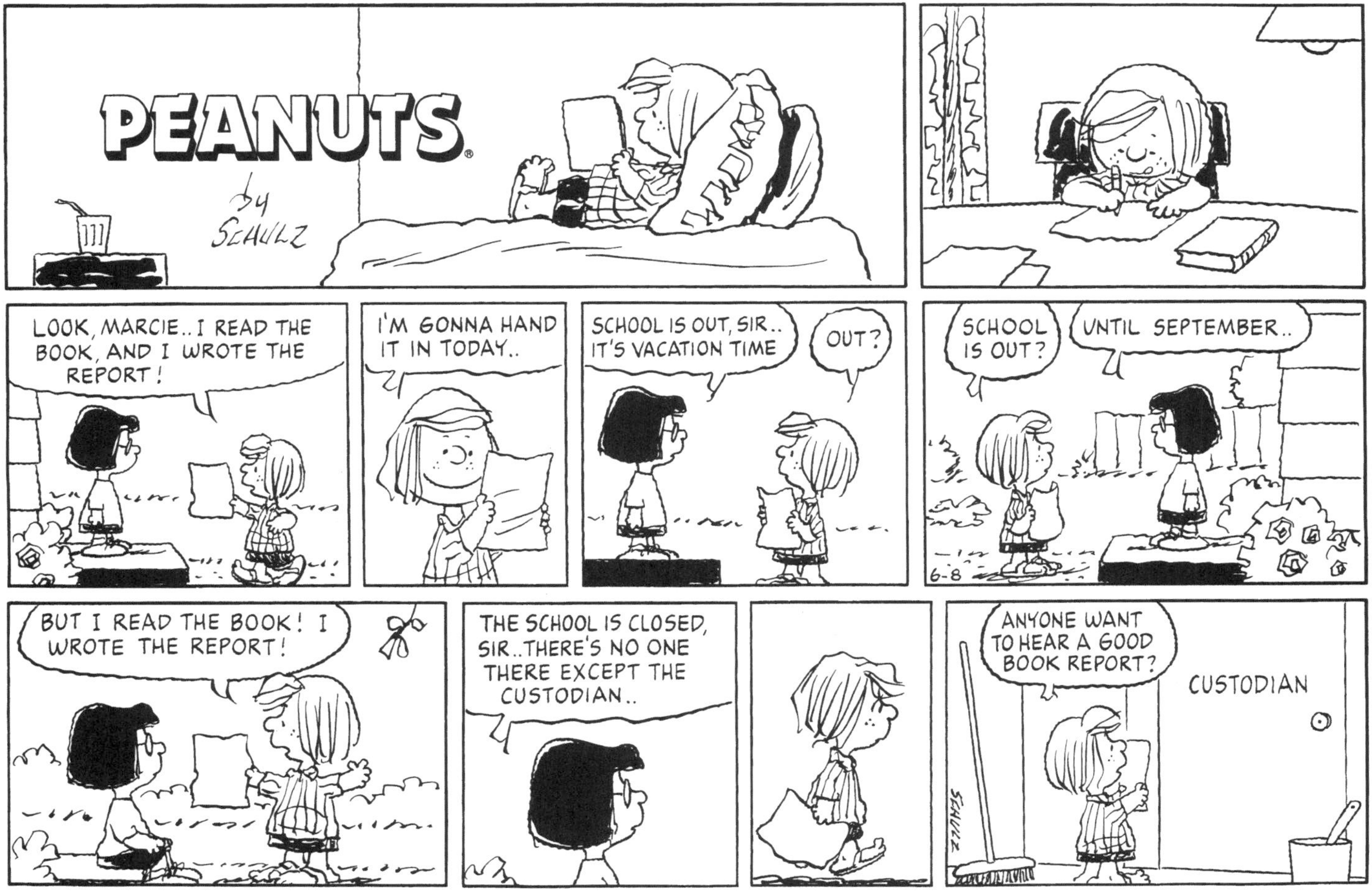
PEANUTS
by SCHULZ
LOOK, MARCIE.. I READ THE BOOK, AND I WROTE THE REPORT!
I'M GONNA HAND IT IN TODAY..
SCHOOL IS OUT, SIR.. IT'S VACATION TIME
OUT?
SCHOOL IS OUT?
UNTIL SEPTEMBER..
6-8
BUT I READ THE BOOK! I WROTE THE REPORT!
THE SCHOOL IS CLOSED, SIR.. THERE'S NO ONE THERE EXCEPT THE CUSTODIAN..
SCHULZ
ANYONE WANT TO HEAR A GOOD BOOK REPORT?
CUSTODIAN

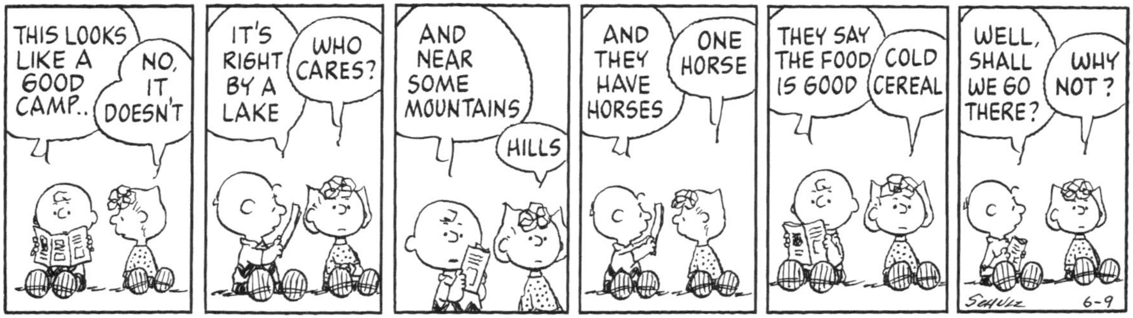
THIS LOOKS LIKE A GOOD CAMP..
NO, IT DOESN'T
IT'S RIGHT BY A LAKE
WHO CARES?
AND NEAR SOME MOUNTAINS
HILLS
AND THEY HAVE HORSES
ONE HORSE
THEY SAY THE FOOD IS GOOD
COLD CEREAL
WELL, SHALL WE GO THERE?
WHY NOT?
SCHULZ
6-9

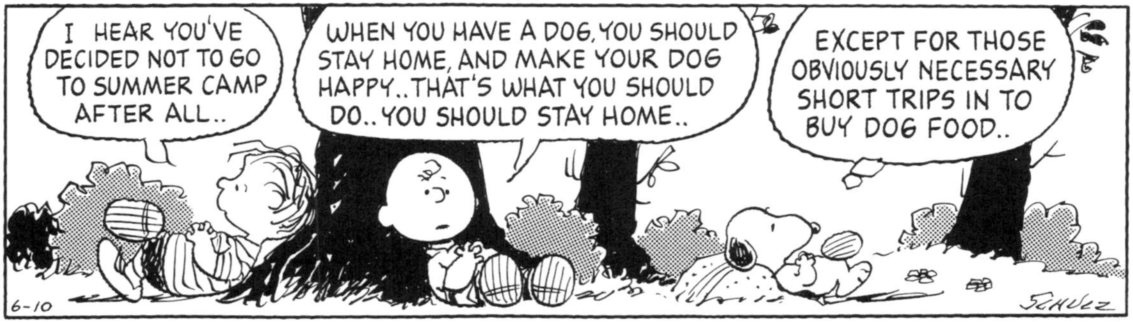
I HEAR YOU'VE DECIDED NOT TO GO TO SUMMER CAMP AFTER ALL..
WHEN YOU HAVE A DOG, YOU SHOULD STAY HOME, AND MAKE YOUR DOG HAPPY..THAT'S WHAT YOU SHOULD DO..YOU SHOULD STAY HOME..
EXCEPT FOR THOSE OBVIOUSLY NECESSARY SHORT TRIPS IN TO BUY DOG FOOD..
6-10
SCHULZ

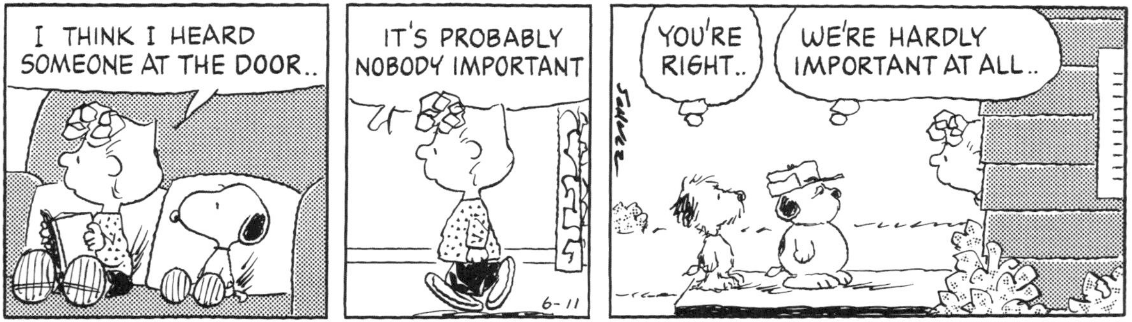
I THINK I HEARD SOMEONE AT THE DOOR..
IT'S PROBABLY NOBODY IMPORTANT
SCHULZ
6-11
YOU'RE RIGHT..
WE'RE HARDLY IMPORTANT AT ALL..

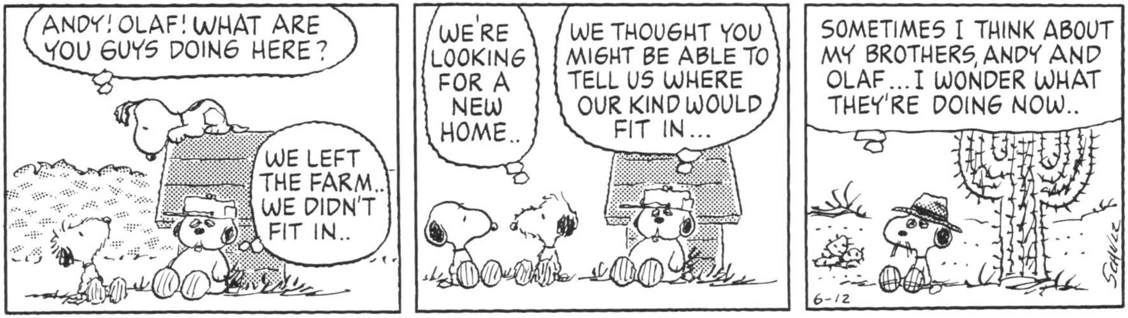
ANDY! OLAF! WHAT ARE YOU GUYS DOING HERE?
WE LEFT THE FARM.. WE DIDN'T FIT IN..
WE'RE LOOKING FOR A NEW HOME..
WE THOUGHT YOU MIGHT BE ABLE TO TELL US WHERE OUR KIND WOULD FIT IN...
SOMETIMES I THINK ABOUT MY BROTHERS, ANDY AND OLAF... I WONDER WHAT THEY'RE DOING NOW..
6-12

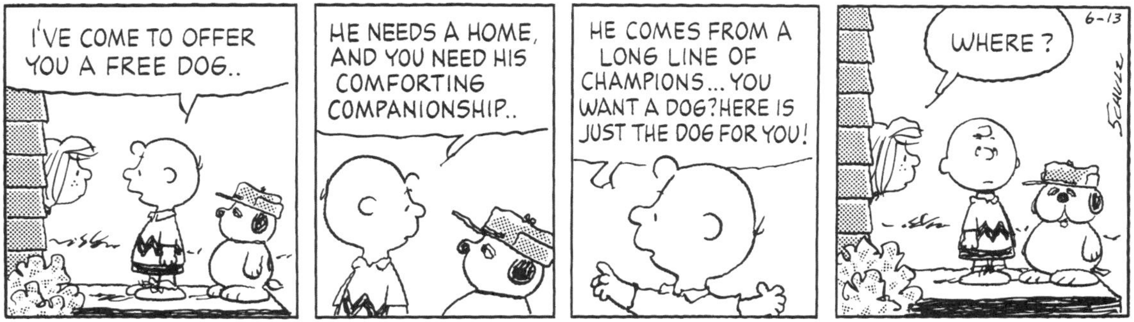
I'VE COME TO OFFER YOU A FREE DOG..
HE NEEDS A HOME, AND YOU NEED HIS COMFORTING COMPANIONSHIP..
HE COMES FROM A LONG LINE OF CHAMPIONS... YOU WANT A DOG? HERE IS JUST THE DOG FOR YOU!
6-13
WHERE?

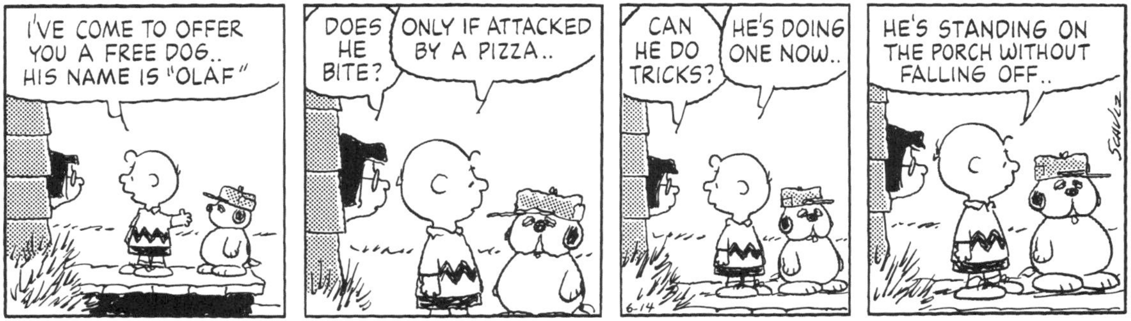
I'VE COME TO OFFER YOU A FREE DOG.. HIS NAME IS "OLAF"
DOES HE BITE?
ONLY IF ATTACKED BY A PIZZA..
CAN HE DO TRICKS?
HE'S DOING ONE NOW..
6-14
HE'S STANDING ON THE PORCH WITHOUT FALLING OFF..

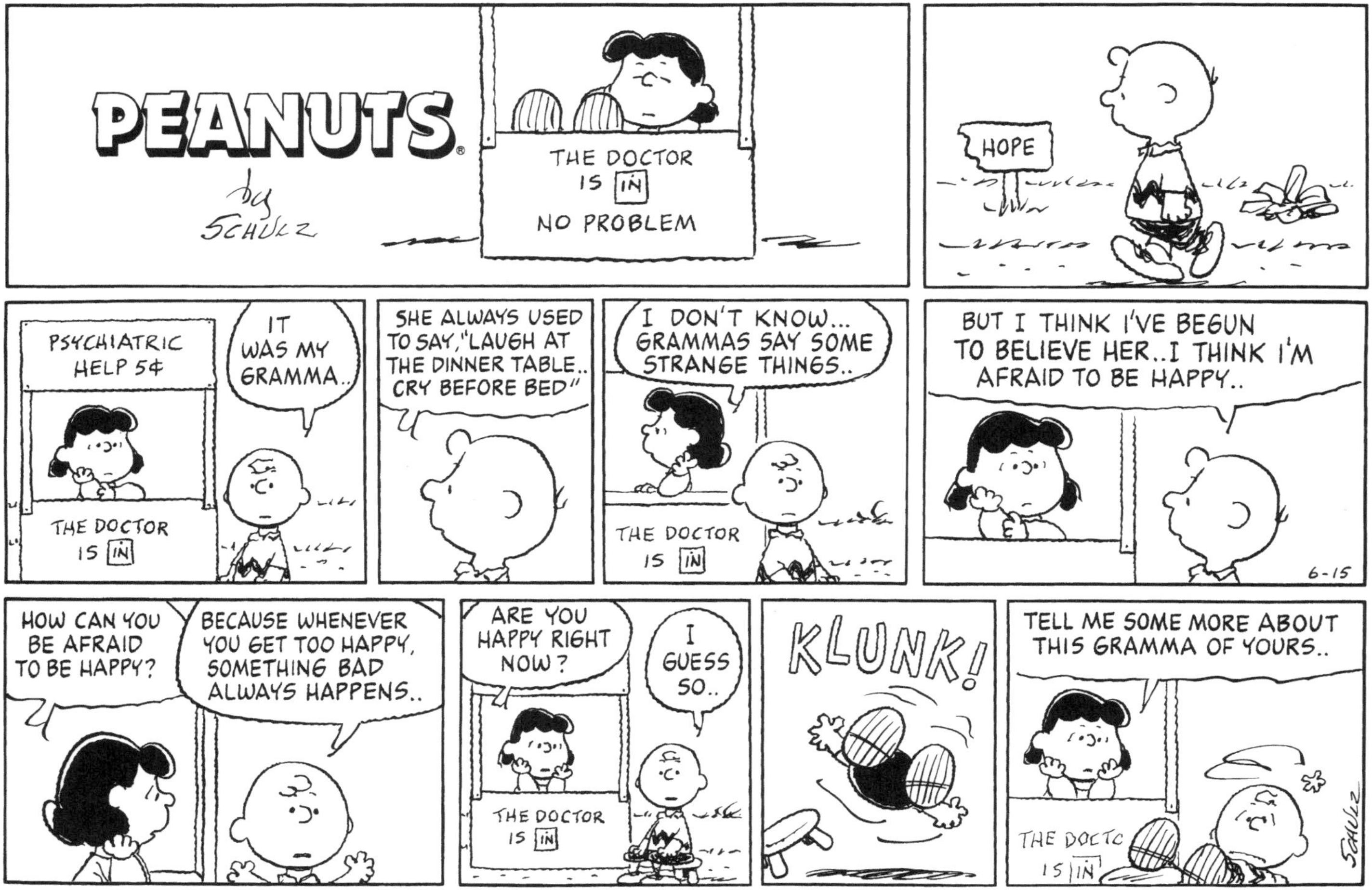
PEANUTS
by SCHULZ
THE DOCTOR IS IN
NO PROBLEM
HOPE
PSYCHIATRIC HELP 5¢
IT WAS MY GRAMMA..
THE DOCTOR IS IN
SHE ALWAYS USED TO SAY, "LAUGH AT THE DINNER TABLE.. CRY BEFORE BED"
I DON'T KNOW... GRAMMAS SAY SOME STRANGE THINGS..
THE DOCTOR IS IN
BUT I THINK I'VE BEGUN TO BELIEVE HER..I THINK I'M AFRAID TO BE HAPPY..
6-15
HOW CAN YOU BE AFRAID TO BE HAPPY?
BECAUSE WHENEVER YOU GET TOO HAPPY, SOMETHING BAD ALWAYS HAPPENS..
ARE YOU HAPPY RIGHT NOW?
I GUESS SO..
THE DOCTOR IS IN
KLUNK!
TELL ME SOME MORE ABOUT THIS GRAMMA OF YOURS..
THE DOCTC IS IN
SCHULZ

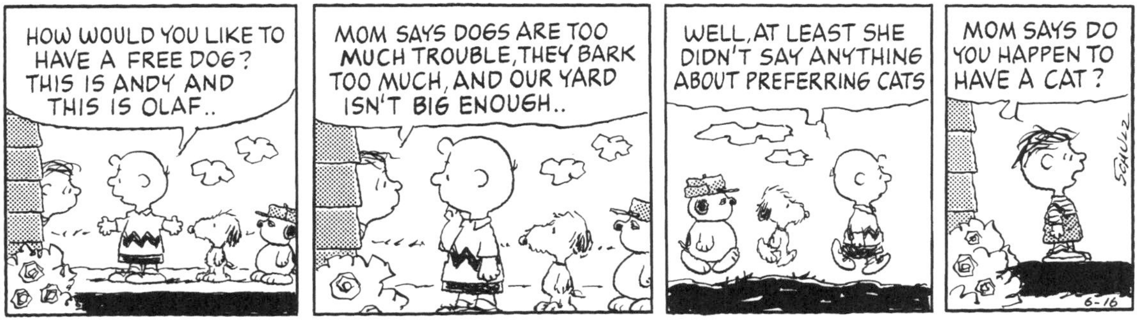
HOW WOULD YOU LIKE TO HAVE A FREE DOG? THIS IS ANDY AND THIS IS OLAF..
MOM SAYS DOGS ARE TOO MUCH TROUBLE, THEY BARK TOO MUCH, AND OUR YARD ISN'T BIG ENOUGH..
WELL, AT LEAST SHE DIDN'T SAY ANYTHING ABOUT PREFERRING CATS
MOM SAYS DO YOU HAPPEN TO HAVE A CAT?
6-16

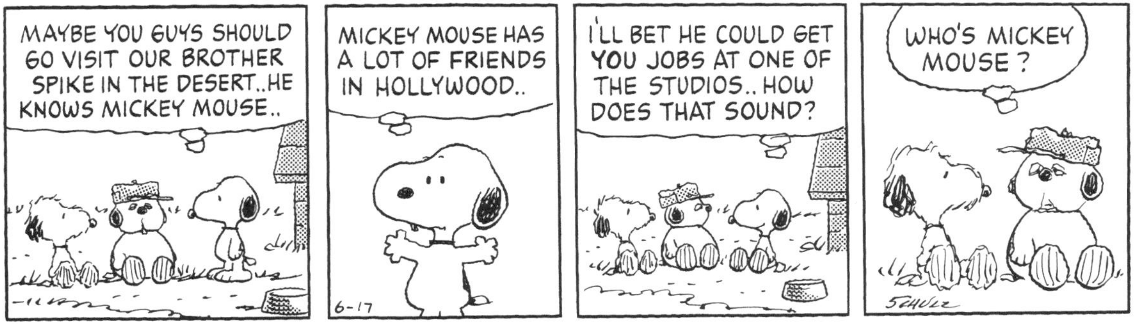
MAYBE YOU GUYS SHOULD GO VISIT OUR BROTHER SPIKE IN THE DESERT..HE KNOWS MICKEY MOUSE..
MICKEY MOUSE HAS A LOT OF FRIENDS IN HOLLYWOOD..
6-17
I'LL BET HE COULD GET YOU JOBS AT ONE OF THE STUDIOS.. HOW DOES THAT SOUND?
WHO'S MICKEY MOUSE?

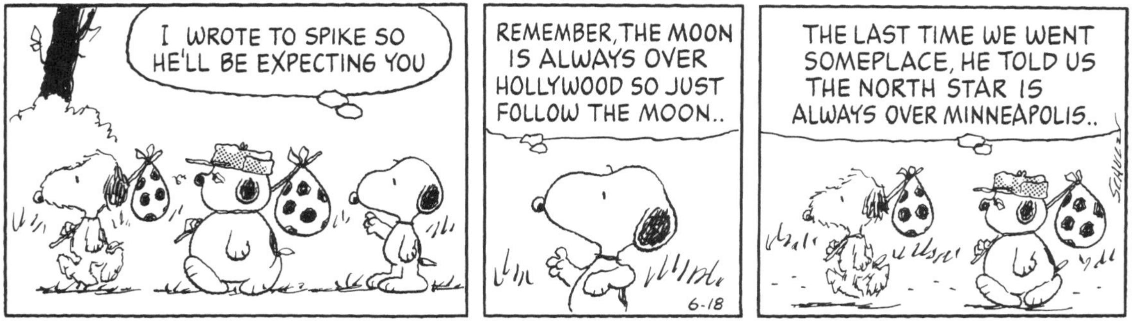
I WROTE TO SPIKE SO HE'LL BE EXPECTING YOU
REMEMBER, THE MOON IS ALWAYS OVER HOLLYWOOD SO JUST FOLLOW THE MOON..
6-18
THE LAST TIME WE WENT SOMEPLACE, HE TOLD US THE NORTH STAR IS ALWAYS OVER MINNEAPOLIS..

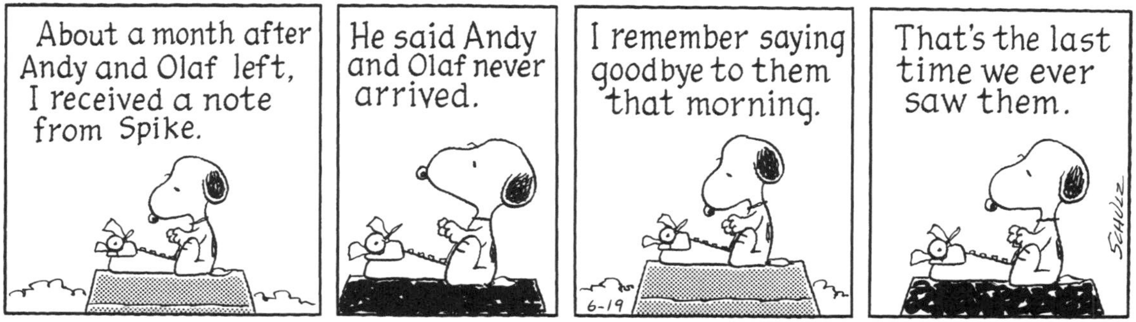
About a month after Andy and Olaf left, I received a note from Spike.
He said Andy and Olaf never arrived.
I remember saying goodbye to them that morning.
6-19
That's the last time we ever saw them.
SCHULZ

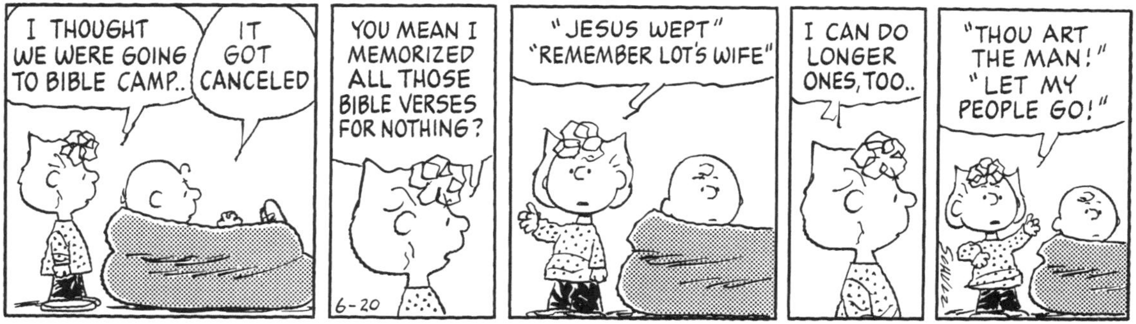
I THOUGHT WE WERE GOING TO BIBLE CAMP..
IT GOT CANCELED
YOU MEAN I MEMORIZED ALL THOSE BIBLE VERSES FOR NOTHING?
6-20
"JESUS WEPT" "REMEMBER LOT'S WIFE"
I CAN DO LONGER ONES, TOO..
"THOU ART THE MAN!" "LET MY PEOPLE GO!"
SCHULZ

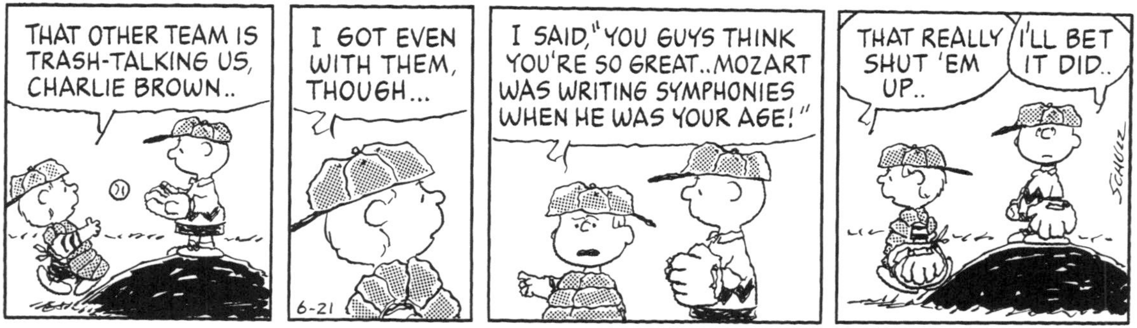
THAT OTHER TEAM IS TRASH-TALKING US, CHARLIE BROWN..
I GOT EVEN WITH THEM, THOUGH...
6-21
I SAID, "YOU GUYS THINK YOU'RE SO GREAT..MOZART WAS WRITING SYMPHONIES WHEN HE WAS YOUR AGE!"
THAT REALLY SHUT 'EM UP..
I'LL BET IT DID..
SCHULZ

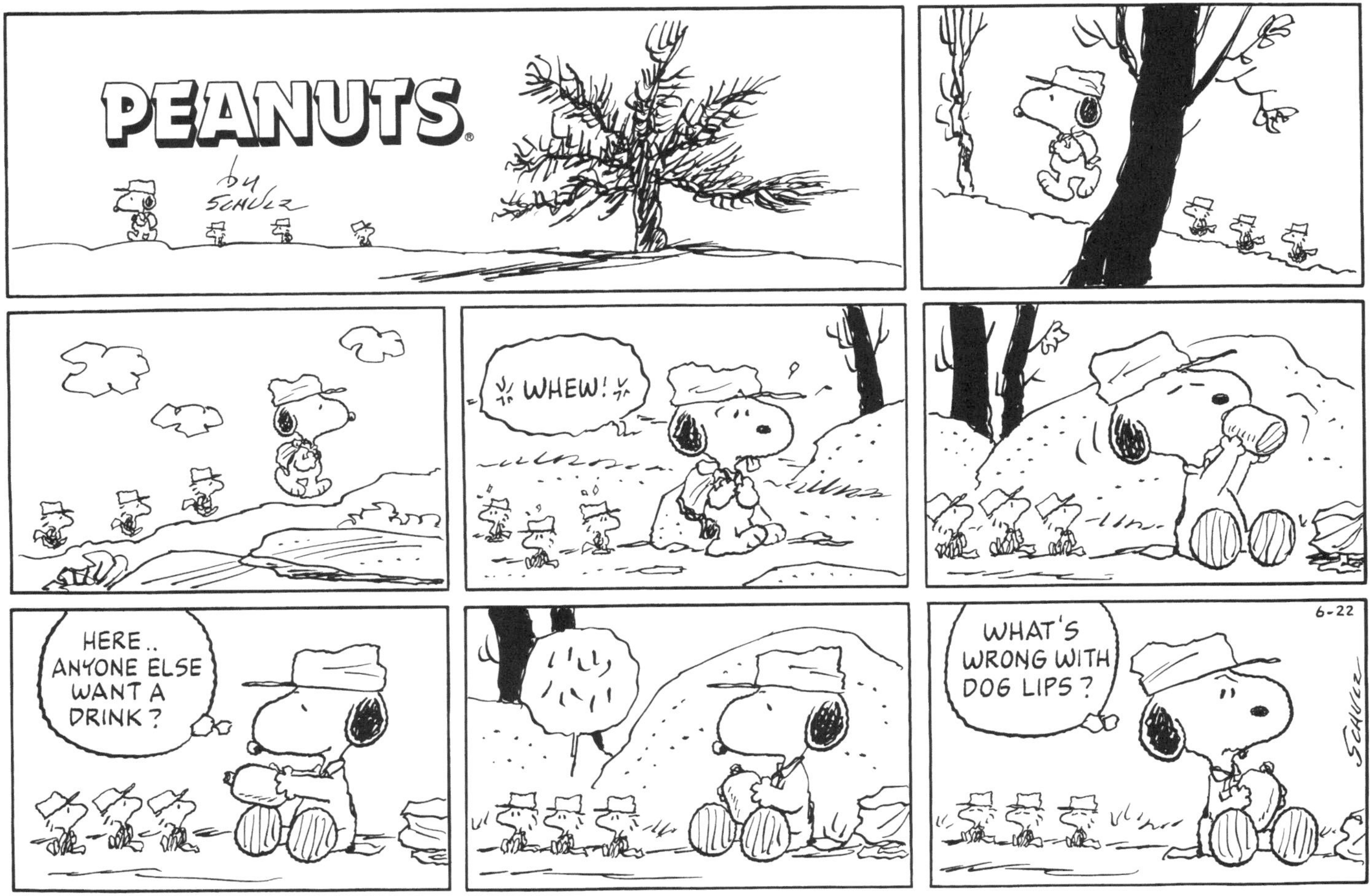
PEANUTS
by Schulz
WHEW!
HERE.. ANYONE ELSE WANT A DRINK?
WHAT'S WRONG WITH DOG LIPS?
6-22
SCHULZ

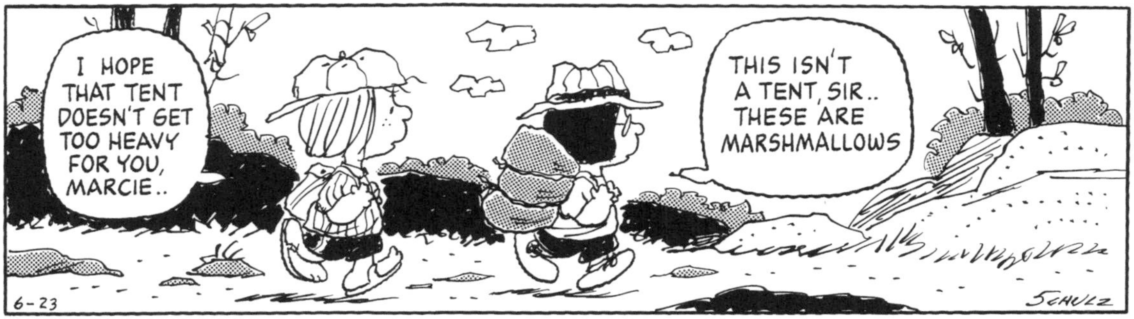
I HOPE THAT TENT DOESN'T GET TOO HEAVY FOR YOU, MARCIE..
THIS ISN'T A TENT, SIR.. THESE ARE MARSHMALLOWS
6-23
SCHULZ

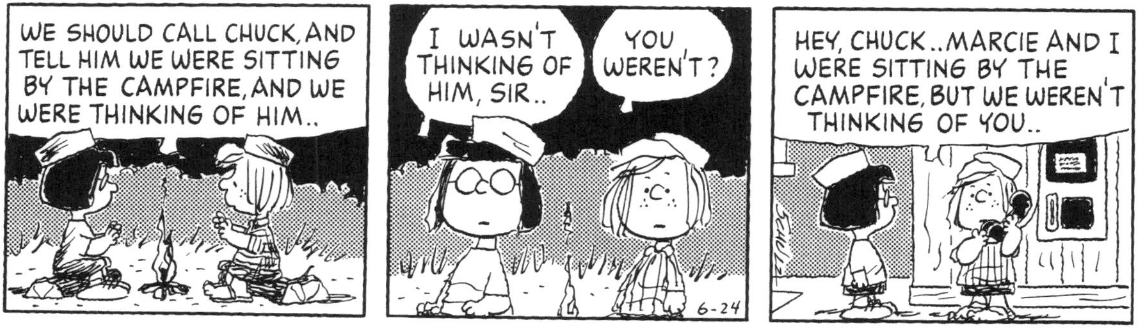
WE SHOULD CALL CHUCK, AND TELL HIM WE WERE SITTING BY THE CAMPFIRE, AND WE WERE THINKING OF HIM..
I WASN'T THINKING OF HIM, SIR..
YOU WEREN'T?
6-24
HEY, CHUCK..MARCIE AND I WERE SITTING BY THE CAMPFIRE, BUT WE WEREN'T THINKING OF YOU..
SCHULZ

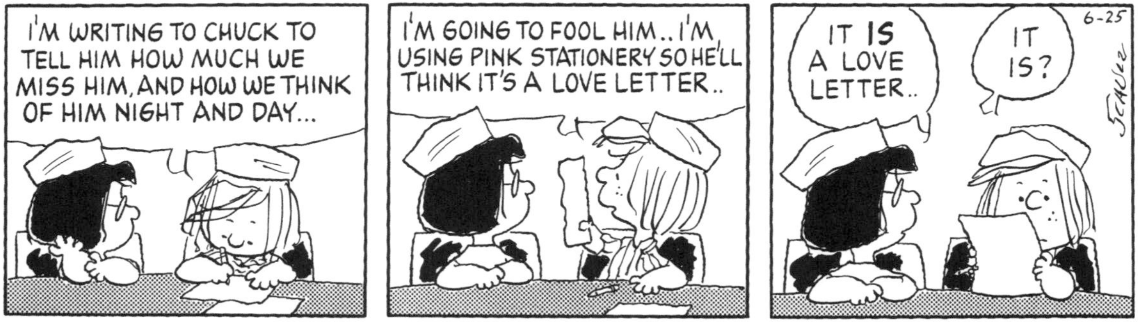
I'M WRITING TO CHUCK TO TELL HIM HOW MUCH WE MISS HIM, AND HOW WE THINK OF HIM NIGHT AND DAY...
I'M GOING TO FOOL HIM.. I'M USING PINK STATIONERY SO HE'LL THINK IT'S A LOVE LETTER..
6-25
IT **IS** A LOVE LETTER..
IT IS?
SCHULZ

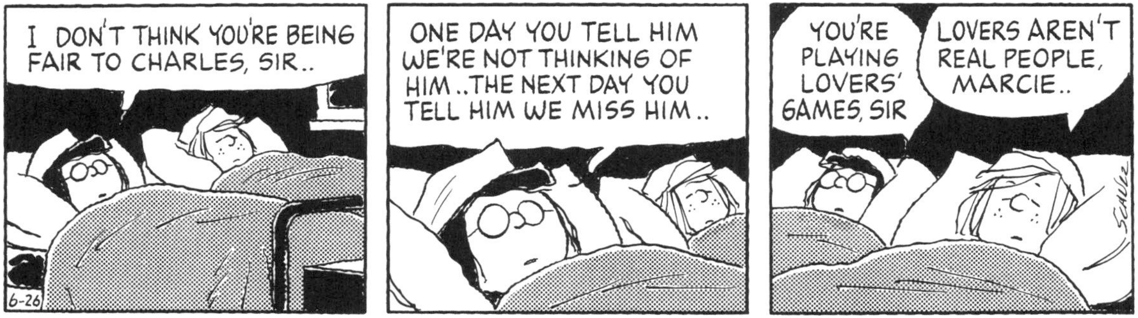
I DON'T THINK YOU'RE BEING FAIR TO CHARLES, SIR..
6-26
ONE DAY YOU TELL HIM WE'RE NOT THINKING OF HIM..THE NEXT DAY YOU TELL HIM WE MISS HIM..
YOU'RE PLAYING LOVERS' GAMES, SIR
LOVERS AREN'T REAL PEOPLE, MARCIE..
SCHULZ

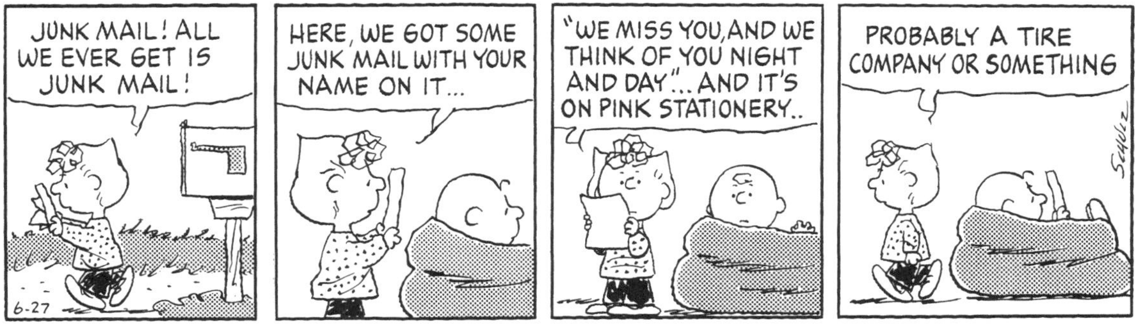
JUNK MAIL! ALL WE EVER GET IS JUNK MAIL!
6-27
HERE, WE GOT SOME JUNK MAIL WITH YOUR NAME ON IT...
"WE MISS YOU, AND WE THINK OF YOU NIGHT AND DAY"... AND IT'S ON PINK STATIONERY..
PROBABLY A TIRE COMPANY OR SOMETHING
SCHULZ

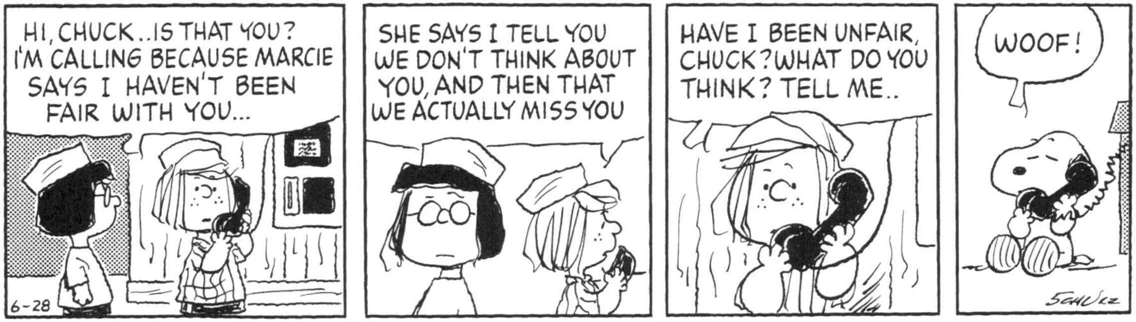
HI, CHUCK..IS THAT YOU? I'M CALLING BECAUSE MARCIE SAYS I HAVEN'T BEEN FAIR WITH YOU...
6-28
SHE SAYS I TELL YOU WE DON'T THINK ABOUT YOU, AND THEN THAT WE ACTUALLY MISS YOU
HAVE I BEEN UNFAIR, CHUCK? WHAT DO YOU THINK? TELL ME..
WOOF!
SCHULZ

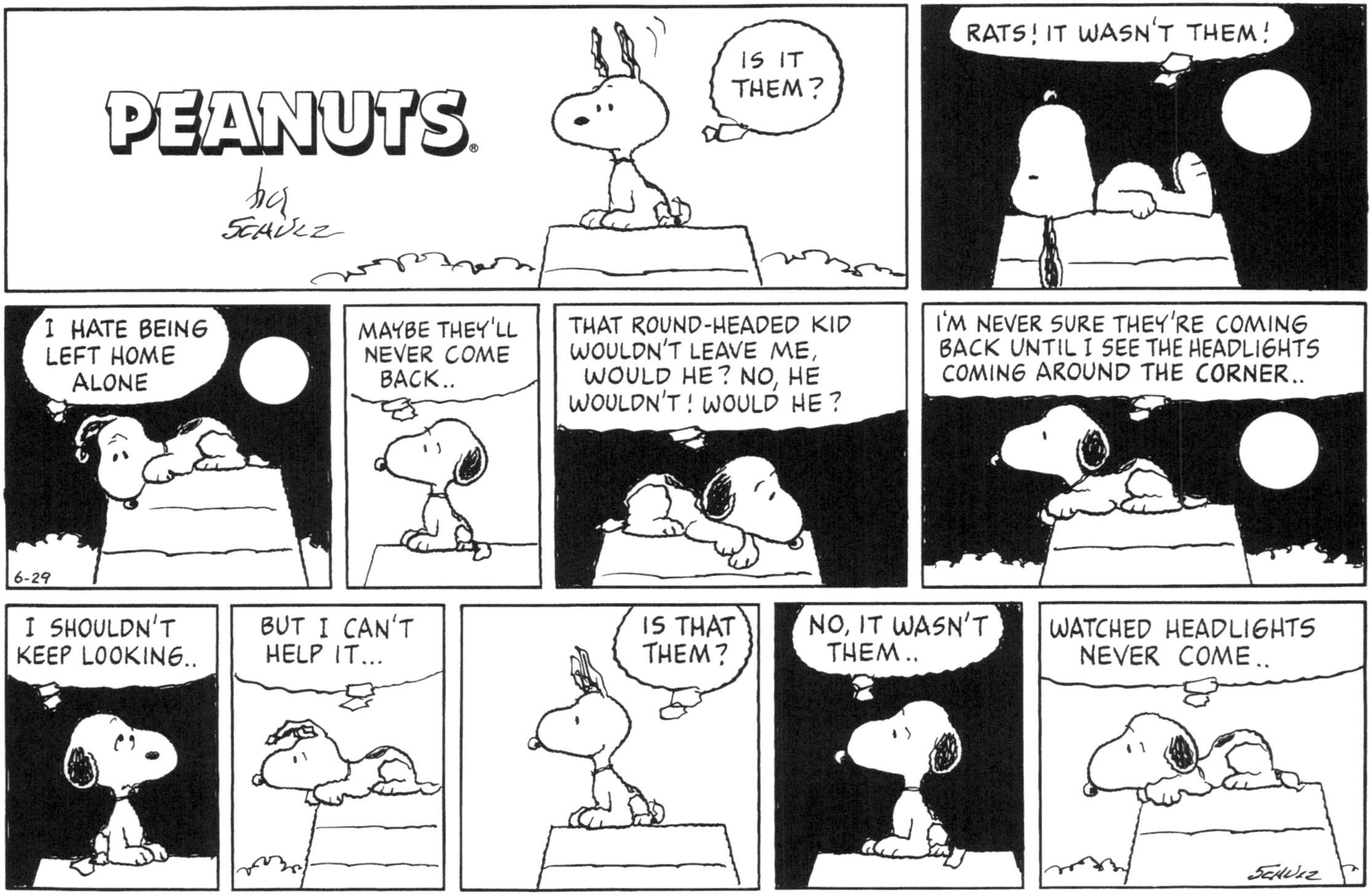
PEANUTS
by SCHULZ
IS IT THEM?
RATS! IT WASN'T THEM!
I HATE BEING LEFT HOME ALONE
6-29
MAYBE THEY'LL NEVER COME BACK..
THAT ROUND-HEADED KID WOULDN'T LEAVE ME, WOULD HE? NO, HE WOULDN'T! WOULD HE?
I'M NEVER SURE THEY'RE COMING BACK UNTIL I SEE THE HEADLIGHTS COMING AROUND THE CORNER..
I SHOULDN'T KEEP LOOKING..
BUT I CAN'T HELP IT...
IS THAT THEM?
NO, IT WASN'T THEM..
WATCHED HEADLIGHTS NEVER COME..
SCHULZ

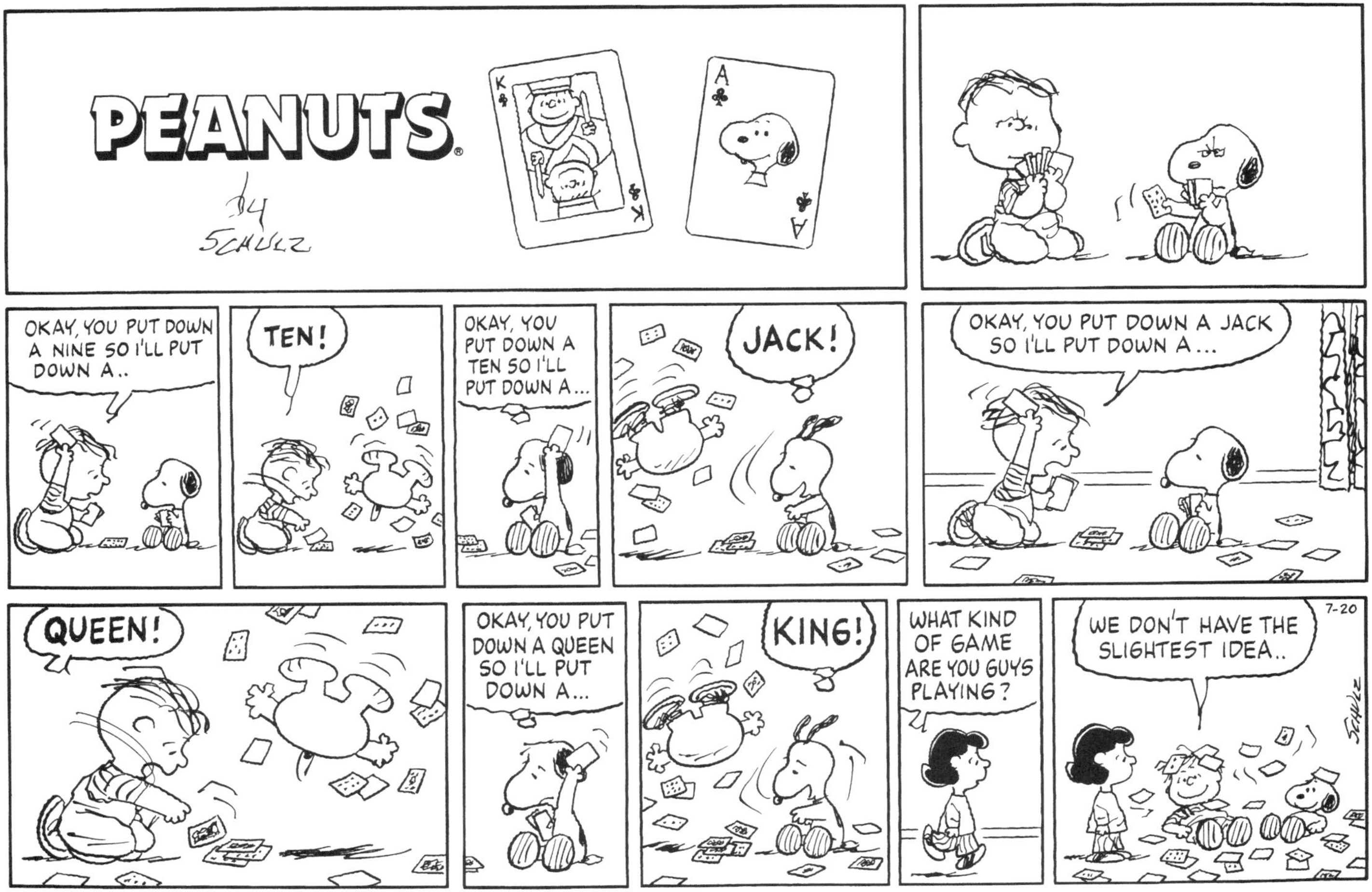
PEANUTS
K
A
OKAY, YOU PUT DOWN A NINE SO I'LL PUT DOWN A..
TEN!
OKAY, YOU PUT DOWN A TEN SO I'LL PUT DOWN A...
JACK!
OKAY, YOU PUT DOWN A JACK SO I'LL PUT DOWN A...
QUEEN!
OKAY, YOU PUT DOWN A QUEEN SO I'LL PUT DOWN A...
KING!
WHAT KIND OF GAME ARE YOU GUYS PLAYING?
WE DON'T HAVE THE SLIGHTEST IDEA..
7-20

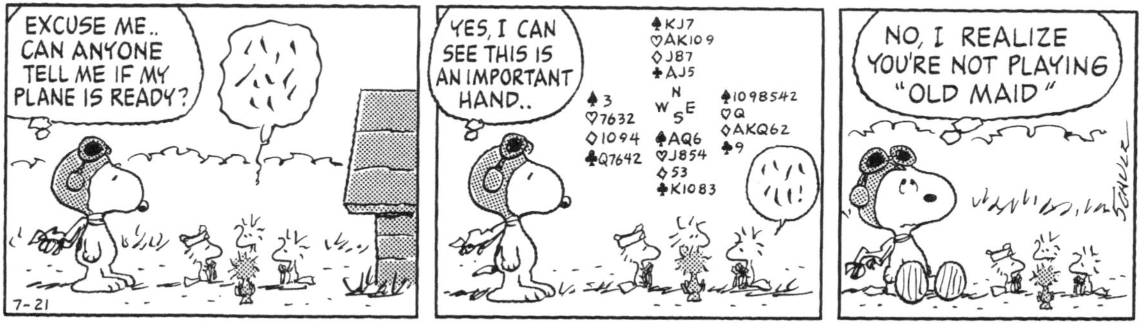
EXCUSE ME.. CAN ANYONE TELL ME IF MY PLANE IS READY?
YES, I CAN SEE THIS IS AN IMPORTANT HAND..
♠KJ7
♡AK109
◊J87
♣AJ5
N
W E
S
♠3
♡7632
◊1094
♣Q7642
♠AQ6
♡J854
◊53
♣K1083
♠1098542
♡Q
◊AKQ62
♣9
NO, I REALIZE YOU'RE NOT PLAYING "OLD MAID"
7-21
SCHULZ

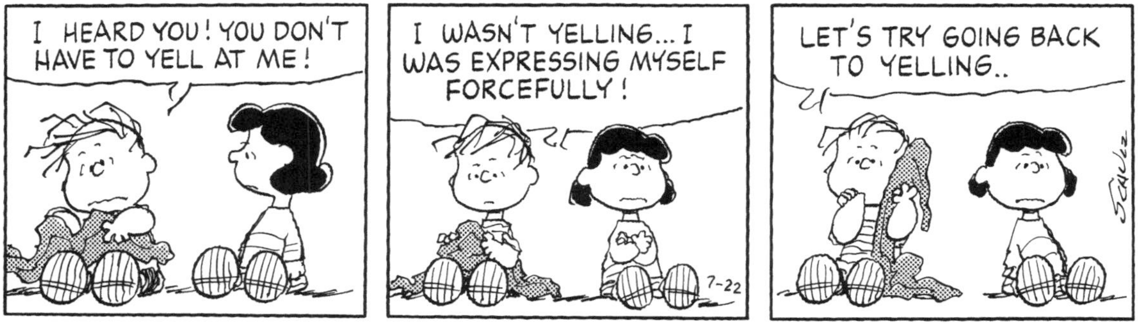
I HEARD YOU! YOU DON'T HAVE TO YELL AT ME!
I WASN'T YELLING... I WAS EXPRESSING MYSELF FORCEFULLY!
LET'S TRY GOING BACK TO YELLING..
7-22
SCHULZ

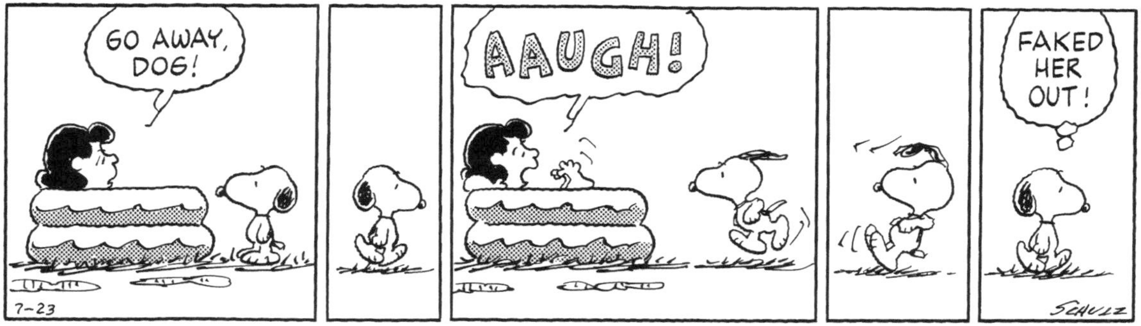
GO AWAY, DOG!
AAUGH!
FAKED HER OUT!
7-23
SCHULZ

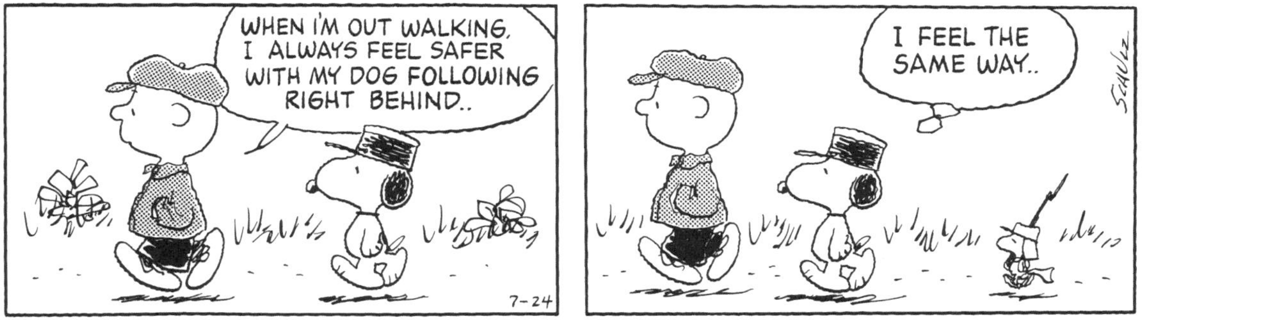
WHEN I'M OUT WALKING, I ALWAYS FEEL SAFER WITH MY DOG FOLLOWING RIGHT BEHIND..
7-24
I FEEL THE SAME WAY..
SCHULZ

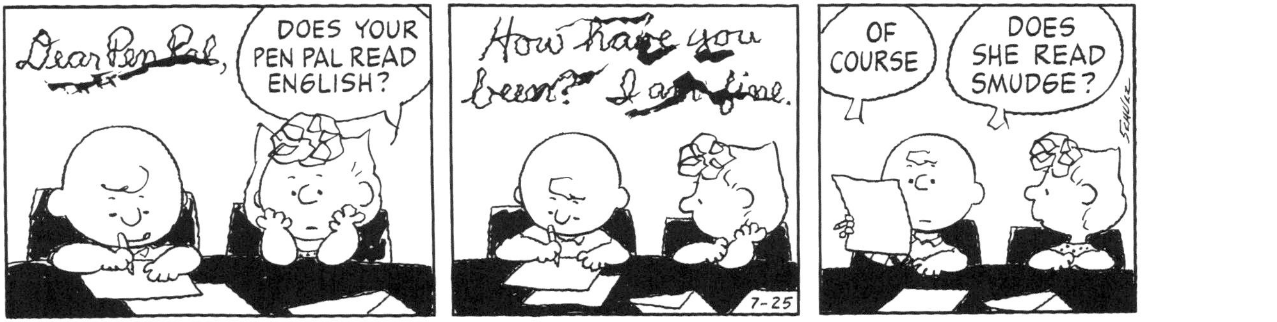
Dear Pen Pal,
DOES YOUR PEN PAL READ ENGLISH?
How have you been? I am fine.
7-25
OF COURSE
DOES SHE READ SMUDGE?
SCHULZ

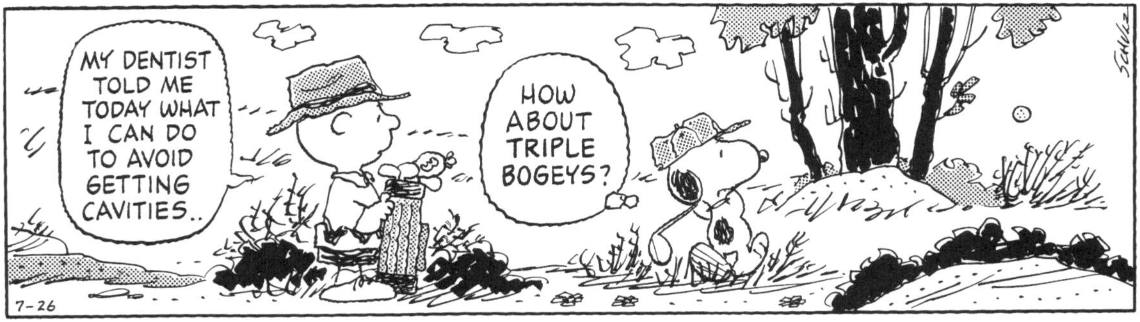
MY DENTIST TOLD ME TODAY WHAT I CAN DO TO AVOID GETTING CAVITIES..
HOW ABOUT TRIPLE BOGEYS?
SCHULZ
7-26

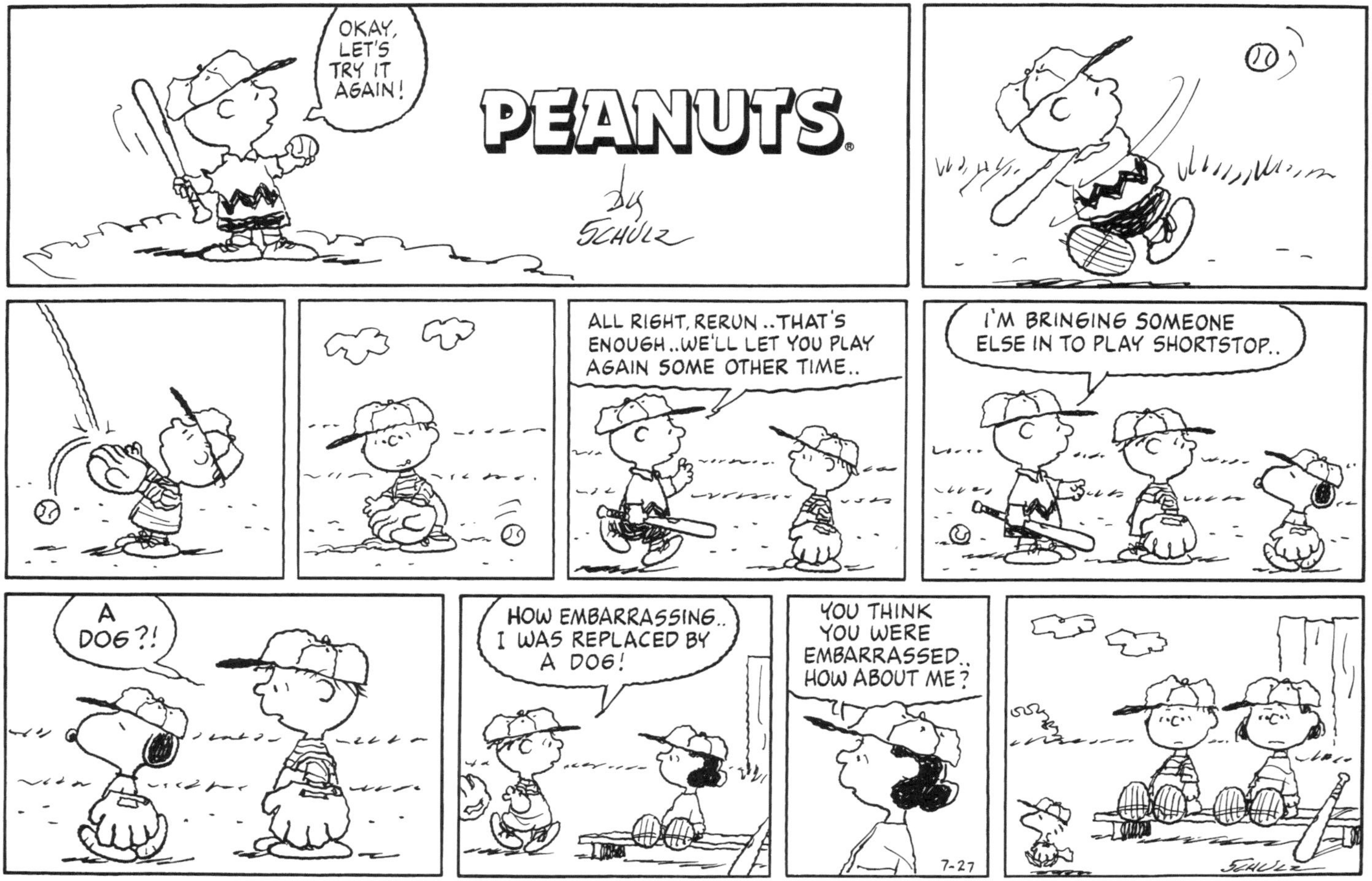
OKAY, LET'S TRY IT AGAIN!
PEANUTS
SCHULZ
ALL RIGHT, RERUN..THAT'S ENOUGH..WE'LL LET YOU PLAY AGAIN SOME OTHER TIME..
I'M BRINGING SOMEONE ELSE IN TO PLAY SHORTSTOP..
A DOG?!
HOW EMBARRASSING.. I WAS REPLACED BY A DOG!
YOU THINK YOU WERE EMBARRASSED.. HOW ABOUT ME?
7-27
SCHULZ

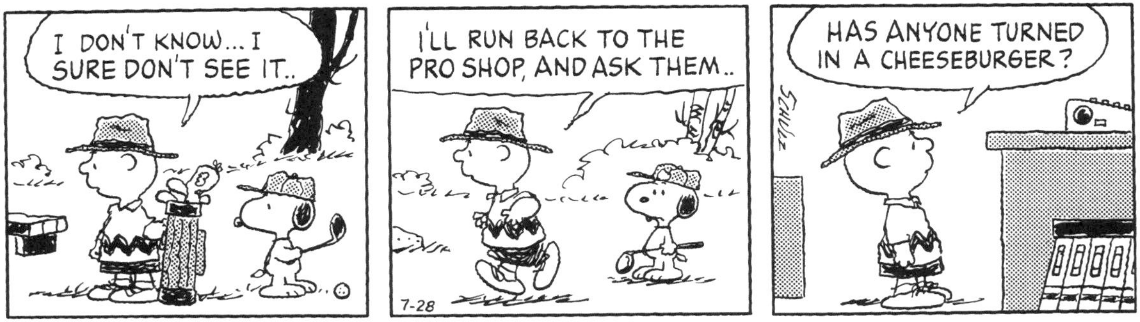
I DON'T KNOW... I SURE DON'T SEE IT..
I'LL RUN BACK TO THE PRO SHOP, AND ASK THEM..
HAS ANYONE TURNED IN A CHEESEBURGER?

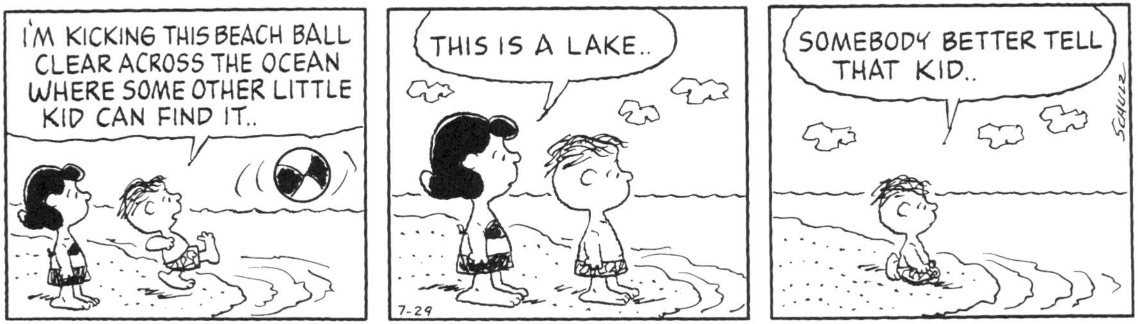
I'M KICKING THIS BEACH BALL CLEAR ACROSS THE OCEAN WHERE SOME OTHER LITTLE KID CAN FIND IT..
THIS IS A LAKE..
SOMEBODY BETTER TELL THAT KID..

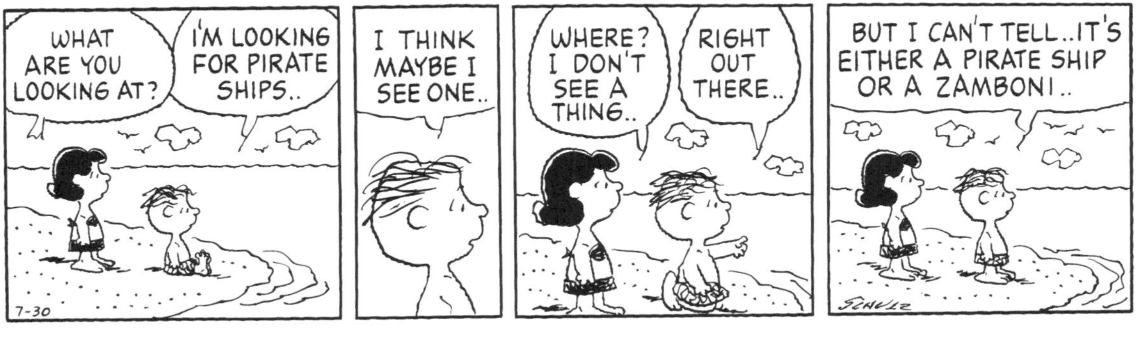
WHAT ARE YOU LOOKING AT?
I'M LOOKING FOR PIRATE SHIPS..
I THINK MAYBE I SEE ONE..
WHERE? I DON'T SEE A THING..
RIGHT OUT THERE..
BUT I CAN'T TELL..IT'S EITHER A PIRATE SHIP OR A ZAMBONI..

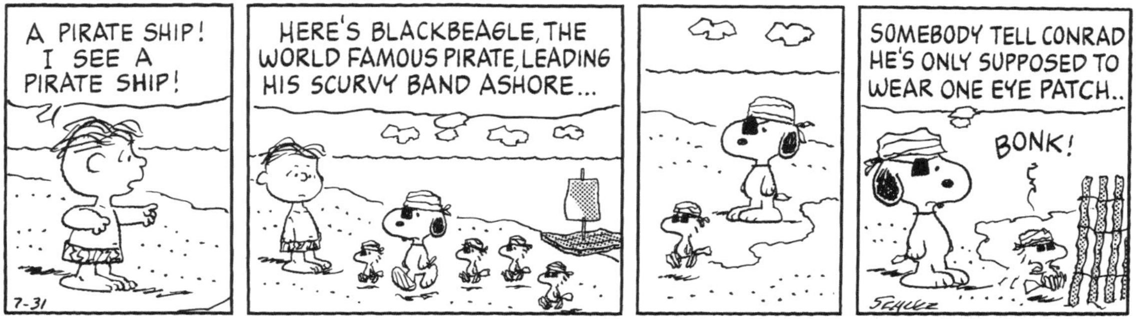
A PIRATE SHIP! I SEE A PIRATE SHIP!
7-31
HERE'S BLACKBEAGLE, THE WORLD FAMOUS PIRATE, LEADING HIS SCURVY BAND ASHORE...
SOMEBODY TELL CONRAD HE'S ONLY SUPPOSED TO WEAR ONE EYE PATCH..
BONK!

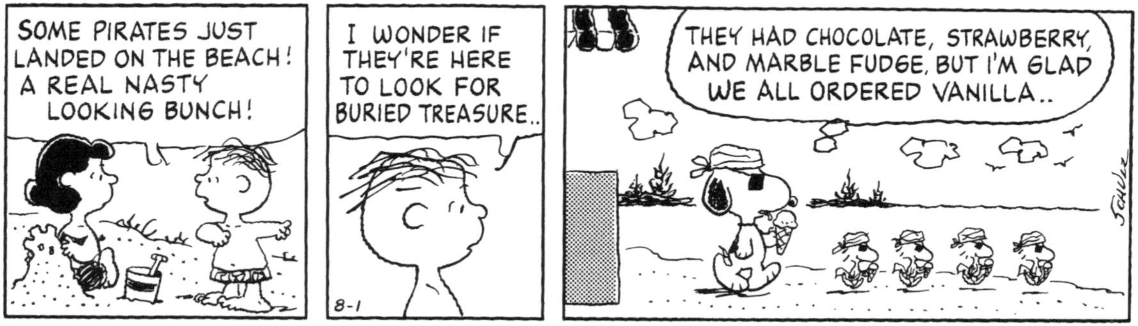
SOME PIRATES JUST LANDED ON THE BEACH! A REAL NASTY LOOKING BUNCH!
I WONDER IF THEY'RE HERE TO LOOK FOR BURIED TREASURE..
8-1
THEY HAD CHOCOLATE, STRAWBERRY, AND MARBLE FUDGE, BUT I'M GLAD WE ALL ORDERED VANILLA..

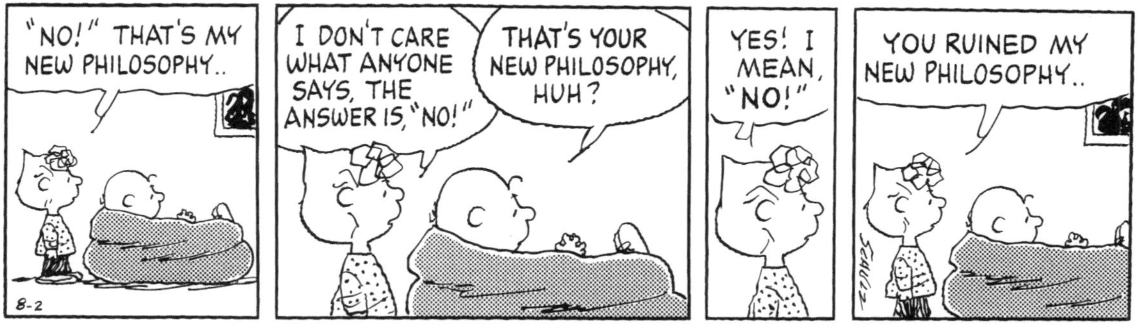
"NO!" THAT'S MY NEW PHILOSOPHY..
8-2
I DON'T CARE WHAT ANYONE SAYS, THE ANSWER IS, "NO!"
THAT'S YOUR NEW PHILOSOPHY, HUH?
YES! I MEAN, "NO!"
YOU RUINED MY NEW PHILOSOPHY..

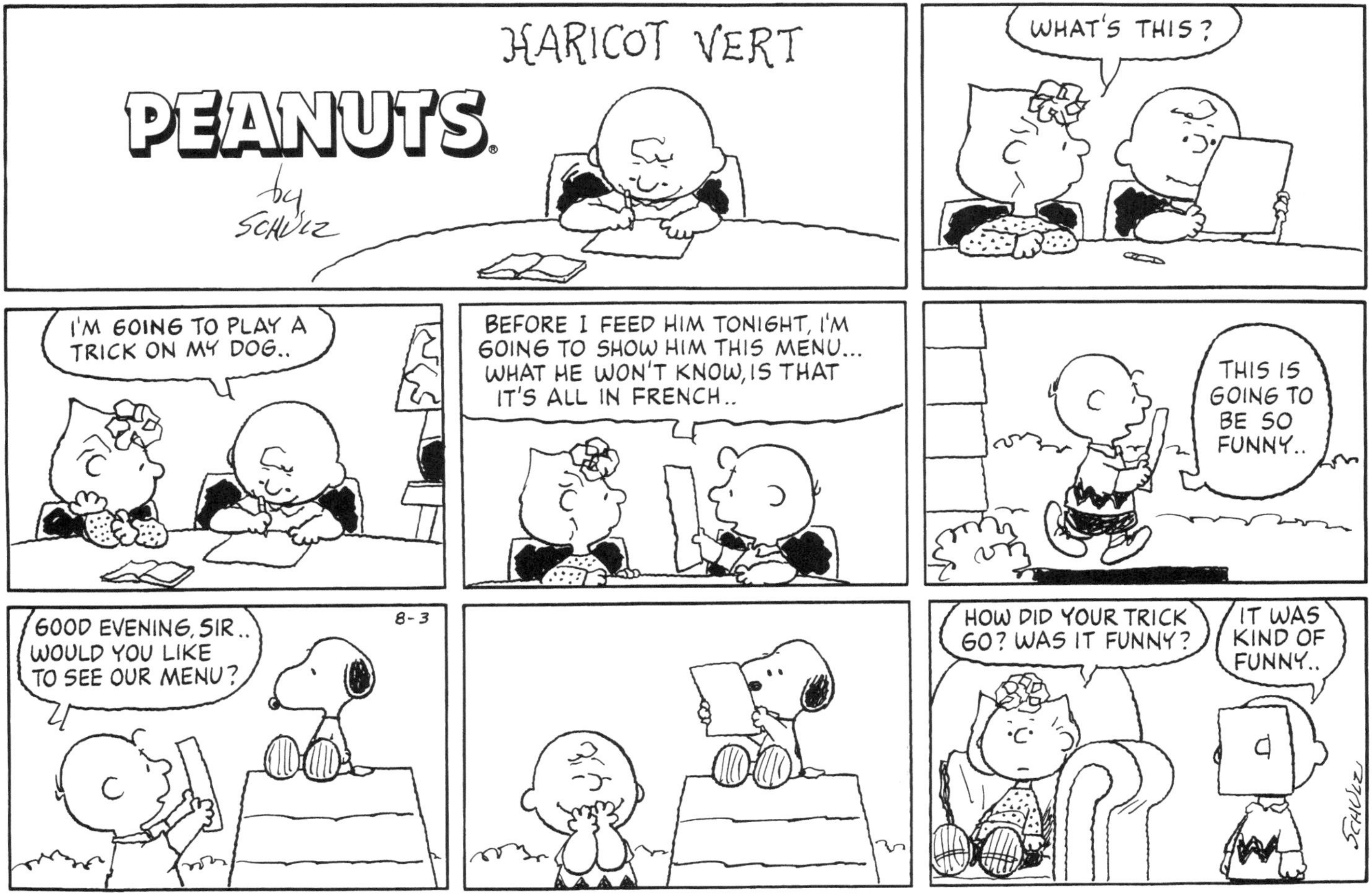
PEANUTS
by SCHULZ
HARICOT VERT
WHAT'S THIS?
I'M GOING TO PLAY A TRICK ON MY DOG..
BEFORE I FEED HIM TONIGHT, I'M GOING TO SHOW HIM THIS MENU... WHAT HE WON'T KNOW, IS THAT IT'S ALL IN FRENCH..
THIS IS GOING TO BE SO FUNNY..
8-3
GOOD EVENING, SIR.. WOULD YOU LIKE TO SEE OUR MENU?
HOW DID YOUR TRICK GO? WAS IT FUNNY?
IT WAS KIND OF FUNNY..
SCHULZ

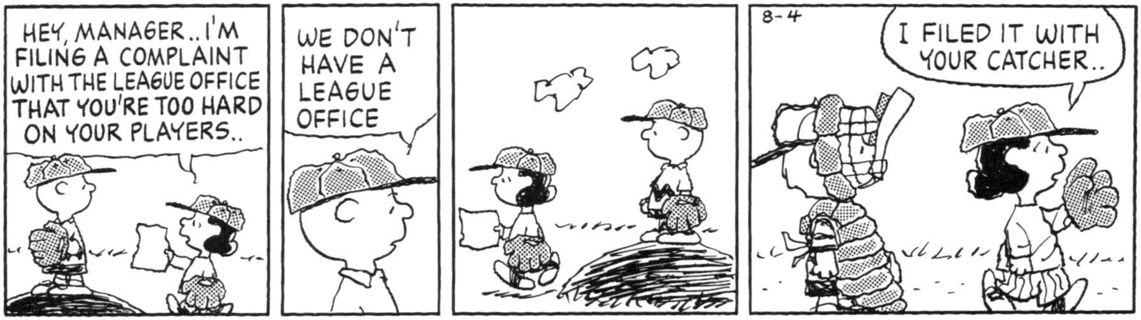
HEY, MANAGER..I'M FILING A COMPLAINT WITH THE LEAGUE OFFICE THAT YOU'RE TOO HARD ON YOUR PLAYERS..
WE DON'T HAVE A LEAGUE OFFICE
8-4
I FILED IT WITH YOUR CATCHER..

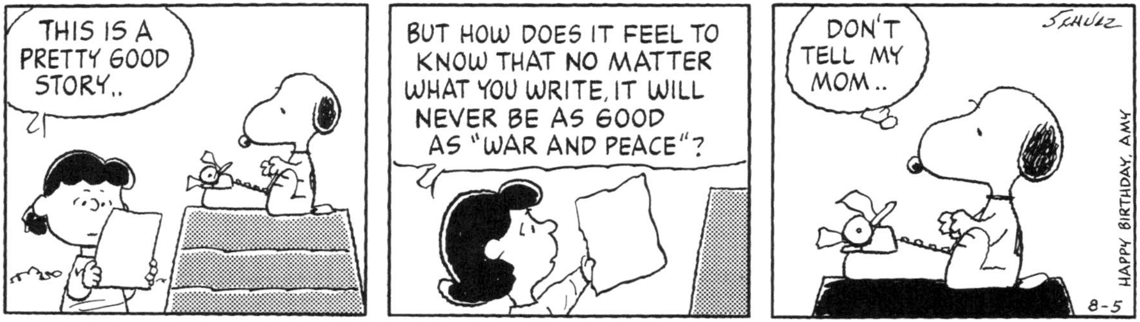
THIS IS A PRETTY GOOD STORY..
BUT HOW DOES IT FEEL TO KNOW THAT NO MATTER WHAT YOU WRITE, IT WILL NEVER BE AS GOOD AS "WAR AND PEACE"?
DON'T TELL MY MOM..
SCHULZ
HAPPY BIRTHDAY, AMY
8-5

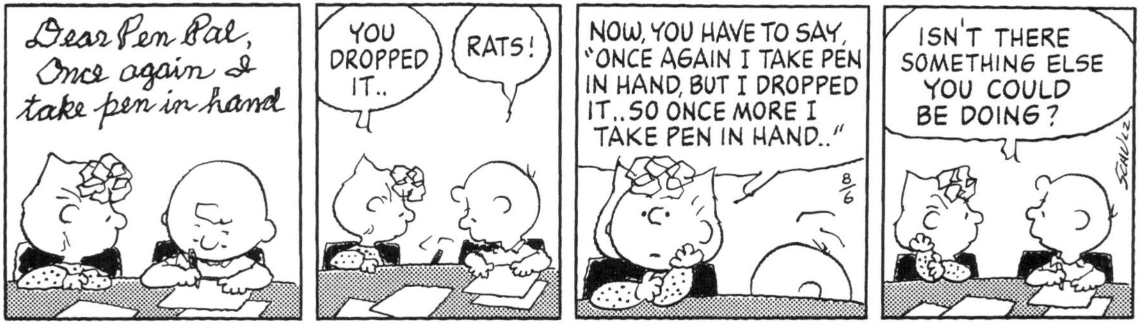
Dear Pen Pal, Once again I take pen in hand
YOU DROPPED IT..
RATS!
NOW, YOU HAVE TO SAY, "ONCE AGAIN I TAKE PEN IN HAND, BUT I DROPPED IT..SO ONCE MORE I TAKE PEN IN HAND.."
8/6
ISN'T THERE SOMETHING ELSE YOU COULD BE DOING?
SCHULZ

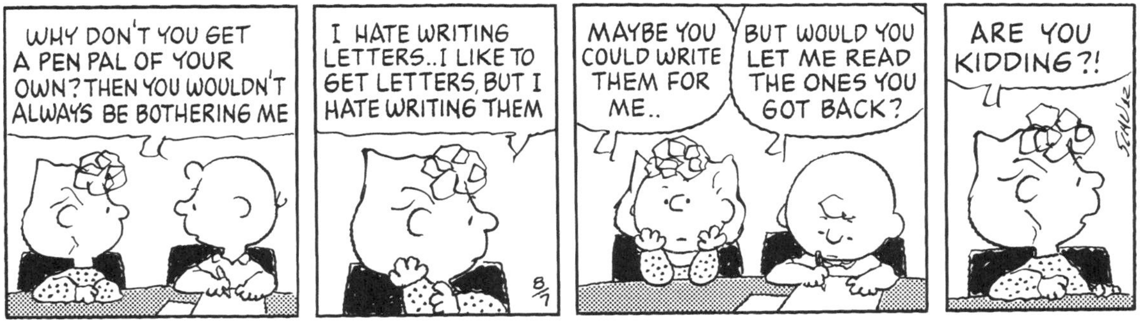
WHY DON'T YOU GET A PEN PAL OF YOUR OWN? THEN YOU WOULDN'T ALWAYS BE BOTHERING ME
I HATE WRITING LETTERS..I LIKE TO GET LETTERS, BUT I HATE WRITING THEM
8/7
MAYBE YOU COULD WRITE THEM FOR ME..
BUT WOULD YOU LET ME READ THE ONES YOU GOT BACK?
ARE YOU KIDDING?!
SCHULZ

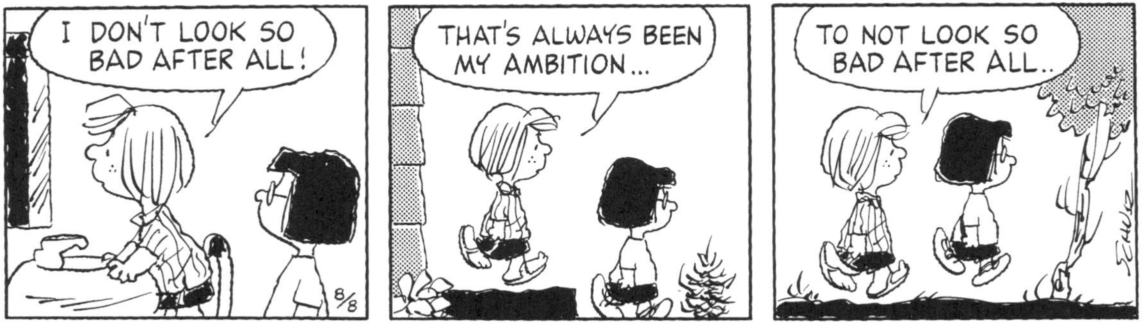
I DON'T LOOK SO BAD AFTER ALL!
8/8
THAT'S ALWAYS BEEN MY AMBITION...
TO NOT LOOK SO BAD AFTER ALL..
SCHULZ

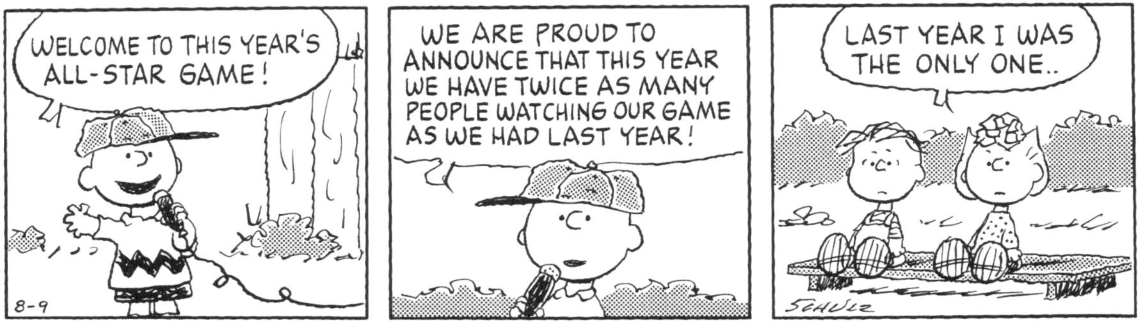
WELCOME TO THIS YEAR'S ALL-STAR GAME!
8-9
WE ARE PROUD TO ANNOUNCE THAT THIS YEAR WE HAVE TWICE AS MANY PEOPLE WATCHING OUR GAME AS WE HAD LAST YEAR!
LAST YEAR I WAS THE ONLY ONE..
SCHULZ

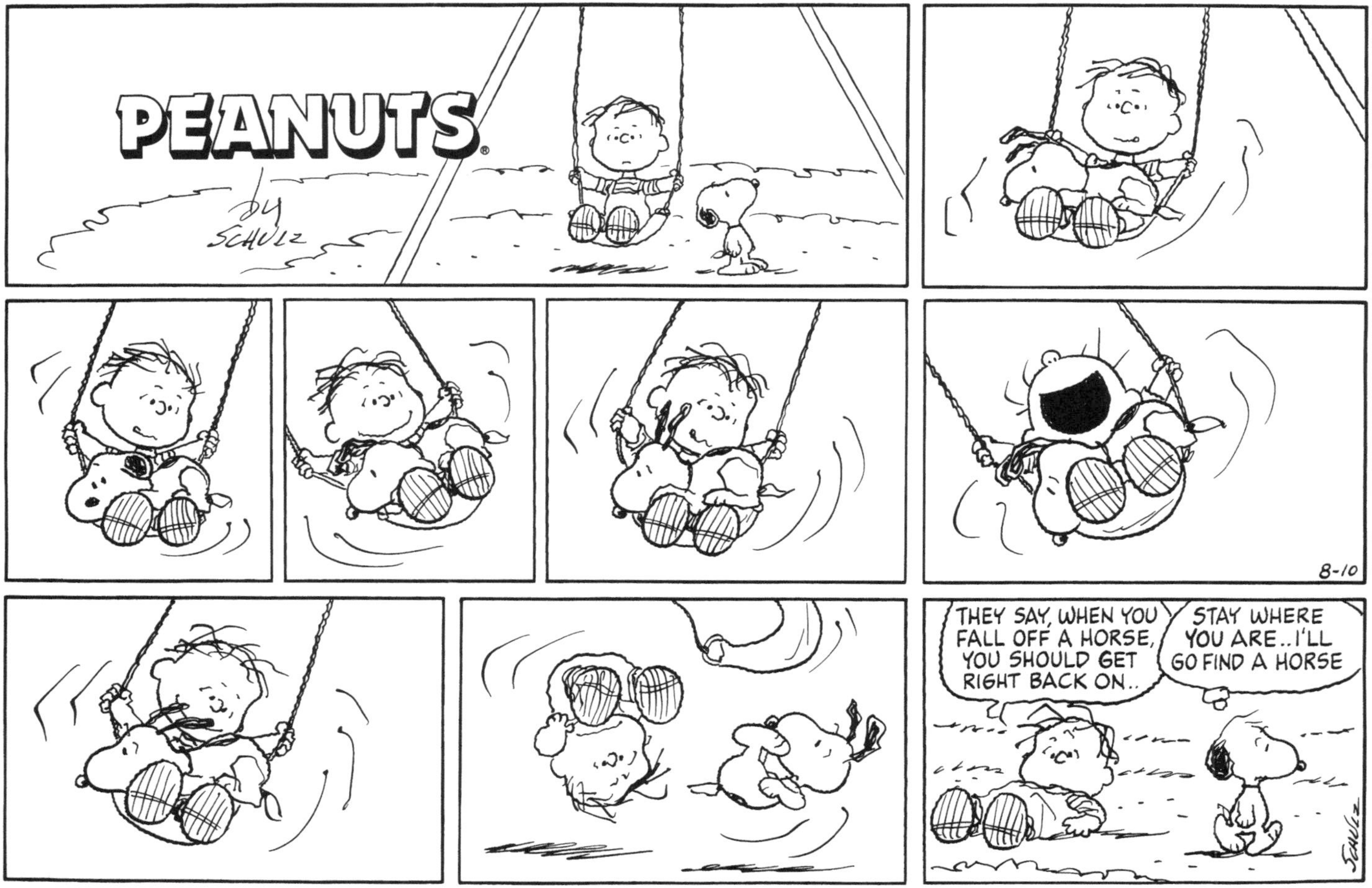
PEANUTS
by SCHULZ
8-10
THEY SAY, WHEN YOU FALL OFF A HORSE, YOU SHOULD GET RIGHT BACK ON..
STAY WHERE YOU ARE..I'LL GO FIND A HORSE
SCHULZ

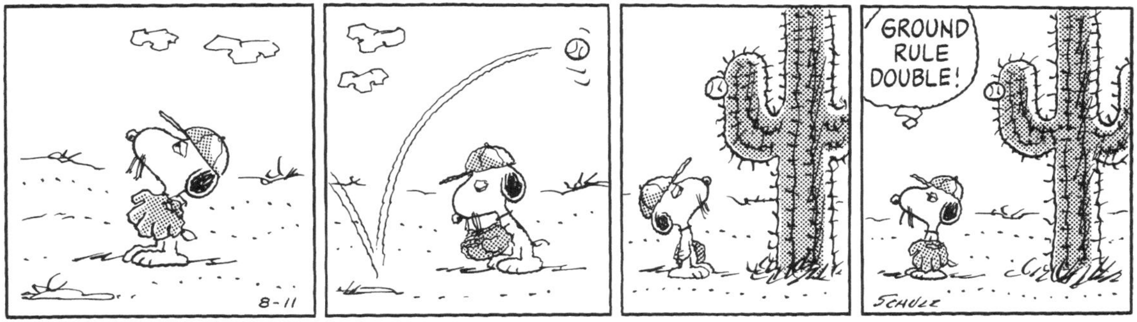
GROUND RULE DOUBLE!

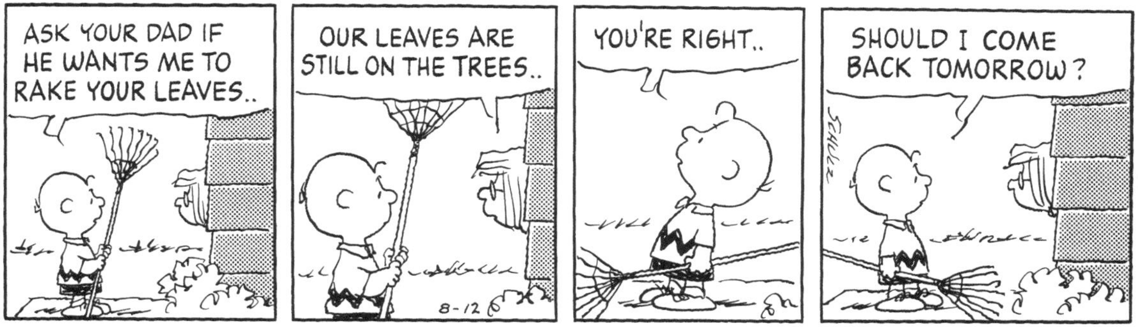
ASK YOUR DAD IF HE WANTS ME TO RAKE YOUR LEAVES..
OUR LEAVES ARE STILL ON THE TREES..
YOU'RE RIGHT..
SHOULD I COME BACK TOMORROW?

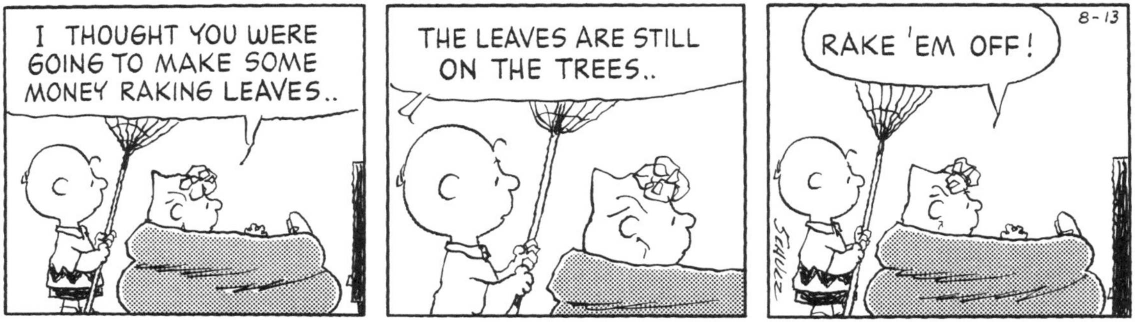
I THOUGHT YOU WERE GOING TO MAKE SOME MONEY RAKING LEAVES..
THE LEAVES ARE STILL ON THE TREES..
RAKE 'EM OFF!

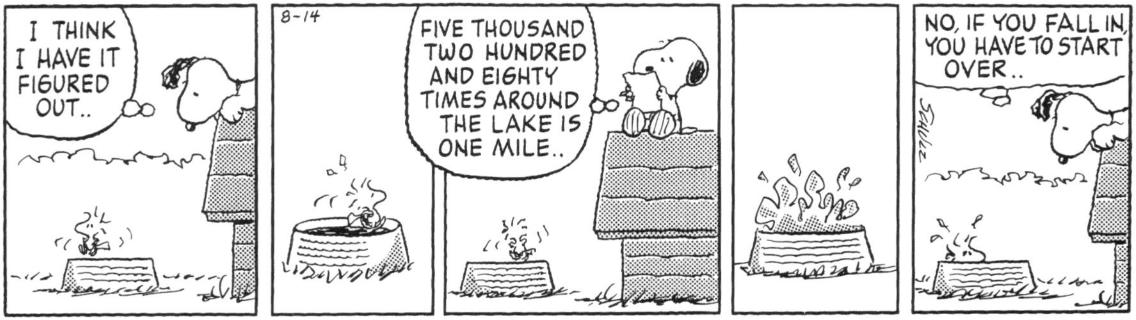
8-14
I THINK I HAVE IT FIGURED OUT..
FIVE THOUSAND TWO HUNDRED AND EIGHTY TIMES AROUND THE LAKE IS ONE MILE..
NO, IF YOU FALL IN, YOU HAVE TO START OVER..
SCHULZ

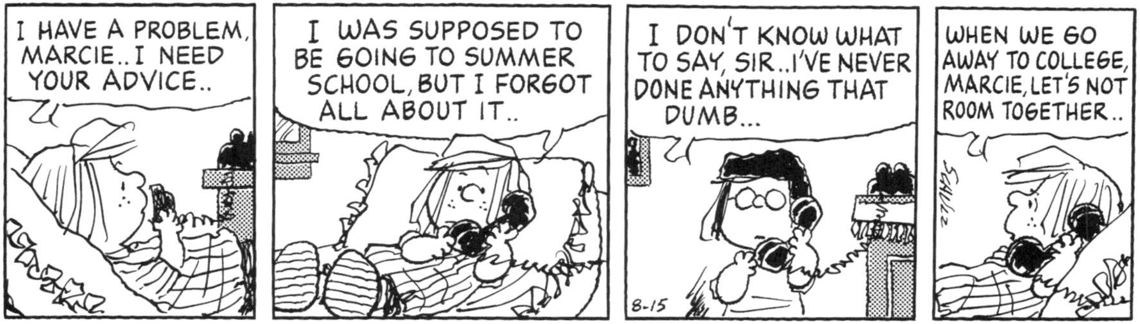
I HAVE A PROBLEM, MARCIE..I NEED YOUR ADVICE..
I WAS SUPPOSED TO BE GOING TO SUMMER SCHOOL, BUT I FORGOT ALL ABOUT IT..
I DON'T KNOW WHAT TO SAY, SIR..I'VE NEVER DONE ANYTHING THAT DUMB...
8-15
WHEN WE GO AWAY TO COLLEGE, MARCIE, LET'S NOT ROOM TOGETHER..
SCHULZ

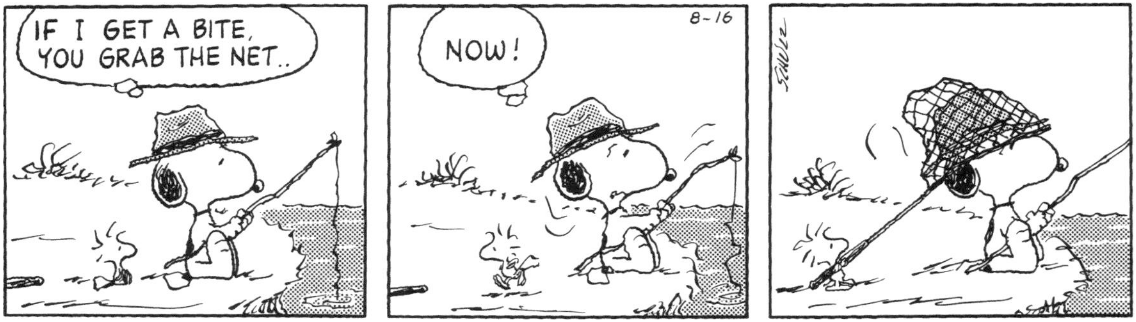
IF I GET A BITE, YOU GRAB THE NET..
8-16
NOW!
SCHULZ

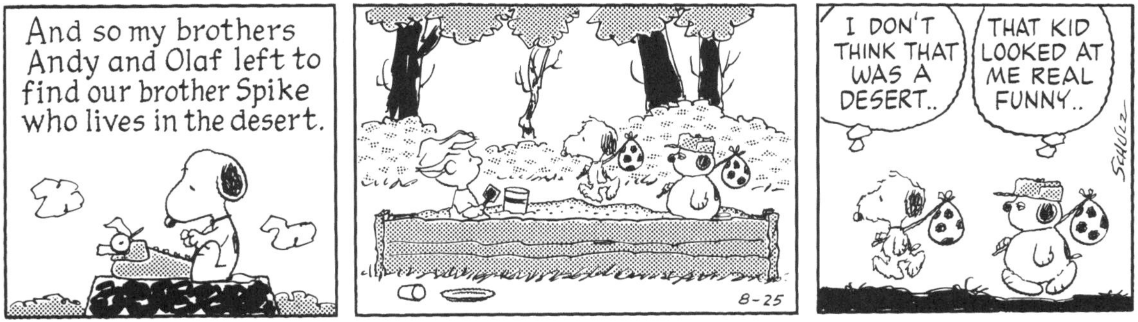
And so my brothers Andy and Olaf left to find our brother Spike who lives in the desert.
8-25
I DON'T THINK THAT WAS A DESERT..
THAT KID LOOKED AT ME REAL FUNNY..
SCHULZ

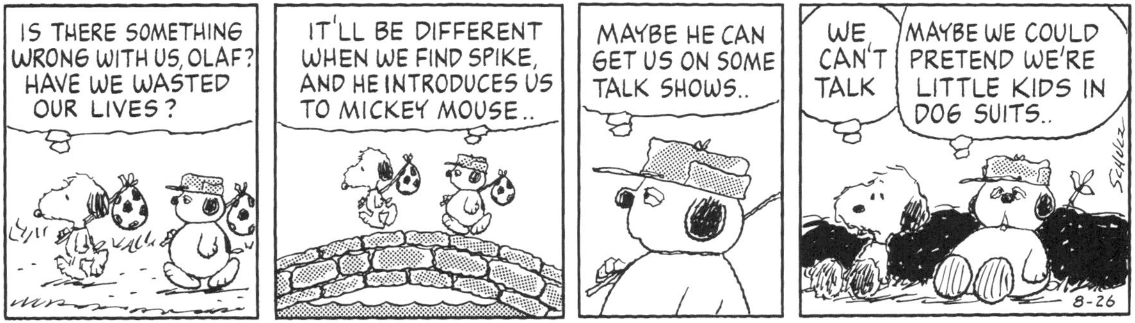
IS THERE SOMETHING WRONG WITH US, OLAF? HAVE WE WASTED OUR LIVES?
IT'LL BE DIFFERENT WHEN WE FIND SPIKE, AND HE INTRODUCES US TO MICKEY MOUSE..
MAYBE HE CAN GET US ON SOME TALK SHOWS..
WE CAN'T TALK
MAYBE WE COULD PRETEND WE'RE LITTLE KIDS IN DOG SUITS..
SCHULZ
8-26

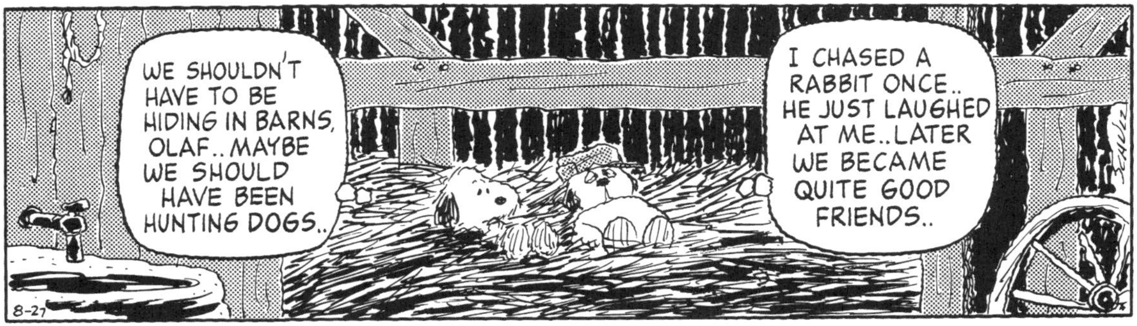
WE SHOULDN'T HAVE TO BE HIDING IN BARNS, OLAF.. MAYBE WE SHOULD HAVE BEEN HUNTING DOGS..
I CHASED A RABBIT ONCE.. HE JUST LAUGHED AT ME.. LATER WE BECAME QUITE GOOD FRIENDS..
SCHULZ
8-27

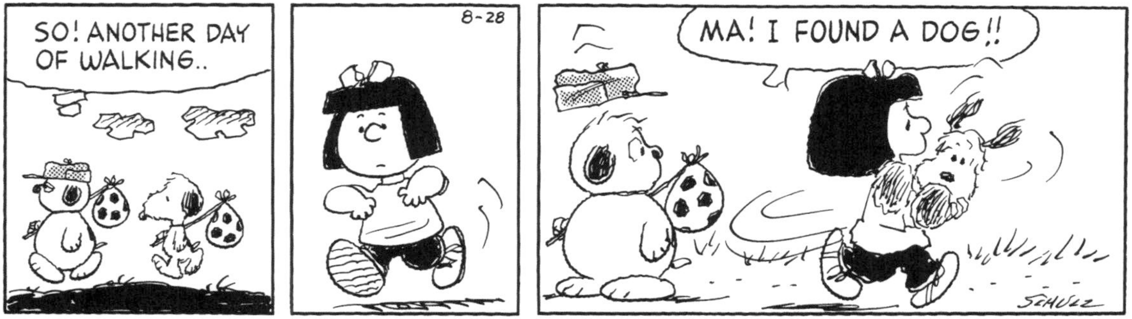
SO! ANOTHER DAY OF WALKING..
8-28
MA! I FOUND A DOG!!
SCHULZ

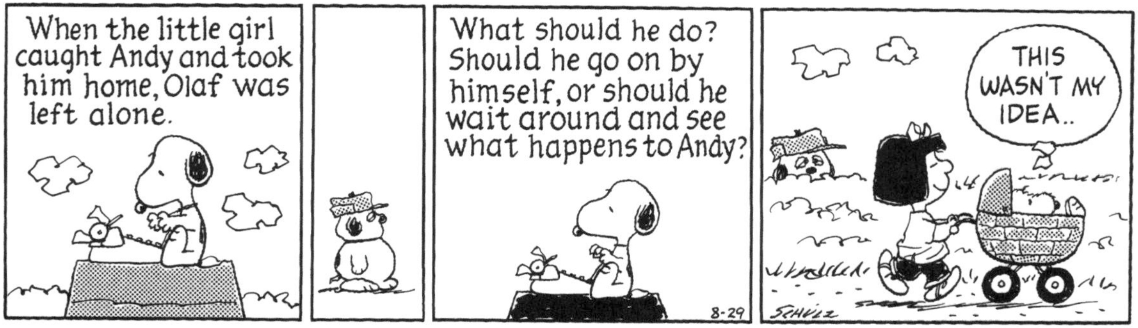
When the little girl caught Andy and took him home, Olaf was left alone.
What should he do? Should he go on by himself, or should he wait around and see what happens to Andy?
8-29
THIS WASN'T MY IDEA..
SCHULZ

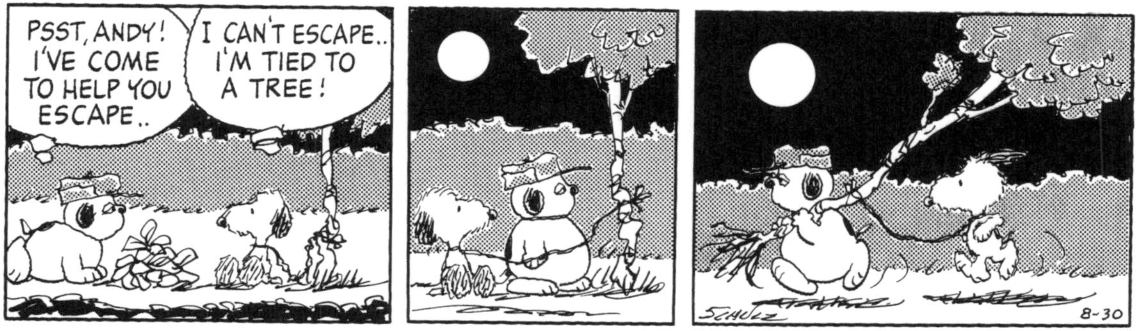
PSST, ANDY! I'VE COME TO HELP YOU ESCAPE..
I CAN'T ESCAPE.. I'M TIED TO A TREE!
SCHULZ
8-30

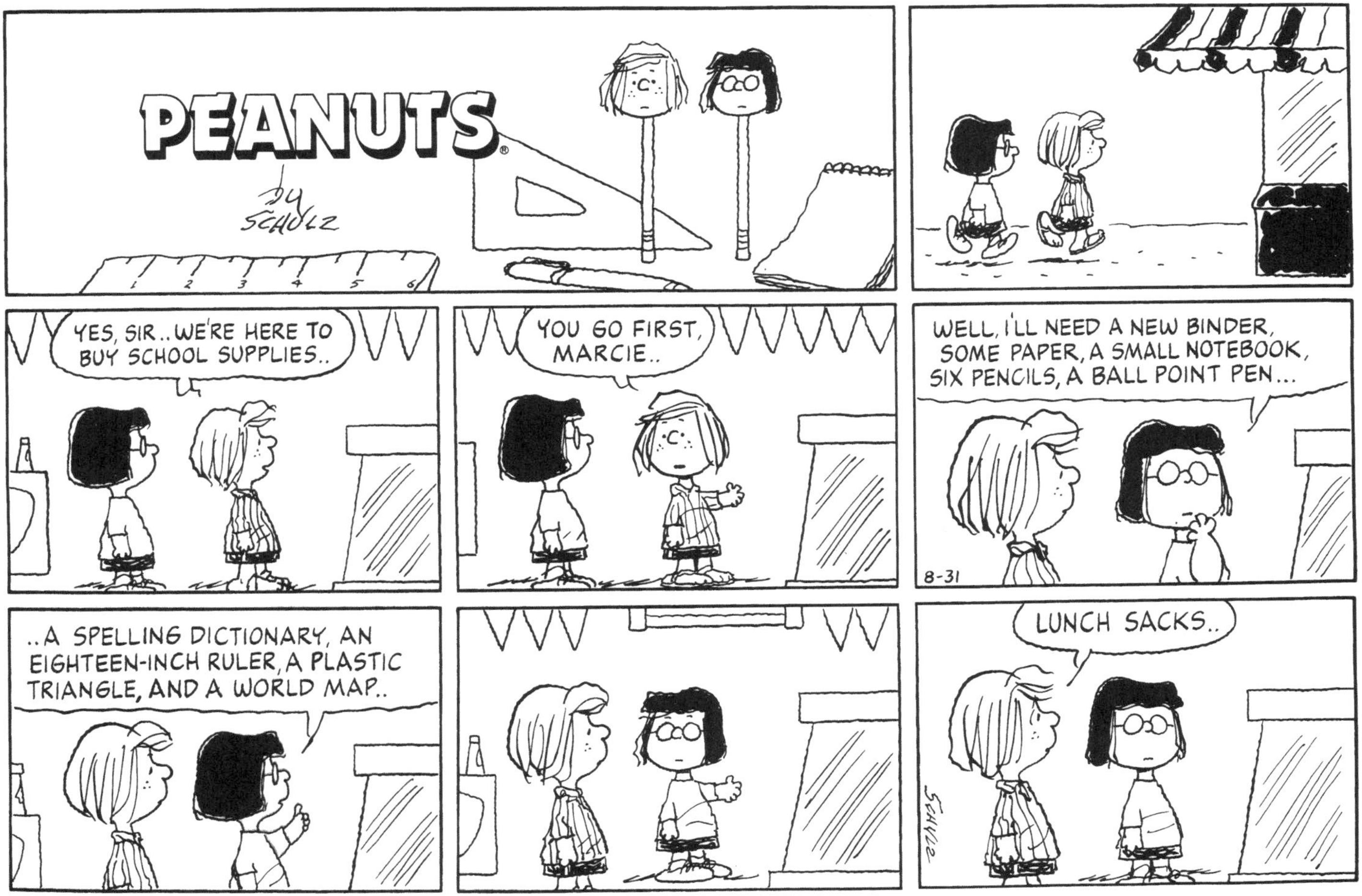
PEANUTS
by SCHULZ
YES, SIR..WE'RE HERE TO BUY SCHOOL SUPPLIES..
YOU GO FIRST, MARCIE..
WELL, I'LL NEED A NEW BINDER, SOME PAPER, A SMALL NOTEBOOK, SIX PENCILS, A BALL POINT PEN...
8-31
..A SPELLING DICTIONARY, AN EIGHTEEN-INCH RULER, A PLASTIC TRIANGLE, AND A WORLD MAP..
LUNCH SACKS..
SCHULZ

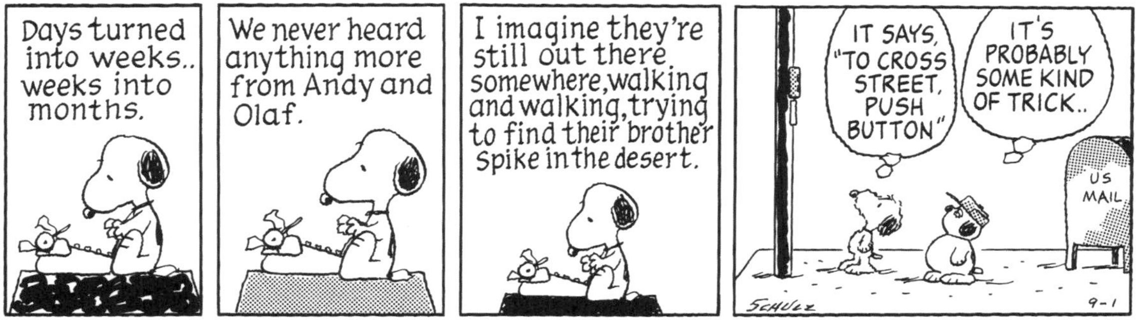
Days turned into weeks.. weeks into months.
We never heard anything more from Andy and Olaf.
I imagine they're still out there somewhere, walking and walking, trying to find their brother Spike in the desert.
IT SAYS, "TO CROSS STREET, PUSH BUTTON"
IT'S PROBABLY SOME KIND OF TRICK..
US MAIL
SCHULZ
9-1

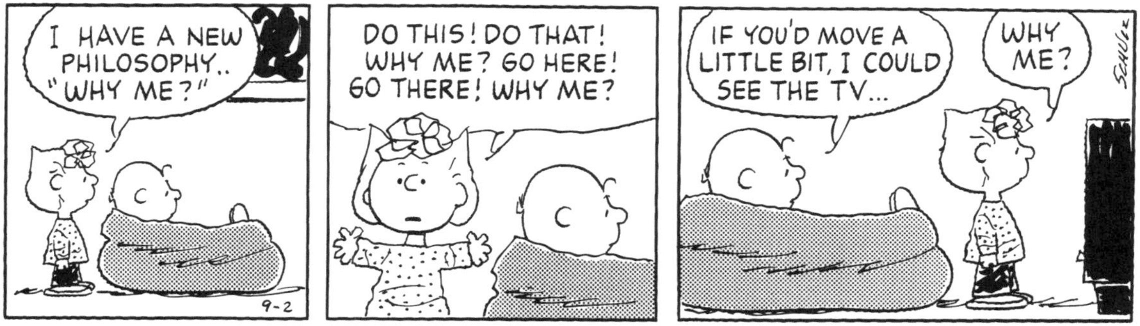
I HAVE A NEW PHILOSOPHY.. "WHY ME?"
9-2
DO THIS! DO THAT! WHY ME? GO HERE! GO THERE! WHY ME?
IF YOU'D MOVE A LITTLE BIT, I COULD SEE THE TV...
WHY ME?
SCHULZ

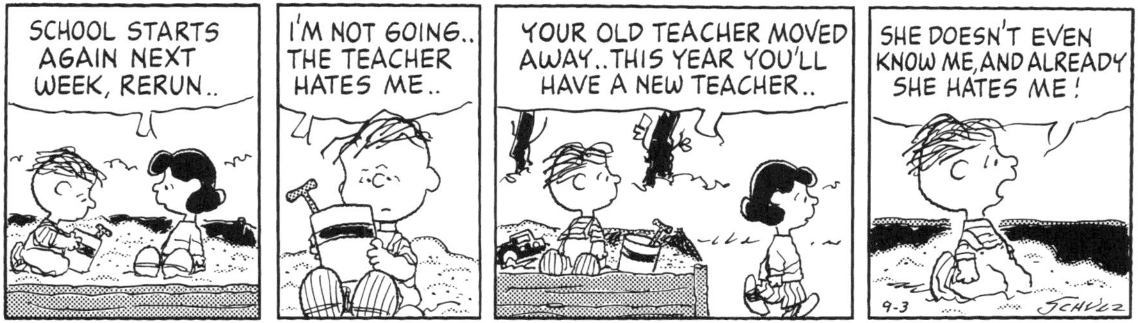
SCHOOL STARTS AGAIN NEXT WEEK, RERUN..
I'M NOT GOING.. THE TEACHER HATES ME..
YOUR OLD TEACHER MOVED AWAY.. THIS YEAR YOU'LL HAVE A NEW TEACHER..
SHE DOESN'T EVEN KNOW ME, AND ALREADY SHE HATES ME!
9-3
SCHULZ

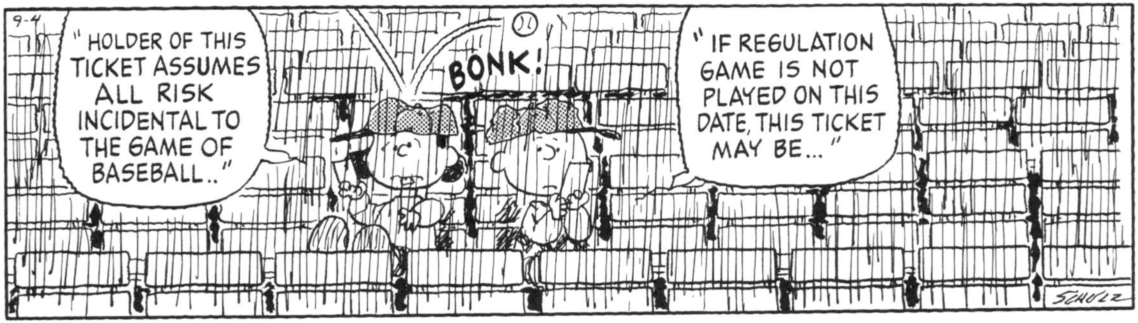

9-4
" HOLDER OF THIS TICKET ASSUMES ALL RISK INCIDENTAL TO THE GAME OF BASEBALL.."
BONK!
" IF REGULATION GAME IS NOT PLAYED ON THIS DATE, THIS TICKET MAY BE..."
SCHULZ

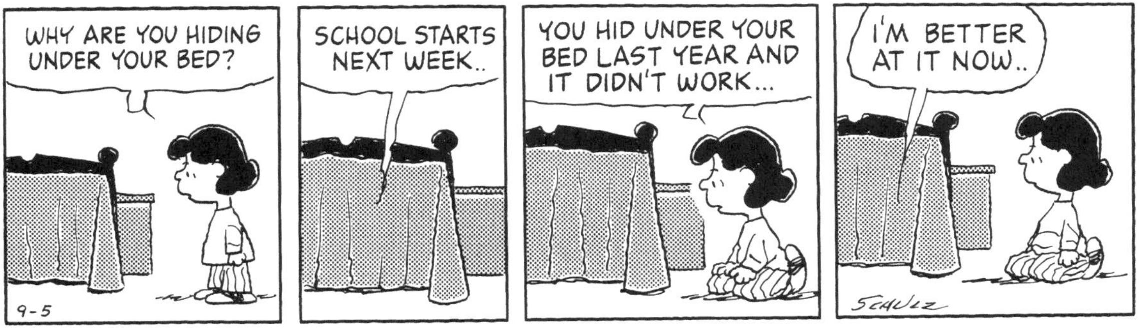

WHY ARE YOU HIDING UNDER YOUR BED?
SCHOOL STARTS NEXT WEEK..
YOU HID UNDER YOUR BED LAST YEAR AND IT DIDN'T WORK...
I'M BETTER AT IT NOW..
9-5
SCHULZ

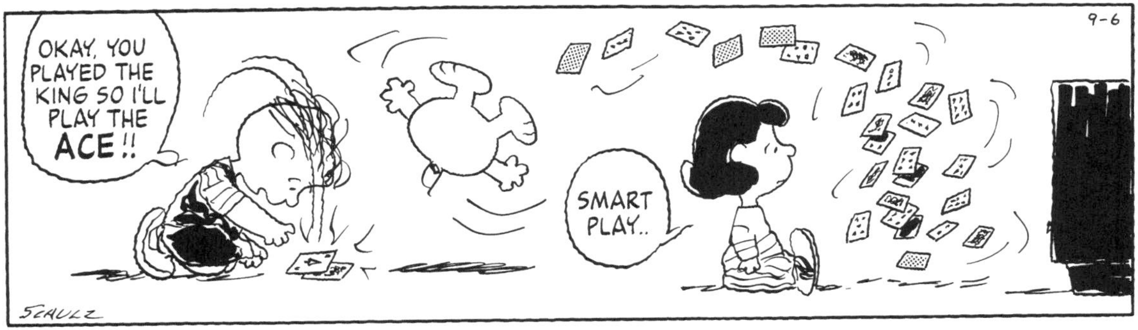

9-6
OKAY, YOU PLAYED THE KING SO I'LL PLAY THE ACE!!
SMART PLAY..
SCHULZ

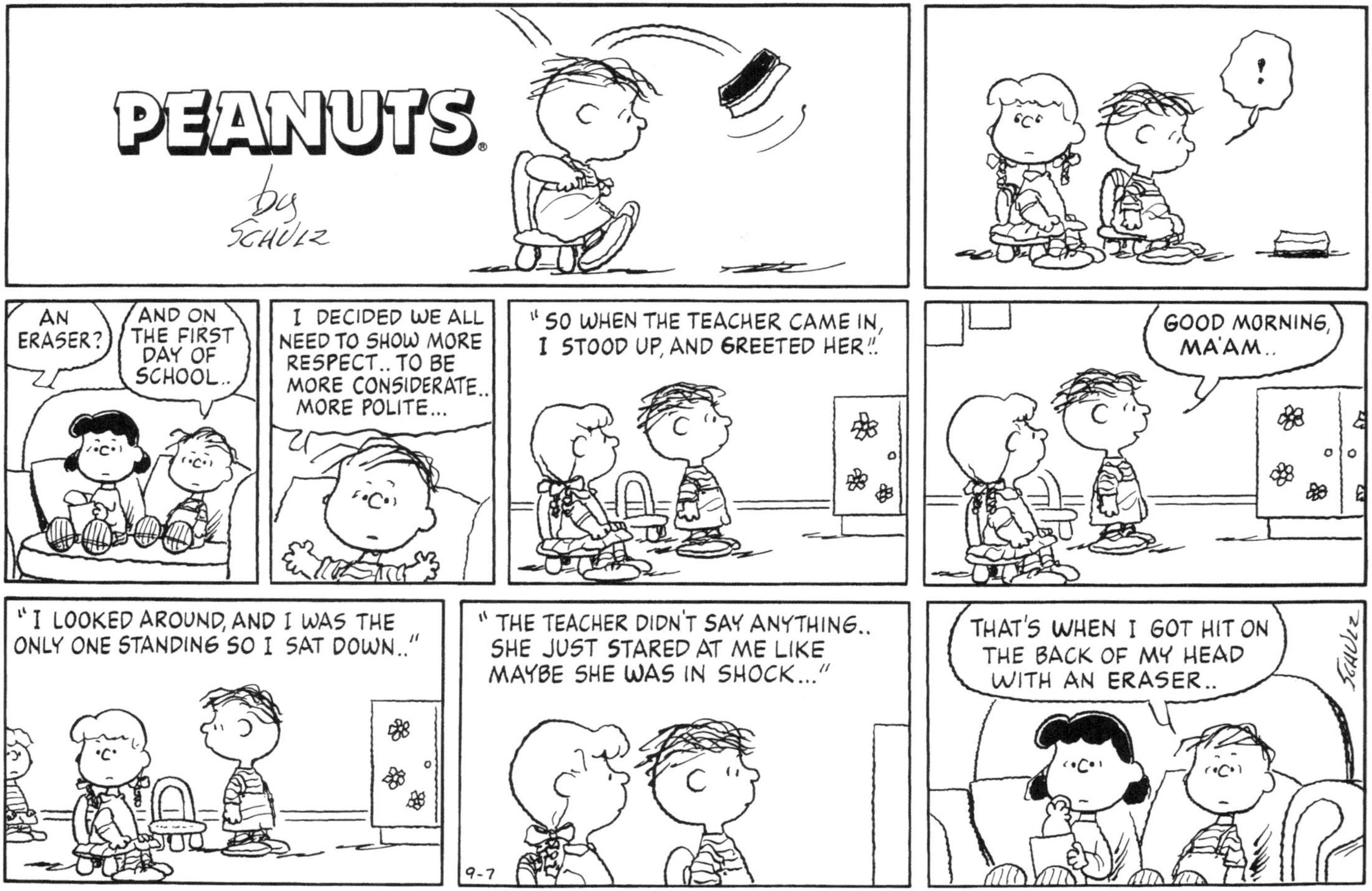
PEANUTS
by SCHULZ
!
AN ERASER?
AND ON THE FIRST DAY OF SCHOOL..
I DECIDED WE ALL NEED TO SHOW MORE RESPECT.. TO BE MORE CONSIDERATE.. MORE POLITE...
"SO WHEN THE TEACHER CAME IN, I STOOD UP, AND GREETED HER"..
GOOD MORNING, MA'AM..
"I LOOKED AROUND, AND I WAS THE ONLY ONE STANDING SO I SAT DOWN.."
"THE TEACHER DIDN'T SAY ANYTHING.. SHE JUST STARED AT ME LIKE MAYBE SHE WAS IN SHOCK..."
9-7
THAT'S WHEN I GOT HIT ON THE BACK OF MY HEAD WITH AN ERASER..
SCHULZ

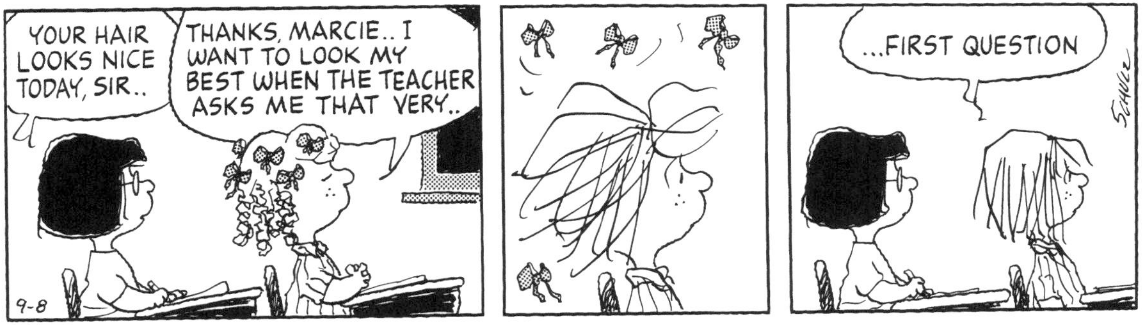
YOUR HAIR LOOKS NICE TODAY, SIR..
THANKS, MARCIE.. I WANT TO LOOK MY BEST WHEN THE TEACHER ASKS ME THAT VERY..
...FIRST QUESTION
SCHULZ

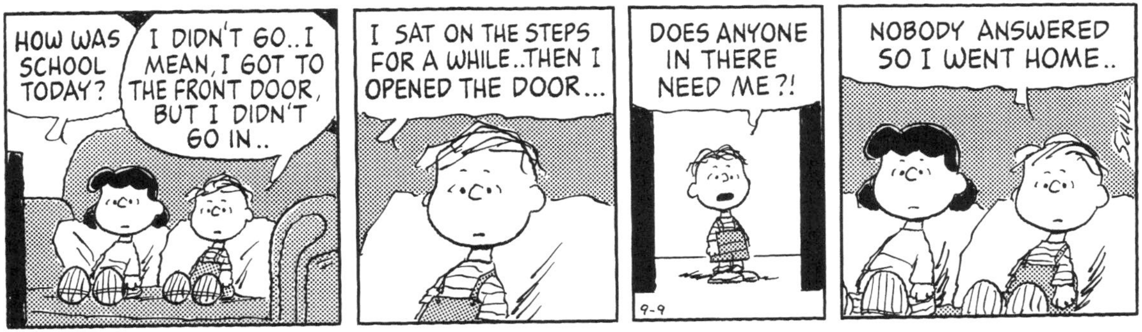
HOW WAS SCHOOL TODAY?
I DIDN'T GO..I MEAN, I GOT TO THE FRONT DOOR, BUT I DIDN'T GO IN..
I SAT ON THE STEPS FOR A WHILE..THEN I OPENED THE DOOR...
DOES ANYONE IN THERE NEED ME?!
NOBODY ANSWERED SO I WENT HOME..
SCHULZ

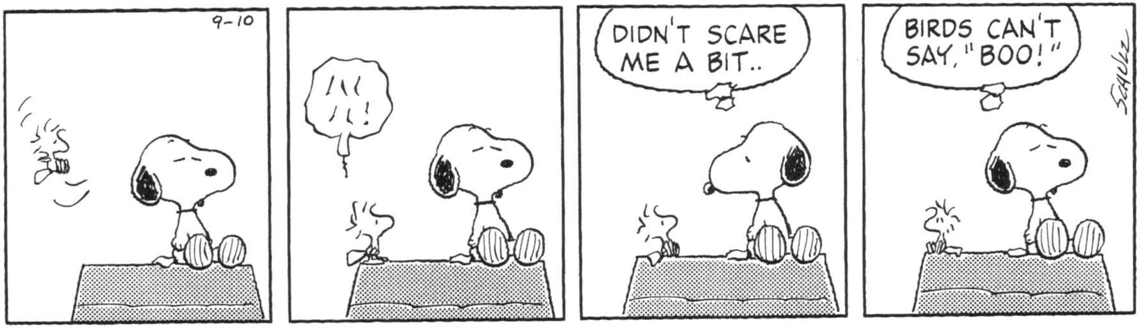
DIDN'T SCARE ME A BIT..
BIRDS CAN'T SAY, "BOO!"
SCHULZ

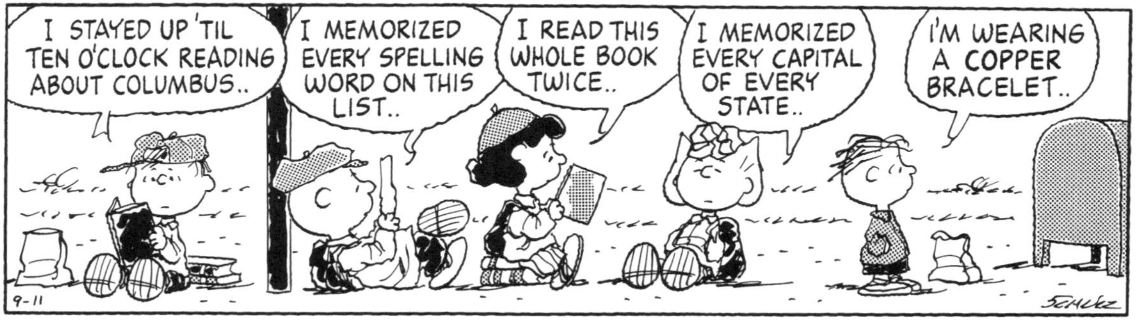
I STAYED UP 'TIL TEN O'CLOCK READING ABOUT COLUMBUS..
I MEMORIZED EVERY SPELLING WORD ON THIS LIST..
I READ THIS WHOLE BOOK TWICE..
I MEMORIZED EVERY CAPITAL OF EVERY STATE..
I'M WEARING A COPPER BRACELET..
9-11
SCHULZ

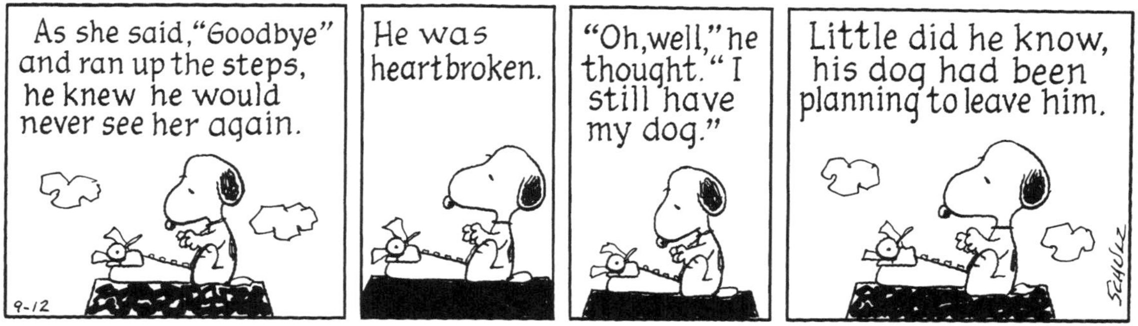
As she said, "Goodbye" and ran up the steps, he knew he would never see her again.
He was heartbroken.
"Oh, well," he thought. "I still have my dog."
Little did he know, his dog had been planning to leave him.
9-12
SCHULZ

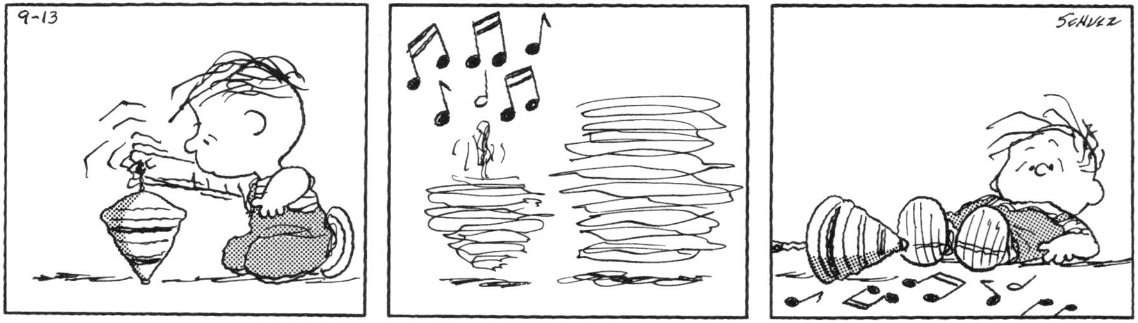
9-13
SCHULZ

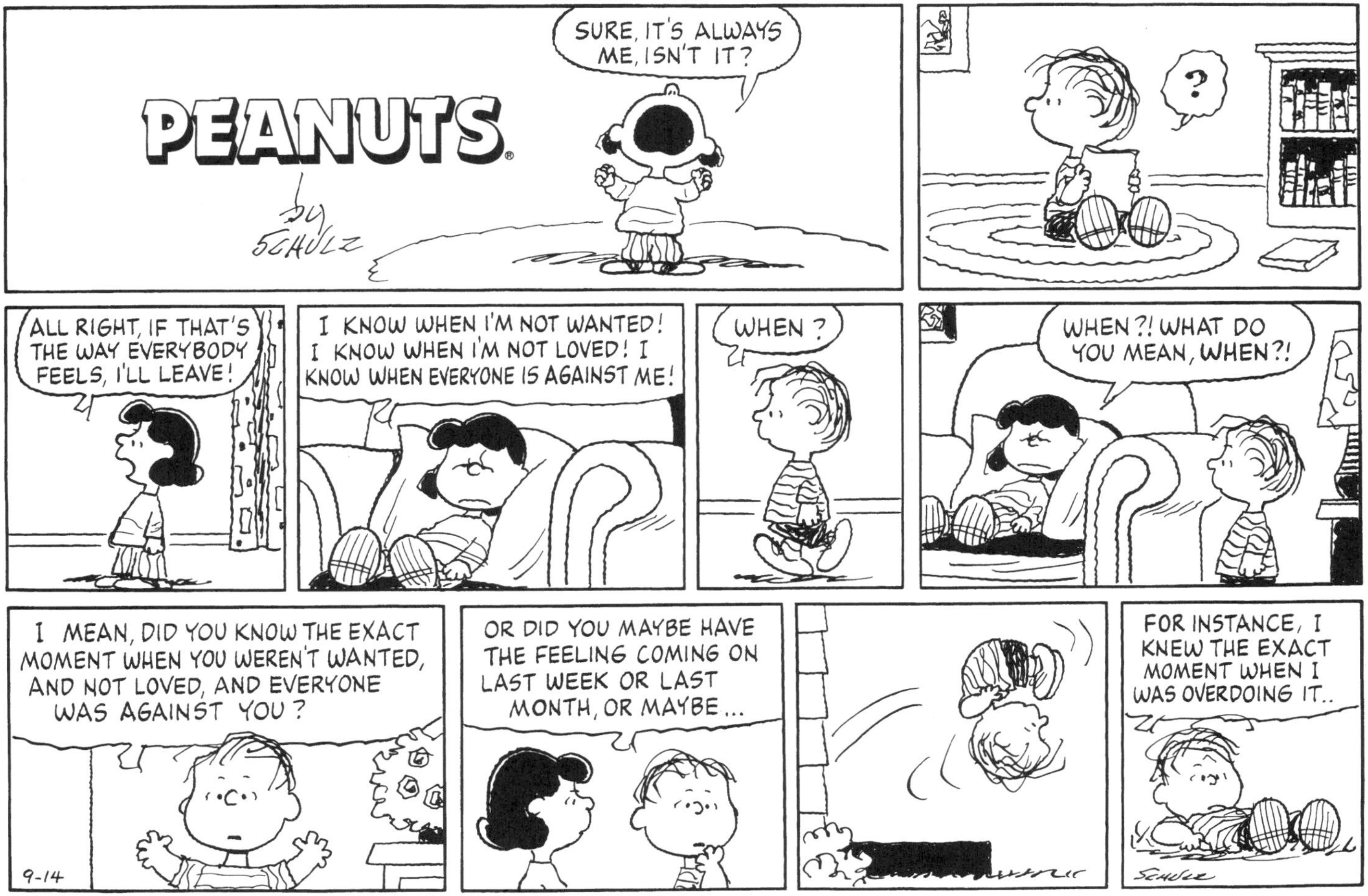
PEANUTS
SURE, IT'S ALWAYS ME, ISN'T IT?
?
ALL RIGHT, IF THAT'S THE WAY EVERYBODY FEELS, I'LL LEAVE!
I KNOW WHEN I'M NOT WANTED! I KNOW WHEN I'M NOT LOVED! I KNOW WHEN EVERYONE IS AGAINST ME!
WHEN?
WHEN?! WHAT DO YOU MEAN, WHEN?!
I MEAN, DID YOU KNOW THE EXACT MOMENT WHEN YOU WEREN'T WANTED, AND NOT LOVED, AND EVERYONE WAS AGAINST YOU?
9-14
OR DID YOU MAYBE HAVE THE FEELING COMING ON LAST WEEK OR LAST MONTH, OR MAYBE...
FOR INSTANCE, I KNEW THE EXACT MOMENT WHEN I WAS OVERDOING IT..

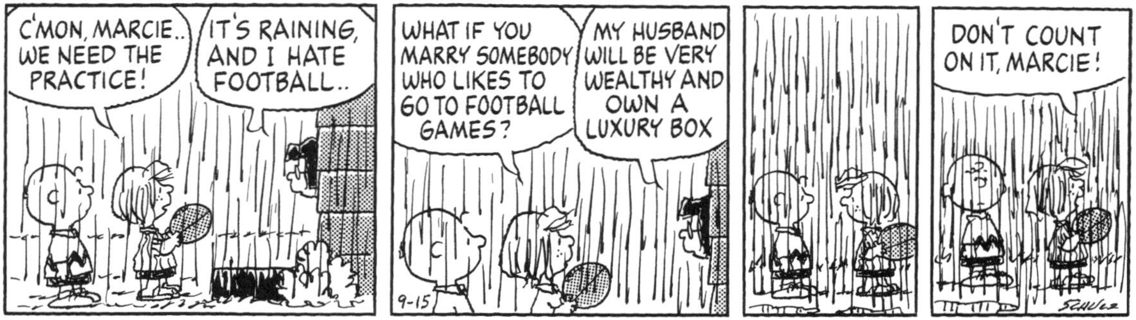
C'MON, MARCIE.. WE NEED THE PRACTICE!
IT'S RAINING, AND I HATE FOOTBALL..
WHAT IF YOU MARRY SOMEBODY WHO LIKES TO GO TO FOOTBALL GAMES?
MY HUSBAND WILL BE VERY WEALTHY AND OWN A LUXURY BOX
9-15
DON'T COUNT ON IT, MARCIE!

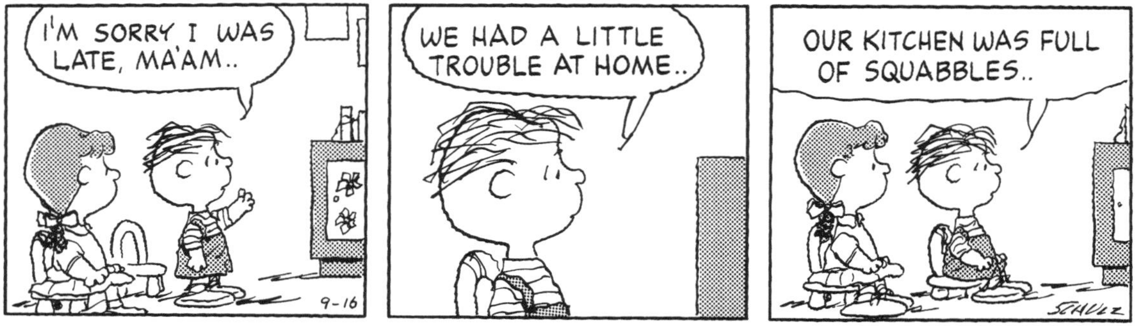
I'M SORRY I WAS LATE, MA'AM..
9-16
WE HAD A LITTLE TROUBLE AT HOME..
OUR KITCHEN WAS FULL OF SQUABBLES..

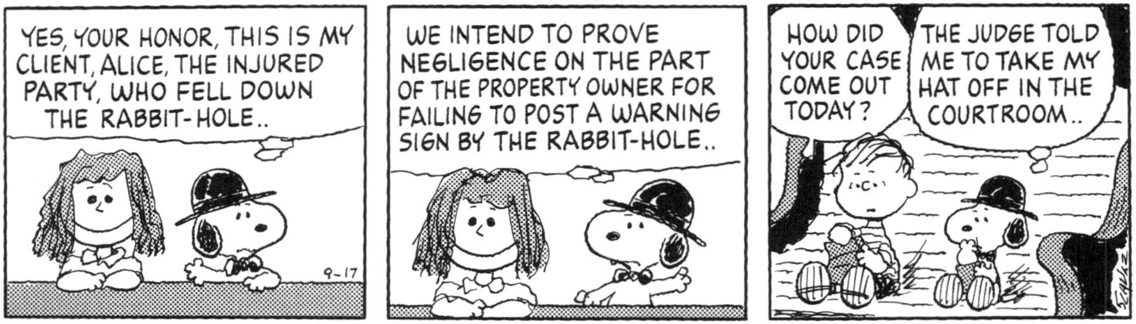
YES, YOUR HONOR, THIS IS MY CLIENT, ALICE, THE INJURED PARTY, WHO FELL DOWN THE RABBIT-HOLE..
9-17
WE INTEND TO PROVE NEGLIGENCE ON THE PART OF THE PROPERTY OWNER FOR FAILING TO POST A WARNING SIGN BY THE RABBIT-HOLE..
HOW DID YOUR CASE COME OUT TODAY?
THE JUDGE TOLD ME TO TAKE MY HAT OFF IN THE COURTROOM..

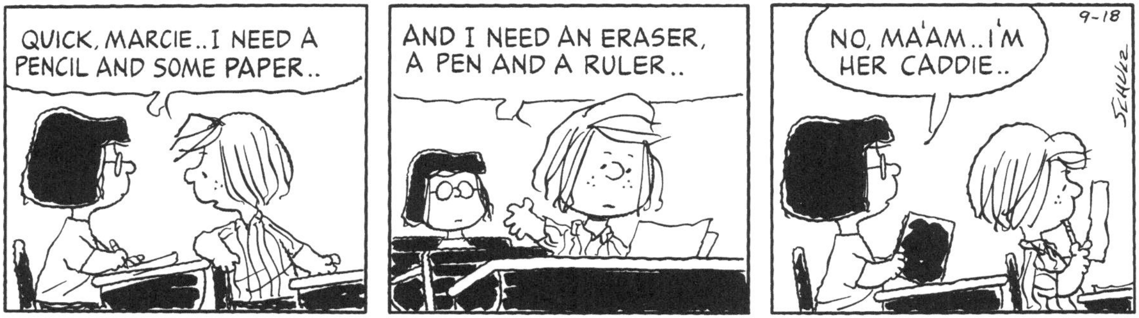
QUICK, MARCIE..I NEED A PENCIL AND SOME PAPER..
AND I NEED AN ERASER, A PEN AND A RULER..
NO, MA'AM..I'M HER CADDIE..
9-18
SCHULZ

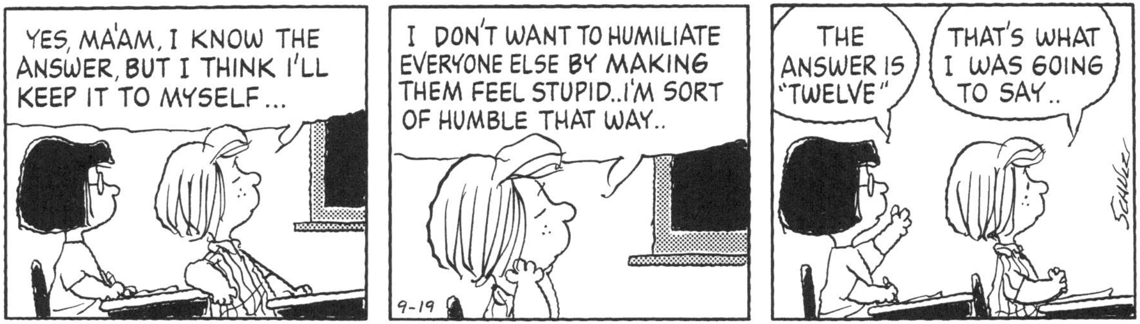
YES, MA'AM, I KNOW THE ANSWER, BUT I THINK I'LL KEEP IT TO MYSELF...
I DON'T WANT TO HUMILIATE EVERYONE ELSE BY MAKING THEM FEEL STUPID..I'M SORT OF HUMBLE THAT WAY..
9-19
THE ANSWER IS "TWELVE"
THAT'S WHAT I WAS GOING TO SAY..
SCHULZ

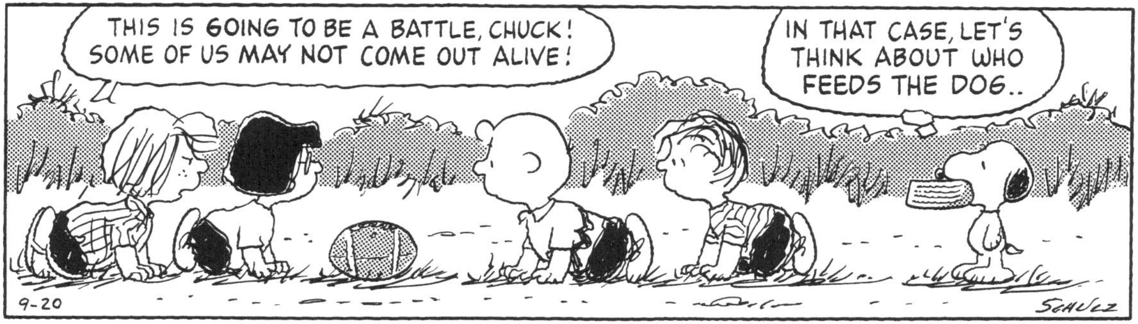
THIS IS GOING TO BE A BATTLE, CHUCK! SOME OF US MAY NOT COME OUT ALIVE!
IN THAT CASE, LET'S THINK ABOUT WHO FEEDS THE DOG..
9-20
SCHULZ

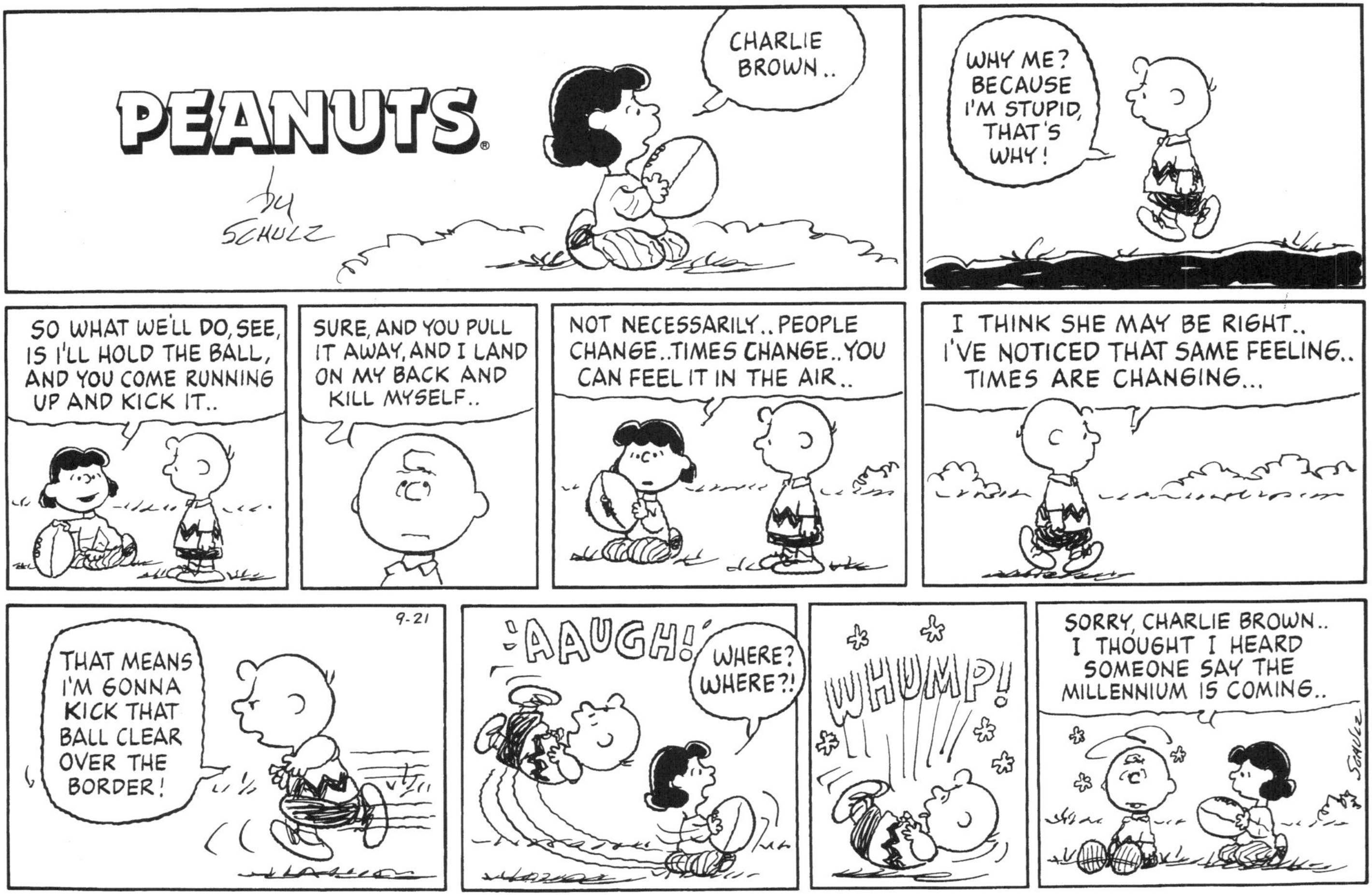
PEANUTS
by SCHULZ
CHARLIE BROWN..
WHY ME? BECAUSE I'M STUPID, THAT'S WHY!
SO WHAT WE'LL DO, SEE, IS I'LL HOLD THE BALL, AND YOU COME RUNNING UP AND KICK IT..
SURE, AND YOU PULL IT AWAY, AND I LAND ON MY BACK AND KILL MYSELF..
NOT NECESSARILY.. PEOPLE CHANGE..TIMES CHANGE..YOU CAN FEEL IT IN THE AIR..
I THINK SHE MAY BE RIGHT.. I'VE NOTICED THAT SAME FEELING.. TIMES ARE CHANGING...
9-21
THAT MEANS I'M GONNA KICK THAT BALL CLEAR OVER THE BORDER!
AAUGH!
WHERE? WHERE?!
WHUMP!
SORRY, CHARLIE BROWN.. I THOUGHT I HEARD SOMEONE SAY THE MILLENNIUM IS COMING..
SCHULZ

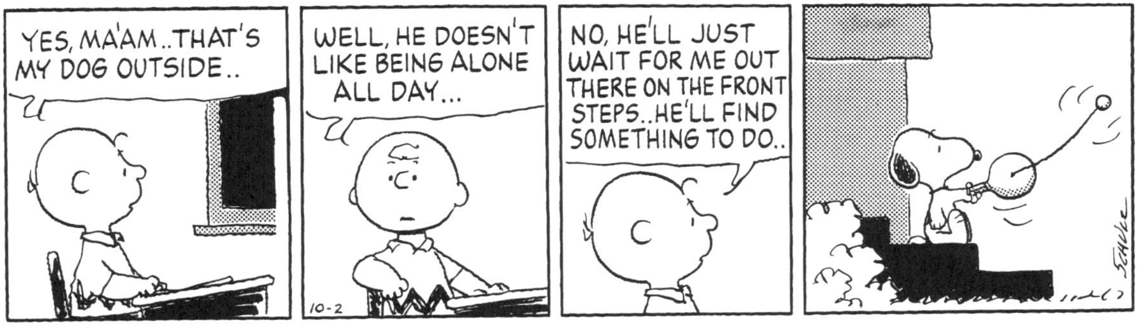
YES, MA'AM..THAT'S MY DOG OUTSIDE..
WELL, HE DOESN'T LIKE BEING ALONE ALL DAY...
NO, HE'LL JUST WAIT FOR ME OUT THERE ON THE FRONT STEPS..HE'LL FIND SOMETHING TO DO..

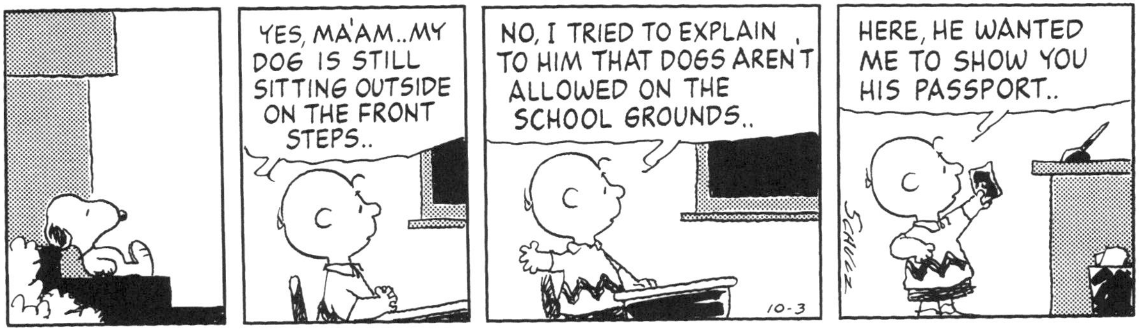
YES, MA'AM..MY DOG IS STILL SITTING OUTSIDE ON THE FRONT STEPS..
NO, I TRIED TO EXPLAIN TO HIM THAT DOGS AREN'T ALLOWED ON THE SCHOOL GROUNDS..
HERE, HE WANTED ME TO SHOW YOU HIS PASSPORT..

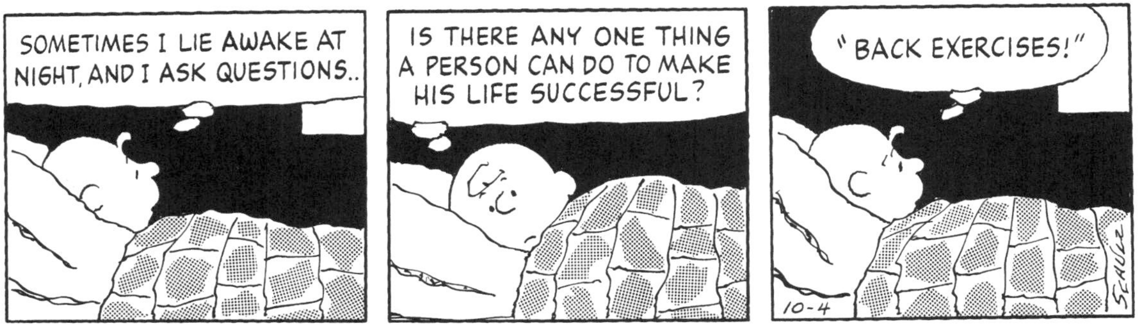
SOMETIMES I LIE AWAKE AT NIGHT, AND I ASK QUESTIONS..
IS THERE ANY ONE THING A PERSON CAN DO TO MAKE HIS LIFE SUCCESSFUL?
"BACK EXERCISES!"

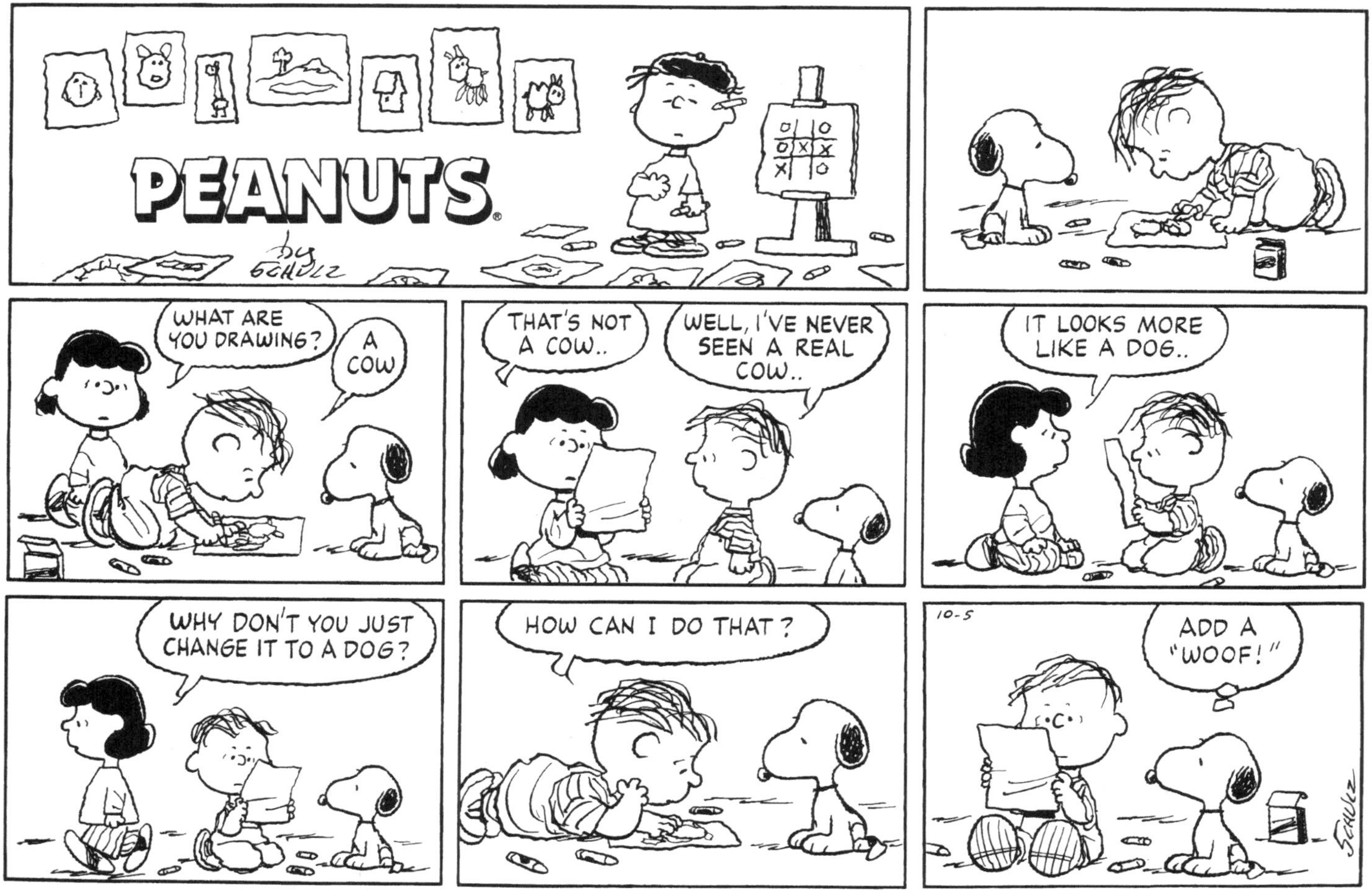
PEANUTS
by SCHULZ
WHAT ARE YOU DRAWING?
A COW
THAT'S NOT A COW..
WELL, I'VE NEVER SEEN A REAL COW..
IT LOOKS MORE LIKE A DOG..
WHY DON'T YOU JUST CHANGE IT TO A DOG?
HOW CAN I DO THAT?
10-5
ADD A "WOOF!"
SCHULZ

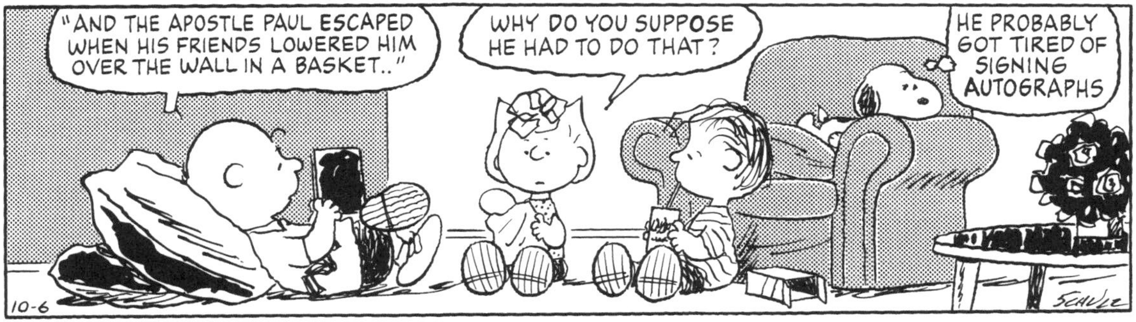
"AND THE APOSTLE PAUL ESCAPED WHEN HIS FRIENDS LOWERED HIM OVER THE WALL IN A BASKET.."
WHY DO YOU SUPPOSE HE HAD TO DO THAT?
HE PROBABLY GOT TIRED OF SIGNING AUTOGRAPHS
10-6
SCHULZ

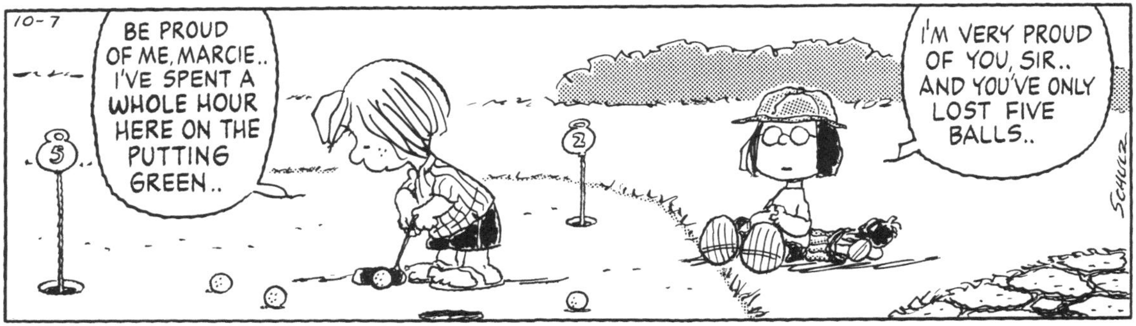
10-7
BE PROUD OF ME, MARCIE.. I'VE SPENT A WHOLE HOUR HERE ON THE PUTTING GREEN..
I'M VERY PROUD OF YOU, SIR.. AND YOU'VE ONLY LOST FIVE BALLS..
SCHULZ

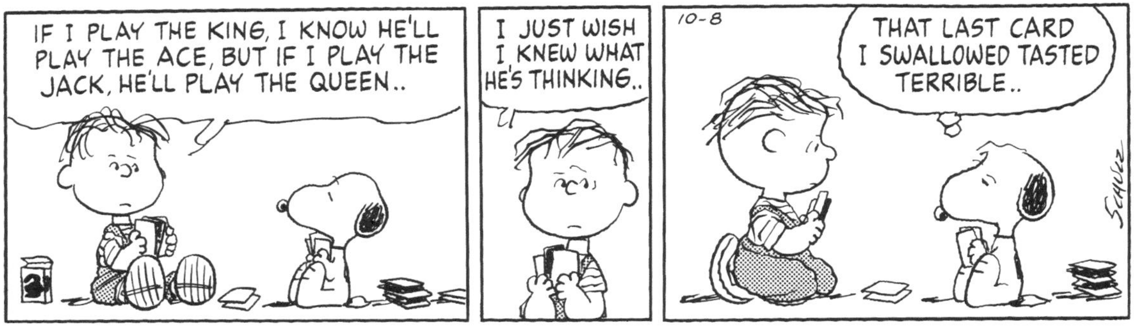
IF I PLAY THE KING, I KNOW HE'LL PLAY THE ACE, BUT IF I PLAY THE JACK, HE'LL PLAY THE QUEEN..
I JUST WISH I KNEW WHAT HE'S THINKING..
10-8
THAT LAST CARD I SWALLOWED TASTED TERRIBLE..
SCHULZ

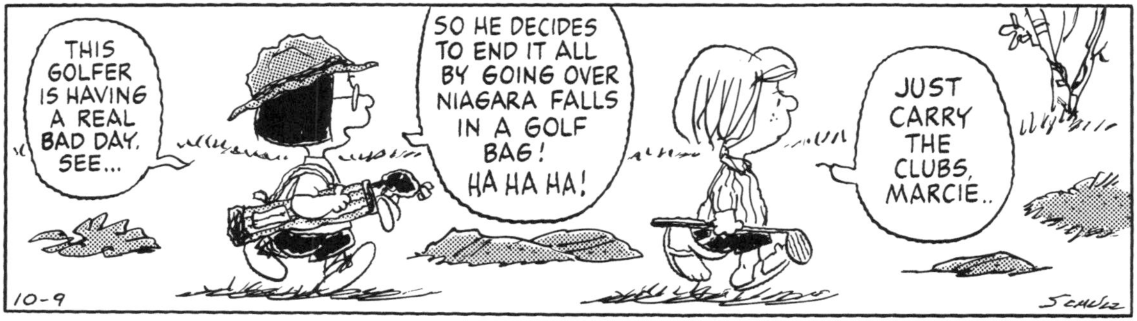
THIS GOLFER IS HAVING A REAL BAD DAY, SEE...
SO HE DECIDES TO END IT ALL BY GOING OVER NIAGARA FALLS IN A GOLF BAG! HA HA HA!
JUST CARRY THE CLUBS, MARCIE..
10-9
SCHULZ

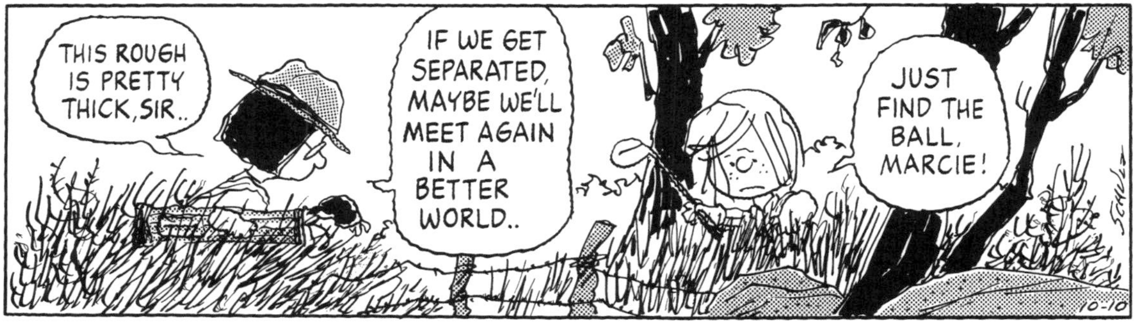
THIS ROUGH IS PRETTY THICK, SIR..
IF WE GET SEPARATED, MAYBE WE'LL MEET AGAIN IN A BETTER WORLD..
JUST FIND THE BALL, MARCIE!
SCHULZ
10-10

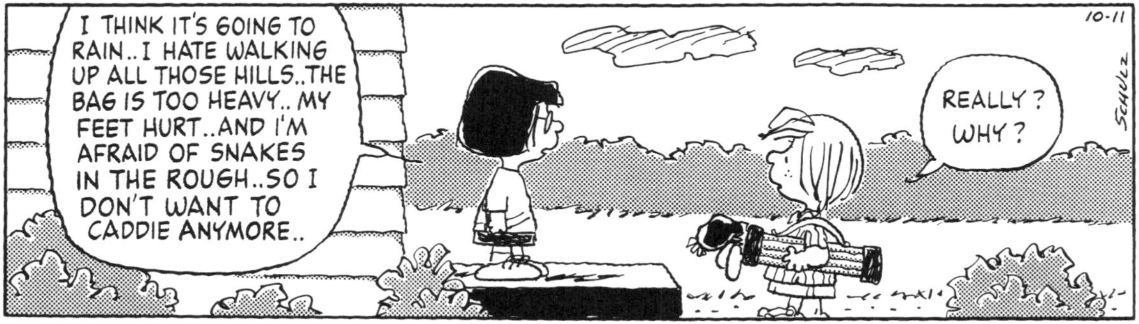
I THINK IT'S GOING TO RAIN..I HATE WALKING UP ALL THOSE HILLS..THE BAG IS TOO HEAVY.. MY FEET HURT..AND I'M AFRAID OF SNAKES IN THE ROUGH..SO I DON'T WANT TO CADDIE ANYMORE..
10-11
SCHULZ
REALLY? WHY?

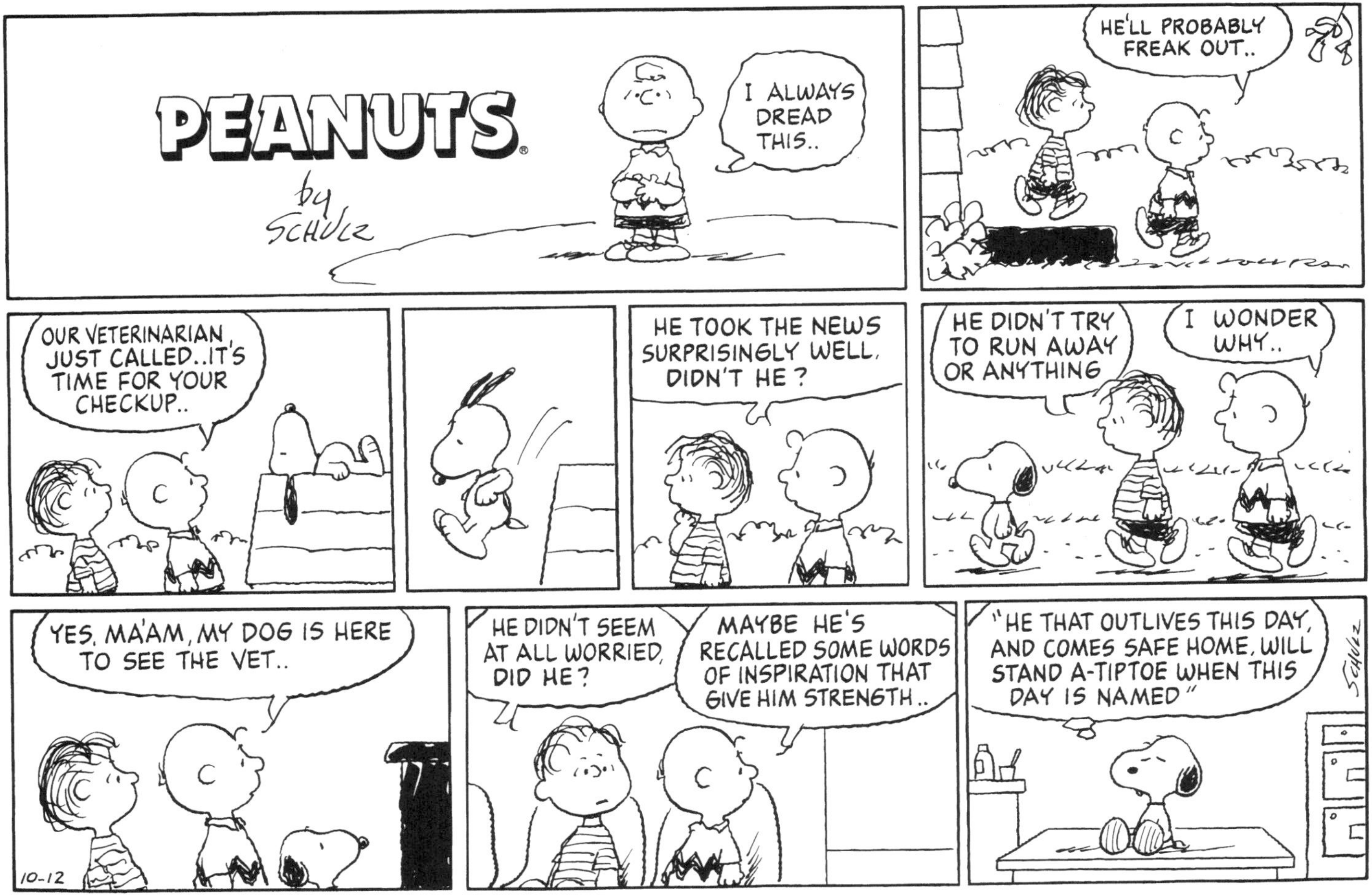
PEANUTS
by SCHULZ
I ALWAYS DREAD THIS..
HE'LL PROBABLY FREAK OUT..
OUR VETERINARIAN JUST CALLED..IT'S TIME FOR YOUR CHECKUP..
HE TOOK THE NEWS SURPRISINGLY WELL, DIDN'T HE?
HE DIDN'T TRY TO RUN AWAY OR ANYTHING
I WONDER WHY..
YES, MA'AM, MY DOG IS HERE TO SEE THE VET..
10-12
HE DIDN'T SEEM AT ALL WORRIED, DID HE?
MAYBE HE'S RECALLED SOME WORDS OF INSPIRATION THAT GIVE HIM STRENGTH..
"HE THAT OUTLIVES THIS DAY, AND COMES SAFE HOME, WILL STAND A-TIPTOE WHEN THIS DAY IS NAMED"
SCHULZ

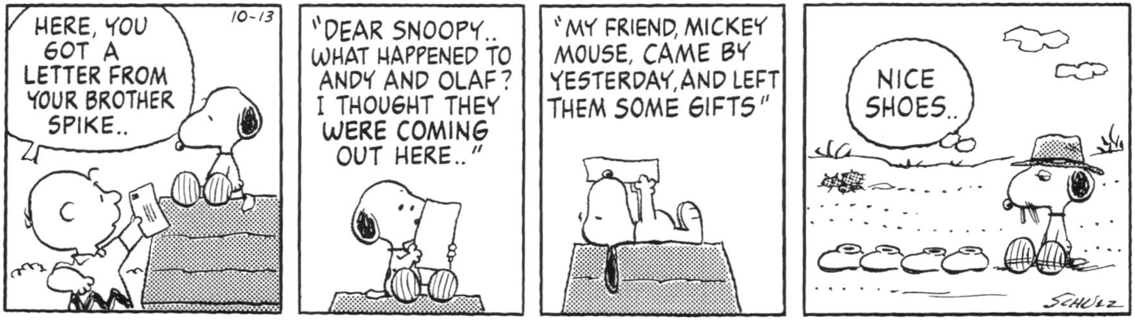
10-13
HERE, YOU GOT A LETTER FROM YOUR BROTHER SPIKE..
"DEAR SNOOPY.. WHAT HAPPENED TO ANDY AND OLAF? I THOUGHT THEY WERE COMING OUT HERE.."
"MY FRIEND, MICKEY MOUSE, CAME BY YESTERDAY, AND LEFT THEM SOME GIFTS"
NICE SHOES..
SCHULZ

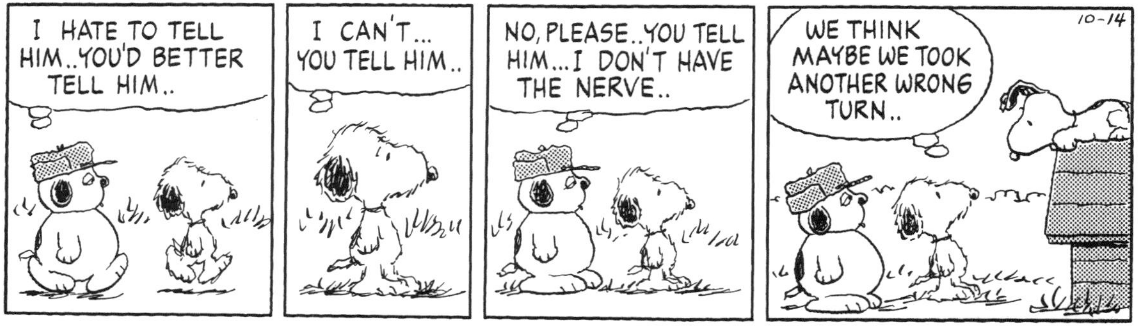
I HATE TO TELL HIM..YOU'D BETTER TELL HIM..
I CAN'T... YOU TELL HIM..
NO, PLEASE..YOU TELL HIM...I DON'T HAVE THE NERVE..
10-14
WE THINK MAYBE WE TOOK ANOTHER WRONG TURN..

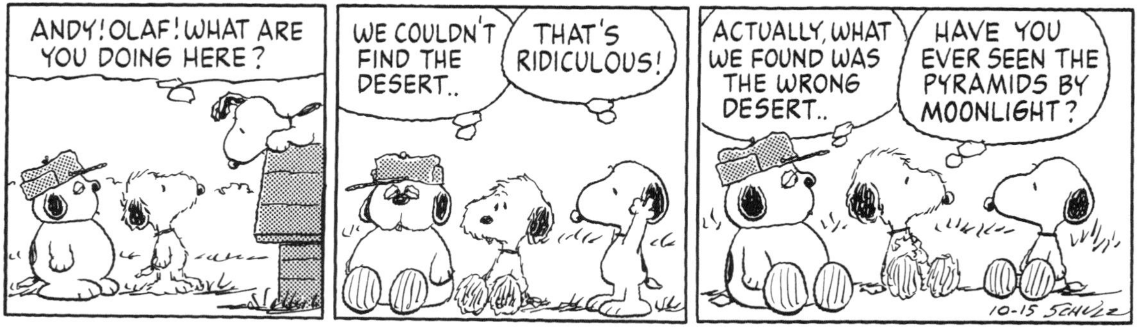
ANDY! OLAF! WHAT ARE YOU DOING HERE?
WE COULDN'T FIND THE DESERT..
THAT'S RIDICULOUS!
ACTUALLY, WHAT WE FOUND WAS THE WRONG DESERT..
HAVE YOU EVER SEEN THE PYRAMIDS BY MOONLIGHT?
10-15 SCHULZ

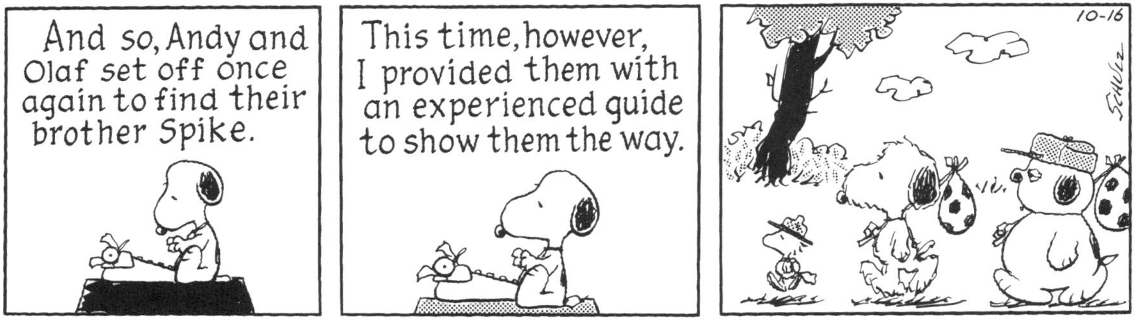
And so, Andy and Olaf set off once again to find their brother Spike.
This time, however, I provided them with an experienced guide to show them the way.
10-16
SCHULZ

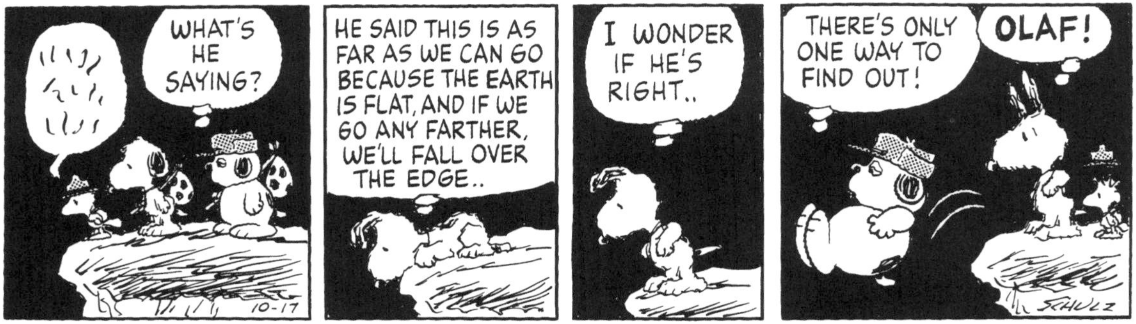
WHAT'S HE SAYING?
HE SAID THIS IS AS FAR AS WE CAN GO BECAUSE THE EARTH IS FLAT, AND IF WE GO ANY FARTHER, WE'LL FALL OVER THE EDGE..
I WONDER IF HE'S RIGHT..
THERE'S ONLY ONE WAY TO FIND OUT!
OLAF!
10-17
SCHULZ

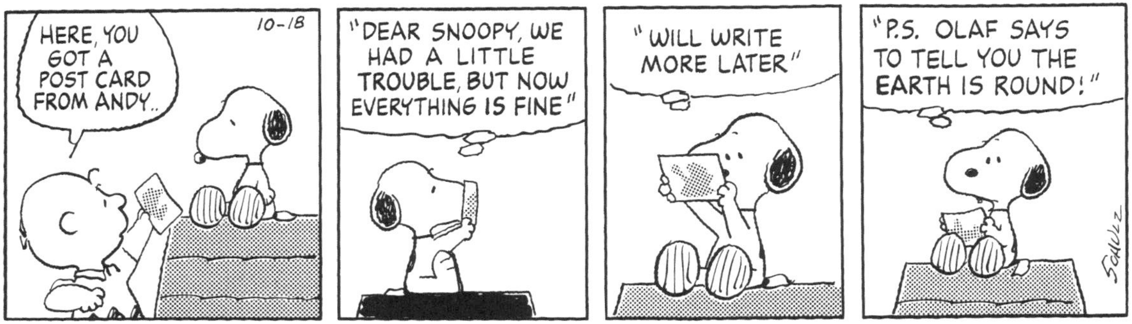
HERE, YOU GOT A POST CARD FROM ANDY..
"DEAR SNOOPY, WE HAD A LITTLE TROUBLE, BUT NOW EVERYTHING IS FINE"
"WILL WRITE MORE LATER"
"P.S. OLAF SAYS TO TELL YOU THE EARTH IS ROUND!"
10-18
SCHULZ

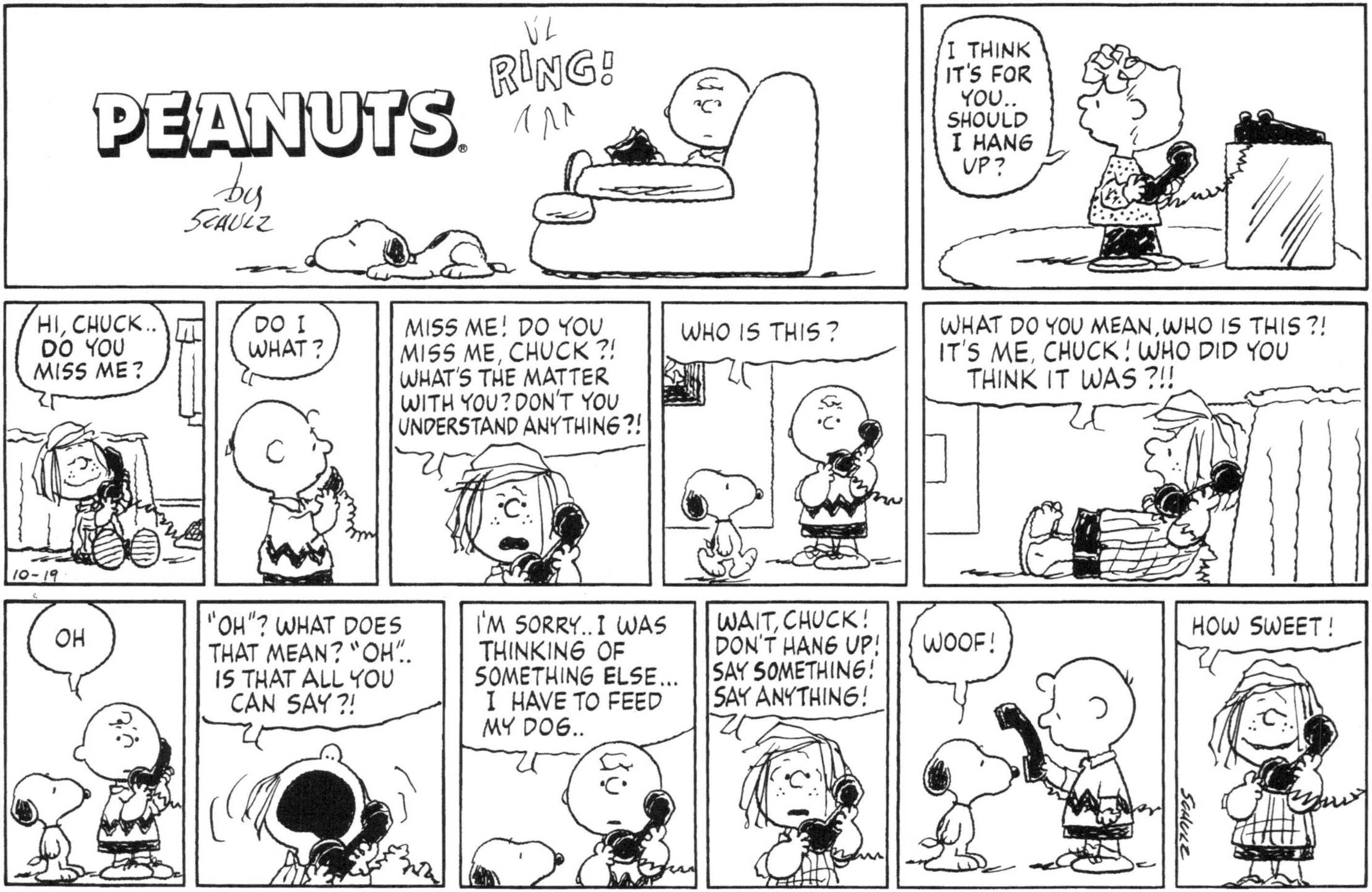
PEANUTS
by SCHULZ
RING!
I THINK IT'S FOR YOU.. SHOULD I HANG UP?
HI, CHUCK.. DO YOU MISS ME?
10-19
DO I WHAT?
MISS ME! DO YOU MISS ME, CHUCK?! WHAT'S THE MATTER WITH YOU? DON'T YOU UNDERSTAND ANYTHING?!
WHO IS THIS?
WHAT DO YOU MEAN, WHO IS THIS?! IT'S ME, CHUCK! WHO DID YOU THINK IT WAS?!!
OH
"OH"? WHAT DOES THAT MEAN? "OH".. IS THAT ALL YOU CAN SAY?!
I'M SORRY.. I WAS THINKING OF SOMETHING ELSE... I HAVE TO FEED MY DOG..
WAIT, CHUCK! DON'T HANG UP! SAY SOMETHING! SAY ANYTHING!
WOOF!
HOW SWEET!
SCHULZ

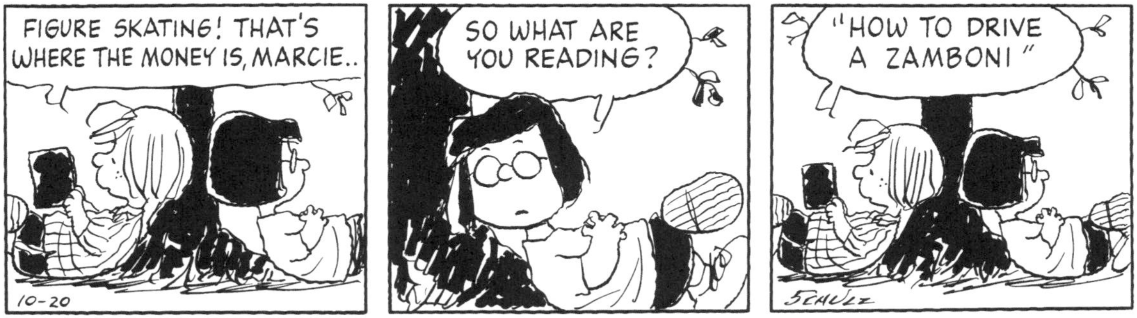
FIGURE SKATING! THAT'S WHERE THE MONEY IS, MARCIE..
10-20
SO WHAT ARE YOU READING?
"HOW TO DRIVE A ZAMBONI"
SCHULZ

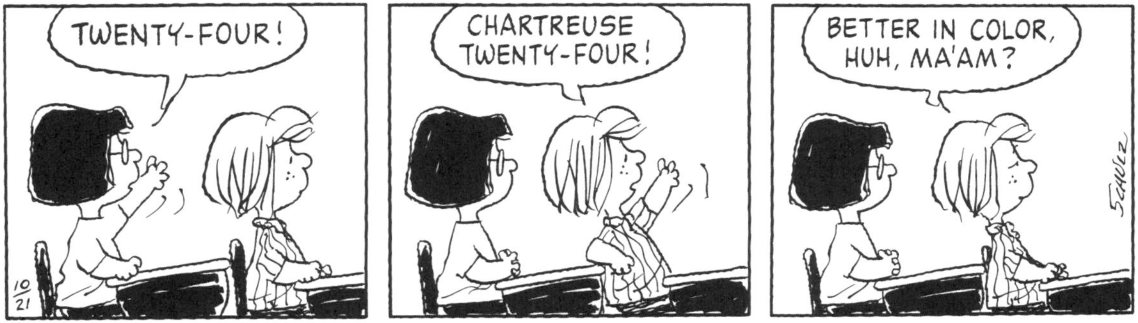
TWENTY-FOUR!
10/21
CHARTREUSE TWENTY-FOUR!
BETTER IN COLOR, HUH, MA'AM?
SCHULZ

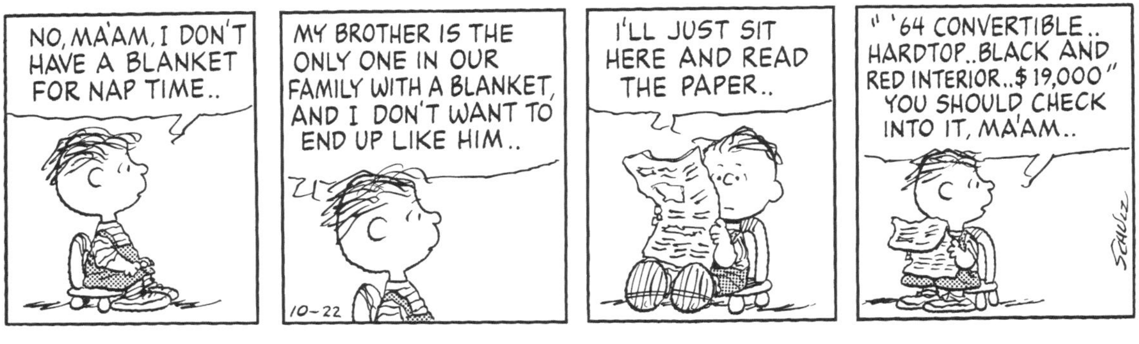
NO, MA'AM, I DON'T HAVE A BLANKET FOR NAP TIME..
MY BROTHER IS THE ONLY ONE IN OUR FAMILY WITH A BLANKET, AND I DON'T WANT TO END UP LIKE HIM..
10-22
I'LL JUST SIT HERE AND READ THE PAPER..
" '64 CONVERTIBLE.. HARDTOP..BLACK AND RED INTERIOR..$ 19,000" YOU SHOULD CHECK INTO IT, MA'AM..
SCHULZ

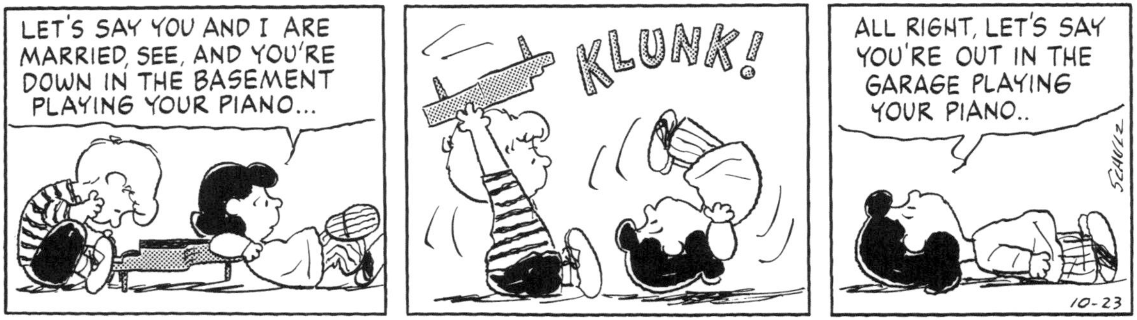
LET'S SAY YOU AND I ARE MARRIED, SEE, AND YOU'RE DOWN IN THE BASEMENT PLAYING YOUR PIANO...
KLUNK!
ALL RIGHT, LET'S SAY YOU'RE OUT IN THE GARAGE PLAYING YOUR PIANO..
SCHULZ
10-23

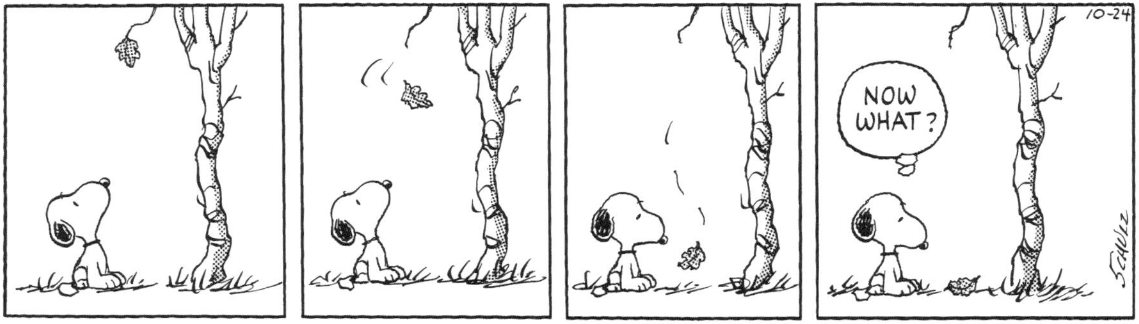
10-24
NOW WHAT?
SCHULZ

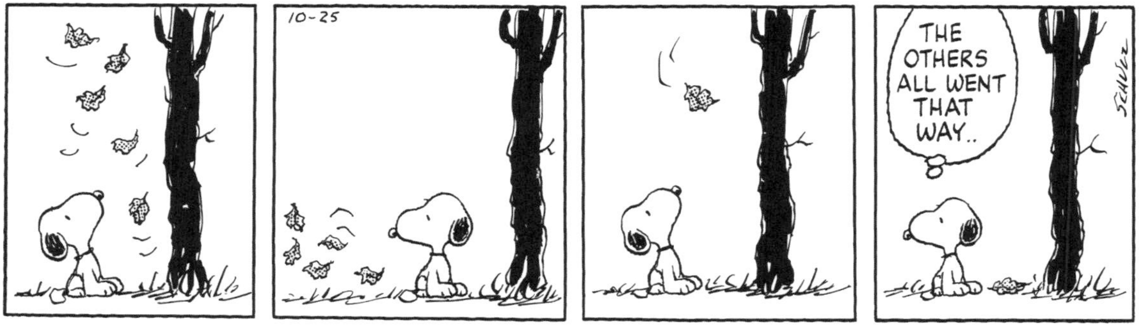
10-25
THE OTHERS ALL WENT THAT WAY..
SCHULZ

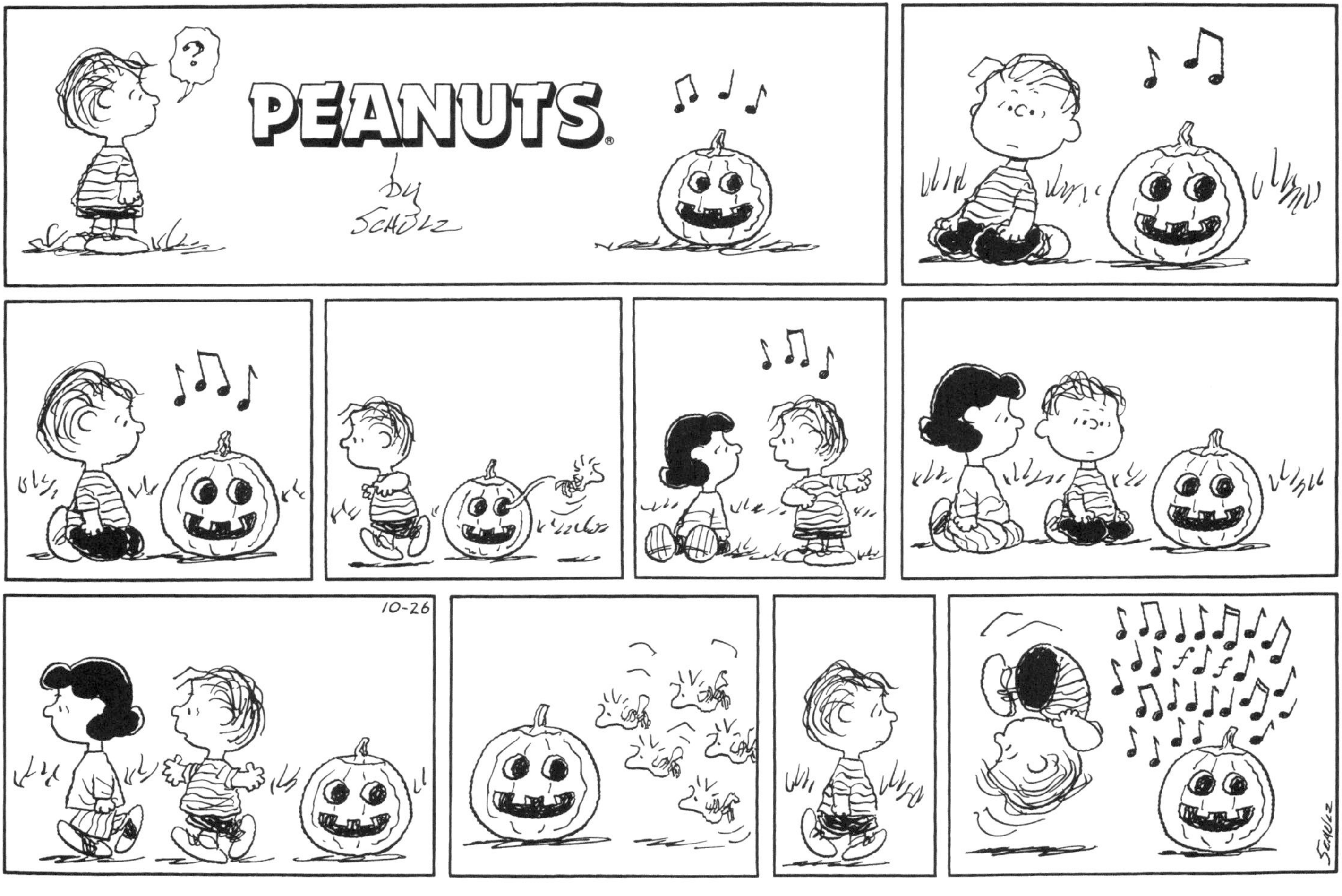
?
PEANUTS®
by SCHULZ
10-26
SCHULZ

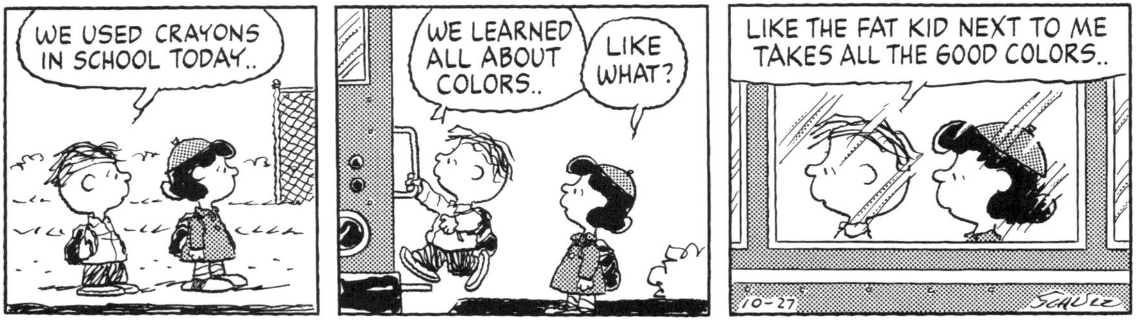
WE USED CRAYONS IN SCHOOL TODAY..
WE LEARNED ALL ABOUT COLORS..
LIKE WHAT?
LIKE THE FAT KID NEXT TO ME TAKES ALL THE GOOD COLORS..
10-27

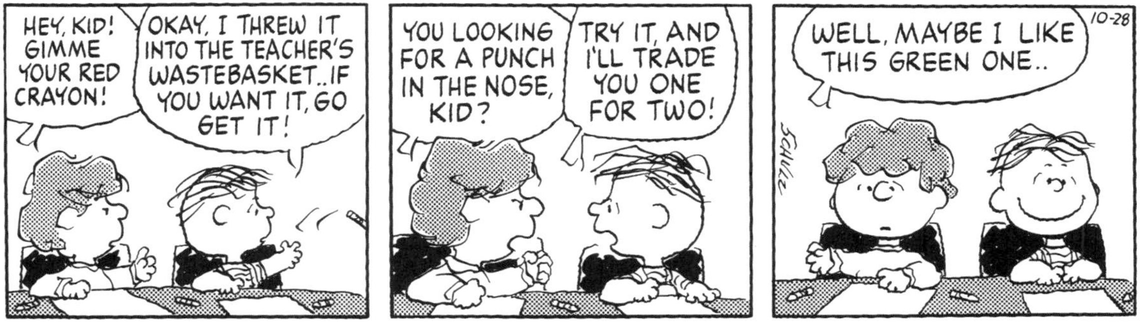
HEY, KID! GIMME YOUR RED CRAYON!
OKAY, I THREW IT INTO THE TEACHER'S WASTEBASKET..IF YOU WANT IT, GO GET IT!
YOU LOOKING FOR A PUNCH IN THE NOSE, KID?
TRY IT, AND I'LL TRADE YOU ONE FOR TWO!
WELL, MAYBE I LIKE THIS GREEN ONE..
10-28

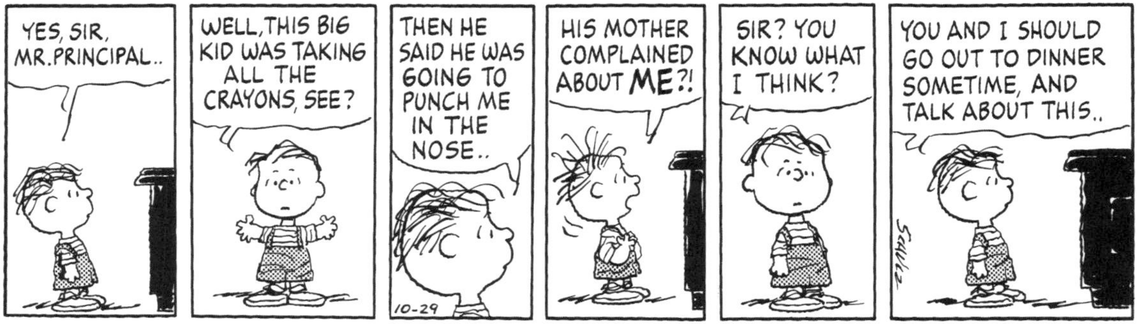
YES, SIR, MR.PRINCIPAL..
WELL, THIS BIG KID WAS TAKING ALL THE CRAYONS, SEE?
THEN HE SAID HE WAS GOING TO PUNCH ME IN THE NOSE..
10-29
HIS MOTHER COMPLAINED ABOUT ME?!
SIR? YOU KNOW WHAT I THINK?
YOU AND I SHOULD GO OUT TO DINNER SOMETIME, AND TALK ABOUT THIS..

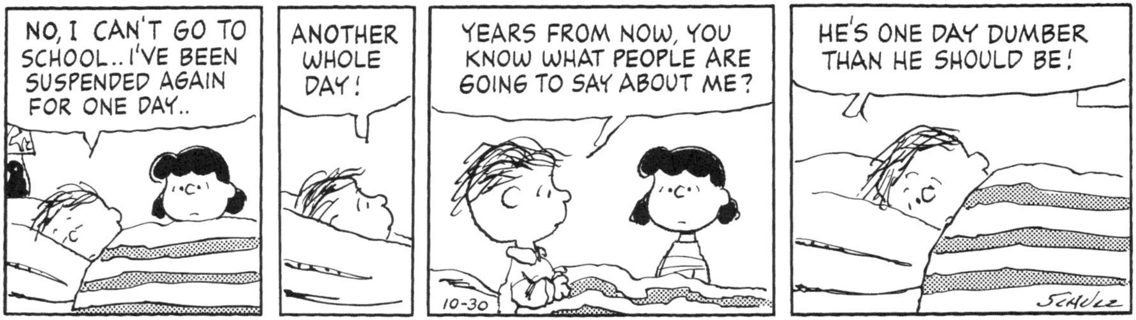
NO, I CAN'T GO TO SCHOOL.. I'VE BEEN SUSPENDED AGAIN FOR ONE DAY..
ANOTHER WHOLE DAY!
YEARS FROM NOW, YOU KNOW WHAT PEOPLE ARE GOING TO SAY ABOUT ME?
HE'S ONE DAY DUMBER THAN HE SHOULD BE!
10-30
SCHULZ

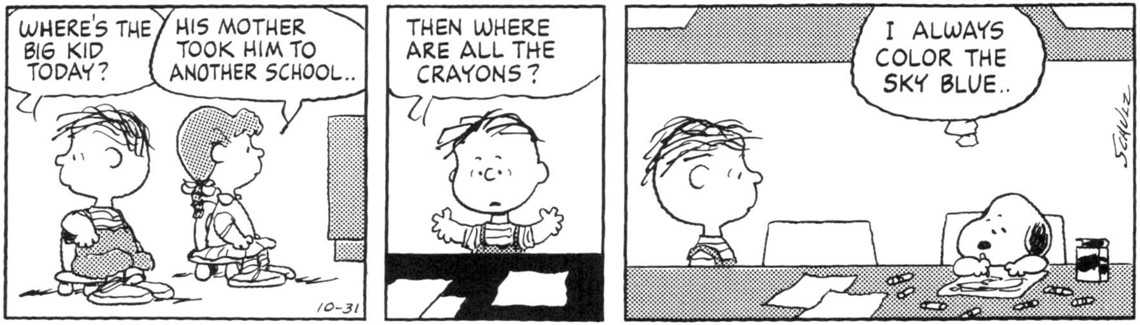
WHERE'S THE BIG KID TODAY?
HIS MOTHER TOOK HIM TO ANOTHER SCHOOL..
10-31
THEN WHERE ARE ALL THE CRAYONS?
I ALWAYS COLOR THE SKY BLUE..
SCHULZ

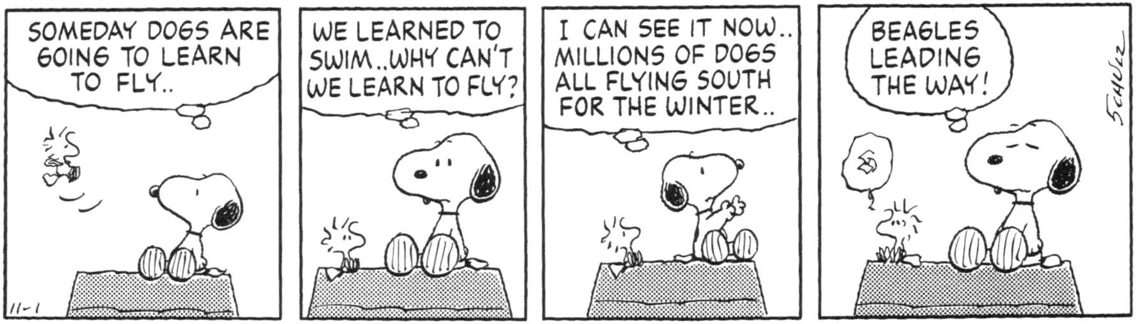
SOMEDAY DOGS ARE GOING TO LEARN TO FLY..
11-1
WE LEARNED TO SWIM.. WHY CAN'T WE LEARN TO FLY?
I CAN SEE IT NOW.. MILLIONS OF DOGS ALL FLYING SOUTH FOR THE WINTER..
BEAGLES LEADING THE WAY!
SCHULZ

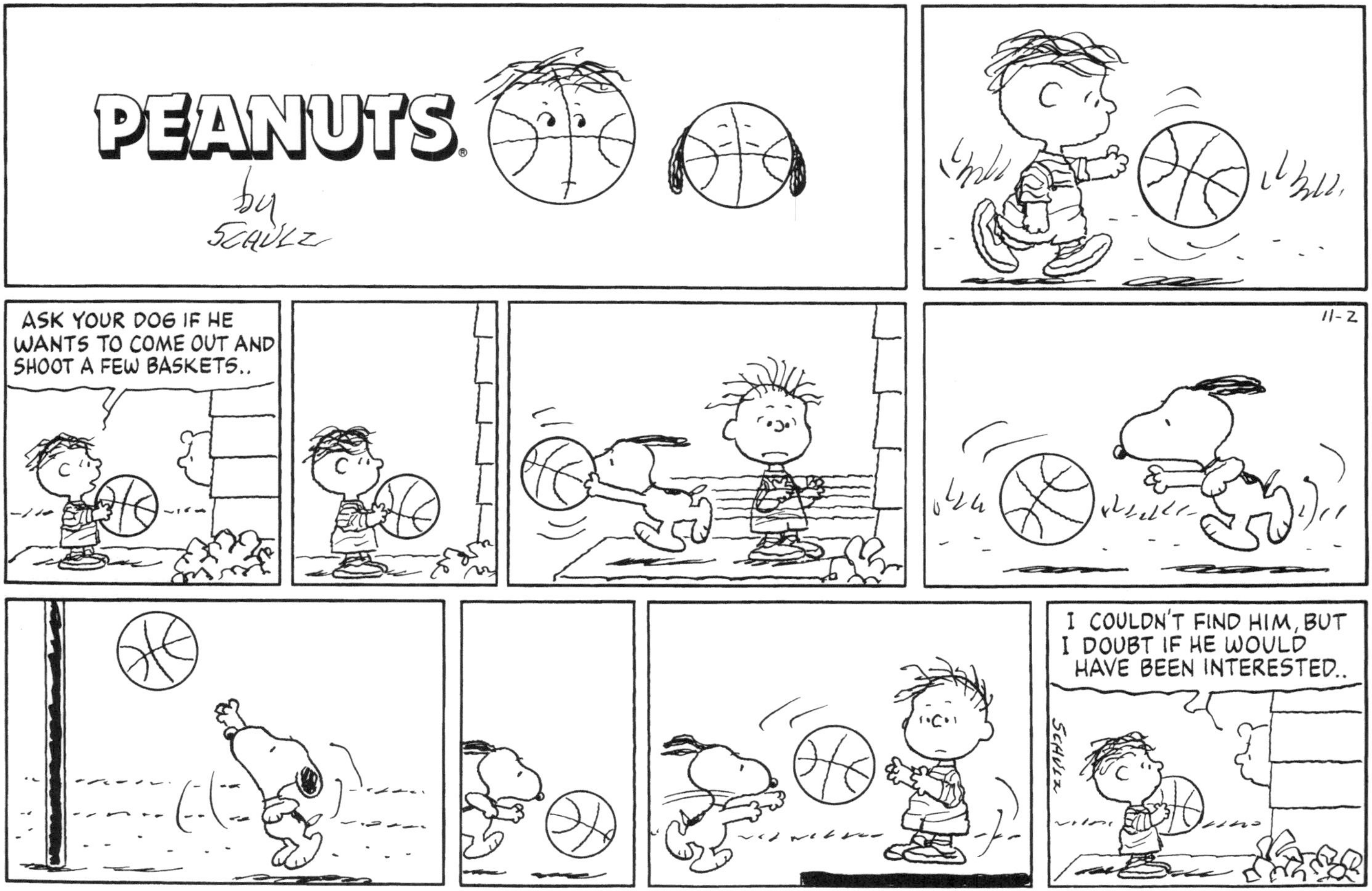
PEANUTS
by SCHULZ
ASK YOUR DOG IF HE WANTS TO COME OUT AND SHOOT A FEW BASKETS..
11-2
I COULDN'T FIND HIM, BUT I DOUBT IF HE WOULD HAVE BEEN INTERESTED..
SCHULZ

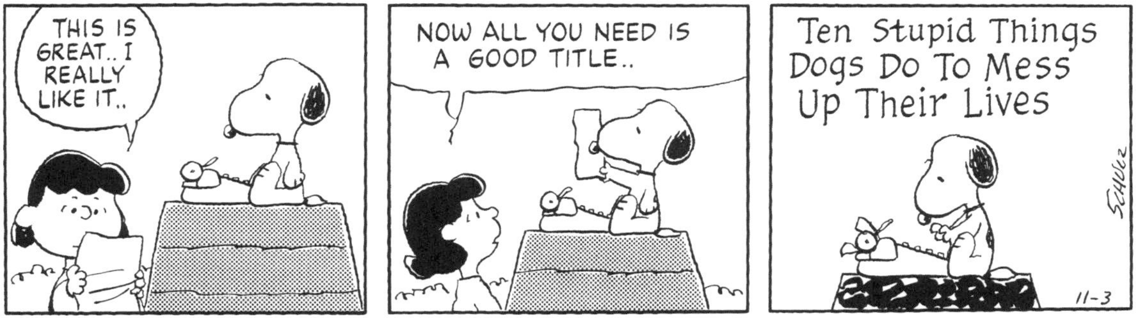
THIS IS GREAT.. I REALLY LIKE IT..
NOW ALL YOU NEED IS A GOOD TITLE..
Ten Stupid Things Dogs Do To Mess Up Their Lives
SCHULZ
11-3

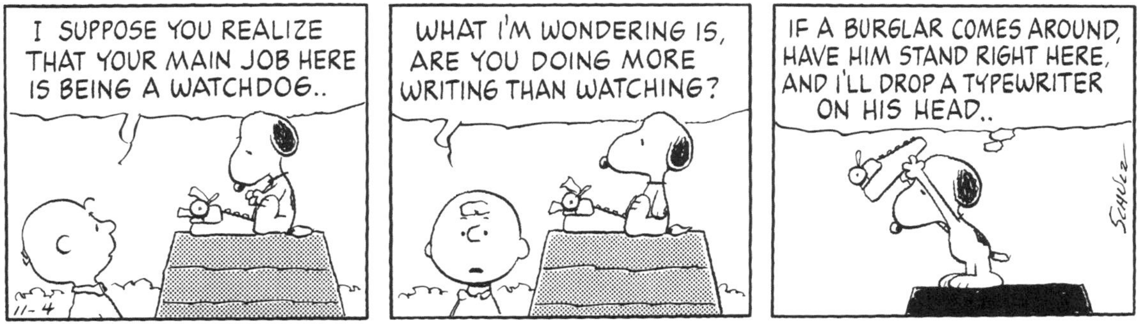
I SUPPOSE YOU REALIZE THAT YOUR MAIN JOB HERE IS BEING A WATCHDOG..
11-4
WHAT I'M WONDERING IS, ARE YOU DOING MORE WRITING THAN WATCHING?
IF A BURGLAR COMES AROUND, HAVE HIM STAND RIGHT HERE, AND I'LL DROP A TYPEWRITER ON HIS HEAD..
SCHULZ

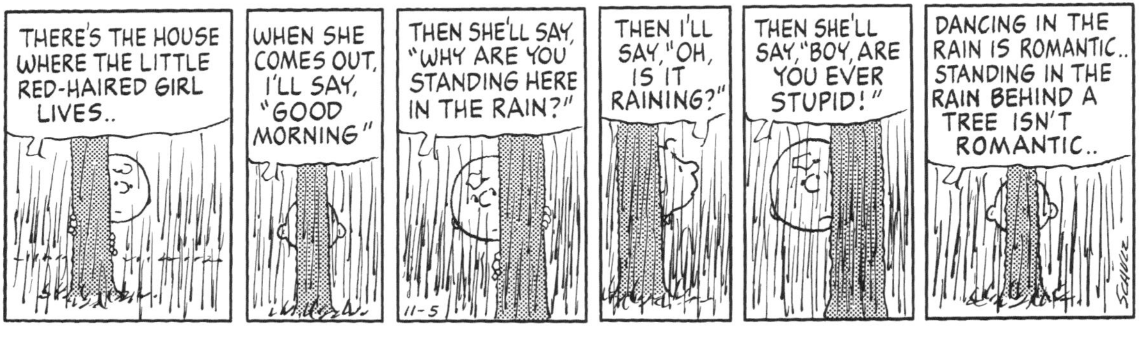
THERE'S THE HOUSE WHERE THE LITTLE RED-HAIRED GIRL LIVES..
WHEN SHE COMES OUT, I'LL SAY, "GOOD MORNING"
THEN SHE'LL SAY, "WHY ARE YOU STANDING HERE IN THE RAIN?"
11-5
THEN I'LL SAY, "OH, IS IT RAINING?"
THEN SHE'LL SAY, "BOY, ARE YOU EVER STUPID!"
DANCING IN THE RAIN IS ROMANTIC.. STANDING IN THE RAIN BEHIND A TREE ISN'T ROMANTIC..
SCHULZ

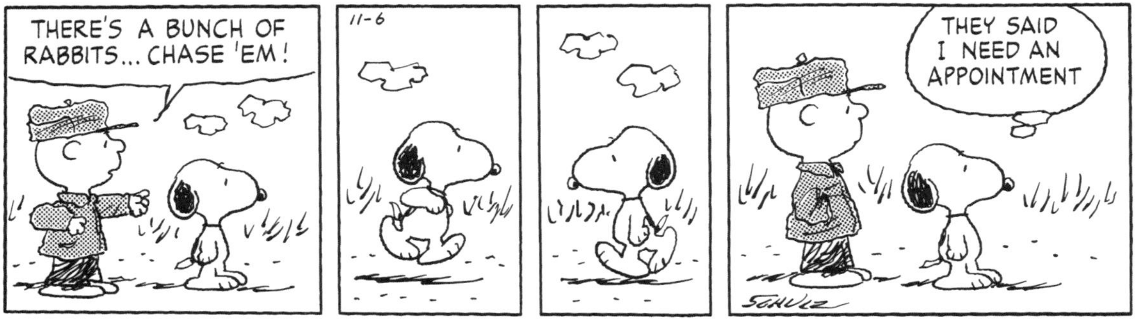
THERE'S A BUNCH OF RABBITS... CHASE 'EM!
11-6
THEY SAID I NEED AN APPOINTMENT
SCHULZ

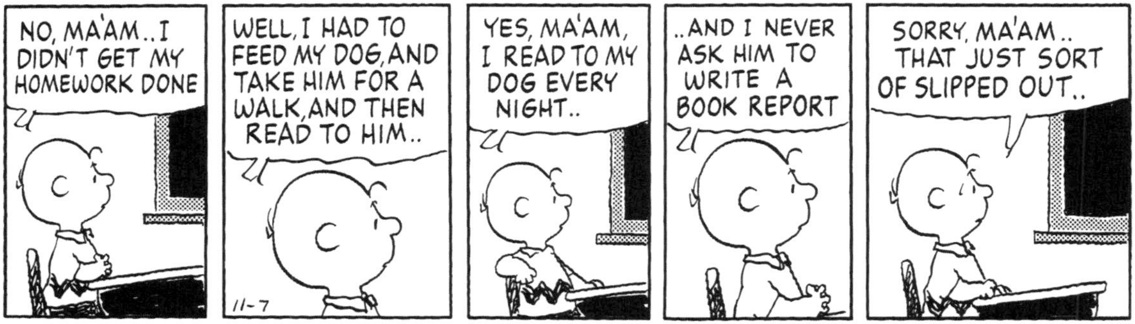
NO, MA'AM..I DIDN'T GET MY HOMEWORK DONE
WELL, I HAD TO FEED MY DOG, AND TAKE HIM FOR A WALK, AND THEN READ TO HIM..
11-7
YES, MA'AM, I READ TO MY DOG EVERY NIGHT..
..AND I NEVER ASK HIM TO WRITE A BOOK REPORT
SORRY, MA'AM.. THAT JUST SORT OF SLIPPED OUT..

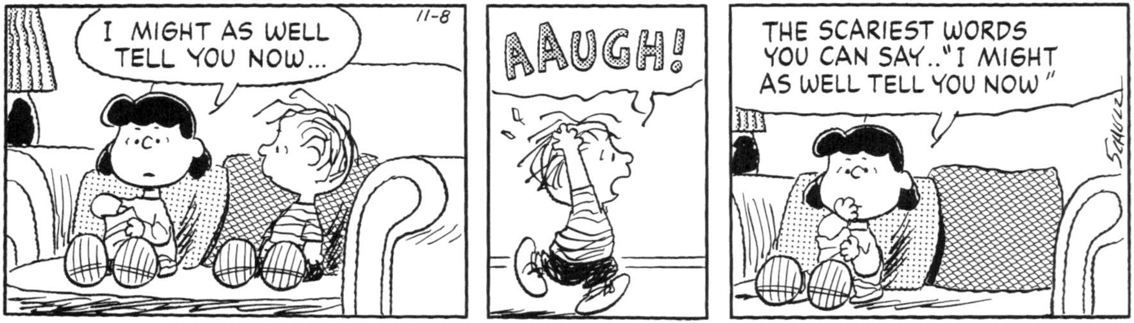
I MIGHT AS WELL TELL YOU NOW...
11-8
AAUGH!
THE SCARIEST WORDS YOU CAN SAY.."I MIGHT AS WELL TELL YOU NOW"
SCHULZ

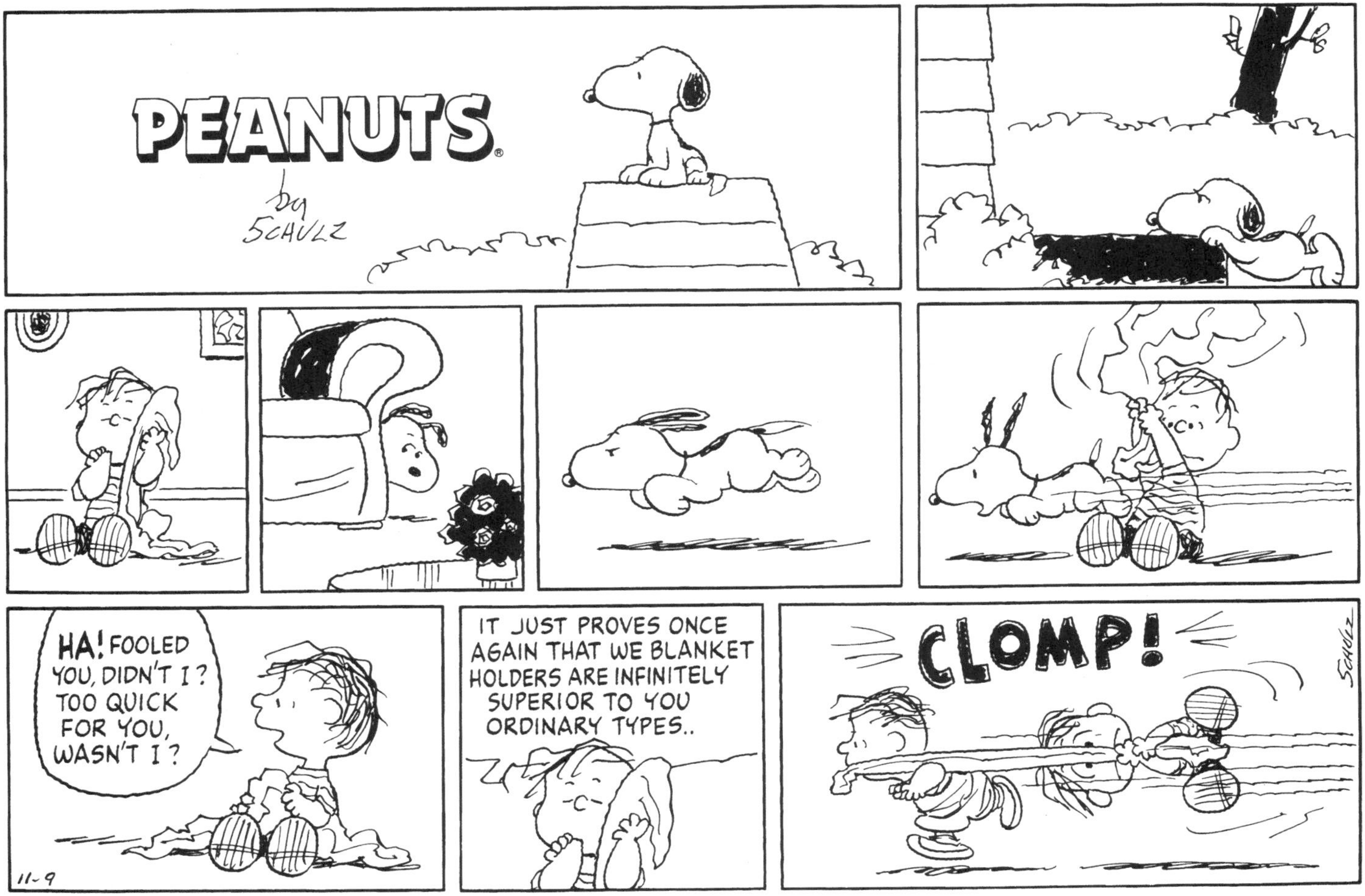
PEANUTS
by SCHULZ
HA! FOOLED YOU, DIDN'T I? TOO QUICK FOR YOU, WASN'T I?
11-9
IT JUST PROVES ONCE AGAIN THAT WE BLANKET HOLDERS ARE INFINITELY SUPERIOR TO YOU ORDINARY TYPES..
CLOMP!
SCHULZ

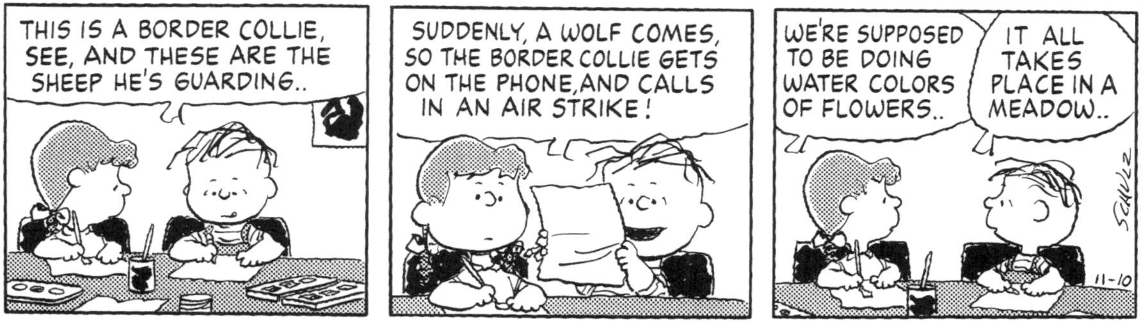
THIS IS A BORDER COLLIE, SEE, AND THESE ARE THE SHEEP HE'S GUARDING..
SUDDENLY, A WOLF COMES, SO THE BORDER COLLIE GETS ON THE PHONE, AND CALLS IN AN AIR STRIKE!
WE'RE SUPPOSED TO BE DOING WATER COLORS OF FLOWERS..
IT ALL TAKES PLACE IN A MEADOW..
SCHULZ
11-10

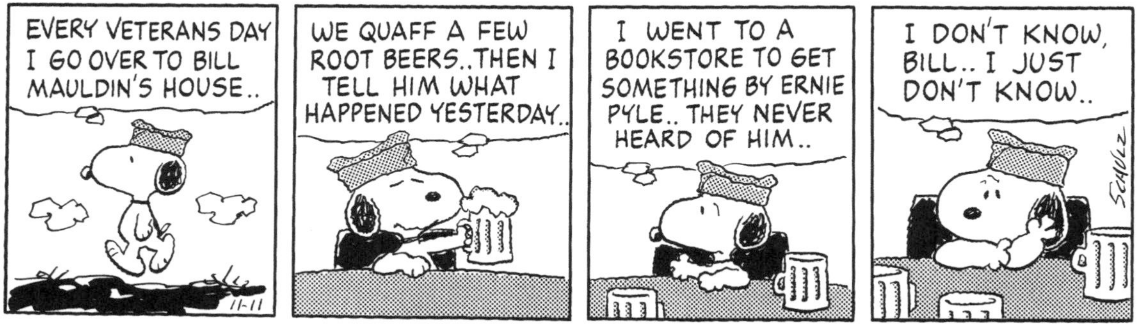
EVERY VETERANS DAY I GO OVER TO BILL MAULDIN'S HOUSE..
11-11
WE QUAFF A FEW ROOT BEERS..THEN I TELL HIM WHAT HAPPENED YESTERDAY..
I WENT TO A BOOKSTORE TO GET SOMETHING BY ERNIE PYLE.. THEY NEVER HEARD OF HIM..
I DON'T KNOW, BILL.. I JUST DON'T KNOW..
SCHULZ

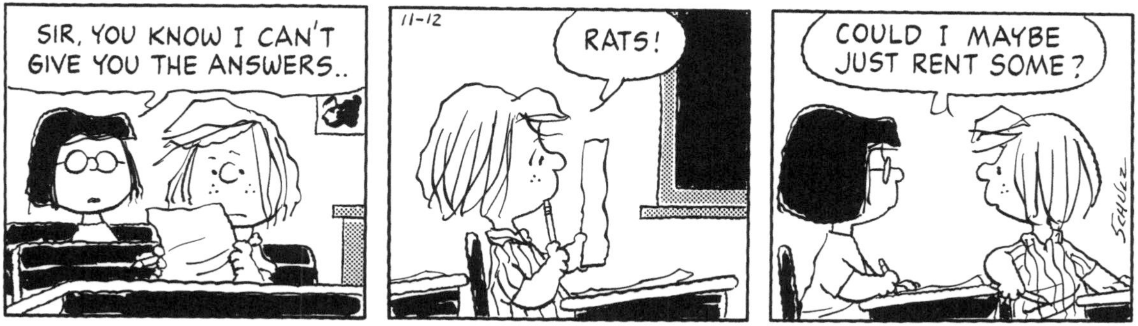
SIR, YOU KNOW I CAN'T GIVE YOU THE ANSWERS..
11-12
RATS!
COULD I MAYBE JUST RENT SOME?
SCHULZ

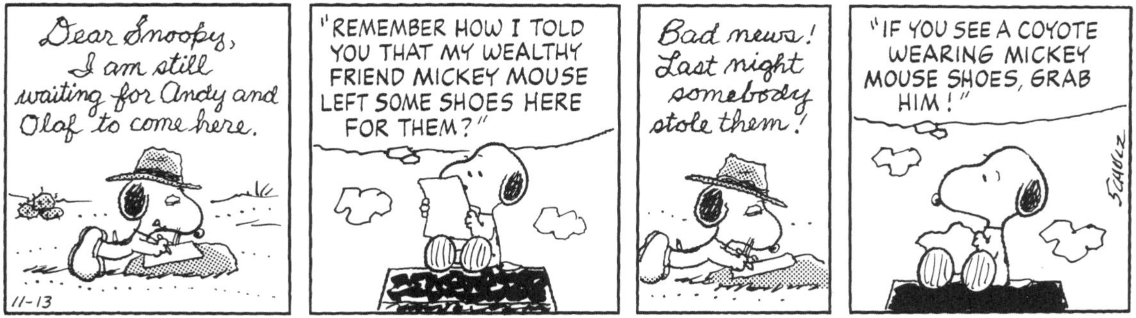
Dear Snoopy, I am still waiting for Andy and Olaf to come here.
"REMEMBER HOW I TOLD YOU THAT MY WEALTHY FRIEND MICKEY MOUSE LEFT SOME SHOES HERE FOR THEM?"
Bad news! Last night somebody stole them!
"IF YOU SEE A COYOTE WEARING MICKEY MOUSE SHOES, GRAB HIM!"
SCHULZ
11-13

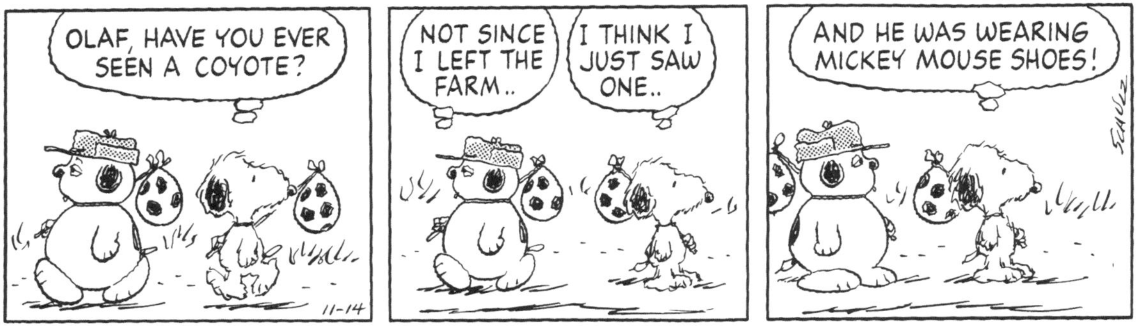
OLAF, HAVE YOU EVER SEEN A COYOTE?
NOT SINCE I LEFT THE FARM..
I THINK I JUST SAW ONE..
AND HE WAS WEARING MICKEY MOUSE SHOES!
SCHULZ
11-14

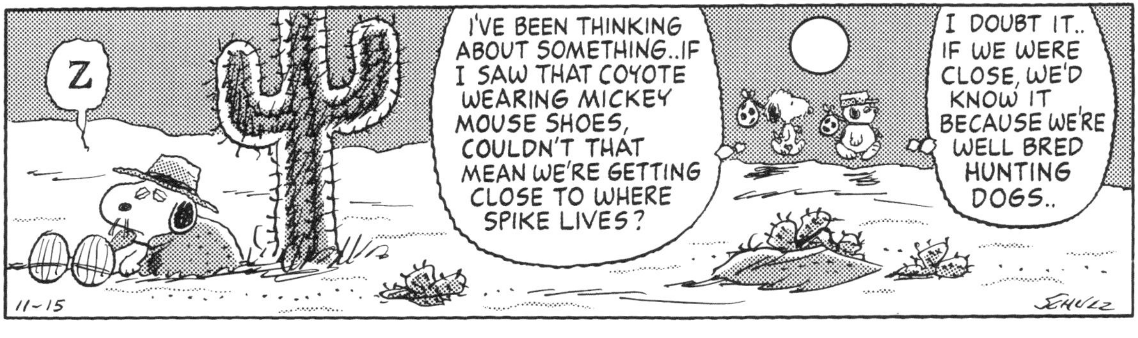
Z
I'VE BEEN THINKING ABOUT SOMETHING..IF I SAW THAT COYOTE WEARING MICKEY MOUSE SHOES, COULDN'T THAT MEAN WE'RE GETTING CLOSE TO WHERE SPIKE LIVES?
I DOUBT IT.. IF WE WERE CLOSE, WE'D KNOW IT BECAUSE WE'RE WELL BRED HUNTING DOGS..
SCHULZ
11-15

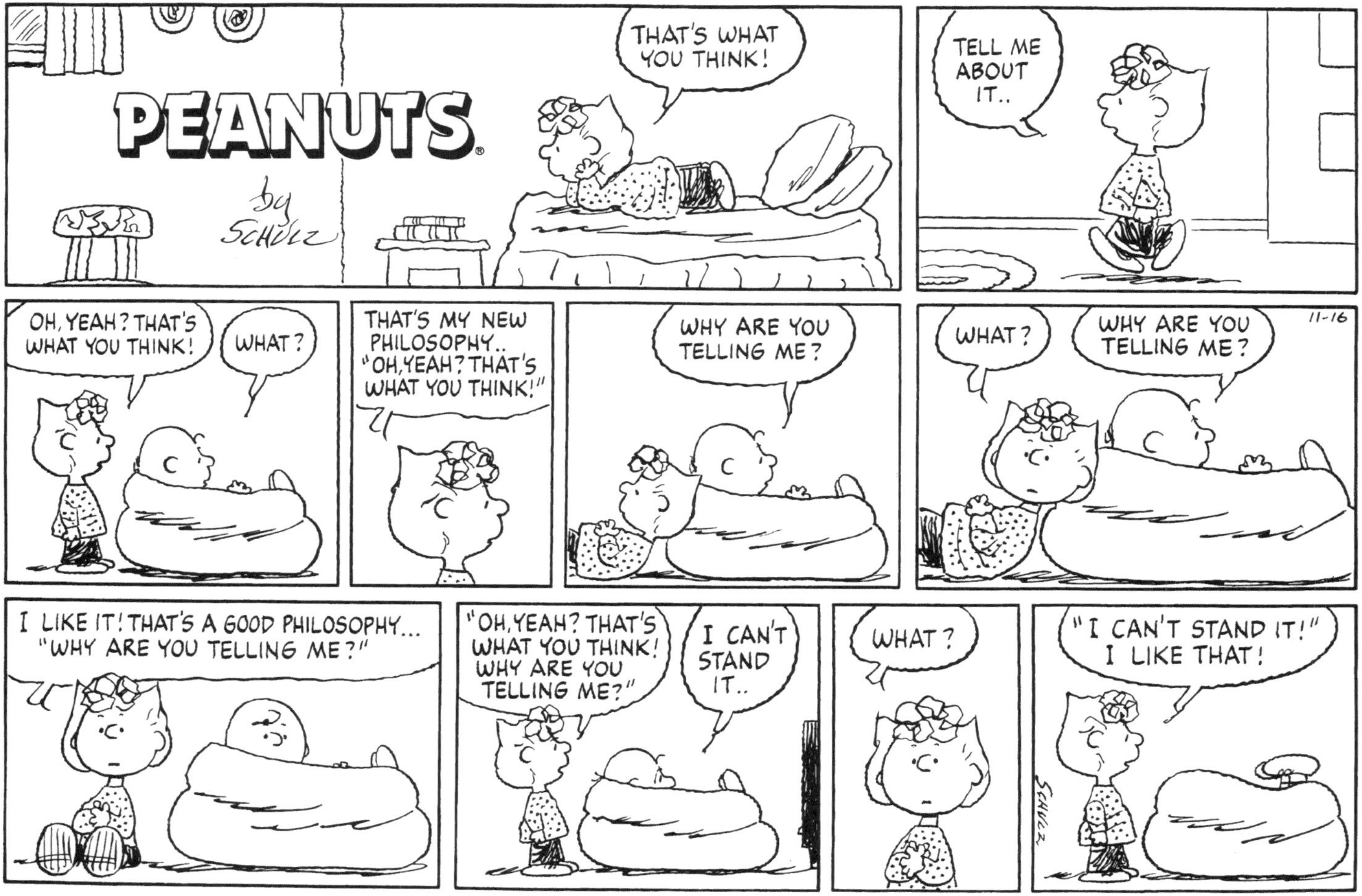
PEANUTS
by SCHULZ
THAT'S WHAT YOU THINK!
TELL ME ABOUT IT..
OH, YEAH? THAT'S WHAT YOU THINK!
WHAT?
THAT'S MY NEW PHILOSOPHY.. "OH, YEAH? THAT'S WHAT YOU THINK!"
WHY ARE YOU TELLING ME?
11-16
WHAT?
WHY ARE YOU TELLING ME?
I LIKE IT! THAT'S A GOOD PHILOSOPHY... "WHY ARE YOU TELLING ME?"
"OH, YEAH? THAT'S WHAT YOU THINK! WHY ARE YOU TELLING ME?"
I CAN'T STAND IT..
WHAT?
"I CAN'T STAND IT!" I LIKE THAT!
SCHULZ

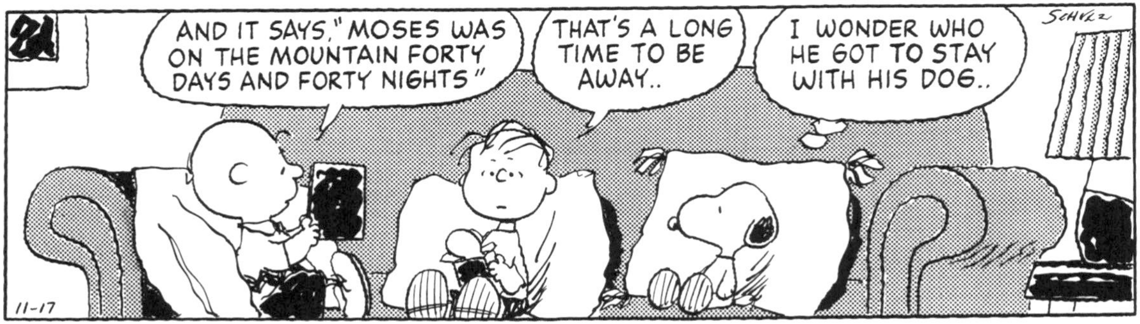
AND IT SAYS, "MOSES WAS ON THE MOUNTAIN FORTY DAYS AND FORTY NIGHTS"
THAT'S A LONG TIME TO BE AWAY..
I WONDER WHO HE GOT TO STAY WITH HIS DOG..
SCHULZ
11-17

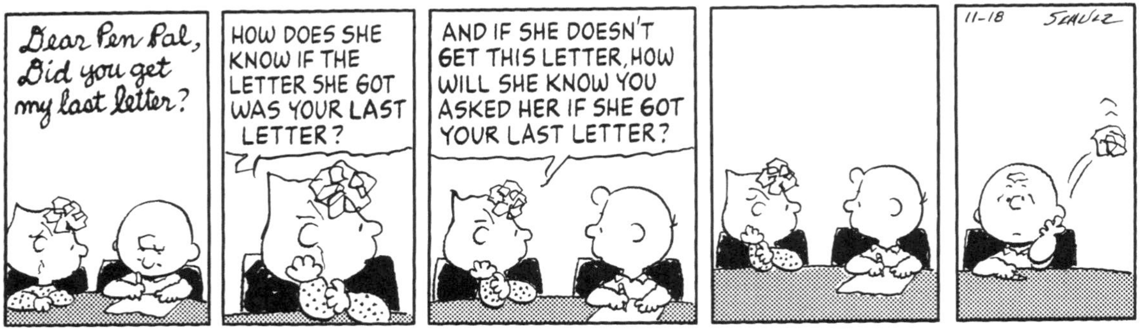
Dear Pen Pal, Did you get my last letter?
HOW DOES SHE KNOW IF THE LETTER SHE GOT WAS YOUR LAST LETTER?
AND IF SHE DOESN'T GET THIS LETTER, HOW WILL SHE KNOW YOU ASKED HER IF SHE GOT YOUR LAST LETTER?
11-18
SCHULZ

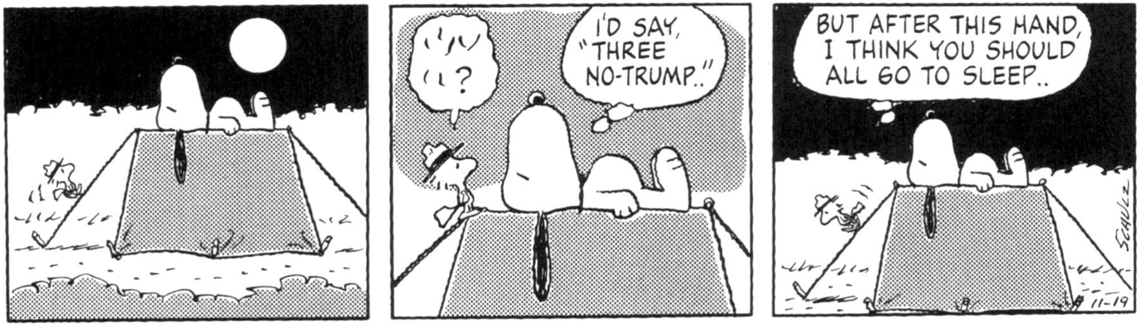
?
I'D SAY, "THREE NO-TRUMP.."
BUT AFTER THIS HAND, I THINK YOU SHOULD ALL GO TO SLEEP..
SCHULZ
11-19

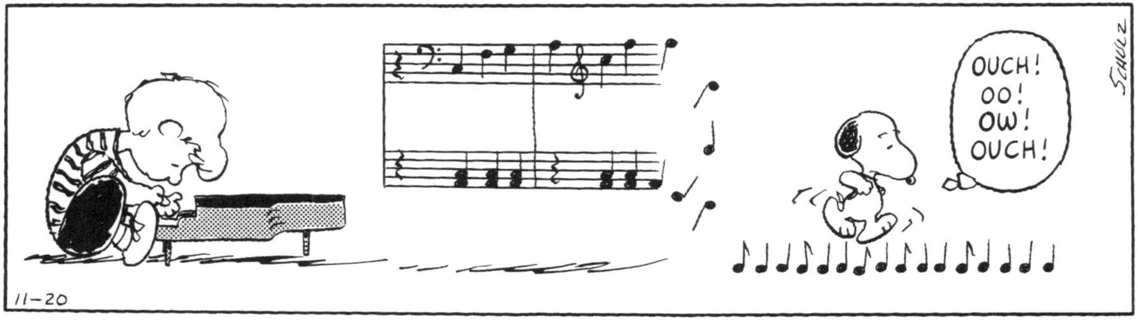
OUCH! OO! OW! OUCH!

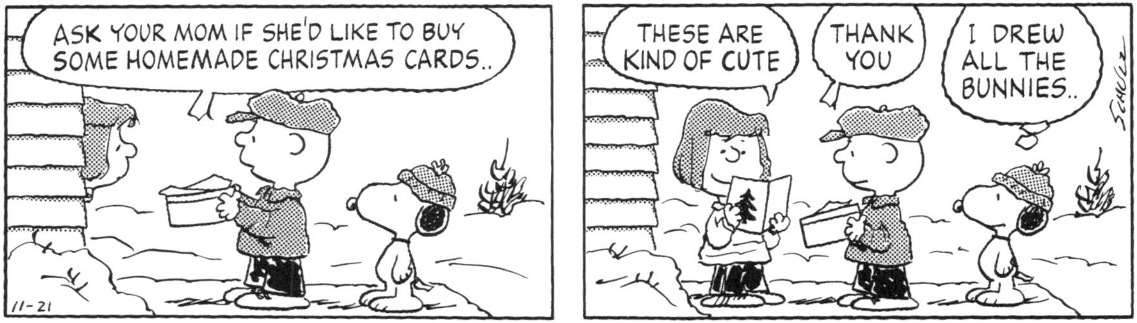
ASK YOUR MOM IF SHE'D LIKE TO BUY SOME HOMEMADE CHRISTMAS CARDS..
THESE ARE KIND OF CUTE
THANK YOU
I DREW ALL THE BUNNIES..

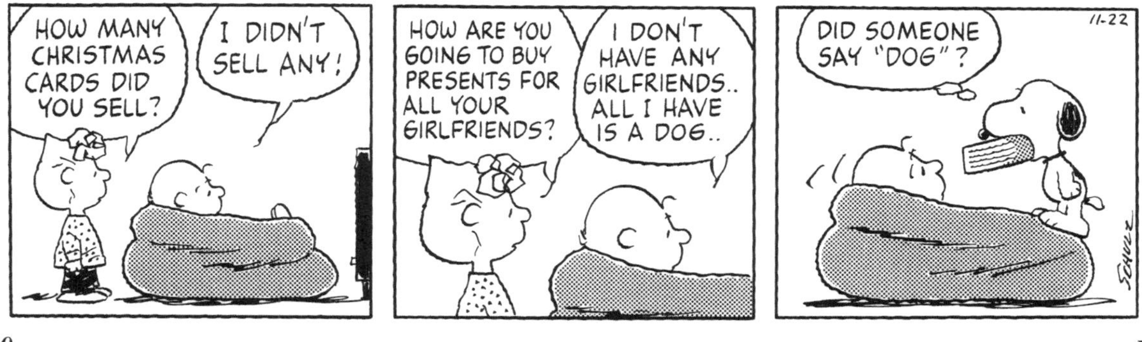
HOW MANY CHRISTMAS CARDS DID YOU SELL?
I DIDN'T SELL ANY!
HOW ARE YOU GOING TO BUY PRESENTS FOR ALL YOUR GIRLFRIENDS?
I DON'T HAVE ANY GIRLFRIENDS.. ALL I HAVE IS A DOG..
DID SOMEONE SAY "DOG"?

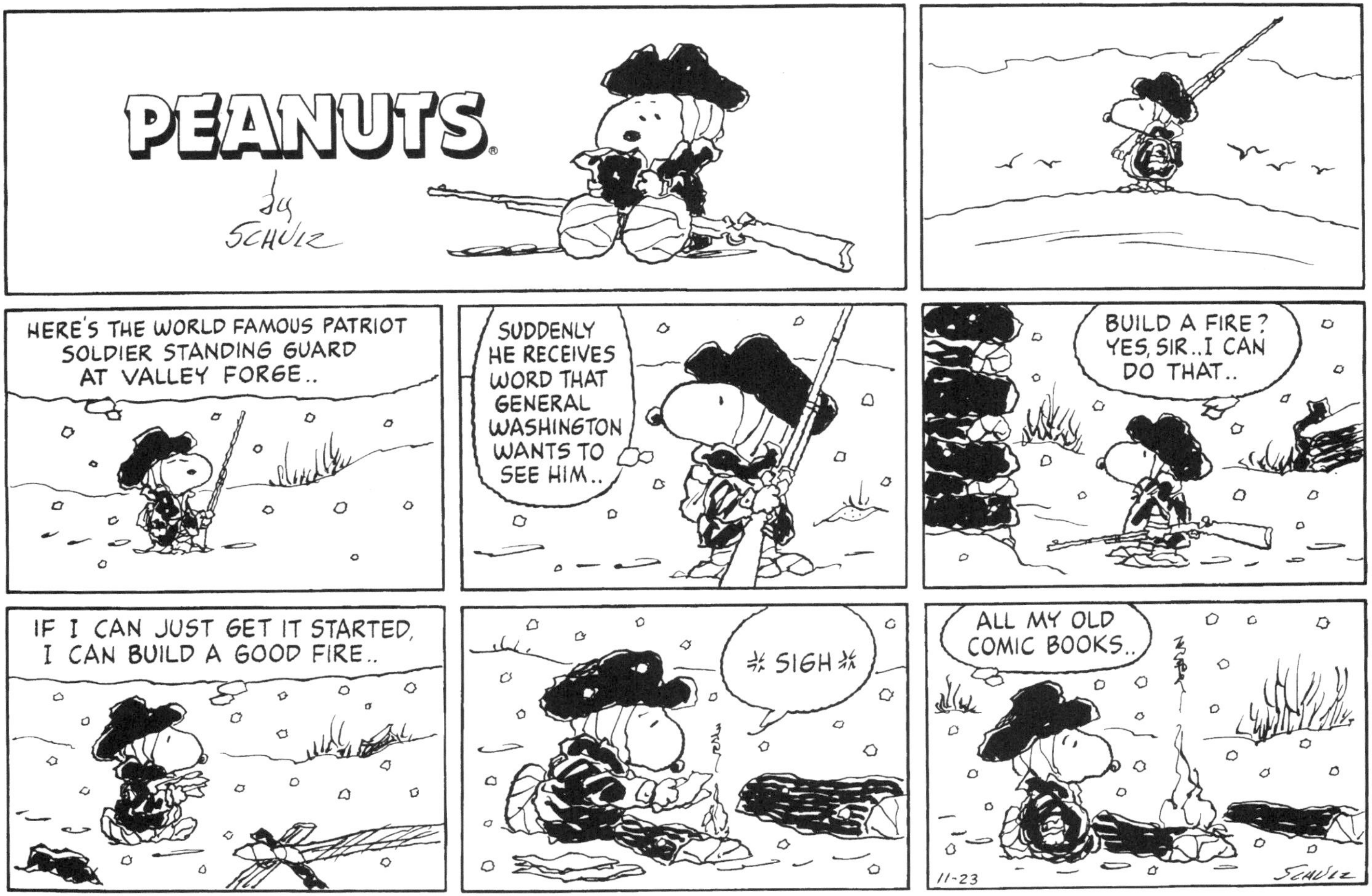
PEANUTS®
by SCHULZ
HERE'S THE WORLD FAMOUS PATRIOT SOLDIER STANDING GUARD AT VALLEY FORGE..
SUDDENLY HE RECEIVES WORD THAT GENERAL WASHINGTON WANTS TO SEE HIM..
BUILD A FIRE? YES, SIR..I CAN DO THAT..
IF I CAN JUST GET IT STARTED, I CAN BUILD A GOOD FIRE..
SIGH
ALL MY OLD COMIC BOOKS..
11-23
SCHULZ

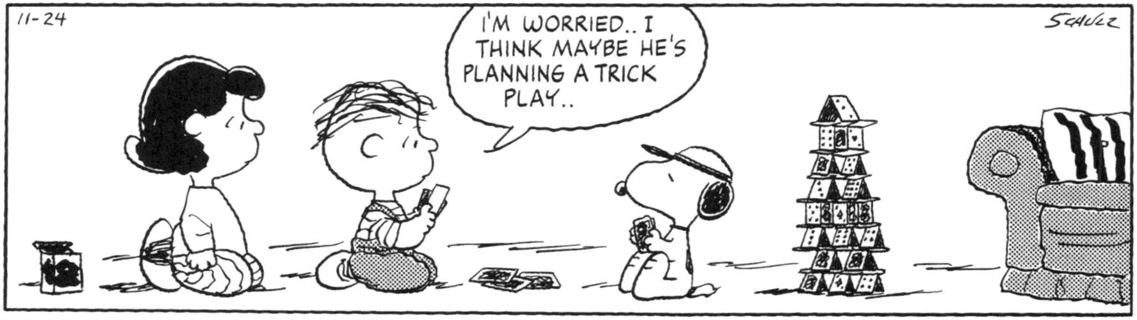
11-24
I'M WORRIED.. I THINK MAYBE HE'S PLANNING A TRICK PLAY..

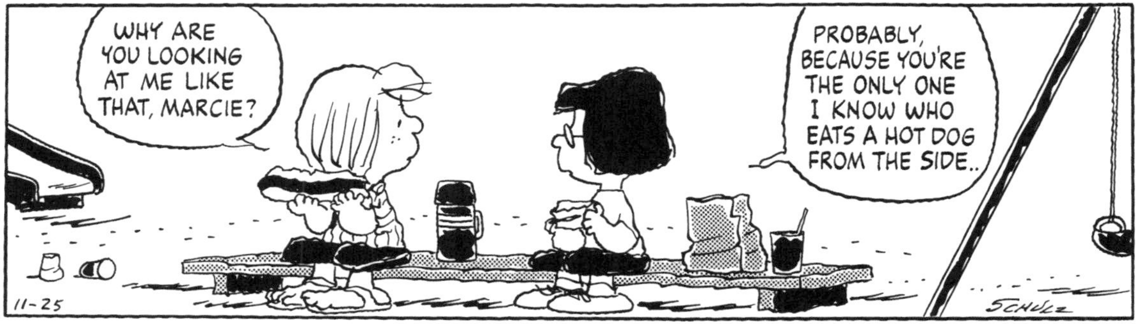
WHY ARE YOU LOOKING AT ME LIKE THAT, MARCIE?
PROBABLY, BECAUSE YOU'RE THE ONLY ONE I KNOW WHO EATS A HOT DOG FROM THE SIDE..
11-25

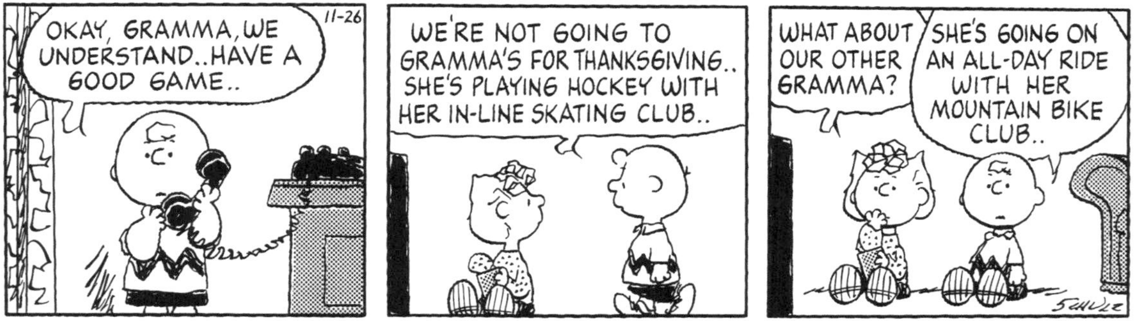
OKAY, GRAMMA, WE UNDERSTAND..HAVE A GOOD GAME..
11-26
WE'RE NOT GOING TO GRAMMA'S FOR THANKSGIVING.. SHE'S PLAYING HOCKEY WITH HER IN-LINE SKATING CLUB..
WHAT ABOUT OUR OTHER GRAMMA?
SHE'S GOING ON AN ALL-DAY RIDE WITH HER MOUNTAIN BIKE CLUB..

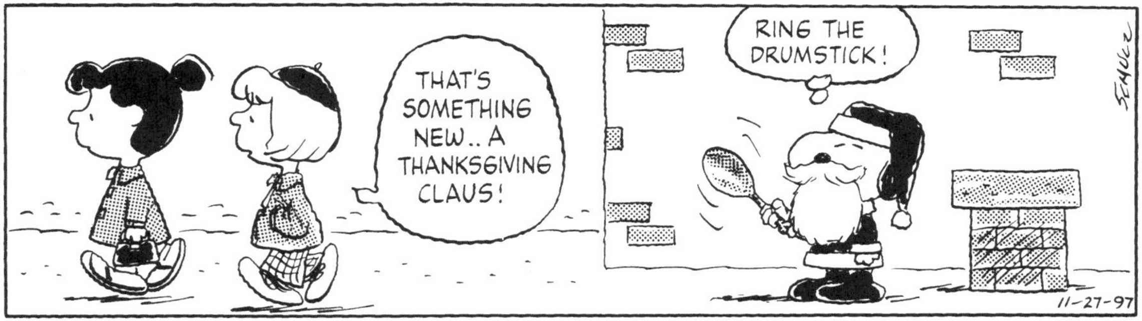
THAT'S SOMETHING NEW.. A THANKSGIVING CLAUS!
RING THE DRUMSTICK!
SCHULZ
11-27-97

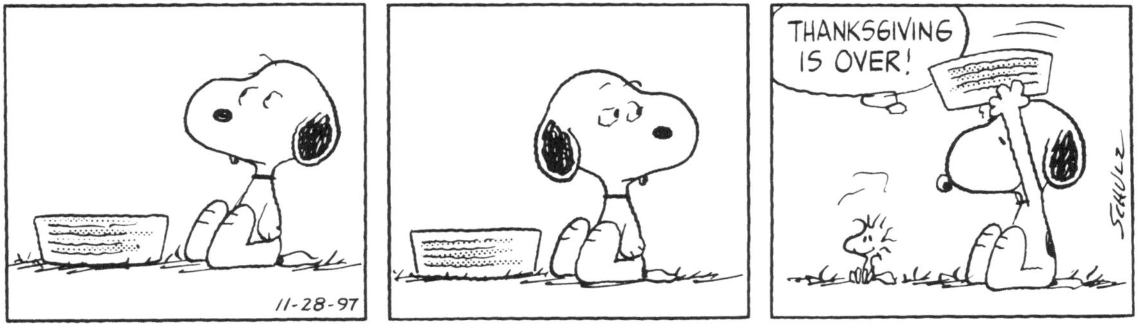
11-28-97
THANKSGIVING IS OVER!
SCHULZ

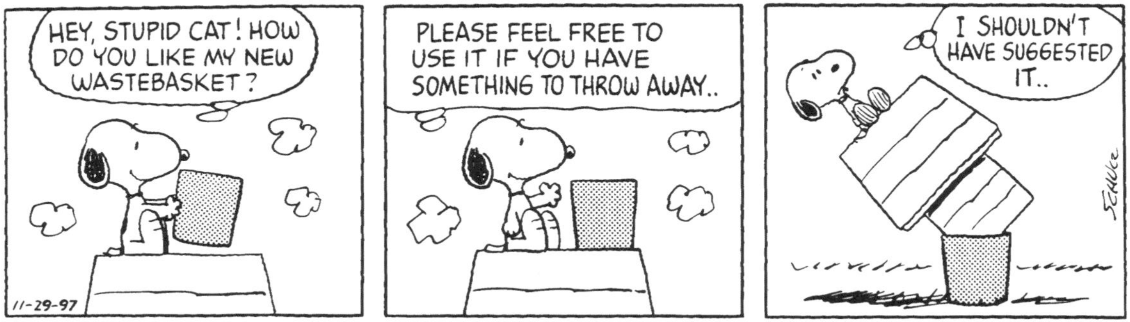
HEY, STUPID CAT! HOW DO YOU LIKE MY NEW WASTEBASKET?
11-29-97
PLEASE FEEL FREE TO USE IT IF YOU HAVE SOMETHING TO THROW AWAY..
I SHOULDN'T HAVE SUGGESTED IT..
SCHULZ

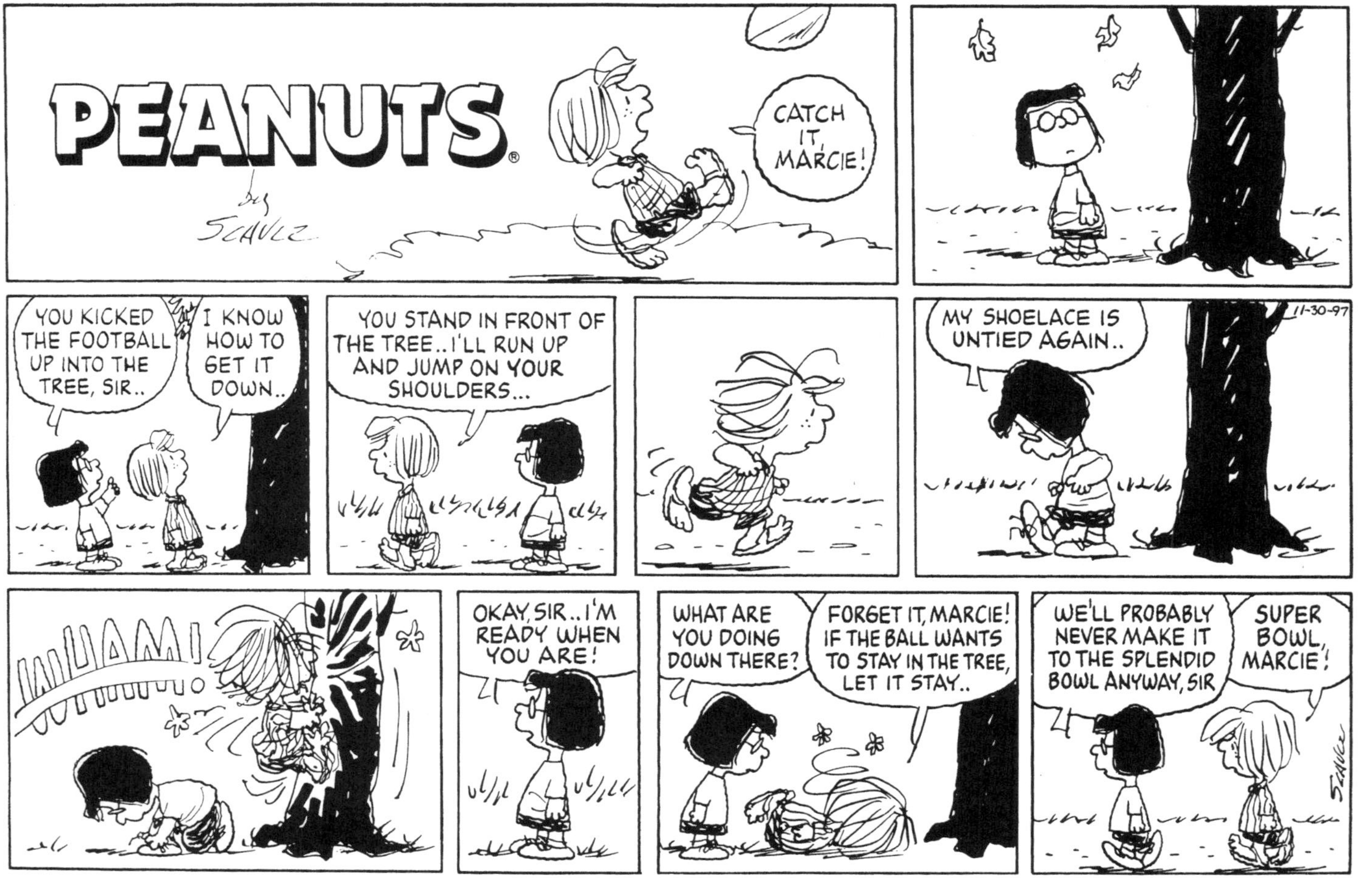
PEANUTS
by SCHULZ
CATCH IT, MARCIE!
YOU KICKED THE FOOTBALL UP INTO THE TREE, SIR..
I KNOW HOW TO GET IT DOWN..
YOU STAND IN FRONT OF THE TREE..I'LL RUN UP AND JUMP ON YOUR SHOULDERS...
MY SHOELACE IS UNTIED AGAIN..
11-30-97
WHAM!
OKAY, SIR..I'M READY WHEN YOU ARE!
WHAT ARE YOU DOING DOWN THERE?
FORGET IT, MARCIE! IF THE BALL WANTS TO STAY IN THE TREE, LET IT STAY..
WE'LL PROBABLY NEVER MAKE IT TO THE SPLENDID BOWL ANYWAY, SIR
SUPER BOWL, MARCIE!
SCHULZ

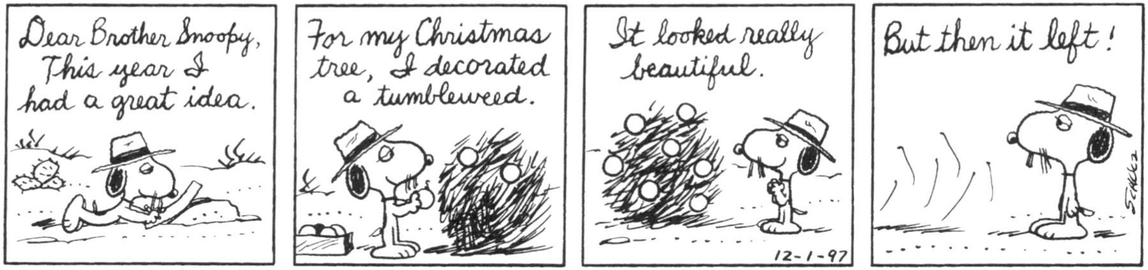
Dear Brother Snoopy, This year I had a great idea.
For my Christmas tree, I decorated a tumbleweed.
It looked really beautiful.
12-1-97
But then it left!

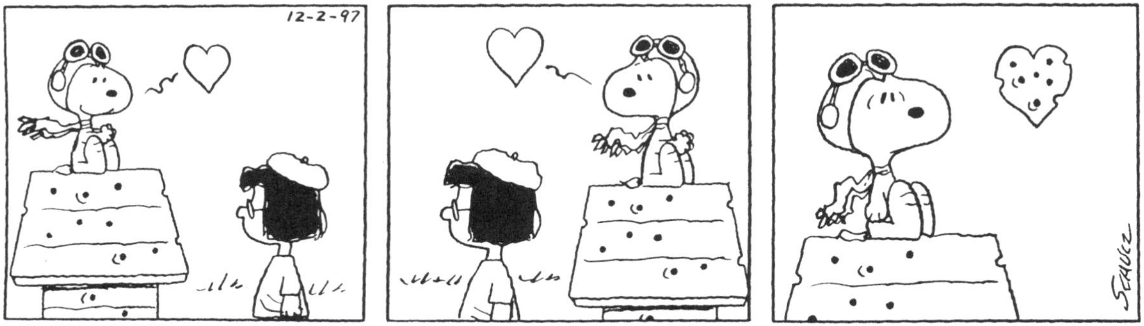
12-2-97

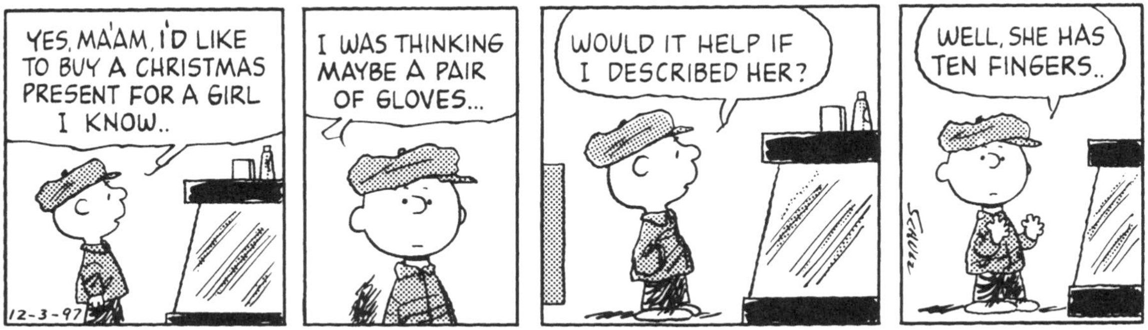
YES, MA'AM, I'D LIKE TO BUY A CHRISTMAS PRESENT FOR A GIRL I KNOW..
12-3-97
I WAS THINKING MAYBE A PAIR OF GLOVES...
WOULD IT HELP IF I DESCRIBED HER?
WELL, SHE HAS TEN FINGERS..

Row 1, Panel 1: I WANTED TO BUY PEGGY JEAN SOME GLOVES FOR CHRISTMAS, BUT THEY COST TWENTY-FIVE DOLLARS

12-4-97

Row 1, Panel 2: SHE'S GOING TO BE DISAPPOINTED WHEN SHE FINDS OUT HER BOYFRIEND IS A CHEAPSKATE

Row 1, Panel 3: I'M NOT A CHEAPSKATE.. I JUST DON'T HAVE TWENTY-FIVE DOLLARS

PUT IT ON YOUR CREDIT CARD..

Row 1, Panel 4: I DON'T HAVE A CREDIT CARD..

SO LONG, PEGGY JEAN!

Row 2, Panel 1: YOU KNOW WHY I WANT TO BUY PEGGY JEAN THOSE GLOVES FOR CHRISTMAS?

Row 2, Panel 2: WHEN I FIRST MET HER THIS SUMMER AT CAMP, I NOTICED WHAT PRETTY HANDS SHE HAD... I WANT THOSE PRETTY HANDS TO BE WARM..

12-5-97

Row 2, Panel 3: BUT I DON'T HAVE TWENTY-FIVE DOLLARS TO BUY THE GLOVES...

Row 2, Panel 4: SEND HER A NICE CARD, AND TELL HER TO KEEP HER HANDS IN HER POCKETS!

Row 3, Panel 1: SEE? THERE THEY ARE... THOSE ARE THE GLOVES I'D LIKE TO BUY PEGGY JEAN FOR CHRISTMAS..

Row 3, Panel 2: WHERE ARE YOU GOING TO GET TWENTY-FIVE DOLLARS?

THAT'S THE PROBLEM

Row 3, Panel 3: MAYBE YOU COULD SELL YOUR DOG...

Row 3, Panel 4: I TAKE IT BACK.. HE'S PROBABLY ONLY WORTH FIFTY CENTS

12-6-97

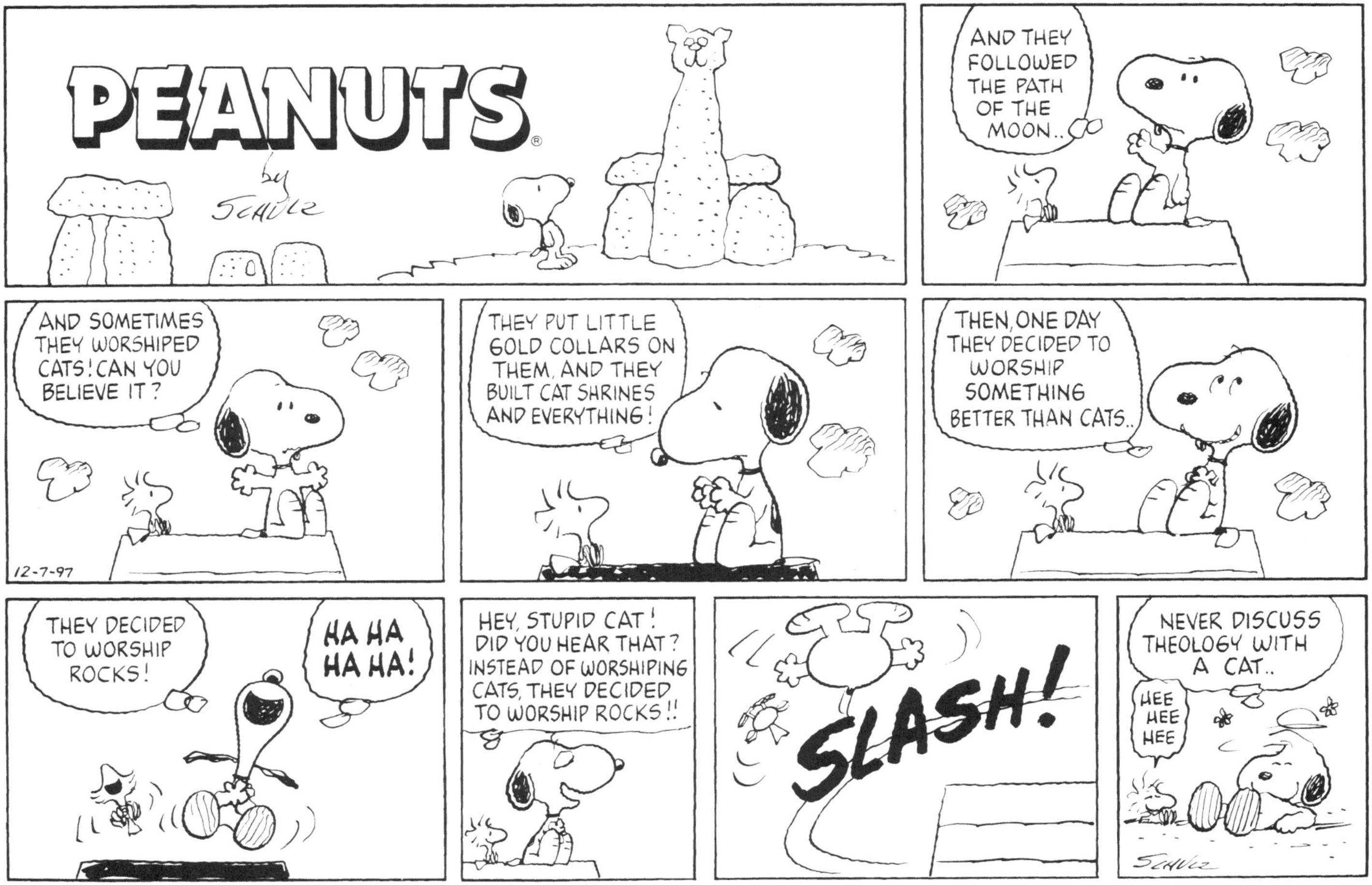
PEANUTS
by SCHULZ
AND THEY FOLLOWED THE PATH OF THE MOON..
AND SOMETIMES THEY WORSHIPED CATS! CAN YOU BELIEVE IT?
12-7-97
THEY PUT LITTLE GOLD COLLARS ON THEM, AND THEY BUILT CAT SHRINES AND EVERYTHING!
THEN, ONE DAY THEY DECIDED TO WORSHIP SOMETHING BETTER THAN CATS..
THEY DECIDED TO WORSHIP ROCKS!
HA HA HA HA!
HEY, STUPID CAT! DID YOU HEAR THAT? INSTEAD OF WORSHIPING CATS, THEY DECIDED TO WORSHIP ROCKS!!
SLASH!
NEVER DISCUSS THEOLOGY WITH A CAT..
HEE HEE HEE
SCHULZ

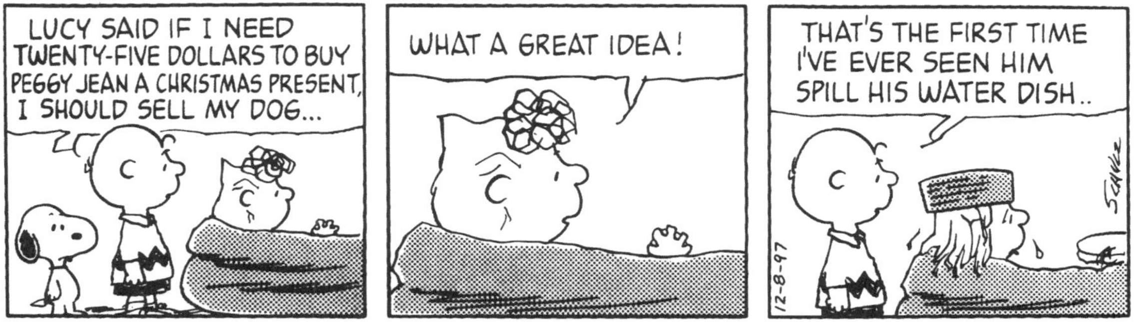
LUCY SAID IF I NEED TWENTY-FIVE DOLLARS TO BUY PEGGY JEAN A CHRISTMAS PRESENT, I SHOULD SELL MY DOG...
WHAT A GREAT IDEA!
THAT'S THE FIRST TIME I'VE EVER SEEN HIM SPILL HIS WATER DISH..
12-8-97
SCHULZ

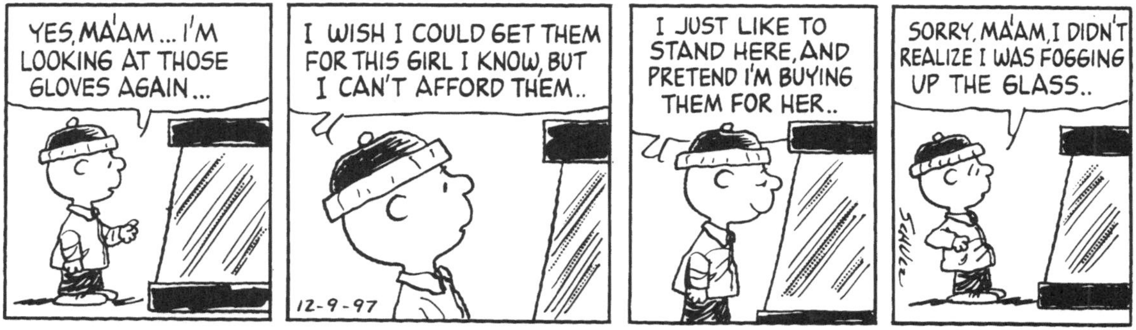
YES, MA'AM ... I'M LOOKING AT THOSE GLOVES AGAIN...
I WISH I COULD GET THEM FOR THIS GIRL I KNOW, BUT I CAN'T AFFORD THEM..
12-9-97
I JUST LIKE TO STAND HERE, AND PRETEND I'M BUYING THEM FOR HER..
SORRY, MA'AM, I DIDN'T REALIZE I WAS FOGGING UP THE GLASS..
SCHULZ

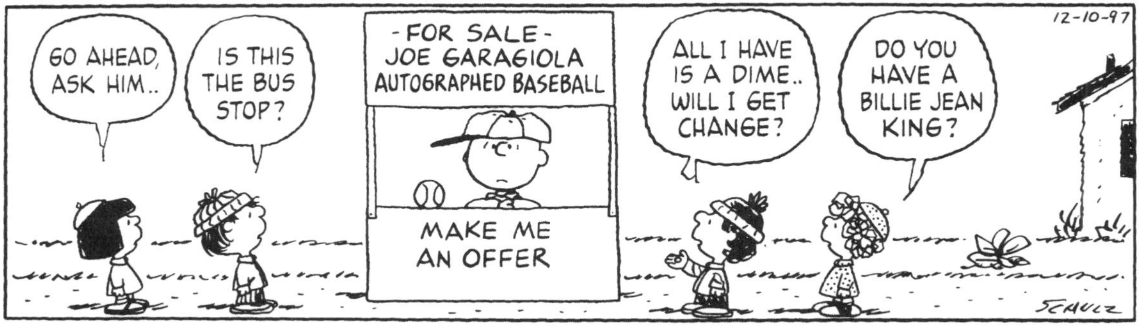
12-10-97
GO AHEAD, ASK HIM..
IS THIS THE BUS STOP?
- FOR SALE -
JOE GARAGIOLA AUTOGRAPHED BASEBALL
MAKE ME AN OFFER
ALL I HAVE IS A DIME.. WILL I GET CHANGE?
DO YOU HAVE A BILLIE JEAN KING?
SCHULZ

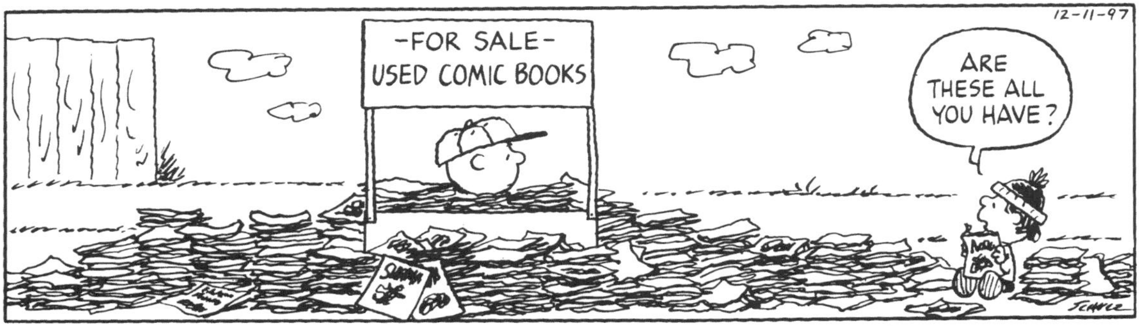
12-11-97
-FOR SALE-
USED COMIC BOOKS
ARE THESE ALL YOU HAVE?
YES, MA'AM.. I SOLD MY WHOLE COLLECTION OF COMIC BOOKS..SEE? HERE'S THE MONEY! NOW, I CAN BUY THOSE GLOVES FOR THAT GIRL I LIKE...

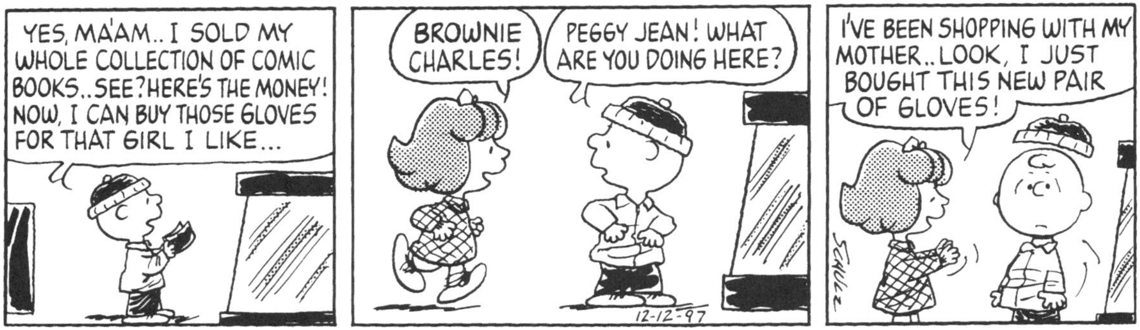
BROWNIE CHARLES!
PEGGY JEAN! WHAT ARE YOU DOING HERE?
I'VE BEEN SHOPPING WITH MY MOTHER.. LOOK, I JUST BOUGHT THIS NEW PAIR OF GLOVES!
12-12-97

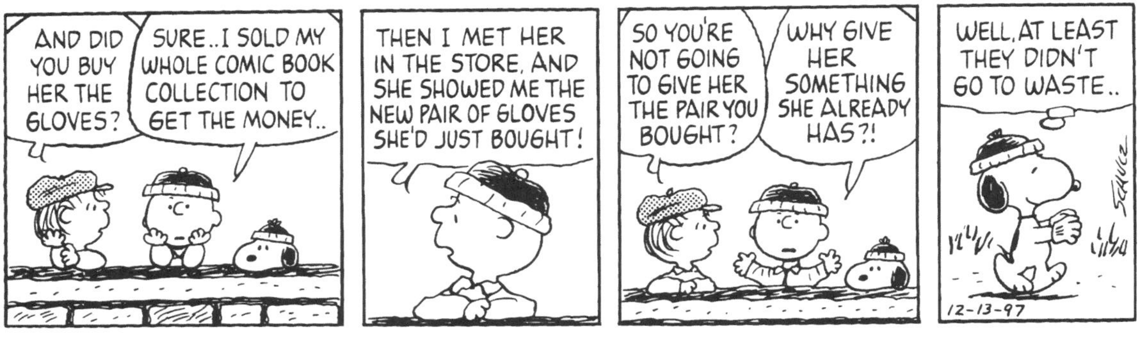
AND DID YOU BUY HER THE GLOVES?
SURE..I SOLD MY WHOLE COMIC BOOK COLLECTION TO GET THE MONEY..
THEN I MET HER IN THE STORE, AND SHE SHOWED ME THE NEW PAIR OF GLOVES SHE'D JUST BOUGHT!
SO YOU'RE NOT GOING TO GIVE HER THE PAIR YOU BOUGHT?
WHY GIVE HER SOMETHING SHE ALREADY HAS?!
WELL, AT LEAST THEY DIDN'T GO TO WASTE..
12-13-97

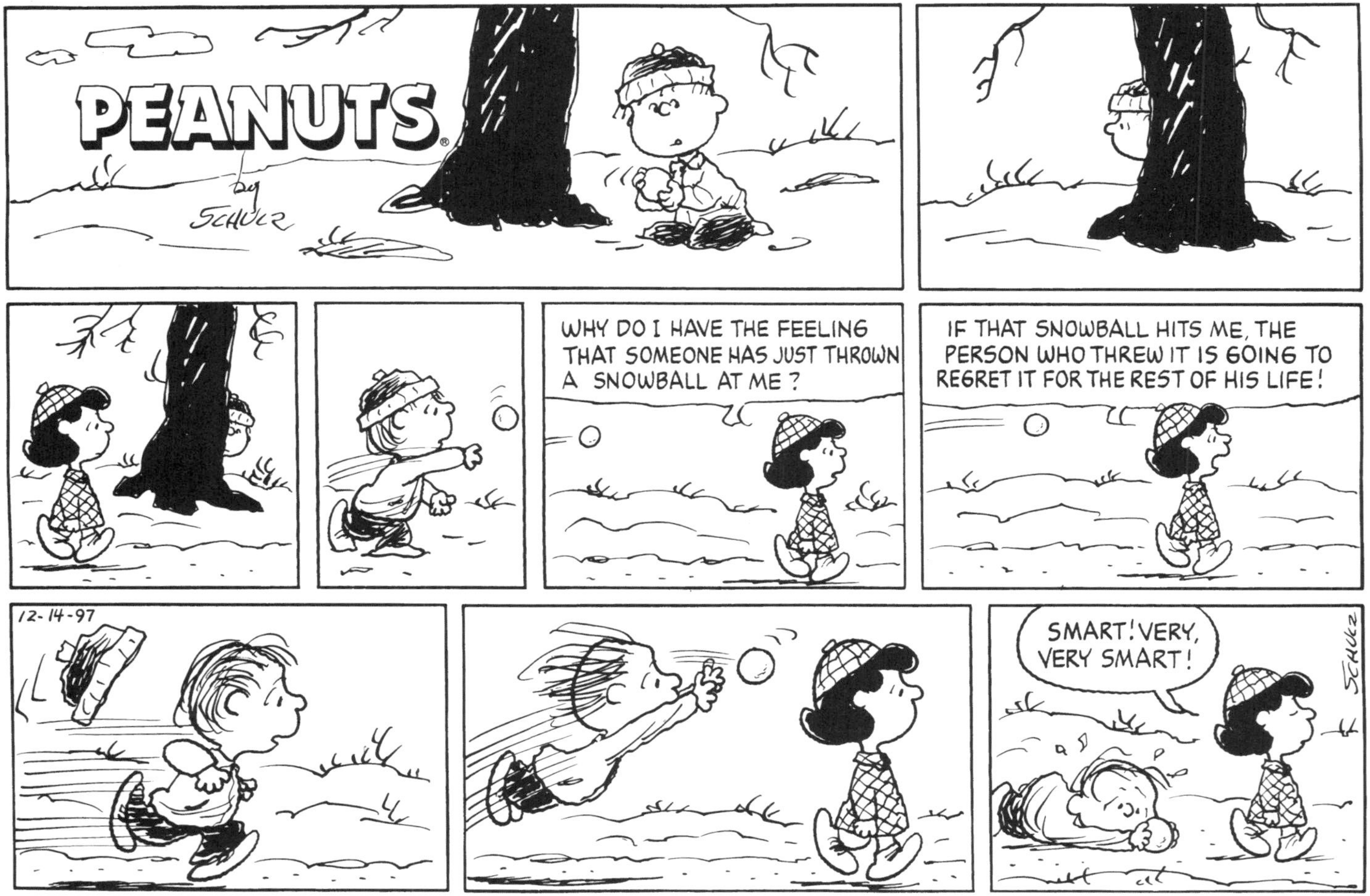
PEANUTS
by SCHULZ
WHY DO I HAVE THE FEELING THAT SOMEONE HAS JUST THROWN A SNOWBALL AT ME ?
IF THAT SNOWBALL HITS ME, THE PERSON WHO THREW IT IS GOING TO REGRET IT FOR THE REST OF HIS LIFE!
12-14-97
SMART! VERY, VERY SMART!
SCHULZ

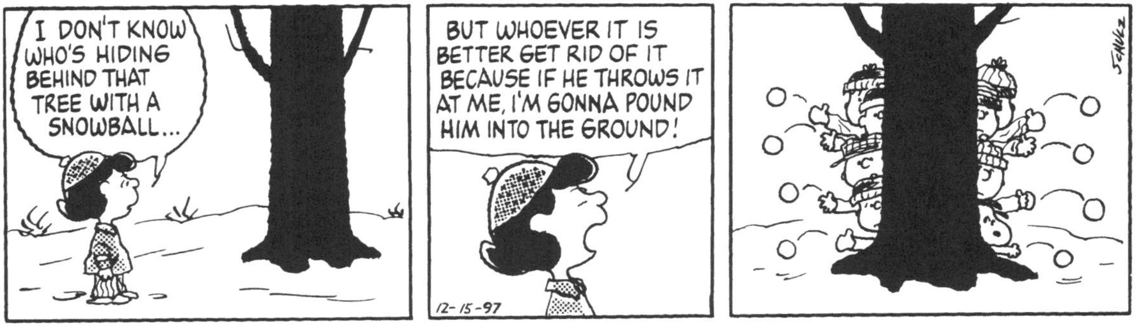
I DON'T KNOW WHO'S HIDING BEHIND THAT TREE WITH A SNOWBALL...
BUT WHOEVER IT IS BETTER GET RID OF IT BECAUSE IF HE THROWS IT AT ME, I'M GONNA POUND HIM INTO THE GROUND!
12-15-97
SCHULZ

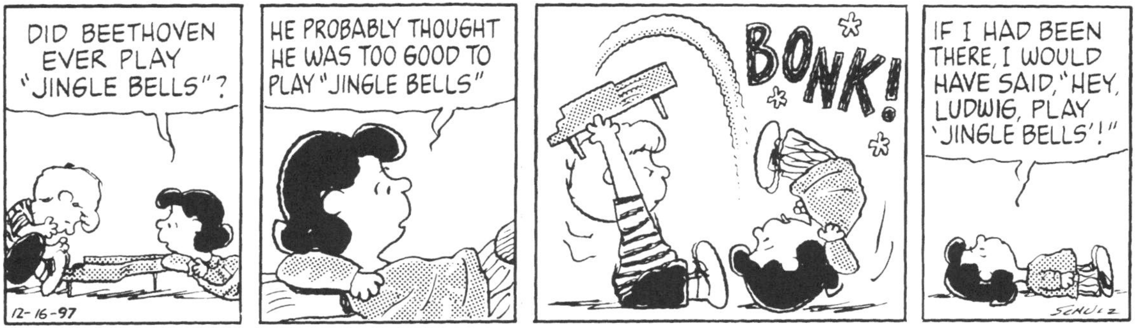
DID BEETHOVEN EVER PLAY "JINGLE BELLS"?
12-16-97
HE PROBABLY THOUGHT HE WAS TOO GOOD TO PLAY "JINGLE BELLS"
BONK!
IF I HAD BEEN THERE, I WOULD HAVE SAID, "HEY, LUDWIG, PLAY 'JINGLE BELLS'!"
SCHULZ

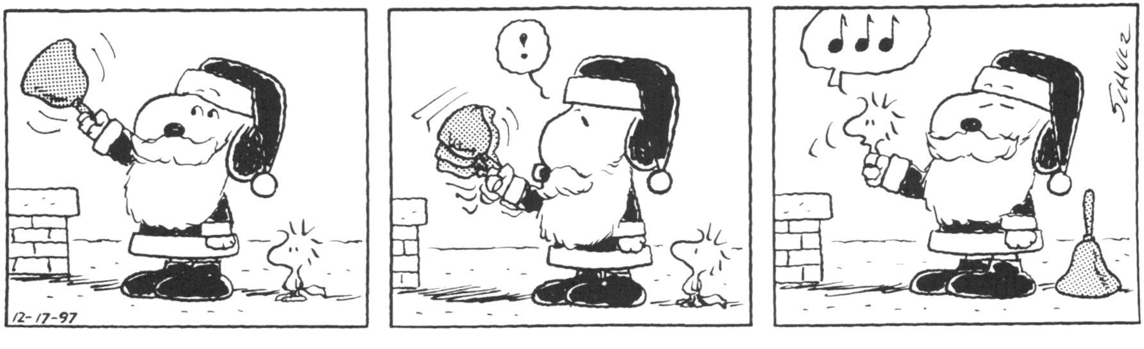
12-17-97
!
SCHULZ

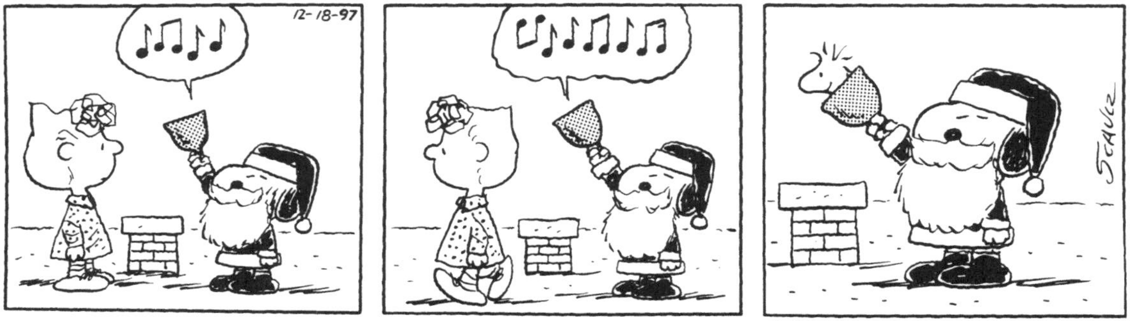
12-18-97
SCHULZ

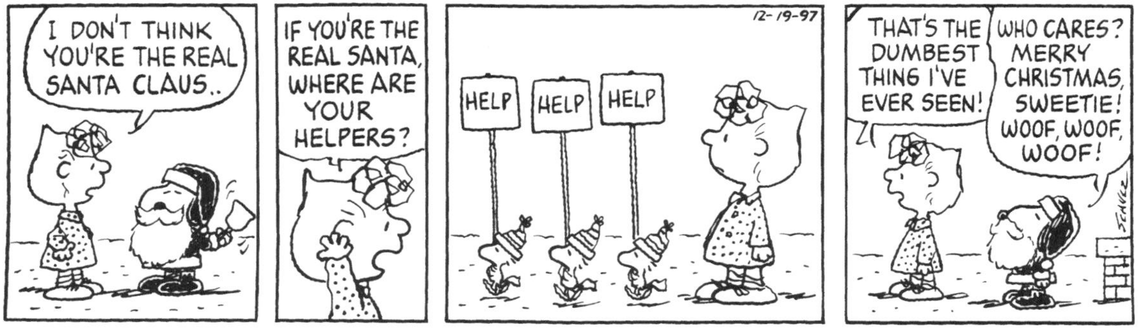
I DON'T THINK YOU'RE THE REAL SANTA CLAUS..
IF YOU'RE THE REAL SANTA, WHERE ARE YOUR HELPERS?
12-19-97
HELP
HELP
HELP
THAT'S THE DUMBEST THING I'VE EVER SEEN!
WHO CARES? MERRY CHRISTMAS, SWEETIE! WOOF, WOOF, WOOF!
SCHULZ

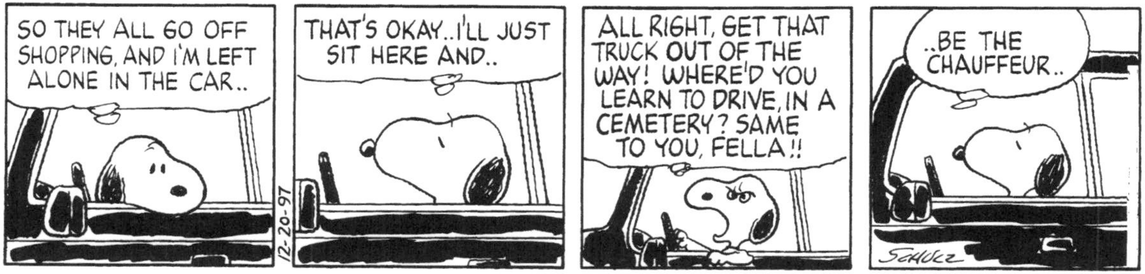
SO THEY ALL GO OFF SHOPPING, AND I'M LEFT ALONE IN THE CAR..
THAT'S OKAY..I'LL JUST SIT HERE AND..
12-20-97
ALL RIGHT, GET THAT TRUCK OUT OF THE WAY! WHERE'D YOU LEARN TO DRIVE, IN A CEMETERY? SAME TO YOU, FELLA!!
..BE THE CHAUFFEUR..
SCHULZ

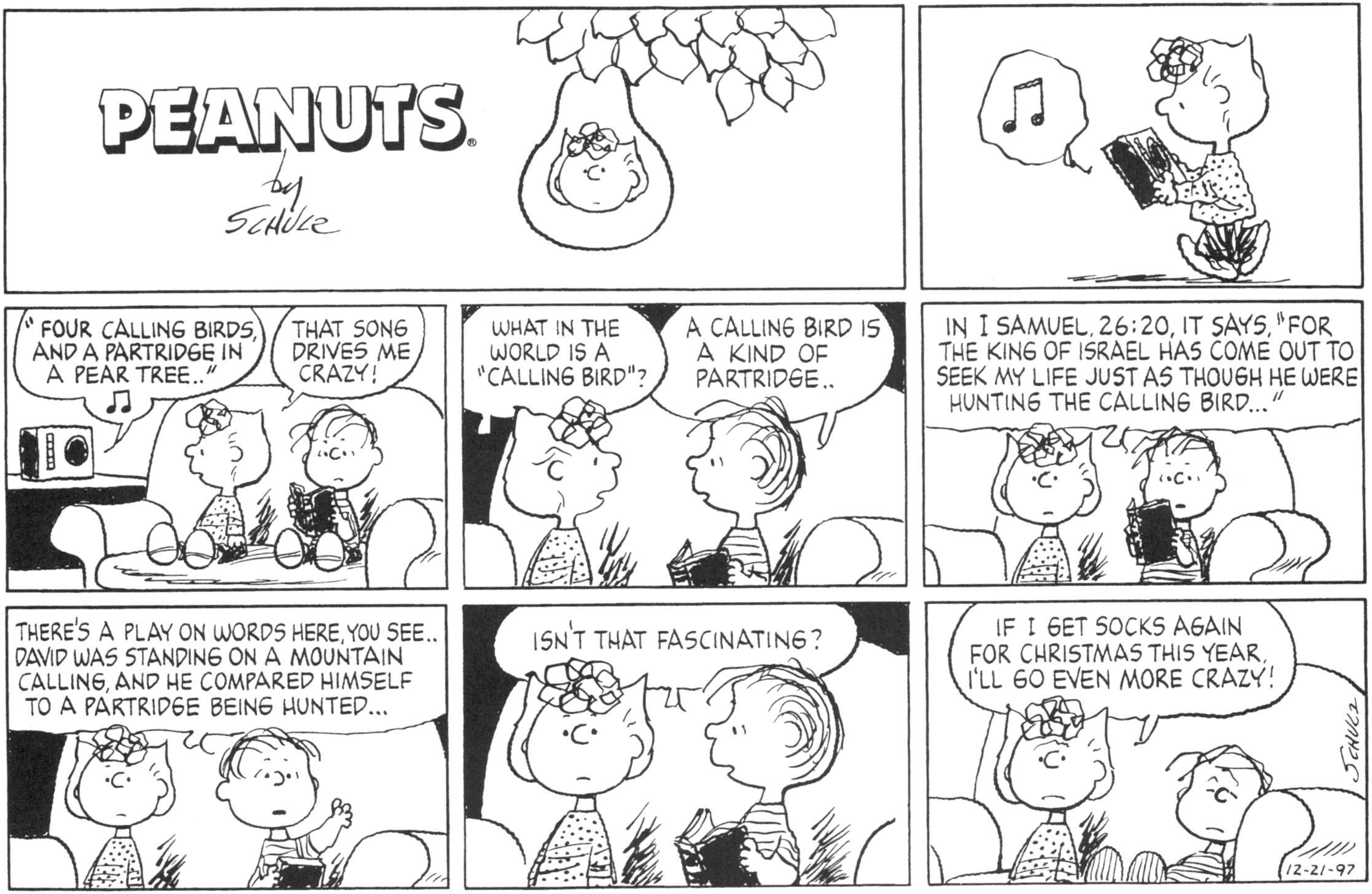
PEANUTS®
by SCHULZ
" FOUR CALLING BIRDS, AND A PARTRIDGE IN A PEAR TREE.."
THAT SONG DRIVES ME CRAZY!
WHAT IN THE WORLD IS A "CALLING BIRD"?
A CALLING BIRD IS A KIND OF PARTRIDGE..
IN I SAMUEL, 26:20, IT SAYS, "FOR THE KING OF ISRAEL HAS COME OUT TO SEEK MY LIFE JUST AS THOUGH HE WERE HUNTING THE CALLING BIRD..."
THERE'S A PLAY ON WORDS HERE, YOU SEE.. DAVID WAS STANDING ON A MOUNTAIN CALLING, AND HE COMPARED HIMSELF TO A PARTRIDGE BEING HUNTED...
ISN'T THAT FASCINATING?
IF I GET SOCKS AGAIN FOR CHRISTMAS THIS YEAR, I'LL GO EVEN MORE CRAZY!
SCHULZ
12-21-97

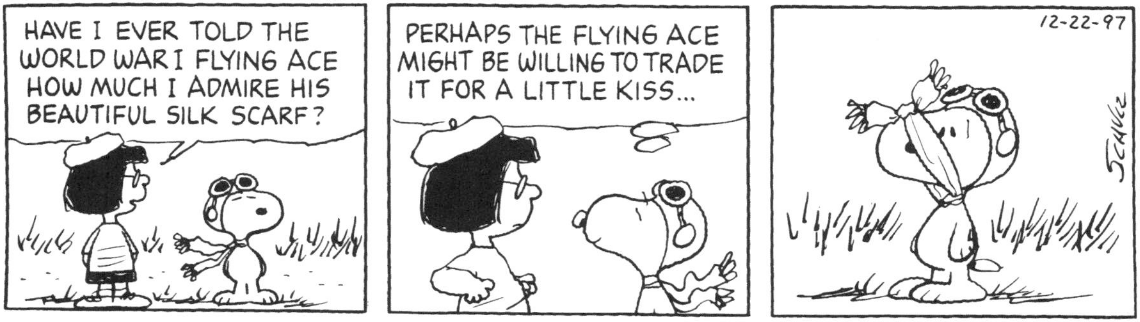
HAVE I EVER TOLD THE WORLD WAR I FLYING ACE HOW MUCH I ADMIRE HIS BEAUTIFUL SILK SCARF?
PERHAPS THE FLYING ACE MIGHT BE WILLING TO TRADE IT FOR A LITTLE KISS...
12-22-97
SCHULZ

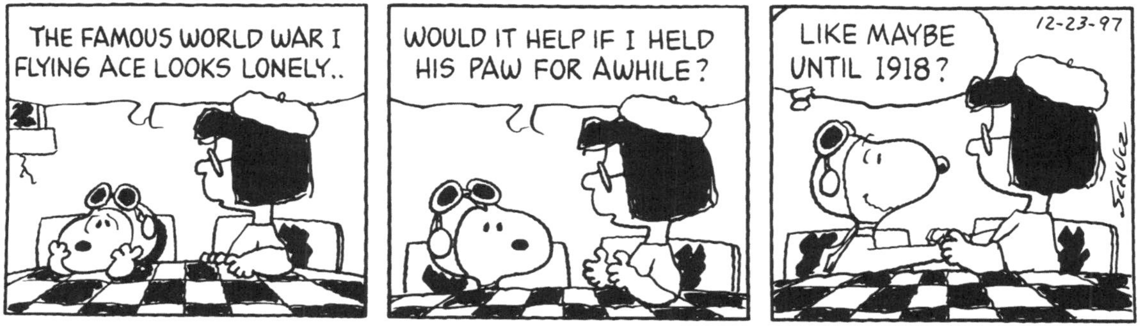
THE FAMOUS WORLD WAR I FLYING ACE LOOKS LONELY..
WOULD IT HELP IF I HELD HIS PAW FOR AWHILE?
12-23-97
LIKE MAYBE UNTIL 1918?
SCHULZ

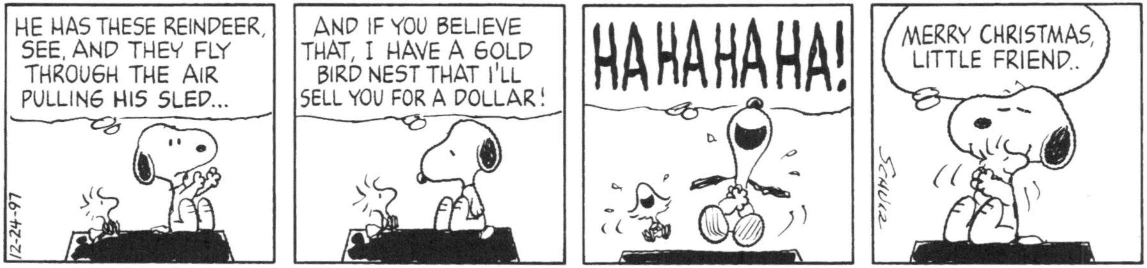
12-24-97
HE HAS THESE REINDEER, SEE, AND THEY FLY THROUGH THE AIR PULLING HIS SLED...
AND IF YOU BELIEVE THAT, I HAVE A GOLD BIRD NEST THAT I'LL SELL YOU FOR A DOLLAR!
HAHAHAHA!
SCHULZ
MERRY CHRISTMAS, LITTLE FRIEND..

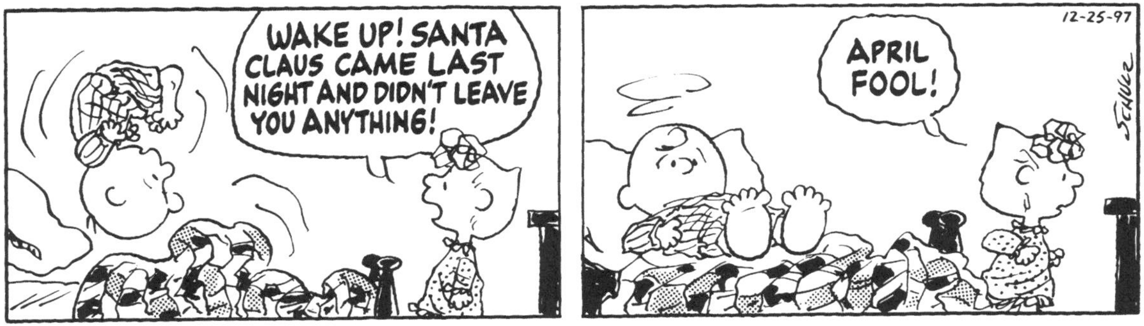
WAKE UP! SANTA CLAUS CAME LAST NIGHT AND DIDN'T LEAVE YOU ANYTHING!
12-25-97
APRIL FOOL!
SCHULZ

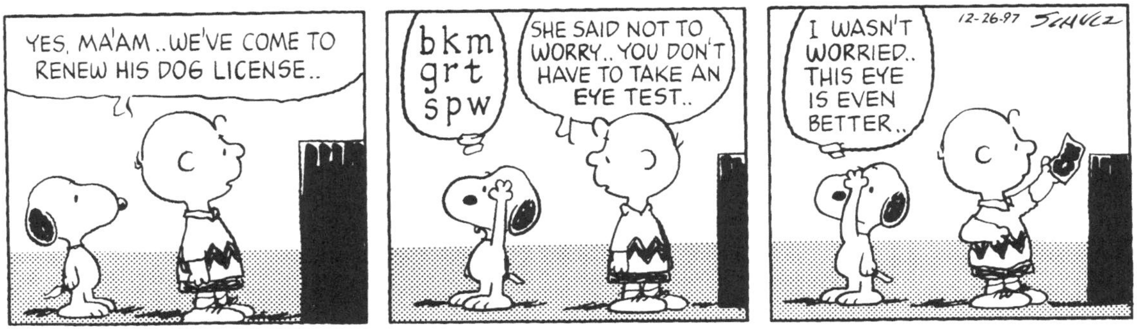
YES, MA'AM..WE'VE COME TO RENEW HIS DOG LICENSE..
bkm grt spw
SHE SAID NOT TO WORRY.. YOU DON'T HAVE TO TAKE AN EYE TEST..
12-26-97 SCHULZ
I WASN'T WORRIED.. THIS EYE IS EVEN BETTER..

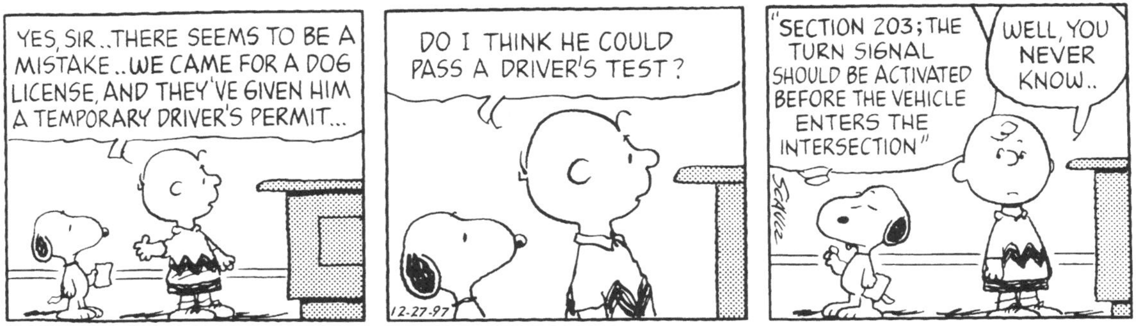
YES, SIR..THERE SEEMS TO BE A MISTAKE..WE CAME FOR A DOG LICENSE, AND THEY'VE GIVEN HIM A TEMPORARY DRIVER'S PERMIT...
DO I THINK HE COULD PASS A DRIVER'S TEST?
12-27-97
"SECTION 203; THE TURN SIGNAL SHOULD BE ACTIVATED BEFORE THE VEHICLE ENTERS THE INTERSECTION"
WELL, YOU NEVER KNOW..
SCHULZ

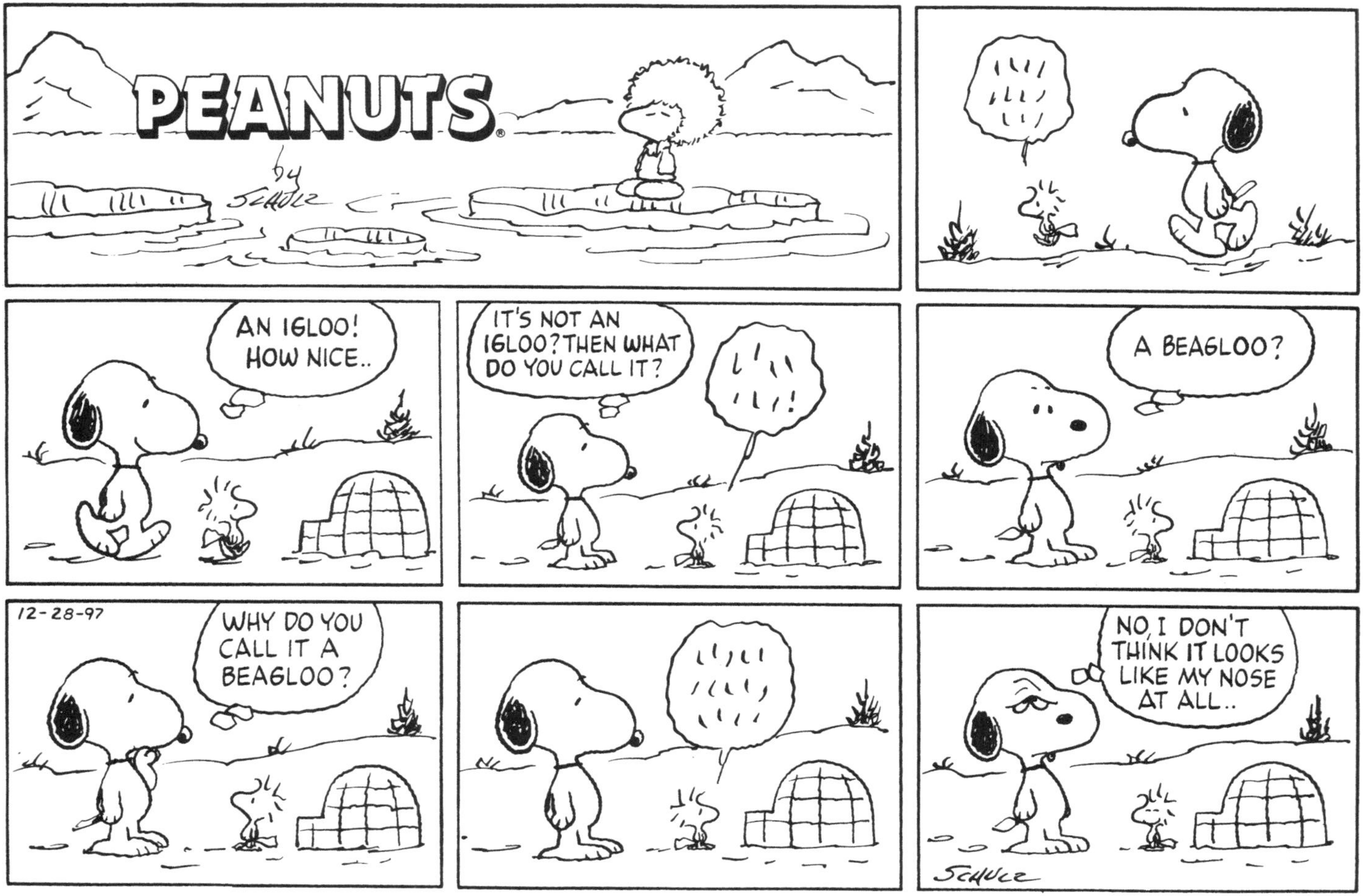
PEANUTS
by SCHULZ
AN IGLOO! HOW NICE..
IT'S NOT AN IGLOO? THEN WHAT DO YOU CALL IT?
A BEAGLOO?
12-28-97
WHY DO YOU CALL IT A BEAGLOO?
NO, I DON'T THINK IT LOOKS LIKE MY NOSE AT ALL..
SCHULZ

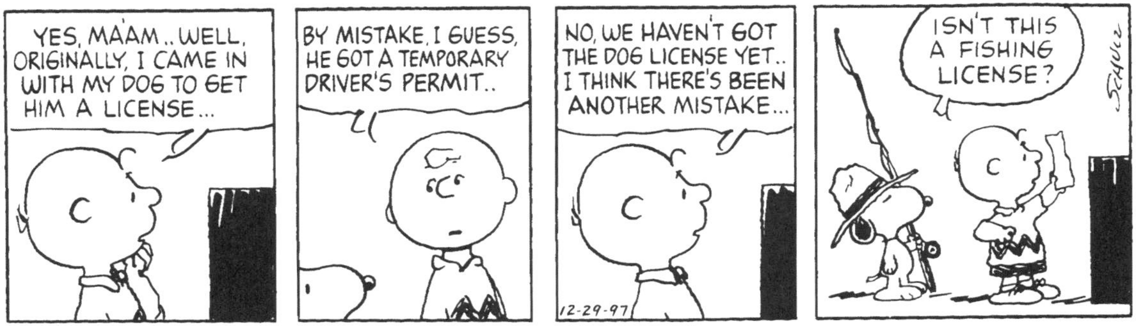
YES, MA'AM .. WELL, ORIGINALLY, I CAME IN WITH MY DOG TO GET HIM A LICENSE...
BY MISTAKE, I GUESS, HE GOT A TEMPORARY DRIVER'S PERMIT..
NO, WE HAVEN'T GOT THE DOG LICENSE YET.. I THINK THERE'S BEEN ANOTHER MISTAKE...
12-29-97
ISN'T THIS A FISHING LICENSE?
SCHULZ

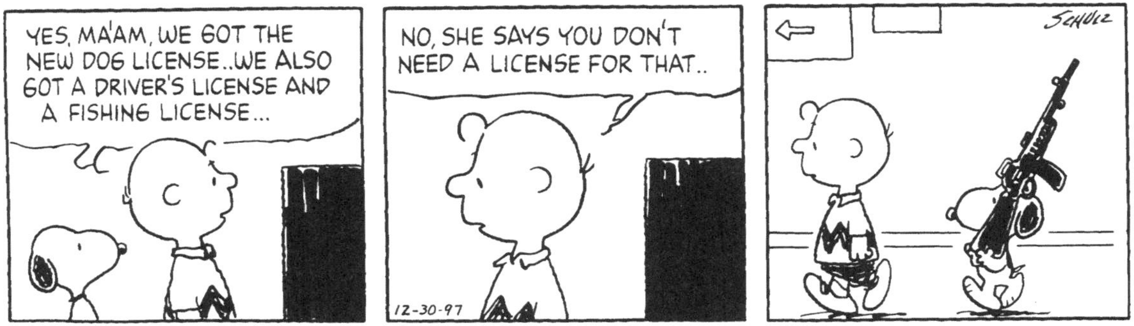
YES, MA'AM, WE GOT THE NEW DOG LICENSE..WE ALSO GOT A DRIVER'S LICENSE AND A FISHING LICENSE...
NO, SHE SAYS YOU DON'T NEED A LICENSE FOR THAT..
12-30-97
SCHULZ

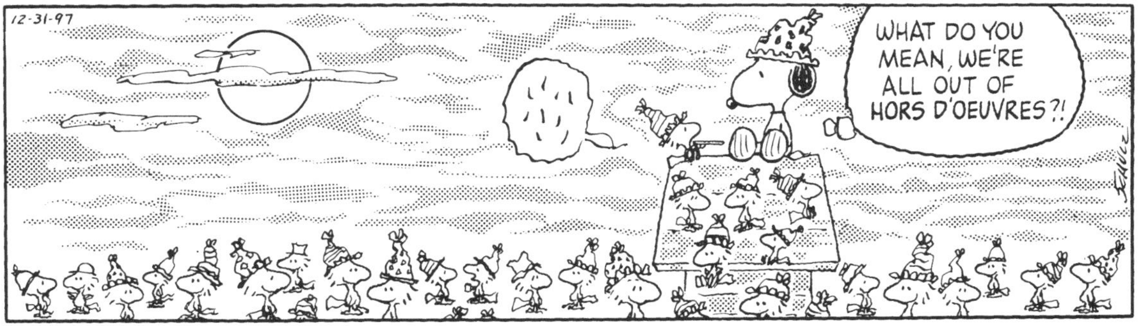
12-31-97
WHAT DO YOU MEAN, WE'RE ALL OUT OF HORS D'OEUVRES?!
SCHULZ

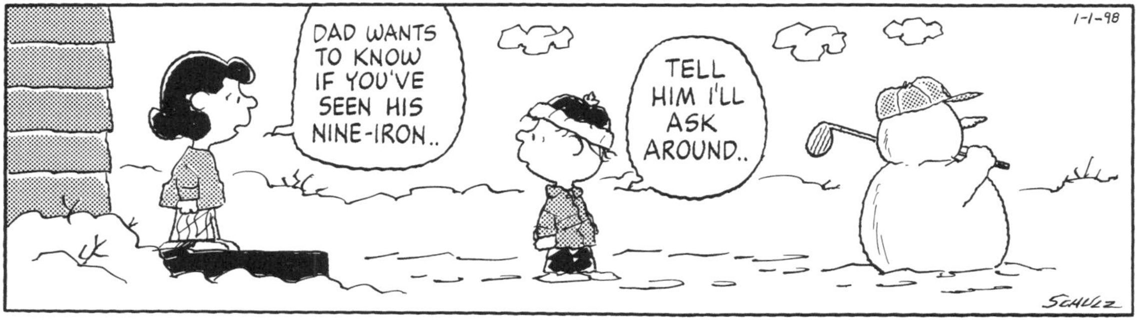
1-1-98
DAD WANTS TO KNOW IF YOU'VE SEEN HIS NINE-IRON..
TELL HIM I'LL ASK AROUND..
SCHULZ

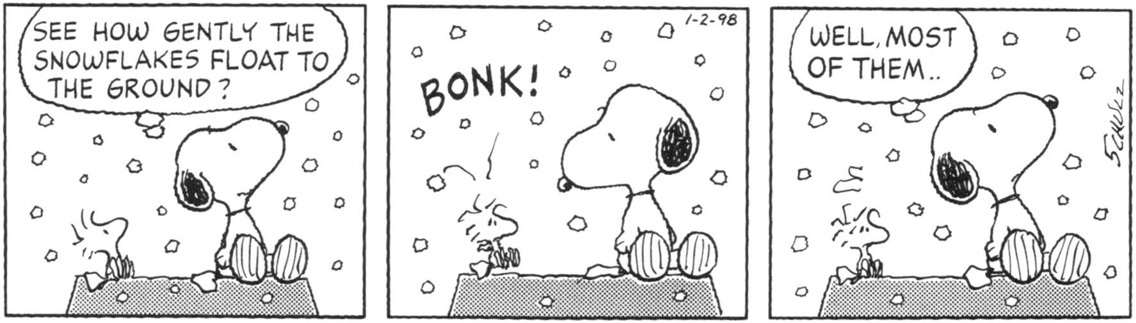
SEE HOW GENTLY THE SNOWFLAKES FLOAT TO THE GROUND?
1-2-98
BONK!
WELL, MOST OF THEM..
SCHULZ

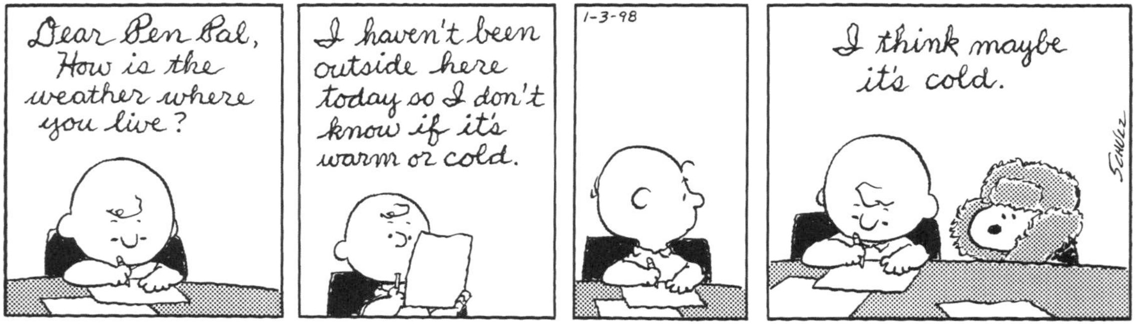
Dear Pen Pal,
How is the weather where you live?
I haven't been outside here today so I don't know if it's warm or cold.
1-3-98
I think maybe it's cold.
SCHULZ

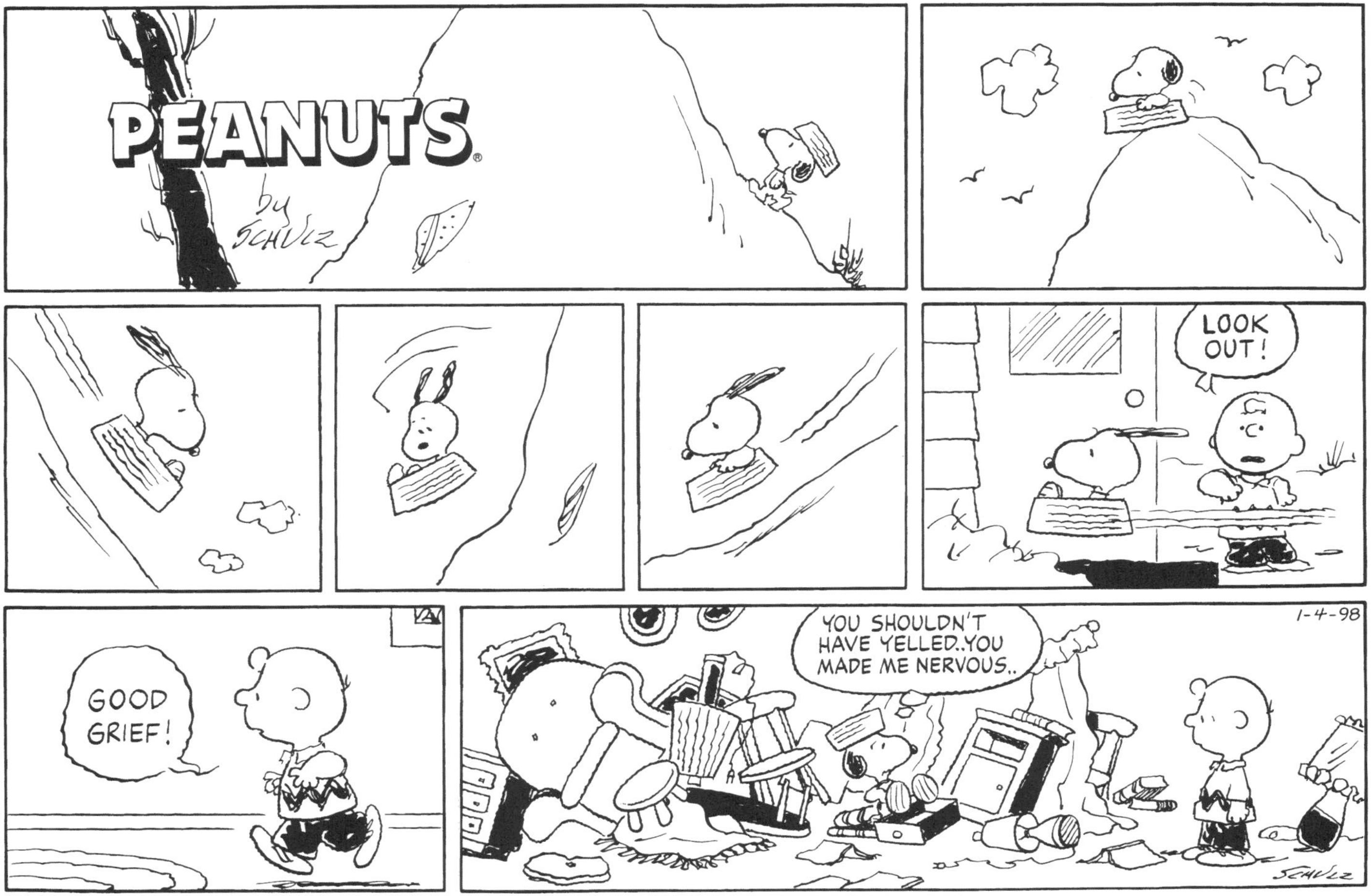
PEANUTS
by SCHULZ
LOOK OUT!
GOOD GRIEF!
YOU SHOULDN'T HAVE YELLED..YOU MADE ME NERVOUS..
1-4-98
SCHULZ

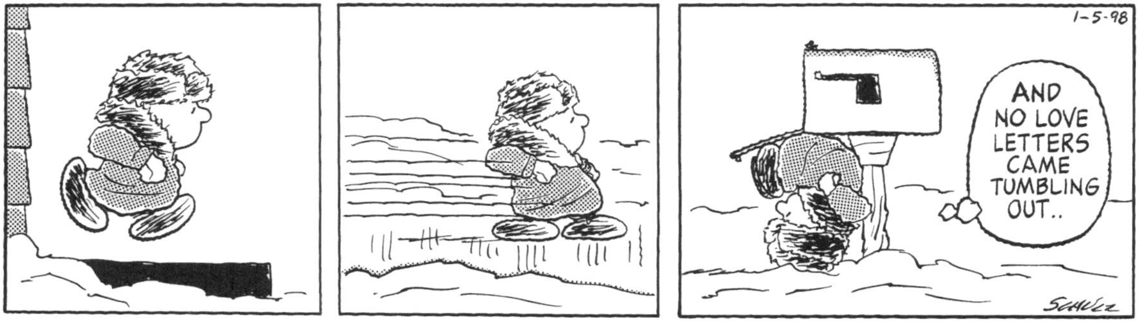
1-5-98
AND NO LOVE LETTERS CAME TUMBLING OUT..
SCHULZ

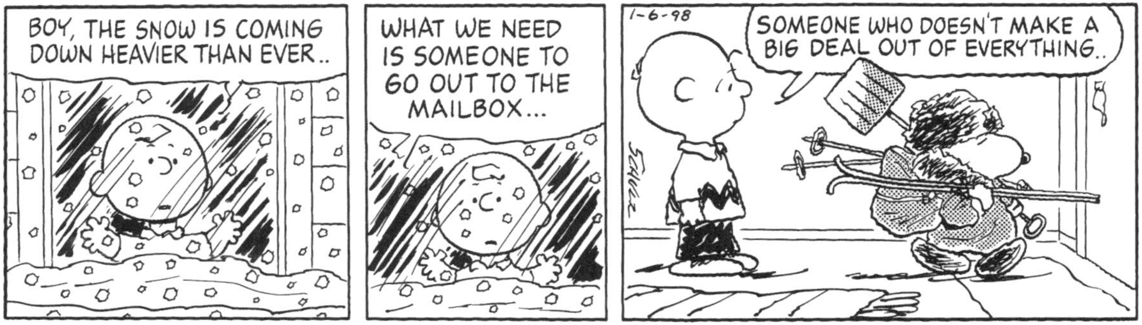
BOY, THE SNOW IS COMING DOWN HEAVIER THAN EVER..
WHAT WE NEED IS SOMEONE TO GO OUT TO THE MAILBOX...
1-6-98
SOMEONE WHO DOESN'T MAKE A BIG DEAL OUT OF EVERYTHING..
SCHULZ

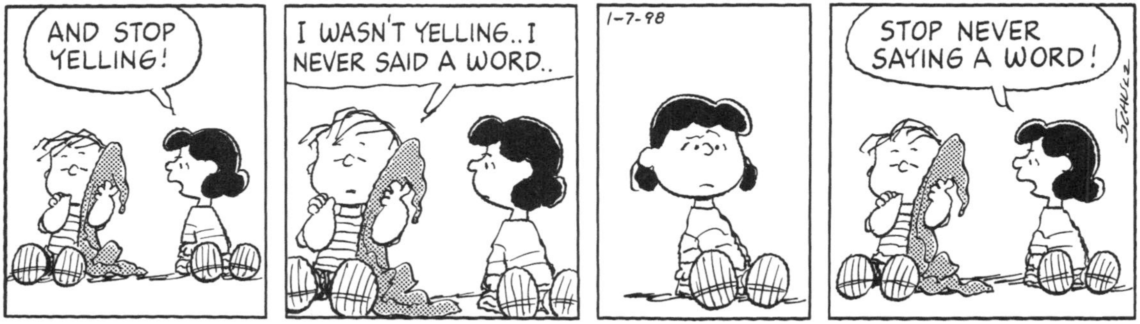
AND STOP YELLING!
I WASN'T YELLING..I NEVER SAID A WORD..
1-7-98
STOP NEVER SAYING A WORD!
SCHULZ

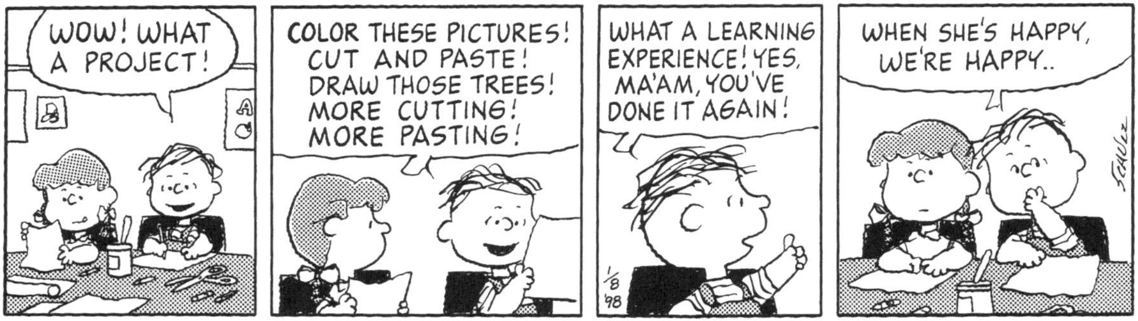
WOW! WHAT A PROJECT!
COLOR THESE PICTURES! CUT AND PASTE! DRAW THOSE TREES! MORE CUTTING! MORE PASTING!
WHAT A LEARNING EXPERIENCE! YES, MA'AM, YOU'VE DONE IT AGAIN!
1/8/98
WHEN SHE'S HAPPY, WE'RE HAPPY..
SCHULZ

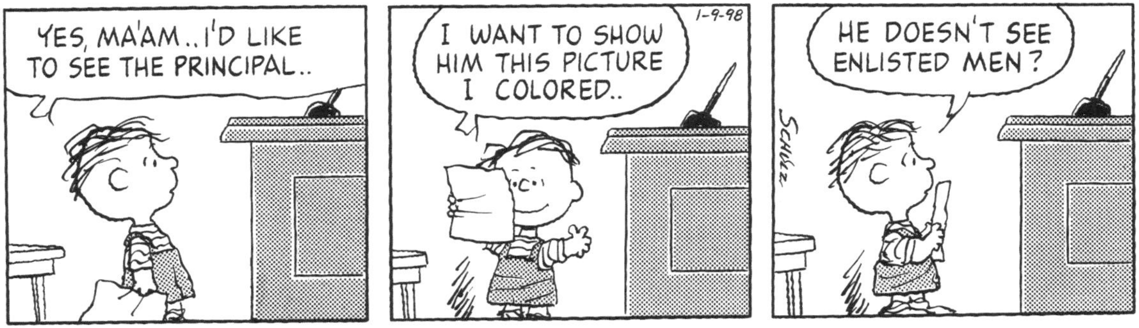
YES, MA'AM.. I'D LIKE TO SEE THE PRINCIPAL..
1-9-98
I WANT TO SHOW HIM THIS PICTURE I COLORED..
SCHULZ
HE DOESN'T SEE ENLISTED MEN?

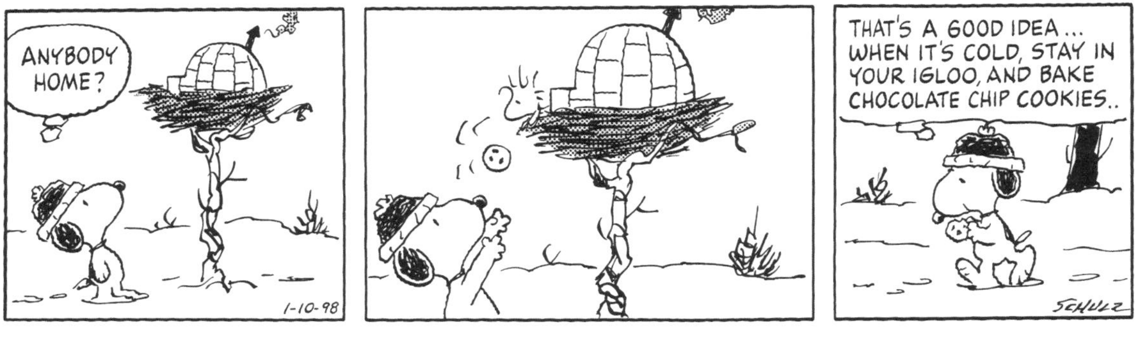
ANYBODY HOME?
1-10-98
THAT'S A GOOD IDEA... WHEN IT'S COLD, STAY IN YOUR IGLOO, AND BAKE CHOCOLATE CHIP COOKIES..
SCHULZ

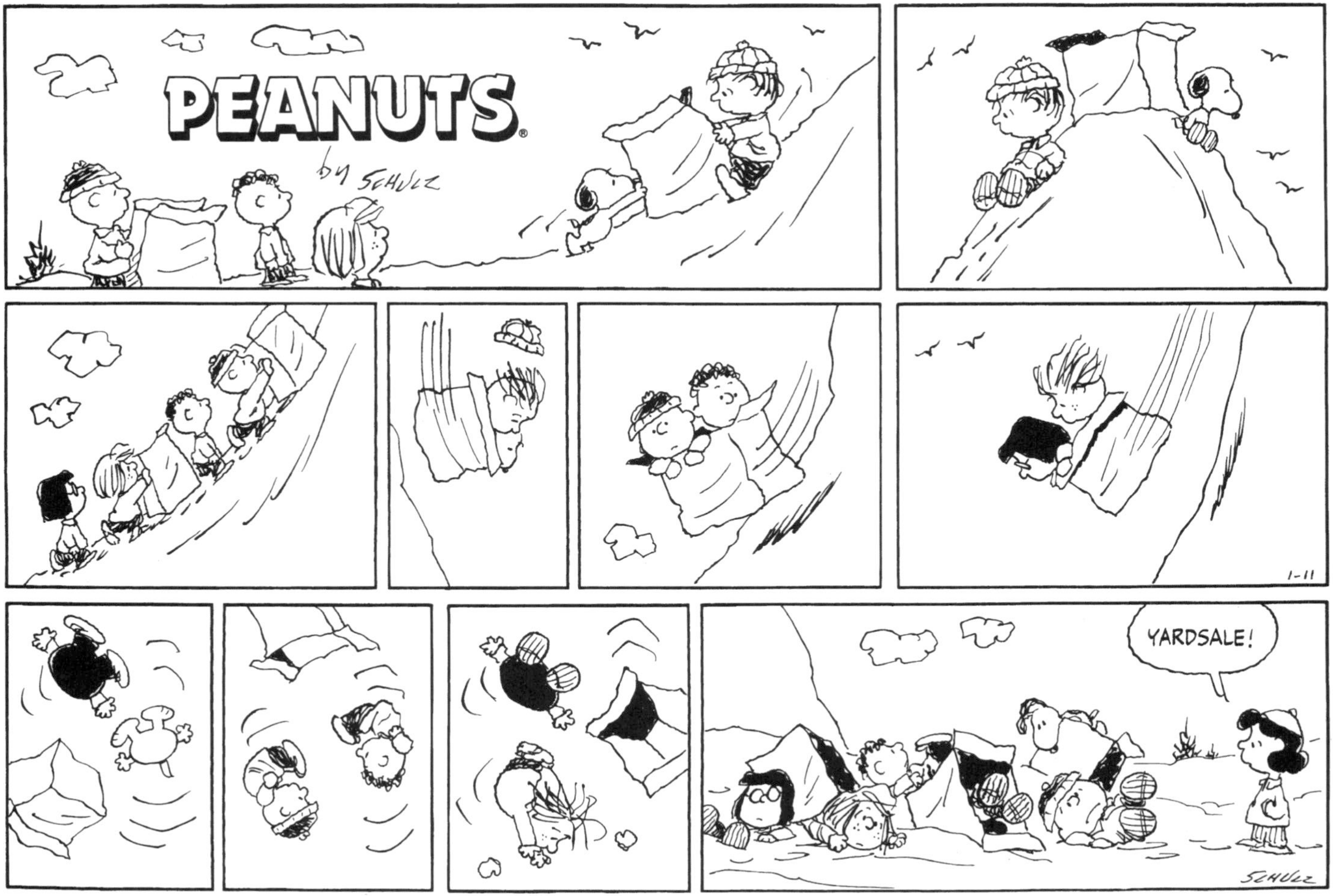
PEANUTS
by SCHULZ
1-11
YARDSALE!
SCHULZ

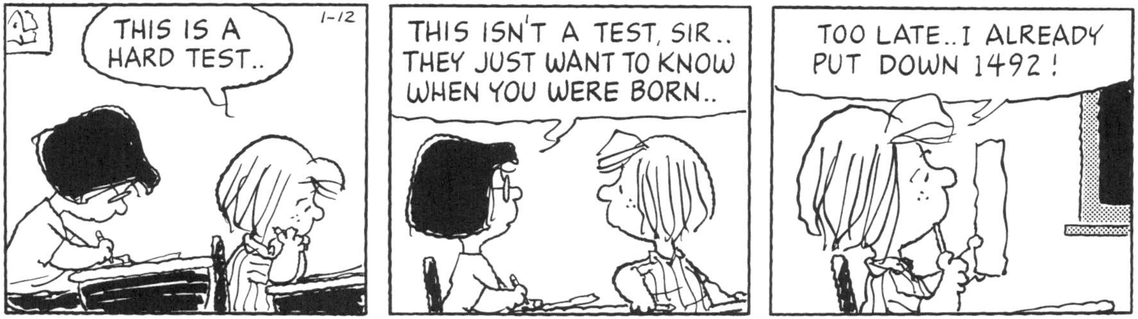
1-12
THIS IS A HARD TEST..
THIS ISN'T A TEST, SIR.. THEY JUST WANT TO KNOW WHEN YOU WERE BORN..
TOO LATE..I ALREADY PUT DOWN 1492!

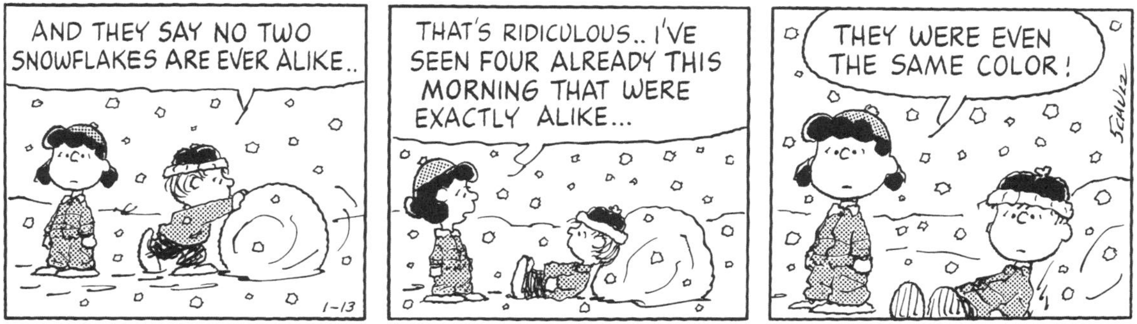
AND THEY SAY NO TWO SNOWFLAKES ARE EVER ALIKE..
1-13
THAT'S RIDICULOUS.. I'VE SEEN FOUR ALREADY THIS MORNING THAT WERE EXACTLY ALIKE...
THEY WERE EVEN THE SAME COLOR!
SCHULZ

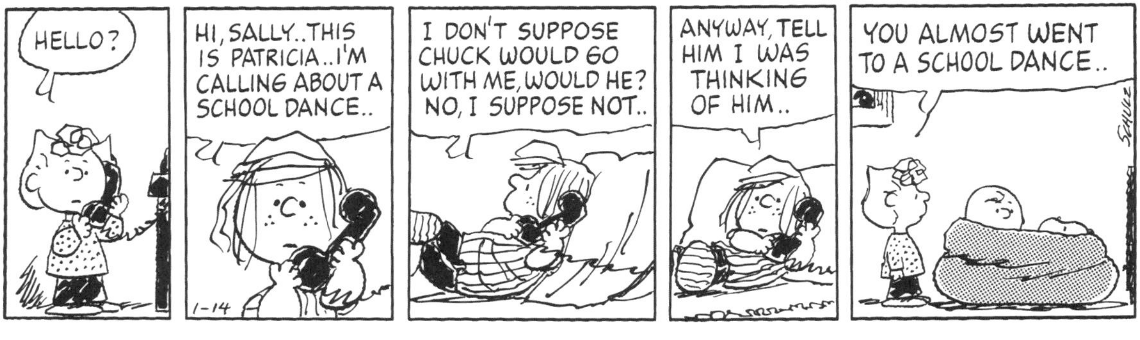
HELLO?
HI, SALLY..THIS IS PATRICIA..I'M CALLING ABOUT A SCHOOL DANCE..
1-14
I DON'T SUPPOSE CHUCK WOULD GO WITH ME, WOULD HE? NO, I SUPPOSE NOT..
ANYWAY, TELL HIM I WAS THINKING OF HIM..
YOU ALMOST WENT TO A SCHOOL DANCE..
SCHULZ

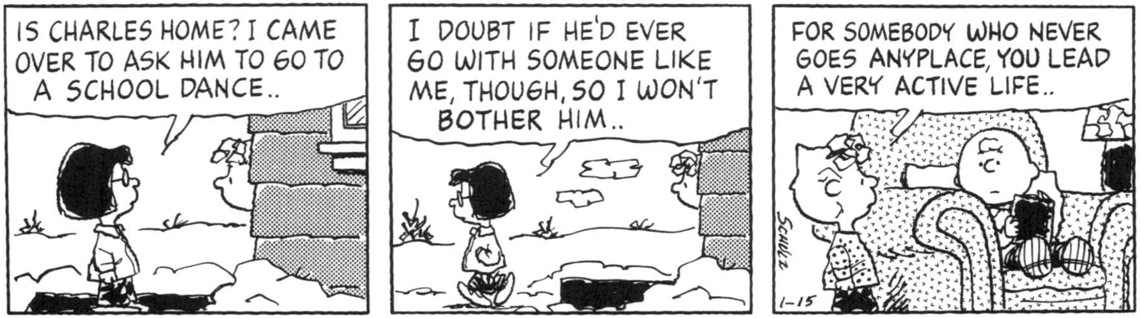
IS CHARLES HOME? I CAME OVER TO ASK HIM TO GO TO A SCHOOL DANCE..
I DOUBT IF HE'D EVER GO WITH SOMEONE LIKE ME, THOUGH, SO I WON'T BOTHER HIM..
FOR SOMEBODY WHO NEVER GOES ANYPLACE, YOU LEAD A VERY ACTIVE LIFE..
1-15

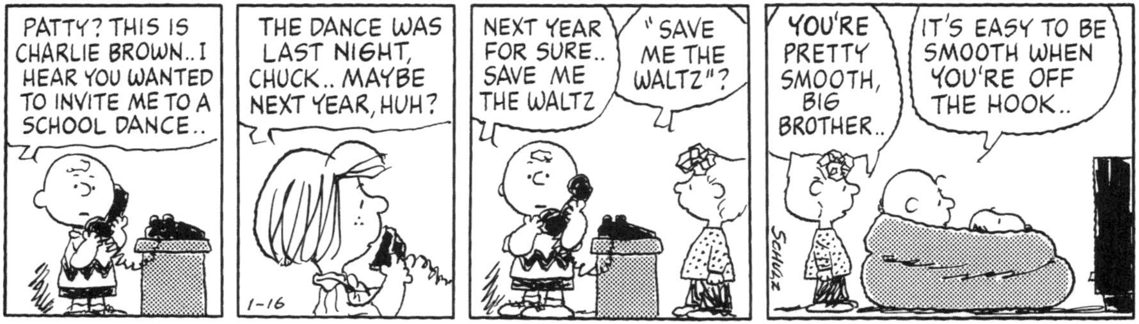
PATTY? THIS IS CHARLIE BROWN.. I HEAR YOU WANTED TO INVITE ME TO A SCHOOL DANCE..
THE DANCE WAS LAST NIGHT, CHUCK.. MAYBE NEXT YEAR, HUH?
1-16
NEXT YEAR FOR SURE.. SAVE ME THE WALTZ
"SAVE ME THE WALTZ"?
YOU'RE PRETTY SMOOTH, BIG BROTHER..
IT'S EASY TO BE SMOOTH WHEN YOU'RE OFF THE HOOK..

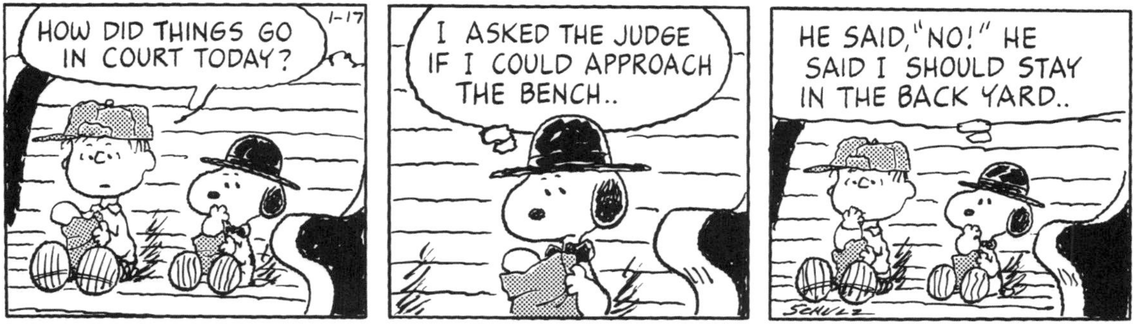
1-17
HOW DID THINGS GO IN COURT TODAY?
I ASKED THE JUDGE IF I COULD APPROACH THE BENCH..
HE SAID, "NO!" HE SAID I SHOULD STAY IN THE BACK YARD..

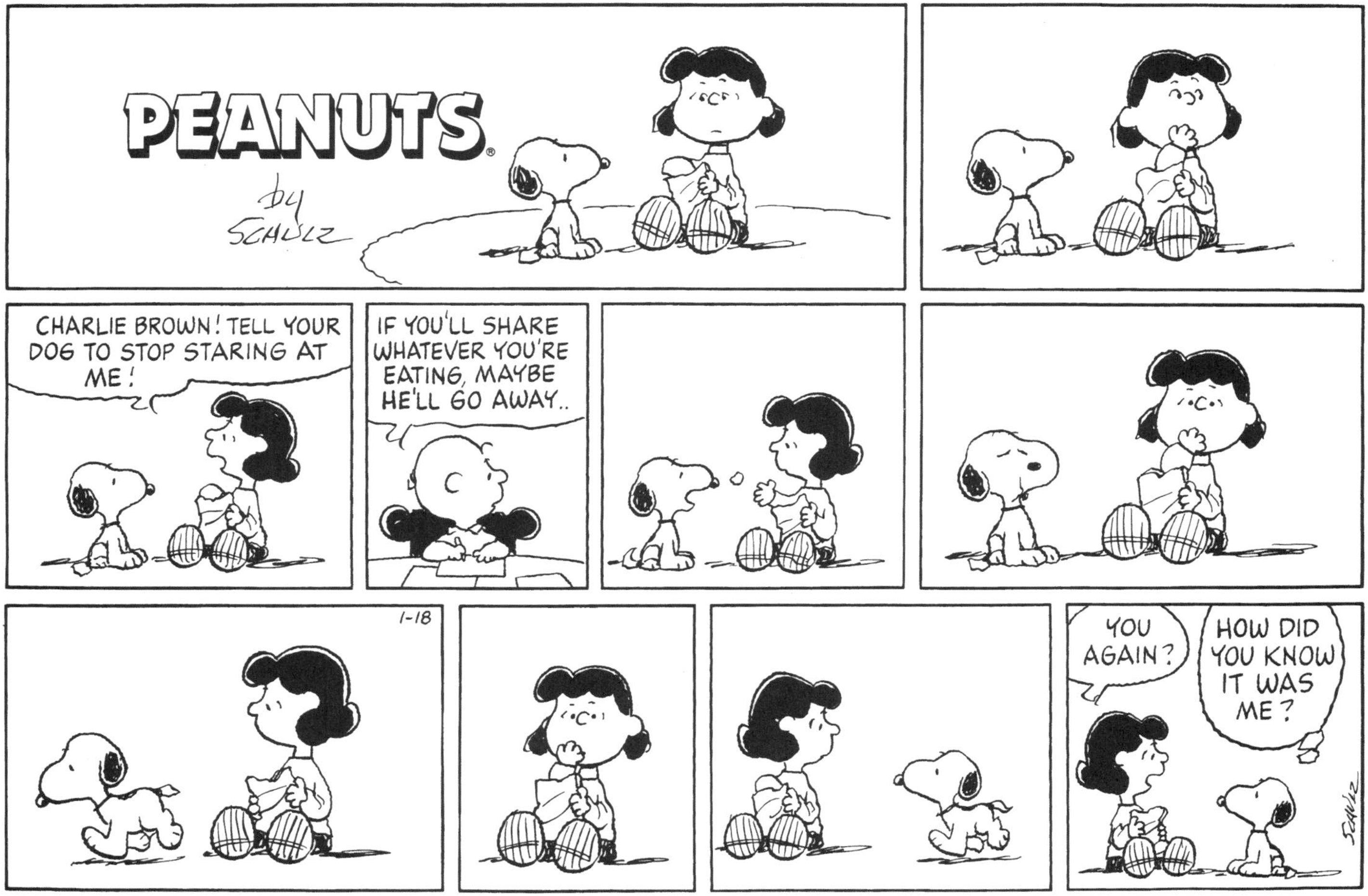
PEANUTS
by SCHULZ
CHARLIE BROWN! TELL YOUR DOG TO STOP STARING AT ME!
IF YOU'LL SHARE WHATEVER YOU'RE EATING, MAYBE HE'LL GO AWAY..
1-18
YOU AGAIN?
HOW DID YOU KNOW IT WAS ME?
SCHULZ

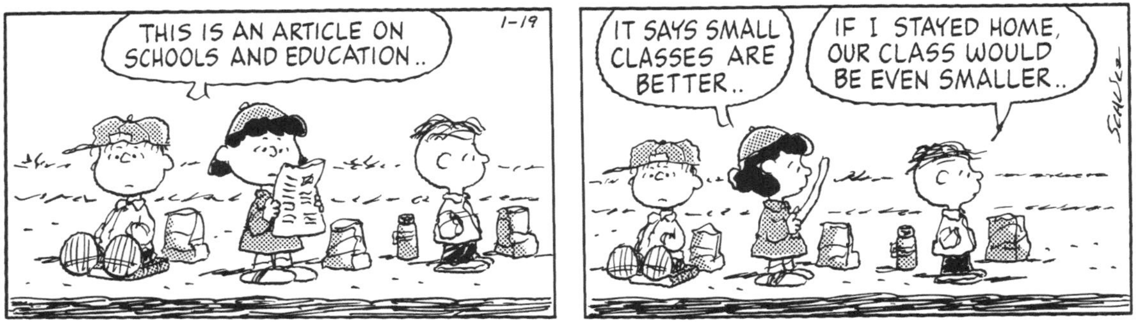
THIS IS AN ARTICLE ON SCHOOLS AND EDUCATION..
IT SAYS SMALL CLASSES ARE BETTER..
IF I STAYED HOME, OUR CLASS WOULD BE EVEN SMALLER..

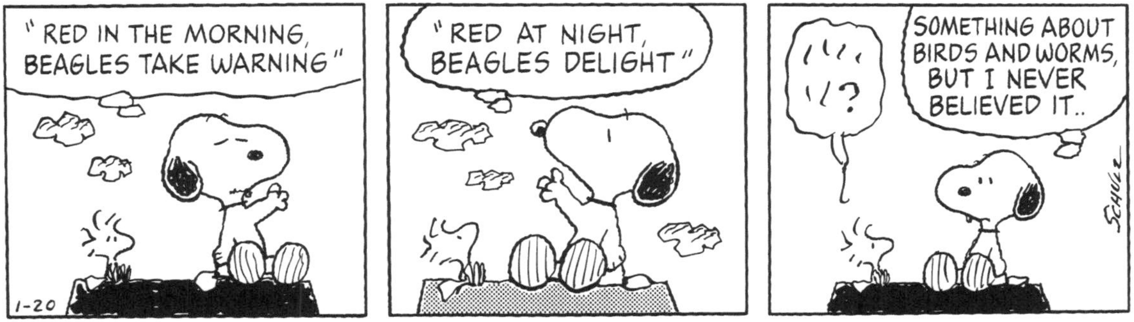
"RED IN THE MORNING, BEAGLES TAKE WARNING"
"RED AT NIGHT, BEAGLES DELIGHT"
?
SOMETHING ABOUT BIRDS AND WORMS, BUT I NEVER BELIEVED IT..

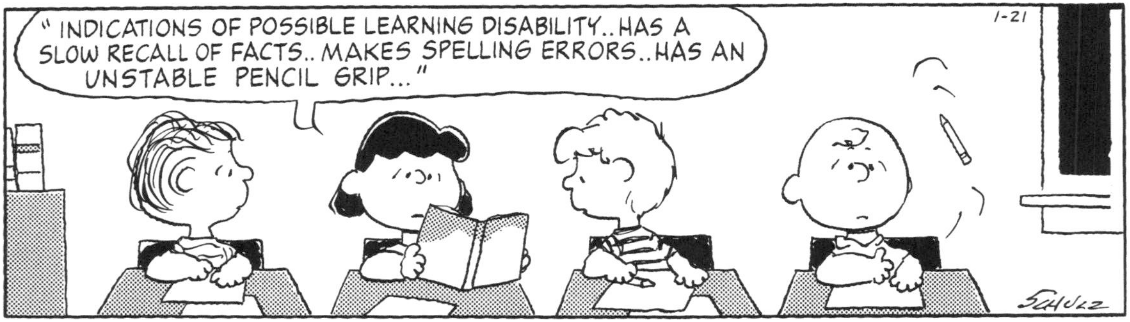
"INDICATIONS OF POSSIBLE LEARNING DISABILITY..HAS A SLOW RECALL OF FACTS..MAKES SPELLING ERRORS..HAS AN UNSTABLE PENCIL GRIP..."

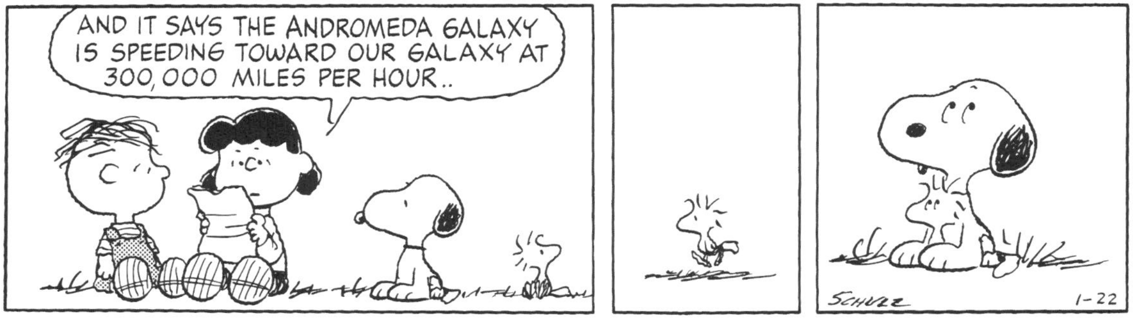
AND IT SAYS THE ANDROMEDA GALAXY IS SPEEDING TOWARD OUR GALAXY AT 300,000 MILES PER HOUR..
SCHULZ
1-22

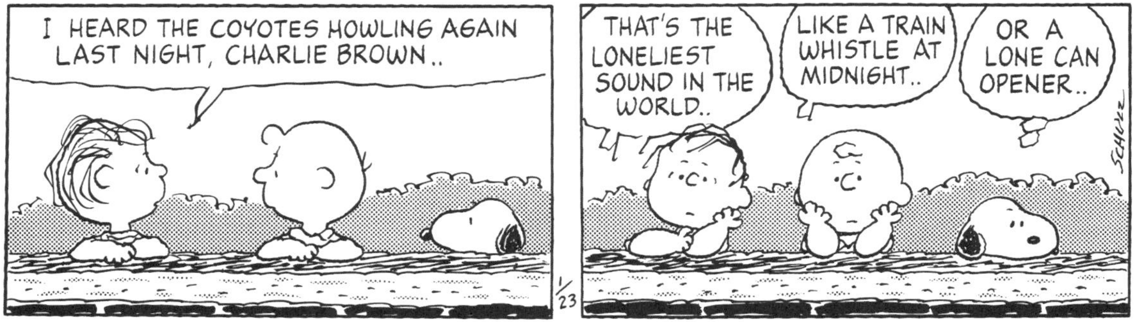
I HEARD THE COYOTES HOWLING AGAIN LAST NIGHT, CHARLIE BROWN..
1/23
THAT'S THE LONELIEST SOUND IN THE WORLD..
LIKE A TRAIN WHISTLE AT MIDNIGHT..
OR A LONE CAN OPENER..
SCHULZ

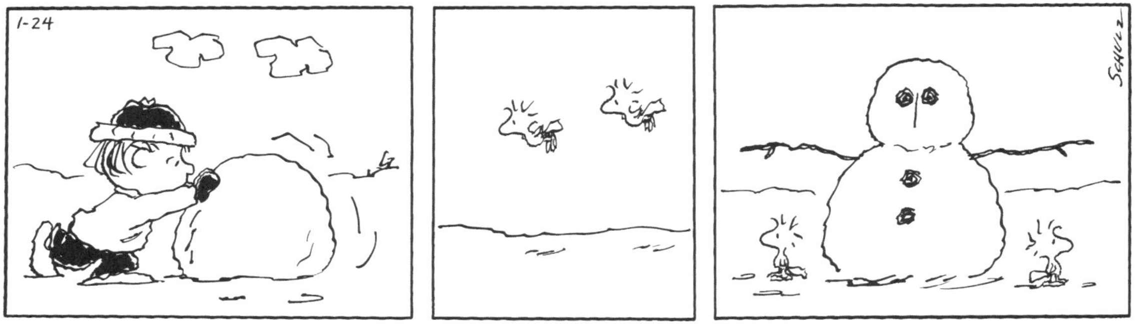
1-24
SCHULZ

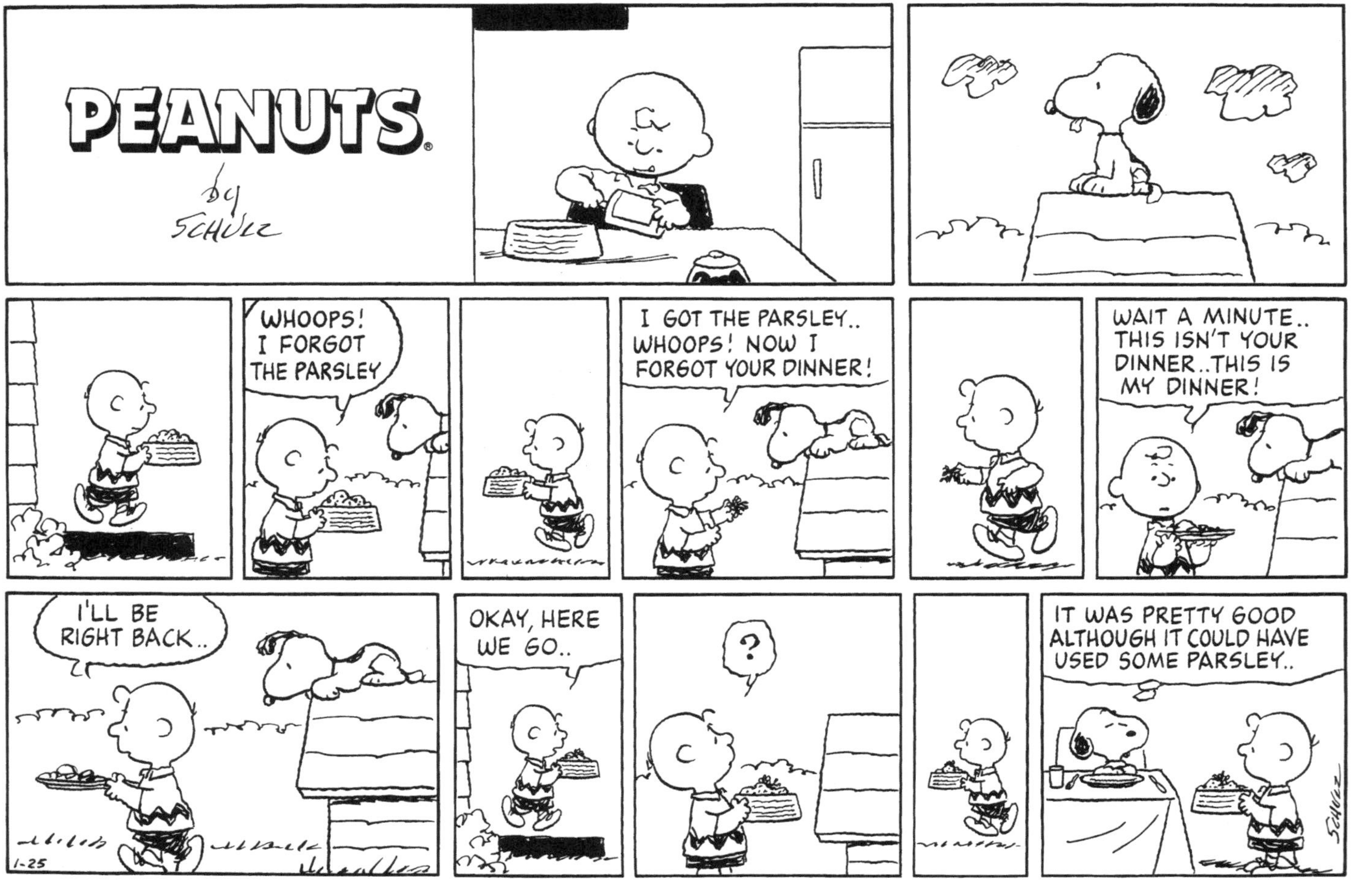
PEANUTS
by SCHULZ
WHOOPS! I FORGOT THE PARSLEY
I GOT THE PARSLEY.. WHOOPS! NOW I FORGOT YOUR DINNER!
WAIT A MINUTE.. THIS ISN'T YOUR DINNER..THIS IS MY DINNER!
I'LL BE RIGHT BACK..
1-25
OKAY, HERE WE GO..
?
IT WAS PRETTY GOOD ALTHOUGH IT COULD HAVE USED SOME PARSLEY..
SCHULZ

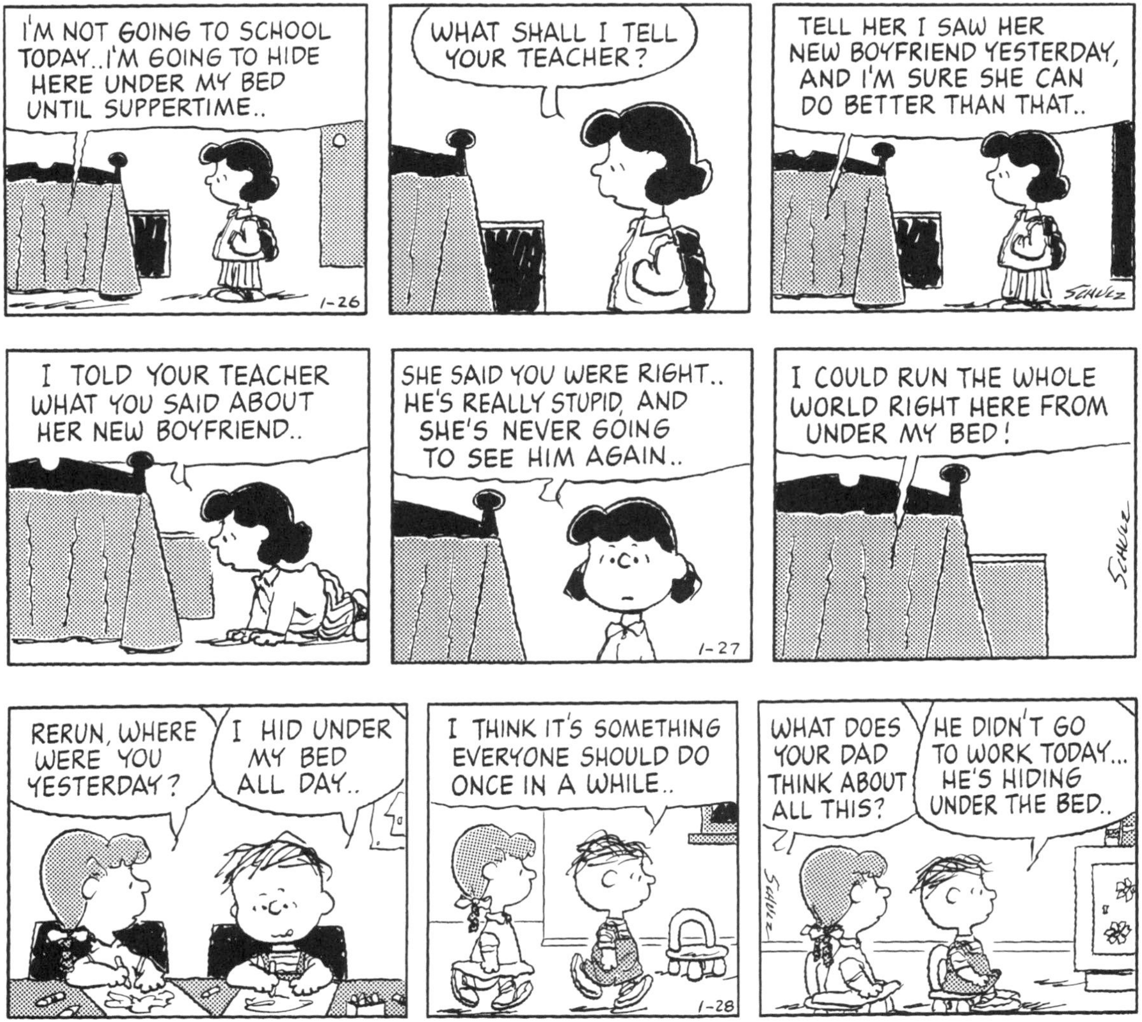
I'M NOT GOING TO SCHOOL TODAY..I'M GOING TO HIDE HERE UNDER MY BED UNTIL SUPPERTIME..
1-26
WHAT SHALL I TELL YOUR TEACHER?
TELL HER I SAW HER NEW BOYFRIEND YESTERDAY, AND I'M SURE SHE CAN DO BETTER THAN THAT..
SCHULZ
I TOLD YOUR TEACHER WHAT YOU SAID ABOUT HER NEW BOYFRIEND..
SHE SAID YOU WERE RIGHT.. HE'S REALLY STUPID, AND SHE'S NEVER GOING TO SEE HIM AGAIN..
1-27
I COULD RUN THE WHOLE WORLD RIGHT HERE FROM UNDER MY BED!
SCHULZ
RERUN, WHERE WERE YOU YESTERDAY?
I HID UNDER MY BED ALL DAY..
I THINK IT'S SOMETHING EVERYONE SHOULD DO ONCE IN A WHILE..
1-28
WHAT DOES YOUR DAD THINK ABOUT ALL THIS?
HE DIDN'T GO TO WORK TODAY... HE'S HIDING UNDER THE BED..
SCHULZ

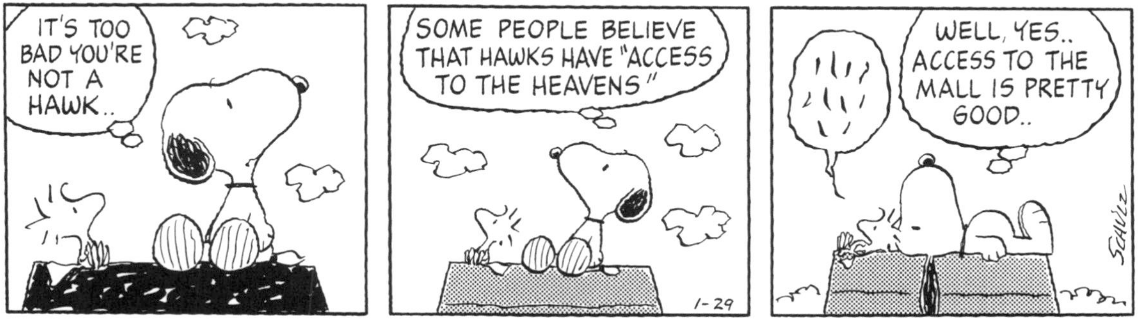
IT'S TOO BAD YOU'RE NOT A HAWK..
SOME PEOPLE BELIEVE THAT HAWKS HAVE "ACCESS TO THE HEAVENS"
WELL, YES.. ACCESS TO THE MALL IS PRETTY GOOD..
1-29

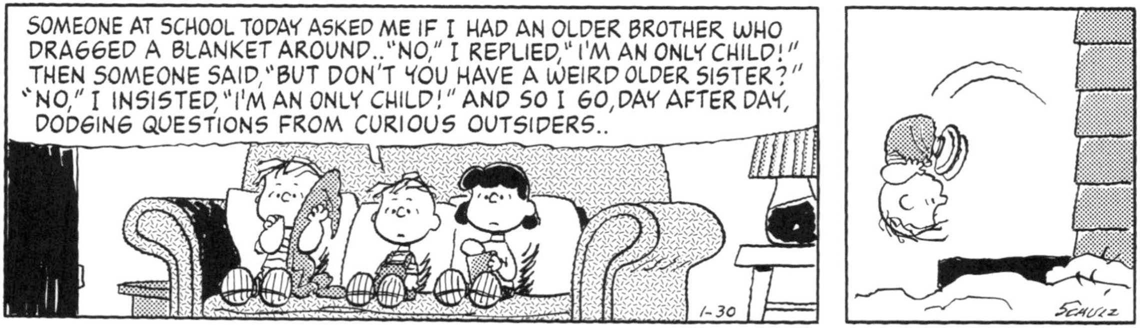
SOMEONE AT SCHOOL TODAY ASKED ME IF I HAD AN OLDER BROTHER WHO DRAGGED A BLANKET AROUND.."NO," I REPLIED, "I'M AN ONLY CHILD!" THEN SOMEONE SAID, "BUT DON'T YOU HAVE A WEIRD OLDER SISTER?" "NO," I INSISTED, "I'M AN ONLY CHILD!" AND SO I GO, DAY AFTER DAY, DODGING QUESTIONS FROM CURIOUS OUTSIDERS..
1-30

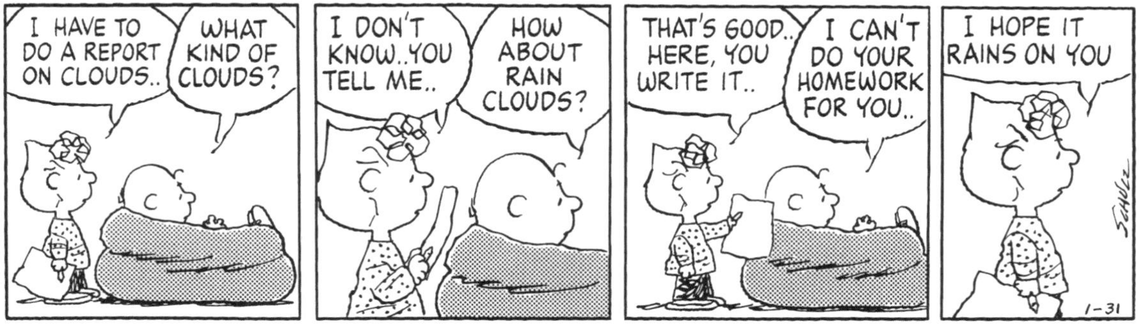
I HAVE TO DO A REPORT ON CLOUDS..
WHAT KIND OF CLOUDS?
I DON'T KNOW..YOU TELL ME..
HOW ABOUT RAIN CLOUDS?
THAT'S GOOD.. HERE, YOU WRITE IT..
I CAN'T DO YOUR HOMEWORK FOR YOU..
I HOPE IT RAINS ON YOU
1-31

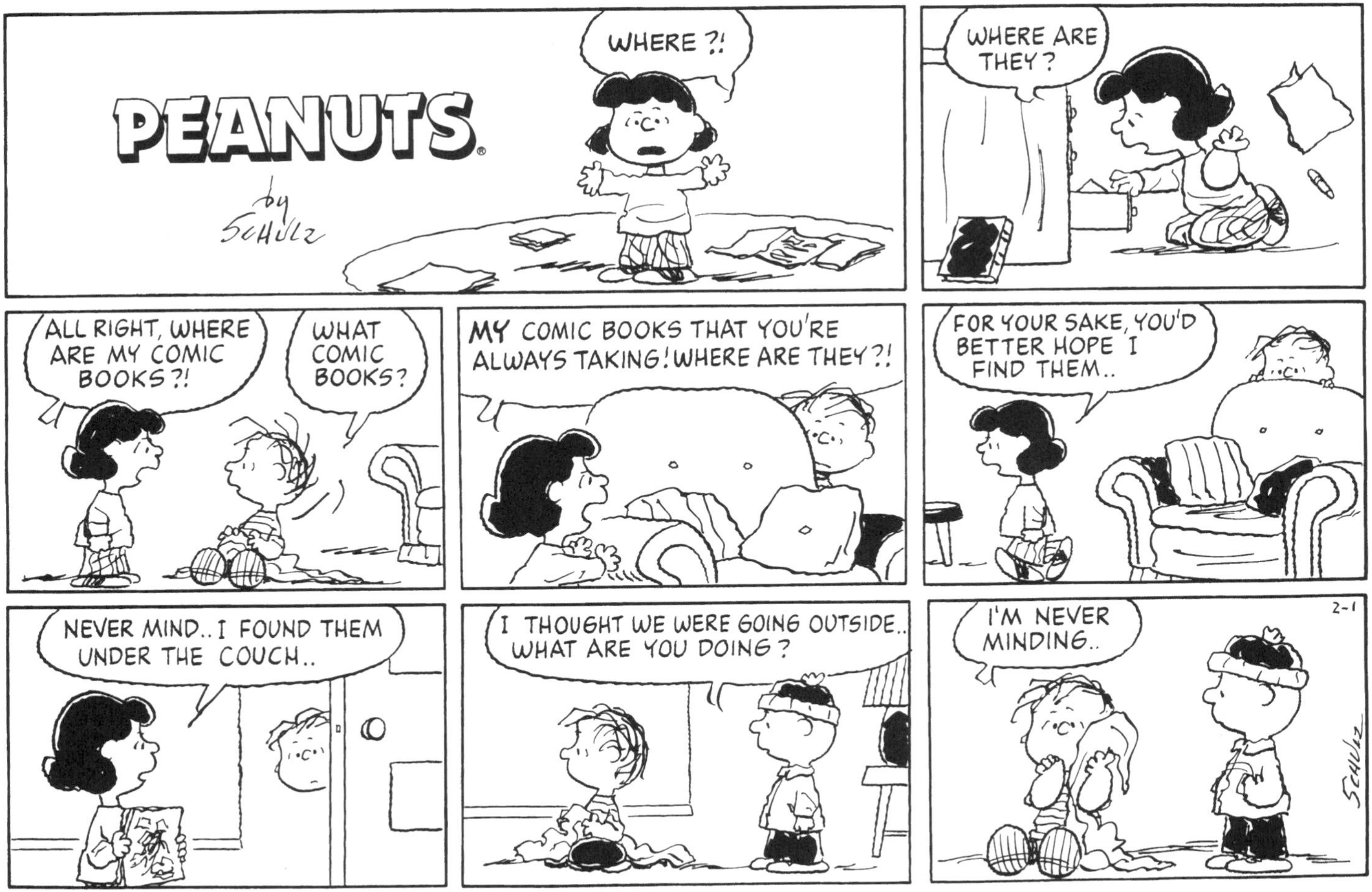
PEANUTS®
by SCHULZ
WHERE ?!
WHERE ARE THEY ?
ALL RIGHT, WHERE ARE MY COMIC BOOKS ?!
WHAT COMIC BOOKS ?
MY COMIC BOOKS THAT YOU'RE ALWAYS TAKING! WHERE ARE THEY ?!
FOR YOUR SAKE, YOU'D BETTER HOPE I FIND THEM..
NEVER MIND.. I FOUND THEM UNDER THE COUCH..
I THOUGHT WE WERE GOING OUTSIDE.. WHAT ARE YOU DOING ?
I'M NEVER MINDING..
2-1
SCHULZ

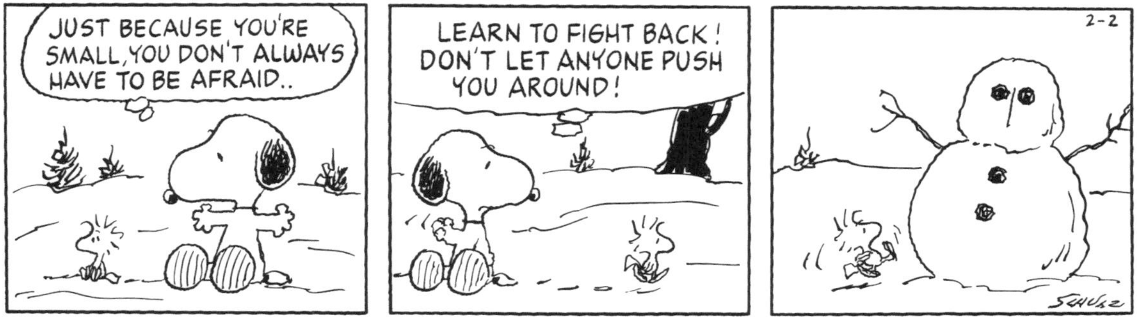
JUST BECAUSE YOU'RE SMALL, YOU DON'T ALWAYS HAVE TO BE AFRAID..
LEARN TO FIGHT BACK! DON'T LET ANYONE PUSH YOU AROUND!
2-2

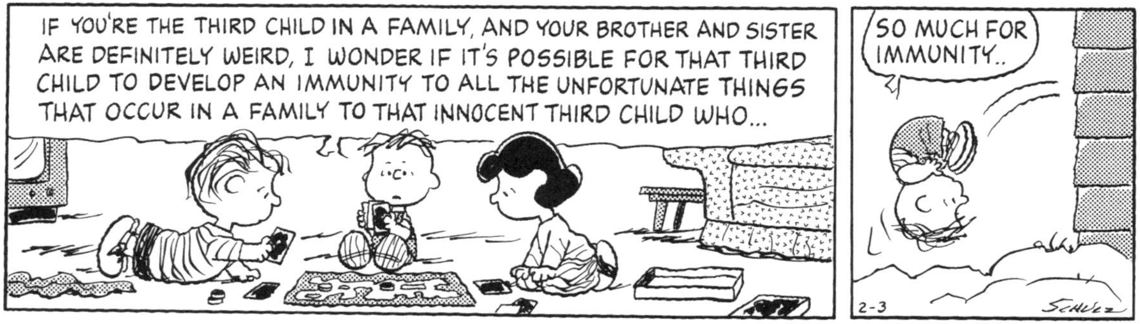
IF YOU'RE THE THIRD CHILD IN A FAMILY, AND YOUR BROTHER AND SISTER ARE DEFINITELY WEIRD, I WONDER IF IT'S POSSIBLE FOR THAT THIRD CHILD TO DEVELOP AN IMMUNITY TO ALL THE UNFORTUNATE THINGS THAT OCCUR IN A FAMILY TO THAT INNOCENT THIRD CHILD WHO...
SO MUCH FOR IMMUNITY..
2-3

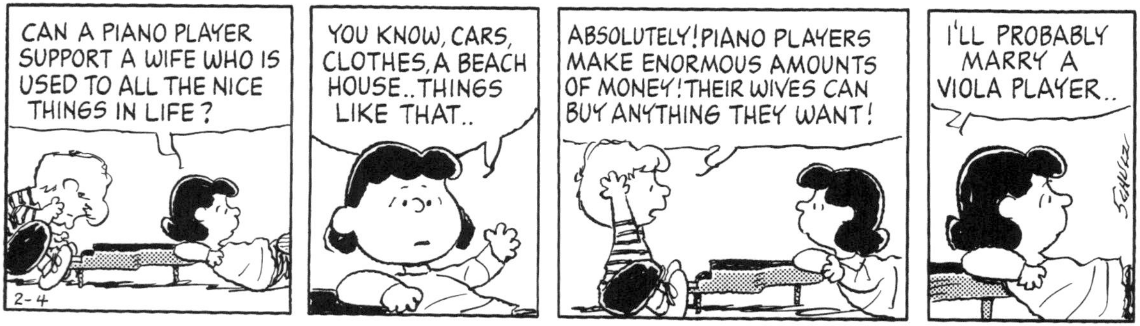
CAN A PIANO PLAYER SUPPORT A WIFE WHO IS USED TO ALL THE NICE THINGS IN LIFE?
YOU KNOW, CARS, CLOTHES, A BEACH HOUSE..THINGS LIKE THAT..
ABSOLUTELY! PIANO PLAYERS MAKE ENORMOUS AMOUNTS OF MONEY! THEIR WIVES CAN BUY ANYTHING THEY WANT!
I'LL PROBABLY MARRY A VIOLA PLAYER..
2-4

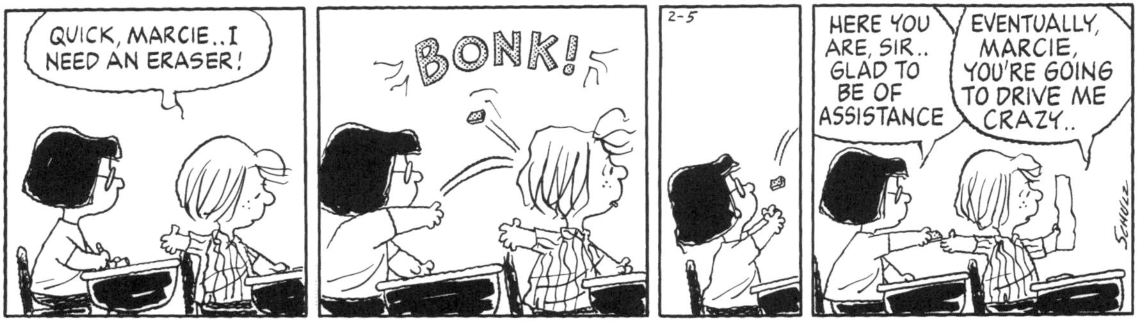
2-5
QUICK, MARCIE..I NEED AN ERASER!
BONK!
HERE YOU ARE, SIR.. GLAD TO BE OF ASSISTANCE
EVENTUALLY, MARCIE, YOU'RE GOING TO DRIVE ME CRAZY..
SCHULZ

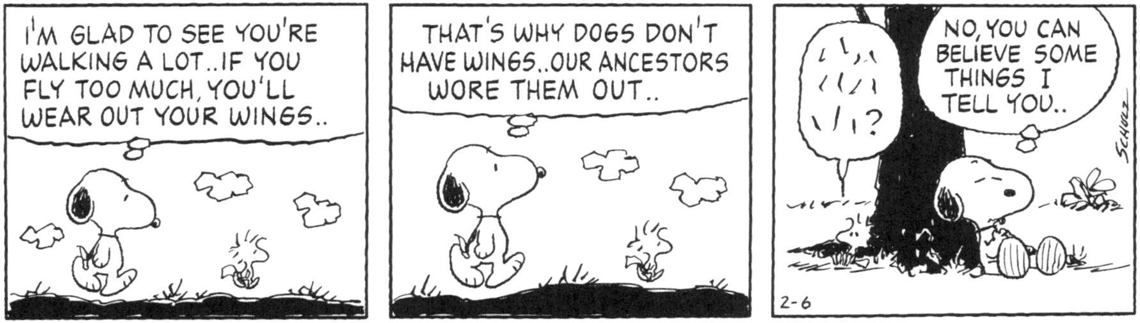
I'M GLAD TO SEE YOU'RE WALKING A LOT..IF YOU FLY TOO MUCH, YOU'LL WEAR OUT YOUR WINGS..
THAT'S WHY DOGS DON'T HAVE WINGS..OUR ANCESTORS WORE THEM OUT..
NO, YOU CAN BELIEVE SOME THINGS I TELL YOU..
SCHULZ
2-6

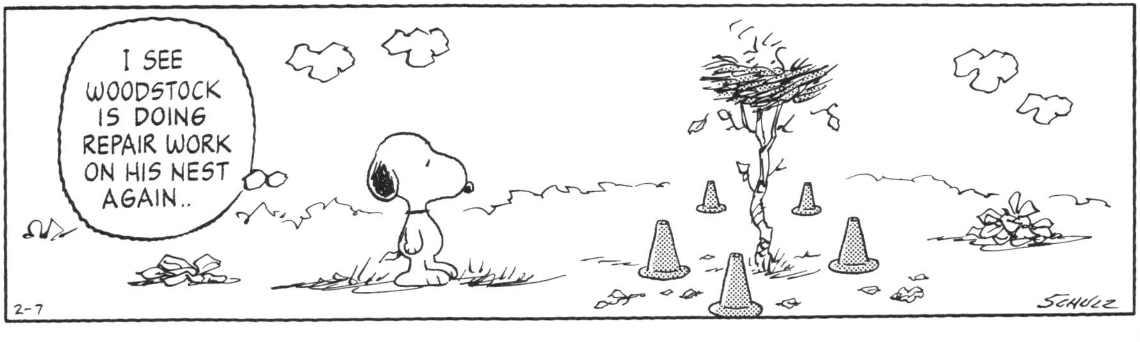
I SEE WOODSTOCK IS DOING REPAIR WORK ON HIS NEST AGAIN..
2-7
SCHULZ

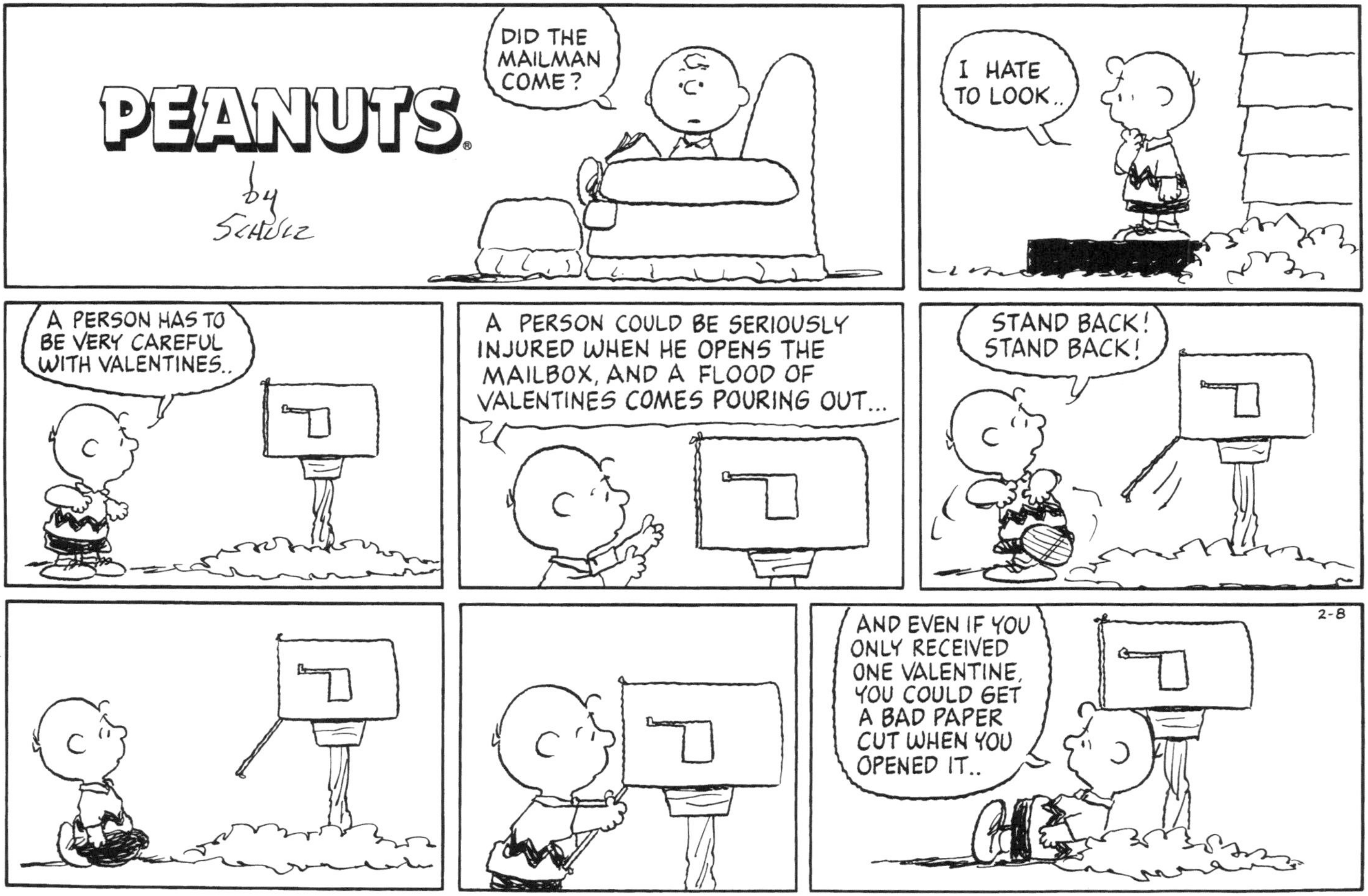
PEANUTS
by SCHULZ
DID THE MAILMAN COME?
I HATE TO LOOK..
A PERSON HAS TO BE VERY CAREFUL WITH VALENTINES..
A PERSON COULD BE SERIOUSLY INJURED WHEN HE OPENS THE MAILBOX, AND A FLOOD OF VALENTINES COMES POURING OUT...
STAND BACK! STAND BACK!
2-8
AND EVEN IF YOU ONLY RECEIVED ONE VALENTINE, YOU COULD GET A BAD PAPER CUT WHEN YOU OPENED IT..

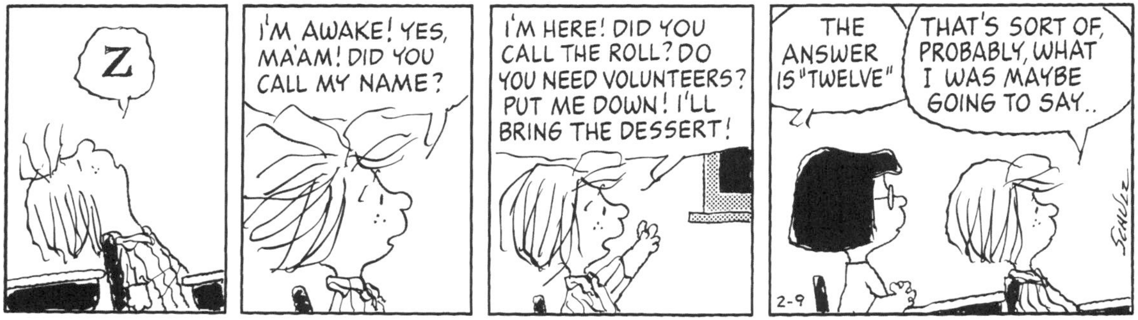
Z
I'M AWAKE! YES, MA'AM! DID YOU CALL MY NAME?
I'M HERE! DID YOU CALL THE ROLL? DO YOU NEED VOLUNTEERS? PUT ME DOWN! I'LL BRING THE DESSERT!
THE ANSWER IS "TWELVE"
THAT'S SORT OF, PROBABLY, WHAT I WAS MAYBE GOING TO SAY..
SCHULZ
2-9

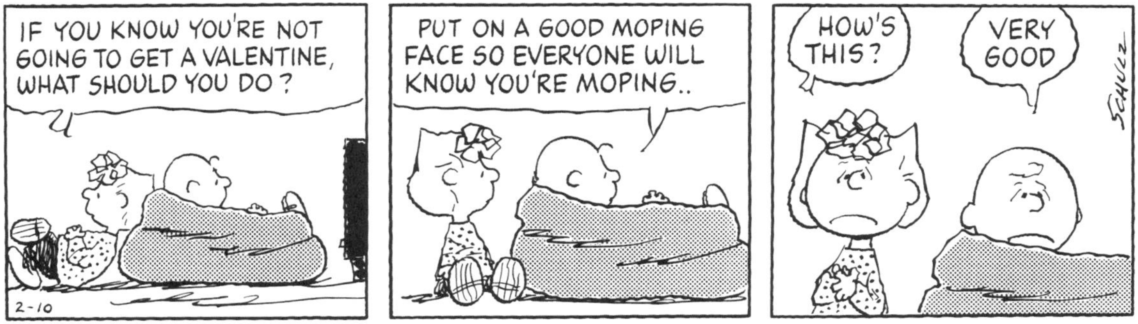
IF YOU KNOW YOU'RE NOT GOING TO GET A VALENTINE, WHAT SHOULD YOU DO?
PUT ON A GOOD MOPING FACE SO EVERYONE WILL KNOW YOU'RE MOPING..
HOW'S THIS?
VERY GOOD
SCHULZ
2-10

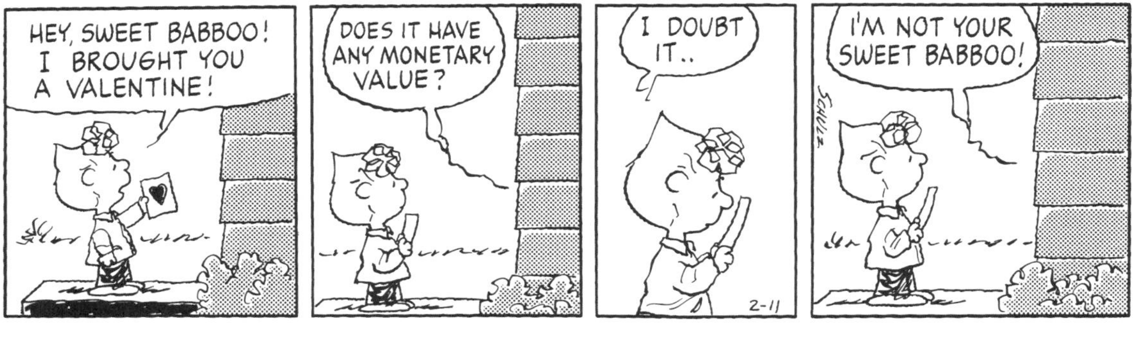
HEY, SWEET BABBOO! I BROUGHT YOU A VALENTINE!
DOES IT HAVE ANY MONETARY VALUE?
I DOUBT IT..
SCHULZ
2-11
I'M NOT YOUR SWEET BABBOO!

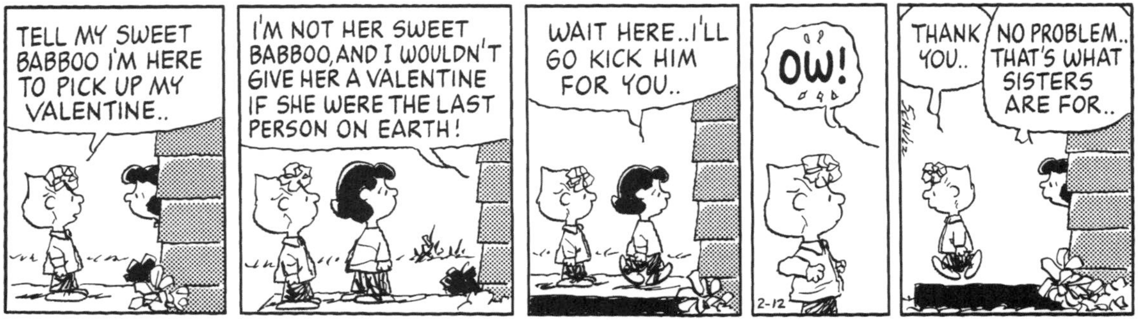
TELL MY SWEET BABBOO I'M HERE TO PICK UP MY VALENTINE..
I'M NOT HER SWEET BABBOO, AND I WOULDN'T GIVE HER A VALENTINE IF SHE WERE THE LAST PERSON ON EARTH!
WAIT HERE..I'LL GO KICK HIM FOR YOU..
OW!
2-12
THANK YOU..
NO PROBLEM.. THAT'S WHAT SISTERS ARE FOR..

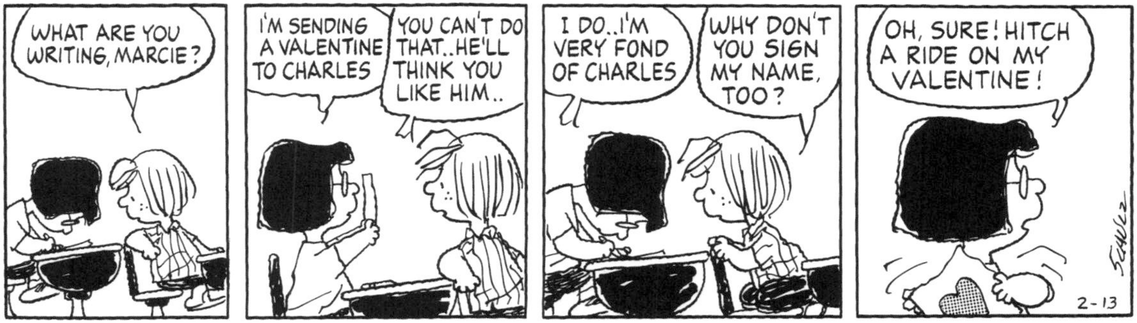
WHAT ARE YOU WRITING, MARCIE?
I'M SENDING A VALENTINE TO CHARLES
YOU CAN'T DO THAT..HE'LL THINK YOU LIKE HIM..
I DO..I'M VERY FOND OF CHARLES
WHY DON'T YOU SIGN MY NAME, TOO?
OH, SURE! HITCH A RIDE ON MY VALENTINE!
2-13

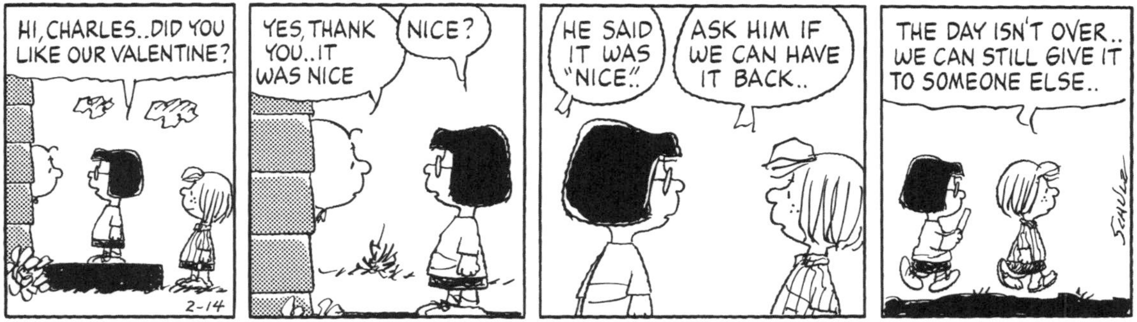
HI, CHARLES..DID YOU LIKE OUR VALENTINE?
2-14
YES, THANK YOU..IT WAS NICE
NICE?
HE SAID IT WAS "NICE"!
ASK HIM IF WE CAN HAVE IT BACK..
THE DAY ISN'T OVER.. WE CAN STILL GIVE IT TO SOMEONE ELSE..

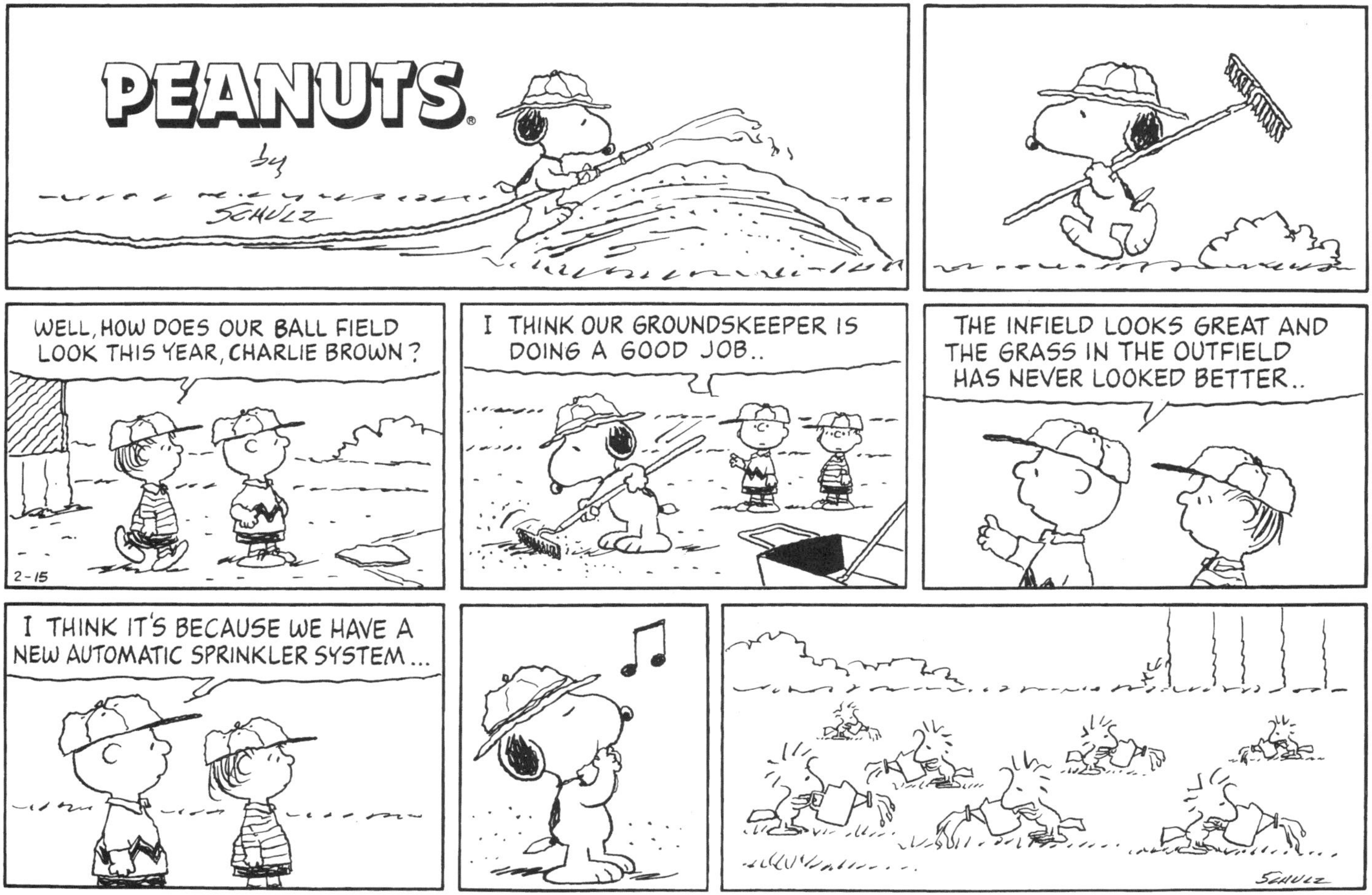
PEANUTS
by SCHULZ
WELL, HOW DOES OUR BALL FIELD LOOK THIS YEAR, CHARLIE BROWN ?
2-15
I THINK OUR GROUNDSKEEPER IS DOING A GOOD JOB..
THE INFIELD LOOKS GREAT AND THE GRASS IN THE OUTFIELD HAS NEVER LOOKED BETTER..
I THINK IT'S BECAUSE WE HAVE A NEW AUTOMATIC SPRINKLER SYSTEM ...
SCHULZ

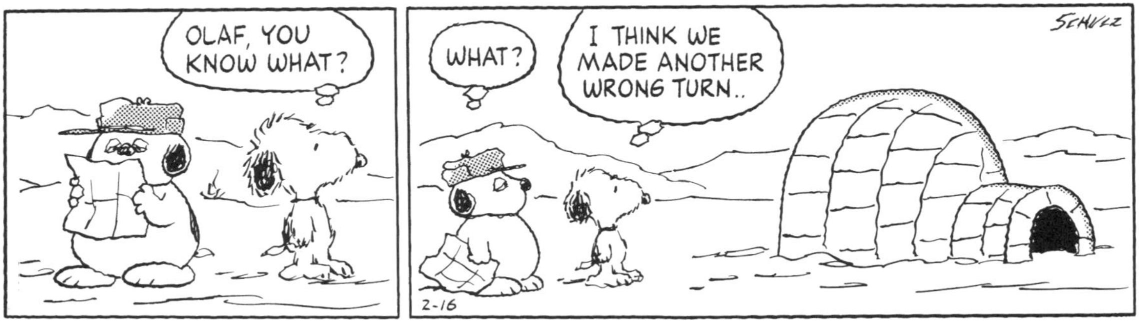
OLAF, YOU KNOW WHAT?
WHAT?
I THINK WE MADE ANOTHER WRONG TURN..
SCHULZ
2-16

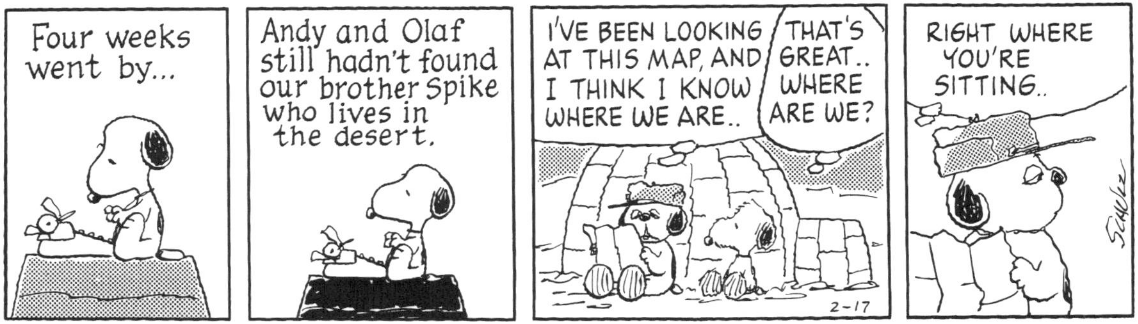
Four weeks went by...
Andy and Olaf still hadn't found our brother Spike who lives in the desert.
I'VE BEEN LOOKING AT THIS MAP, AND I THINK I KNOW WHERE WE ARE..
THAT'S GREAT.. WHERE ARE WE?
2-17
RIGHT WHERE YOU'RE SITTING..
SCHULZ

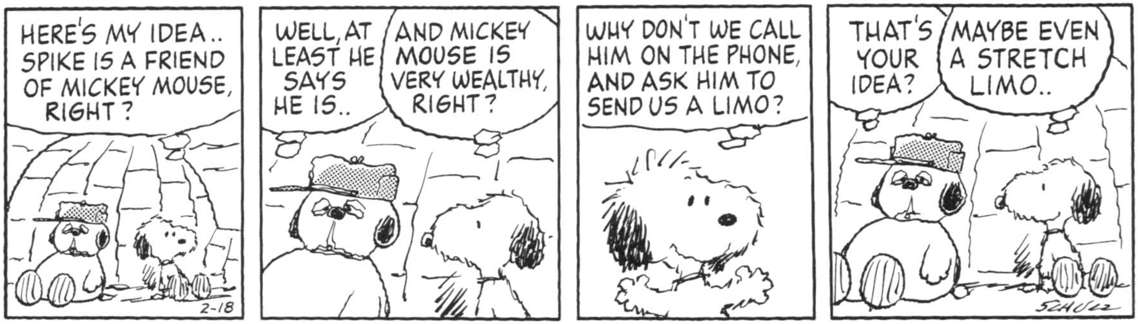
HERE'S MY IDEA.. SPIKE IS A FRIEND OF MICKEY MOUSE, RIGHT?
2-18
WELL, AT LEAST HE SAYS HE IS..
AND MICKEY MOUSE IS VERY WEALTHY, RIGHT?
WHY DON'T WE CALL HIM ON THE PHONE, AND ASK HIM TO SEND US A LIMO?
THAT'S YOUR IDEA?
MAYBE EVEN A STRETCH LIMO..
SCHULZ

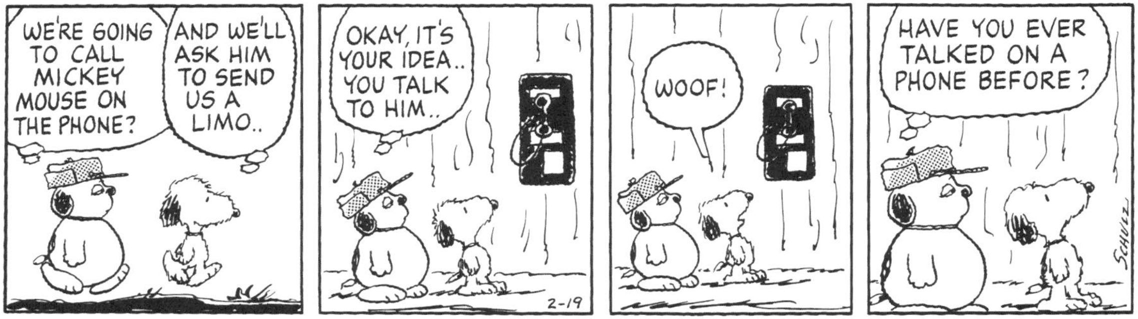
WE'RE GOING TO CALL MICKEY MOUSE ON THE PHONE?
AND WE'LL ASK HIM TO SEND US A LIMO..
OKAY, IT'S YOUR IDEA.. YOU TALK TO HIM..
2-19
WOOF!
HAVE YOU EVER TALKED ON A PHONE BEFORE?
SCHULZ

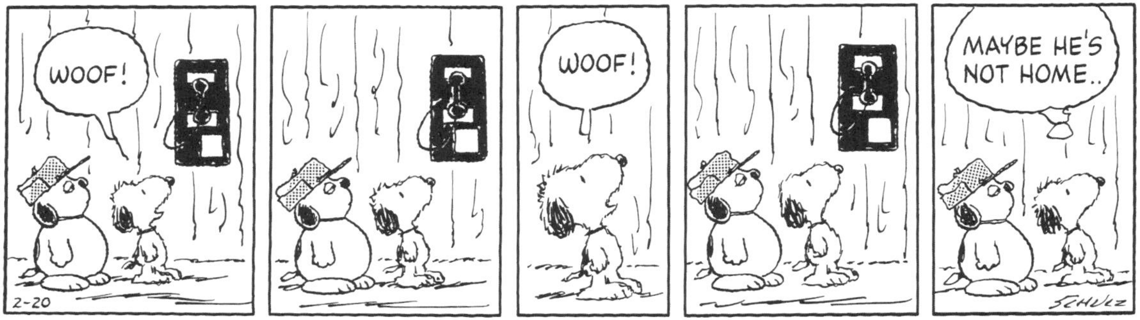
WOOF!
2-20
WOOF!
MAYBE HE'S NOT HOME..
SCHULZ

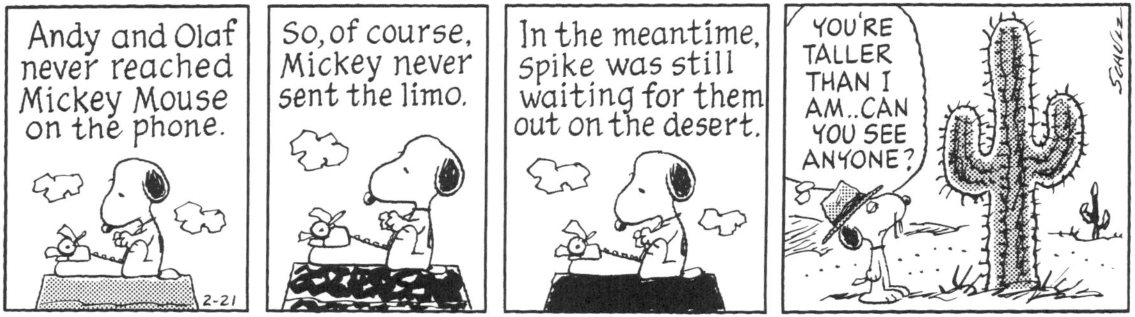
Andy and Olaf never reached Mickey Mouse on the phone.
2-21
So, of course, Mickey never sent the limo.
In the meantime, Spike was still waiting for them out on the desert.
YOU'RE TALLER THAN I AM..CAN YOU SEE ANYONE?
SCHULZ

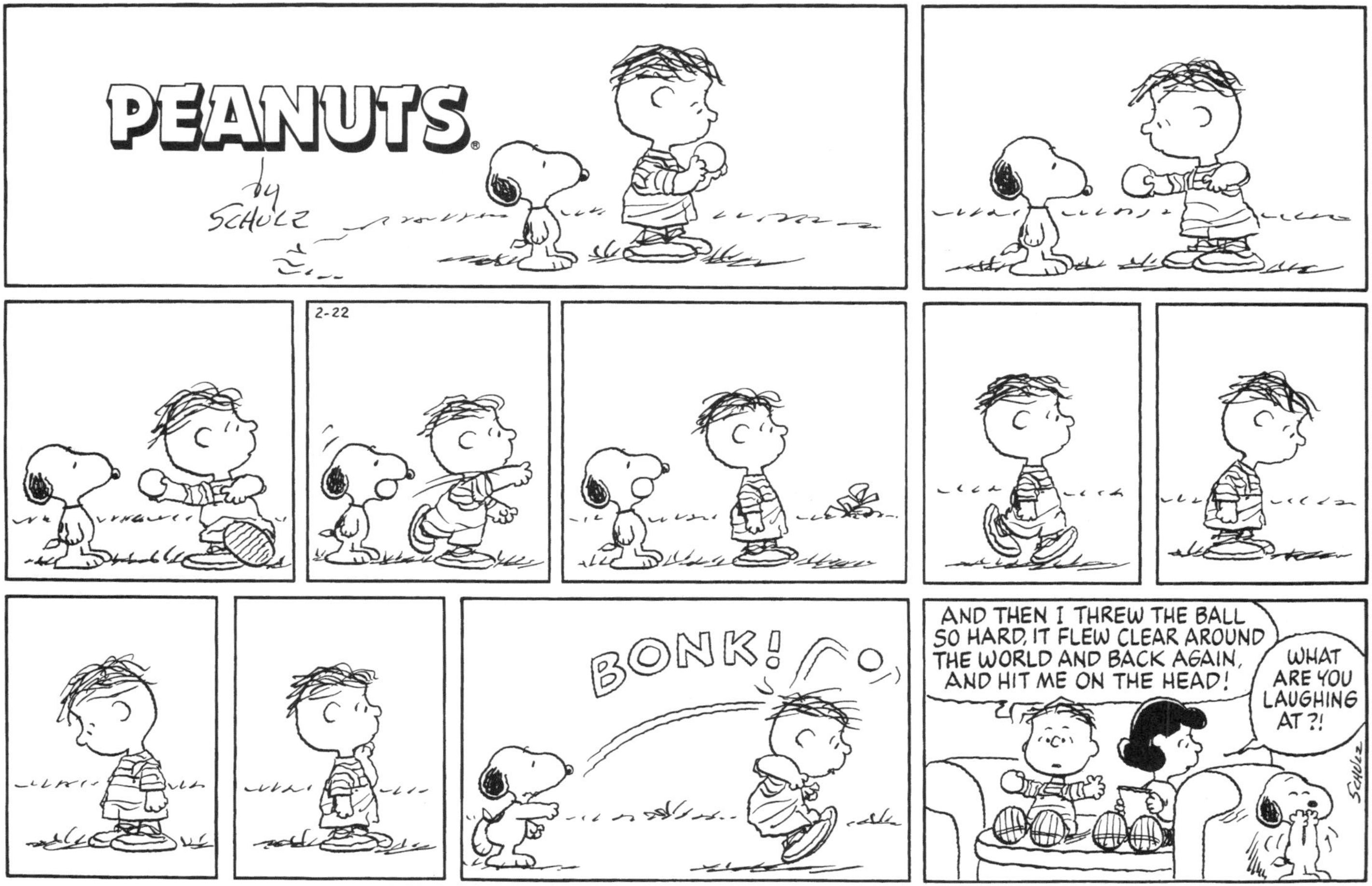
PEANUTS
by SCHULZ
2-22
BONK!
AND THEN I THREW THE BALL SO HARD, IT FLEW CLEAR AROUND THE WORLD AND BACK AGAIN, AND HIT ME ON THE HEAD!
WHAT ARE YOU LAUGHING AT ?!
SCHULZ

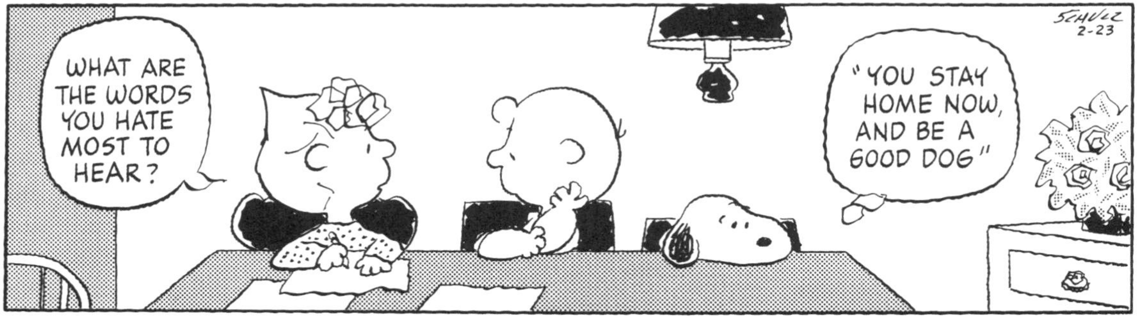
SCHULZ 2-23
WHAT ARE THE WORDS YOU HATE MOST TO HEAR?
"YOU STAY HOME NOW, AND BE A GOOD DOG"

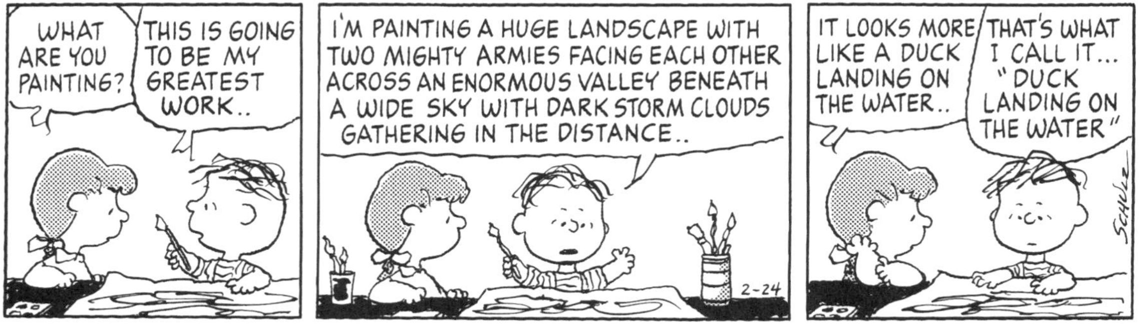
WHAT ARE YOU PAINTING?
THIS IS GOING TO BE MY GREATEST WORK..
I'M PAINTING A HUGE LANDSCAPE WITH TWO MIGHTY ARMIES FACING EACH OTHER ACROSS AN ENORMOUS VALLEY BENEATH A WIDE SKY WITH DARK STORM CLOUDS GATHERING IN THE DISTANCE..
2-24
IT LOOKS MORE LIKE A DUCK LANDING ON THE WATER..
THAT'S WHAT I CALL IT... "DUCK LANDING ON THE WATER"
SCHULZ

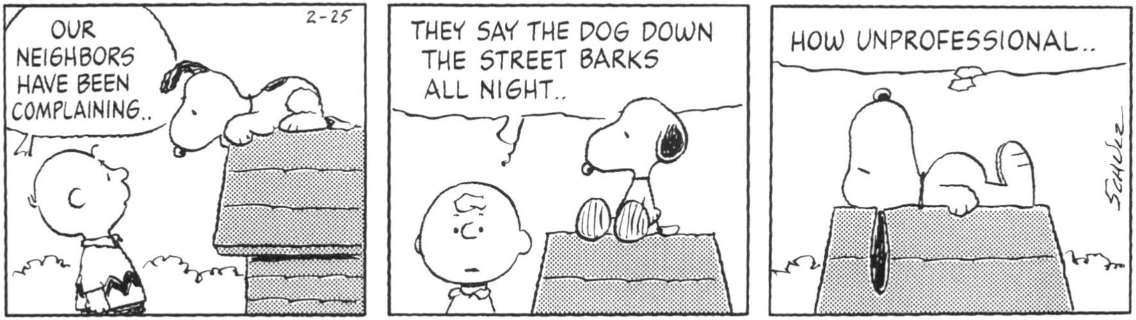
2-25
OUR NEIGHBORS HAVE BEEN COMPLAINING..
THEY SAY THE DOG DOWN THE STREET BARKS ALL NIGHT..
HOW UNPROFESSIONAL..
SCHULZ

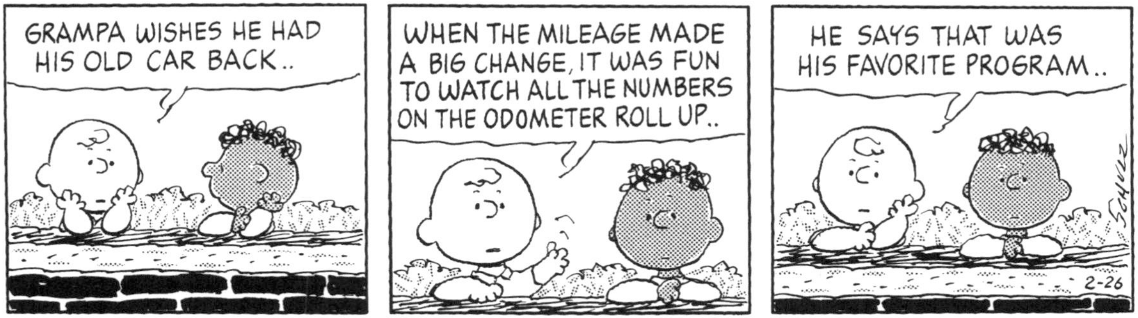
GRAMPA WISHES HE HAD HIS OLD CAR BACK..
WHEN THE MILEAGE MADE A BIG CHANGE, IT WAS FUN TO WATCH ALL THE NUMBERS ON THE ODOMETER ROLL UP..
HE SAYS THAT WAS HIS FAVORITE PROGRAM..
SCHULZ
2-26

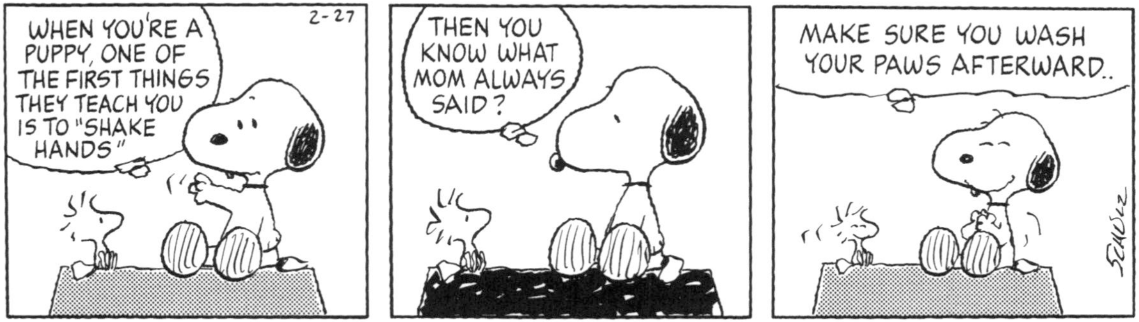
2-27
WHEN YOU'RE A PUPPY, ONE OF THE FIRST THINGS THEY TEACH YOU IS TO "SHAKE HANDS"
THEN YOU KNOW WHAT MOM ALWAYS SAID?
MAKE SURE YOU WASH YOUR PAWS AFTERWARD..
SCHULZ

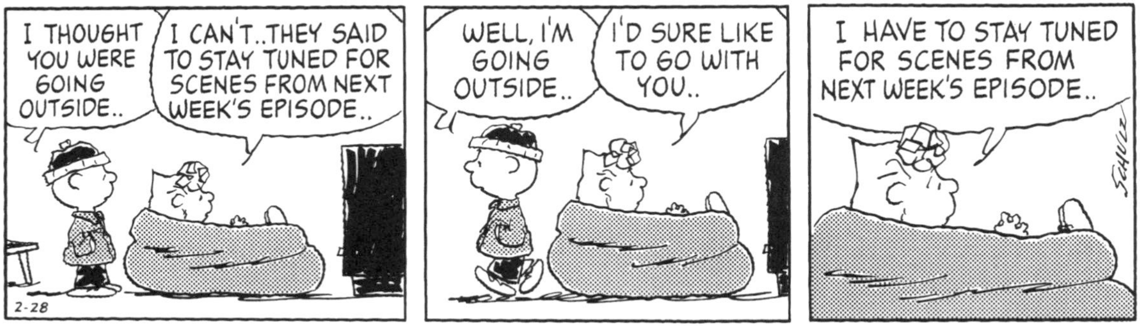
I THOUGHT YOU WERE GOING OUTSIDE..
I CAN'T..THEY SAID TO STAY TUNED FOR SCENES FROM NEXT WEEK'S EPISODE..
2-28
WELL, I'M GOING OUTSIDE..
I'D SURE LIKE TO GO WITH YOU..
I HAVE TO STAY TUNED FOR SCENES FROM NEXT WEEK'S EPISODE..
SCHULZ

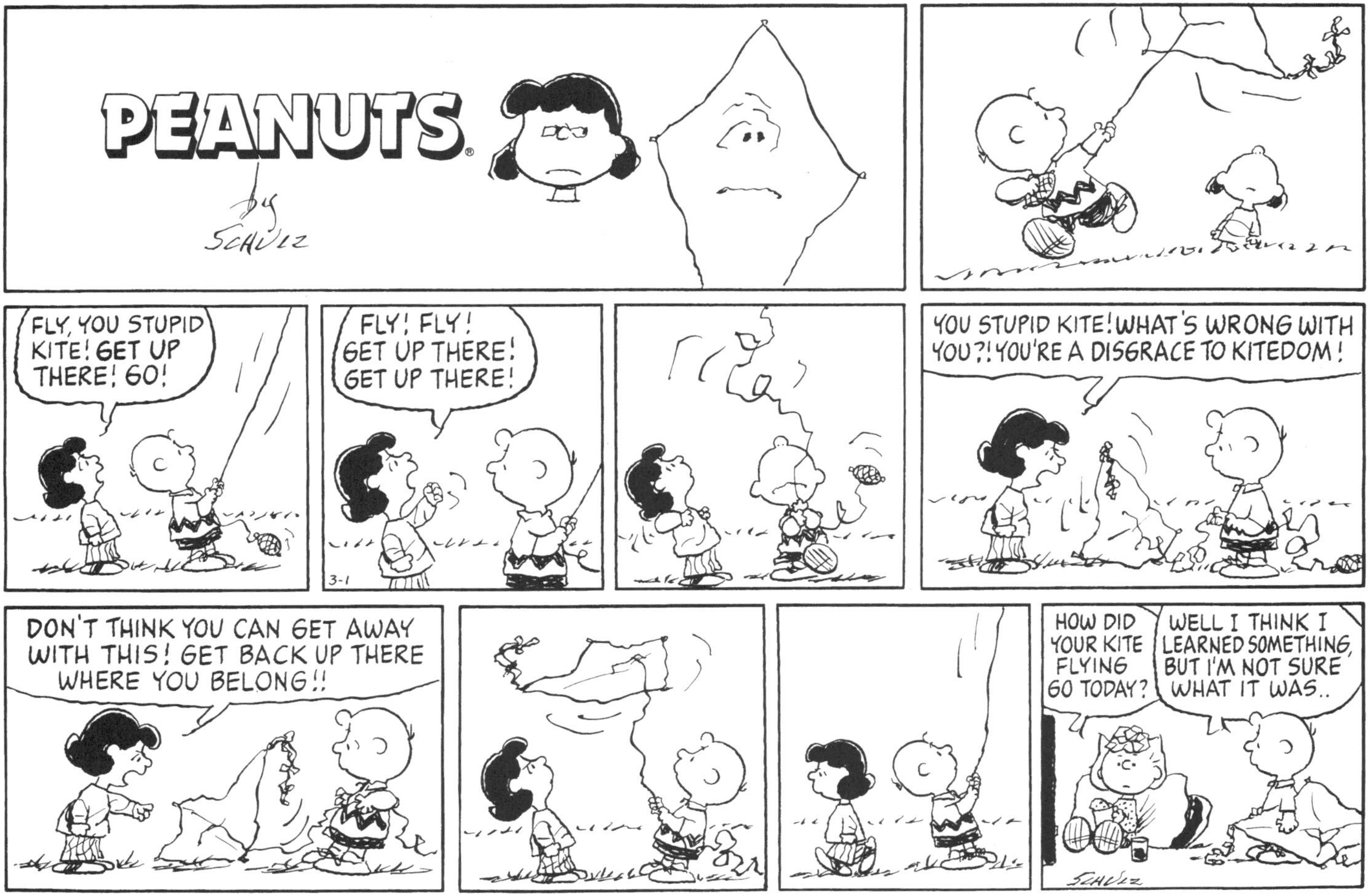
PEANUTS
by SCHULZ
FLY, YOU STUPID KITE! GET UP THERE! GO!
FLY! FLY! GET UP THERE! GET UP THERE!
3-1
YOU STUPID KITE! WHAT'S WRONG WITH YOU?! YOU'RE A DISGRACE TO KITEDOM!
DON'T THINK YOU CAN GET AWAY WITH THIS! GET BACK UP THERE WHERE YOU BELONG!!
HOW DID YOUR KITE FLYING GO TODAY?
WELL I THINK I LEARNED SOMETHING, BUT I'M NOT SURE WHAT IT WAS..
SCHULZ

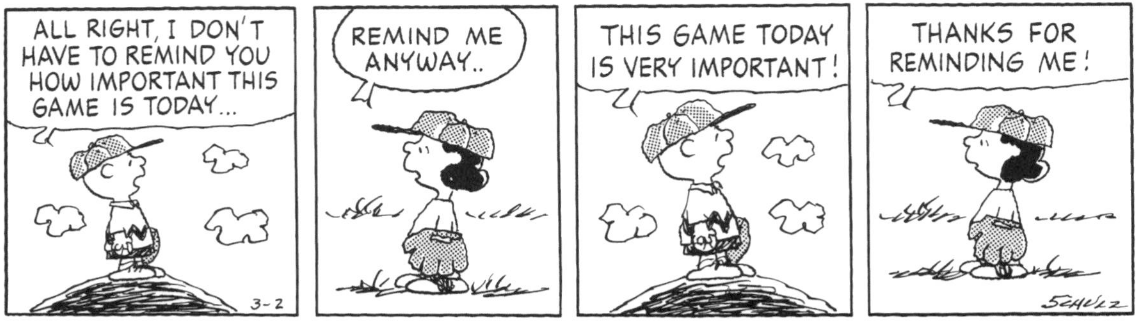
ALL RIGHT, I DON'T HAVE TO REMIND YOU HOW IMPORTANT THIS GAME IS TODAY...
REMIND ME ANYWAY..
THIS GAME TODAY IS VERY IMPORTANT!
THANKS FOR REMINDING ME!
3-2
SCHULZ

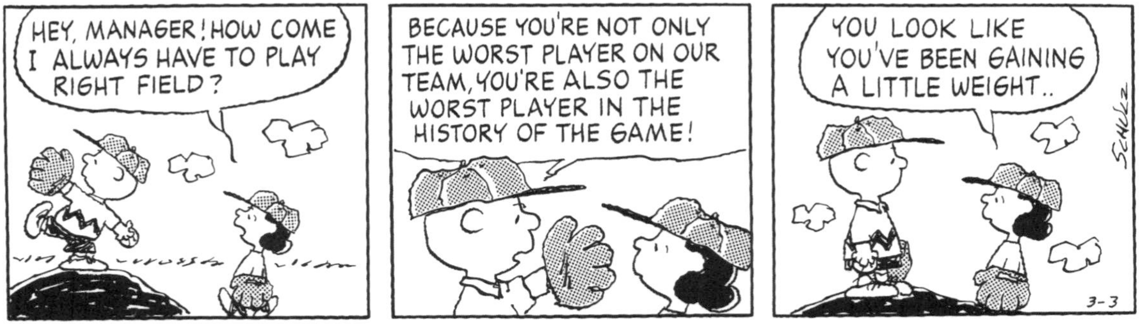
HEY, MANAGER! HOW COME I ALWAYS HAVE TO PLAY RIGHT FIELD?
BECAUSE YOU'RE NOT ONLY THE WORST PLAYER ON OUR TEAM, YOU'RE ALSO THE WORST PLAYER IN THE HISTORY OF THE GAME!
YOU LOOK LIKE YOU'VE BEEN GAINING A LITTLE WEIGHT..
SCHULZ
3-3

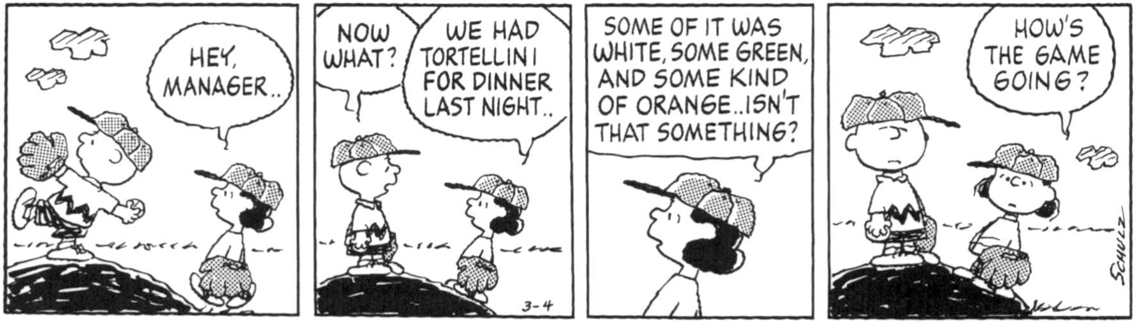
HEY, MANAGER..
NOW WHAT?
WE HAD TORTELLINI FOR DINNER LAST NIGHT..
3-4
SOME OF IT WAS WHITE, SOME GREEN, AND SOME KIND OF ORANGE..ISN'T THAT SOMETHING?
HOW'S THE GAME GOING?
SCHULZ

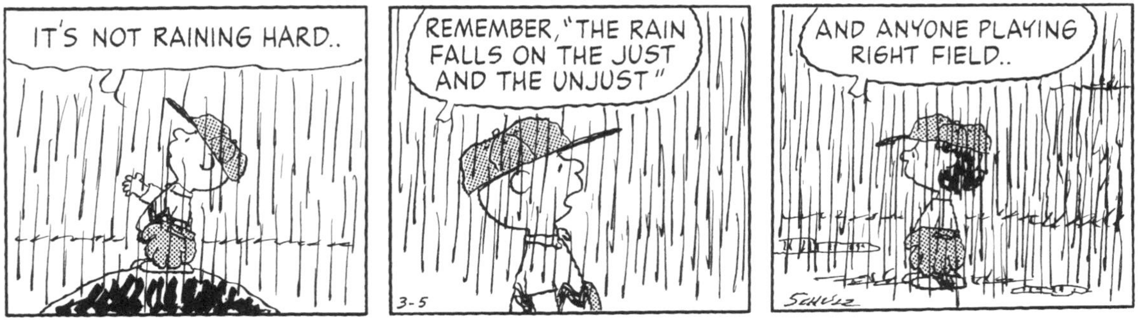
IT'S NOT RAINING HARD..
REMEMBER, "THE RAIN FALLS ON THE JUST AND THE UNJUST"
3-5
AND ANYONE PLAYING RIGHT FIELD..

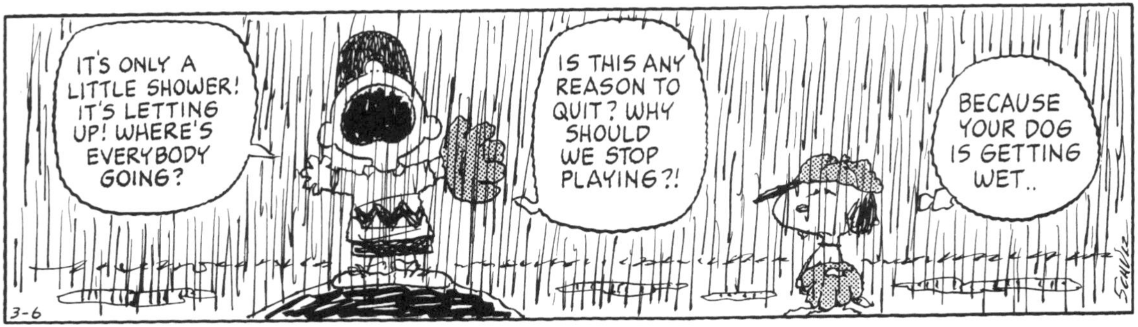
IT'S ONLY A LITTLE SHOWER! IT'S LETTING UP! WHERE'S EVERYBODY GOING?
IS THIS ANY REASON TO QUIT? WHY SHOULD WE STOP PLAYING?!
BECAUSE YOUR DOG IS GETTING WET..
3-6

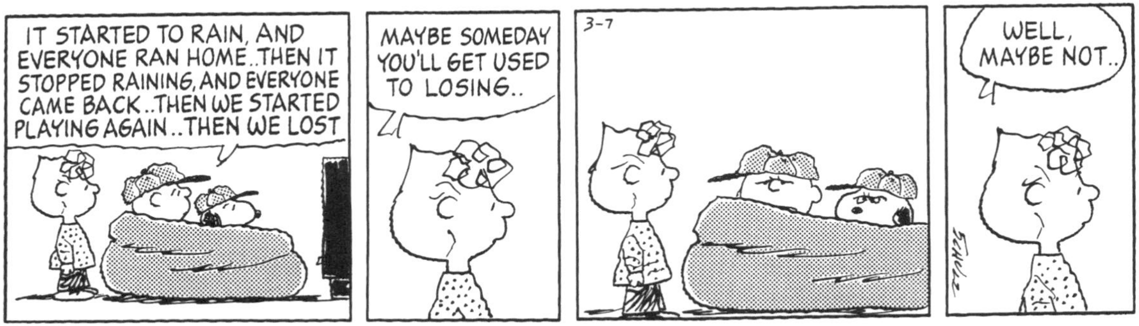
IT STARTED TO RAIN, AND EVERYONE RAN HOME..THEN IT STOPPED RAINING, AND EVERYONE CAME BACK..THEN WE STARTED PLAYING AGAIN..THEN WE LOST
MAYBE SOMEDAY YOU'LL GET USED TO LOSING..
3-7
WELL, MAYBE NOT..

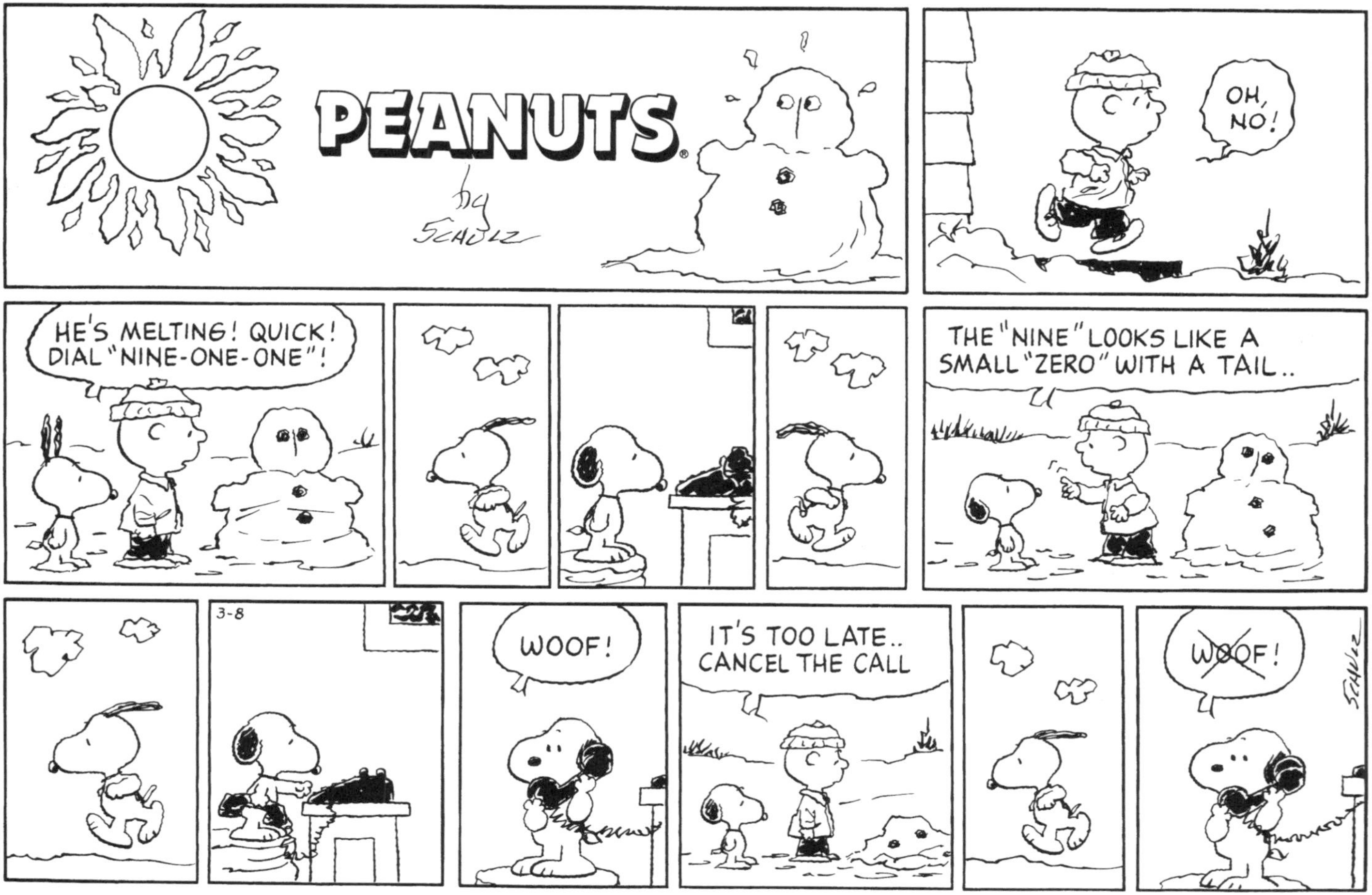
PEANUTS
by SCHULZ
OH, NO!
HE'S MELTING! QUICK! DIAL "NINE-ONE-ONE"!
THE "NINE" LOOKS LIKE A SMALL "ZERO" WITH A TAIL..
3-8
WOOF!
IT'S TOO LATE.. CANCEL THE CALL
WOOF!
SCHULZ

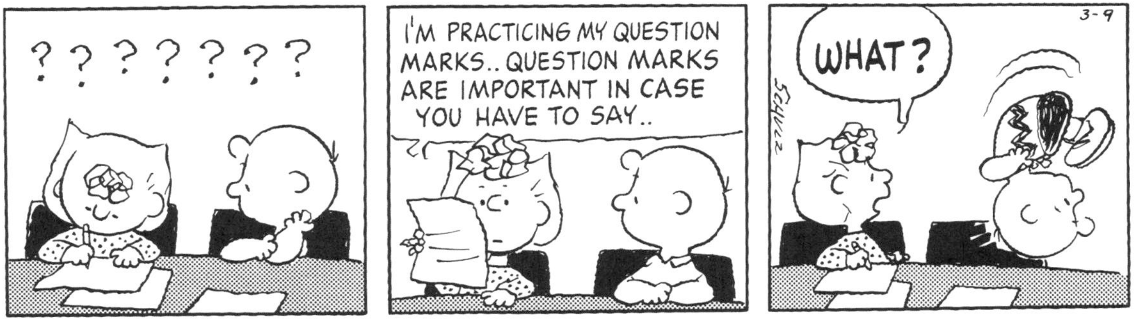
? ? ? ? ? ? ?
I'M PRACTICING MY QUESTION MARKS.. QUESTION MARKS ARE IMPORTANT IN CASE YOU HAVE TO SAY..
3-9
SCHULZ
WHAT?

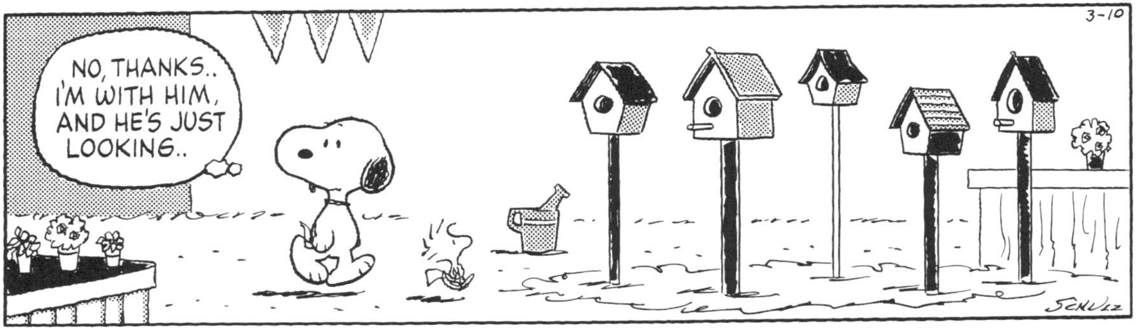
3-10
NO, THANKS.. I'M WITH HIM, AND HE'S JUST LOOKING..
SCHULZ

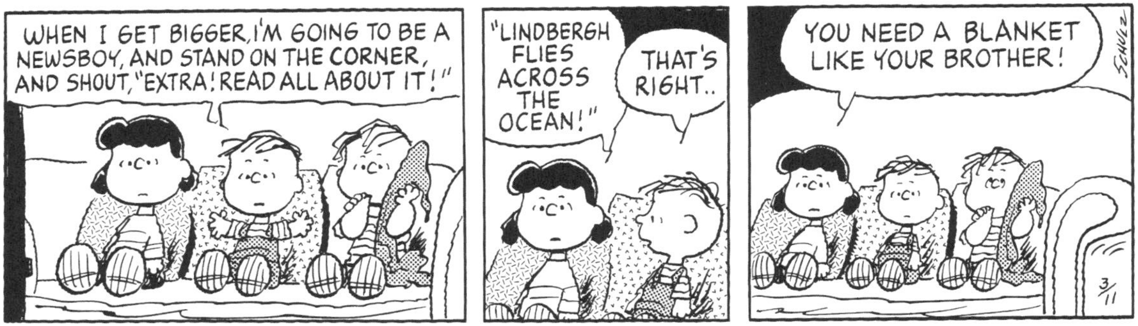
WHEN I GET BIGGER, I'M GOING TO BE A NEWSBOY, AND STAND ON THE CORNER, AND SHOUT, "EXTRA! READ ALL ABOUT IT!"
"LINDBERGH FLIES ACROSS THE OCEAN!"
THAT'S RIGHT..
YOU NEED A BLANKET LIKE YOUR BROTHER!
SCHULZ
3/11

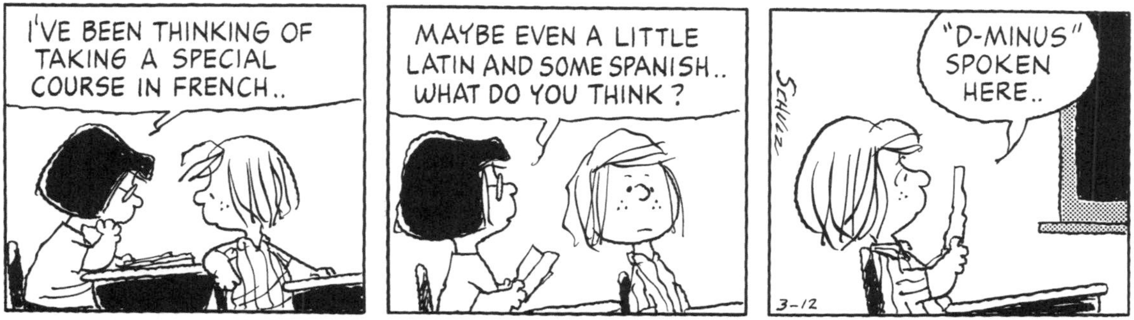
I'VE BEEN THINKING OF TAKING A SPECIAL COURSE IN FRENCH..
MAYBE EVEN A LITTLE LATIN AND SOME SPANISH.. WHAT DO YOU THINK?
"D-MINUS" SPOKEN HERE..
SCHULZ
3-12

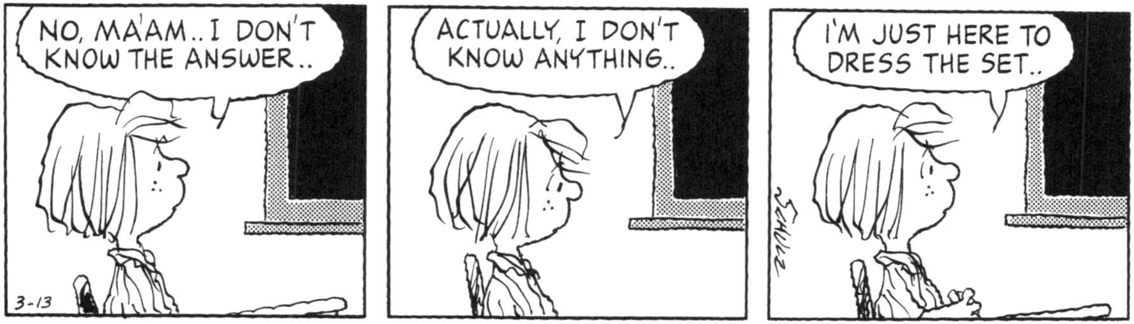
NO, MA'AM.. I DON'T KNOW THE ANSWER..
ACTUALLY, I DON'T KNOW ANYTHING..
I'M JUST HERE TO DRESS THE SET..
SCHULZ
3-13

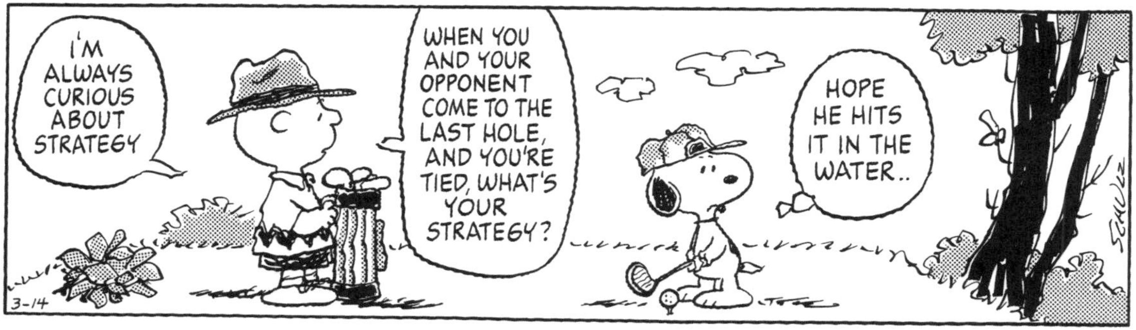
I'M ALWAYS CURIOUS ABOUT STRATEGY
WHEN YOU AND YOUR OPPONENT COME TO THE LAST HOLE, AND YOU'RE TIED, WHAT'S YOUR STRATEGY?
HOPE HE HITS IT IN THE WATER..
SCHULZ
3-14

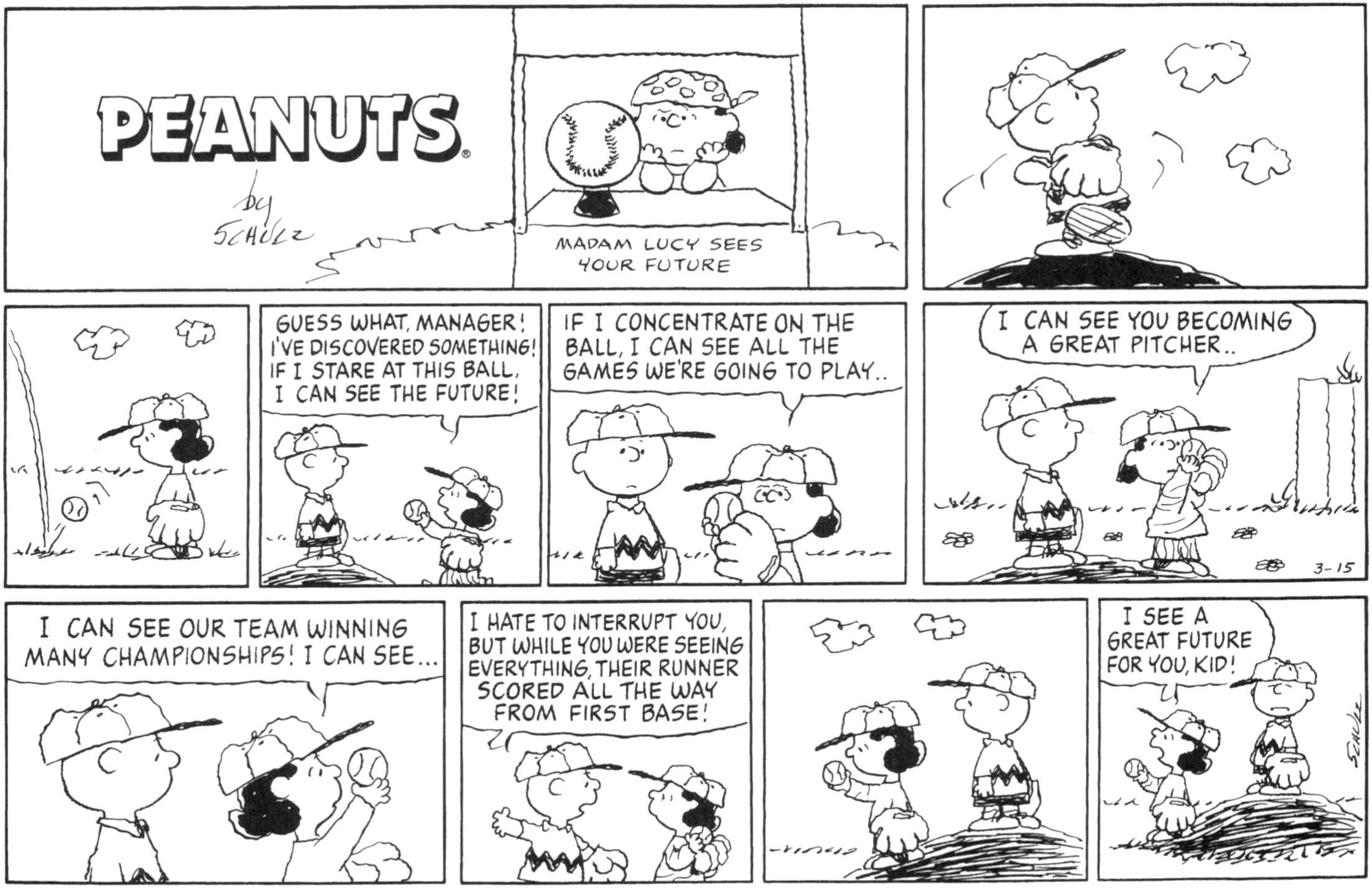
PEANUTS
by SCHULZ
MADAM LUCY SEES YOUR FUTURE
GUESS WHAT, MANAGER! I'VE DISCOVERED SOMETHING! IF I STARE AT THIS BALL, I CAN SEE THE FUTURE!
IF I CONCENTRATE ON THE BALL, I CAN SEE ALL THE GAMES WE'RE GOING TO PLAY..
I CAN SEE YOU BECOMING A GREAT PITCHER..
3-15
I CAN SEE OUR TEAM WINNING MANY CHAMPIONSHIPS! I CAN SEE...
I HATE TO INTERRUPT YOU, BUT WHILE YOU WERE SEEING EVERYTHING, THEIR RUNNER SCORED ALL THE WAY FROM FIRST BASE!
I SEE A GREAT FUTURE FOR YOU, KID!
SCHULZ

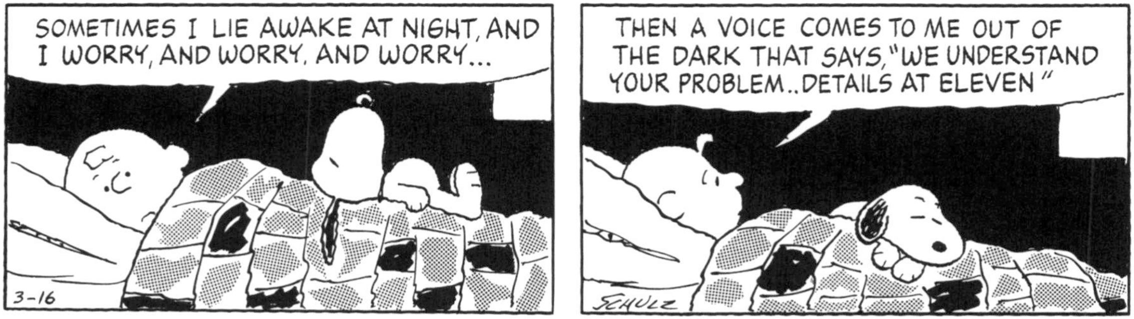
SOMETIMES I LIE AWAKE AT NIGHT, AND I WORRY, AND WORRY, AND WORRY...
THEN A VOICE COMES TO ME OUT OF THE DARK THAT SAYS, "WE UNDERSTAND YOUR PROBLEM..DETAILS AT ELEVEN"
3-16
SCHULZ

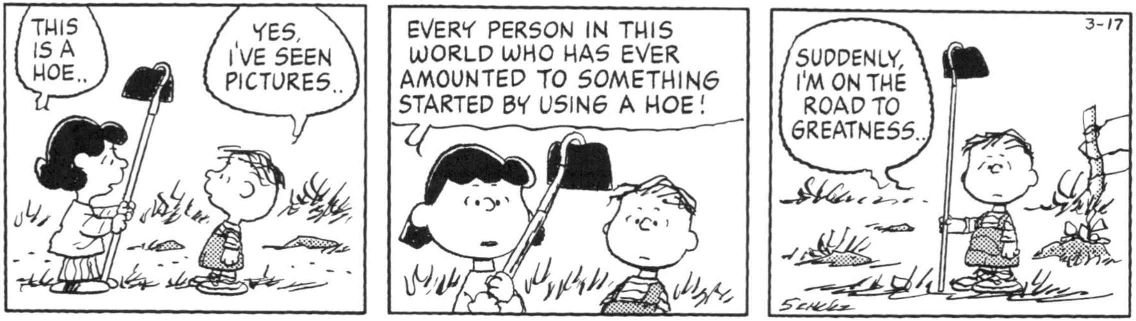
THIS IS A HOE..
YES, I'VE SEEN PICTURES..
EVERY PERSON IN THIS WORLD WHO HAS EVER AMOUNTED TO SOMETHING STARTED BY USING A HOE!
3-17
SUDDENLY, I'M ON THE ROAD TO GREATNESS..
SCHULZ

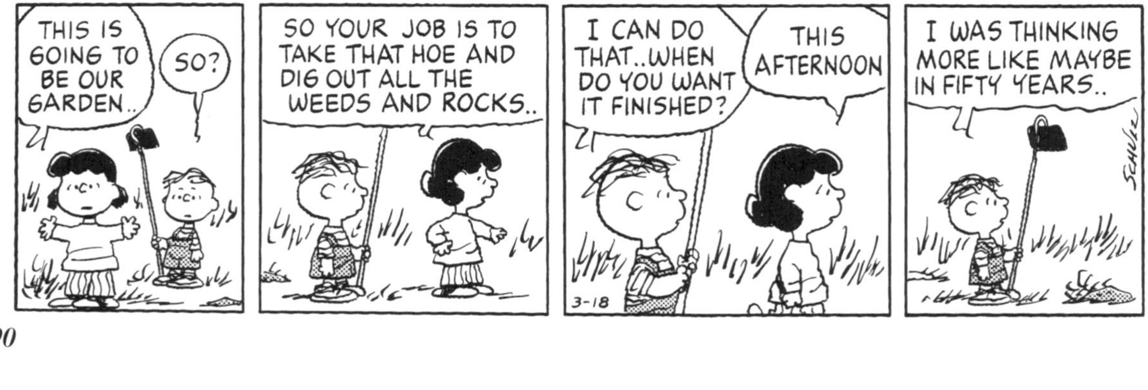
THIS IS GOING TO BE OUR GARDEN..
SO?
SO YOUR JOB IS TO TAKE THAT HOE AND DIG OUT ALL THE WEEDS AND ROCKS..
I CAN DO THAT..WHEN DO YOU WANT IT FINISHED?
THIS AFTERNOON
3-18
I WAS THINKING MORE LIKE MAYBE IN FIFTY YEARS..
SCHULZ

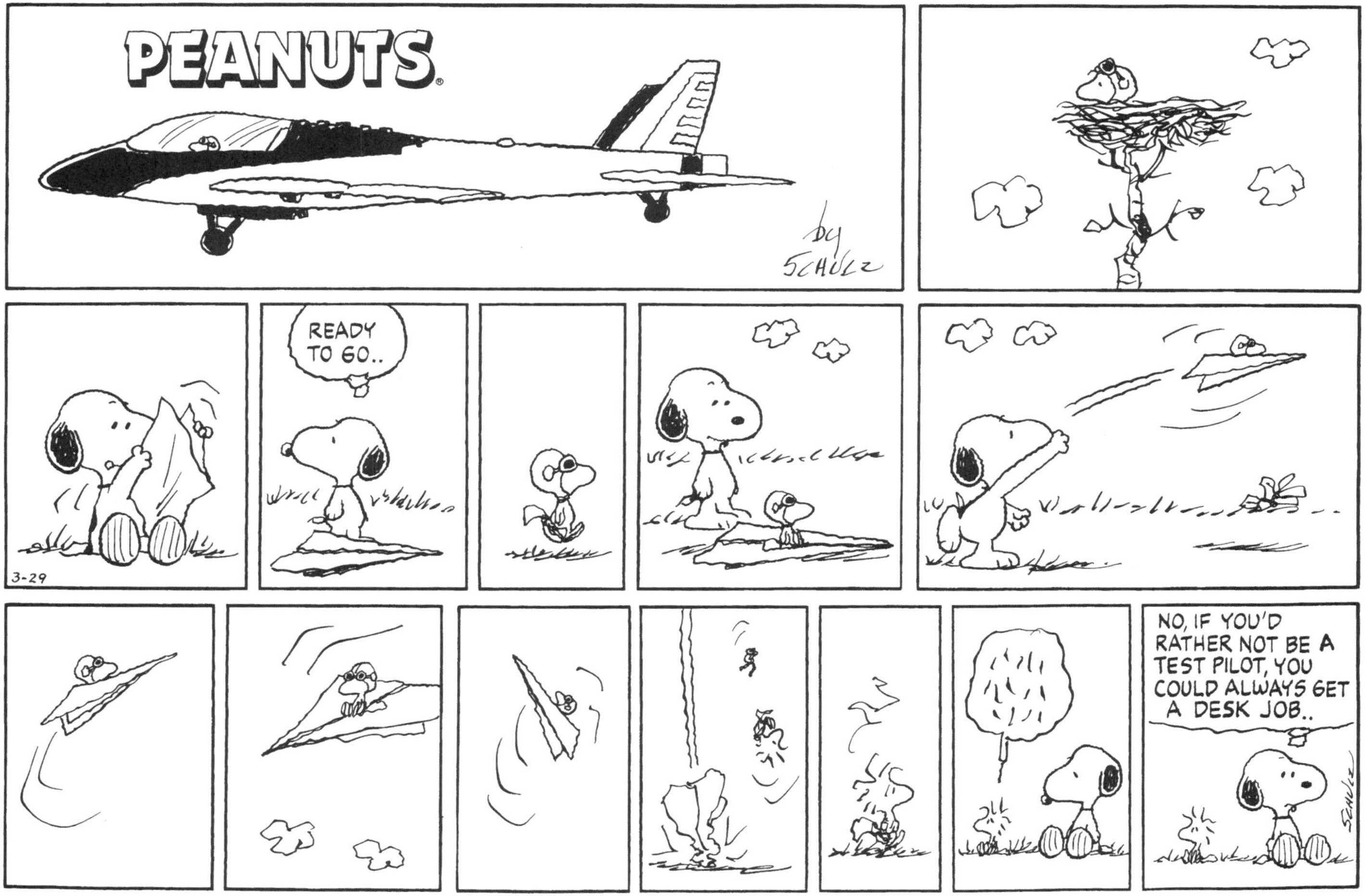
PEANUTS
by SCHULZ
3-29
READY TO GO..
NO, IF YOU'D RATHER NOT BE A TEST PILOT, YOU COULD ALWAYS GET A DESK JOB..
SCHULZ

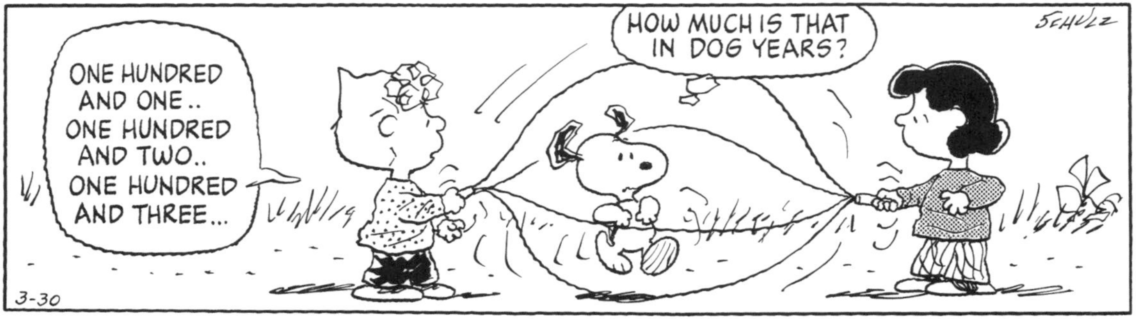
ONE HUNDRED AND ONE.. ONE HUNDRED AND TWO.. ONE HUNDRED AND THREE...
HOW MUCH IS THAT IN DOG YEARS?
3-30

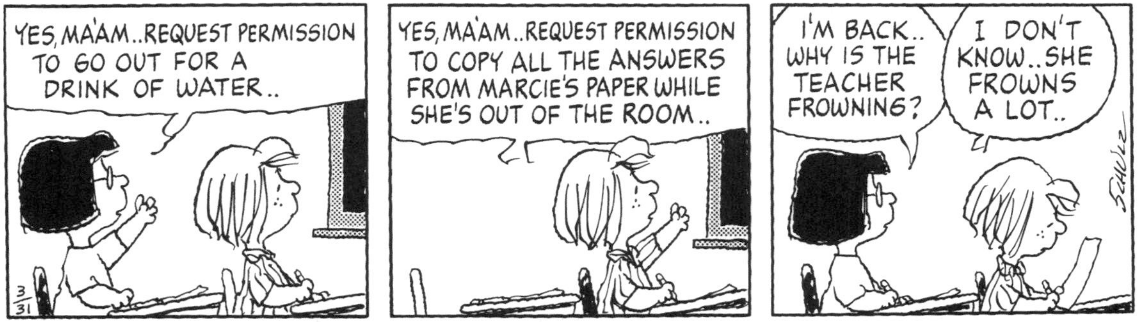
YES, MA'AM..REQUEST PERMISSION TO GO OUT FOR A DRINK OF WATER..
YES, MA'AM..REQUEST PERMISSION TO COPY ALL THE ANSWERS FROM MARCIE'S PAPER WHILE SHE'S OUT OF THE ROOM..
I'M BACK.. WHY IS THE TEACHER FROWNING?
I DON'T KNOW..SHE FROWNS A LOT..
3/31

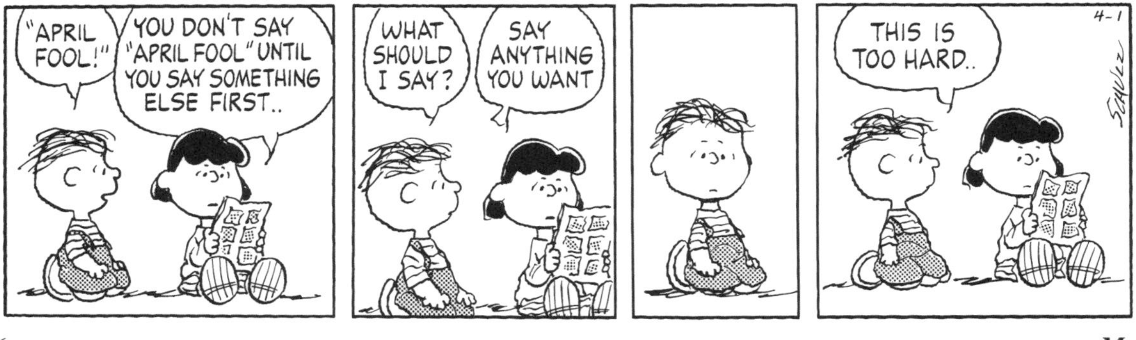
"APRIL FOOL!"
YOU DON'T SAY "APRIL FOOL" UNTIL YOU SAY SOMETHING ELSE FIRST..
WHAT SHOULD I SAY?
SAY ANYTHING YOU WANT
THIS IS TOO HARD..
4-1

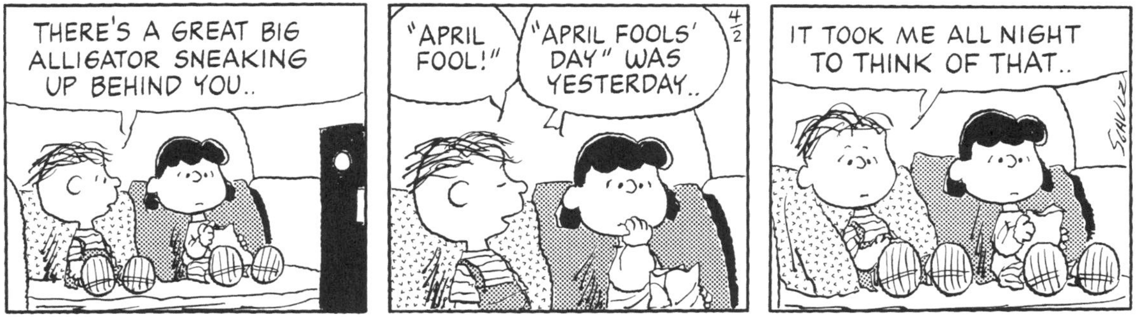
THERE'S A GREAT BIG ALLIGATOR SNEAKING UP BEHIND YOU..
"APRIL FOOL!"
"APRIL FOOLS' DAY" WAS YESTERDAY..
4/2
IT TOOK ME ALL NIGHT TO THINK OF THAT..
SCHULZ

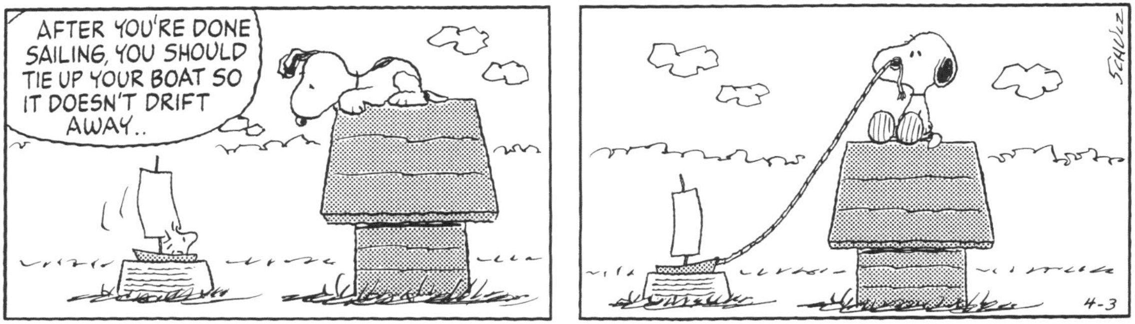
AFTER YOU'RE DONE SAILING, YOU SHOULD TIE UP YOUR BOAT SO IT DOESN'T DRIFT AWAY..
SCHULZ
4-3

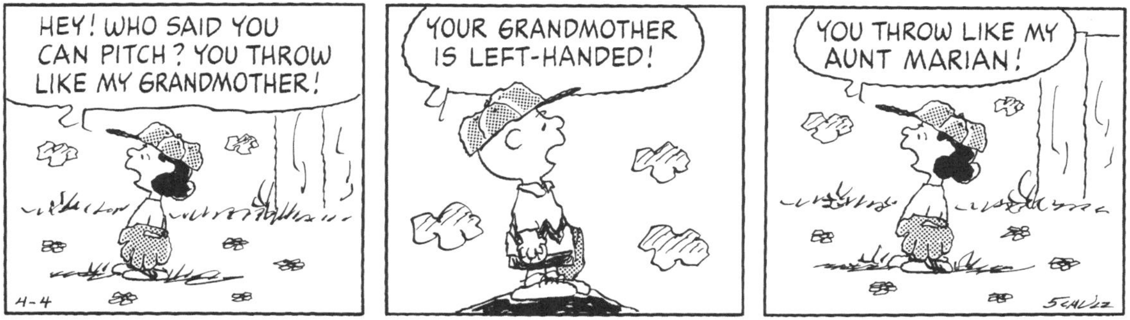
HEY! WHO SAID YOU CAN PITCH? YOU THROW LIKE MY GRANDMOTHER!
4-4
YOUR GRANDMOTHER IS LEFT-HANDED!
YOU THROW LIKE MY AUNT MARIAN!
SCHULZ

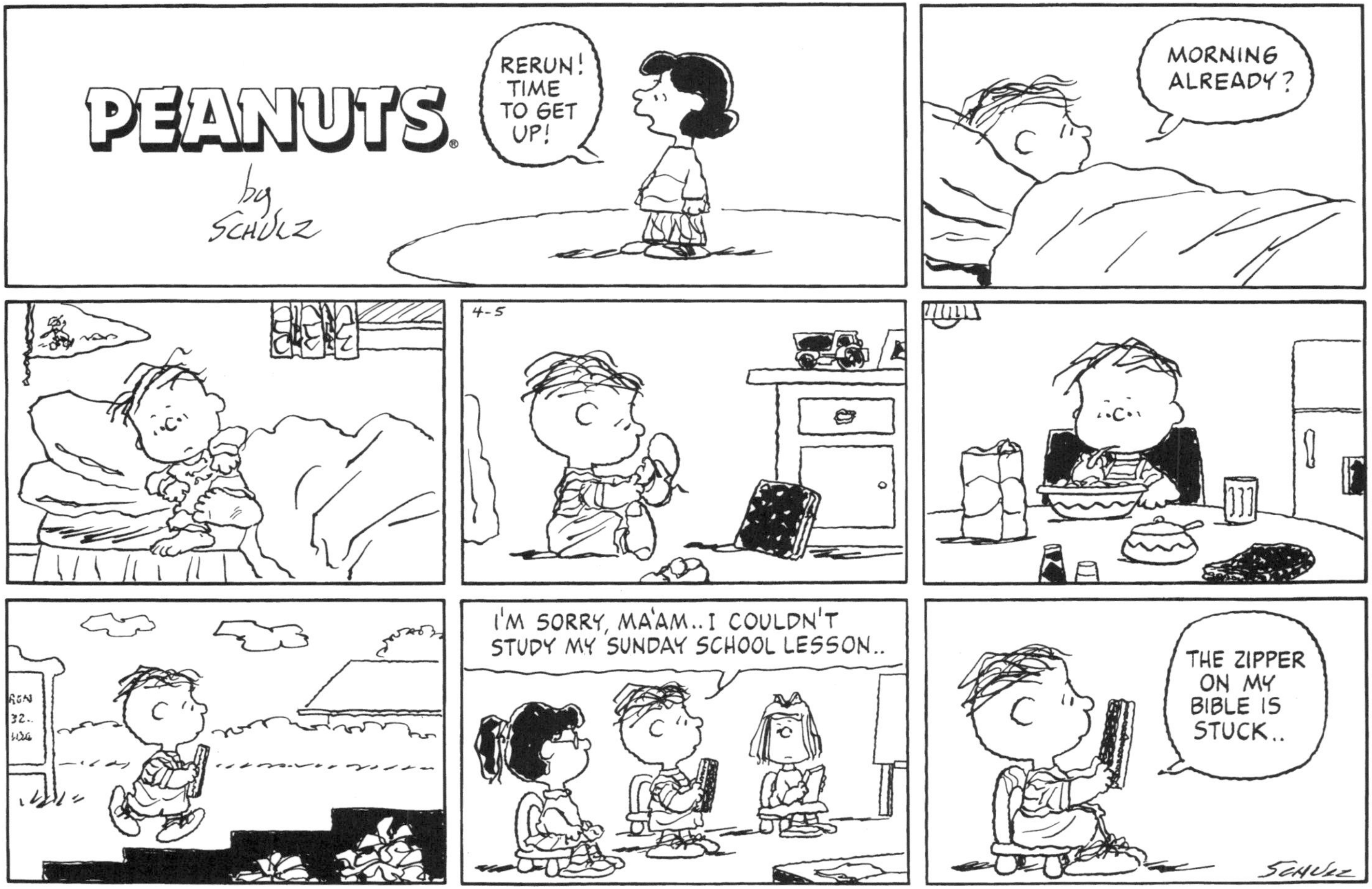
PEANUTS
by SCHULZ
RERUN! TIME TO GET UP!
MORNING ALREADY?
4-5
I'M SORRY, MA'AM.. I COULDN'T STUDY MY SUNDAY SCHOOL LESSON..
THE ZIPPER ON MY BIBLE IS STUCK..
SCHULZ

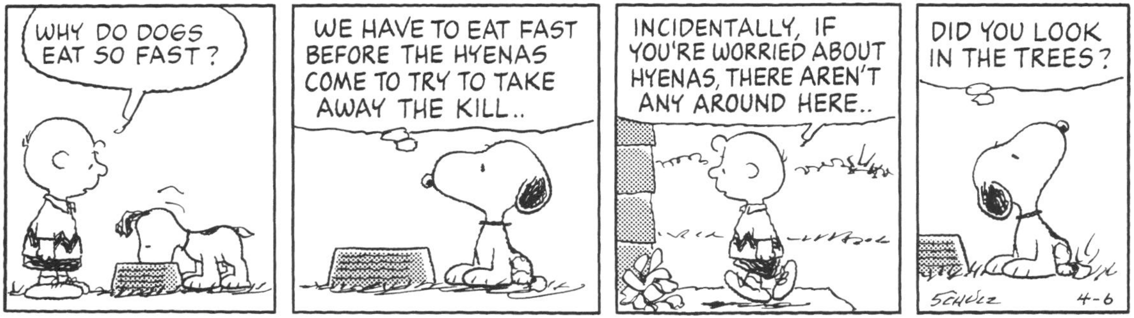
WHY DO DOGS EAT SO FAST?
WE HAVE TO EAT FAST BEFORE THE HYENAS COME TO TRY TO TAKE AWAY THE KILL..
INCIDENTALLY, IF YOU'RE WORRIED ABOUT HYENAS, THERE AREN'T ANY AROUND HERE..
DID YOU LOOK IN THE TREES?
SCHULZ
4-6

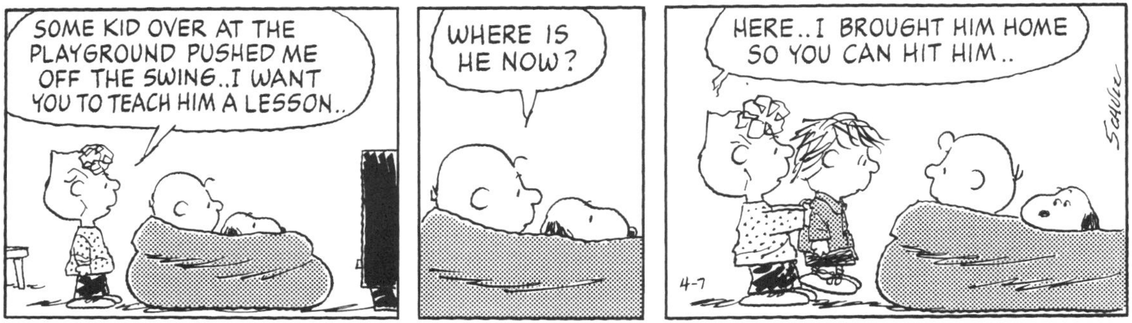
SOME KID OVER AT THE PLAYGROUND PUSHED ME OFF THE SWING..I WANT YOU TO TEACH HIM A LESSON..
WHERE IS HE NOW?
HERE..I BROUGHT HIM HOME SO YOU CAN HIT HIM..
SCHULZ
4-7

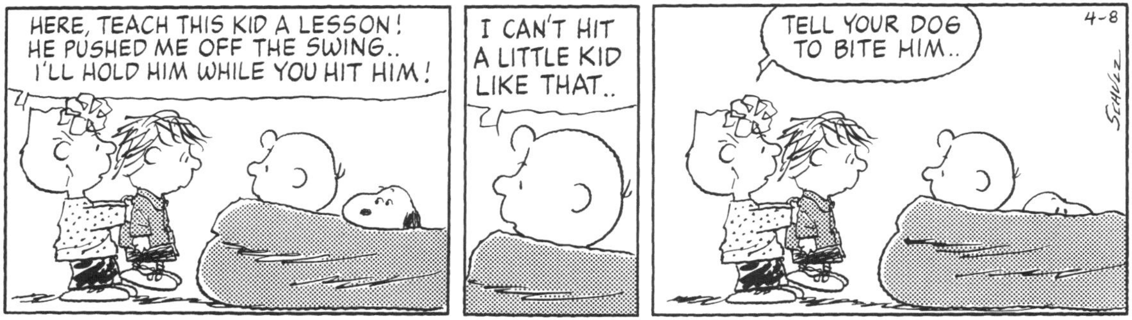
HERE, TEACH THIS KID A LESSON! HE PUSHED ME OFF THE SWING.. I'LL HOLD HIM WHILE YOU HIT HIM!
I CAN'T HIT A LITTLE KID LIKE THAT..
TELL YOUR DOG TO BITE HIM..
4-8
SCHULZ

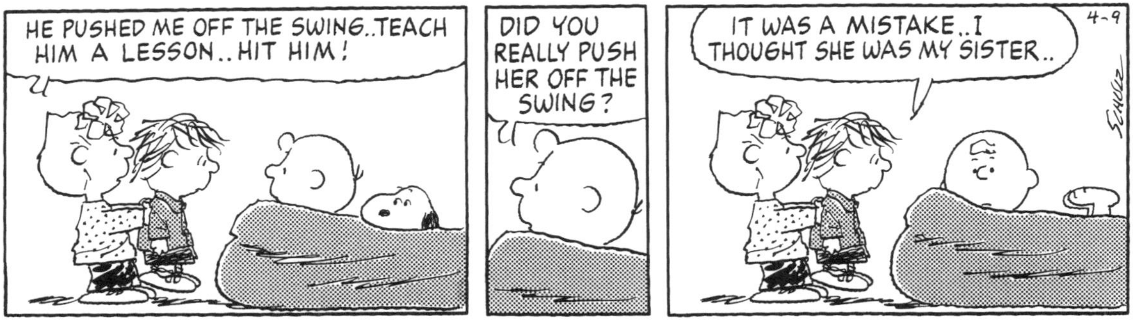
HE PUSHED ME OFF THE SWING..TEACH HIM A LESSON..HIT HIM!
DID YOU REALLY PUSH HER OFF THE SWING?
IT WAS A MISTAKE..I THOUGHT SHE WAS MY SISTER..
4-9
SCHULZ

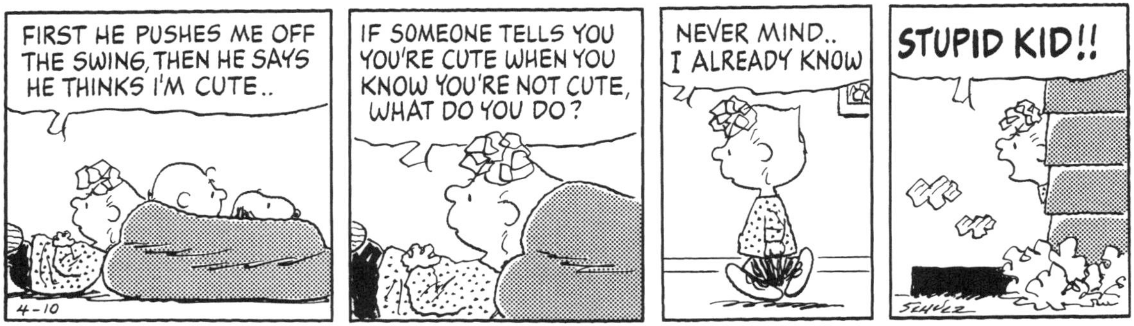
FIRST HE PUSHES ME OFF THE SWING, THEN HE SAYS HE THINKS I'M CUTE..
4-10
IF SOMEONE TELLS YOU YOU'RE CUTE WHEN YOU KNOW YOU'RE NOT CUTE, WHAT DO YOU DO?
NEVER MIND.. I ALREADY KNOW
STUPID KID!!
SCHULZ

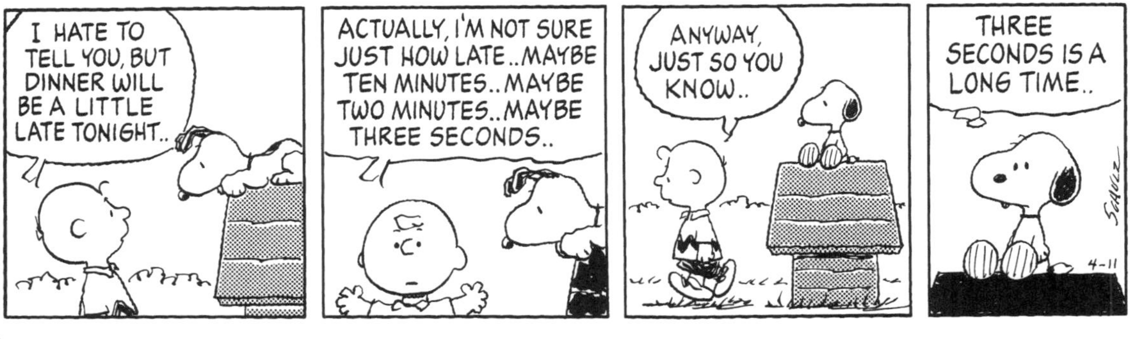
I HATE TO TELL YOU, BUT DINNER WILL BE A LITTLE LATE TONIGHT..
ACTUALLY, I'M NOT SURE JUST HOW LATE..MAYBE TEN MINUTES..MAYBE TWO MINUTES..MAYBE THREE SECONDS..
ANYWAY, JUST SO YOU KNOW..
THREE SECONDS IS A LONG TIME..
SCHULZ
4-11

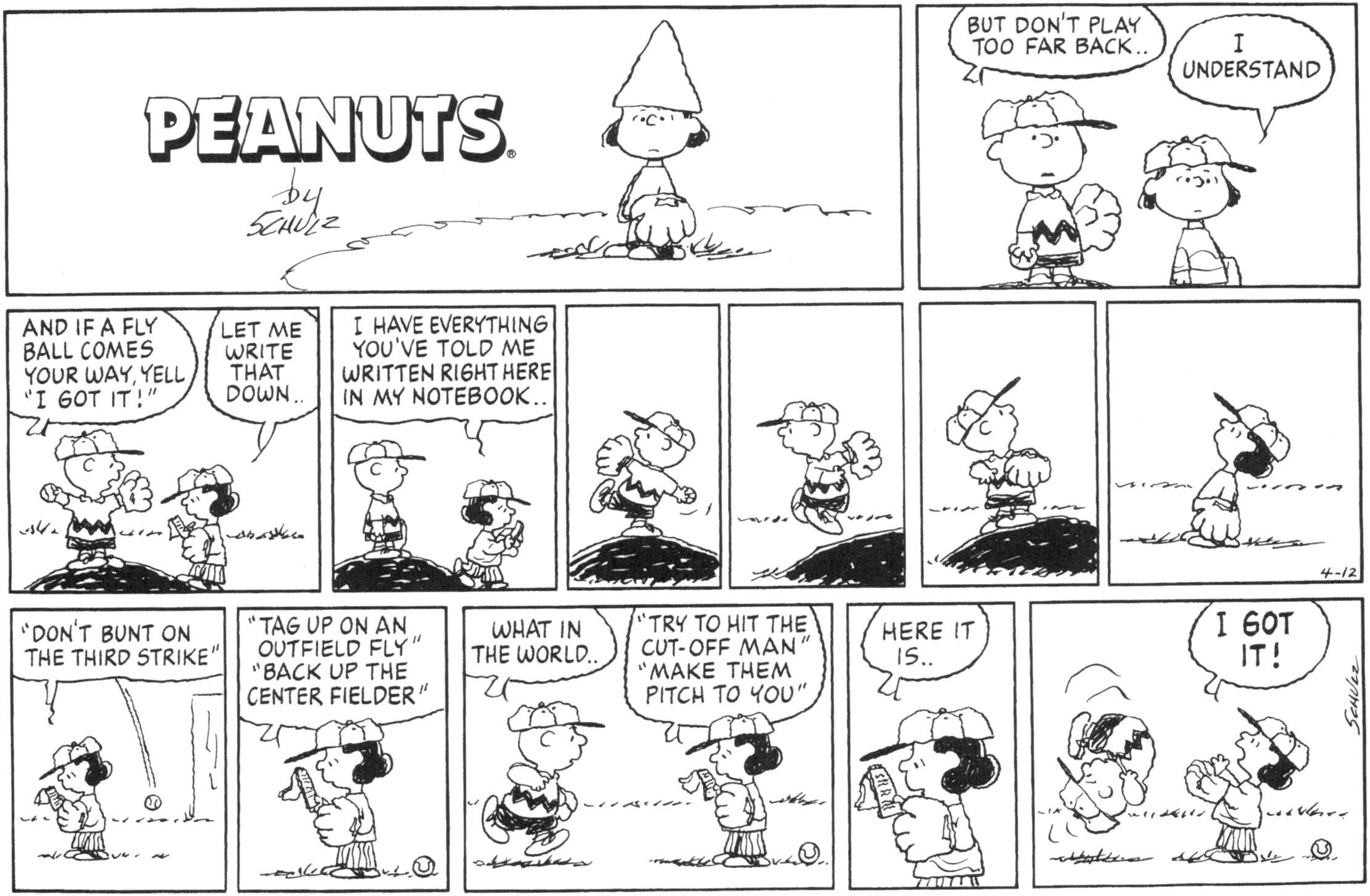
PEANUTS
by SCHULZ
BUT DON'T PLAY TOO FAR BACK..
I UNDERSTAND
AND IF A FLY BALL COMES YOUR WAY, YELL "I GOT IT!"
LET ME WRITE THAT DOWN..
I HAVE EVERYTHING YOU'VE TOLD ME WRITTEN RIGHT HERE IN MY NOTEBOOK..
4-12
"DON'T BUNT ON THE THIRD STRIKE"
"TAG UP ON AN OUTFIELD FLY" "BACK UP THE CENTER FIELDER"
WHAT IN THE WORLD..
"TRY TO HIT THE CUT-OFF MAN" "MAKE THEM PITCH TO YOU"
HERE IT IS..
I GOT IT!
SCHULZ

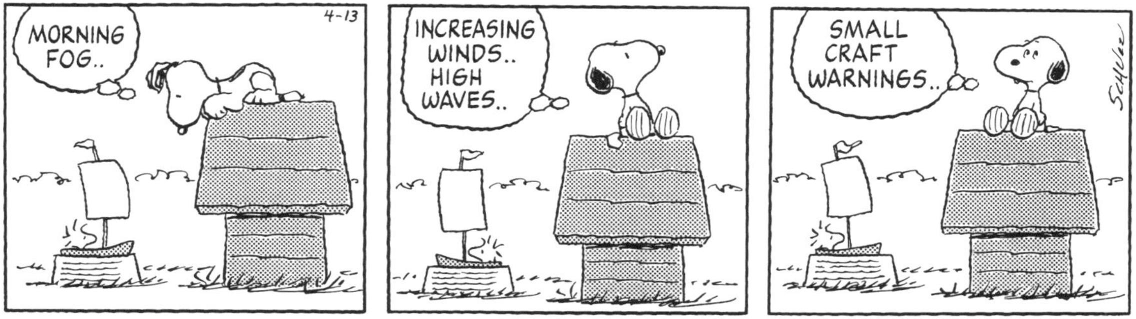
4-13
MORNING FOG..
INCREASING WINDS.. HIGH WAVES..
SMALL CRAFT WARNINGS..
SCHULZ

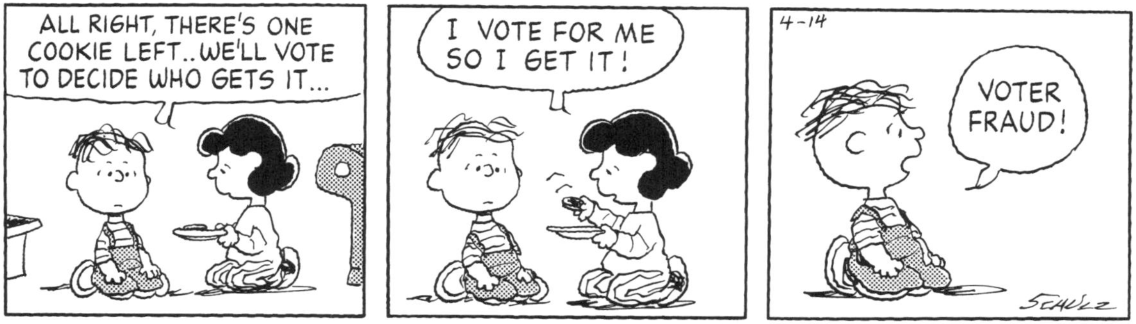
ALL RIGHT, THERE'S ONE COOKIE LEFT..WE'LL VOTE TO DECIDE WHO GETS IT...
I VOTE FOR ME SO I GET IT!
4-14
VOTER FRAUD!
SCHULZ

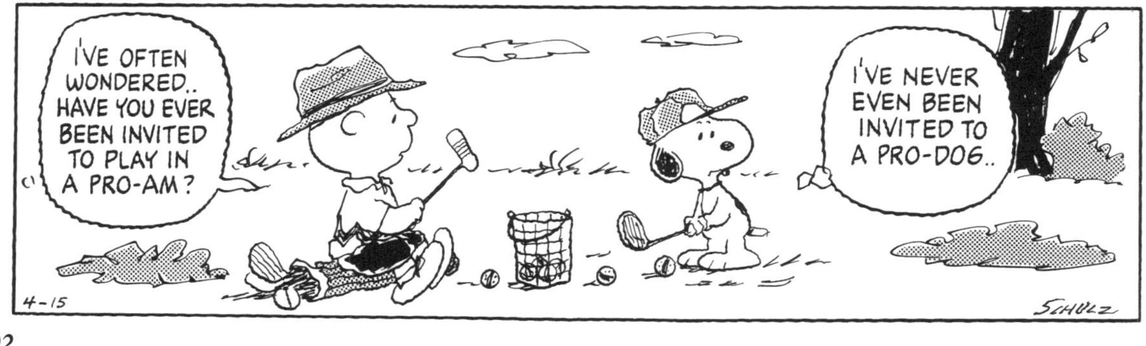
I'VE OFTEN WONDERED.. HAVE YOU EVER BEEN INVITED TO PLAY IN A PRO-AM?
I'VE NEVER EVEN BEEN INVITED TO A PRO-DOG..
4-15
SCHULZ

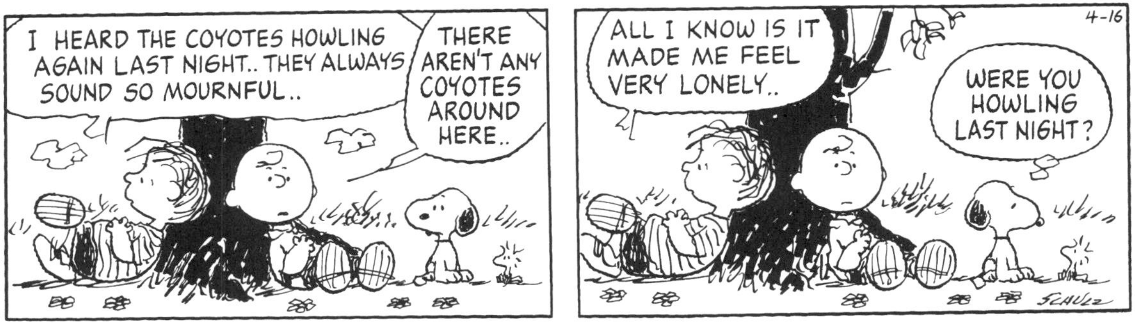
I HEARD THE COYOTES HOWLING AGAIN LAST NIGHT.. THEY ALWAYS SOUND SO MOURNFUL..
THERE AREN'T ANY COYOTES AROUND HERE..
4-16
ALL I KNOW IS IT MADE ME FEEL VERY LONELY..
WERE YOU HOWLING LAST NIGHT?
SCHULZ

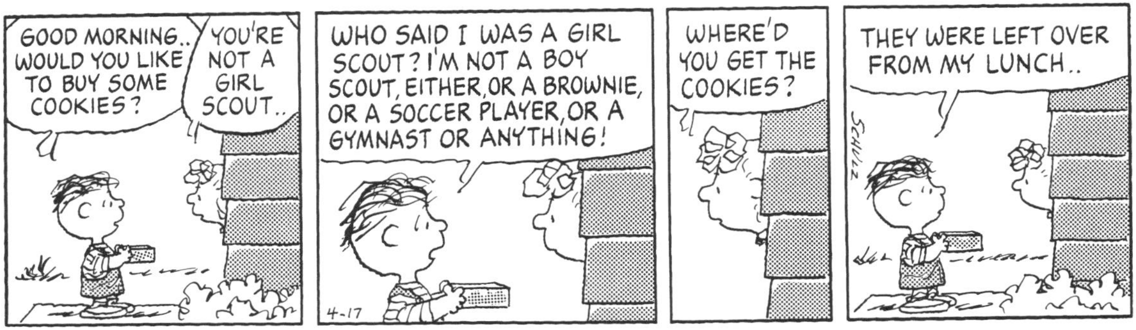
GOOD MORNING.. WOULD YOU LIKE TO BUY SOME COOKIES?
YOU'RE NOT A GIRL SCOUT..
WHO SAID I WAS A GIRL SCOUT? I'M NOT A BOY SCOUT, EITHER, OR A BROWNIE, OR A SOCCER PLAYER, OR A GYMNAST OR ANYTHING!
4-17
WHERE'D YOU GET THE COOKIES?
THEY WERE LEFT OVER FROM MY LUNCH..
SCHULZ

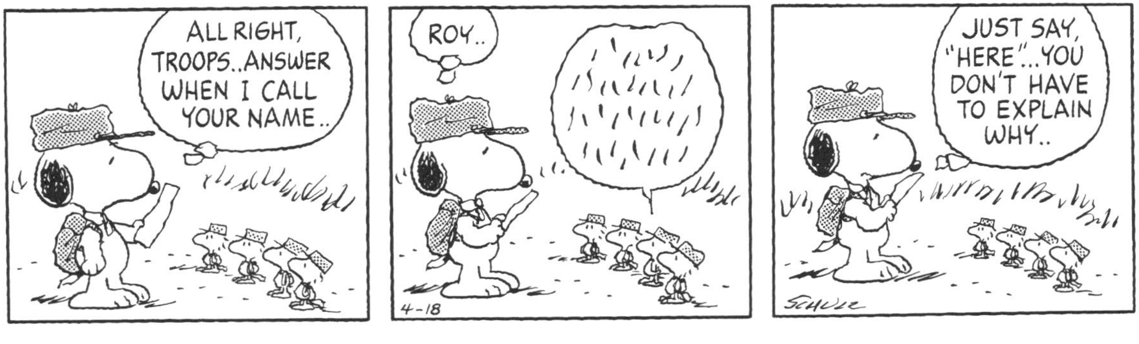
ALL RIGHT, TROOPS..ANSWER WHEN I CALL YOUR NAME..
ROY..
4-18
JUST SAY, "HERE"...YOU DON'T HAVE TO EXPLAIN WHY..
SCHULZ

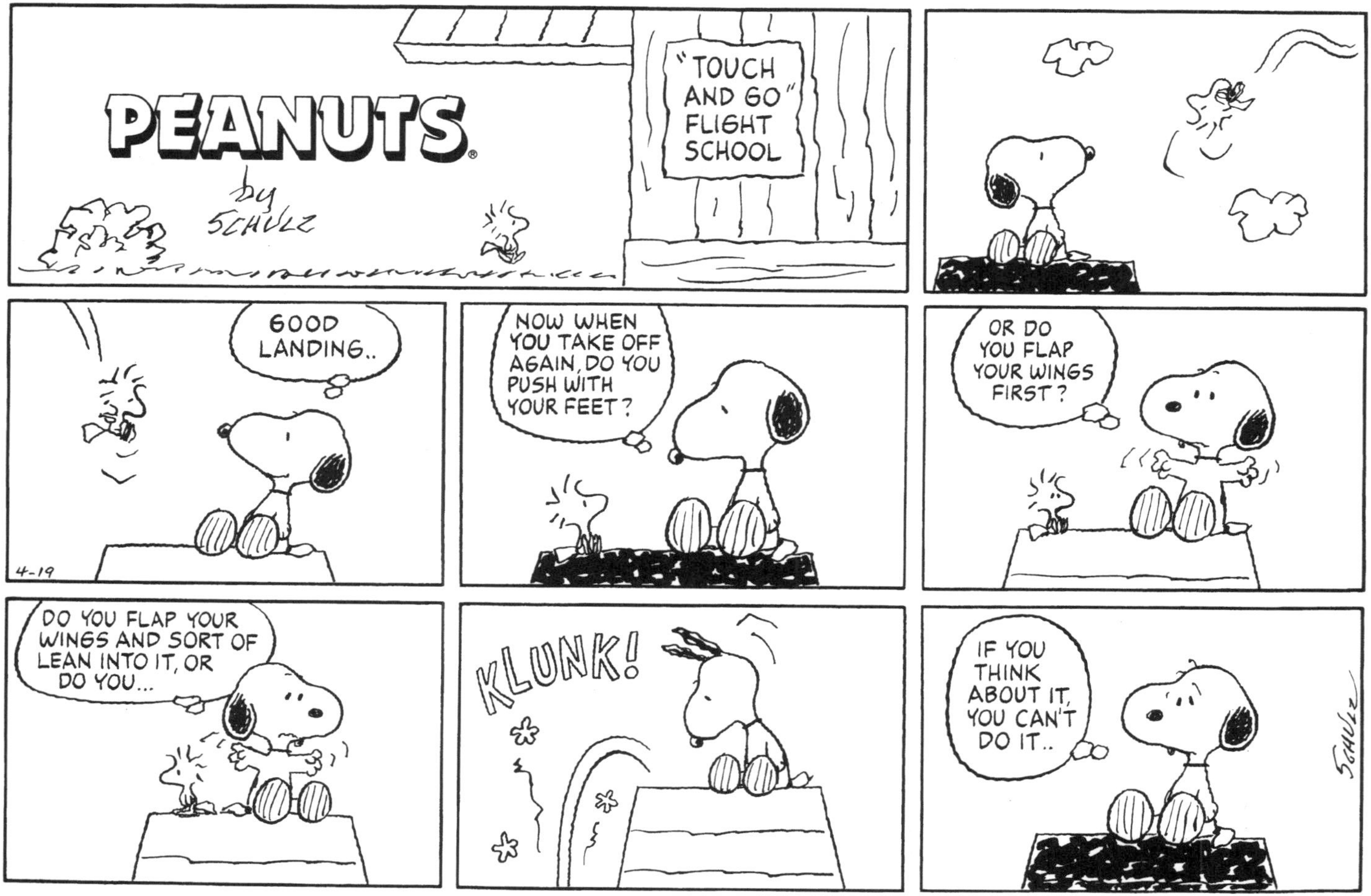
PEANUTS®
by SCHULZ
"TOUCH AND GO" FLIGHT SCHOOL
GOOD LANDING..
4-19
NOW WHEN YOU TAKE OFF AGAIN, DO YOU PUSH WITH YOUR FEET?
OR DO YOU FLAP YOUR WINGS FIRST?
DO YOU FLAP YOUR WINGS AND SORT OF LEAN INTO IT, OR DO YOU...
KLUNK!
IF YOU THINK ABOUT IT, YOU CAN'T DO IT..
SCHULZ

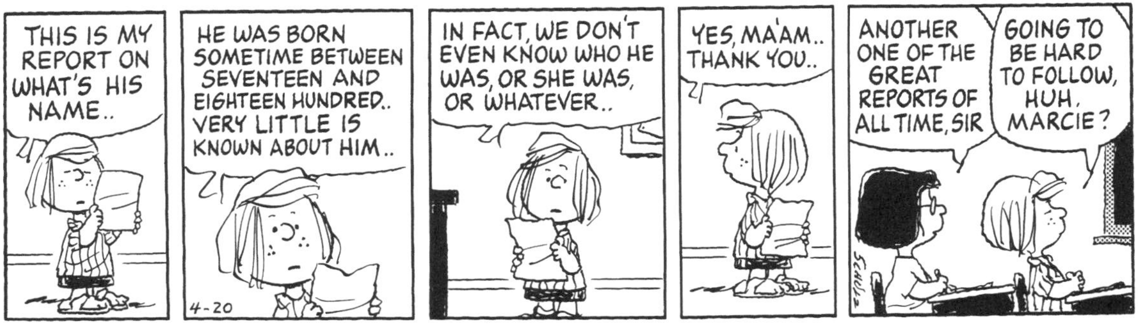
THIS IS MY REPORT ON WHAT'S HIS NAME..
HE WAS BORN SOMETIME BETWEEN SEVENTEEN AND EIGHTEEN HUNDRED.. VERY LITTLE IS KNOWN ABOUT HIM..
4-20
IN FACT, WE DON'T EVEN KNOW WHO HE WAS, OR SHE WAS, OR WHATEVER..
YES, MA'AM.. THANK YOU..
ANOTHER ONE OF THE GREAT REPORTS OF ALL TIME, SIR
GOING TO BE HARD TO FOLLOW, HUH, MARCIE?

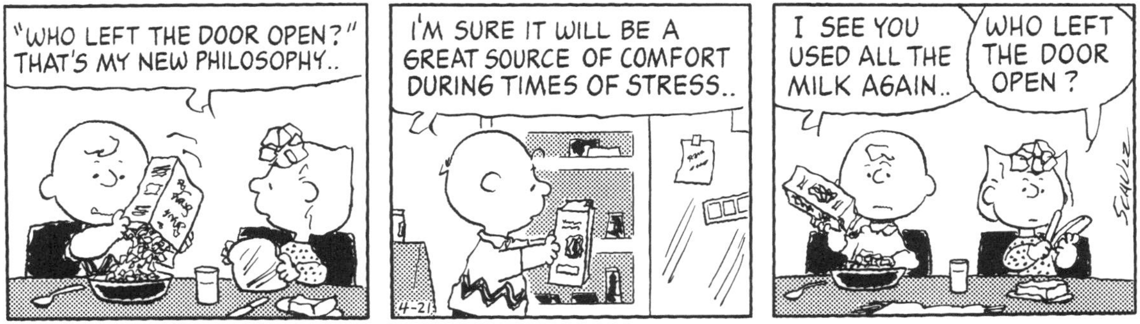
"WHO LEFT THE DOOR OPEN?" THAT'S MY NEW PHILOSOPHY..
I'M SURE IT WILL BE A GREAT SOURCE OF COMFORT DURING TIMES OF STRESS..
4-21
I SEE YOU USED ALL THE MILK AGAIN..
WHO LEFT THE DOOR OPEN?

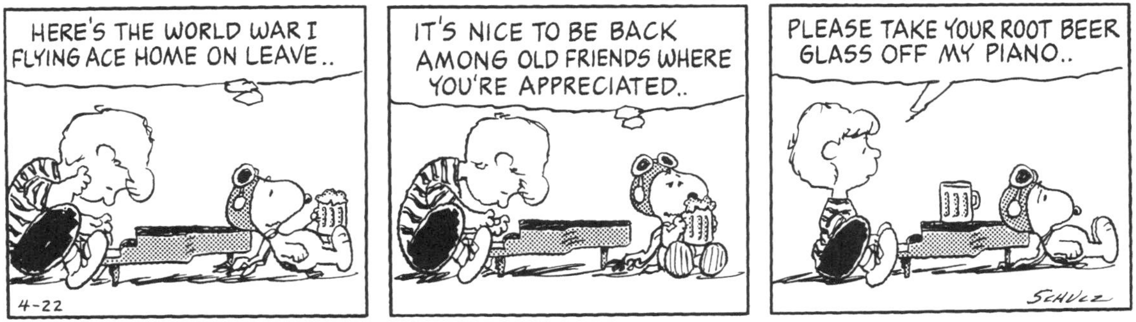
HERE'S THE WORLD WAR I FLYING ACE HOME ON LEAVE..
4-22
IT'S NICE TO BE BACK AMONG OLD FRIENDS WHERE YOU'RE APPRECIATED..
PLEASE TAKE YOUR ROOT BEER GLASS OFF MY PIANO..

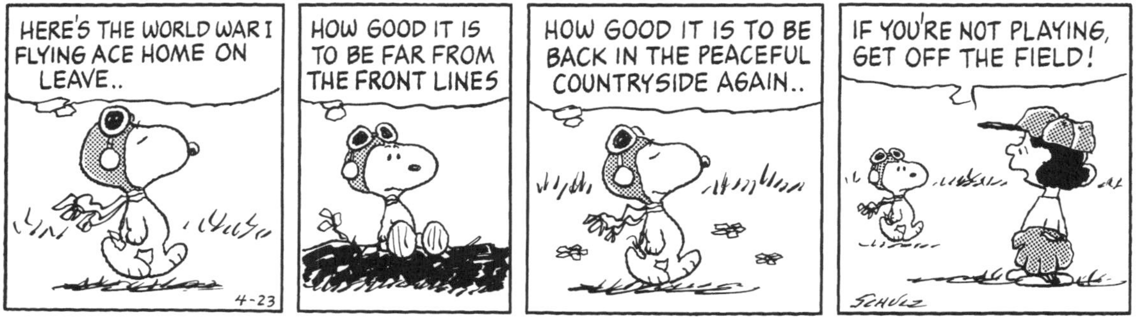
HERE'S THE WORLD WAR I FLYING ACE HOME ON LEAVE..
4-23
HOW GOOD IT IS TO BE FAR FROM THE FRONT LINES
HOW GOOD IT IS TO BE BACK IN THE PEACEFUL COUNTRYSIDE AGAIN..
IF YOU'RE NOT PLAYING, GET OFF THE FIELD!
SCHULZ

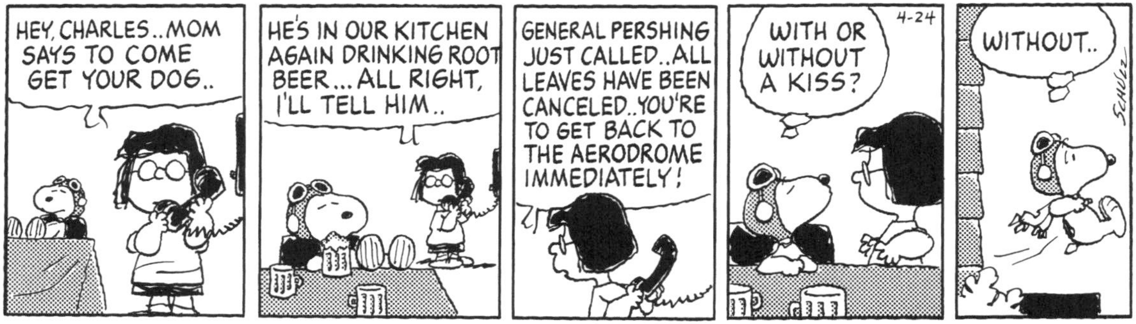
HEY, CHARLES..MOM SAYS TO COME GET YOUR DOG..
HE'S IN OUR KITCHEN AGAIN DRINKING ROOT BEER....ALL RIGHT, I'LL TELL HIM..
GENERAL PERSHING JUST CALLED..ALL LEAVES HAVE BEEN CANCELED..YOU'RE TO GET BACK TO THE AERODROME IMMEDIATELY!
4-24
WITH OR WITHOUT A KISS?
WITHOUT..
SCHULZ

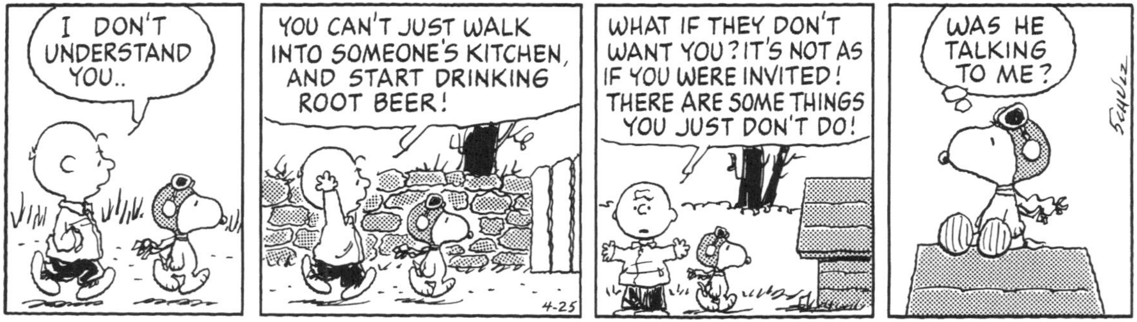
I DON'T UNDERSTAND YOU..
YOU CAN'T JUST WALK INTO SOMEONE'S KITCHEN, AND START DRINKING ROOT BEER!
4-25
WHAT IF THEY DON'T WANT YOU? IT'S NOT AS IF YOU WERE INVITED! THERE ARE SOME THINGS YOU JUST DON'T DO!
WAS HE TALKING TO ME?
SCHULZ

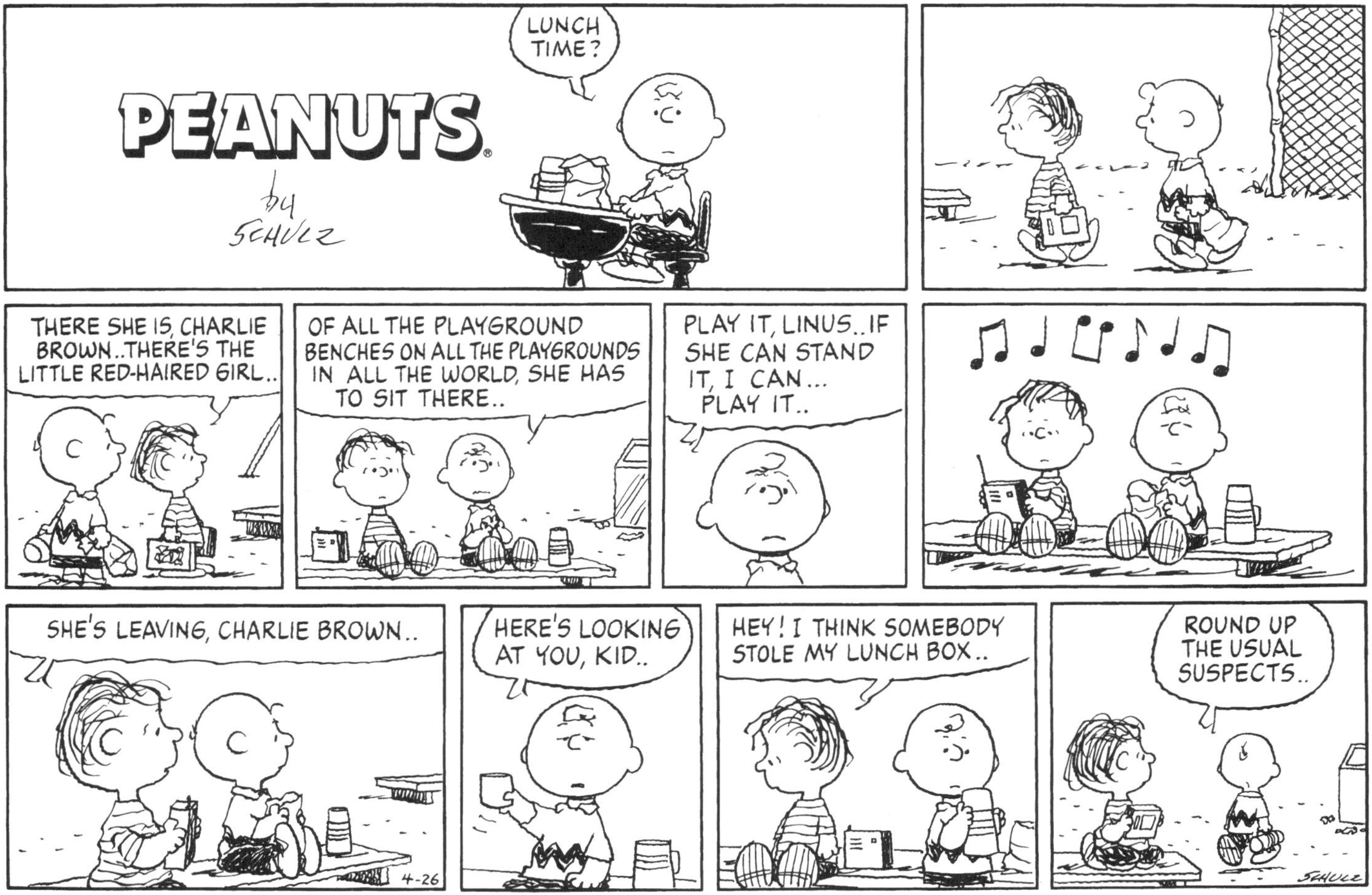
PEANUTS
by SCHULZ
LUNCH TIME?
THERE SHE IS, CHARLIE BROWN..THERE'S THE LITTLE RED-HAIRED GIRL..
OF ALL THE PLAYGROUND BENCHES ON ALL THE PLAYGROUNDS IN ALL THE WORLD, SHE HAS TO SIT THERE..
PLAY IT, LINUS..IF SHE CAN STAND IT, I CAN... PLAY IT..
SHE'S LEAVING, CHARLIE BROWN..
4-26
HERE'S LOOKING AT YOU, KID..
HEY! I THINK SOMEBODY STOLE MY LUNCH BOX..
ROUND UP THE USUAL SUSPECTS..
SCHULZ

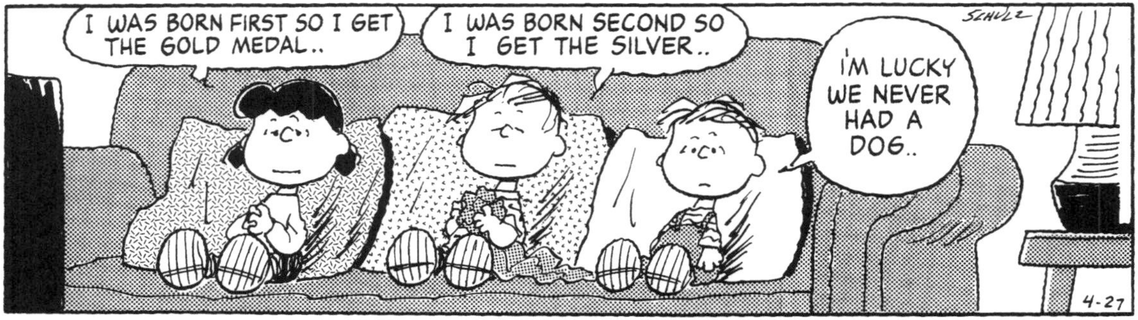
I WAS BORN FIRST SO I GET THE GOLD MEDAL..
I WAS BORN SECOND SO I GET THE SILVER..
I'M LUCKY WE NEVER HAD A DOG..

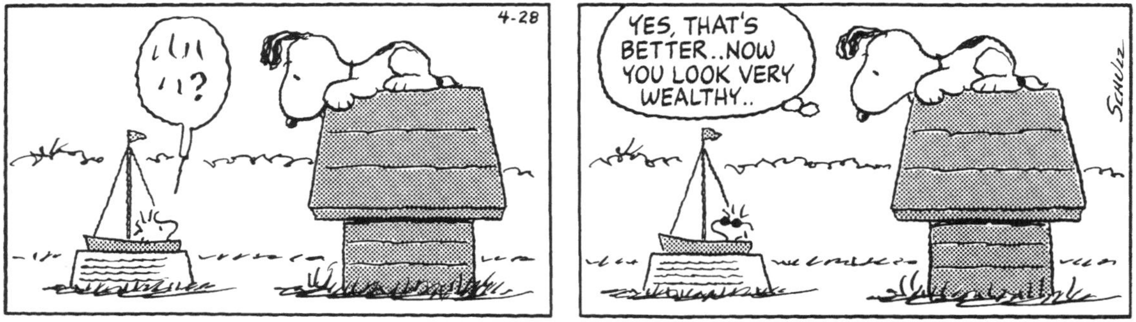
YES, THAT'S BETTER..NOW YOU LOOK VERY WEALTHY..

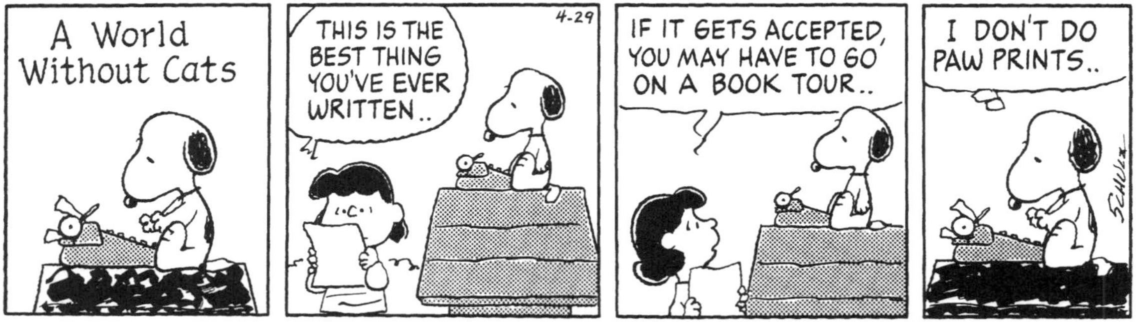
A World Without Cats
THIS IS THE BEST THING YOU'VE EVER WRITTEN..
IF IT GETS ACCEPTED, YOU MAY HAVE TO GO ON A BOOK TOUR..
I DON'T DO PAW PRINTS..

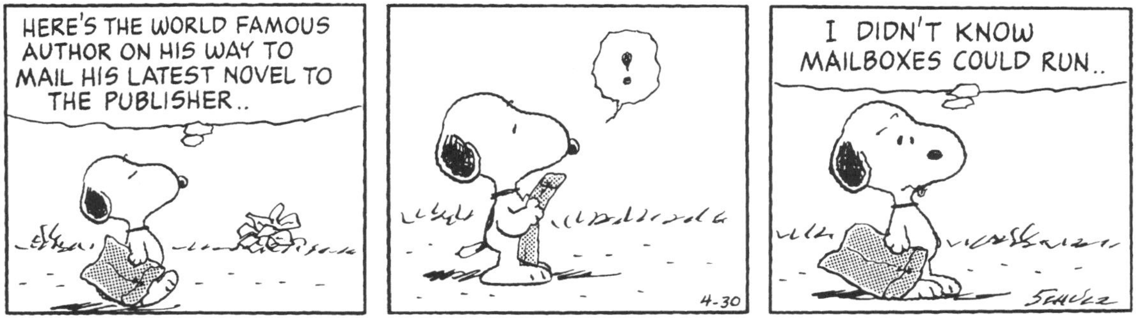
HERE'S THE WORLD FAMOUS AUTHOR ON HIS WAY TO MAIL HIS LATEST NOVEL TO THE PUBLISHER..
!
4-30
I DIDN'T KNOW MAILBOXES COULD RUN..
SCHULZ

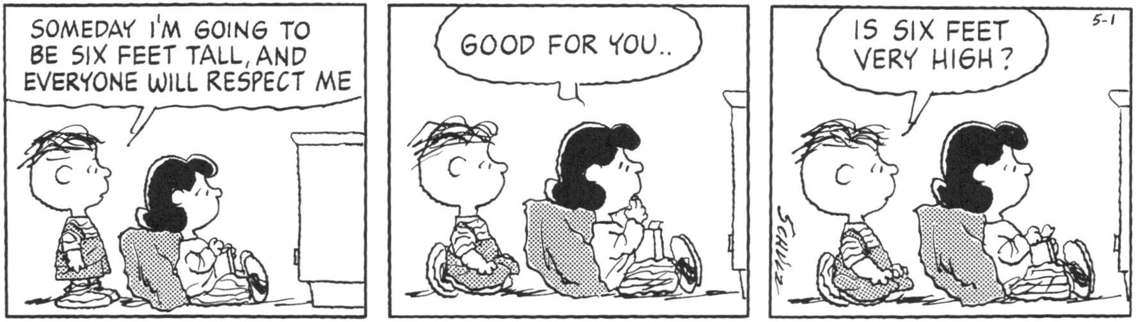
SOMEDAY I'M GOING TO BE SIX FEET TALL, AND EVERYONE WILL RESPECT ME
GOOD FOR YOU..
5-1
IS SIX FEET VERY HIGH?
SCHULZ

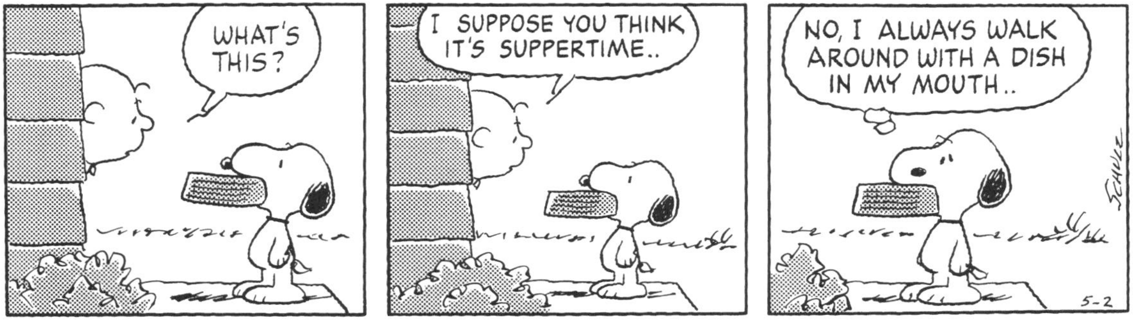
WHAT'S THIS?
I SUPPOSE YOU THINK IT'S SUPPERTIME..
NO, I ALWAYS WALK AROUND WITH A DISH IN MY MOUTH..
SCHULZ
5-2

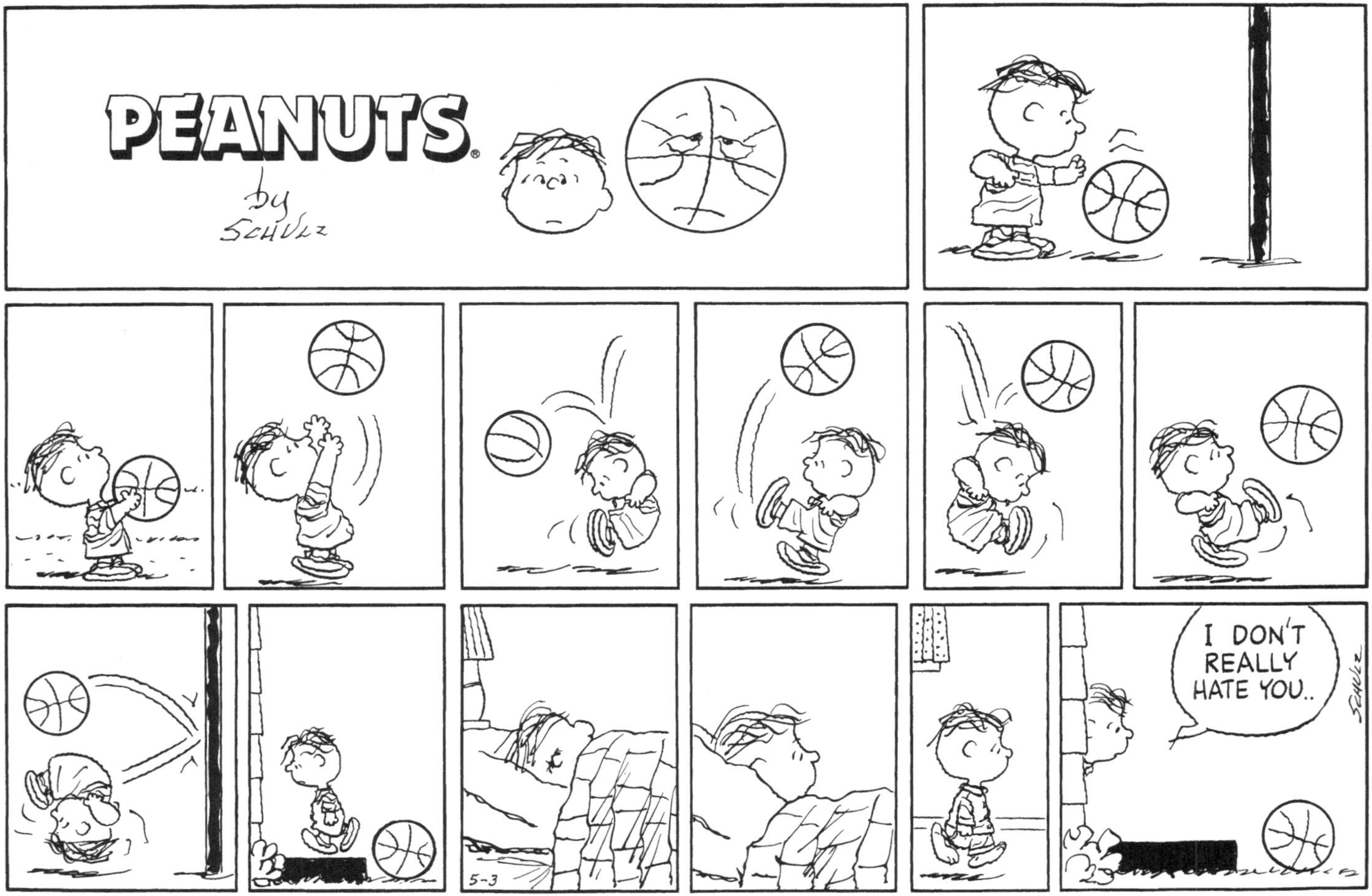
PEANUTS
by SCHULZ
5-3
I DON'T REALLY HATE YOU..
SCHULZ

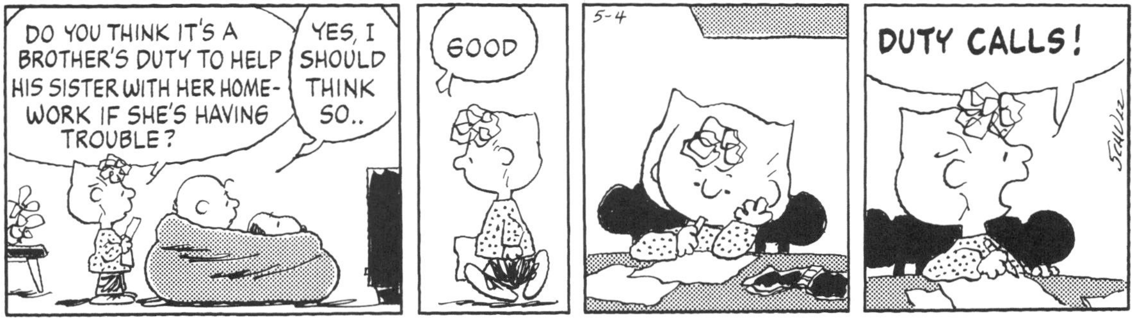
DO YOU THINK IT'S A BROTHER'S DUTY TO HELP HIS SISTER WITH HER HOME-WORK IF SHE'S HAVING TROUBLE?
YES, I SHOULD THINK SO..
GOOD
5-4
DUTY CALLS!
SCHULZ

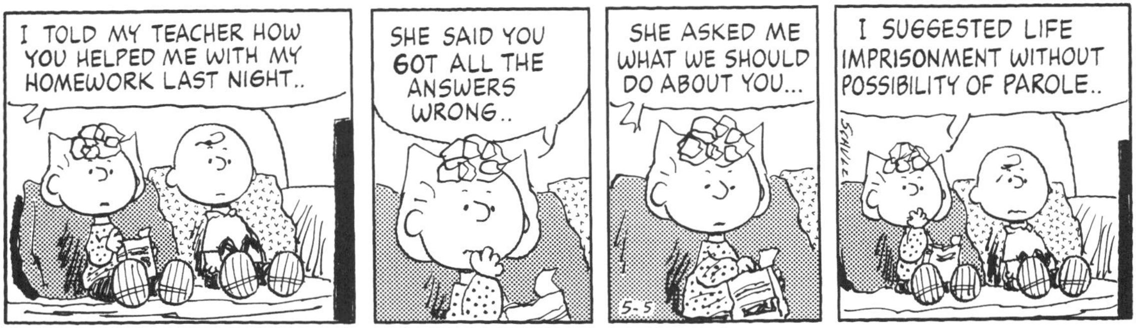
I TOLD MY TEACHER HOW YOU HELPED ME WITH MY HOMEWORK LAST NIGHT..
SHE SAID YOU GOT ALL THE ANSWERS WRONG..
SHE ASKED ME WHAT WE SHOULD DO ABOUT YOU...
5-5
I SUGGESTED LIFE IMPRISONMENT WITHOUT POSSIBILITY OF PAROLE..
SCHULZ

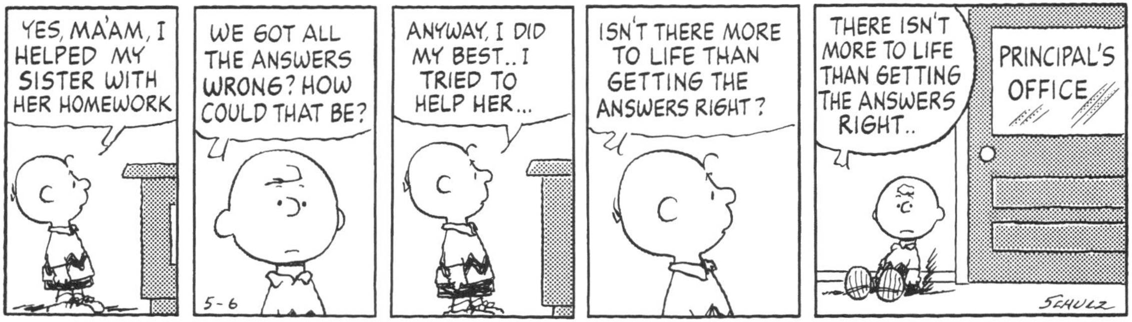
YES, MA'AM, I HELPED MY SISTER WITH HER HOMEWORK
WE GOT ALL THE ANSWERS WRONG? HOW COULD THAT BE?
5-6
ANYWAY, I DID MY BEST.. I TRIED TO HELP HER...
ISN'T THERE MORE TO LIFE THAN GETTING THE ANSWERS RIGHT?
THERE ISN'T MORE TO LIFE THAN GETTING THE ANSWERS RIGHT..
PRINCIPAL'S OFFICE
SCHULZ

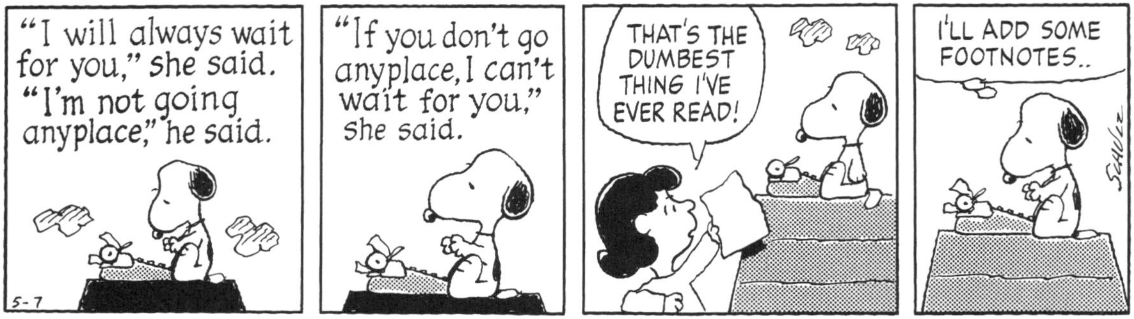
"I will always wait for you," she said. "I'm not going anyplace," he said.
"If you don't go anyplace, I can't wait for you," she said.
THAT'S THE DUMBEST THING I'VE EVER READ!
I'LL ADD SOME FOOTNOTES..

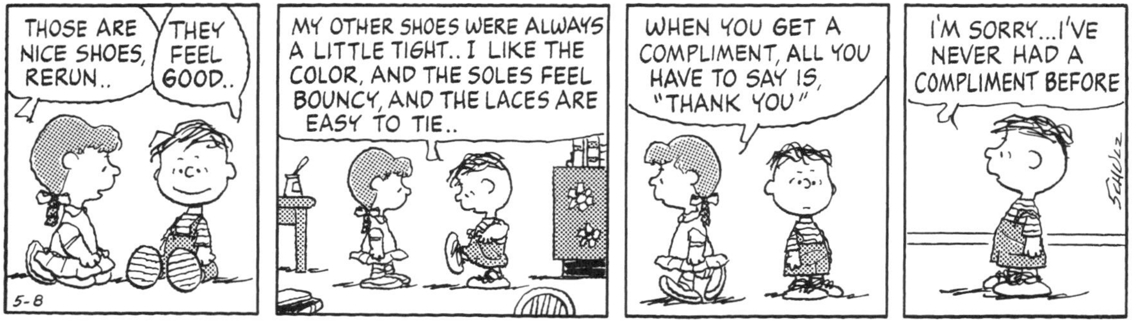
THOSE ARE NICE SHOES, RERUN..
THEY FEEL GOOD..
MY OTHER SHOES WERE ALWAYS A LITTLE TIGHT.. I LIKE THE COLOR, AND THE SOLES FEEL BOUNCY, AND THE LACES ARE EASY TO TIE..
WHEN YOU GET A COMPLIMENT, ALL YOU HAVE TO SAY IS, "THANK YOU"
I'M SORRY...I'VE NEVER HAD A COMPLIMENT BEFORE

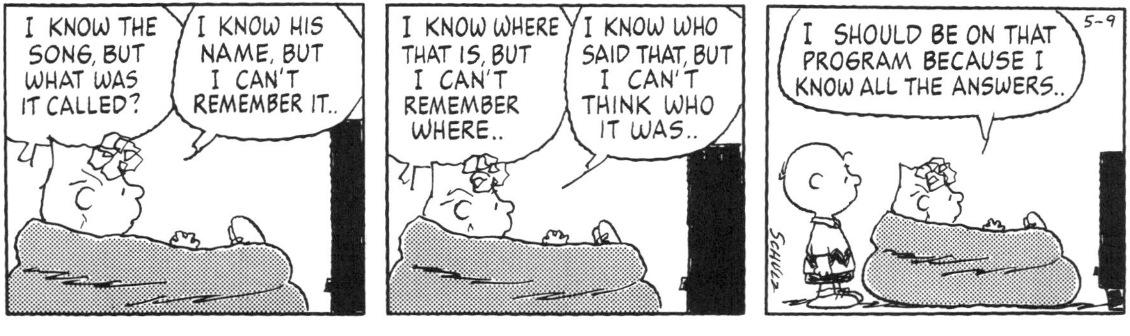
I KNOW THE SONG, BUT WHAT WAS IT CALLED?
I KNOW HIS NAME, BUT I CAN'T REMEMBER IT..
I KNOW WHERE THAT IS, BUT I CAN'T REMEMBER WHERE..
I KNOW WHO SAID THAT, BUT I CAN'T THINK WHO IT WAS..
I SHOULD BE ON THAT PROGRAM BECAUSE I KNOW ALL THE ANSWERS..

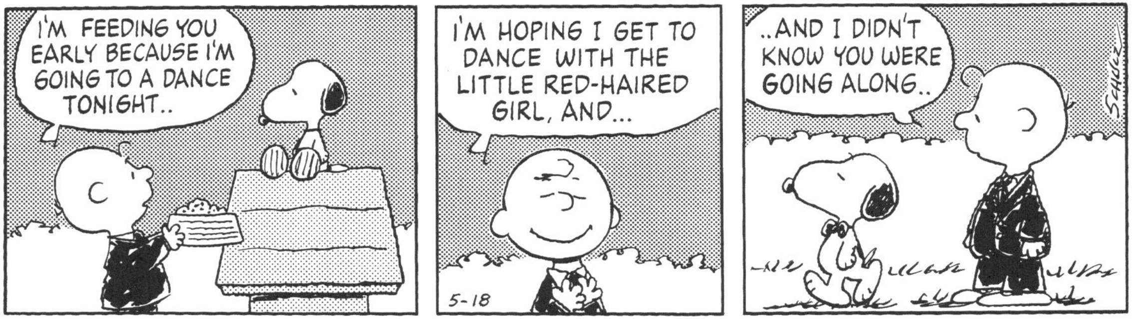
I'M FEEDING YOU EARLY BECAUSE I'M GOING TO A DANCE TONIGHT..
I'M HOPING I GET TO DANCE WITH THE LITTLE RED-HAIRED GIRL, AND...
5-18
..AND I DIDN'T KNOW YOU WERE GOING ALONG..
SCHULZ

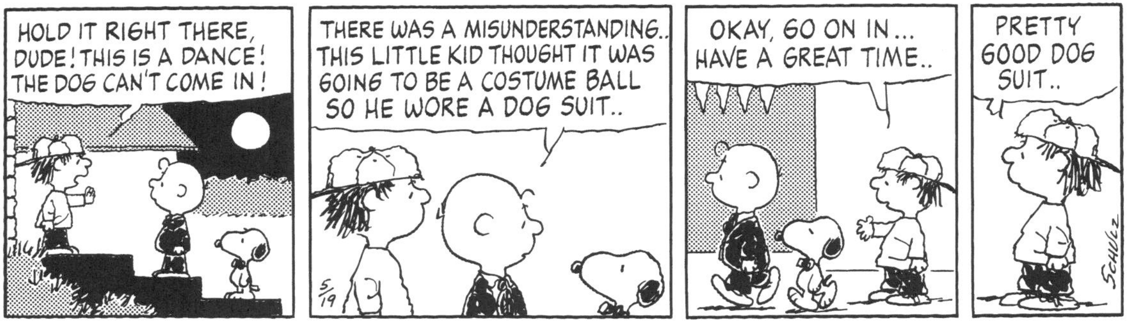
HOLD IT RIGHT THERE, DUDE! THIS IS A DANCE! THE DOG CAN'T COME IN!
THERE WAS A MISUNDERSTANDING.. THIS LITTLE KID THOUGHT IT WAS GOING TO BE A COSTUME BALL SO HE WORE A DOG SUIT..
5/19
OKAY, GO ON IN... HAVE A GREAT TIME..
PRETTY GOOD DOG SUIT..
SCHULZ

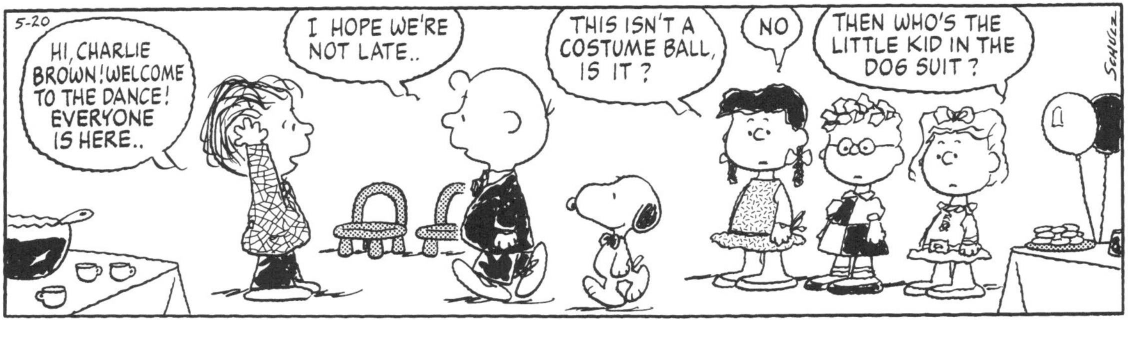
5-20
HI, CHARLIE BROWN! WELCOME TO THE DANCE! EVERYONE IS HERE..
I HOPE WE'RE NOT LATE..
THIS ISN'T A COSTUME BALL, IS IT?
NO
THEN WHO'S THE LITTLE KID IN THE DOG SUIT?
SCHULZ

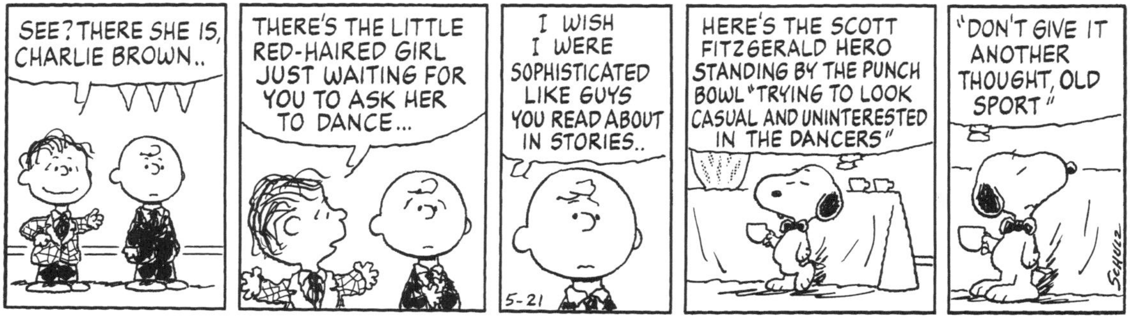
SEE? THERE SHE IS, CHARLIE BROWN..
THERE'S THE LITTLE RED-HAIRED GIRL JUST WAITING FOR YOU TO ASK HER TO DANCE...
I WISH I WERE SOPHISTICATED LIKE GUYS YOU READ ABOUT IN STORIES..
5-21
HERE'S THE SCOTT FITZGERALD HERO STANDING BY THE PUNCH BOWL "TRYING TO LOOK CASUAL AND UNINTERESTED IN THE DANCERS"
"DON'T GIVE IT ANOTHER THOUGHT, OLD SPORT"
SCHULZ

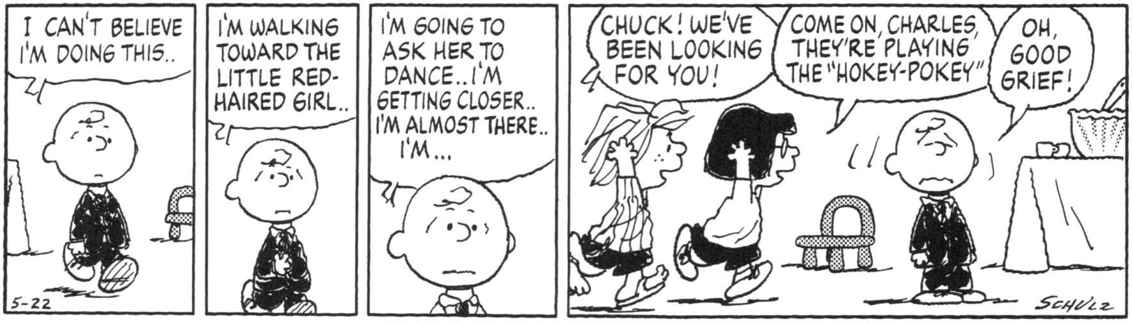
I CAN'T BELIEVE I'M DOING THIS..
5-22
I'M WALKING TOWARD THE LITTLE RED-HAIRED GIRL..
I'M GOING TO ASK HER TO DANCE..I'M GETTING CLOSER.. I'M ALMOST THERE.. I'M...
CHUCK! WE'VE BEEN LOOKING FOR YOU!
COME ON, CHARLES, THEY'RE PLAYING THE "HOKEY-POKEY"
OH, GOOD GRIEF!
SCHULZ

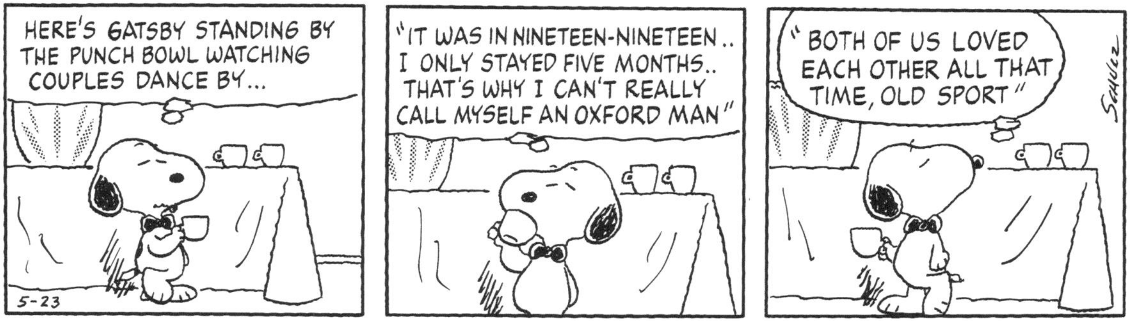
HERE'S GATSBY STANDING BY THE PUNCH BOWL WATCHING COUPLES DANCE BY...
5-23
"IT WAS IN NINETEEN-NINETEEN.. I ONLY STAYED FIVE MONTHS.. THAT'S WHY I CAN'T REALLY CALL MYSELF AN OXFORD MAN"
"BOTH OF US LOVED EACH OTHER ALL THAT TIME, OLD SPORT"
SCHULZ

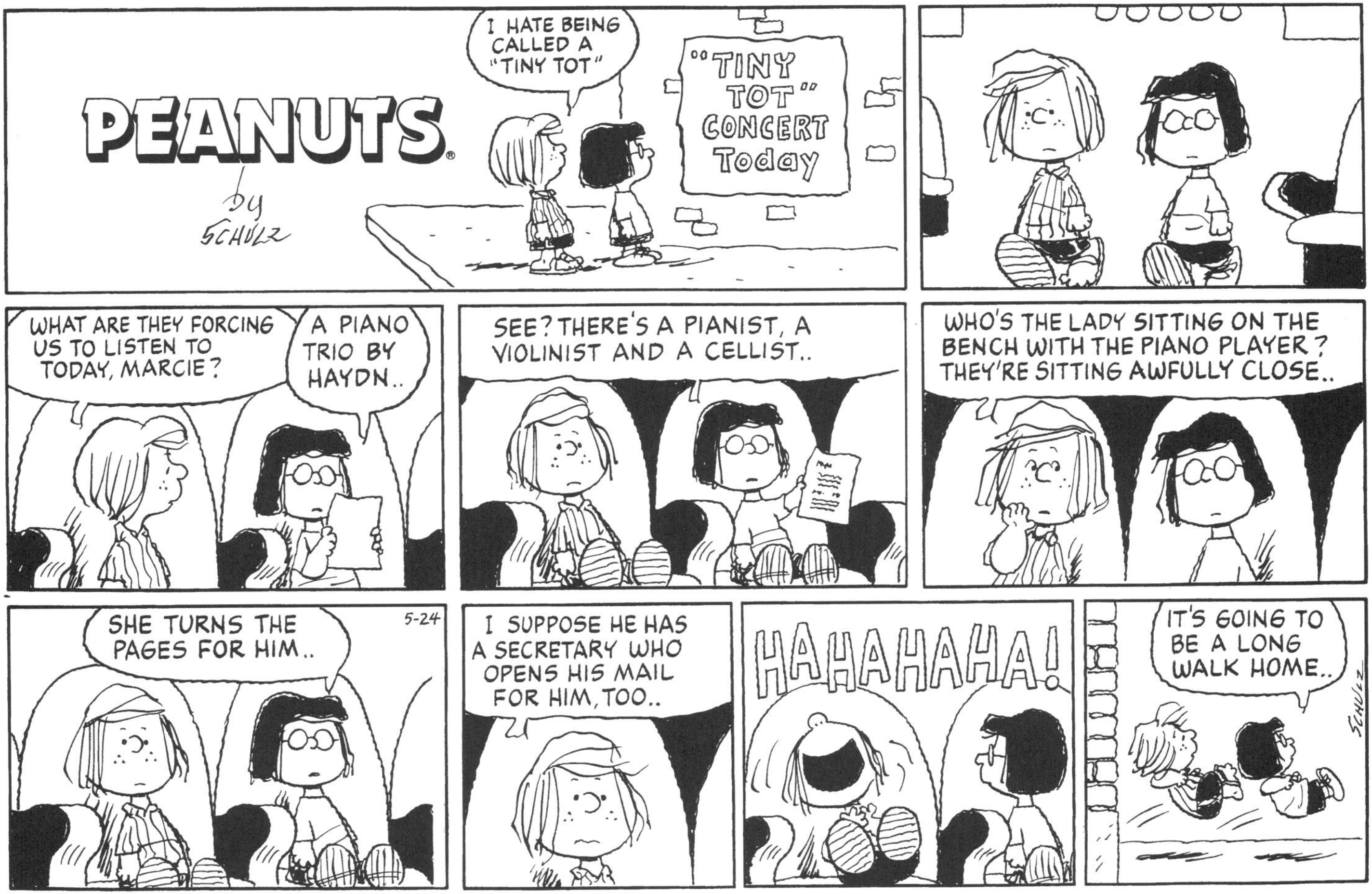
PEANUTS
by SCHULZ
I HATE BEING CALLED A "TINY TOT"
"TINY TOT" CONCERT Today
WHAT ARE THEY FORCING US TO LISTEN TO TODAY, MARCIE?
A PIANO TRIO BY HAYDN..
SEE? THERE'S A PIANIST, A VIOLINIST AND A CELLIST..
WHO'S THE LADY SITTING ON THE BENCH WITH THE PIANO PLAYER? THEY'RE SITTING AWFULLY CLOSE..
5-24
SHE TURNS THE PAGES FOR HIM..
I SUPPOSE HE HAS A SECRETARY WHO OPENS HIS MAIL FOR HIM, TOO..
HAHAHAHAHA!
IT'S GOING TO BE A LONG WALK HOME..
SCHULZ

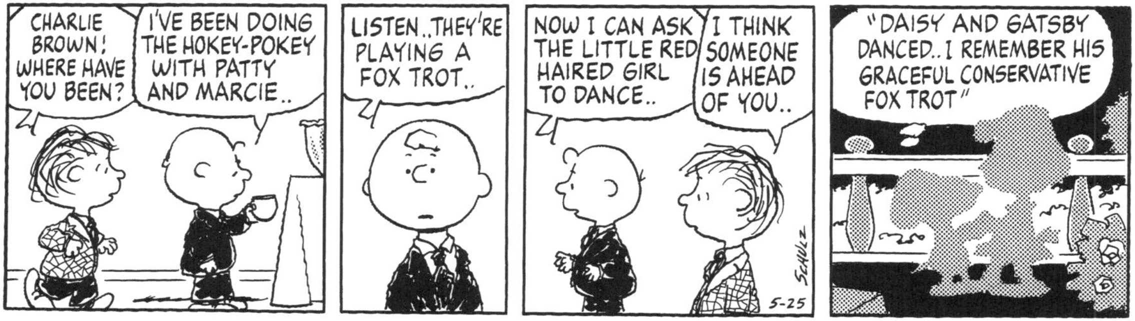
CHARLIE BROWN! WHERE HAVE YOU BEEN?
I'VE BEEN DOING THE HOKEY-POKEY WITH PATTY AND MARCIE..
LISTEN..THEY'RE PLAYING A FOX TROT..
NOW I CAN ASK THE LITTLE RED HAIRED GIRL TO DANCE..
I THINK SOMEONE IS AHEAD OF YOU..
SCHULZ
5-25
"DAISY AND GATSBY DANCED..I REMEMBER HIS GRACEFUL CONSERVATIVE FOX TROT"

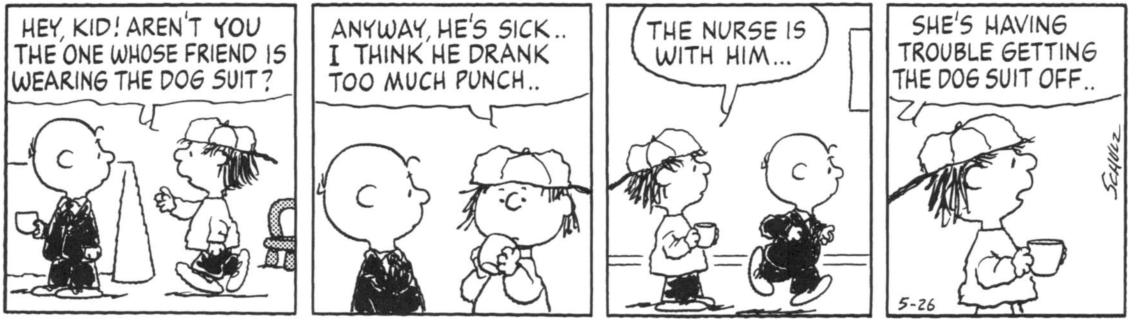
HEY, KID! AREN'T YOU THE ONE WHOSE FRIEND IS WEARING THE DOG SUIT?
ANYWAY, HE'S SICK.. I THINK HE DRANK TOO MUCH PUNCH..
THE NURSE IS WITH HIM...
SHE'S HAVING TROUBLE GETTING THE DOG SUIT OFF..
SCHULZ
5-26

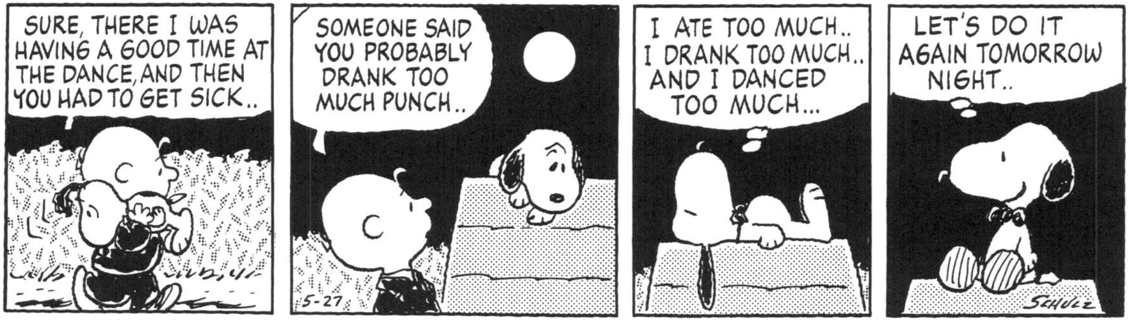
SURE, THERE I WAS HAVING A GOOD TIME AT THE DANCE, AND THEN YOU HAD TO GET SICK..
SOMEONE SAID YOU PROBABLY DRANK TOO MUCH PUNCH..
5-27
I ATE TOO MUCH.. I DRANK TOO MUCH.. AND I DANCED TOO MUCH...
LET'S DO IT AGAIN TOMORROW NIGHT..
SCHULZ

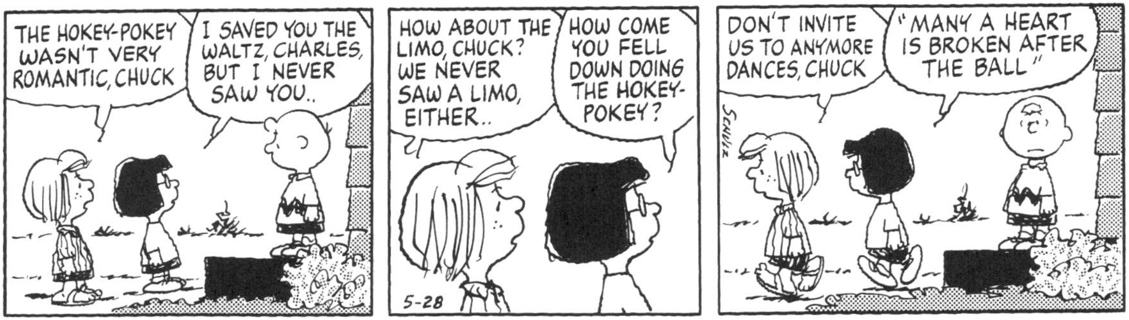
THE HOKEY-POKEY WASN'T VERY ROMANTIC, CHUCK
I SAVED YOU THE WALTZ, CHARLES, BUT I NEVER SAW YOU..
HOW ABOUT THE LIMO, CHUCK? WE NEVER SAW A LIMO, EITHER..
HOW COME YOU FELL DOWN DOING THE HOKEY-POKEY?
5-28
DON'T INVITE US TO ANYMORE DANCES, CHUCK
"MANY A HEART IS BROKEN AFTER THE BALL"
SCHULZ

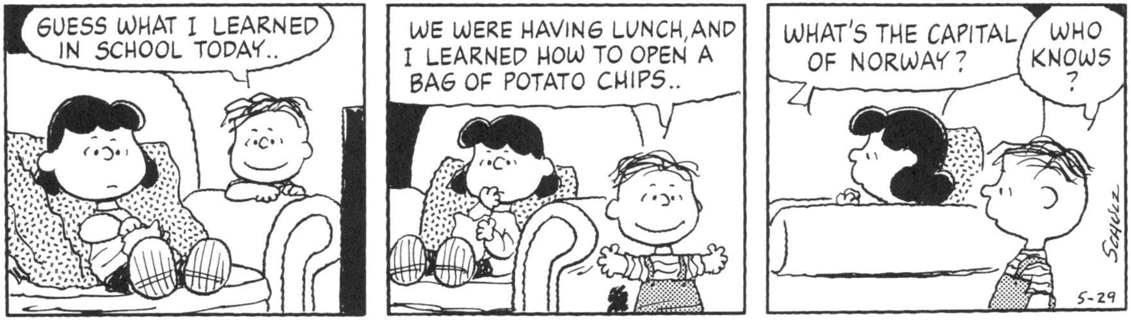
GUESS WHAT I LEARNED IN SCHOOL TODAY..
WE WERE HAVING LUNCH, AND I LEARNED HOW TO OPEN A BAG OF POTATO CHIPS..
WHAT'S THE CAPITAL OF NORWAY?
WHO KNOWS?
SCHULZ
5-29

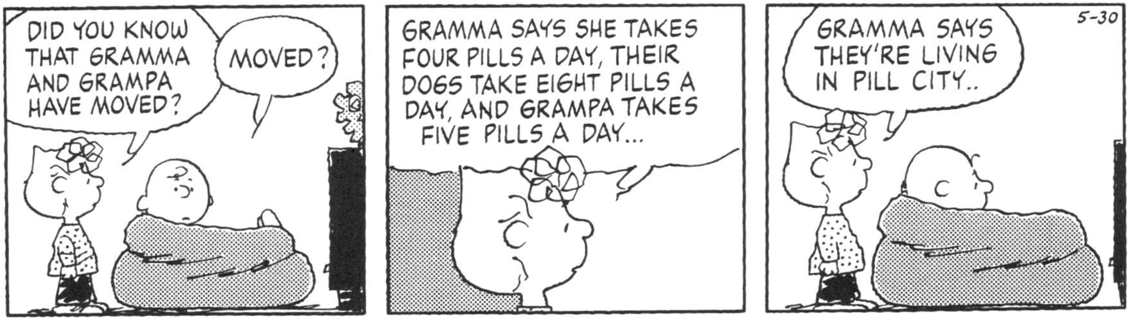
DID YOU KNOW THAT GRAMMA AND GRAMPA HAVE MOVED?
MOVED?
GRAMMA SAYS SHE TAKES FOUR PILLS A DAY, THEIR DOGS TAKE EIGHT PILLS A DAY, AND GRAMPA TAKES FIVE PILLS A DAY...
5-30
GRAMMA SAYS THEY'RE LIVING IN PILL CITY..

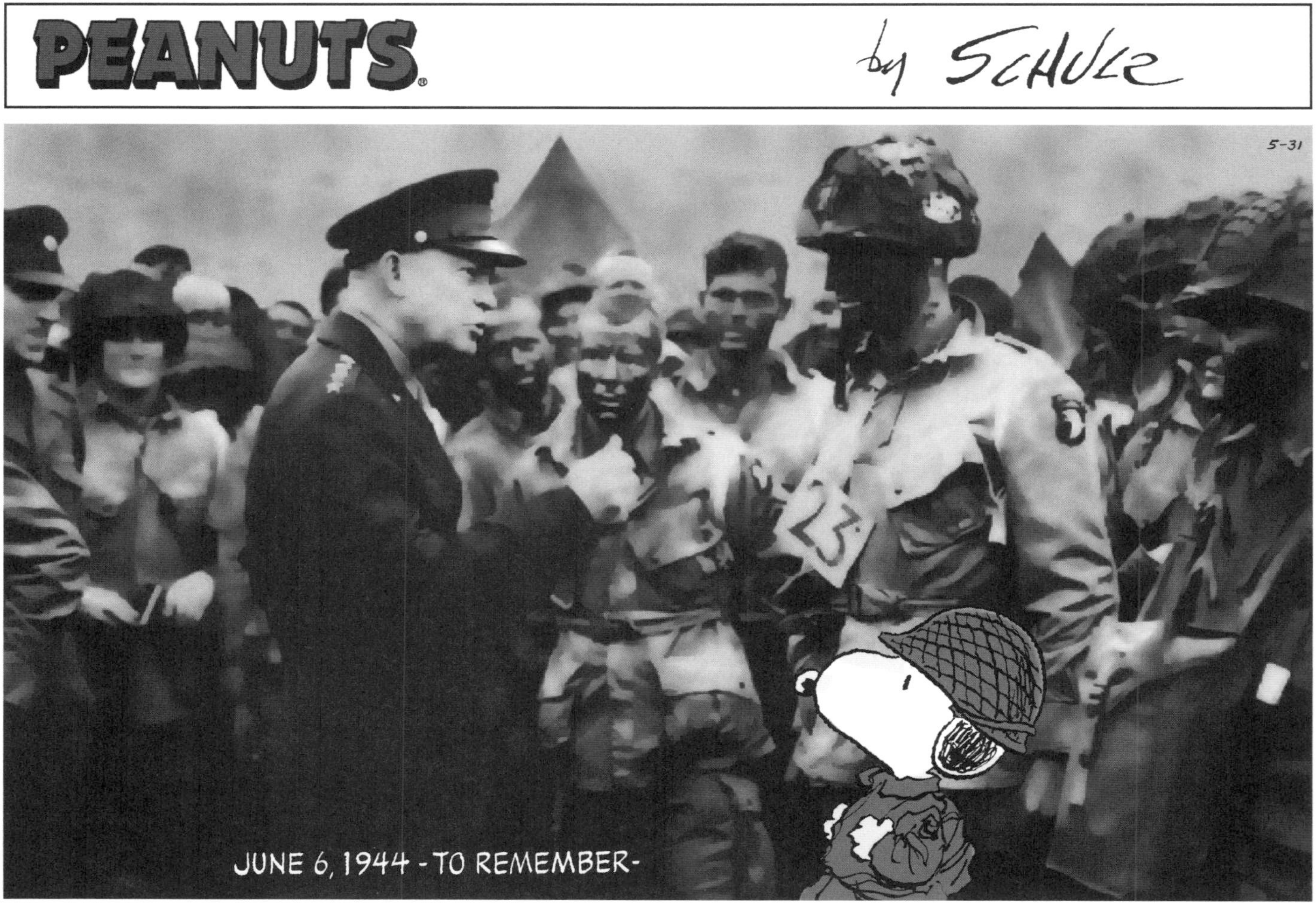

PEANUTS
by SCHULZ
5-31
JUNE 6, 1944 - TO REMEMBER-

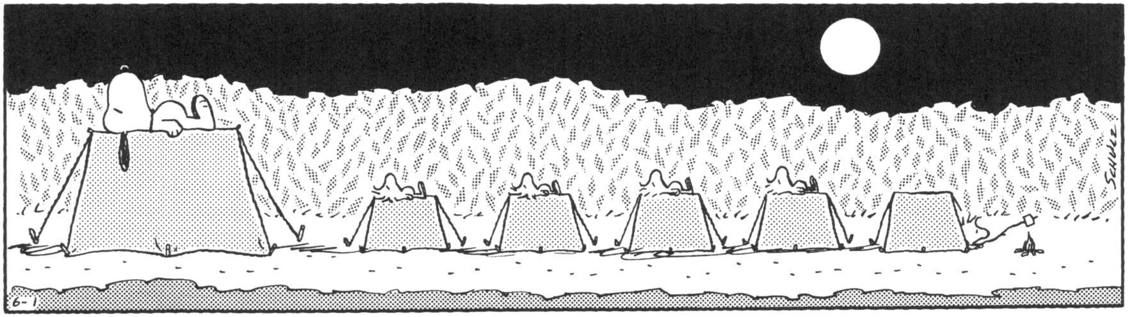

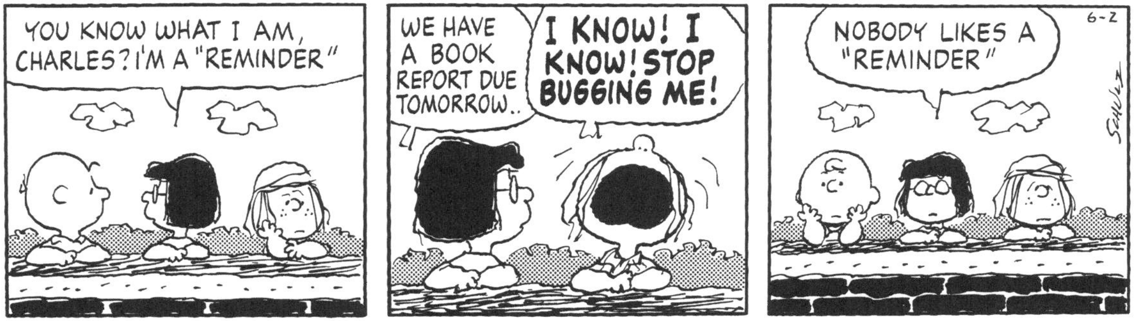
YOU KNOW WHAT I AM, CHARLES? I'M A "REMINDER"
WE HAVE A BOOK REPORT DUE TOMORROW..
I KNOW! I KNOW! STOP BUGGING ME!
NOBODY LIKES A "REMINDER"

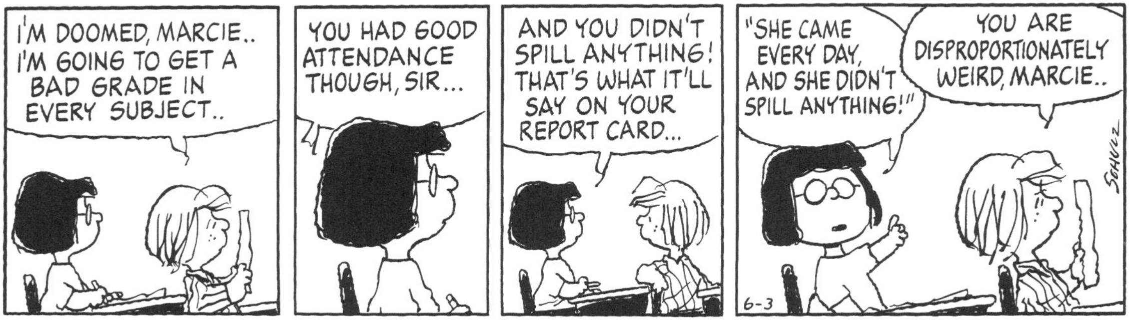
I'M DOOMED, MARCIE.. I'M GOING TO GET A BAD GRADE IN EVERY SUBJECT..
YOU HAD GOOD ATTENDANCE THOUGH, SIR...
AND YOU DIDN'T SPILL ANYTHING! THAT'S WHAT IT'LL SAY ON YOUR REPORT CARD...
"SHE CAME EVERY DAY, AND SHE DIDN'T SPILL ANYTHING!"
YOU ARE DISPROPORTIONATELY WEIRD, MARCIE..

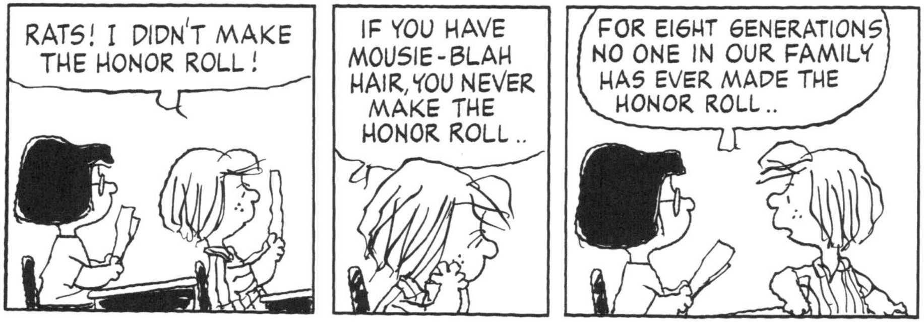
RATS! I DIDN'T MAKE THE HONOR ROLL!
IF YOU HAVE MOUSIE-BLAH HAIR, YOU NEVER MAKE THE HONOR ROLL..
FOR EIGHT GENERATIONS NO ONE IN OUR FAMILY HAS EVER MADE THE HONOR ROLL..
THEY ALL HAD MOUSIE-BLAH HAIR..
6-4

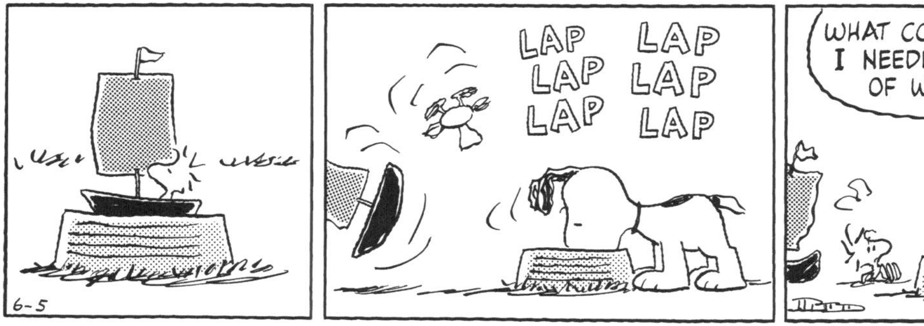
6-5
LAP LAP LAP
LAP LAP LAP
WHAT COULD I DO? I NEEDED A DRINK OF WATER..

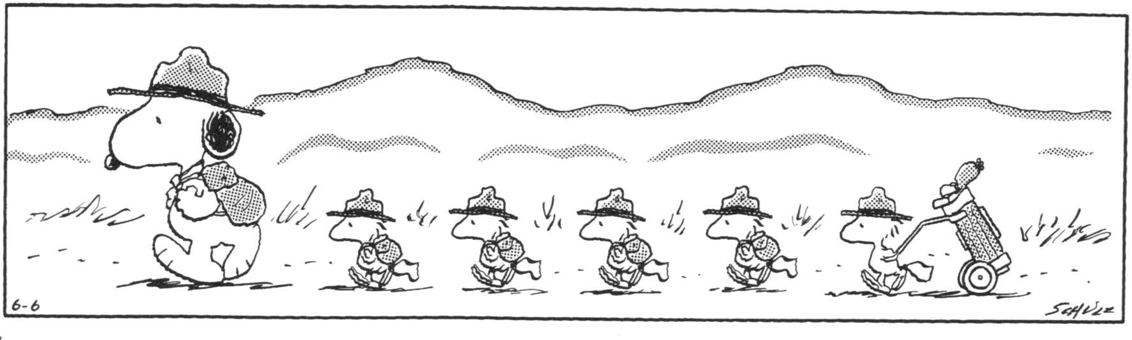
6-6

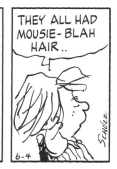

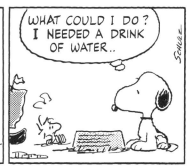

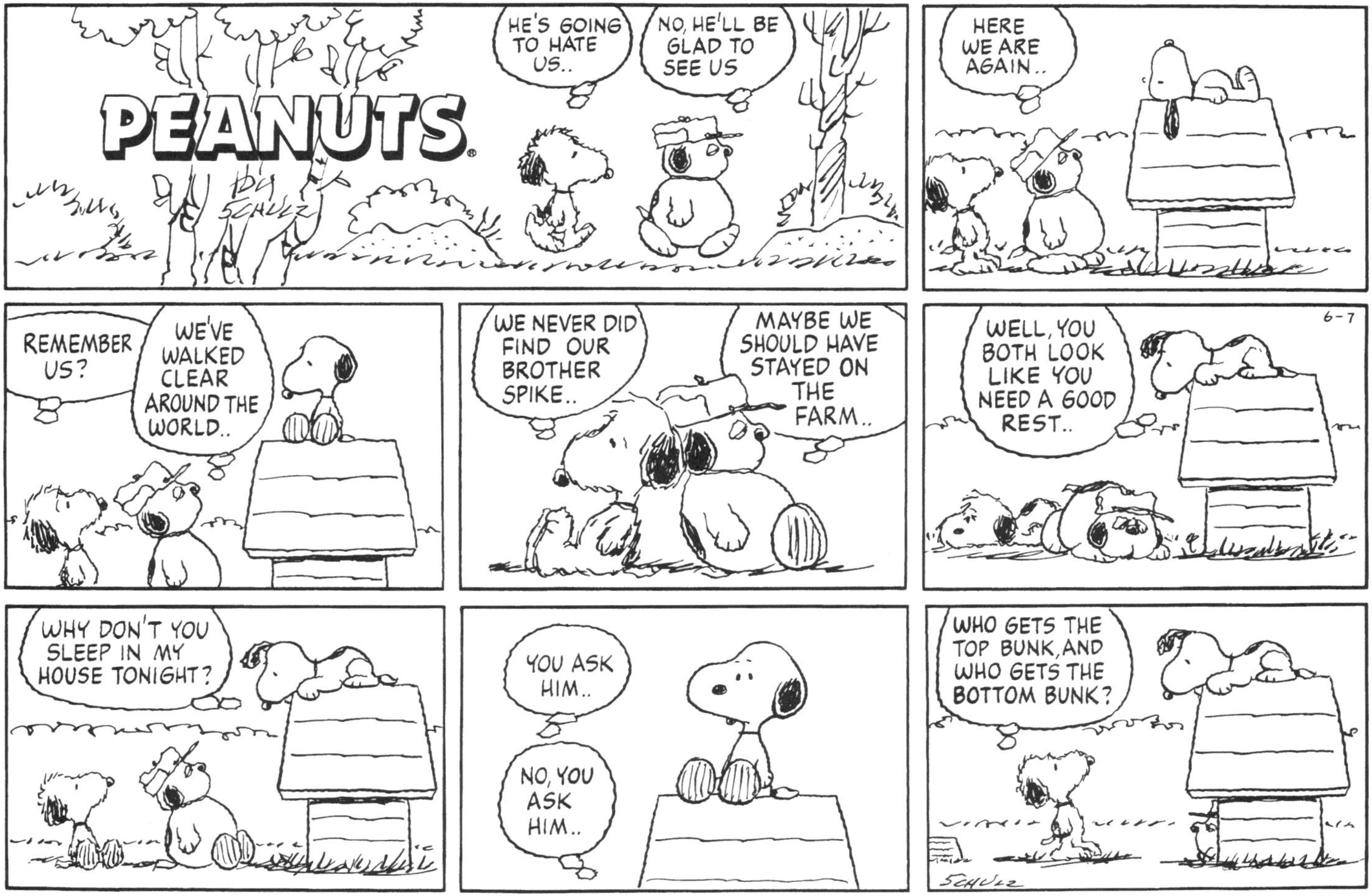
PEANUTS
by SCHULZ
HE'S GOING TO HATE US..
NO, HE'LL BE GLAD TO SEE US
HERE WE ARE AGAIN..
REMEMBER US?
WE'VE WALKED CLEAR AROUND THE WORLD..
WE NEVER DID FIND OUR BROTHER SPIKE..
MAYBE WE SHOULD HAVE STAYED ON THE FARM..
WELL, YOU BOTH LOOK LIKE YOU NEED A GOOD REST..
6-7
WHY DON'T YOU SLEEP IN MY HOUSE TONIGHT?
YOU ASK HIM..
NO, YOU ASK HIM..
WHO GETS THE TOP BUNK, AND WHO GETS THE BOTTOM BUNK?
SCHULZ

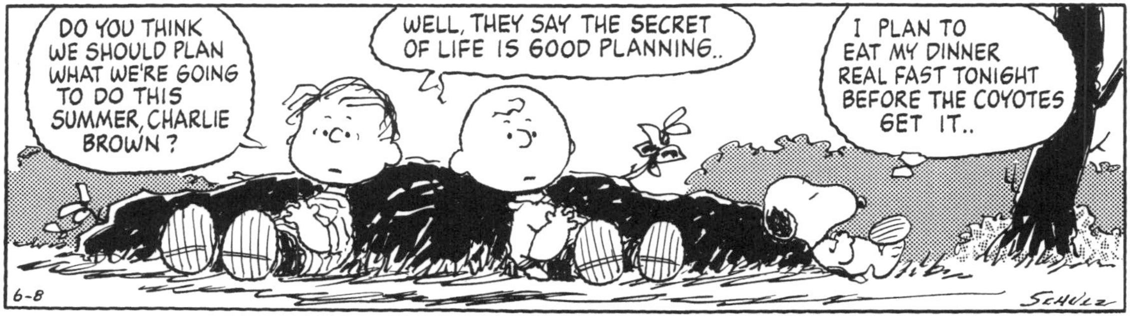
DO YOU THINK WE SHOULD PLAN WHAT WE'RE GOING TO DO THIS SUMMER, CHARLIE BROWN?
WELL, THEY SAY THE SECRET OF LIFE IS GOOD PLANNING..
I PLAN TO EAT MY DINNER REAL FAST TONIGHT BEFORE THE COYOTES GET IT..
6-8
SCHULZ

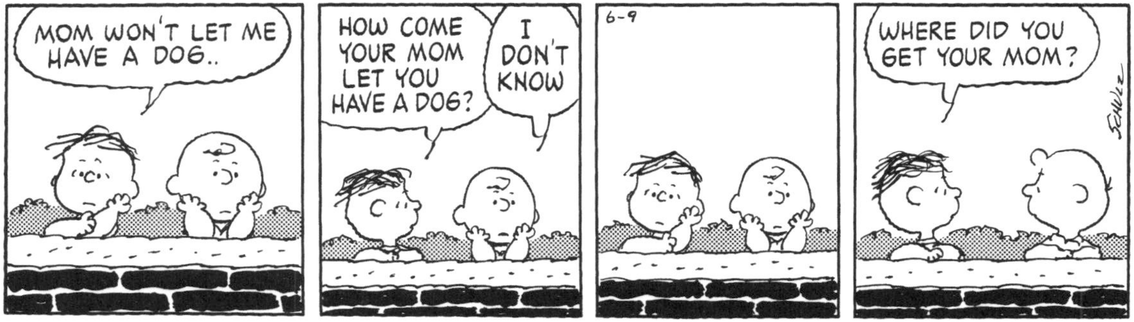
MOM WON'T LET ME HAVE A DOG..
HOW COME YOUR MOM LET YOU HAVE A DOG?
I DON'T KNOW
6-9
WHERE DID YOU GET YOUR MOM?
SCHULZ

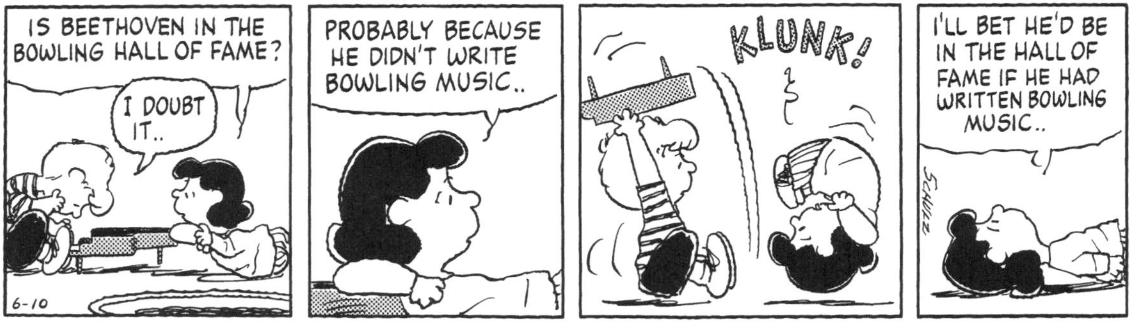
IS BEETHOVEN IN THE BOWLING HALL OF FAME?
I DOUBT IT..
6-10
PROBABLY BECAUSE HE DIDN'T WRITE BOWLING MUSIC..
KLUNK!
I'LL BET HE'D BE IN THE HALL OF FAME IF HE HAD WRITTEN BOWLING MUSIC..
SCHULZ

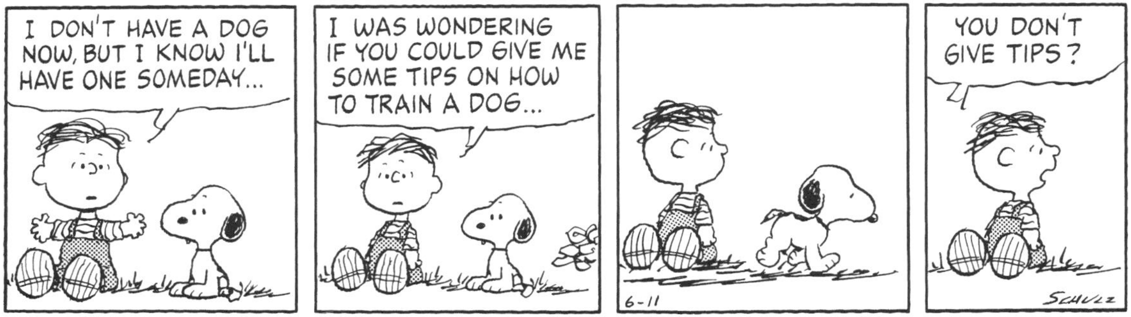
I DON'T HAVE A DOG NOW, BUT I KNOW I'LL HAVE ONE SOMEDAY...
I WAS WONDERING IF YOU COULD GIVE ME SOME TIPS ON HOW TO TRAIN A DOG...
6-11
YOU DON'T GIVE TIPS?

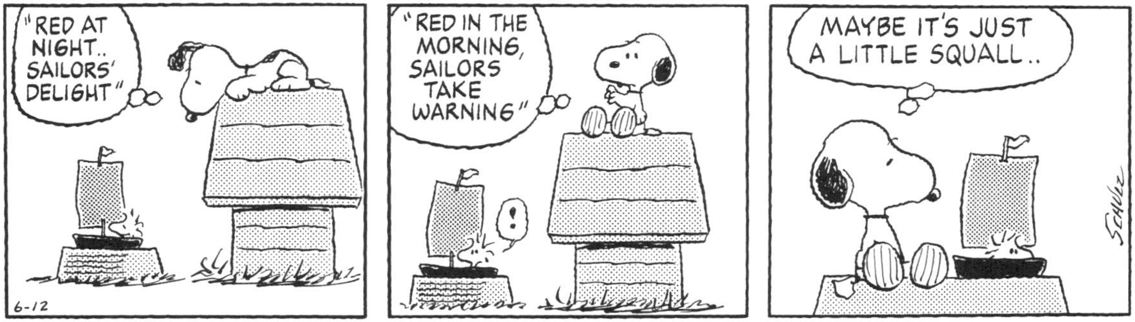
"RED AT NIGHT.. SAILORS' DELIGHT"
6-12
"RED IN THE MORNING, SAILORS TAKE WARNING"
!
MAYBE IT'S JUST A LITTLE SQUALL..

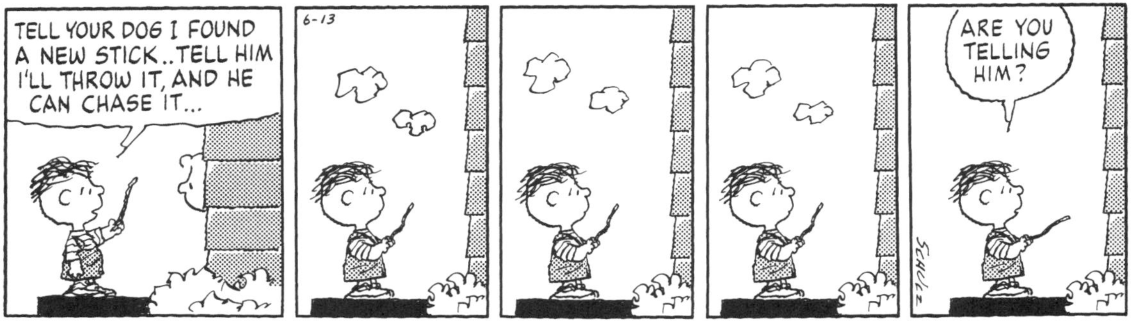
TELL YOUR DOG I FOUND A NEW STICK..TELL HIM I'LL THROW IT, AND HE CAN CHASE IT...
6-13
ARE YOU TELLING HIM?

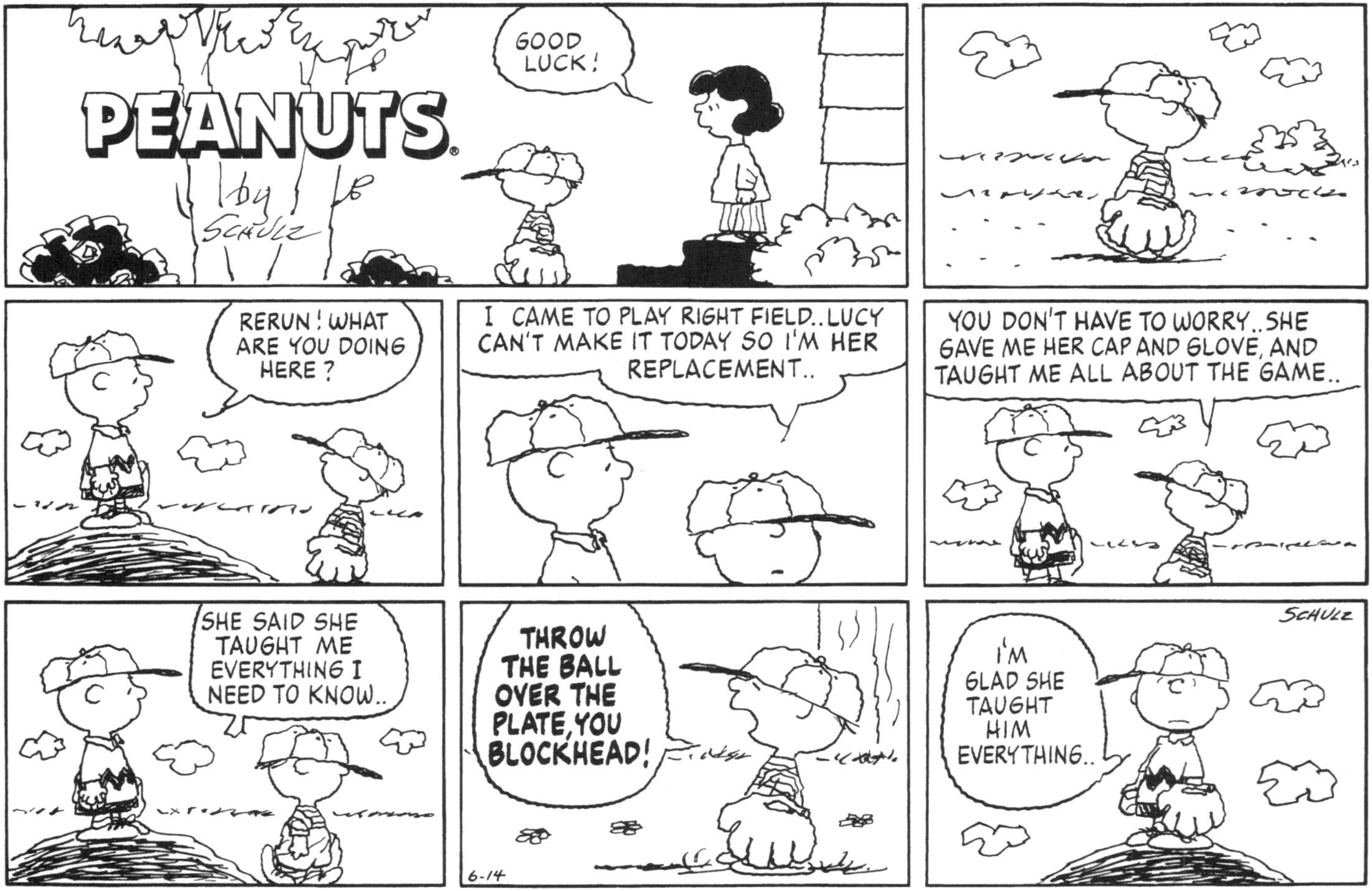
PEANUTS®
by SCHULZ
GOOD LUCK!
RERUN! WHAT ARE YOU DOING HERE?
I CAME TO PLAY RIGHT FIELD..LUCY CAN'T MAKE IT TODAY SO I'M HER REPLACEMENT..
YOU DON'T HAVE TO WORRY..SHE GAVE ME HER CAP AND GLOVE, AND TAUGHT ME ALL ABOUT THE GAME..
SHE SAID SHE TAUGHT ME EVERYTHING I NEED TO KNOW..
THROW THE BALL OVER THE PLATE, YOU BLOCKHEAD!
6-14
SCHULZ
I'M GLAD SHE TAUGHT HIM EVERYTHING..

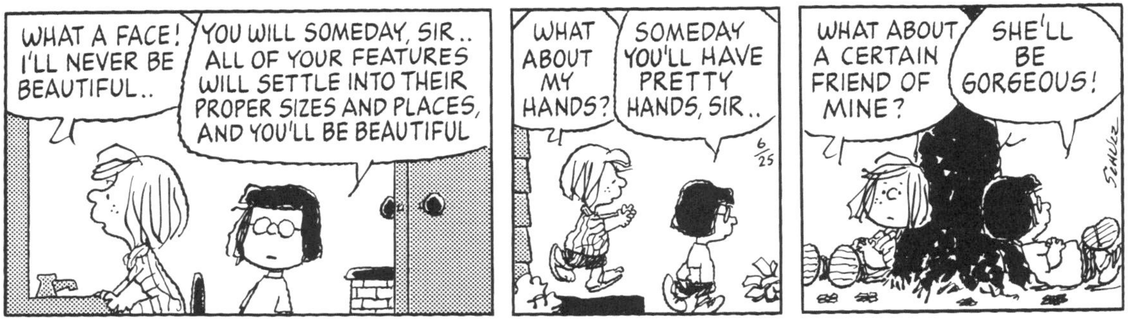
WHAT A FACE! I'LL NEVER BE BEAUTIFUL..
YOU WILL SOMEDAY, SIR.. ALL OF YOUR FEATURES WILL SETTLE INTO THEIR PROPER SIZES AND PLACES, AND YOU'LL BE BEAUTIFUL
WHAT ABOUT MY HANDS?
SOMEDAY YOU'LL HAVE PRETTY HANDS, SIR..
6/25
WHAT ABOUT A CERTAIN FRIEND OF MINE?
SHE'LL BE GORGEOUS!
SCHULZ

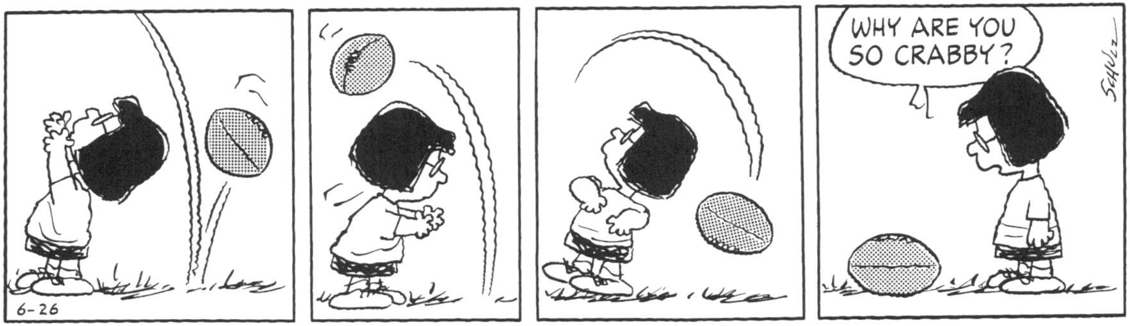
6-26
WHY ARE YOU SO CRABBY?
SCHULZ

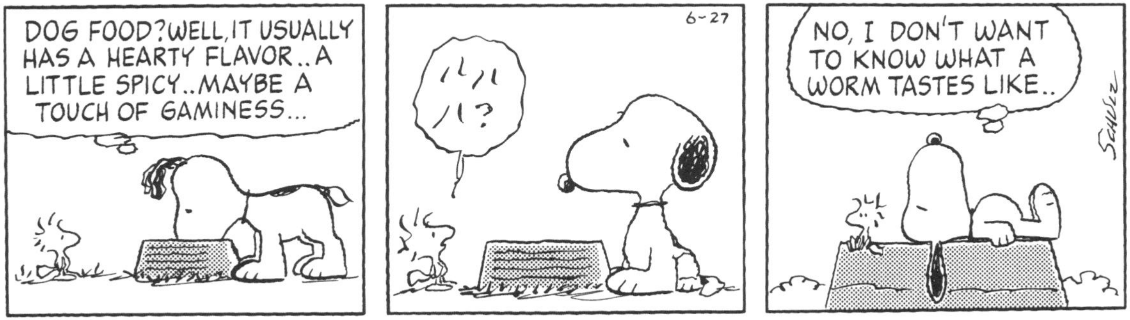
DOG FOOD? WELL, IT USUALLY HAS A HEARTY FLAVOR.. A LITTLE SPICY.. MAYBE A TOUCH OF GAMINESS...
6-27
NO, I DON'T WANT TO KNOW WHAT A WORM TASTES LIKE..
SCHULZ

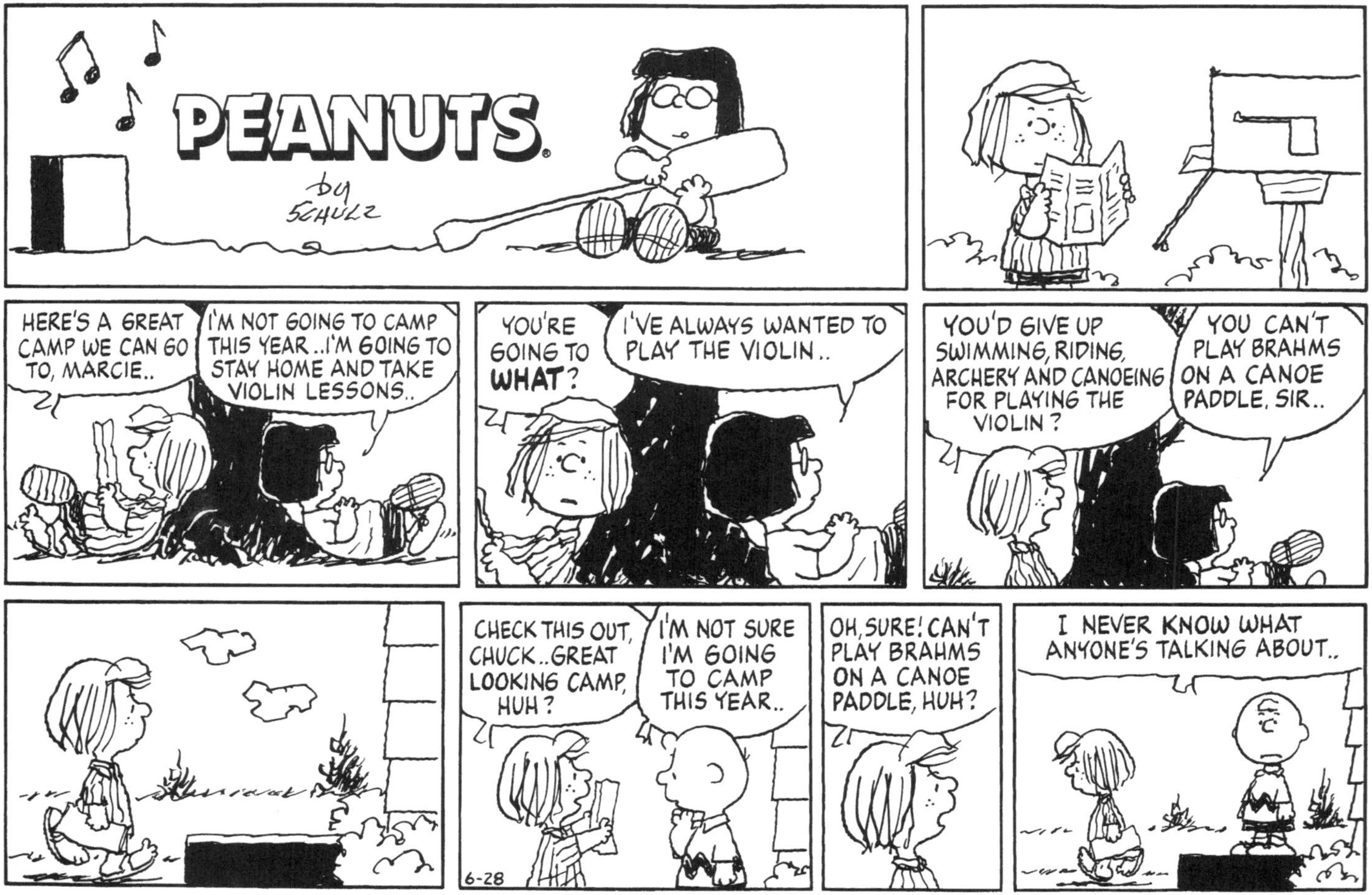
PEANUTS
by SCHULZ
HERE'S A GREAT CAMP WE CAN GO TO, MARCIE..
I'M NOT GOING TO CAMP THIS YEAR..I'M GOING TO STAY HOME AND TAKE VIOLIN LESSONS..
YOU'RE GOING TO **WHAT**?
I'VE ALWAYS WANTED TO PLAY THE VIOLIN..
YOU'D GIVE UP SWIMMING, RIDING, ARCHERY AND CANOEING FOR PLAYING THE VIOLIN?
YOU CAN'T PLAY BRAHMS ON A CANOE PADDLE, SIR..
CHECK THIS OUT, CHUCK..GREAT LOOKING CAMP, HUH?
I'M NOT SURE I'M GOING TO CAMP THIS YEAR..
6-28
OH, SURE! CAN'T PLAY BRAHMS ON A CANOE PADDLE, HUH?
I NEVER KNOW WHAT ANYONE'S TALKING ABOUT..

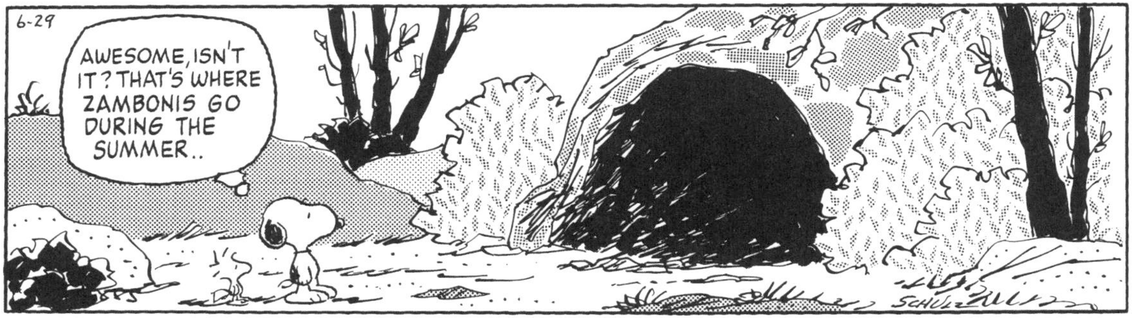
6-29
AWESOME, ISN'T IT? THAT'S WHERE ZAMBONIS GO DURING THE SUMMER..
SCHULZ

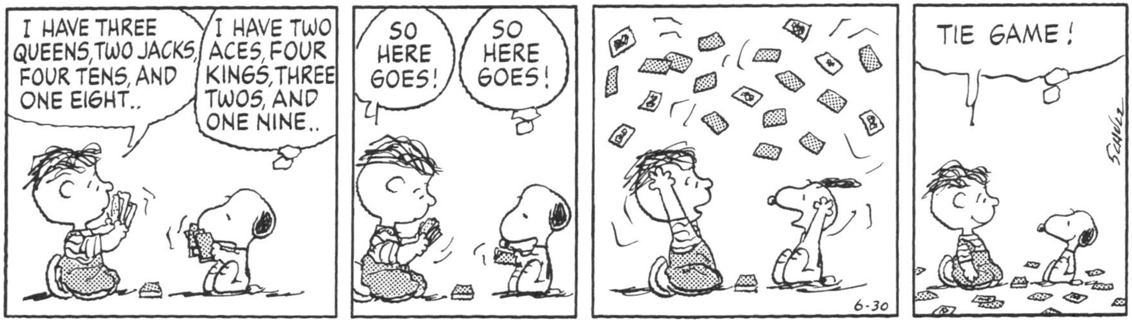
I HAVE THREE QUEENS, TWO JACKS, FOUR TENS, AND ONE EIGHT..
I HAVE TWO ACES, FOUR KINGS, THREE TWOS, AND ONE NINE..
SO HERE GOES!
SO HERE GOES!
6-30
TIE GAME!
SCHULZ

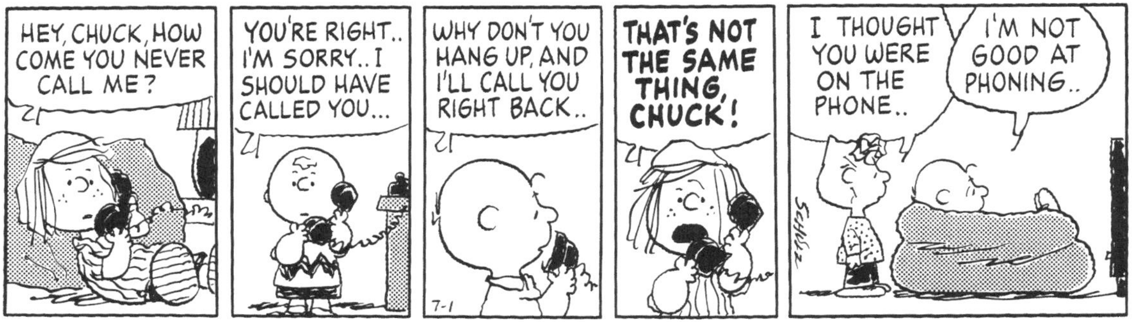
HEY, CHUCK, HOW COME YOU NEVER CALL ME?
YOU'RE RIGHT.. I'M SORRY.. I SHOULD HAVE CALLED YOU...
WHY DON'T YOU HANG UP, AND I'LL CALL YOU RIGHT BACK..
7-1
THAT'S NOT THE SAME THING, CHUCK!
SCHULZ
I THOUGHT YOU WERE ON THE PHONE..
I'M NOT GOOD AT PHONING..

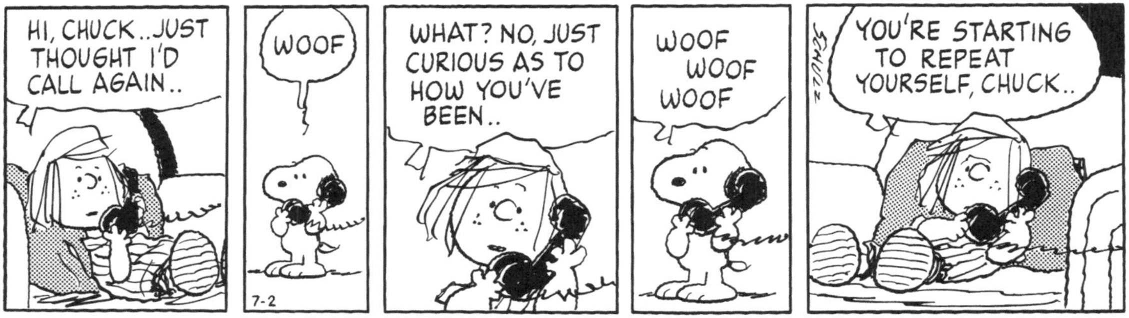
HI, CHUCK.. JUST THOUGHT I'D CALL AGAIN..
WOOF
7-2
WHAT? NO, JUST CURIOUS AS TO HOW YOU'VE BEEN..
WOOF WOOF WOOF
SCHULZ
YOU'RE STARTING TO REPEAT YOURSELF, CHUCK..

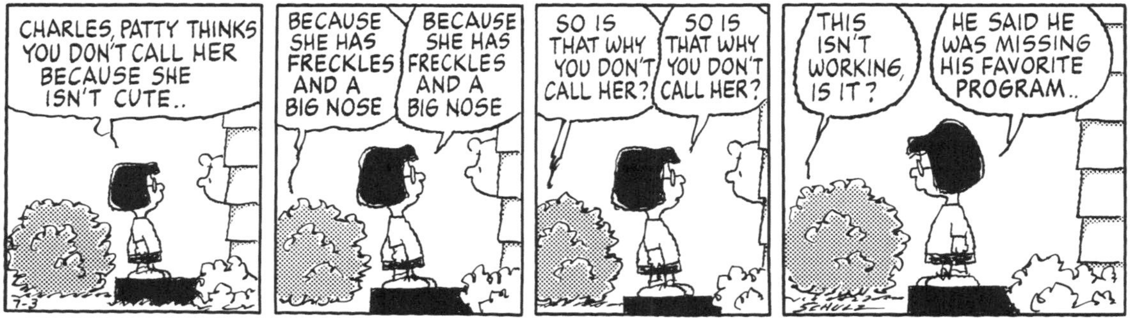
CHARLES, PATTY THINKS YOU DON'T CALL HER BECAUSE SHE ISN'T CUTE..
7-3
BECAUSE SHE HAS FRECKLES AND A BIG NOSE
BECAUSE SHE HAS FRECKLES AND A BIG NOSE
SO IS THAT WHY YOU DON'T CALL HER?
SO IS THAT WHY YOU DON'T CALL HER?
THIS ISN'T WORKING, IS IT?
HE SAID HE WAS MISSING HIS FAVORITE PROGRAM..
SCHULZ

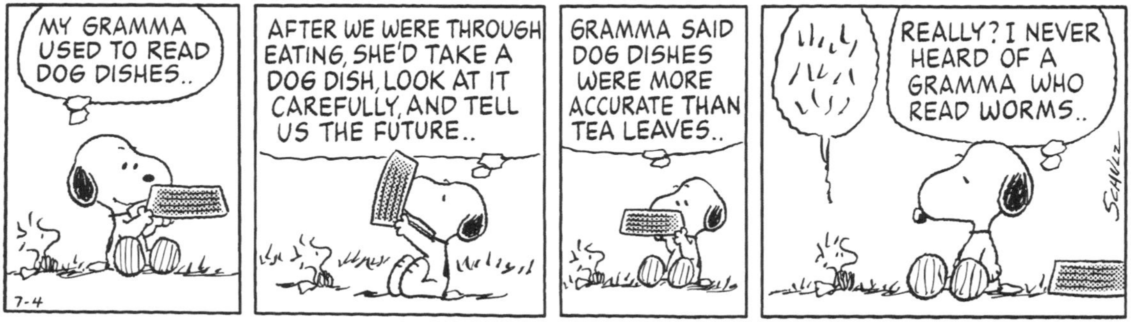
MY GRAMMA USED TO READ DOG DISHES..
7-4
AFTER WE WERE THROUGH EATING, SHE'D TAKE A DOG DISH, LOOK AT IT CAREFULLY, AND TELL US THE FUTURE..
GRAMMA SAID DOG DISHES WERE MORE ACCURATE THAN TEA LEAVES..
REALLY? I NEVER HEARD OF A GRAMMA WHO READ WORMS..
SCHULZ

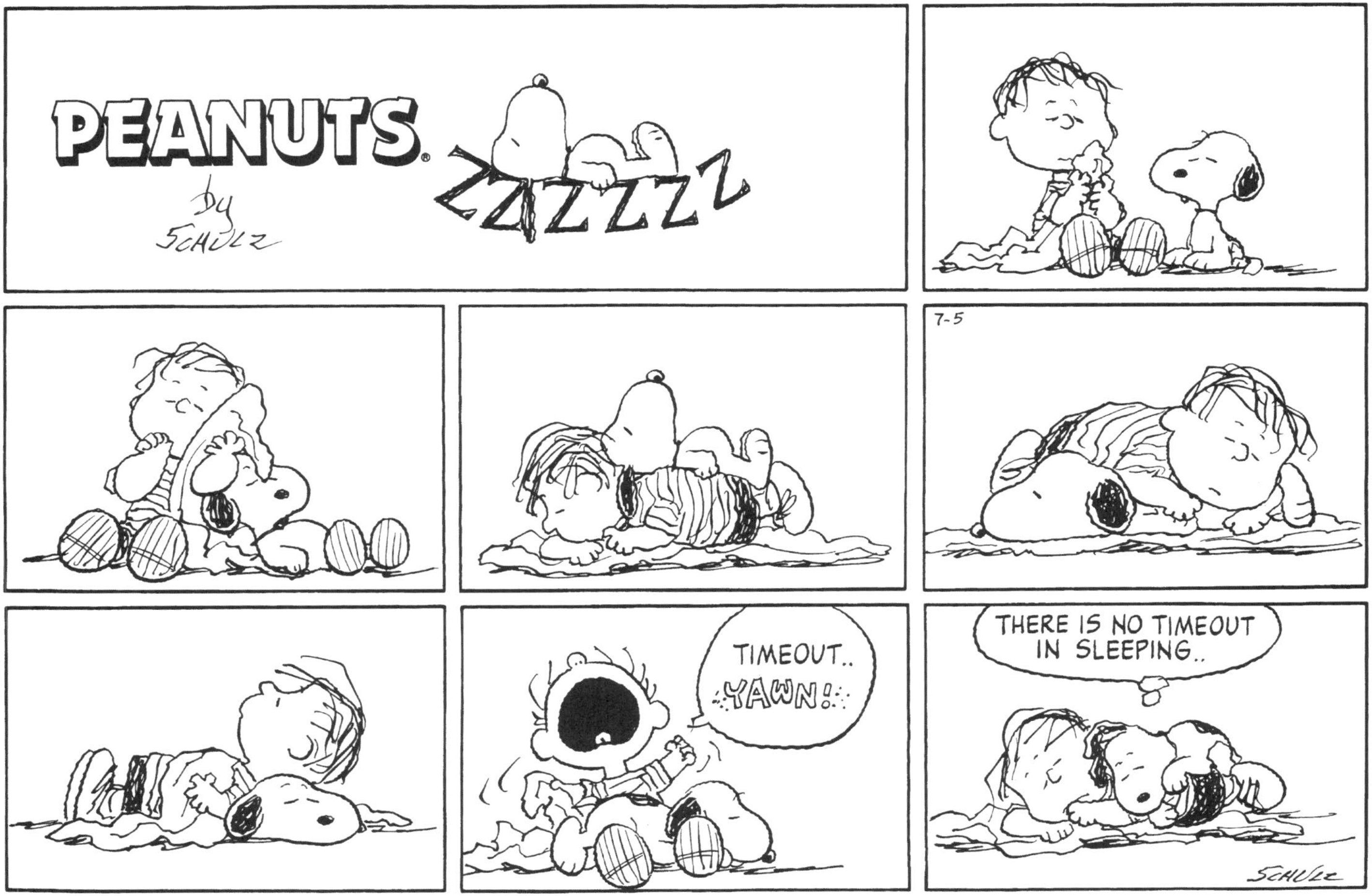
PEANUTS
by SCHULZ
ZZZZZZ
7-5
TIMEOUT..
YAWN!
THERE IS NO TIMEOUT IN SLEEPING..
SCHULZ

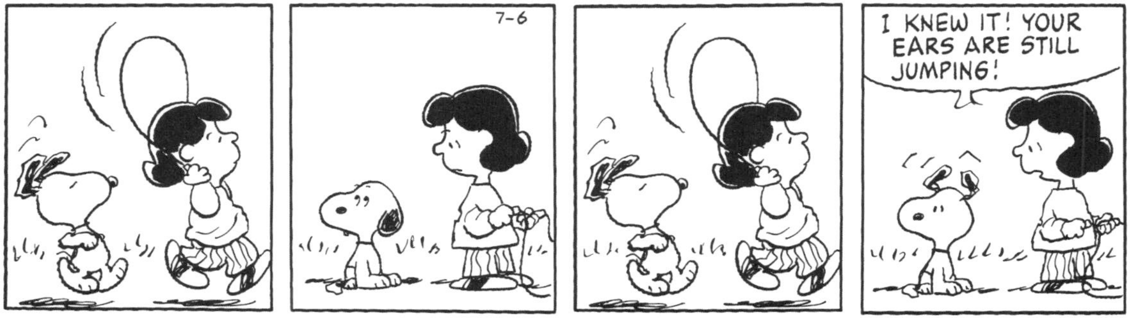
7-6
I KNEW IT! YOUR EARS ARE STILL JUMPING!

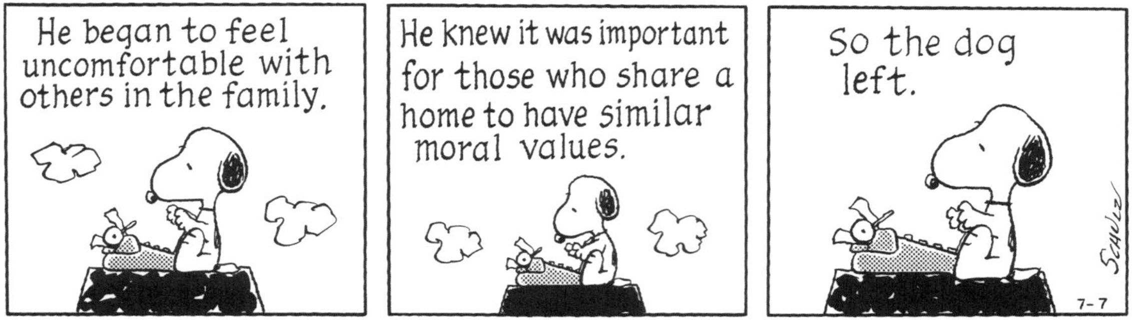
He began to feel uncomfortable with others in the family.
He knew it was important for those who share a home to have similar moral values.
So the dog left.
SCHULZ
7-7

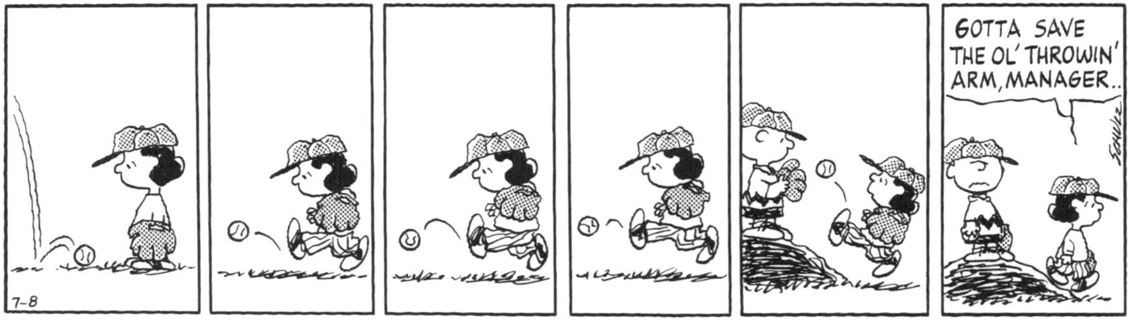
7-8
GOTTA SAVE THE OL' THROWIN' ARM, MANAGER..
SCHULZ

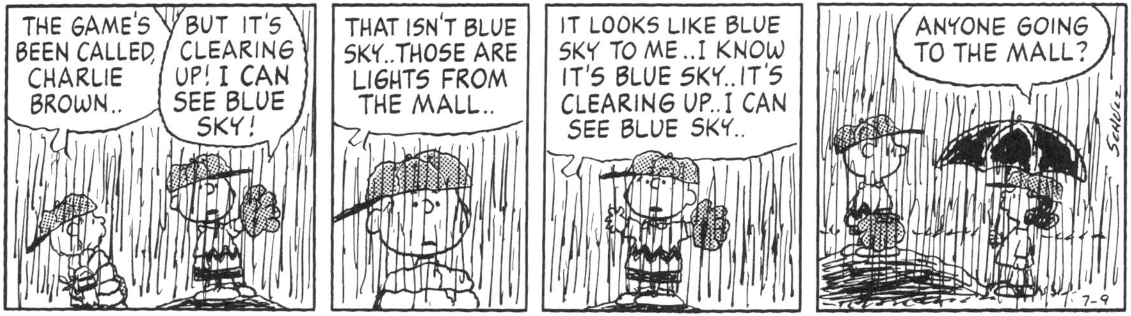
THE GAME'S BEEN CALLED, CHARLIE BROWN..
BUT IT'S CLEARING UP! I CAN SEE BLUE SKY!
THAT ISN'T BLUE SKY..THOSE ARE LIGHTS FROM THE MALL..
IT LOOKS LIKE BLUE SKY TO ME..I KNOW IT'S BLUE SKY..IT'S CLEARING UP..I CAN SEE BLUE SKY..
ANYONE GOING TO THE MALL?
SCHULZ
7-9

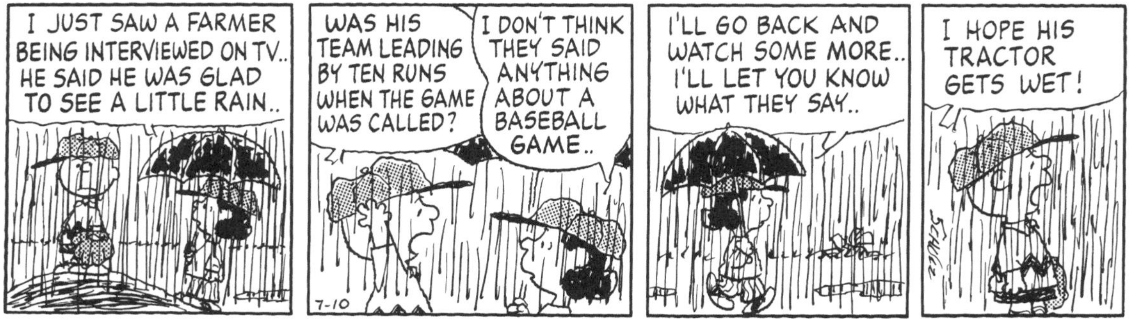
I JUST SAW A FARMER BEING INTERVIEWED ON TV.. HE SAID HE WAS GLAD TO SEE A LITTLE RAIN..
WAS HIS TEAM LEADING BY TEN RUNS WHEN THE GAME WAS CALLED?
I DON'T THINK THEY SAID ANYTHING ABOUT A BASEBALL GAME..
7-10
I'LL GO BACK AND WATCH SOME MORE.. I'LL LET YOU KNOW WHAT THEY SAY..
SCHULZ
I HOPE HIS TRACTOR GETS WET!

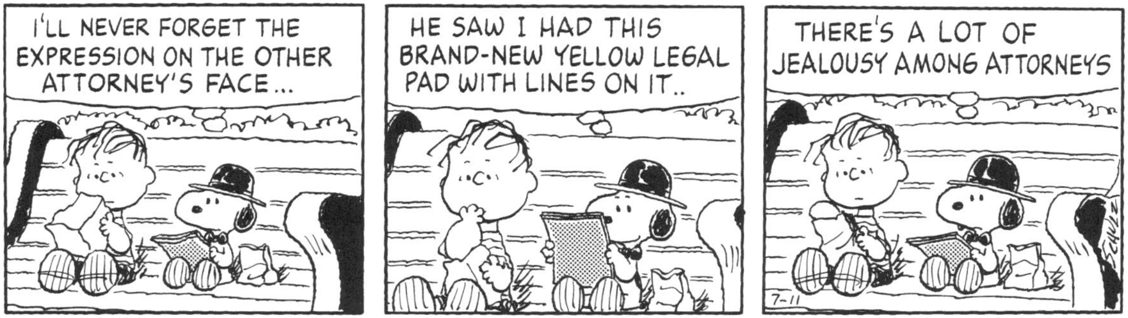
I'LL NEVER FORGET THE EXPRESSION ON THE OTHER ATTORNEY'S FACE...
HE SAW I HAD THIS BRAND-NEW YELLOW LEGAL PAD WITH LINES ON IT..
THERE'S A LOT OF JEALOUSY AMONG ATTORNEYS
SCHULZ
7-11

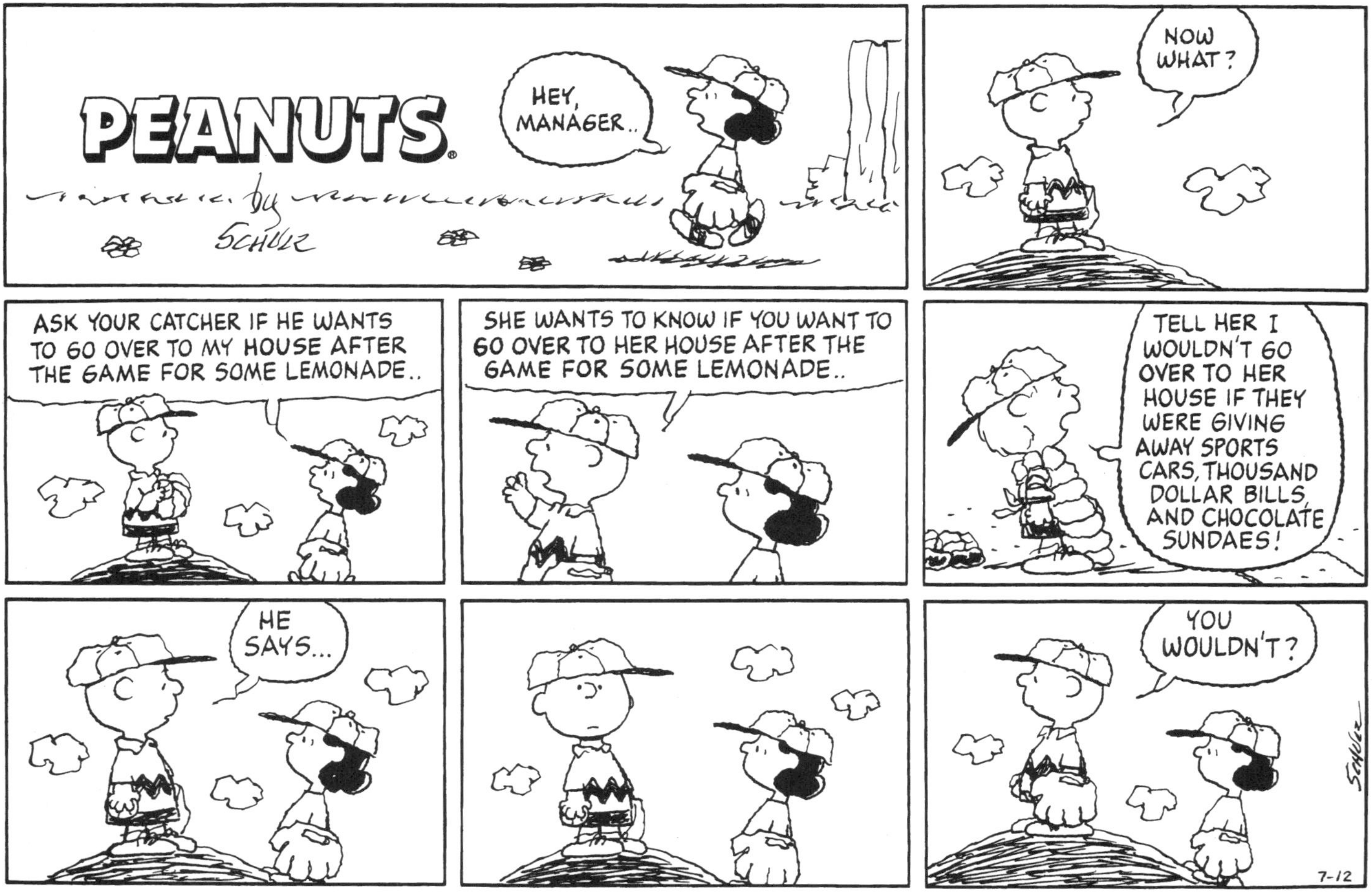
PEANUTS
by Schulz
HEY, MANAGER..
NOW WHAT?
ASK YOUR CATCHER IF HE WANTS TO GO OVER TO MY HOUSE AFTER THE GAME FOR SOME LEMONADE..
SHE WANTS TO KNOW IF YOU WANT TO GO OVER TO HER HOUSE AFTER THE GAME FOR SOME LEMONADE..
TELL HER I WOULDN'T GO OVER TO HER HOUSE IF THEY WERE GIVING AWAY SPORTS CARS, THOUSAND DOLLAR BILLS, AND CHOCOLATE SUNDAES!
HE SAYS...
YOU WOULDN'T?
SCHULZ
7-12

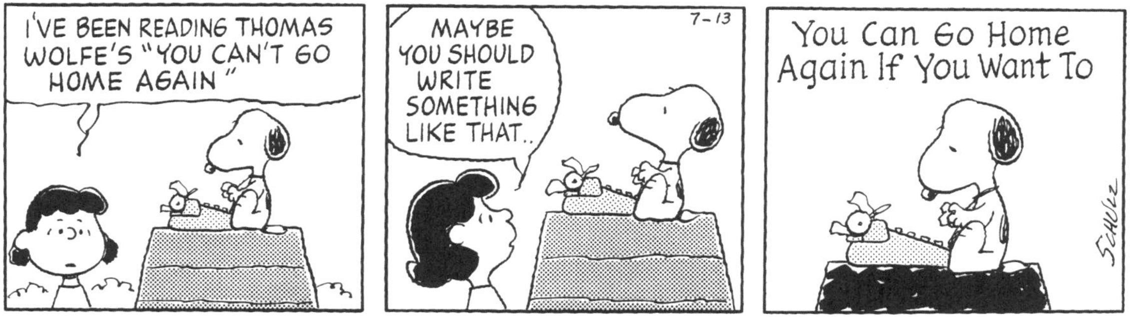
I'VE BEEN READING THOMAS WOLFE'S "YOU CAN'T GO HOME AGAIN"
MAYBE YOU SHOULD WRITE SOMETHING LIKE THAT..
7-13
You Can Go Home Again If You Want To
SCHULZ

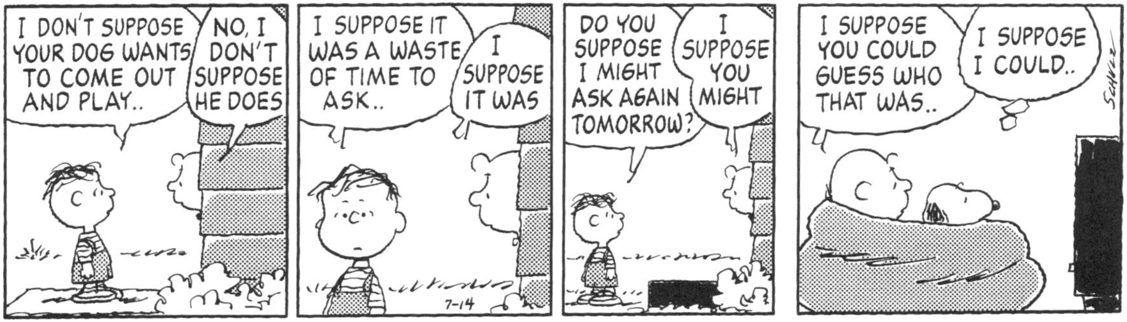
I DON'T SUPPOSE YOUR DOG WANTS TO COME OUT AND PLAY..
NO, I DON'T SUPPOSE HE DOES
I SUPPOSE IT WAS A WASTE OF TIME TO ASK..
I SUPPOSE IT WAS
7-14
DO YOU SUPPOSE I MIGHT ASK AGAIN TOMORROW?
I SUPPOSE YOU MIGHT
I SUPPOSE YOU COULD GUESS WHO THAT WAS..
I SUPPOSE I COULD..
SCHULZ

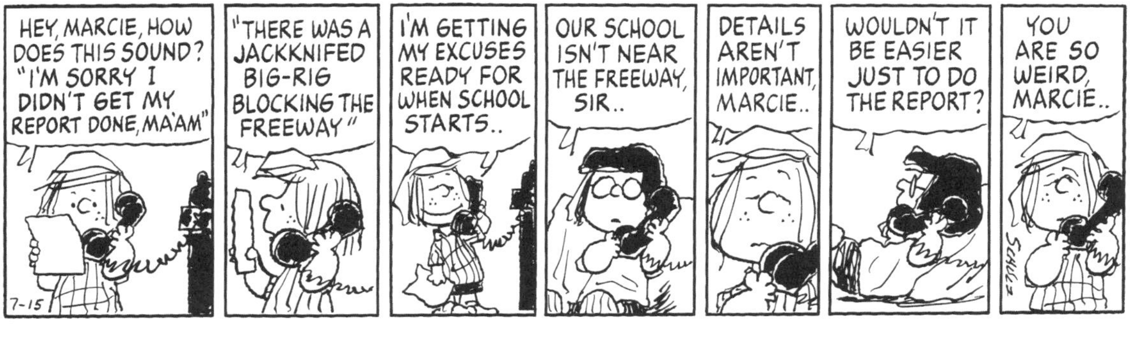
HEY, MARCIE, HOW DOES THIS SOUND? "I'M SORRY I DIDN'T GET MY REPORT DONE, MA'AM"
7-15
"THERE WAS A JACKKNIFED BIG-RIG BLOCKING THE FREEWAY"
I'M GETTING MY EXCUSES READY FOR WHEN SCHOOL STARTS..
OUR SCHOOL ISN'T NEAR THE FREEWAY, SIR..
DETAILS AREN'T IMPORTANT, MARCIE..
WOULDN'T IT BE EASIER JUST TO DO THE REPORT?
YOU ARE SO WEIRD, MARCIE..
SCHULZ

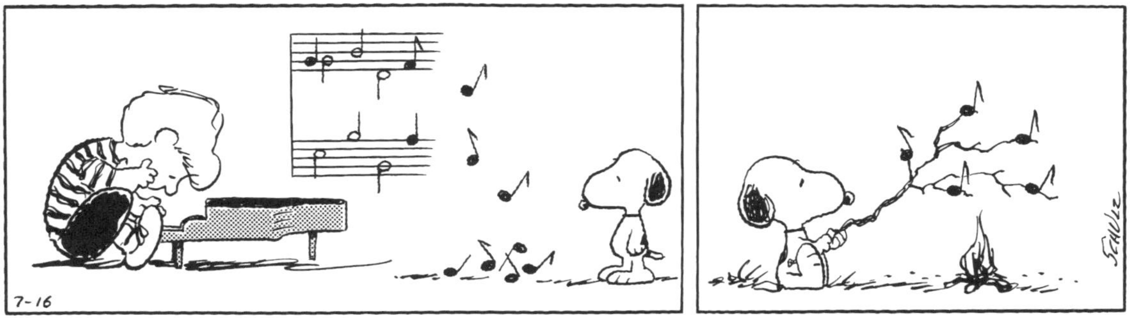

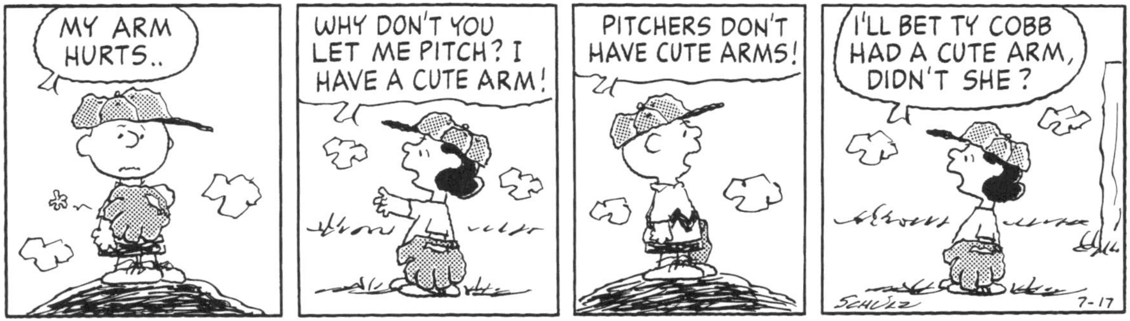
MY ARM HURTS..
WHY DON'T YOU LET ME PITCH? I HAVE A CUTE ARM!
PITCHERS DON'T HAVE CUTE ARMS!
I'LL BET TY COBB HAD A CUTE ARM, DIDN'T SHE?

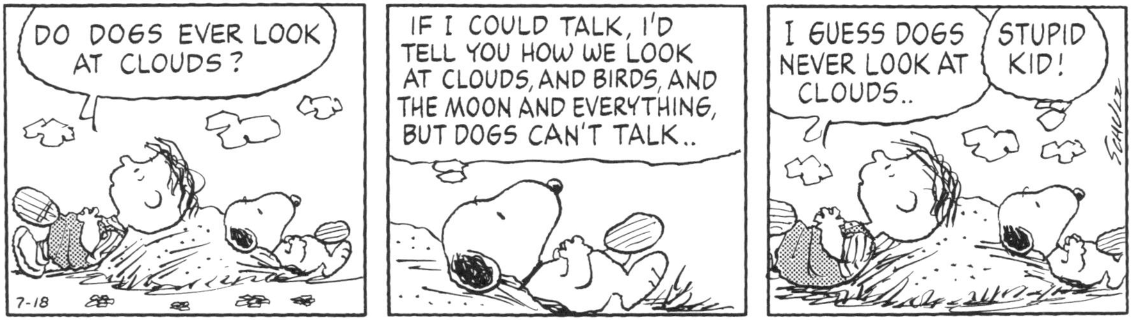
DO DOGS EVER LOOK AT CLOUDS?
IF I COULD TALK, I'D TELL YOU HOW WE LOOK AT CLOUDS, AND BIRDS, AND THE MOON AND EVERYTHING, BUT DOGS CAN'T TALK..
I GUESS DOGS NEVER LOOK AT CLOUDS..
STUPID KID!

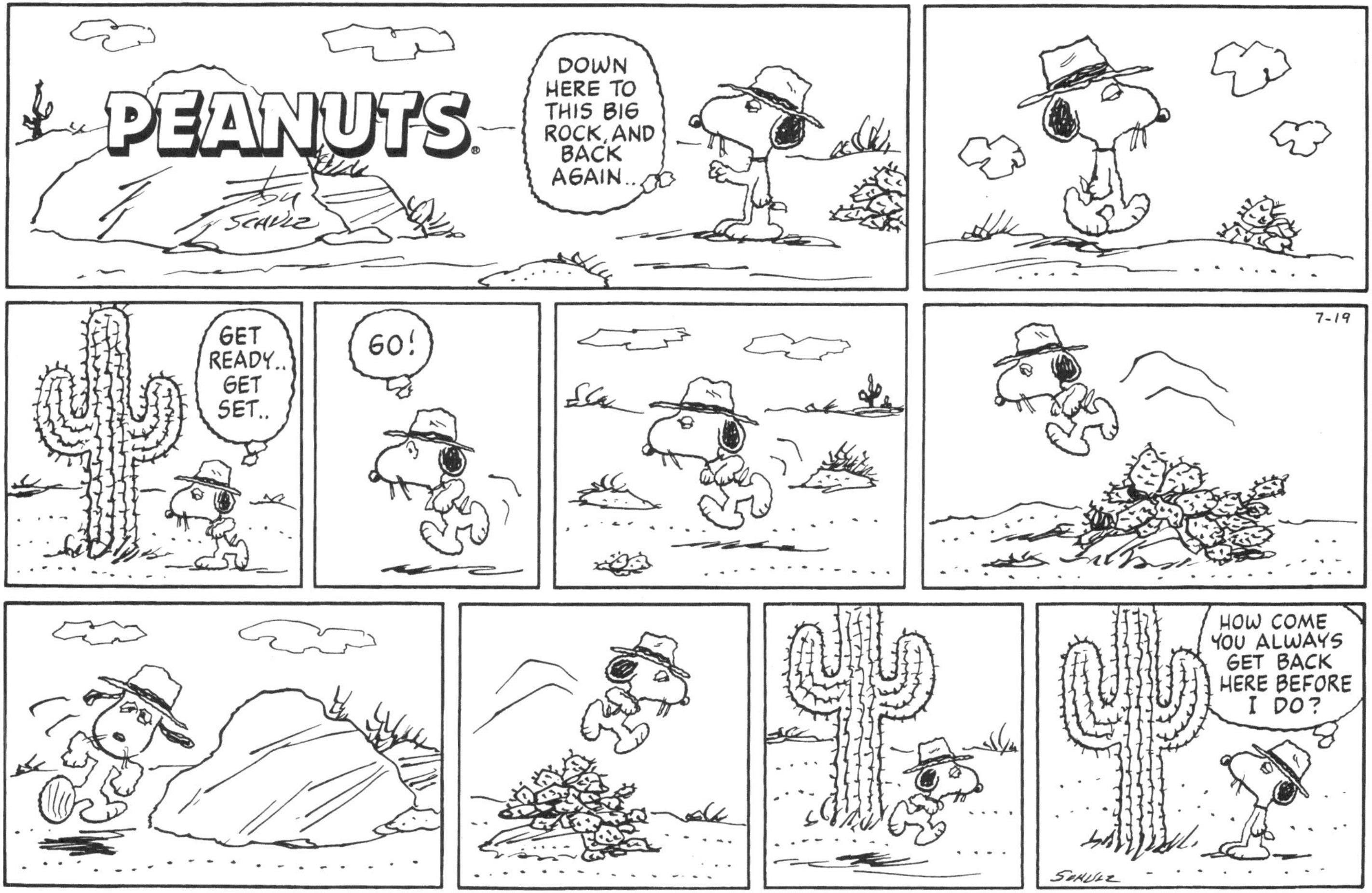
PEANUTS
DOWN HERE TO THIS BIG ROCK, AND BACK AGAIN..
GET READY.. GET SET..
GO!
7-19
HOW COME YOU ALWAYS GET BACK HERE BEFORE I DO?
SCHULZ

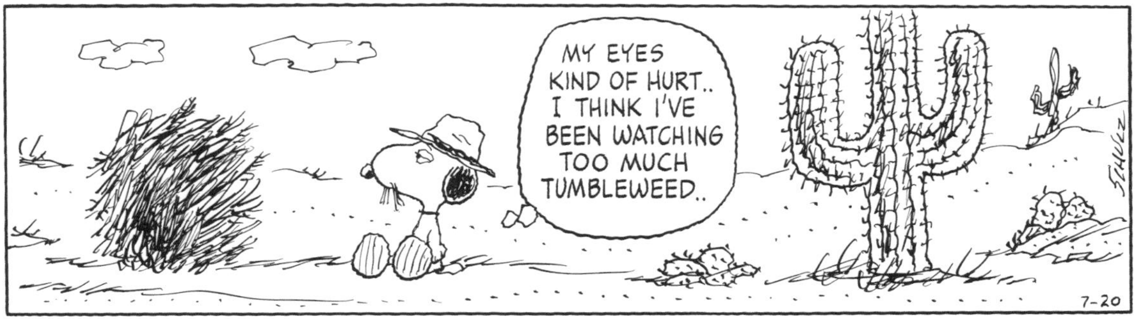
MY EYES KIND OF HURT.. I THINK I'VE BEEN WATCHING TOO MUCH TUMBLEWEED..

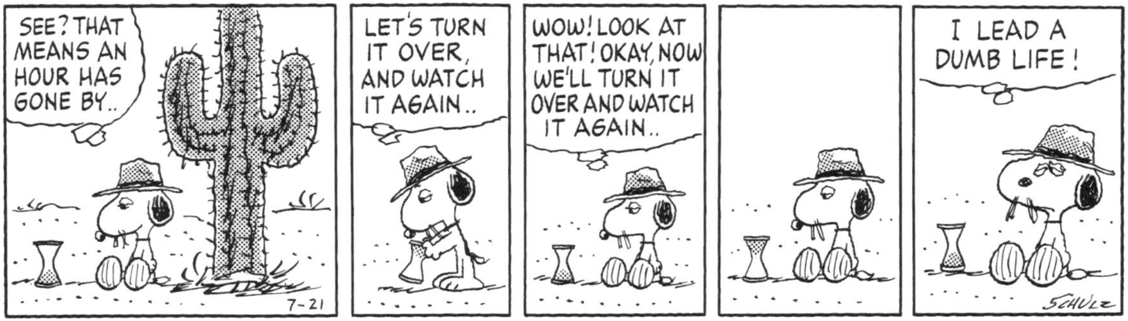
SEE? THAT MEANS AN HOUR HAS GONE BY..
LET'S TURN IT OVER, AND WATCH IT AGAIN..
WOW! LOOK AT THAT! OKAY, NOW WE'LL TURN IT OVER AND WATCH IT AGAIN..
I LEAD A DUMB LIFE!

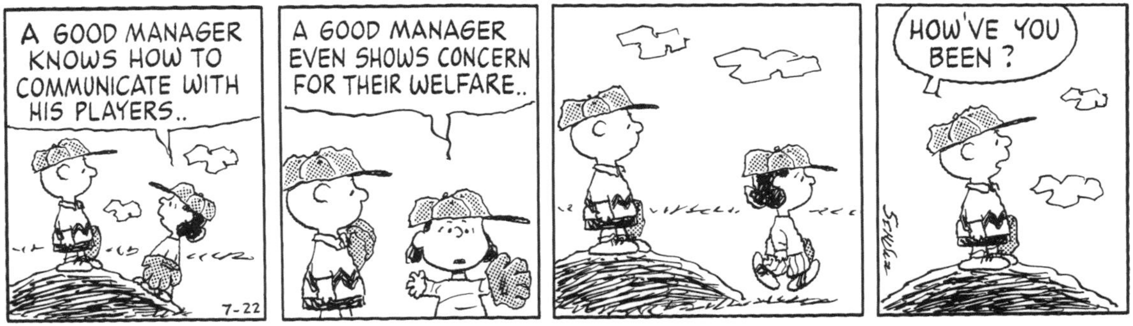
A GOOD MANAGER KNOWS HOW TO COMMUNICATE WITH HIS PLAYERS..
A GOOD MANAGER EVEN SHOWS CONCERN FOR THEIR WELFARE..
HOW'VE YOU BEEN?

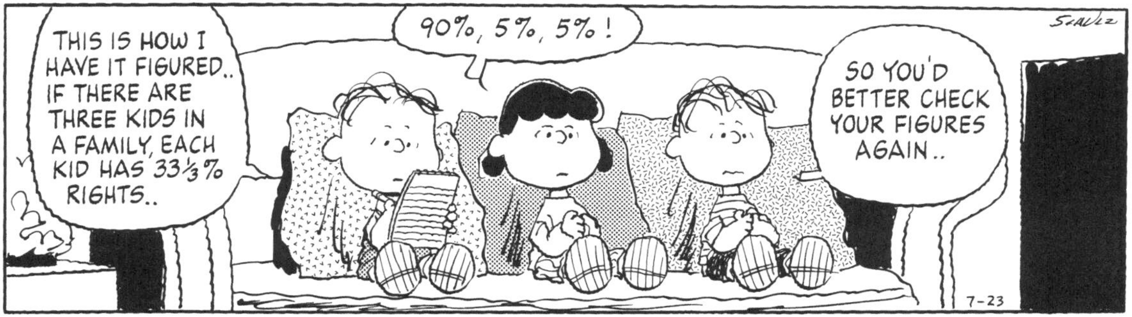
THIS IS HOW I HAVE IT FIGURED.. IF THERE ARE THREE KIDS IN A FAMILY, EACH KID HAS 33⅓% RIGHTS..
90%, 5%, 5%!
SO YOU'D BETTER CHECK YOUR FIGURES AGAIN..

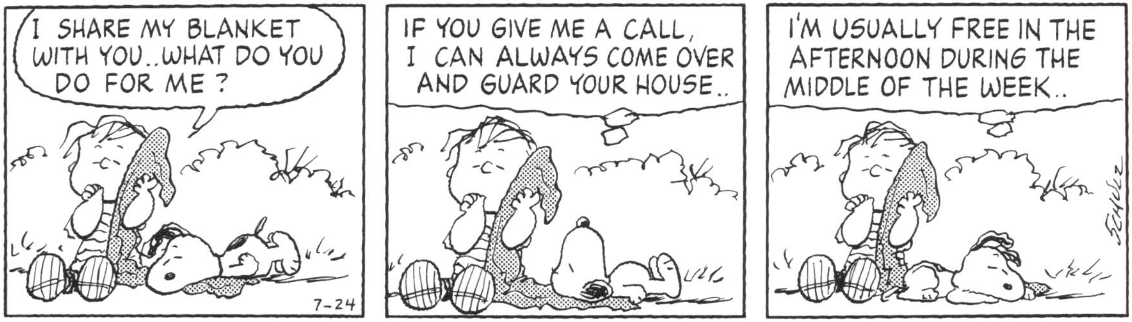
I SHARE MY BLANKET WITH YOU..WHAT DO YOU DO FOR ME?
IF YOU GIVE ME A CALL, I CAN ALWAYS COME OVER AND GUARD YOUR HOUSE..
I'M USUALLY FREE IN THE AFTERNOON DURING THE MIDDLE OF THE WEEK..

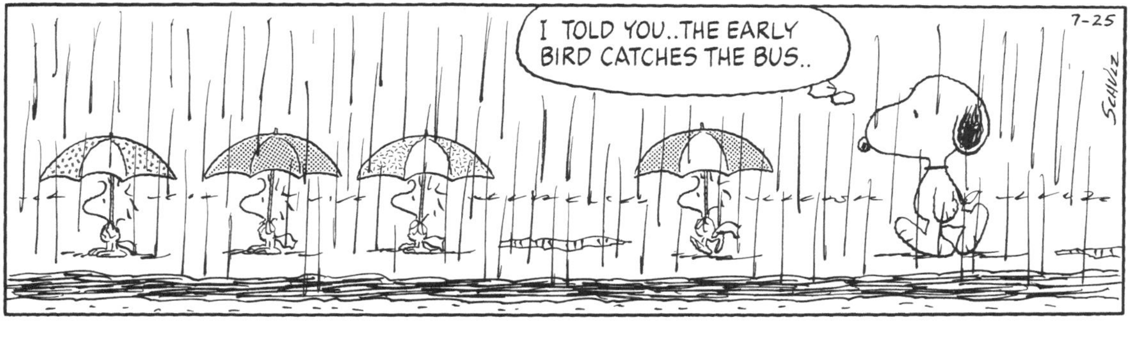
I TOLD YOU..THE EARLY BIRD CATCHES THE BUS..

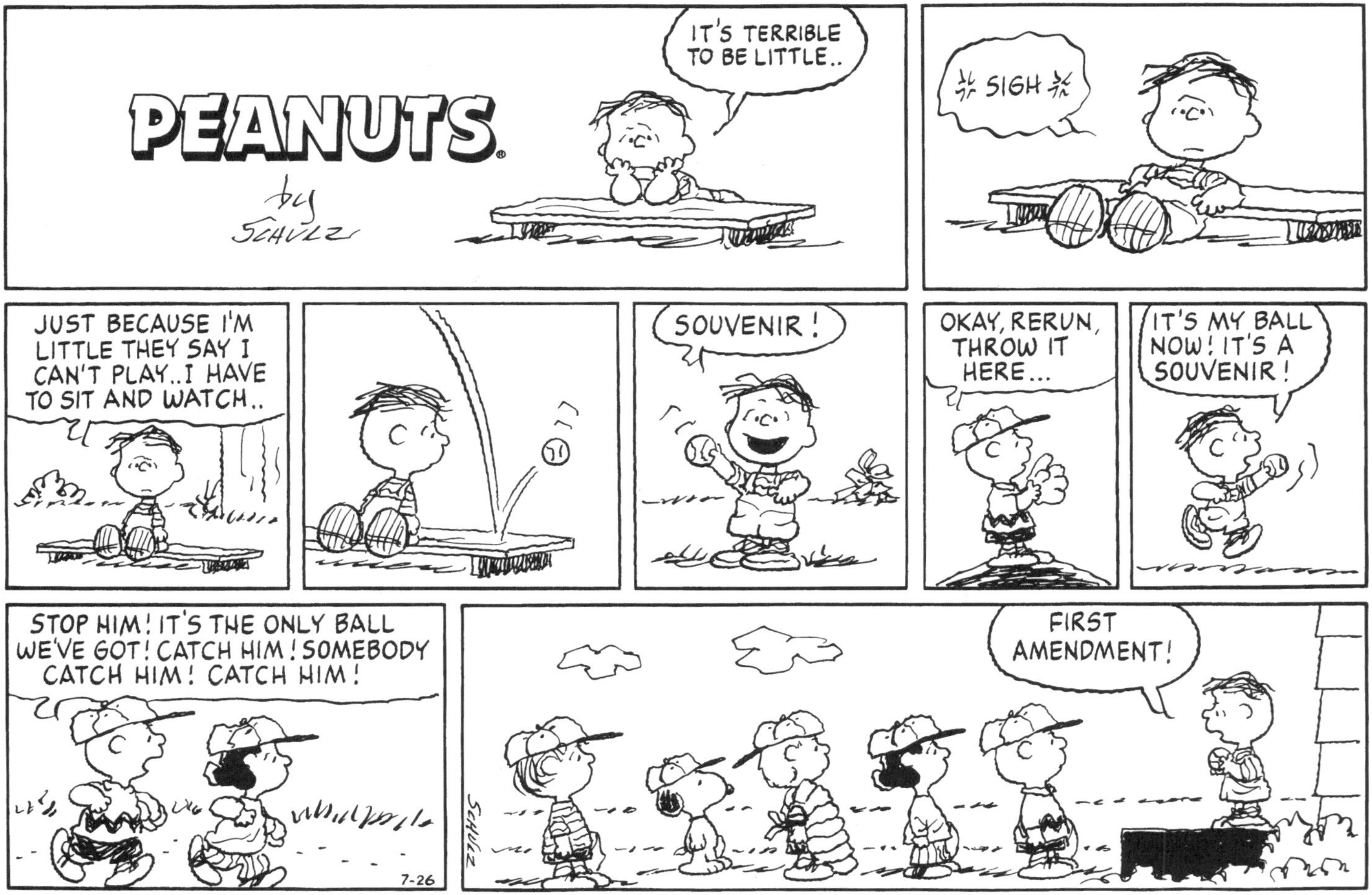
PEANUTS
by SCHULZ
IT'S TERRIBLE TO BE LITTLE..
SIGH
JUST BECAUSE I'M LITTLE THEY SAY I CAN'T PLAY..I HAVE TO SIT AND WATCH..
SOUVENIR!
OKAY, RERUN, THROW IT HERE...
IT'S MY BALL NOW! IT'S A SOUVENIR!
STOP HIM! IT'S THE ONLY BALL WE'VE GOT! CATCH HIM! SOMEBODY CATCH HIM! CATCH HIM!
7-26
SCHULZ
FIRST AMENDMENT!

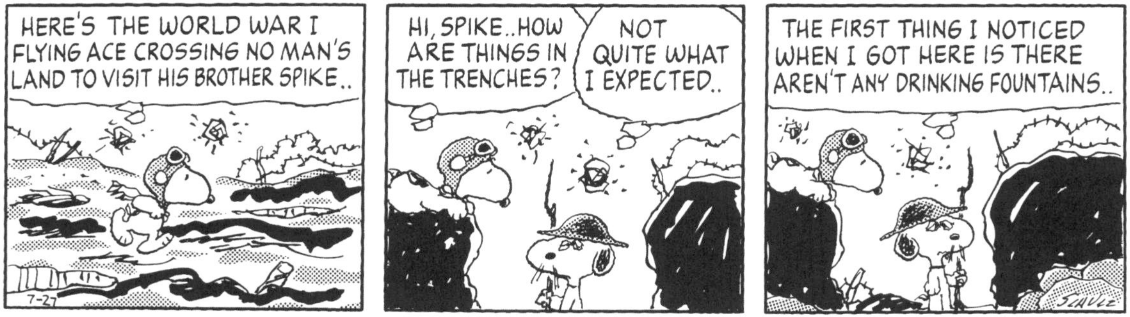
HERE'S THE WORLD WAR I FLYING ACE CROSSING NO MAN'S LAND TO VISIT HIS BROTHER SPIKE..
HI, SPIKE..HOW ARE THINGS IN THE TRENCHES?
NOT QUITE WHAT I EXPECTED..
THE FIRST THING I NOTICED WHEN I GOT HERE IS THERE AREN'T ANY DRINKING FOUNTAINS..

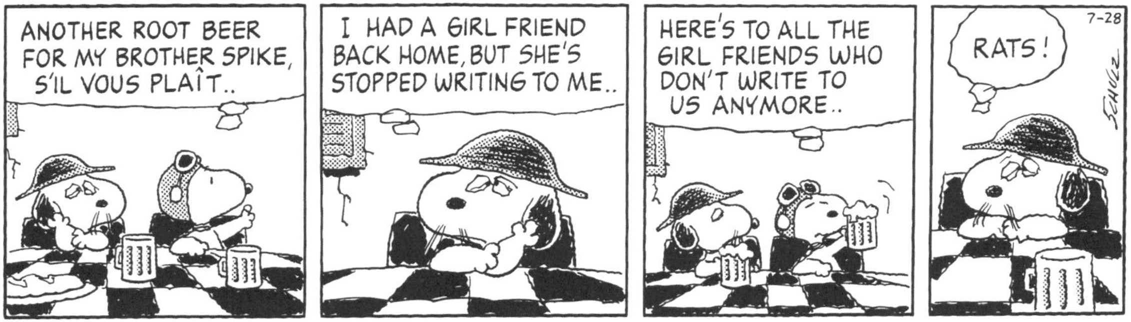
ANOTHER ROOT BEER FOR MY BROTHER SPIKE, S'IL VOUS PLAÎT..
I HAD A GIRL FRIEND BACK HOME, BUT SHE'S STOPPED WRITING TO ME..
HERE'S TO ALL THE GIRL FRIENDS WHO DON'T WRITE TO US ANYMORE..
RATS!

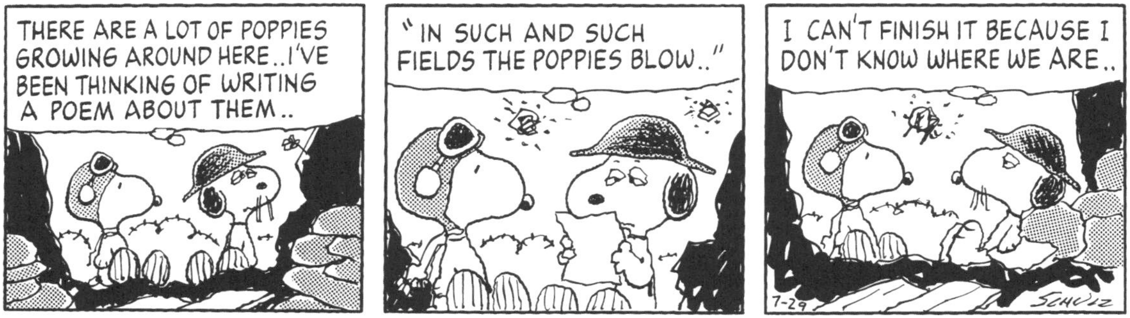
THERE ARE A LOT OF POPPIES GROWING AROUND HERE..I'VE BEEN THINKING OF WRITING A POEM ABOUT THEM..
"IN SUCH AND SUCH FIELDS THE POPPIES BLOW.."
I CAN'T FINISH IT BECAUSE I DON'T KNOW WHERE WE ARE..

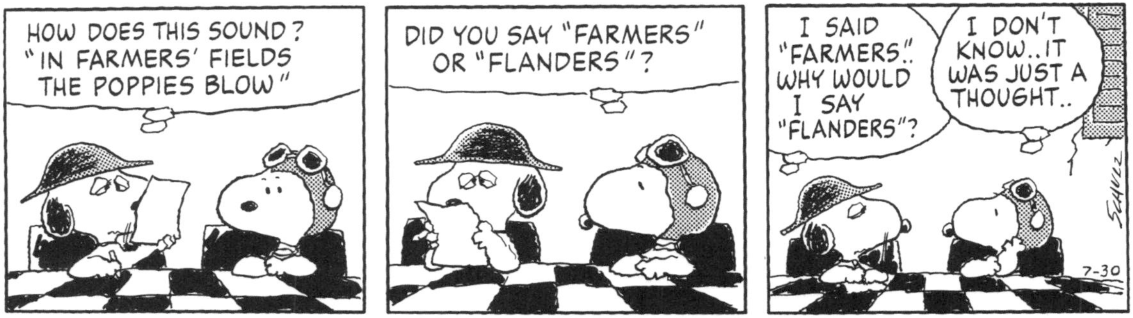
HOW DOES THIS SOUND? "IN FARMERS' FIELDS THE POPPIES BLOW"
DID YOU SAY "FARMERS" OR "FLANDERS"?
I SAID "FARMERS". WHY WOULD I SAY "FLANDERS"?
I DON'T KNOW..IT WAS JUST A THOUGHT..
SCHULZ
7-30

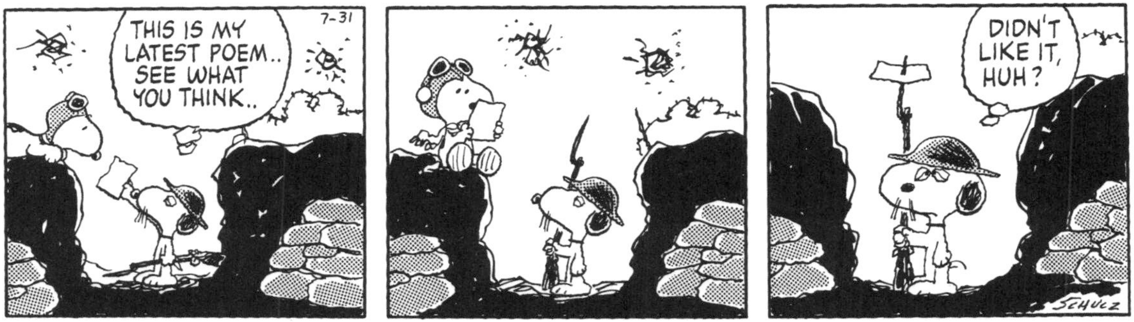
7-31
THIS IS MY LATEST POEM.. SEE WHAT YOU THINK..
DIDN'T LIKE IT, HUH?
SCHULZ

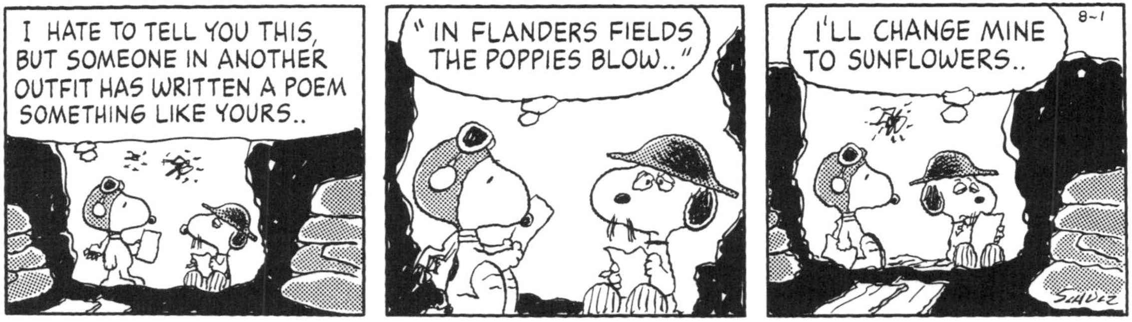
I HATE TO TELL YOU THIS, BUT SOMEONE IN ANOTHER OUTFIT HAS WRITTEN A POEM SOMETHING LIKE YOURS..
"IN FLANDERS FIELDS THE POPPIES BLOW.."
8-1
I'LL CHANGE MINE TO SUNFLOWERS..
SCHULZ

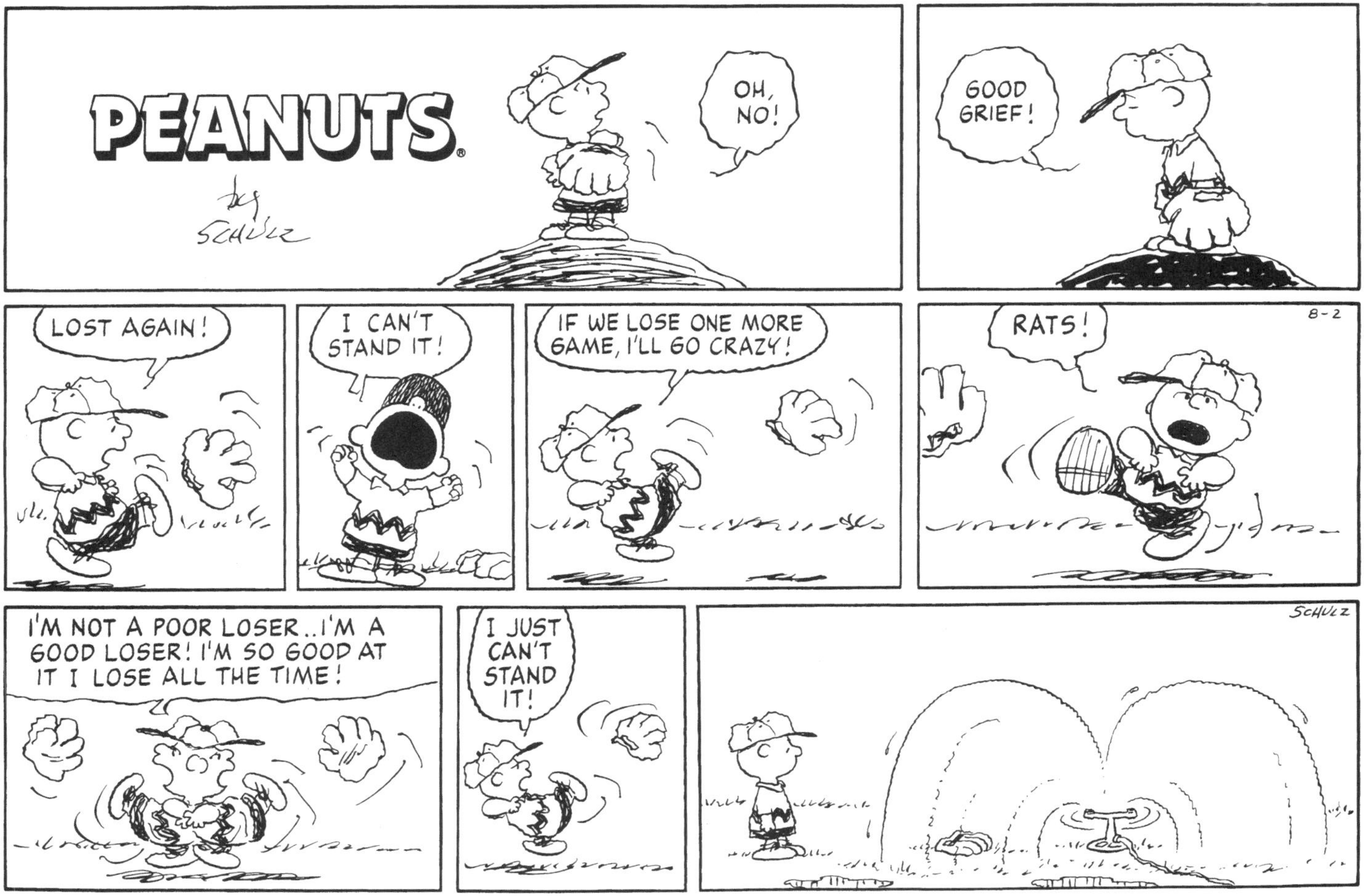
PEANUTS
Schulz
OH, NO!
GOOD GRIEF!
LOST AGAIN!
I CAN'T STAND IT!
IF WE LOSE ONE MORE GAME, I'LL GO CRAZY!
RATS!
8-2
I'M NOT A POOR LOSER..I'M A GOOD LOSER! I'M SO GOOD AT IT I LOSE ALL THE TIME!
I JUST CAN'T STAND IT!
SCHULZ

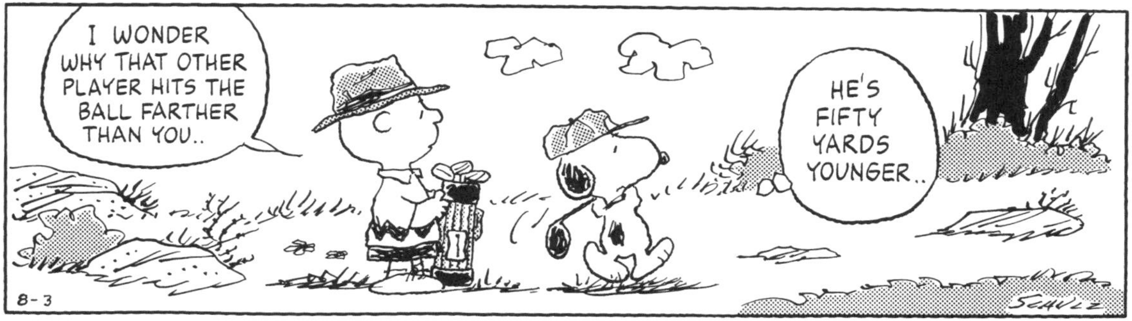
I WONDER WHY THAT OTHER PLAYER HITS THE BALL FARTHER THAN YOU..
HE'S FIFTY YARDS YOUNGER..
8-3
SCHULZ

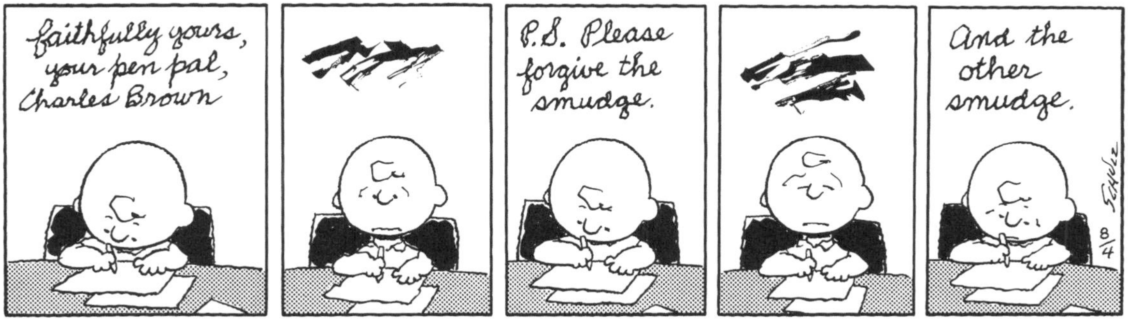
faithfully yours, your pen pal, Charles Brown
P.S. Please forgive the smudge.
And the other smudge.
SCHULZ
8/4

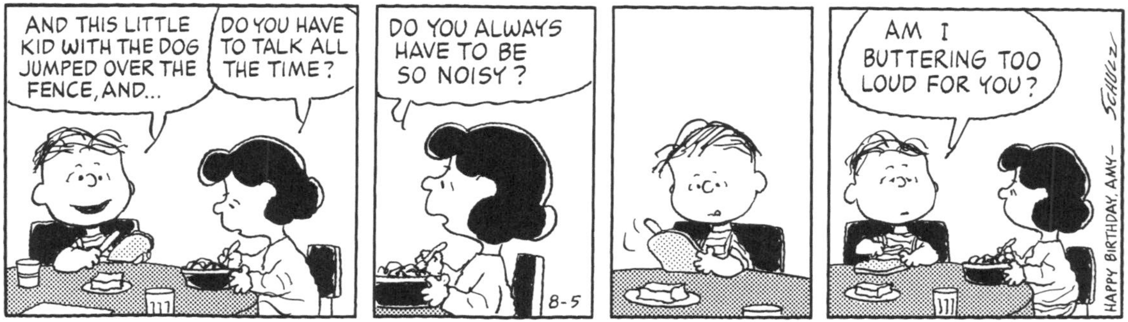
AND THIS LITTLE KID WITH THE DOG JUMPED OVER THE FENCE, AND...
DO YOU HAVE TO TALK ALL THE TIME?
DO YOU ALWAYS HAVE TO BE SO NOISY?
AM I BUTTERING TOO LOUD FOR YOU?
8-5
SCHULZ
HAPPY BIRTHDAY, AMY—

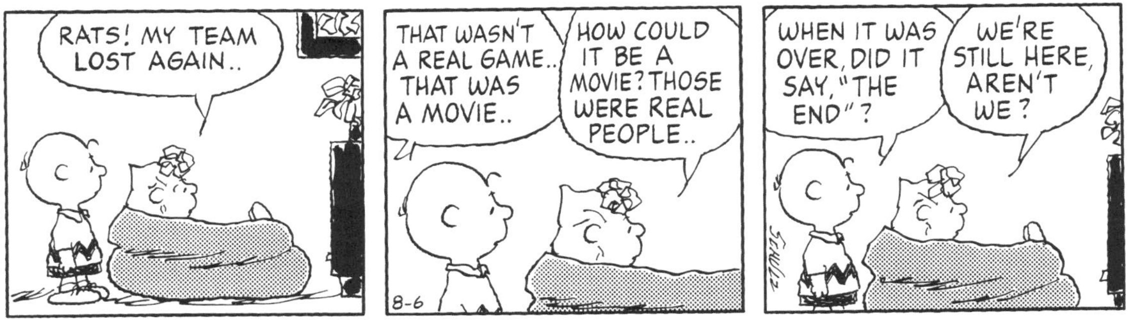
RATS! MY TEAM LOST AGAIN..
THAT WASN'T A REAL GAME.. THAT WAS A MOVIE..
HOW COULD IT BE A MOVIE? THOSE WERE REAL PEOPLE..
WHEN IT WAS OVER, DID IT SAY, "THE END"?
WE'RE STILL HERE, AREN'T WE?
8-6
SCHULZ

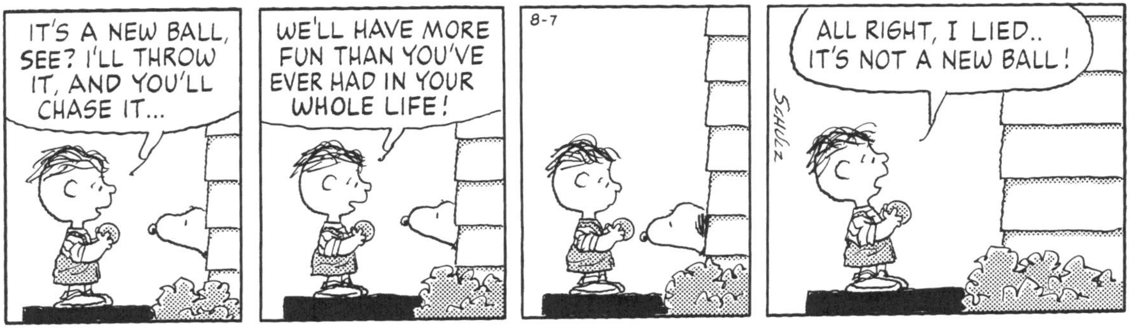
IT'S A NEW BALL, SEE? I'LL THROW IT, AND YOU'LL CHASE IT...
WE'LL HAVE MORE FUN THAN YOU'VE EVER HAD IN YOUR WHOLE LIFE!
8-7
SCHULZ
ALL RIGHT, I LIED.. IT'S NOT A NEW BALL!

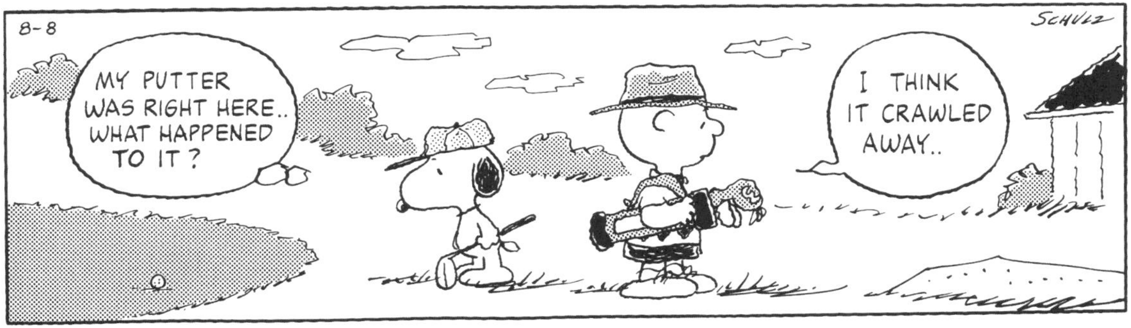
8-8
SCHULZ
MY PUTTER WAS RIGHT HERE.. WHAT HAPPENED TO IT?
I THINK IT CRAWLED AWAY..

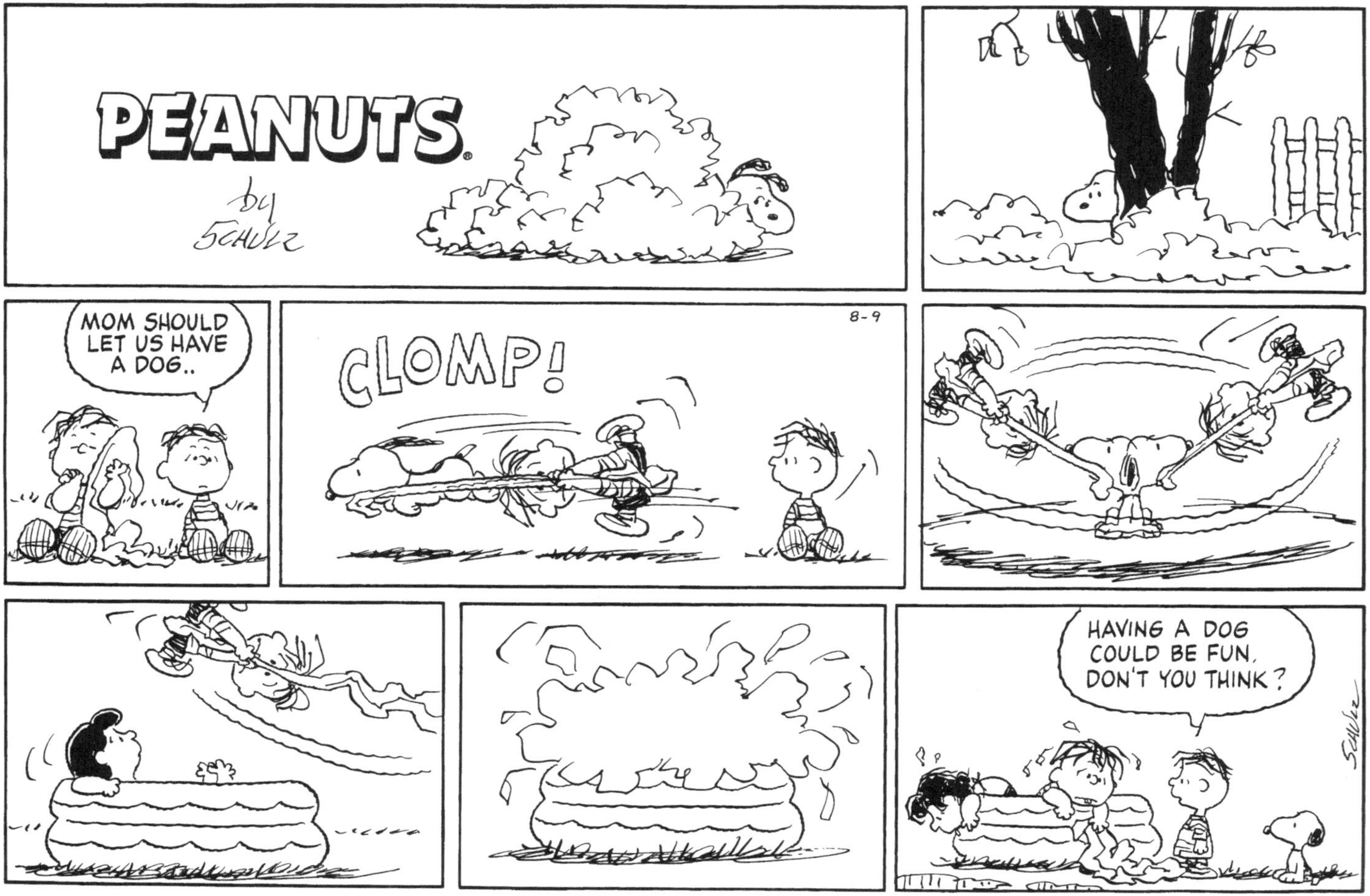
PEANUTS
by SCHULZ
MOM SHOULD LET US HAVE A DOG..
8-9
CLOMP!
HAVING A DOG COULD BE FUN, DON'T YOU THINK?
SCHULZ

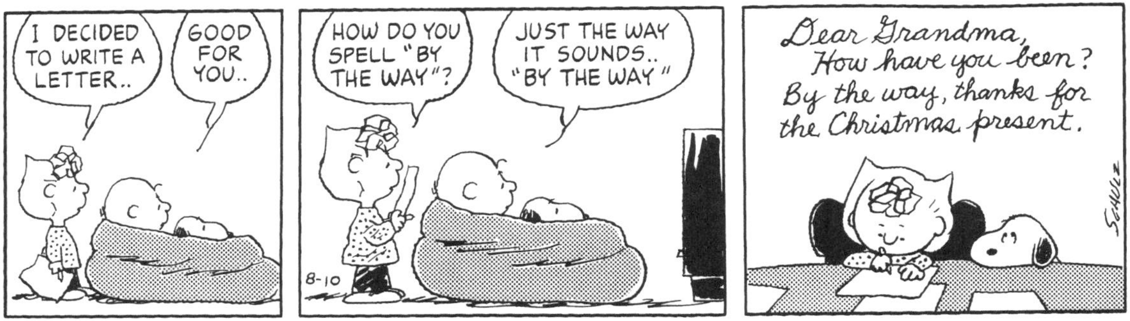
I DECIDED TO WRITE A LETTER..
GOOD FOR YOU..
HOW DO YOU SPELL "BY THE WAY"?
JUST THE WAY IT SOUNDS.. "BY THE WAY"
8-10
Dear Grandma,
How have you been?
By the way, thanks for the Christmas present.
SCHULZ

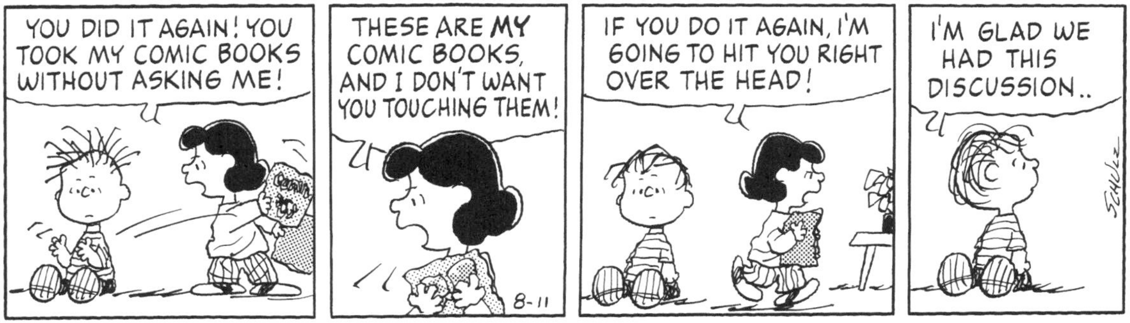
YOU DID IT AGAIN! YOU TOOK MY COMIC BOOKS WITHOUT ASKING ME!
THESE ARE MY COMIC BOOKS, AND I DON'T WANT YOU TOUCHING THEM!
8-11
IF YOU DO IT AGAIN, I'M GOING TO HIT YOU RIGHT OVER THE HEAD!
I'M GLAD WE HAD THIS DISCUSSION..
SCHULZ

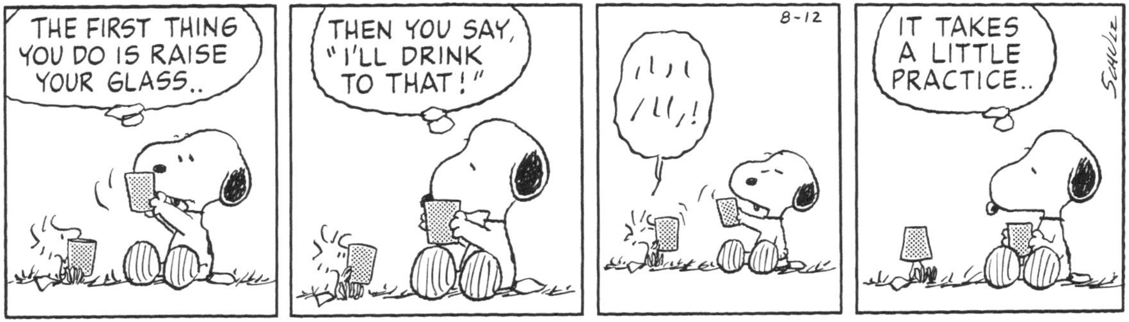
THE FIRST THING YOU DO IS RAISE YOUR GLASS..
THEN YOU SAY, "I'LL DRINK TO THAT!"
8-12
IT TAKES A LITTLE PRACTICE..
SCHULZ

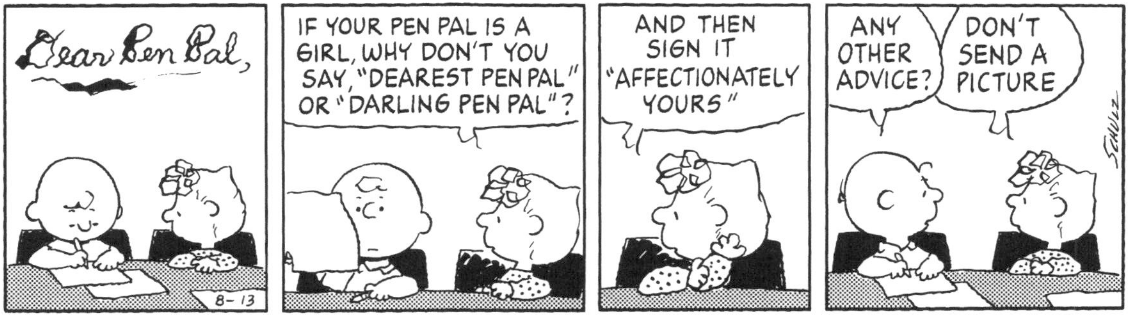
Dear Pen Pal,
IF YOUR PEN PAL IS A GIRL, WHY DON'T YOU SAY, "DEAREST PEN PAL" OR "DARLING PEN PAL"?
AND THEN SIGN IT "AFFECTIONATELY YOURS"
ANY OTHER ADVICE?
DON'T SEND A PICTURE
SCHULZ
8-13

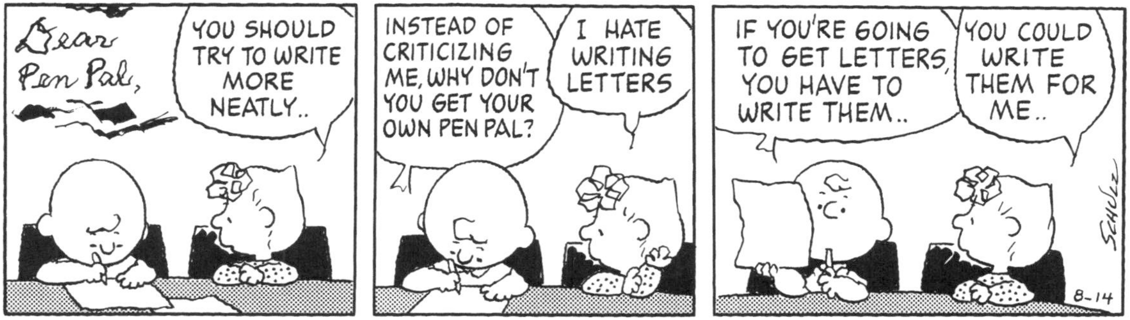
Dear Pen Pal,
YOU SHOULD TRY TO WRITE MORE NEATLY..
INSTEAD OF CRITICIZING ME, WHY DON'T YOU GET YOUR OWN PEN PAL?
I HATE WRITING LETTERS
IF YOU'RE GOING TO GET LETTERS, YOU HAVE TO WRITE THEM..
YOU COULD WRITE THEM FOR ME..
SCHULZ
8-14

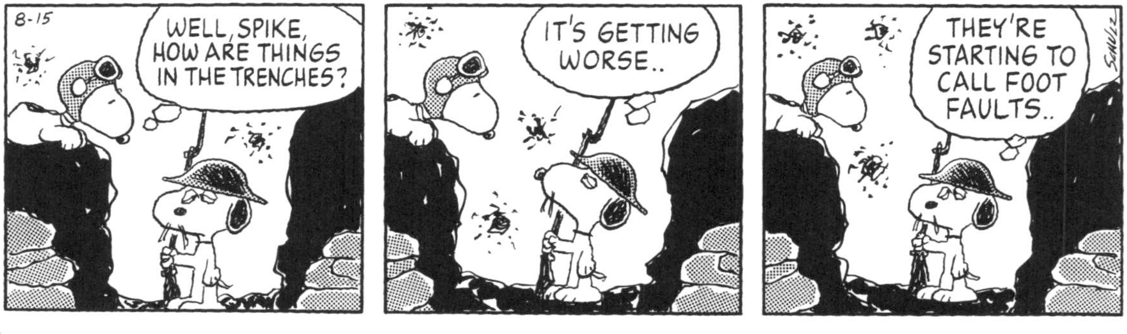
8-15
WELL, SPIKE, HOW ARE THINGS IN THE TRENCHES?
IT'S GETTING WORSE..
THEY'RE STARTING TO CALL FOOT FAULTS..
SCHULZ

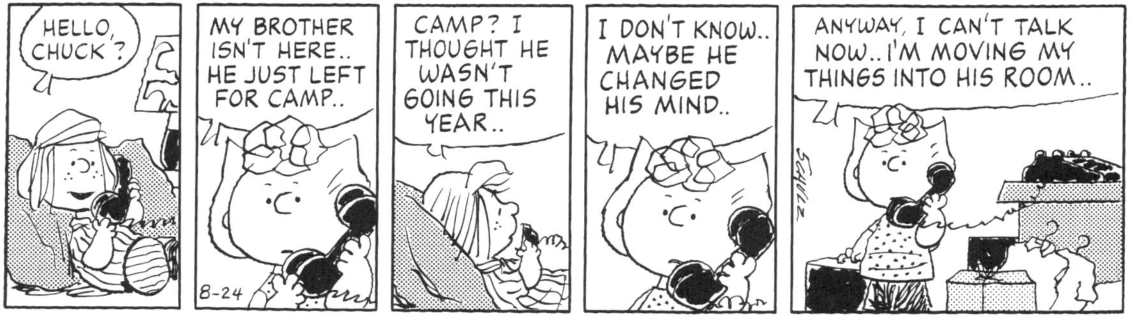
HELLO, CHUCK?
MY BROTHER ISN'T HERE.. HE JUST LEFT FOR CAMP..
8-24
CAMP? I THOUGHT HE WASN'T GOING THIS YEAR..
I DON'T KNOW.. MAYBE HE CHANGED HIS MIND..
ANYWAY, I CAN'T TALK NOW.. I'M MOVING MY THINGS INTO HIS ROOM..
SCHULZ

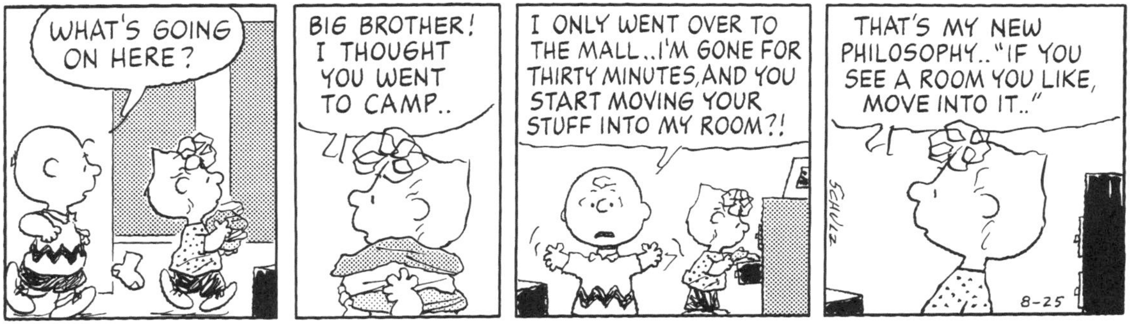
WHAT'S GOING ON HERE?
BIG BROTHER! I THOUGHT YOU WENT TO CAMP..
I ONLY WENT OVER TO THE MALL.. I'M GONE FOR THIRTY MINUTES, AND YOU START MOVING YOUR STUFF INTO MY ROOM?!
THAT'S MY NEW PHILOSOPHY.. "IF YOU SEE A ROOM YOU LIKE, MOVE INTO IT.."
SCHULZ
8-25

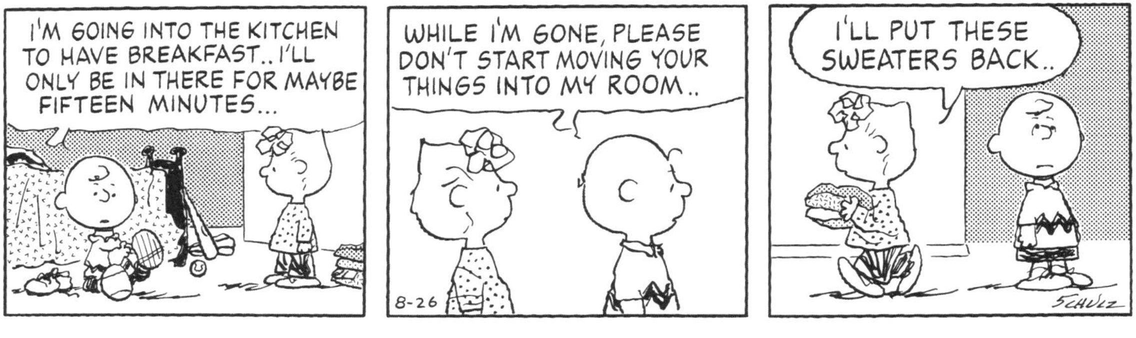
I'M GOING INTO THE KITCHEN TO HAVE BREAKFAST.. I'LL ONLY BE IN THERE FOR MAYBE FIFTEEN MINUTES...
WHILE I'M GONE, PLEASE DON'T START MOVING YOUR THINGS INTO MY ROOM..
8-26
I'LL PUT THESE SWEATERS BACK..
SCHULZ

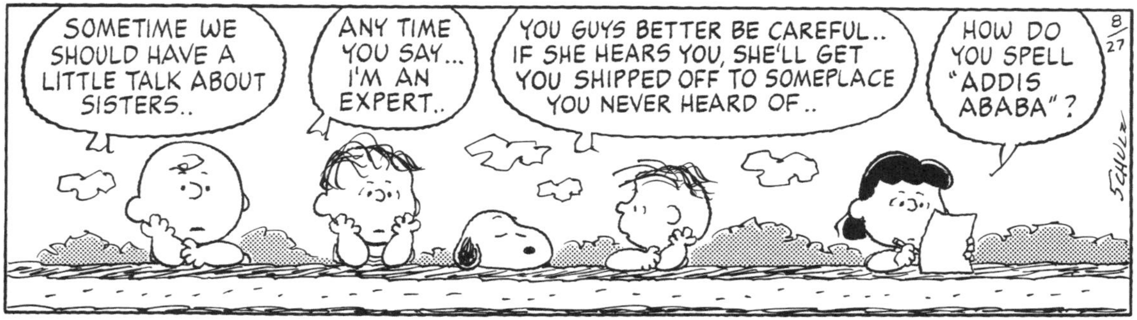
SOMETIME WE SHOULD HAVE A LITTLE TALK ABOUT SISTERS..
ANY TIME YOU SAY... I'M AN EXPERT..
YOU GUYS BETTER BE CAREFUL.. IF SHE HEARS YOU, SHE'LL GET YOU SHIPPED OFF TO SOMEPLACE YOU NEVER HEARD OF..
HOW DO YOU SPELL "ADDIS ABABA"?
8/27
SCHULZ

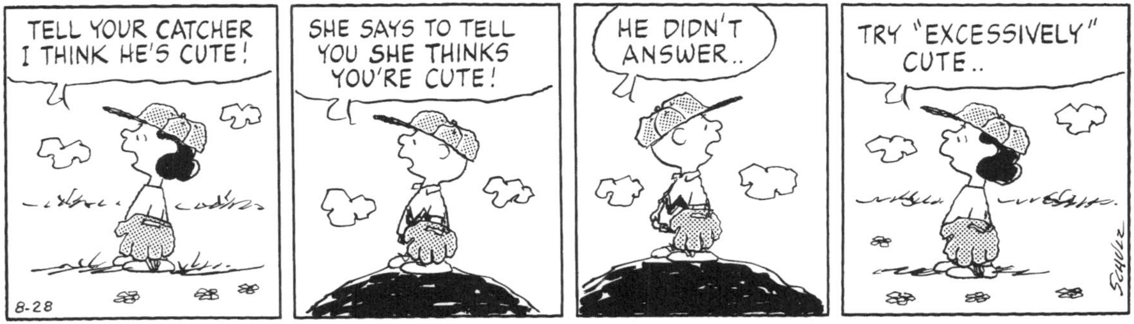
TELL YOUR CATCHER I THINK HE'S CUTE!
8-28
SHE SAYS TO TELL YOU SHE THINKS YOU'RE CUTE!
HE DIDN'T ANSWER..
TRY "EXCESSIVELY" CUTE..
SCHULZ

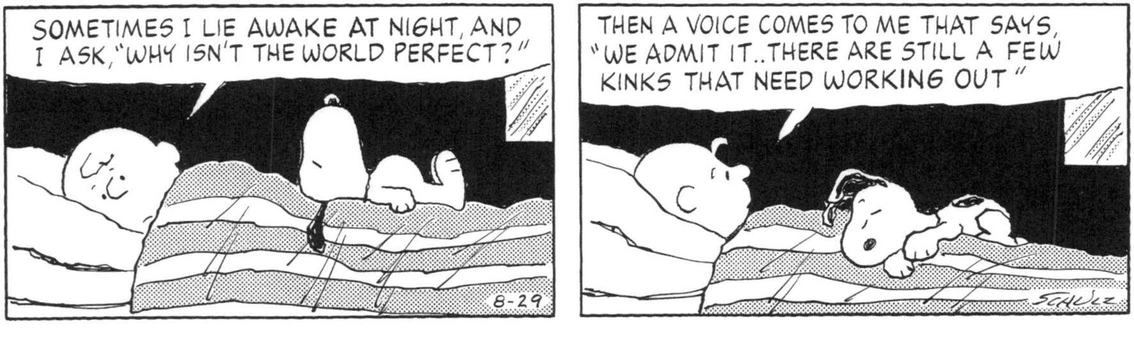
SOMETIMES I LIE AWAKE AT NIGHT, AND I ASK, "WHY ISN'T THE WORLD PERFECT?"
8-29
THEN A VOICE COMES TO ME THAT SAYS, "WE ADMIT IT..THERE ARE STILL A FEW KINKS THAT NEED WORKING OUT"
SCHULZ

PEANUTS.
by Schulz

PSYCHIATRIC HELP 5¢
THE DOCTOR IS IN OUT AND ABOUT

HELP 5¢
THE DOCTOR IS IN

SEE?

WHAT WE'RE TALKING ABOUT HERE, CHARLIE BROWN, IS COMMUNICATION

THE DOCTOR IS IN

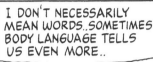

I DON'T NECESSARILY MEAN WORDS..SOMETIMES BODY LANGUAGE TELLS US EVEN MORE..

BODY LANGUAGE?

THAT'S INTERESTING..BODY LANGUAGE..COMMUNICATION..

THE DOCTOR IS IN

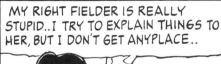

MY RIGHT FIELDER IS REALLY STUPID..I TRY TO EXPLAIN THINGS TO HER, BUT I DON'T GET ANYPLACE..

MAYBE IT'S COMMUNICATION.. WHAT DO YOU THINK?

HELP 5¢
8-30
THE DOCTOR IS IN

PSYCHIATRISTS ARE BIG ON BODY LANGUAGE..

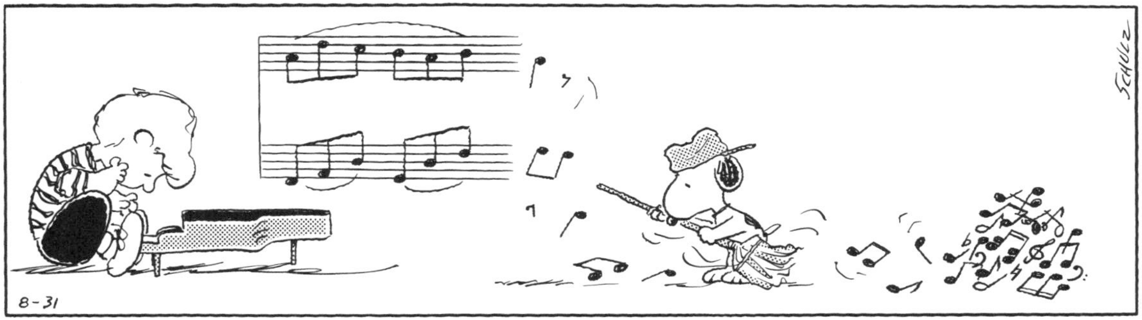
SCHULZ
8-31

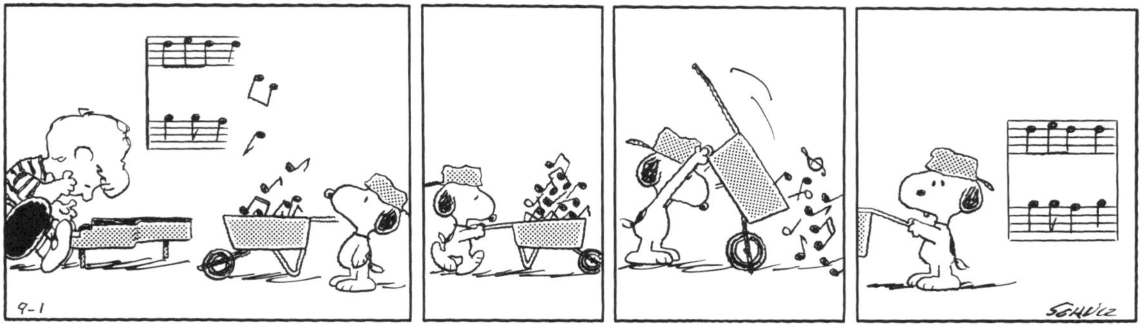
9-1
SCHULZ

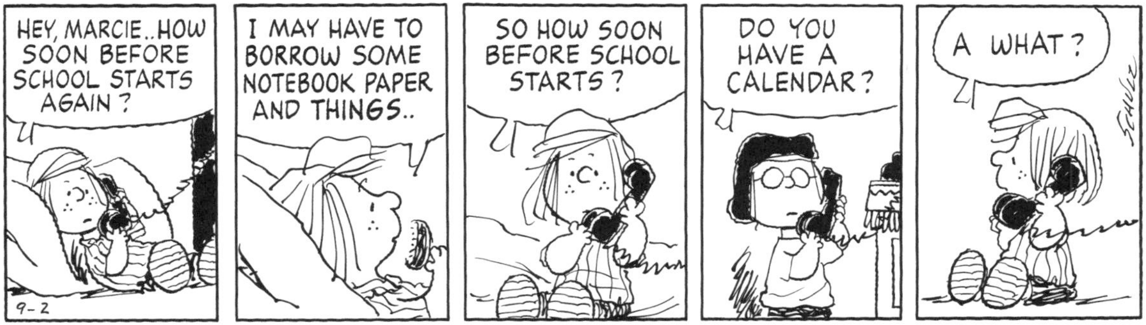
HEY, MARCIE..HOW SOON BEFORE SCHOOL STARTS AGAIN ?
I MAY HAVE TO BORROW SOME NOTEBOOK PAPER AND THINGS..
SO HOW SOON BEFORE SCHOOL STARTS ?
DO YOU HAVE A CALENDAR ?
A WHAT ?
SCHULZ
9-2

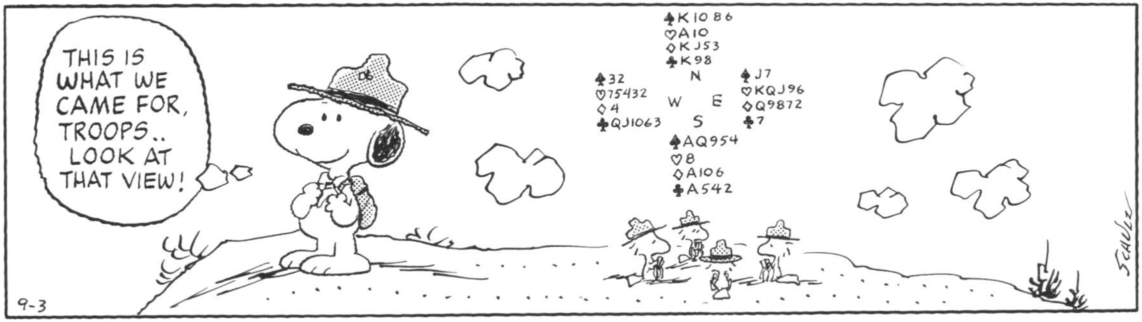
THIS IS WHAT WE CAME FOR, TROOPS.. LOOK AT THAT VIEW!
♠K1086
♡A10
◇KJ53
♣K98
N
♠32
♡75432
◇4
♣QJ1063
W
E
♠J7
♡KQJ96
◇Q9872
♣7
S
♠AQ954
♡8
◇A106
♣A542
9-3
SCHULZ

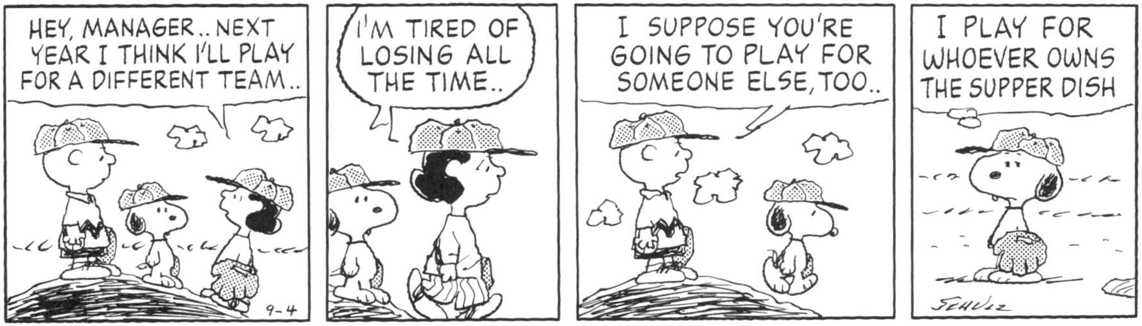
HEY, MANAGER.. NEXT YEAR I THINK I'LL PLAY FOR A DIFFERENT TEAM..
9-4
I'M TIRED OF LOSING ALL THE TIME..
I SUPPOSE YOU'RE GOING TO PLAY FOR SOMEONE ELSE, TOO..
I PLAY FOR WHOEVER OWNS THE SUPPER DISH
SCHULZ

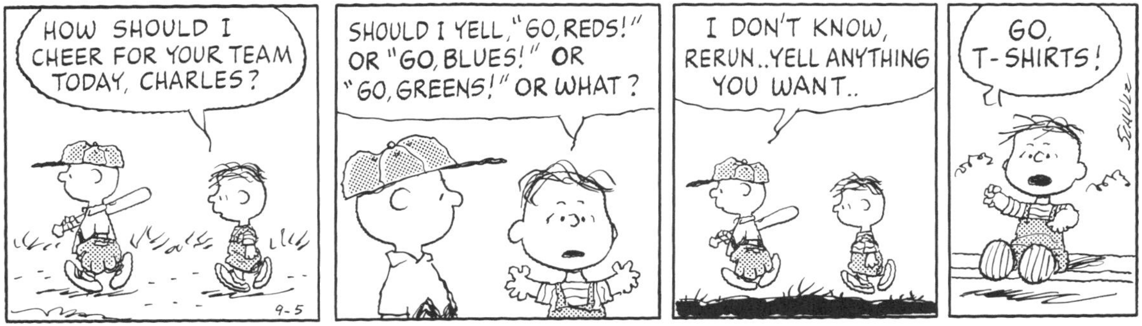
HOW SHOULD I CHEER FOR YOUR TEAM TODAY, CHARLES?
9-5
SHOULD I YELL, "GO, REDS!" OR "GO, BLUES!" OR "GO, GREENS!" OR WHAT?
I DON'T KNOW, RERUN.. YELL ANYTHING YOU WANT..
GO, T-SHIRTS!
SCHULZ

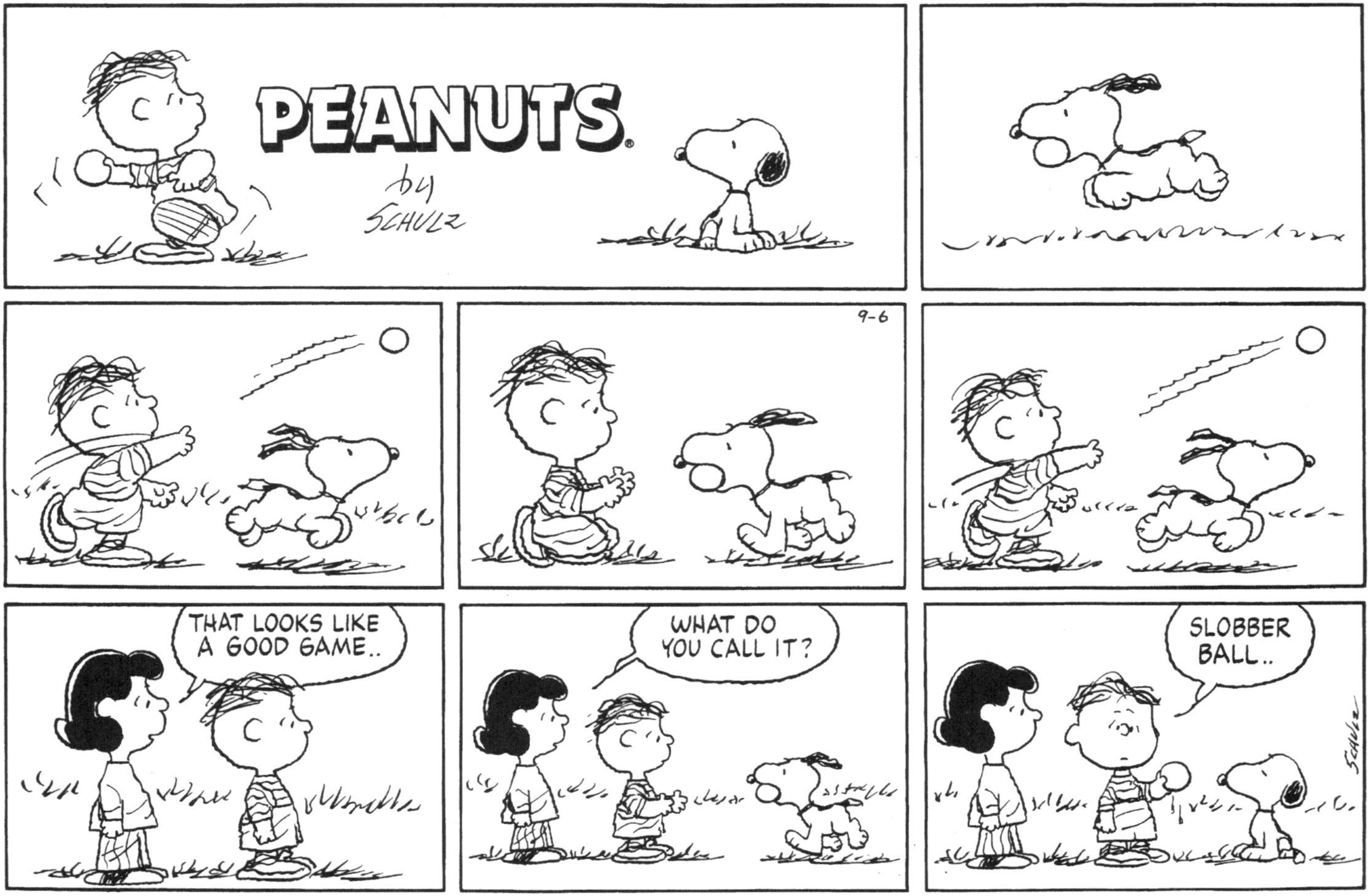
PEANUTS
by SCHULZ
9-6
THAT LOOKS LIKE A GOOD GAME..
WHAT DO YOU CALL IT?
SLOBBER BALL..
SCHULZ

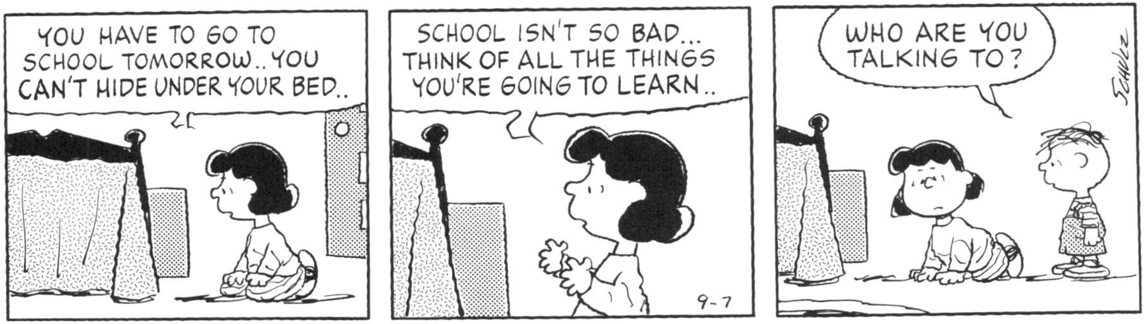
YOU HAVE TO GO TO SCHOOL TOMORROW.. YOU CAN'T HIDE UNDER YOUR BED..
SCHOOL ISN'T SO BAD... THINK OF ALL THE THINGS YOU'RE GOING TO LEARN..
9-7
WHO ARE YOU TALKING TO?
SCHULZ

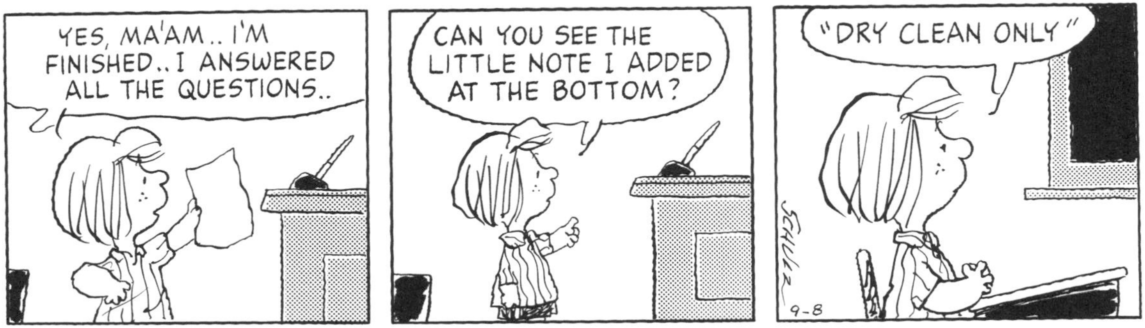
YES, MA'AM.. I'M FINISHED.. I ANSWERED ALL THE QUESTIONS..
CAN YOU SEE THE LITTLE NOTE I ADDED AT THE BOTTOM?
SCHULZ
9-8
"DRY CLEAN ONLY"

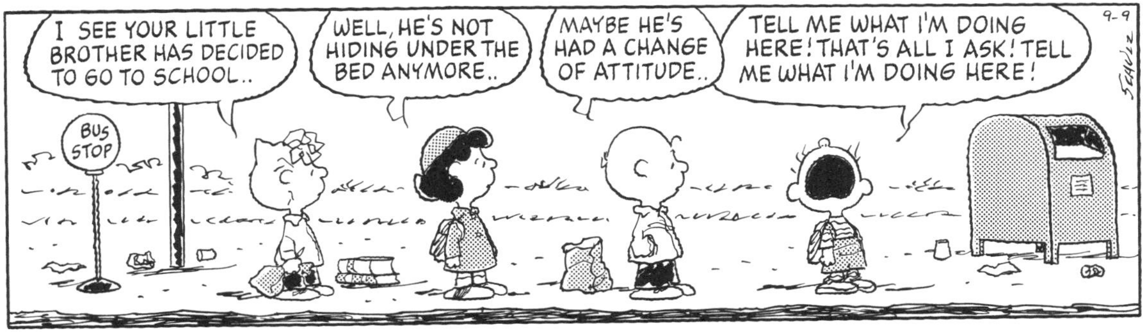
I SEE YOUR LITTLE BROTHER HAS DECIDED TO GO TO SCHOOL..
WELL, HE'S NOT HIDING UNDER THE BED ANYMORE..
MAYBE HE'S HAD A CHANGE OF ATTITUDE..
TELL ME WHAT I'M DOING HERE! THAT'S ALL I ASK! TELL ME WHAT I'M DOING HERE!
9-9
SCHULZ
BUS STOP

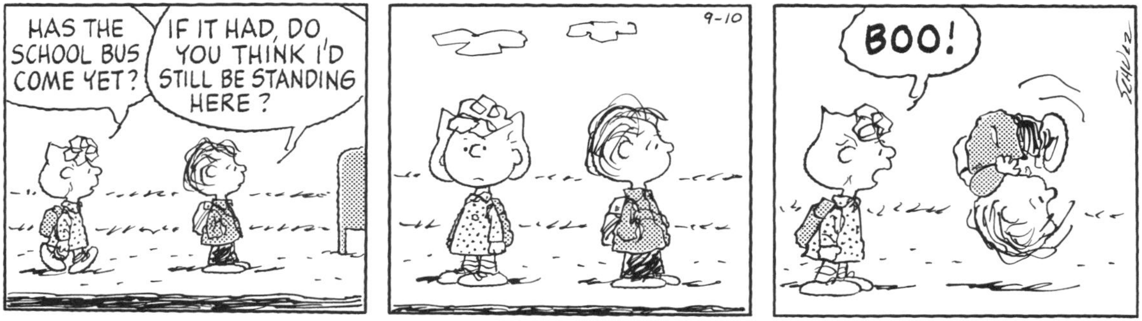
HAS THE SCHOOL BUS COME YET?
IF IT HAD, DO YOU THINK I'D STILL BE STANDING HERE?
9-10
BOO!

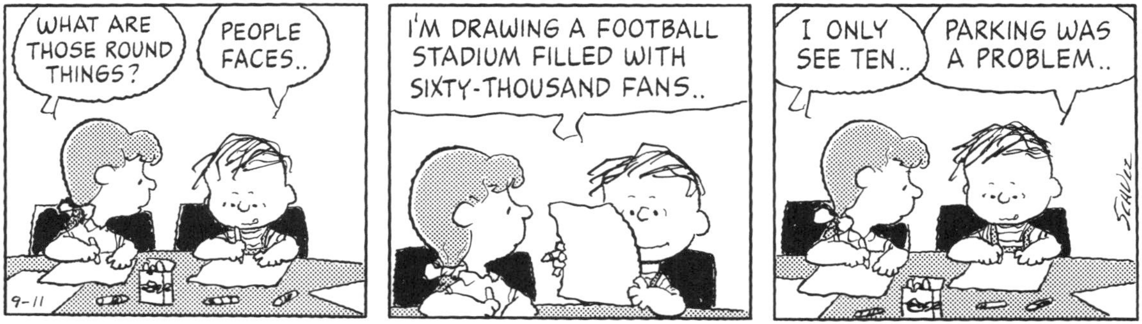
WHAT ARE THOSE ROUND THINGS?
PEOPLE FACES..
9-11
I'M DRAWING A FOOTBALL STADIUM FILLED WITH SIXTY-THOUSAND FANS..
I ONLY SEE TEN..
PARKING WAS A PROBLEM..

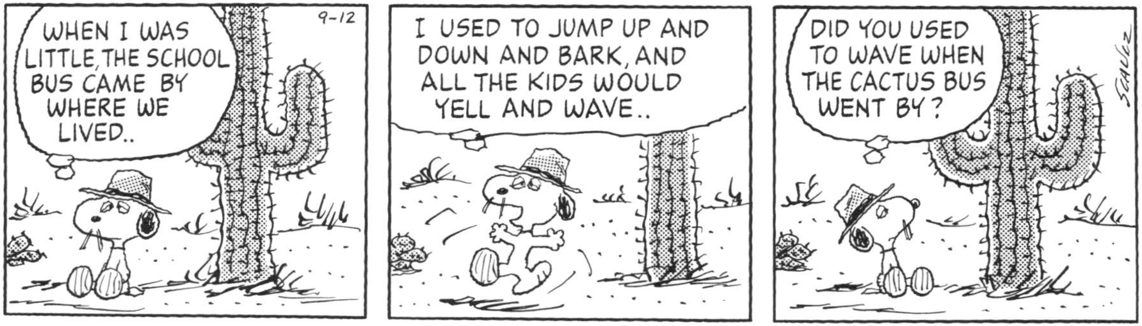
WHEN I WAS LITTLE, THE SCHOOL BUS CAME BY WHERE WE LIVED..
9-12
I USED TO JUMP UP AND DOWN AND BARK, AND ALL THE KIDS WOULD YELL AND WAVE..
DID YOU USED TO WAVE WHEN THE CACTUS BUS WENT BY?

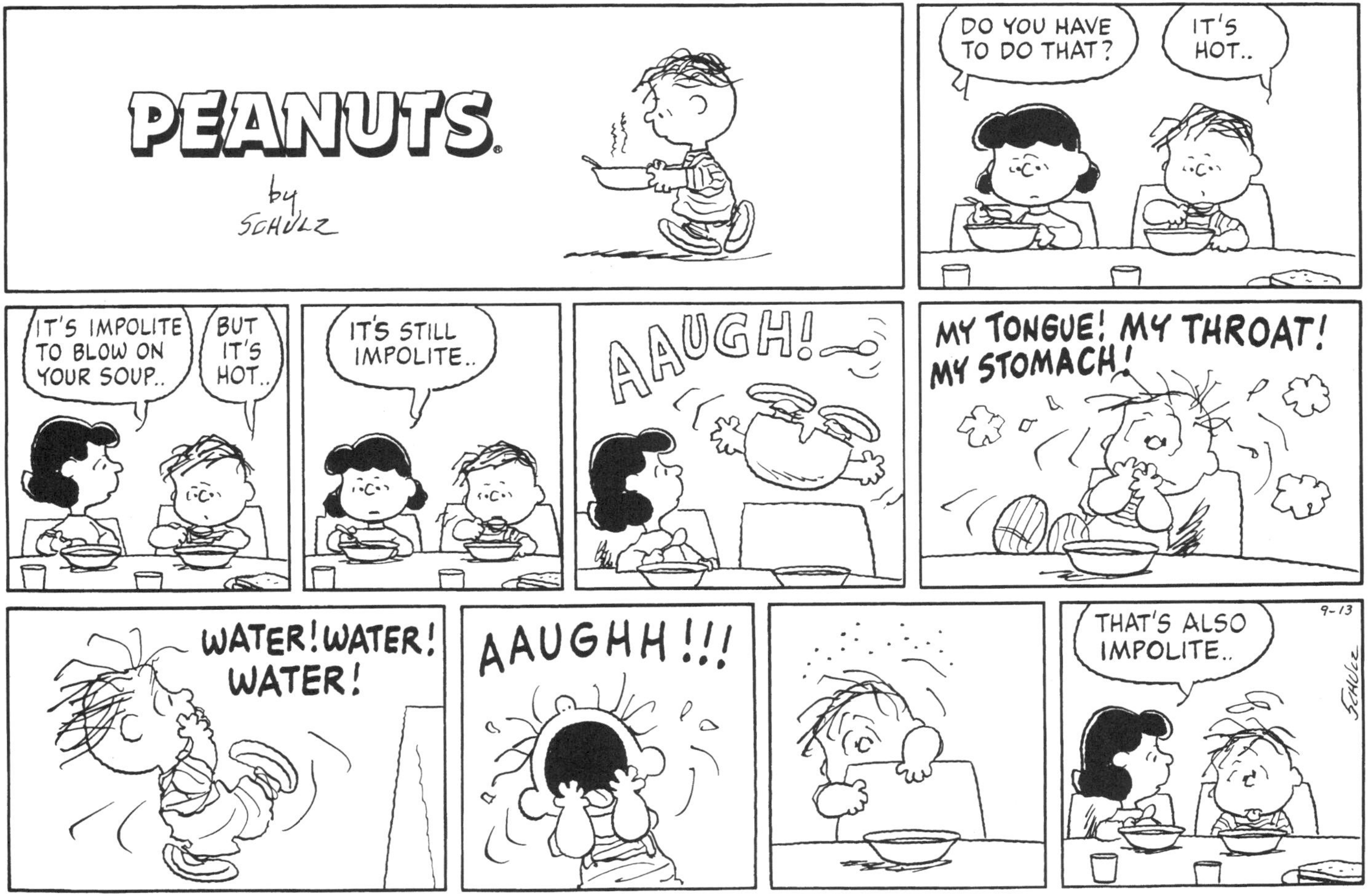
PEANUTS
by SCHULZ
DO YOU HAVE TO DO THAT?
IT'S HOT..
IT'S IMPOLITE TO BLOW ON YOUR SOUP..
BUT IT'S HOT..
IT'S STILL IMPOLITE..
AAUGH!
MY TONGUE! MY THROAT! MY STOMACH!
WATER! WATER! WATER!
AAUGHH!!!
THAT'S ALSO IMPOLITE..
9-13
SCHULZ

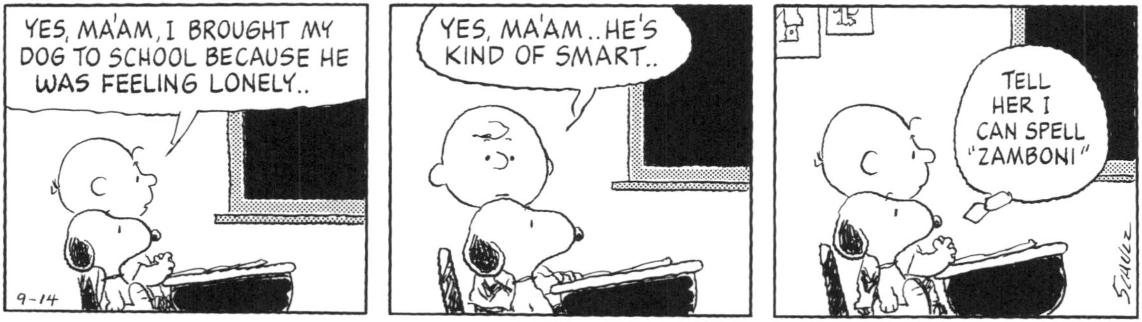
YES, MA'AM, I BROUGHT MY DOG TO SCHOOL BECAUSE HE WAS FEELING LONELY..
9-14
YES, MA'AM..HE'S KIND OF SMART..
TELL HER I CAN SPELL "ZAMBONI"
SCHULZ

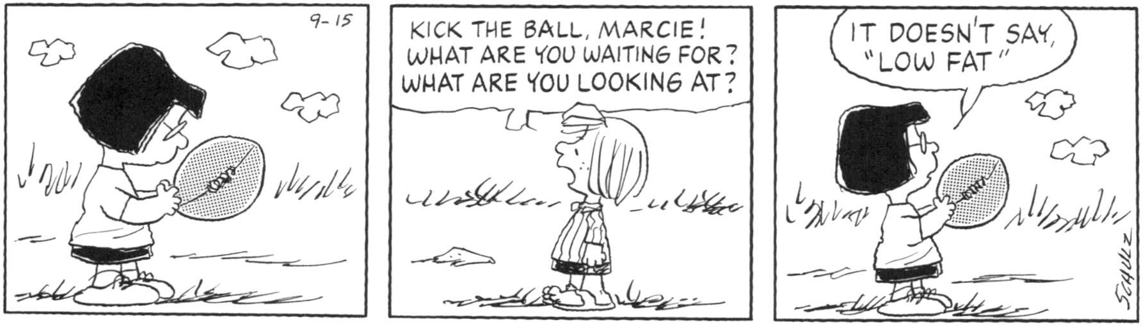
9-15
KICK THE BALL, MARCIE! WHAT ARE YOU WAITING FOR? WHAT ARE YOU LOOKING AT?
IT DOESN'T SAY, "LOW FAT"
SCHULZ

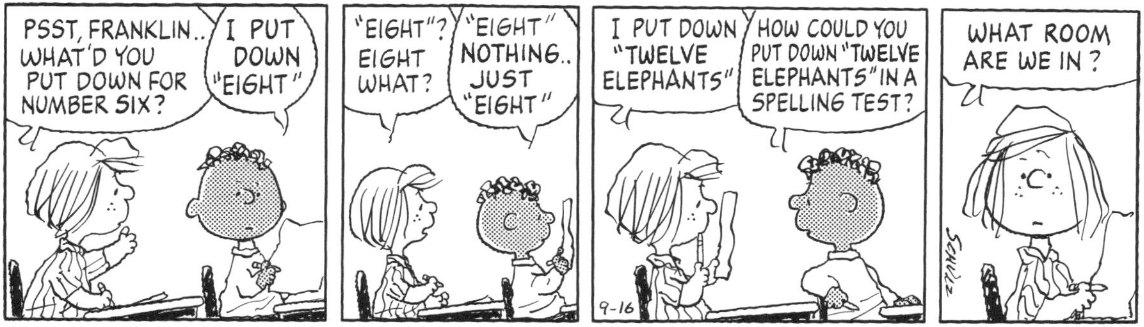
PSST, FRANKLIN.. WHAT'D YOU PUT DOWN FOR NUMBER SIX?
I PUT DOWN "EIGHT"
"EIGHT"? EIGHT WHAT?
"EIGHT" NOTHING.. JUST "EIGHT"
I PUT DOWN "TWELVE ELEPHANTS"
HOW COULD YOU PUT DOWN "TWELVE ELEPHANTS" IN A SPELLING TEST?
9-16
SCHULZ
WHAT ROOM ARE WE IN?

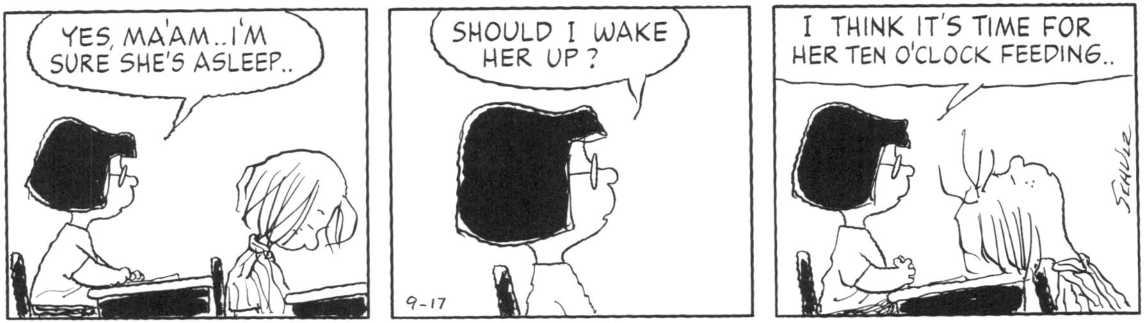
YES, MA'AM..I'M SURE SHE'S ASLEEP..
SHOULD I WAKE HER UP ?
9-17
I THINK IT'S TIME FOR HER TEN O'CLOCK FEEDING..
SCHULZ

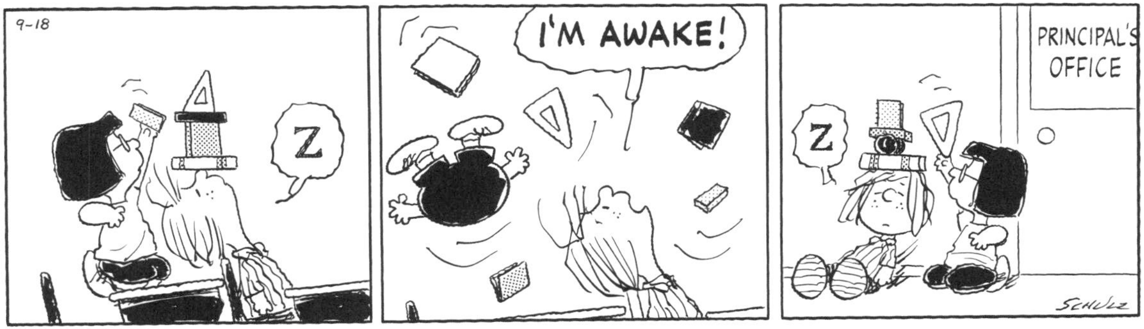
9-18
Z
I'M AWAKE!
PRINCIPAL'S OFFICE
Z
SCHULZ

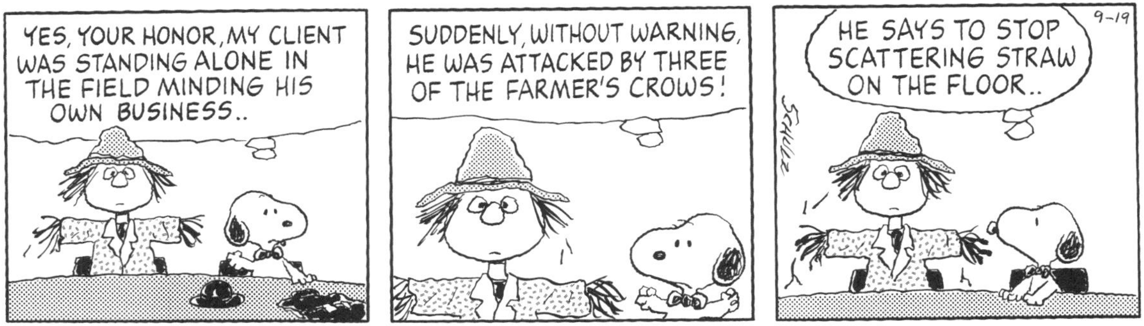
YES, YOUR HONOR, MY CLIENT WAS STANDING ALONE IN THE FIELD MINDING HIS OWN BUSINESS..
SUDDENLY, WITHOUT WARNING, HE WAS ATTACKED BY THREE OF THE FARMER'S CROWS!
SCHULZ
9-19
HE SAYS TO STOP SCATTERING STRAW ON THE FLOOR..

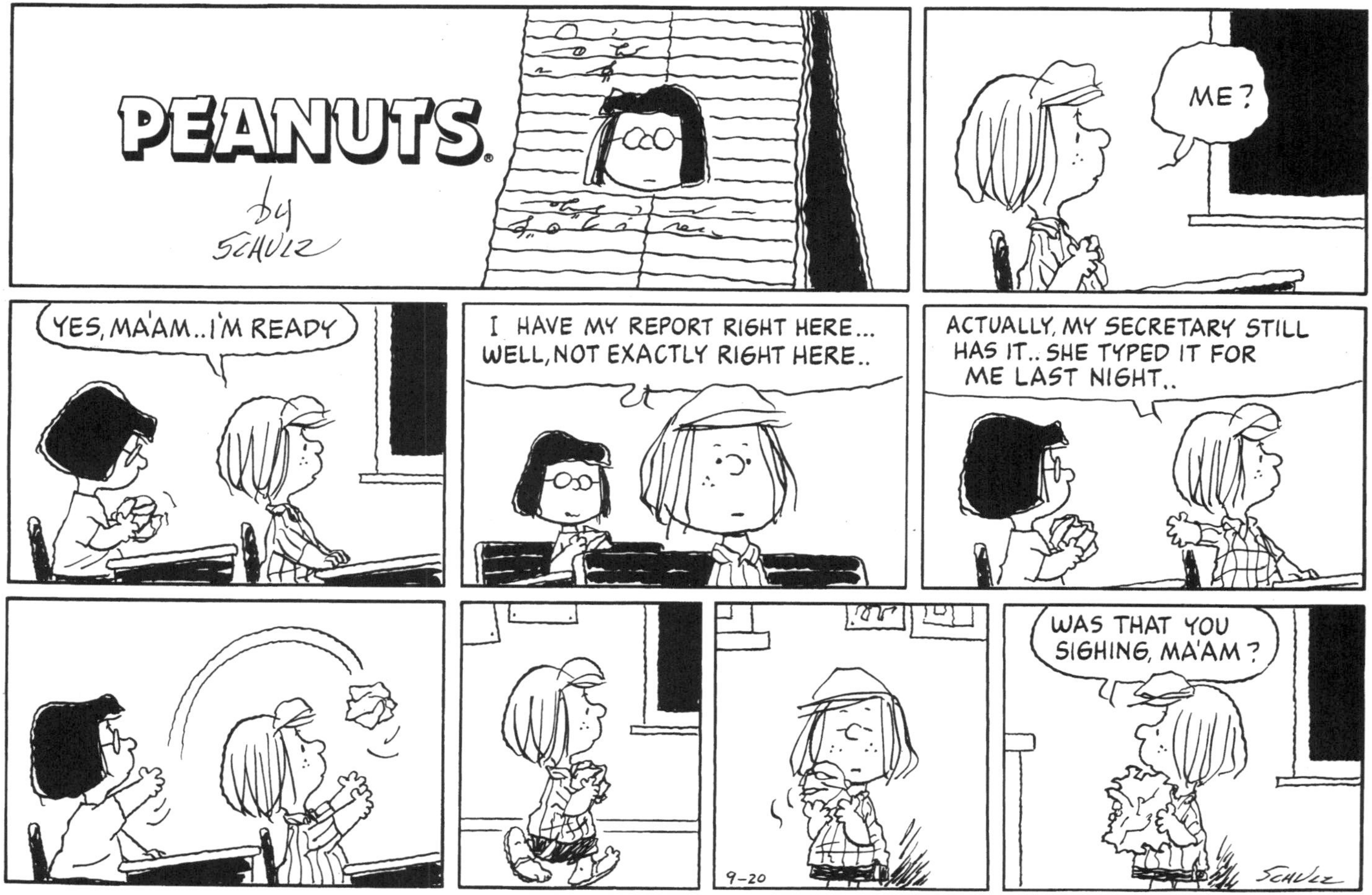
PEANUTS
by SCHULZ
ME?
YES, MA'AM..I'M READY
I HAVE MY REPORT RIGHT HERE... WELL, NOT EXACTLY RIGHT HERE..
ACTUALLY, MY SECRETARY STILL HAS IT.. SHE TYPED IT FOR ME LAST NIGHT..
9-20
WAS THAT YOU SIGHING, MA'AM?
SCHULZ

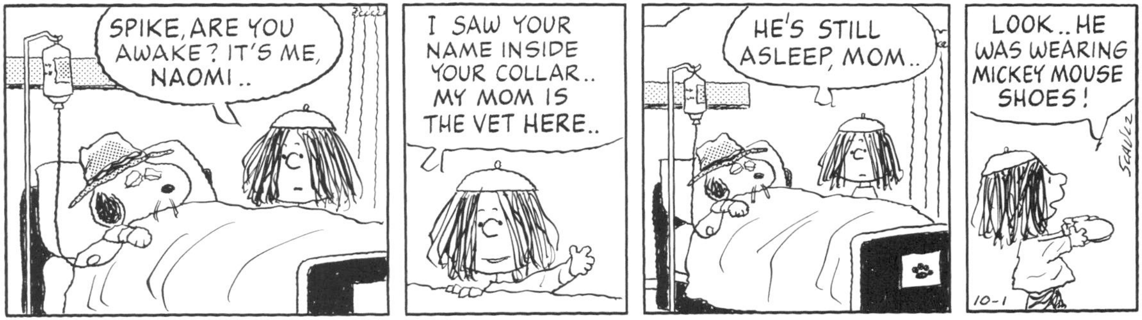
SPIKE, ARE YOU AWAKE? IT'S ME, NAOMI..
I SAW YOUR NAME INSIDE YOUR COLLAR.. MY MOM IS THE VET HERE..
HE'S STILL ASLEEP, MOM..
LOOK.. HE WAS WEARING MICKEY MOUSE SHOES!
SCHULZ
10-1

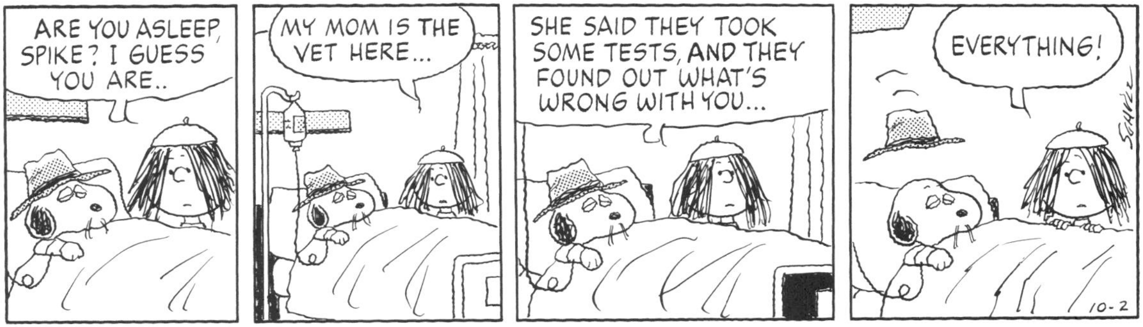
ARE YOU ASLEEP, SPIKE? I GUESS YOU ARE..
MY MOM IS THE VET HERE...
SHE SAID THEY TOOK SOME TESTS, AND THEY FOUND OUT WHAT'S WRONG WITH YOU...
EVERYTHING!
SCHULZ
10-2

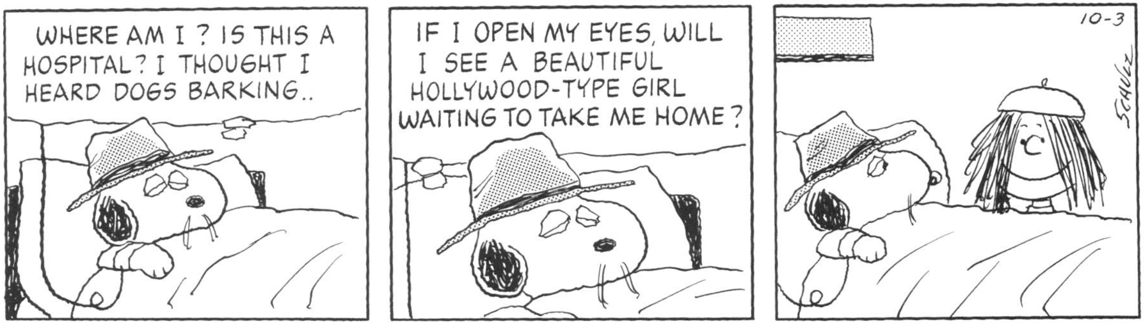
WHERE AM I? IS THIS A HOSPITAL? I THOUGHT I HEARD DOGS BARKING..
IF I OPEN MY EYES, WILL I SEE A BEAUTIFUL HOLLYWOOD-TYPE GIRL WAITING TO TAKE ME HOME?
10-3
SCHULZ

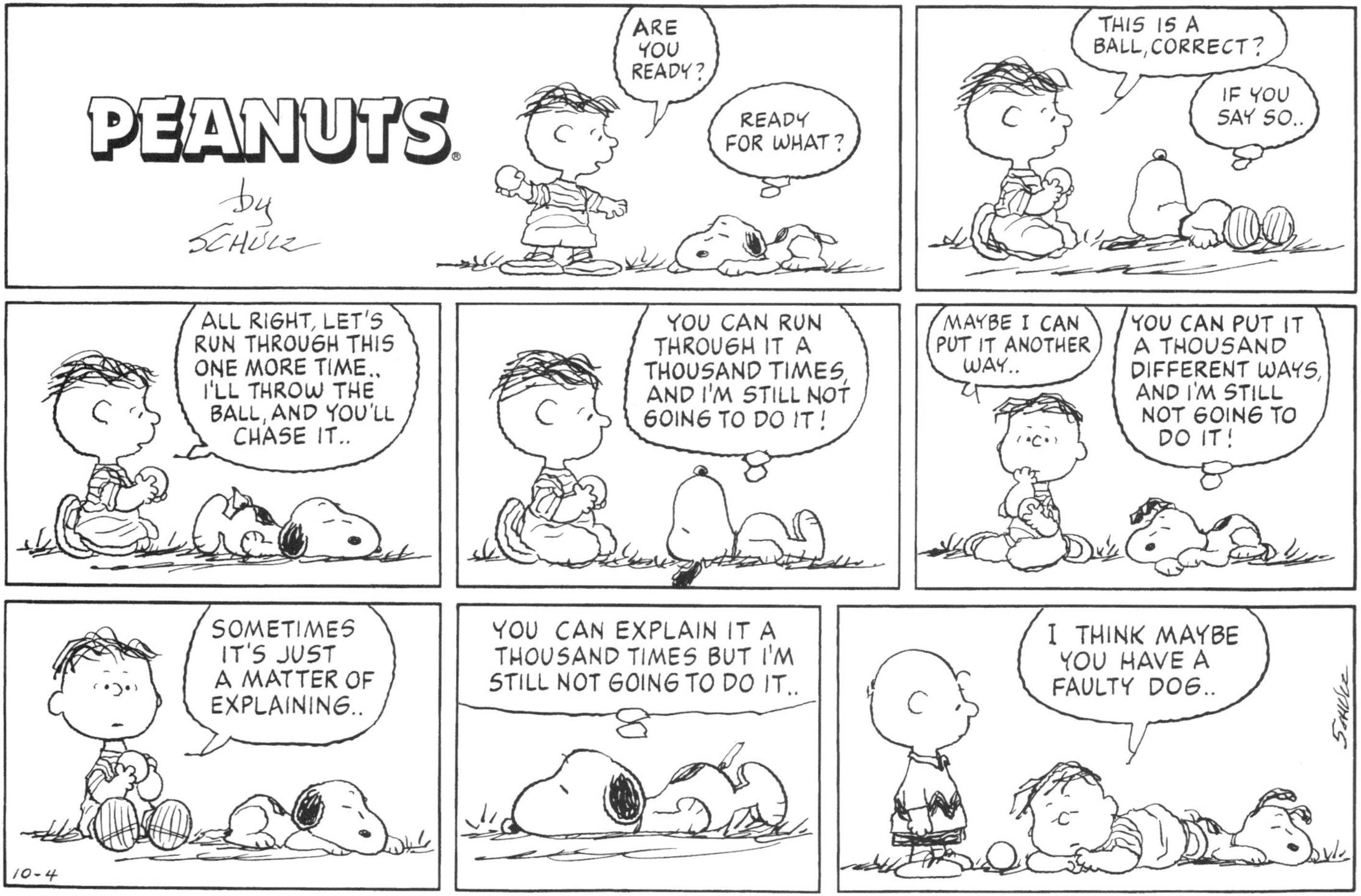
PEANUTS
by SCHULZ
ARE YOU READY?
READY FOR WHAT?
THIS IS A BALL, CORRECT?
IF YOU SAY SO..
ALL RIGHT, LET'S RUN THROUGH THIS ONE MORE TIME.. I'LL THROW THE BALL, AND YOU'LL CHASE IT..
YOU CAN RUN THROUGH IT A THOUSAND TIMES, AND I'M STILL NOT GOING TO DO IT!
MAYBE I CAN PUT IT ANOTHER WAY..
YOU CAN PUT IT A THOUSAND DIFFERENT WAYS, AND I'M STILL NOT GOING TO DO IT!
SOMETIMES IT'S JUST A MATTER OF EXPLAINING..
10-4
YOU CAN EXPLAIN IT A THOUSAND TIMES BUT I'M STILL NOT GOING TO DO IT..
I THINK MAYBE YOU HAVE A FAULTY DOG..
SCHULZ

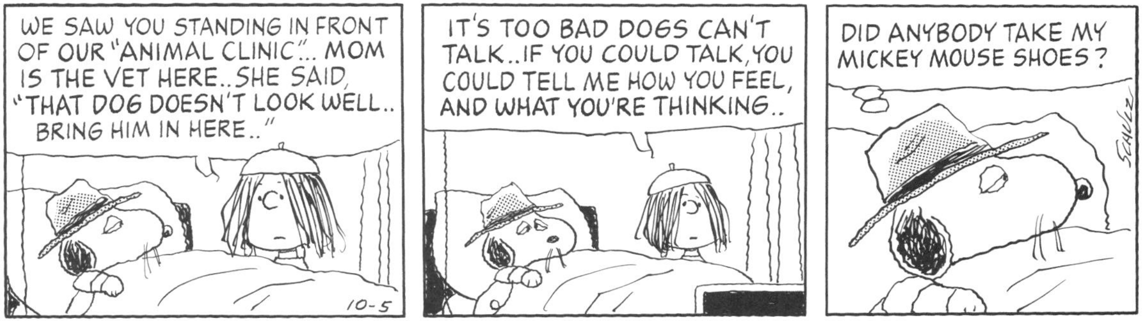
WE SAW YOU STANDING IN FRONT OF OUR "ANIMAL CLINIC".. MOM IS THE VET HERE..SHE SAID, "THAT DOG DOESN'T LOOK WELL.. BRING HIM IN HERE.."
IT'S TOO BAD DOGS CAN'T TALK..IF YOU COULD TALK, YOU COULD TELL ME HOW YOU FEEL, AND WHAT YOU'RE THINKING..
DID ANYBODY TAKE MY MICKEY MOUSE SHOES?
10-5
SCHULZ

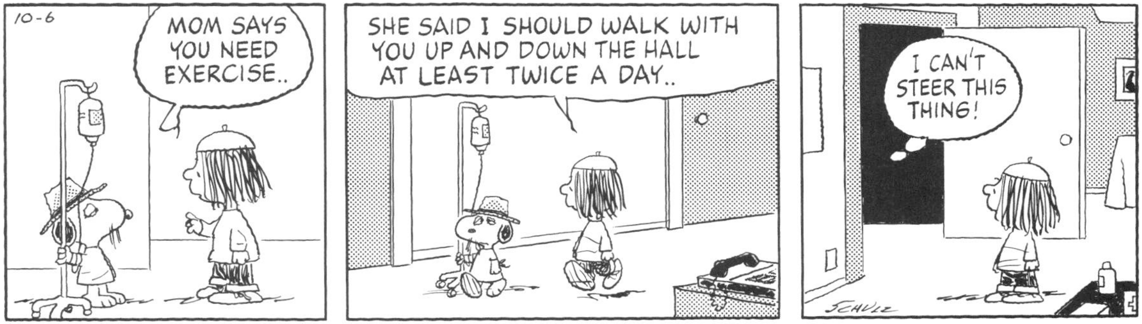
10-6
MOM SAYS YOU NEED EXERCISE..
SHE SAID I SHOULD WALK WITH YOU UP AND DOWN THE HALL AT LEAST TWICE A DAY..
I CAN'T STEER THIS THING!
SCHULZ

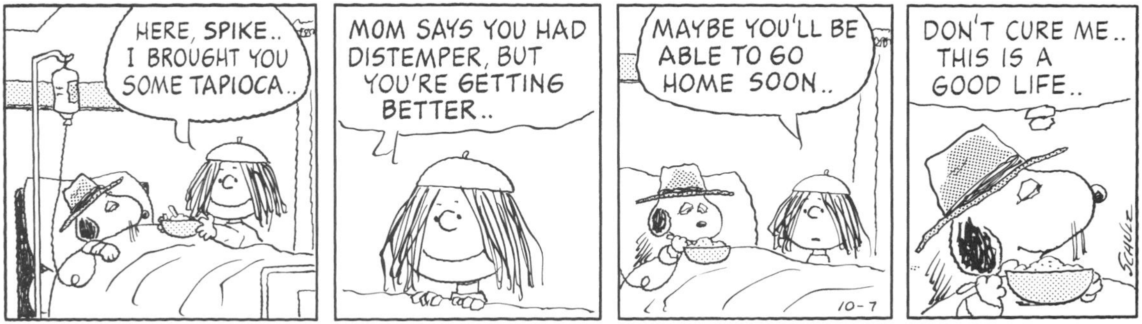
HERE, SPIKE.. I BROUGHT YOU SOME TAPIOCA..
MOM SAYS YOU HAD DISTEMPER, BUT YOU'RE GETTING BETTER..
MAYBE YOU'LL BE ABLE TO GO HOME SOON..
DON'T CURE ME.. THIS IS A GOOD LIFE..
10-7
SCHULZ

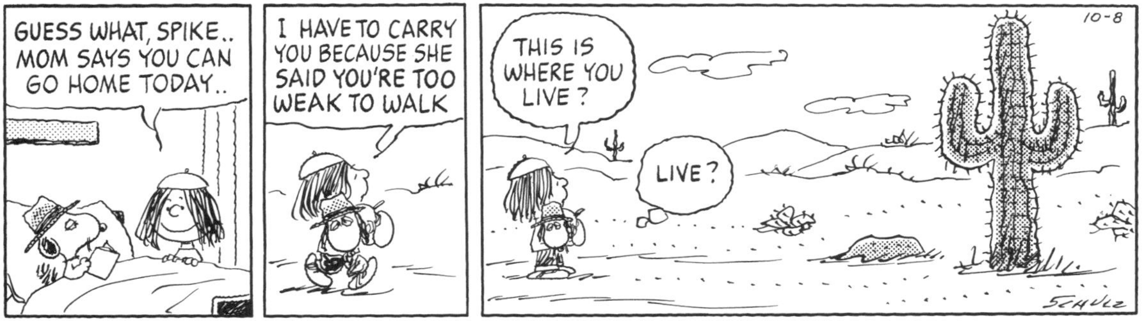
GUESS WHAT, SPIKE.. MOM SAYS YOU CAN GO HOME TODAY..
I HAVE TO CARRY YOU BECAUSE SHE SAID YOU'RE TOO WEAK TO WALK
10-8
THIS IS WHERE YOU LIVE ?
LIVE ?
SCHULZ

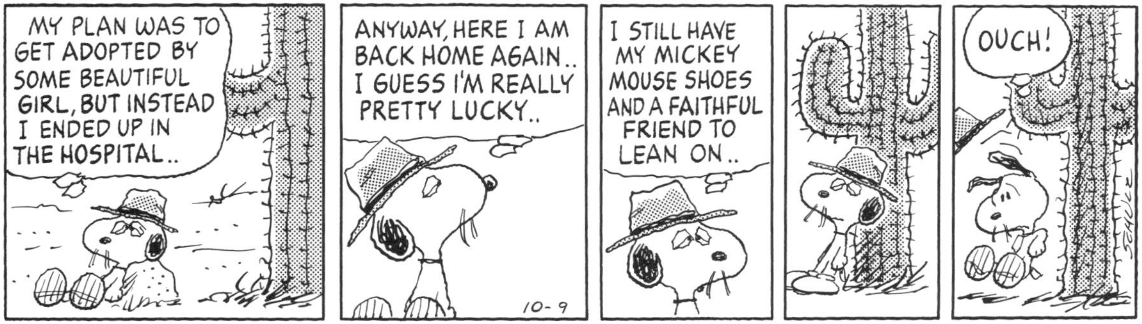
MY PLAN WAS TO GET ADOPTED BY SOME BEAUTIFUL GIRL, BUT INSTEAD I ENDED UP IN THE HOSPITAL..
ANYWAY, HERE I AM BACK HOME AGAIN.. I GUESS I'M REALLY PRETTY LUCKY..
10-9
I STILL HAVE MY MICKEY MOUSE SHOES AND A FAITHFUL FRIEND TO LEAN ON..
OUCH!
SCHULZ

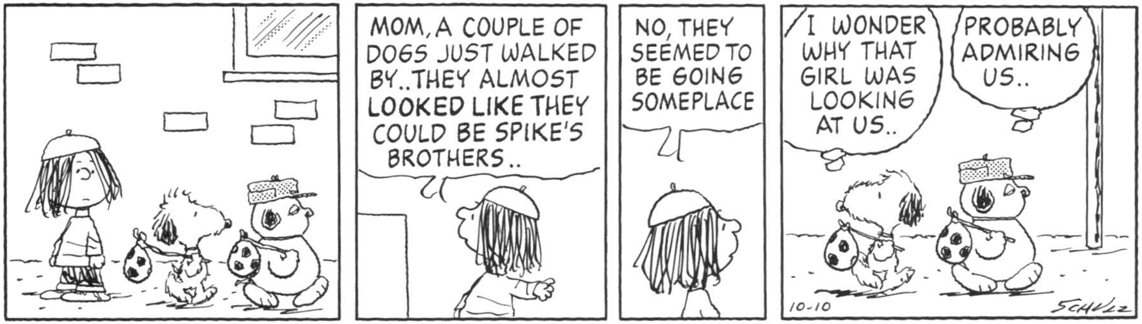
MOM, A COUPLE OF DOGS JUST WALKED BY.. THEY ALMOST LOOKED LIKE THEY COULD BE SPIKE'S BROTHERS..
NO, THEY SEEMED TO BE GOING SOMEPLACE
I WONDER WHY THAT GIRL WAS LOOKING AT US..
PROBABLY ADMIRING US..
10-10
SCHULZ

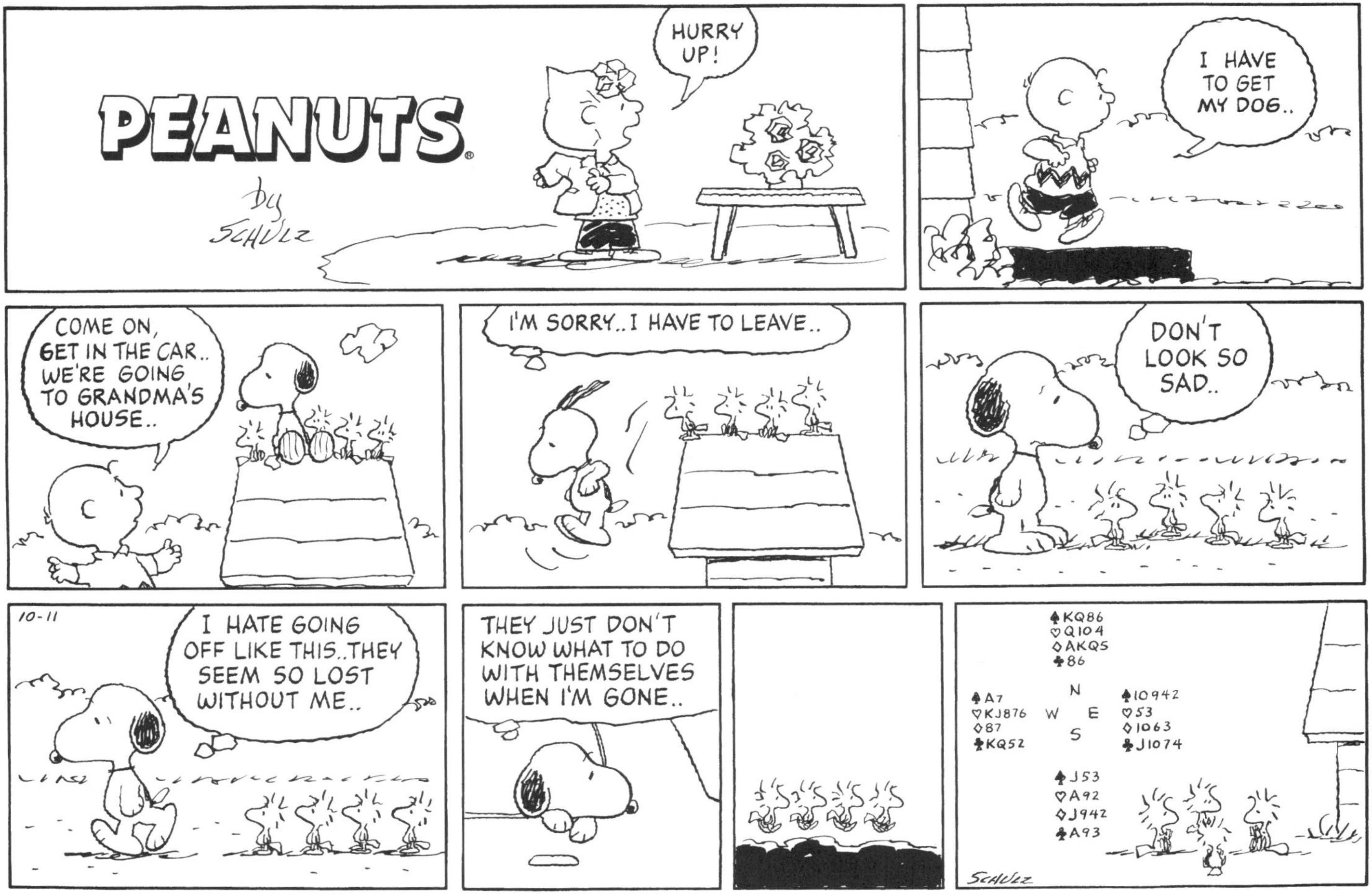
PEANUTS
by SCHULZ
HURRY UP!
I HAVE TO GET MY DOG..
COME ON, GET IN THE CAR.. WE'RE GOING TO GRANDMA'S HOUSE..
I'M SORRY..I HAVE TO LEAVE..
DON'T LOOK SO SAD..
10-11
I HATE GOING OFF LIKE THIS..THEY SEEM SO LOST WITHOUT ME..
THEY JUST DON'T KNOW WHAT TO DO WITH THEMSELVES WHEN I'M GONE..
♠KQ86 ♡Q104 ◊AKQ5 ♣86
N W E S
♠A7 ♡KJ876 ◊87 ♣KQ52
♠10942 ♡53 ◊1063 ♣J1074
♠J53 ♡A92 ◊J942 ♣A93
SCHULZ

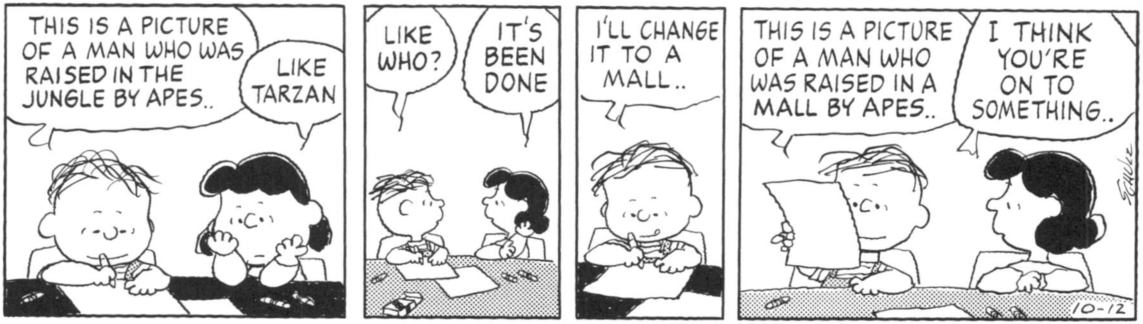
THIS IS A PICTURE OF A MAN WHO WAS RAISED IN THE JUNGLE BY APES..
LIKE TARZAN
LIKE WHO?
IT'S BEEN DONE
I'LL CHANGE IT TO A MALL..
THIS IS A PICTURE OF A MAN WHO WAS RAISED IN A MALL BY APES..
I THINK YOU'RE ON TO SOMETHING..
SCHULZ
10-12

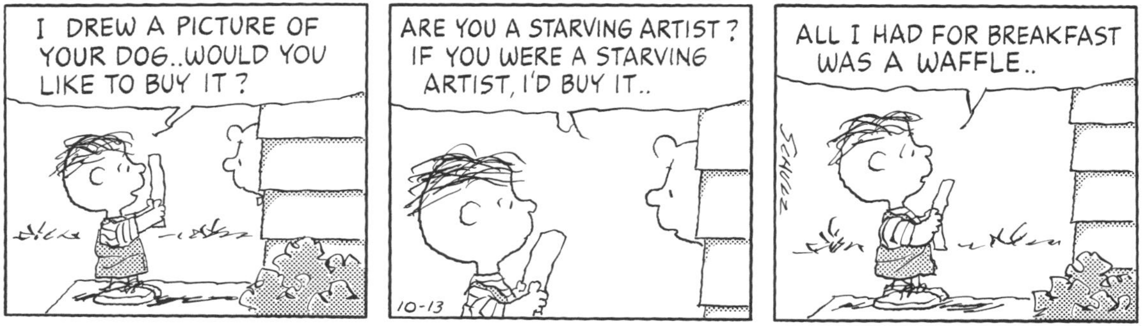
I DREW A PICTURE OF YOUR DOG..WOULD YOU LIKE TO BUY IT?
ARE YOU A STARVING ARTIST? IF YOU WERE A STARVING ARTIST, I'D BUY IT..
10-13
ALL I HAD FOR BREAKFAST WAS A WAFFLE..
SCHULZ

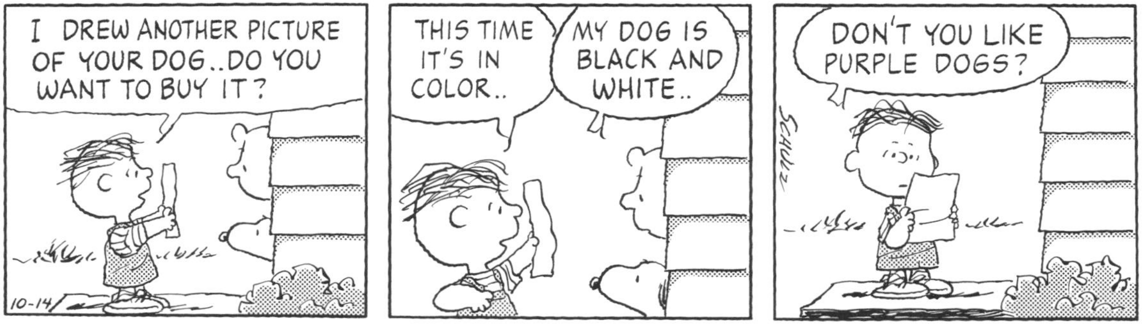
I DREW ANOTHER PICTURE OF YOUR DOG..DO YOU WANT TO BUY IT?
10-14
THIS TIME IT'S IN COLOR..
MY DOG IS BLACK AND WHITE..
DON'T YOU LIKE PURPLE DOGS?
SCHULZ

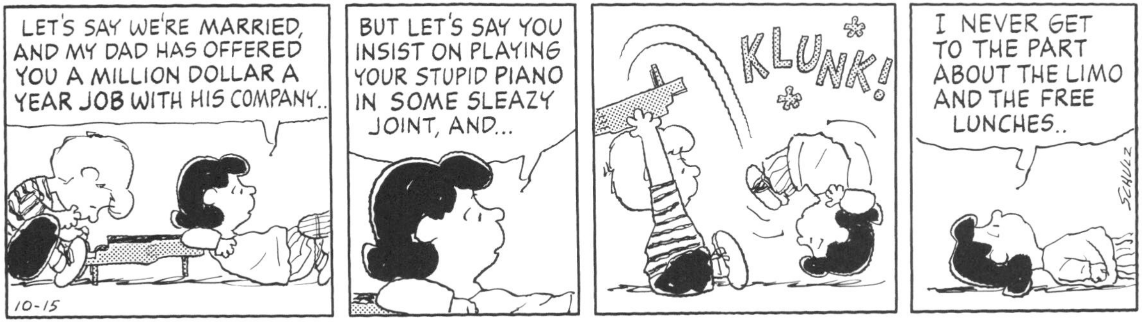
LET'S SAY WE'RE MARRIED, AND MY DAD HAS OFFERED YOU A MILLION DOLLAR A YEAR JOB WITH HIS COMPANY..
10-15
BUT LET'S SAY YOU INSIST ON PLAYING YOUR STUPID PIANO IN SOME SLEAZY JOINT, AND...
KLUNK!
I NEVER GET TO THE PART ABOUT THE LIMO AND THE FREE LUNCHES..
SCHULZ

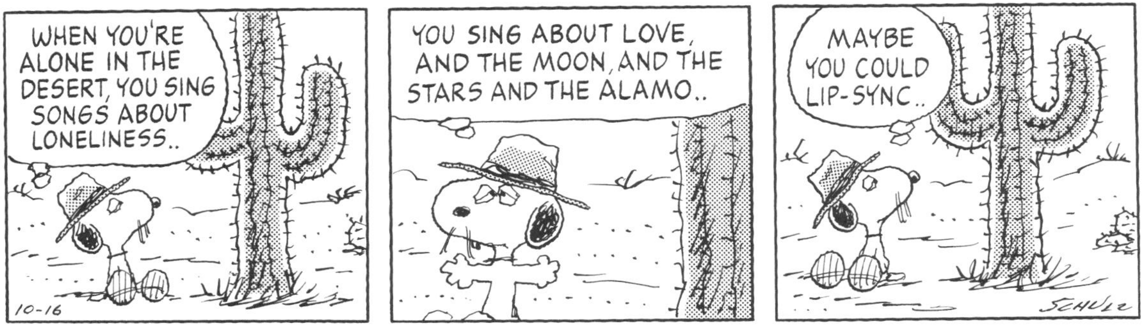
WHEN YOU'RE ALONE IN THE DESERT, YOU SING SONGS ABOUT LONELINESS..
10-16
YOU SING ABOUT LOVE, AND THE MOON, AND THE STARS AND THE ALAMO..
MAYBE YOU COULD LIP-SYNC..
SCHULZ

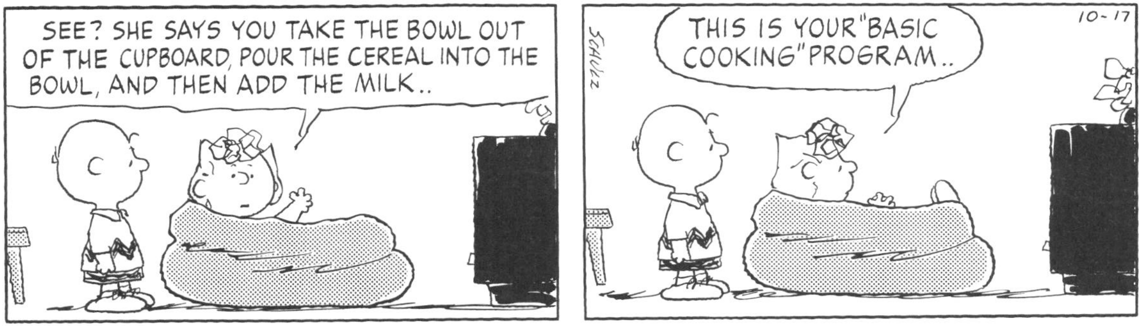
SEE? SHE SAYS YOU TAKE THE BOWL OUT OF THE CUPBOARD, POUR THE CEREAL INTO THE BOWL, AND THEN ADD THE MILK..
SCHULZ
10-17
THIS IS YOUR "BASIC COOKING" PROGRAM..

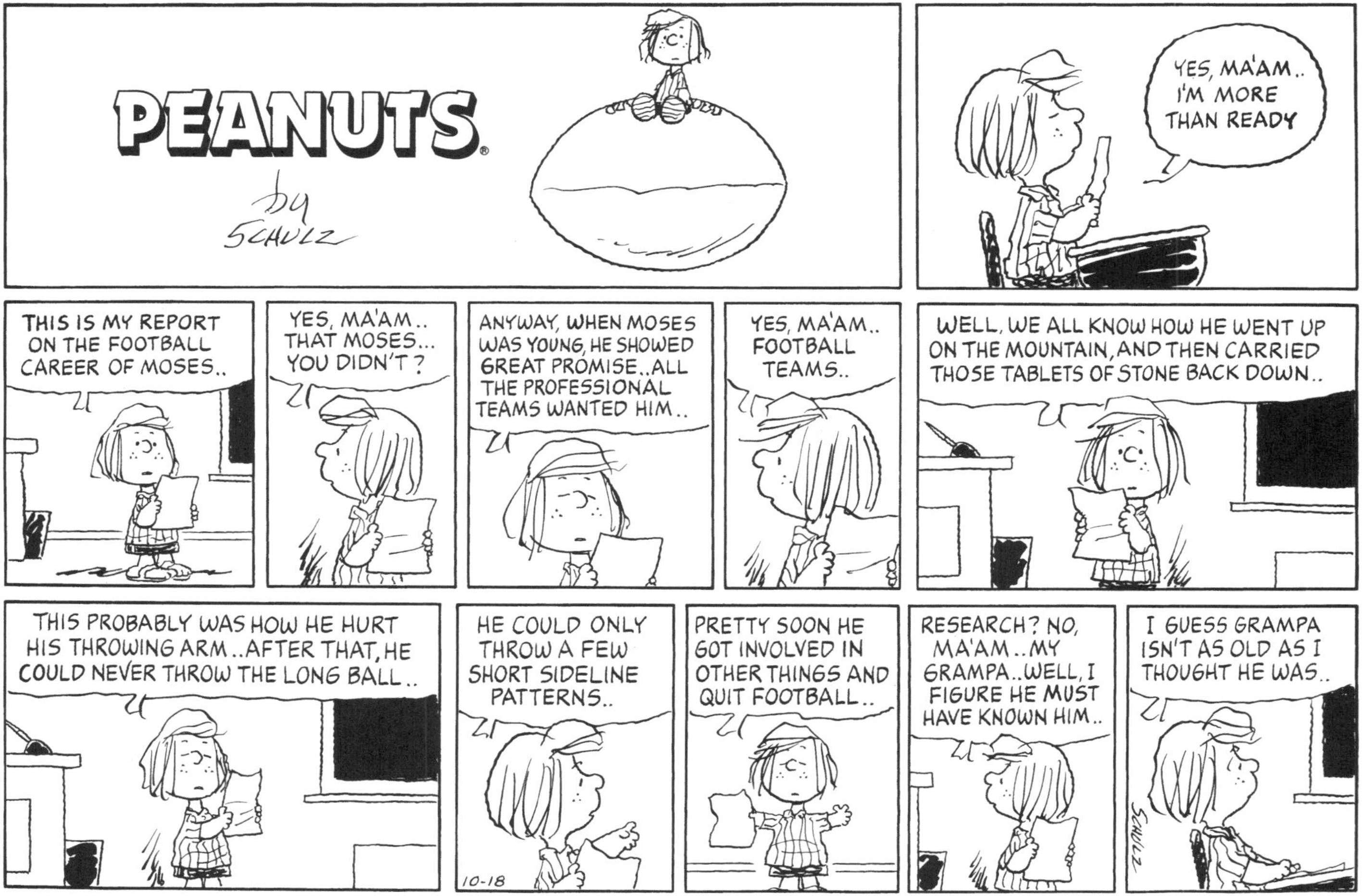
PEANUTS
by SCHULZ
YES, MA'AM.. I'M MORE THAN READY
THIS IS MY REPORT ON THE FOOTBALL CAREER OF MOSES..
YES, MA'AM.. THAT MOSES... YOU DIDN'T?
ANYWAY, WHEN MOSES WAS YOUNG, HE SHOWED GREAT PROMISE..ALL THE PROFESSIONAL TEAMS WANTED HIM..
YES, MA'AM.. FOOTBALL TEAMS..
WELL, WE ALL KNOW HOW HE WENT UP ON THE MOUNTAIN, AND THEN CARRIED THOSE TABLETS OF STONE BACK DOWN..
THIS PROBABLY WAS HOW HE HURT HIS THROWING ARM..AFTER THAT, HE COULD NEVER THROW THE LONG BALL..
HE COULD ONLY THROW A FEW SHORT SIDELINE PATTERNS..
10-18
PRETTY SOON HE GOT INVOLVED IN OTHER THINGS AND QUIT FOOTBALL..
RESEARCH? NO, MA'AM..MY GRAMPA..WELL, I FIGURE HE MUST HAVE KNOWN HIM..
SCHULZ
I GUESS GRAMPA ISN'T AS OLD AS I THOUGHT HE WAS..

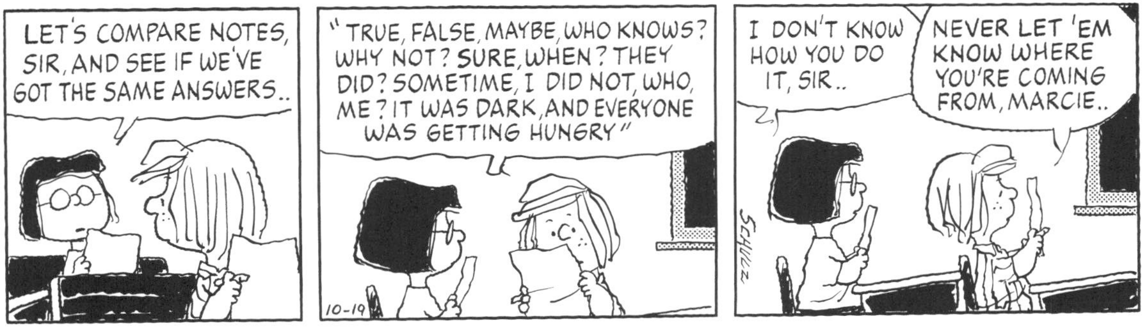
LET'S COMPARE NOTES, SIR, AND SEE IF WE'VE GOT THE SAME ANSWERS..
"TRUE, FALSE, MAYBE, WHO KNOWS? WHY NOT? SURE, WHEN? THEY DID? SOMETIME, I DID NOT, WHO, ME? IT WAS DARK, AND EVERYONE WAS GETTING HUNGRY"
10-19
I DON'T KNOW HOW YOU DO IT, SIR..
NEVER LET 'EM KNOW WHERE YOU'RE COMING FROM, MARCIE..
SCHULZ

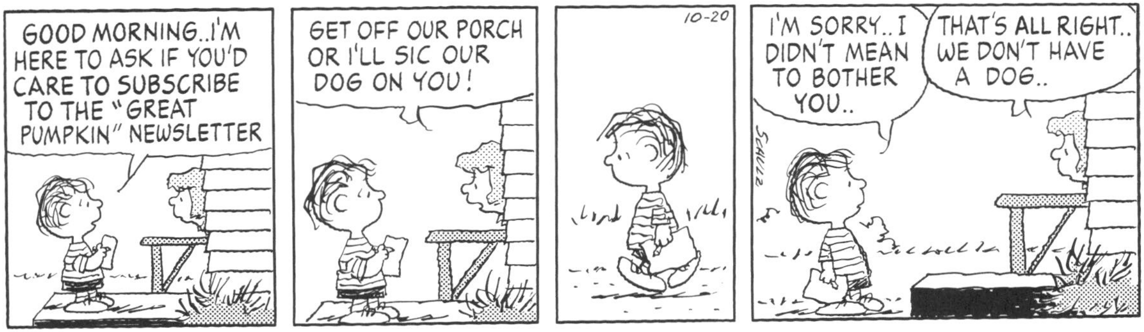
GOOD MORNING..I'M HERE TO ASK IF YOU'D CARE TO SUBSCRIBE TO THE "GREAT PUMPKIN" NEWSLETTER
GET OFF OUR PORCH OR I'LL SIC OUR DOG ON YOU!
10-20
I'M SORRY.. I DIDN'T MEAN TO BOTHER YOU..
THAT'S ALL RIGHT.. WE DON'T HAVE A DOG..
SCHULZ

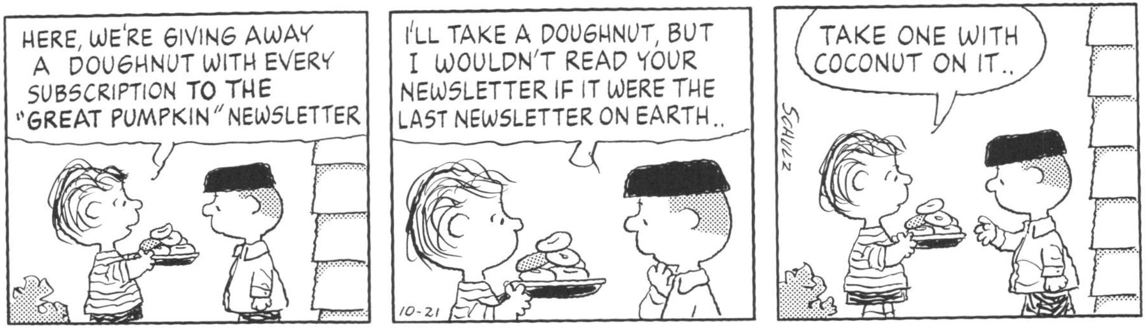
HERE, WE'RE GIVING AWAY A DOUGHNUT WITH EVERY SUBSCRIPTION TO THE "GREAT PUMPKIN" NEWSLETTER
I'LL TAKE A DOUGHNUT, BUT I WOULDN'T READ YOUR NEWSLETTER IF IT WERE THE LAST NEWSLETTER ON EARTH..
10-21
TAKE ONE WITH COCONUT ON IT..
SCHULZ

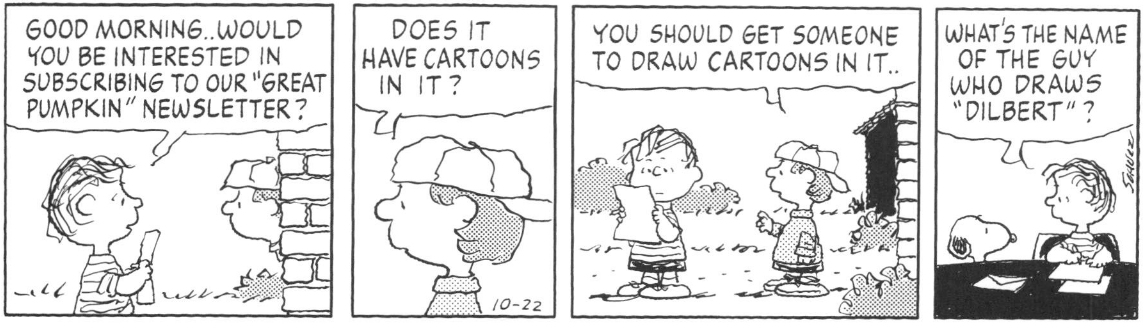
GOOD MORNING..WOULD YOU BE INTERESTED IN SUBSCRIBING TO OUR "GREAT PUMPKIN" NEWSLETTER?
DOES IT HAVE CARTOONS IN IT?
YOU SHOULD GET SOMEONE TO DRAW CARTOONS IN IT..
WHAT'S THE NAME OF THE GUY WHO DRAWS "DILBERT"?
10-22
SCHULZ

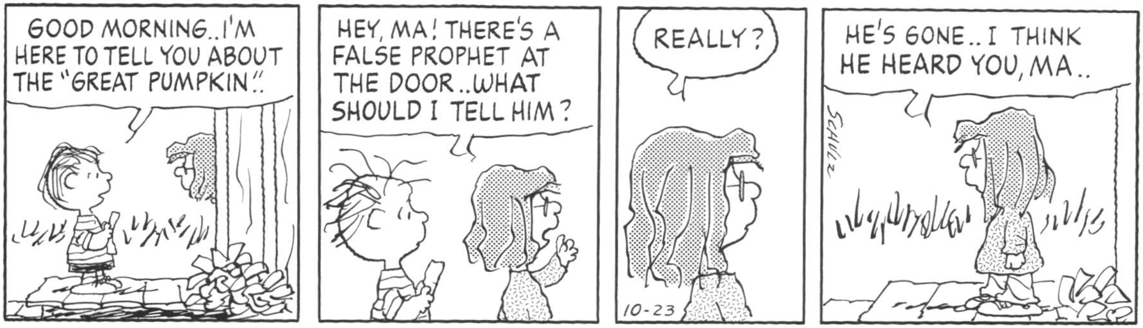
GOOD MORNING..I'M HERE TO TELL YOU ABOUT THE "GREAT PUMPKIN"..
HEY, MA! THERE'S A FALSE PROPHET AT THE DOOR..WHAT SHOULD I TELL HIM?
REALLY?
HE'S GONE..I THINK HE HEARD YOU, MA..
10-23
SCHULZ

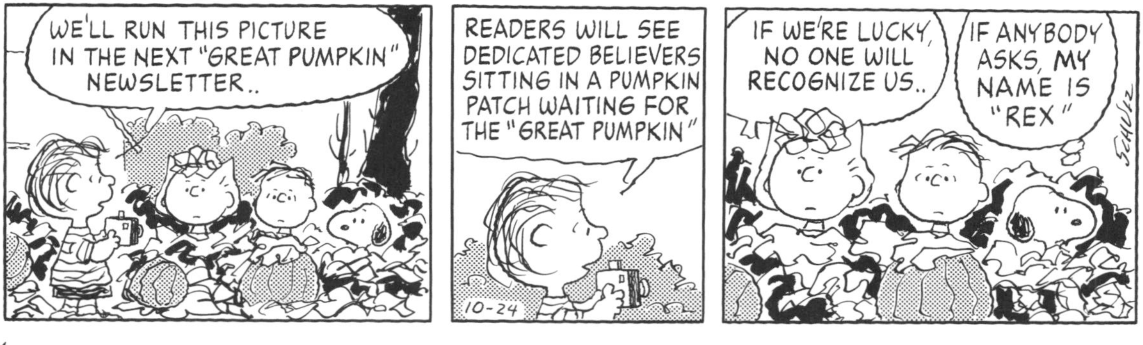
WE'LL RUN THIS PICTURE IN THE NEXT "GREAT PUMPKIN" NEWSLETTER..
READERS WILL SEE DEDICATED BELIEVERS SITTING IN A PUMPKIN PATCH WAITING FOR THE "GREAT PUMPKIN"
IF WE'RE LUCKY, NO ONE WILL RECOGNIZE US..
IF ANYBODY ASKS, MY NAME IS "REX"
10-24
SCHULZ

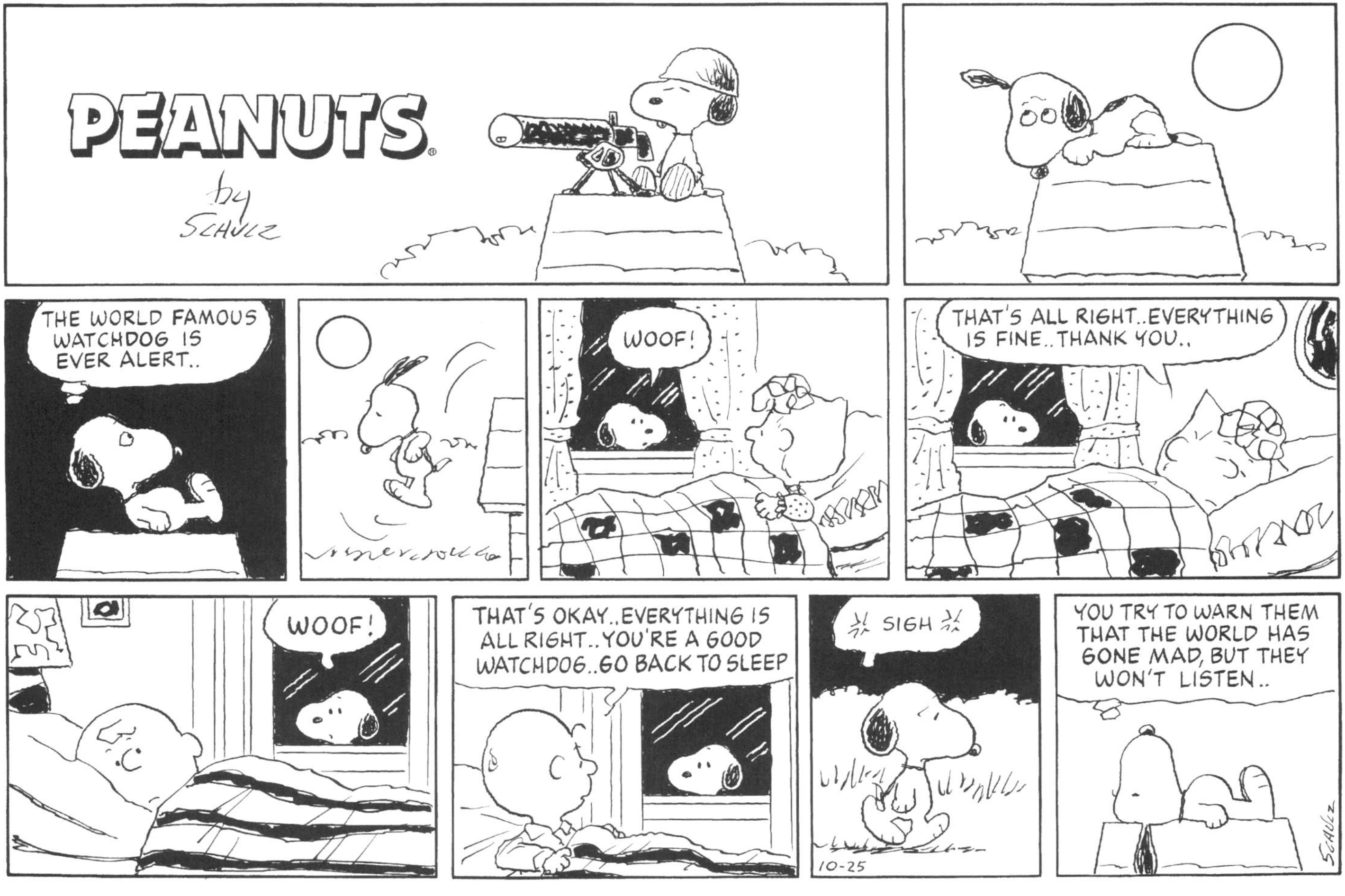
PEANUTS
by SCHULZ
THE WORLD FAMOUS WATCHDOG IS EVER ALERT..
WOOF!
THAT'S ALL RIGHT..EVERYTHING IS FINE..THANK YOU..
WOOF!
THAT'S OKAY..EVERYTHING IS ALL RIGHT..YOU'RE A GOOD WATCHDOG..GO BACK TO SLEEP
SIGH
10-25
YOU TRY TO WARN THEM THAT THE WORLD HAS GONE MAD, BUT THEY WON'T LISTEN..
SCHULZ

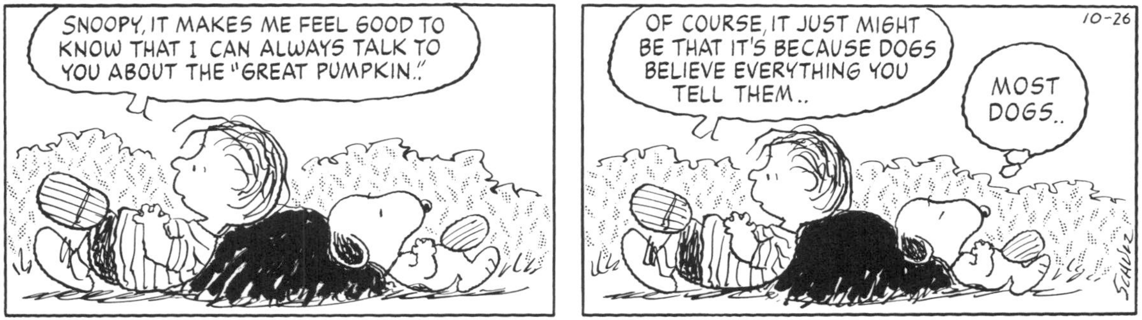
SNOOPY, IT MAKES ME FEEL GOOD TO KNOW THAT I CAN ALWAYS TALK TO YOU ABOUT THE "GREAT PUMPKIN."
10-26
OF COURSE, IT JUST MIGHT BE THAT IT'S BECAUSE DOGS BELIEVE EVERYTHING YOU TELL THEM..
MOST DOGS..
SCHULZ

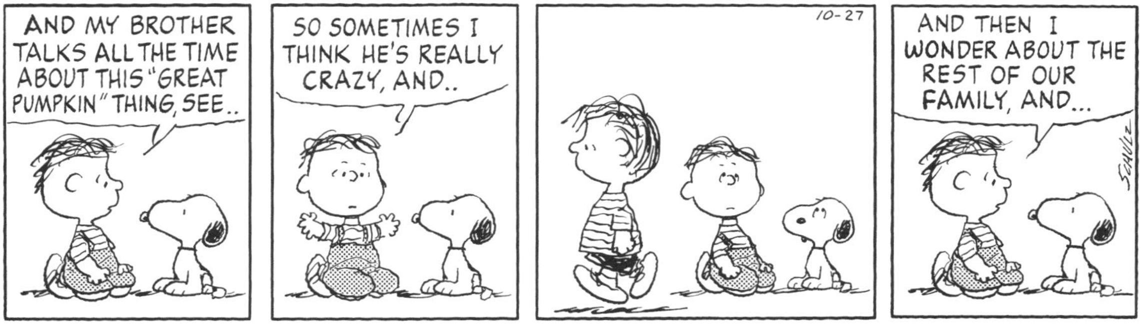
AND MY BROTHER TALKS ALL THE TIME ABOUT THIS "GREAT PUMPKIN" THING, SEE..
SO SOMETIMES I THINK HE'S REALLY CRAZY, AND..
10-27
AND THEN I WONDER ABOUT THE REST OF OUR FAMILY, AND...
SCHULZ

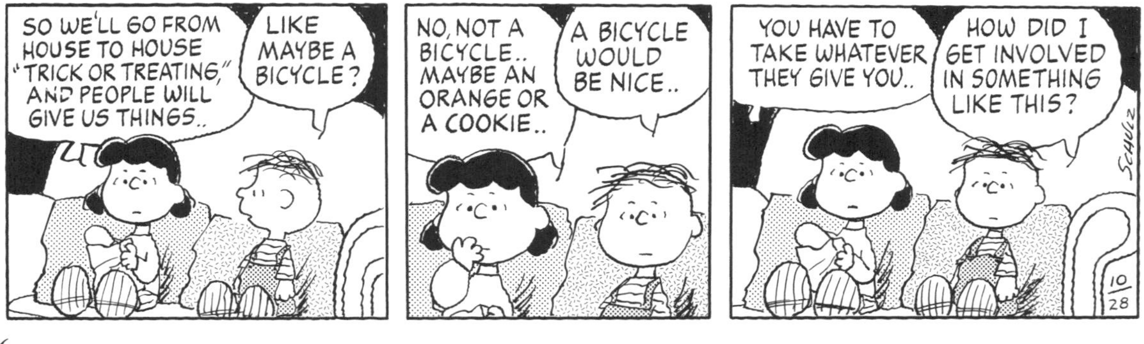
SO WE'LL GO FROM HOUSE TO HOUSE "TRICK OR TREATING," AND PEOPLE WILL GIVE US THINGS..
LIKE MAYBE A BICYCLE?
NO, NOT A BICYCLE.. MAYBE AN ORANGE OR A COOKIE..
A BICYCLE WOULD BE NICE..
YOU HAVE TO TAKE WHATEVER THEY GIVE YOU..
HOW DID I GET INVOLVED IN SOMETHING LIKE THIS?
SCHULZ
10/28

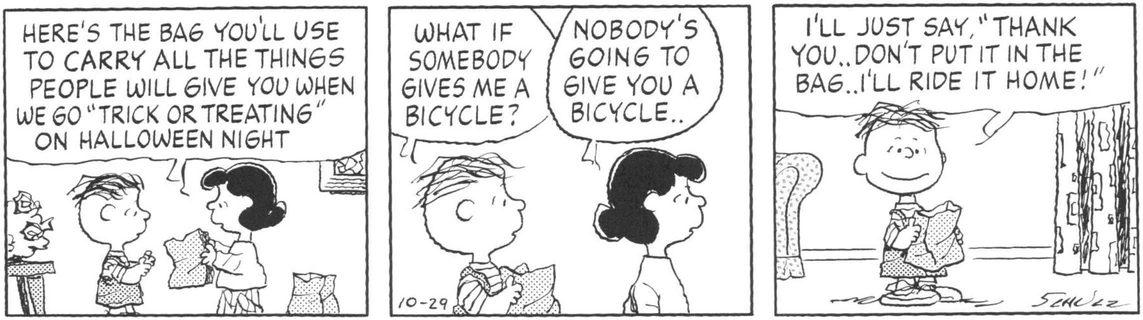
HERE'S THE BAG YOU'LL USE TO CARRY ALL THE THINGS PEOPLE WILL GIVE YOU WHEN WE GO "TRICK OR TREATING" ON HALLOWEEN NIGHT
WHAT IF SOMEBODY GIVES ME A BICYCLE?
NOBODY'S GOING TO GIVE YOU A BICYCLE..
10-29
I'LL JUST SAY, "THANK YOU..DON'T PUT IT IN THE BAG..I'LL RIDE IT HOME!"
SCHULZ

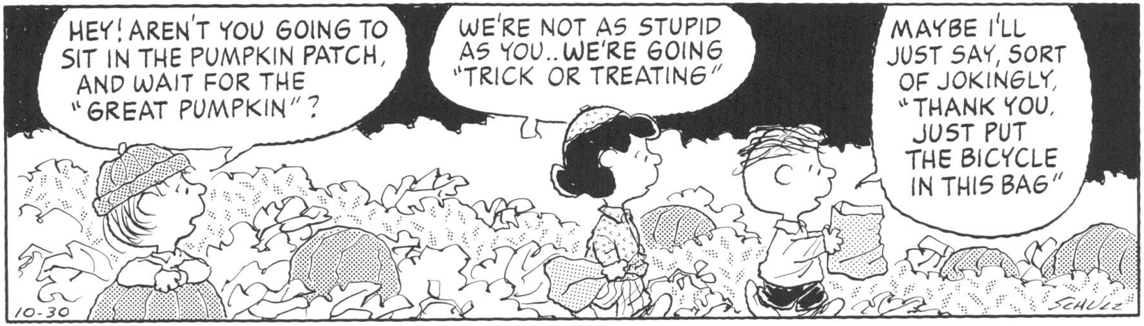
HEY! AREN'T YOU GOING TO SIT IN THE PUMPKIN PATCH, AND WAIT FOR THE "GREAT PUMPKIN"?
WE'RE NOT AS STUPID AS YOU..WE'RE GOING "TRICK OR TREATING"
MAYBE I'LL JUST SAY, SORT OF JOKINGLY, "THANK YOU. JUST PUT THE BICYCLE IN THIS BAG"
10-30
SCHULZ

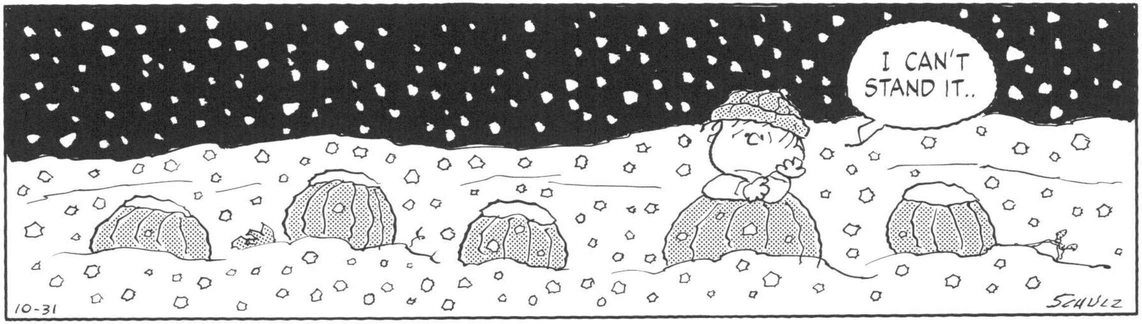
I CAN'T STAND IT..
10-31
SCHULZ

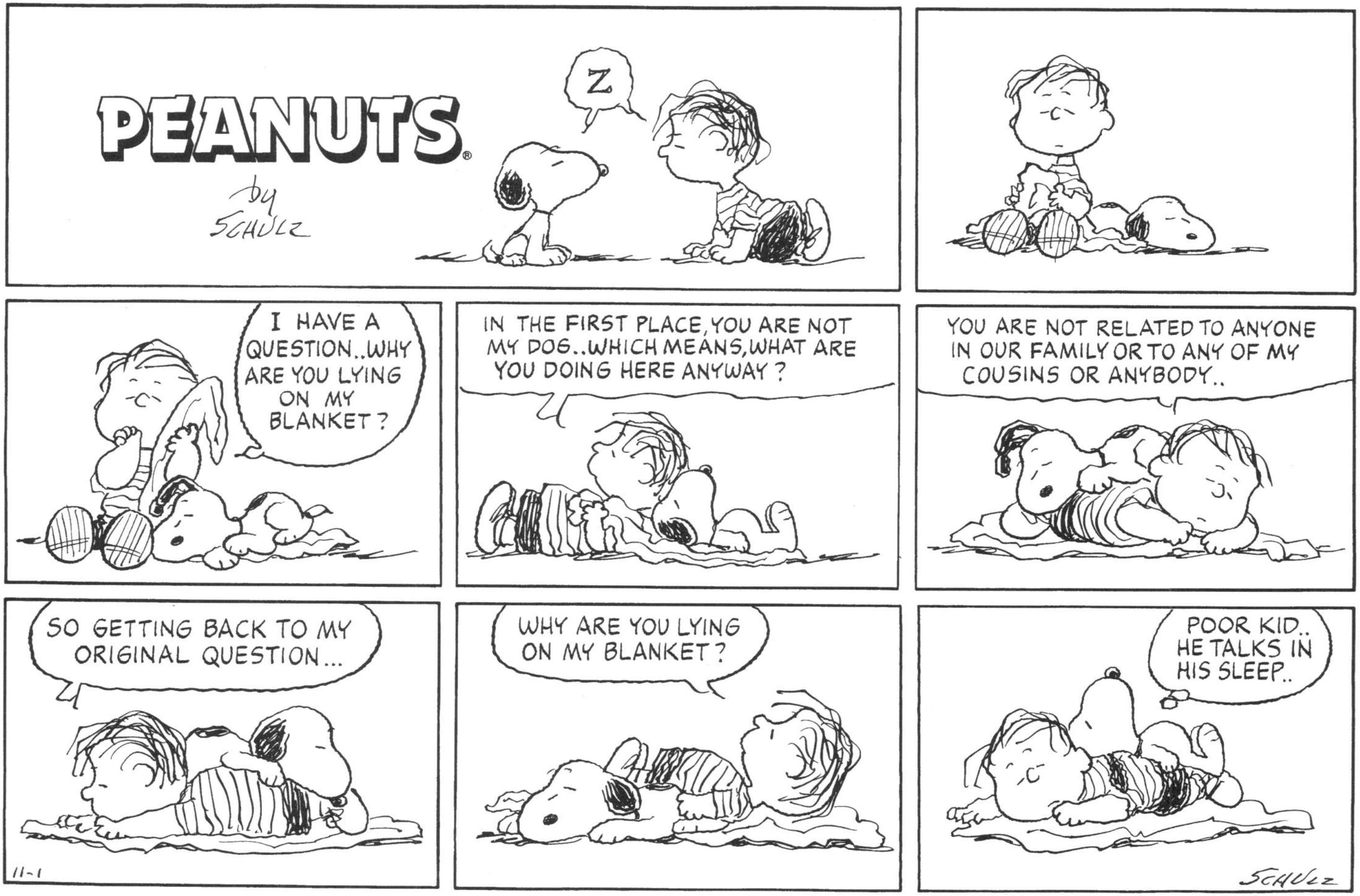
PEANUTS
by SCHULZ
Z
I HAVE A QUESTION..WHY ARE YOU LYING ON MY BLANKET?
IN THE FIRST PLACE, YOU ARE NOT MY DOG..WHICH MEANS, WHAT ARE YOU DOING HERE ANYWAY?
YOU ARE NOT RELATED TO ANYONE IN OUR FAMILY OR TO ANY OF MY COUSINS OR ANYBODY..
SO GETTING BACK TO MY ORIGINAL QUESTION...
WHY ARE YOU LYING ON MY BLANKET?
POOR KID.. HE TALKS IN HIS SLEEP..
11-1
SCHULZ

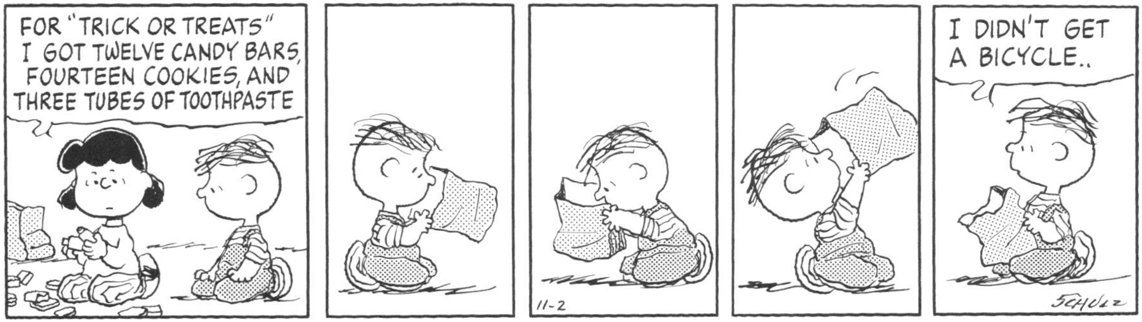
FOR "TRICK OR TREATS" I GOT TWELVE CANDY BARS, FOURTEEN COOKIES, AND THREE TUBES OF TOOTHPASTE
11-2
I DIDN'T GET A BICYCLE..
SCHULZ

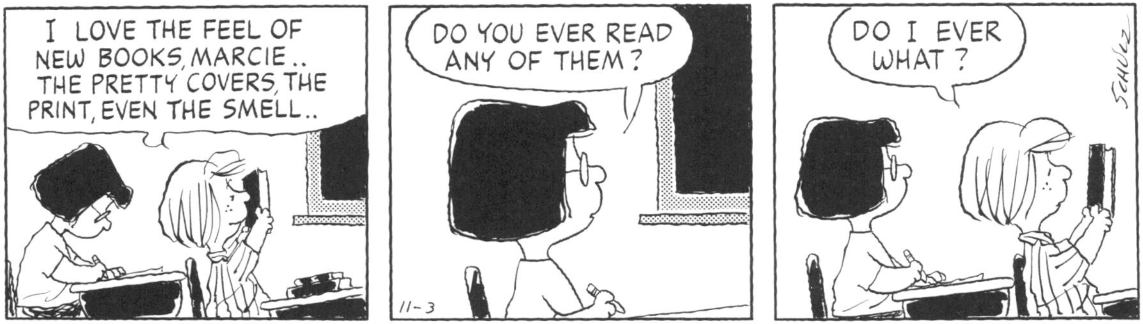
I LOVE THE FEEL OF NEW BOOKS, MARCIE.. THE PRETTY COVERS, THE PRINT, EVEN THE SMELL..
DO YOU EVER READ ANY OF THEM?
11-3
DO I EVER WHAT?
SCHULZ

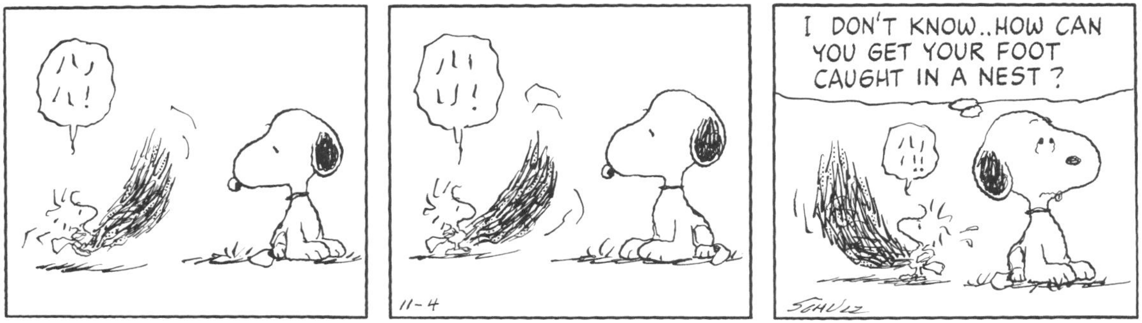
11-4
I DON'T KNOW..HOW CAN YOU GET YOUR FOOT CAUGHT IN A NEST?
SCHULZ

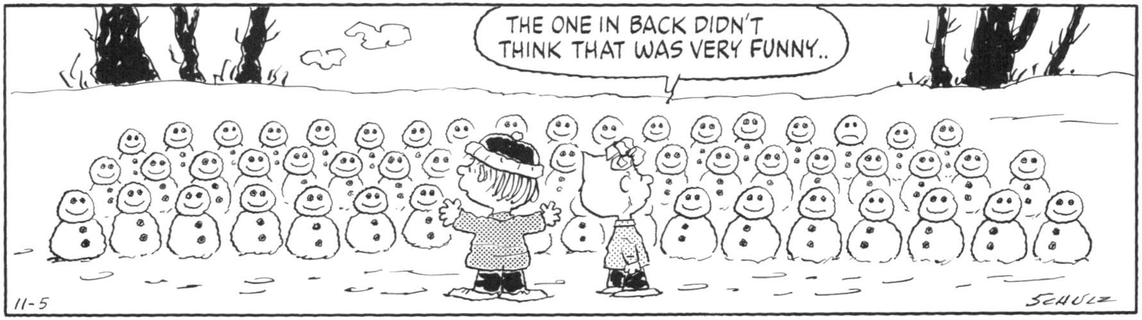
THE ONE IN BACK DIDN'T THINK THAT WAS VERY FUNNY..
11-5
SCHULZ

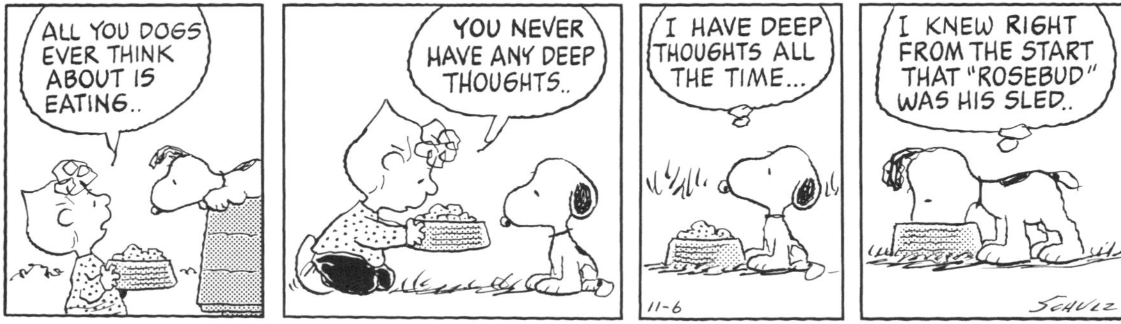
ALL YOU DOGS EVER THINK ABOUT IS EATING..
YOU NEVER HAVE ANY DEEP THOUGHTS..
I HAVE DEEP THOUGHTS ALL THE TIME...
I KNEW RIGHT FROM THE START THAT "ROSEBUD" WAS HIS SLED..
11-6
SCHULZ

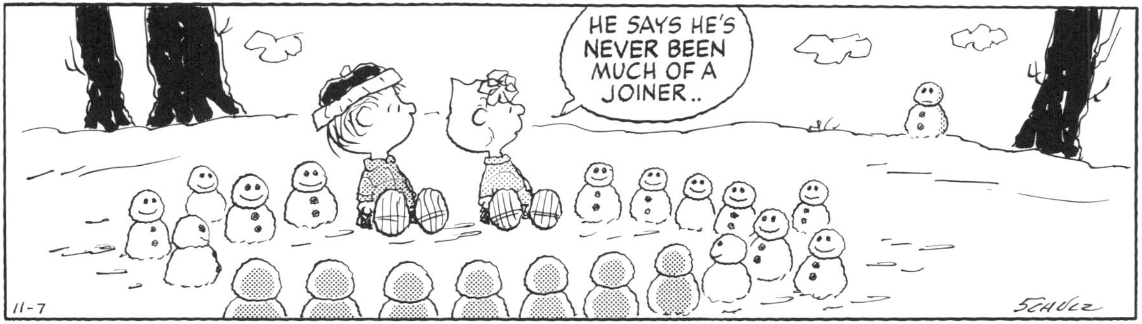
HE SAYS HE'S NEVER BEEN MUCH OF A JOINER..
11-7
SCHULZ

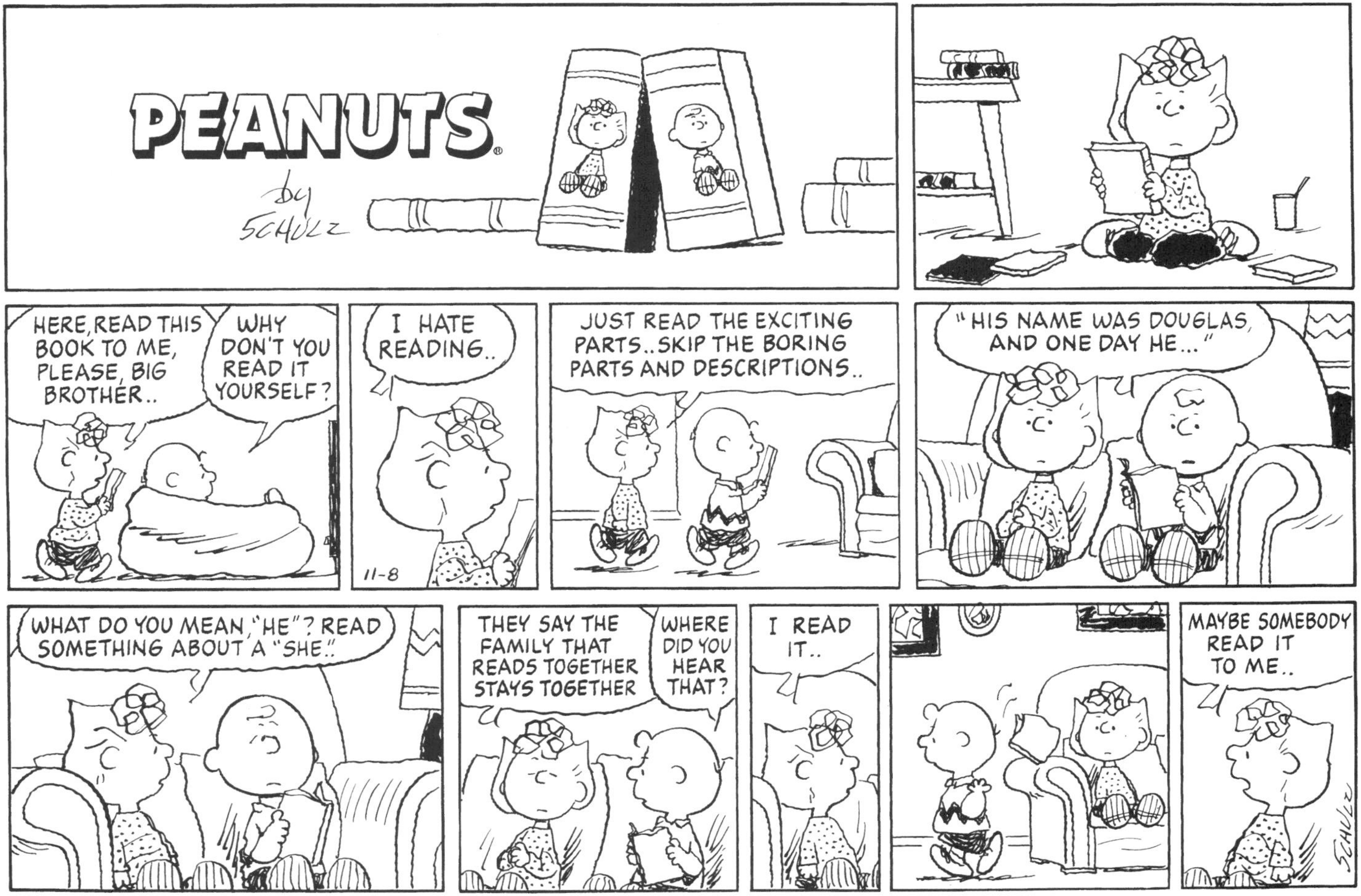
PEANUTS
by SCHULZ
HERE, READ THIS BOOK TO ME, PLEASE, BIG BROTHER..
WHY DON'T YOU READ IT YOURSELF?
I HATE READING..
11-8
JUST READ THE EXCITING PARTS..SKIP THE BORING PARTS AND DESCRIPTIONS..
"HIS NAME WAS DOUGLAS, AND ONE DAY HE..."
WHAT DO YOU MEAN, "HE"? READ SOMETHING ABOUT A "SHE."
THEY SAY THE FAMILY THAT READS TOGETHER STAYS TOGETHER
WHERE DID YOU HEAR THAT?
I READ IT..
MAYBE SOMEBODY READ IT TO ME..
SCHULZ

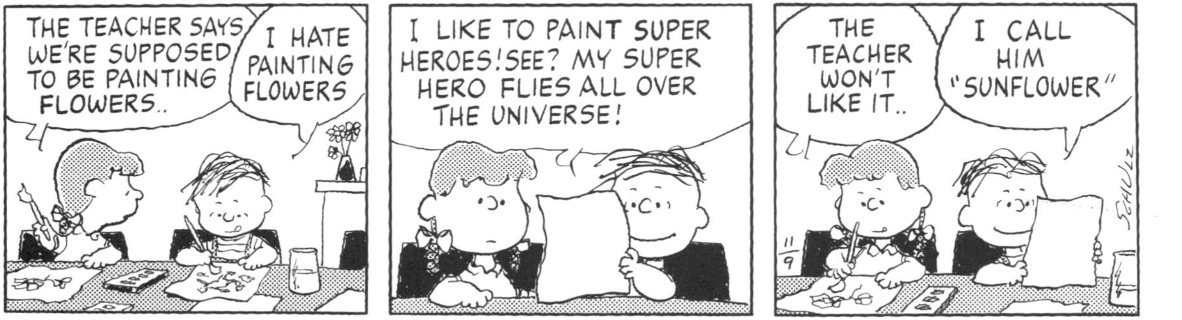
THE TEACHER SAYS WE'RE SUPPOSED TO BE PAINTING FLOWERS..
I HATE PAINTING FLOWERS
I LIKE TO PAINT SUPER HEROES! SEE? MY SUPER HERO FLIES ALL OVER THE UNIVERSE!
THE TEACHER WON'T LIKE IT..
I CALL HIM "SUNFLOWER"
SCHULZ
11/9

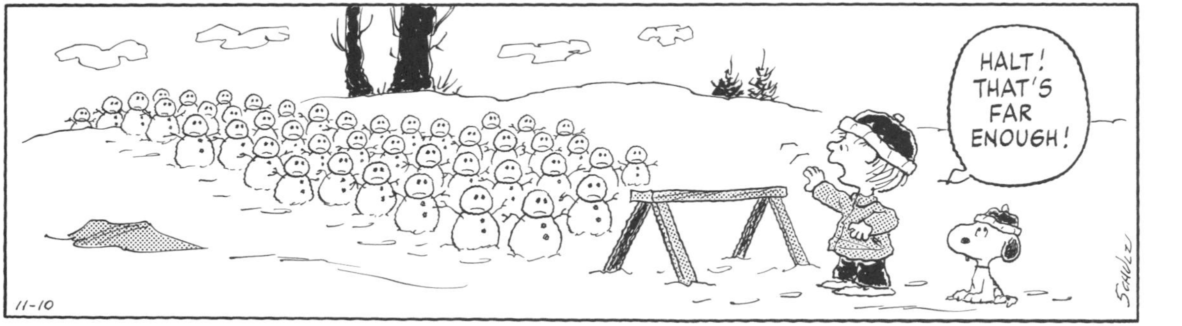
HALT! THAT'S FAR ENOUGH!
SCHULZ
11-10

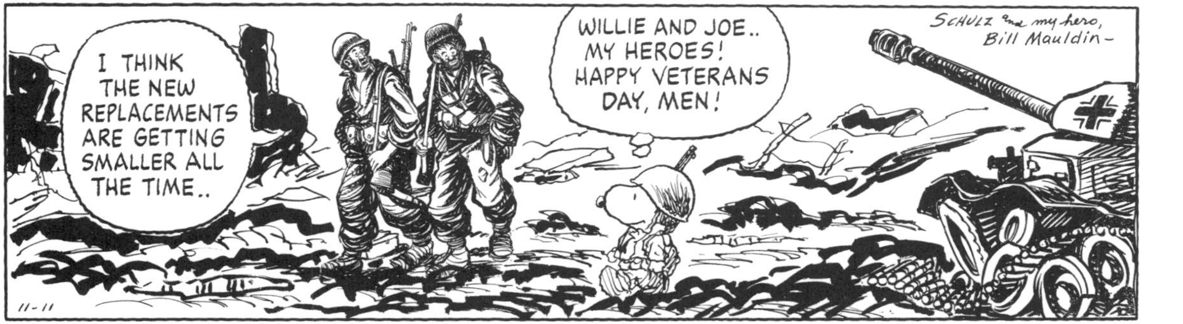
SCHULZ and my hero, Bill Mauldin-
I THINK THE NEW REPLACEMENTS ARE GETTING SMALLER ALL THE TIME..
WILLIE AND JOE.. MY HEROES! HAPPY VETERANS DAY, MEN!
11-11

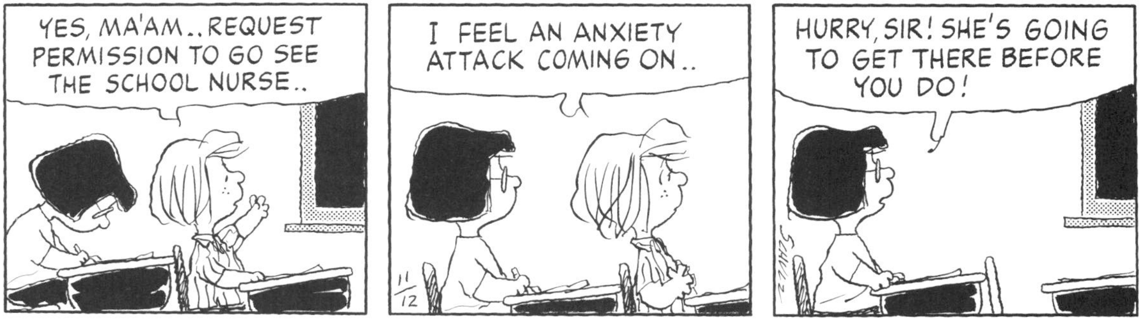
YES, MA'AM..REQUEST PERMISSION TO GO SEE THE SCHOOL NURSE..
I FEEL AN ANXIETY ATTACK COMING ON..
11/12
HURRY, SIR! SHE'S GOING TO GET THERE BEFORE YOU DO!
SCHULZ

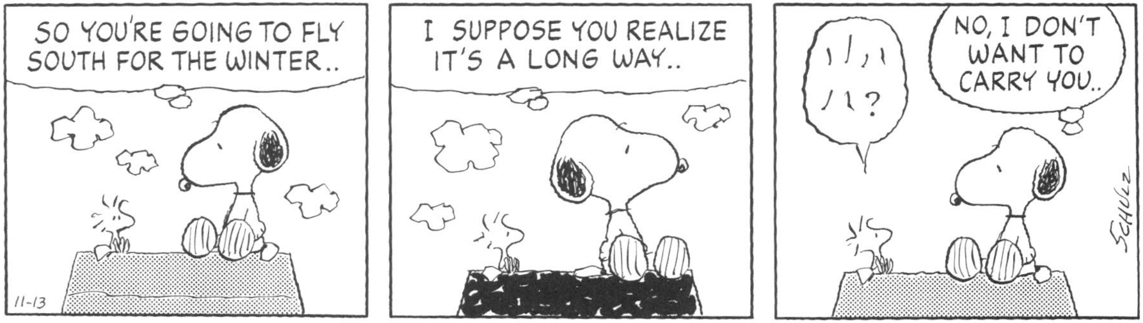
SO YOU'RE GOING TO FLY SOUTH FOR THE WINTER..
11-13
I SUPPOSE YOU REALIZE IT'S A LONG WAY..
NO, I DON'T WANT TO CARRY YOU..
SCHULZ

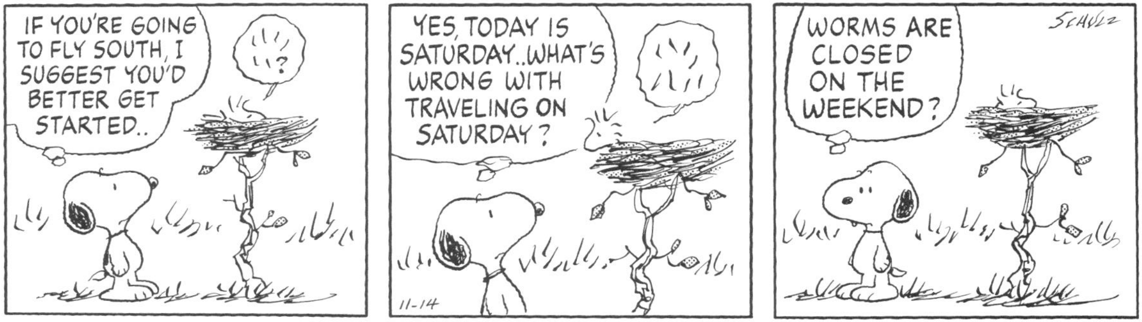
IF YOU'RE GOING TO FLY SOUTH, I SUGGEST YOU'D BETTER GET STARTED..
YES, TODAY IS SATURDAY..WHAT'S WRONG WITH TRAVELING ON SATURDAY?
11-14
SCHULZ
WORMS ARE CLOSED ON THE WEEKEND?

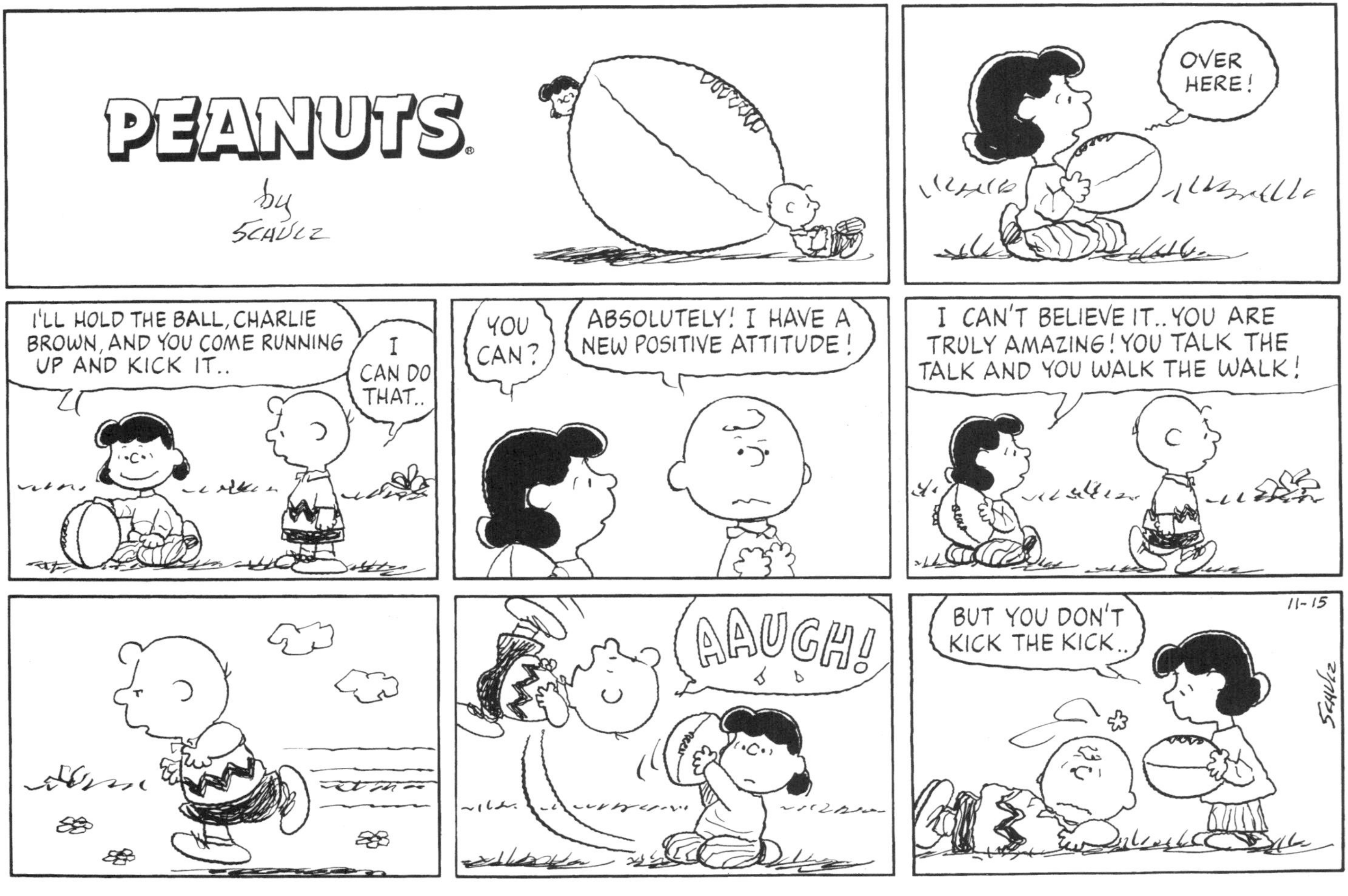
PEANUTS
by SCHULZ
OVER HERE!
I'LL HOLD THE BALL, CHARLIE BROWN, AND YOU COME RUNNING UP AND KICK IT..
I CAN DO THAT..
YOU CAN?
ABSOLUTELY! I HAVE A NEW POSITIVE ATTITUDE!
I CAN'T BELIEVE IT.. YOU ARE TRULY AMAZING! YOU TALK THE TALK AND YOU WALK THE WALK!
AAUGH!
11-15
BUT YOU DON'T KICK THE KICK..
SCHULZ

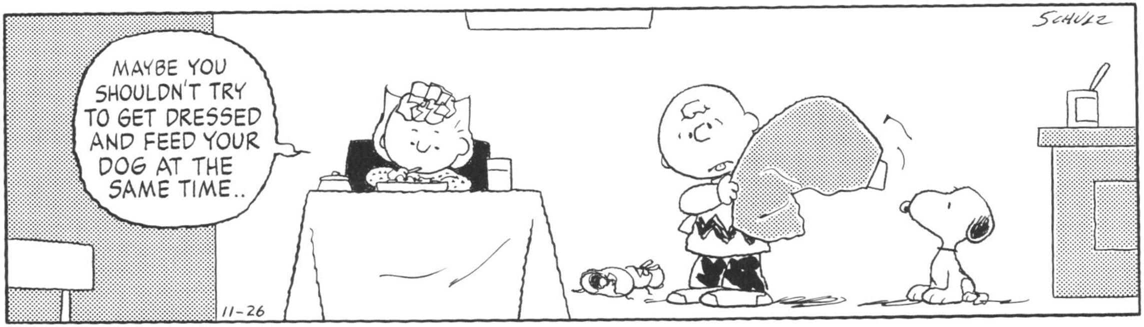
SCHULZ
MAYBE YOU SHOULDN'T TRY TO GET DRESSED AND FEED YOUR DOG AT THE SAME TIME..
11-26

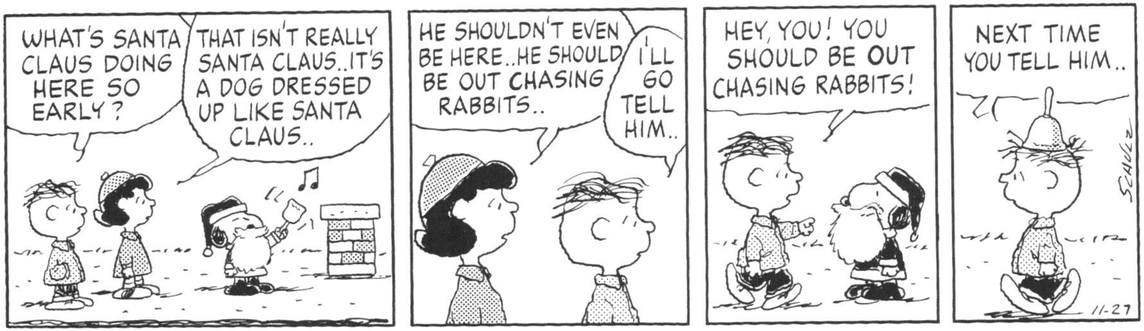
WHAT'S SANTA CLAUS DOING HERE SO EARLY?
THAT ISN'T REALLY SANTA CLAUS..IT'S A DOG DRESSED UP LIKE SANTA CLAUS..
HE SHOULDN'T EVEN BE HERE..HE SHOULD BE OUT CHASING RABBITS..
I'LL GO TELL HIM..
HEY, YOU! YOU SHOULD BE OUT CHASING RABBITS!
NEXT TIME YOU TELL HIM..
SCHULZ
11-27

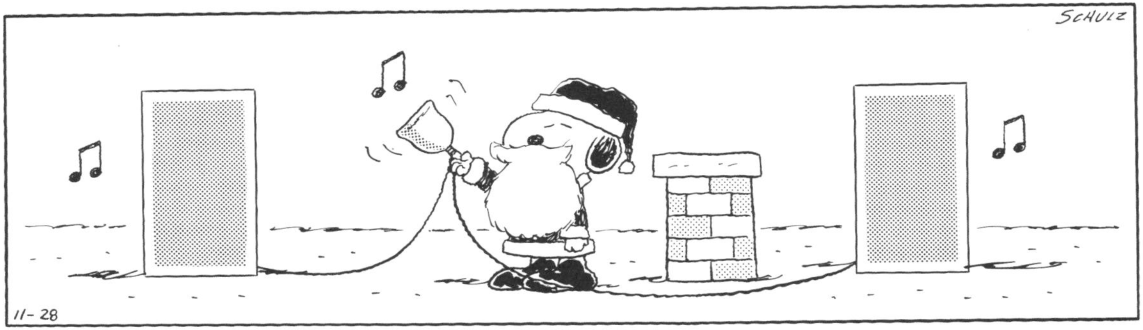
SCHULZ
11-28

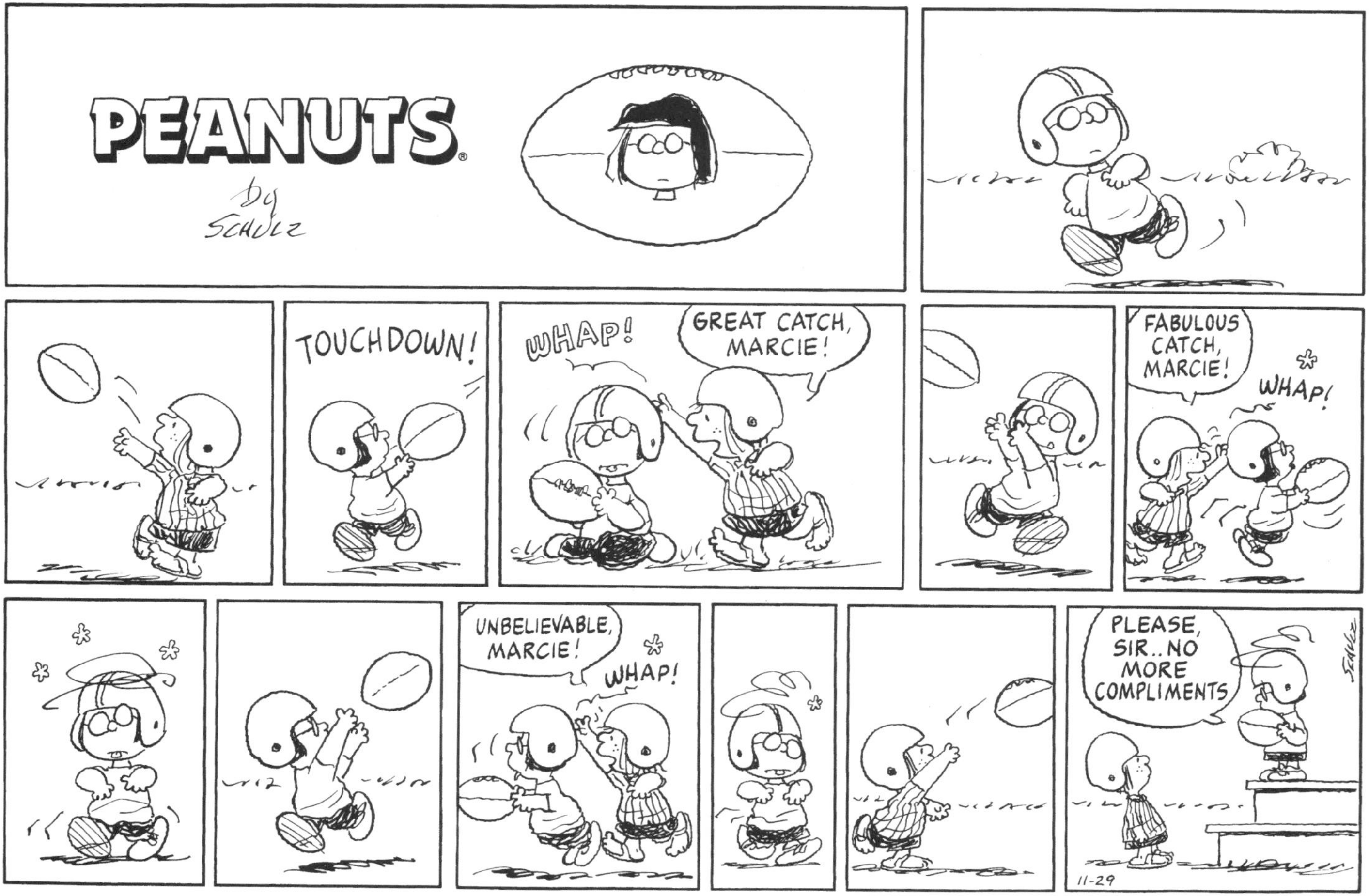
PEANUTS
by SCHULZ
TOUCHDOWN!
WHAP!
GREAT CATCH, MARCIE!
FABULOUS CATCH, MARCIE!
WHAP!
UNBELIEVABLE, MARCIE!
WHAP!
PLEASE, SIR..NO MORE COMPLIMENTS
SCHULZ
11-29

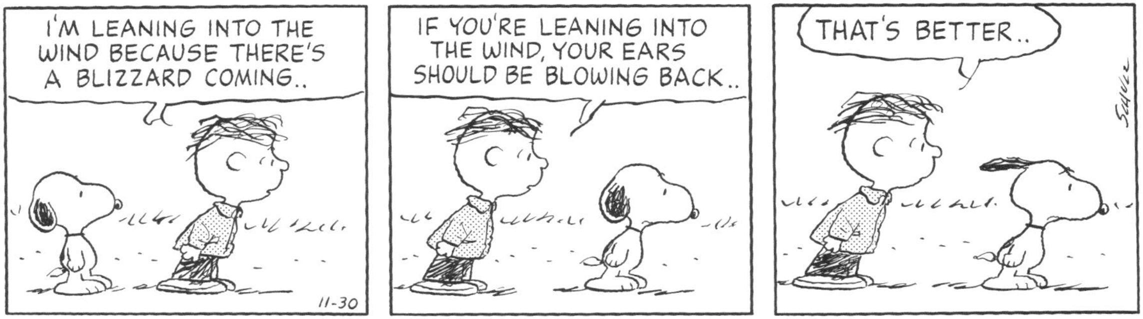
I'M LEANING INTO THE WIND BECAUSE THERE'S A BLIZZARD COMING..
IF YOU'RE LEANING INTO THE WIND, YOUR EARS SHOULD BE BLOWING BACK..
THAT'S BETTER..
11-30
SCHULZ

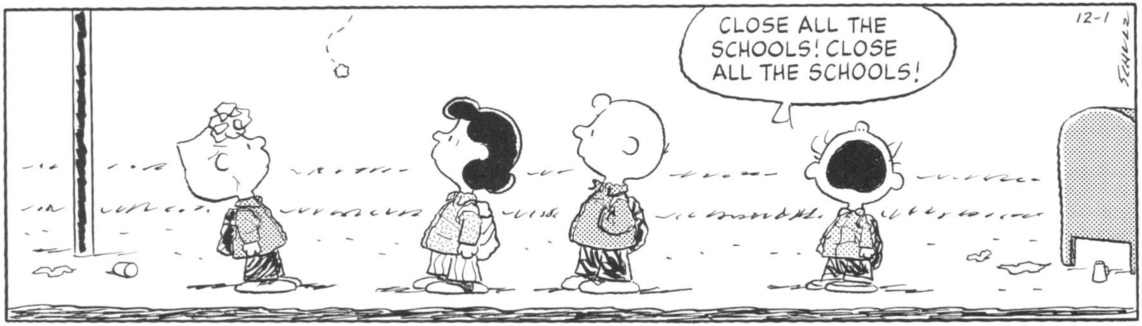
CLOSE ALL THE SCHOOLS! CLOSE ALL THE SCHOOLS!
12-1
SCHULZ

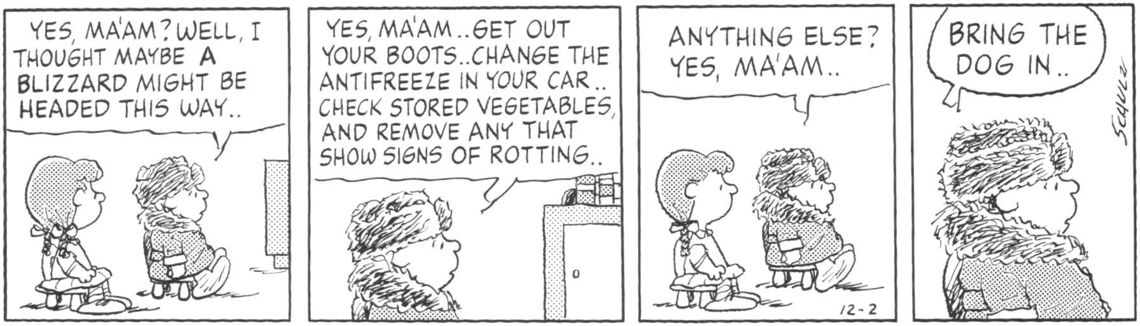
YES, MA'AM? WELL, I THOUGHT MAYBE A BLIZZARD MIGHT BE HEADED THIS WAY..
YES, MA'AM..GET OUT YOUR BOOTS..CHANGE THE ANTIFREEZE IN YOUR CAR.. CHECK STORED VEGETABLES, AND REMOVE ANY THAT SHOW SIGNS OF ROTTING..
ANYTHING ELSE? YES, MA'AM..
12-2
BRING THE DOG IN..
SCHULZ

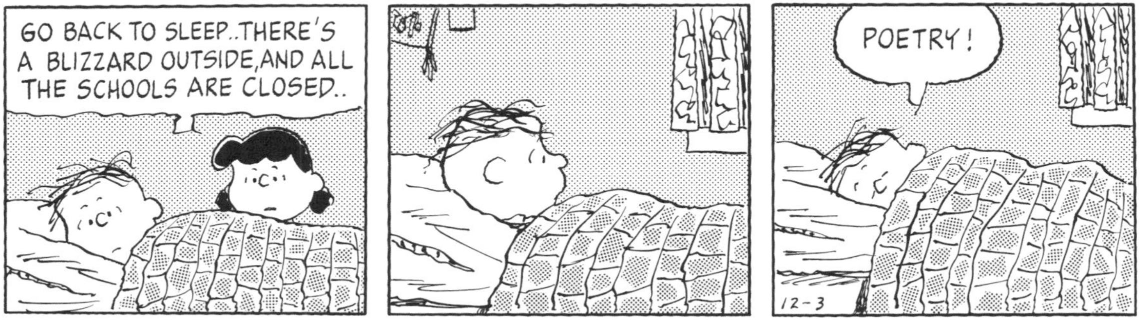
GO BACK TO SLEEP..THERE'S A BLIZZARD OUTSIDE, AND ALL THE SCHOOLS ARE CLOSED..
POETRY!
12-3

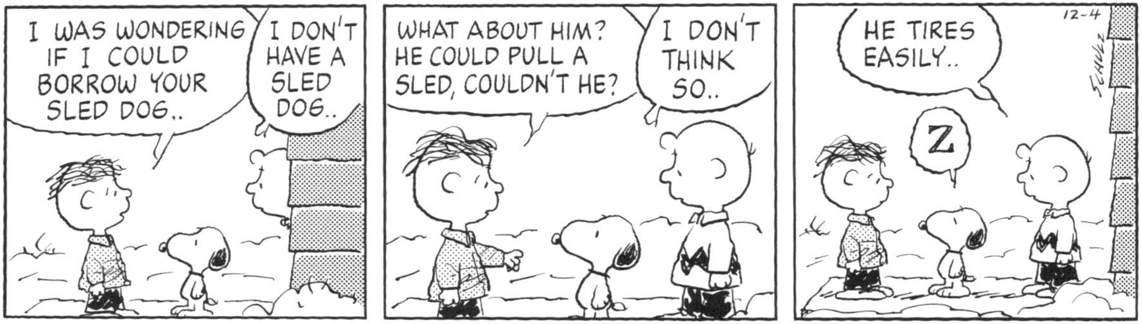
I WAS WONDERING IF I COULD BORROW YOUR SLED DOG..
I DON'T HAVE A SLED DOG..
WHAT ABOUT HIM? HE COULD PULL A SLED, COULDN'T HE?
I DON'T THINK SO..
HE TIRES EASILY..
Z
12-4
SCHULZ

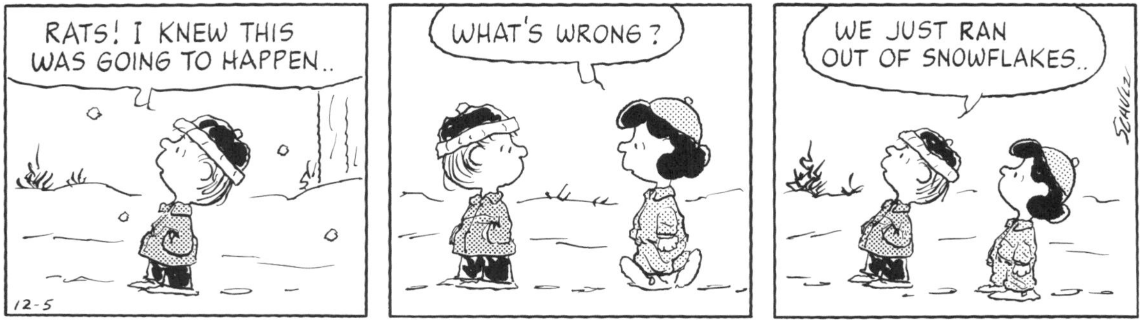
RATS! I KNEW THIS WAS GOING TO HAPPEN..
WHAT'S WRONG?
WE JUST RAN OUT OF SNOWFLAKES..
12-5
SCHULZ

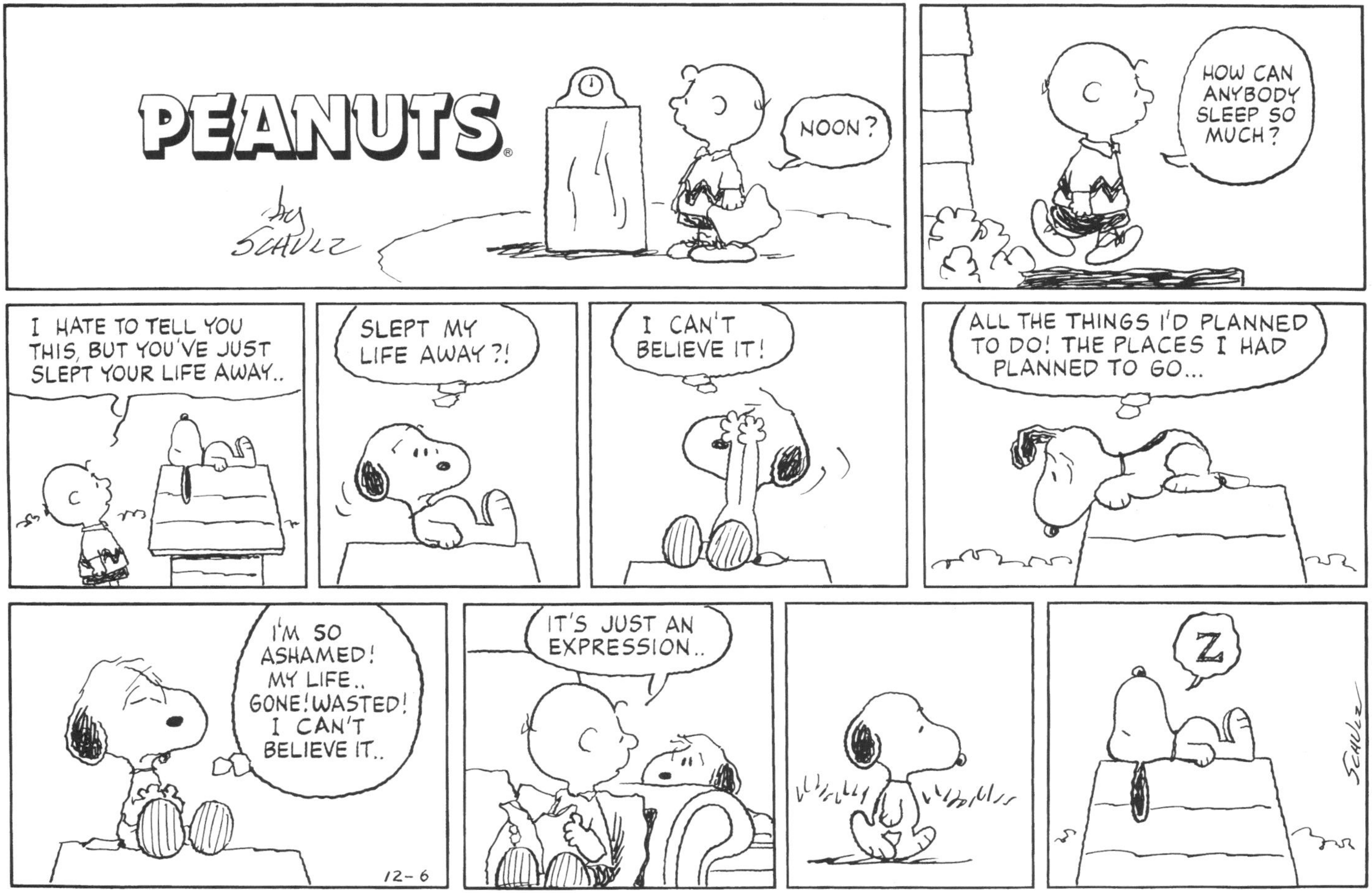
PEANUTS
by SCHULZ
NOON?
HOW CAN ANYBODY SLEEP SO MUCH?
I HATE TO TELL YOU THIS, BUT YOU'VE JUST SLEPT YOUR LIFE AWAY..
SLEPT MY LIFE AWAY?!
I CAN'T BELIEVE IT!
ALL THE THINGS I'D PLANNED TO DO! THE PLACES I HAD PLANNED TO GO...
I'M SO ASHAMED! MY LIFE.. GONE! WASTED! I CAN'T BELIEVE IT..
12-6
IT'S JUST AN EXPRESSION..
Z
SCHULZ

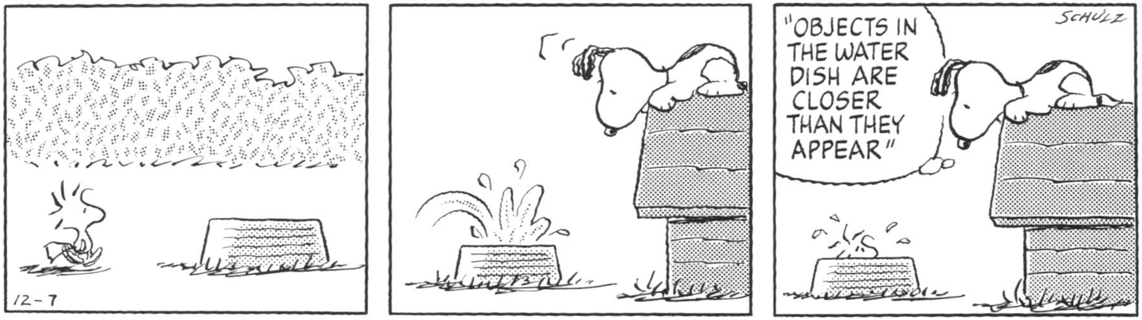
"OBJECTS IN THE WATER DISH ARE CLOSER THAN THEY APPEAR"
SCHULZ
12-7

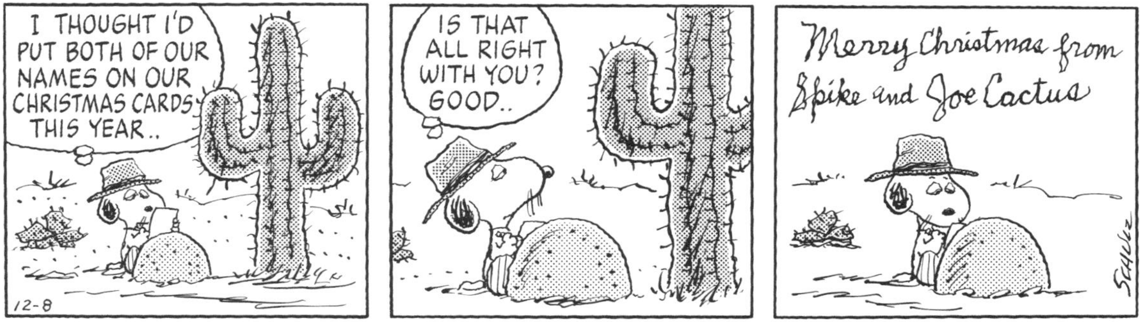
I THOUGHT I'D PUT BOTH OF OUR NAMES ON OUR CHRISTMAS CARDS THIS YEAR..
IS THAT ALL RIGHT WITH YOU? GOOD..
Merry Christmas from Spike and Joe Cactus
SCHULZ
12-8

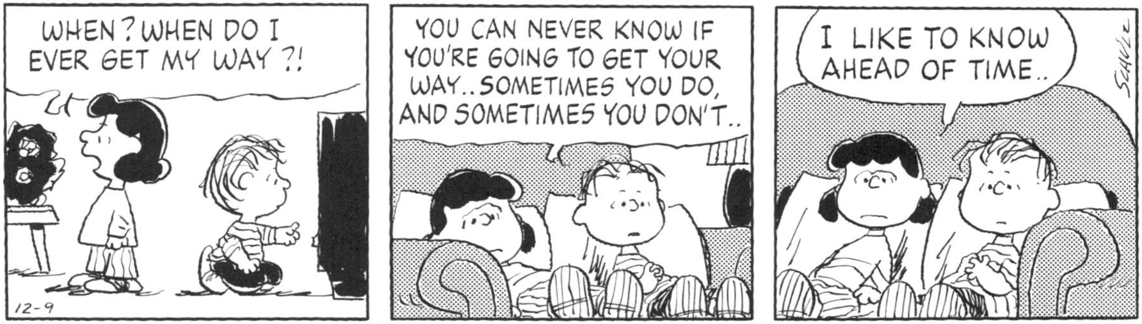
WHEN? WHEN DO I EVER GET MY WAY ?!
YOU CAN NEVER KNOW IF YOU'RE GOING TO GET YOUR WAY.. SOMETIMES YOU DO, AND SOMETIMES YOU DON'T..
I LIKE TO KNOW AHEAD OF TIME..
SCHULZ
12-9

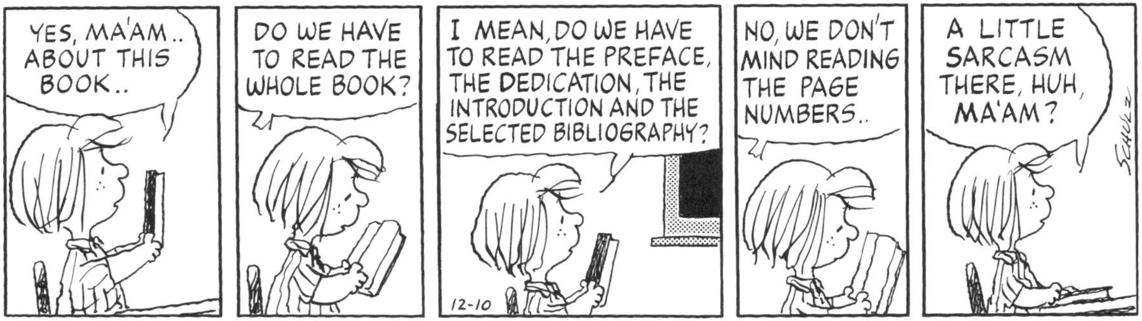
YES, MA'AM.. ABOUT THIS BOOK..
DO WE HAVE TO READ THE WHOLE BOOK?
I MEAN, DO WE HAVE TO READ THE PREFACE, THE DEDICATION, THE INTRODUCTION AND THE SELECTED BIBLIOGRAPHY?
12-10
NO, WE DON'T MIND READING THE PAGE NUMBERS..
A LITTLE SARCASM THERE, HUH, MA'AM?
SCHULZ

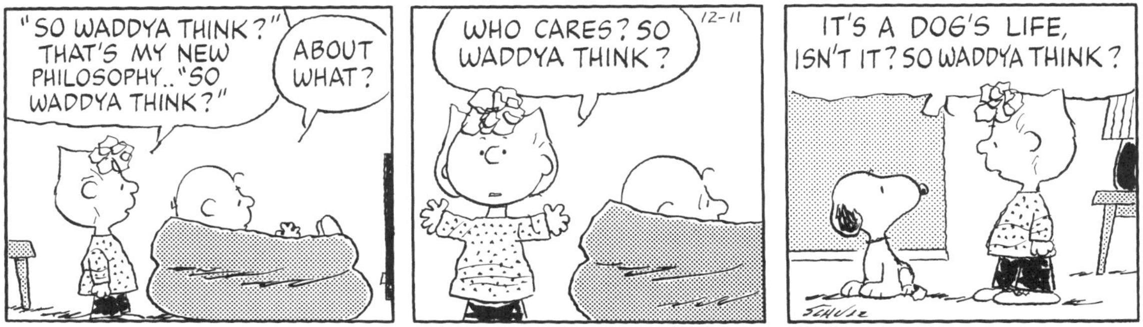
"SO WADDYA THINK?" THAT'S MY NEW PHILOSOPHY.."SO WADDYA THINK?"
ABOUT WHAT?
WHO CARES? SO WADDYA THINK?
12-11
IT'S A DOG'S LIFE, ISN'T IT? SO WADDYA THINK?
SCHULZ

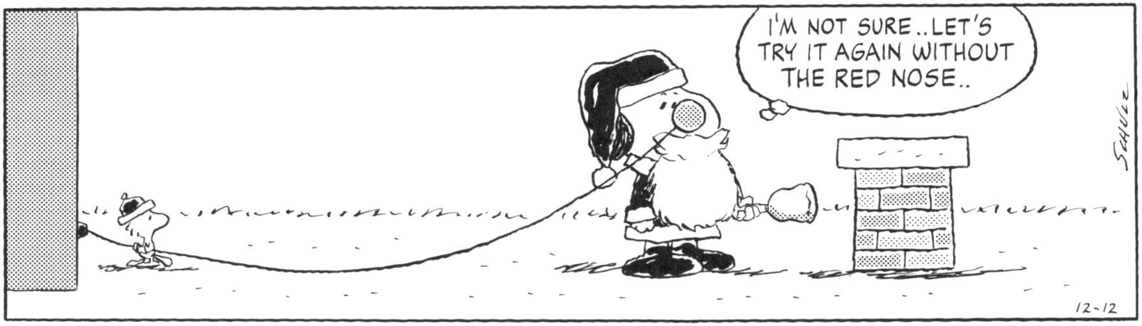
I'M NOT SURE..LET'S TRY IT AGAIN WITHOUT THE RED NOSE..
SCHULZ
12-12

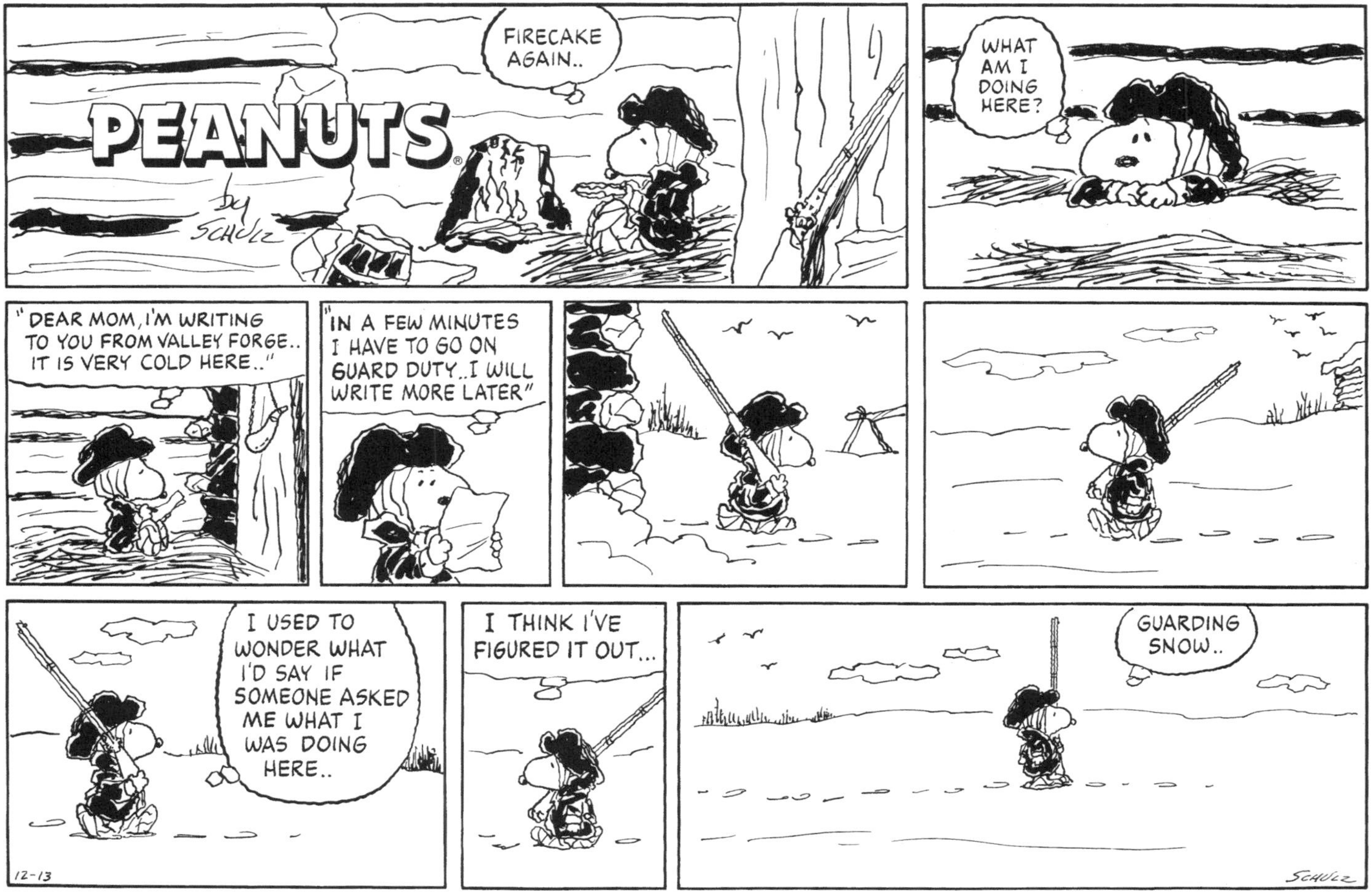
PEANUTS®
by SCHULZ
FIRECAKE AGAIN..
WHAT AM I DOING HERE?
"DEAR MOM, I'M WRITING TO YOU FROM VALLEY FORGE.. IT IS VERY COLD HERE.."
"IN A FEW MINUTES I HAVE TO GO ON GUARD DUTY..I WILL WRITE MORE LATER"
I USED TO WONDER WHAT I'D SAY IF SOMEONE ASKED ME WHAT I WAS DOING HERE..
I THINK I'VE FIGURED IT OUT...
GUARDING SNOW..
12-13
SCHULZ

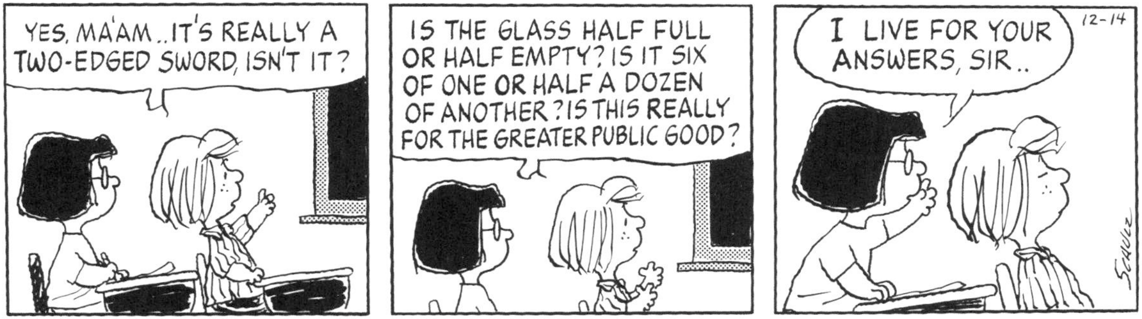
YES, MA'AM..IT'S REALLY A TWO-EDGED SWORD, ISN'T IT?
IS THE GLASS HALF FULL OR HALF EMPTY? IS IT SIX OF ONE OR HALF A DOZEN OF ANOTHER? IS THIS REALLY FOR THE GREATER PUBLIC GOOD?
12-14
I LIVE FOR YOUR ANSWERS, SIR..
SCHULZ

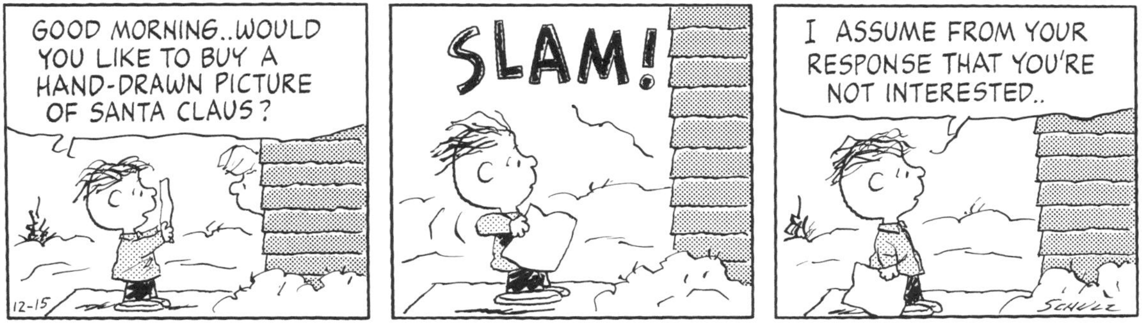
GOOD MORNING..WOULD YOU LIKE TO BUY A HAND-DRAWN PICTURE OF SANTA CLAUS?
12-15
SLAM!
I ASSUME FROM YOUR RESPONSE THAT YOU'RE NOT INTERESTED..
SCHULZ

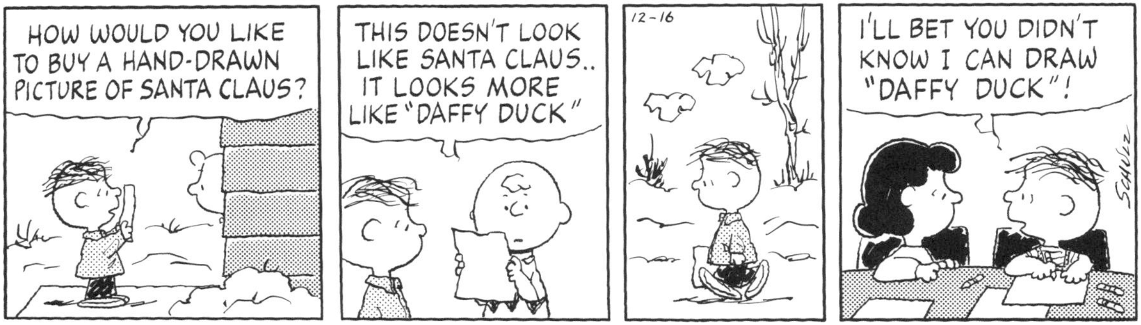
HOW WOULD YOU LIKE TO BUY A HAND-DRAWN PICTURE OF SANTA CLAUS?
THIS DOESN'T LOOK LIKE SANTA CLAUS.. IT LOOKS MORE LIKE "DAFFY DUCK"
12-16
I'LL BET YOU DIDN'T KNOW I CAN DRAW "DAFFY DUCK"!
SCHULZ

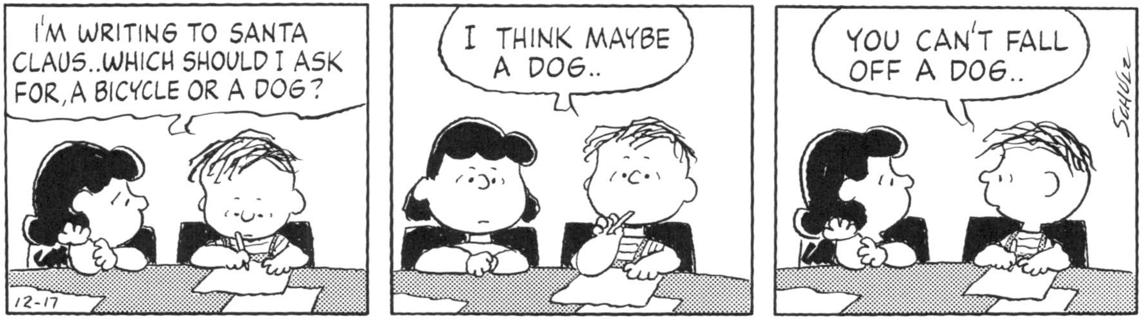
I'M WRITING TO SANTA CLAUS..WHICH SHOULD I ASK FOR, A BICYCLE OR A DOG?
12-17
I THINK MAYBE A DOG..
YOU CAN'T FALL OFF A DOG..
SCHULZ

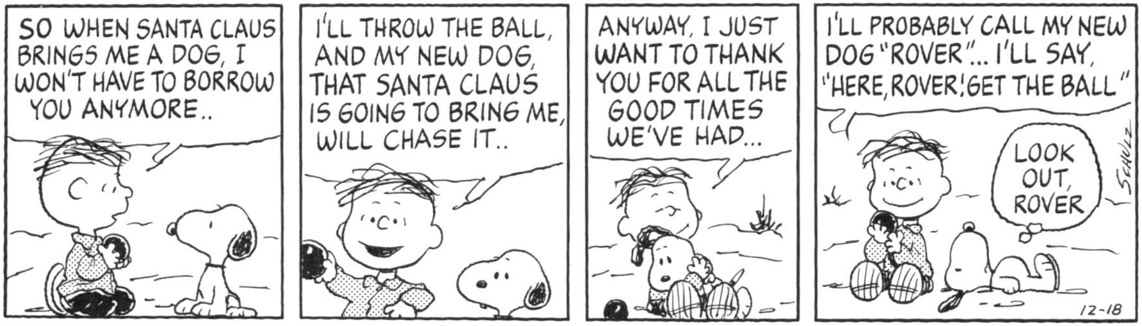
SO WHEN SANTA CLAUS BRINGS ME A DOG, I WON'T HAVE TO BORROW YOU ANYMORE..
I'LL THROW THE BALL, AND MY NEW DOG, THAT SANTA CLAUS IS GOING TO BRING ME, WILL CHASE IT..
ANYWAY, I JUST WANT TO THANK YOU FOR ALL THE GOOD TIMES WE'VE HAD...
I'LL PROBABLY CALL MY NEW DOG "ROVER"... I'LL SAY, "HERE, ROVER! GET THE BALL"
LOOK OUT, ROVER
SCHULZ
12-18

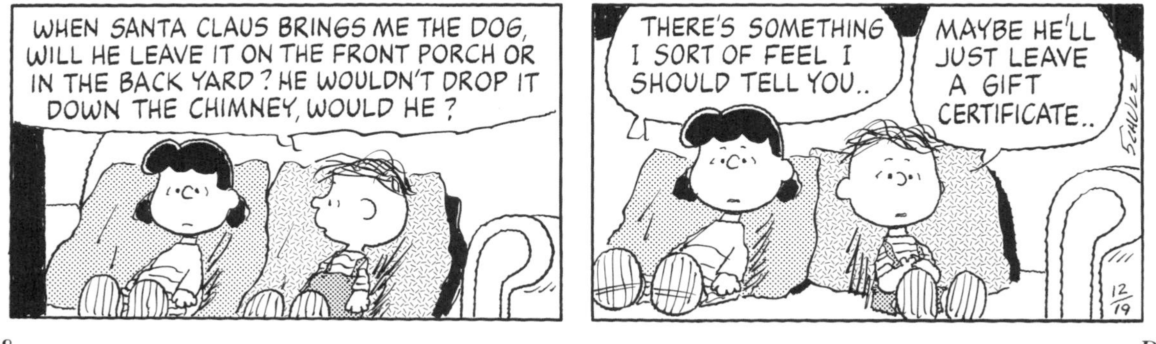
WHEN SANTA CLAUS BRINGS ME THE DOG, WILL HE LEAVE IT ON THE FRONT PORCH OR IN THE BACK YARD? HE WOULDN'T DROP IT DOWN THE CHIMNEY, WOULD HE?
THERE'S SOMETHING I SORT OF FEEL I SHOULD TELL YOU..
MAYBE HE'LL JUST LEAVE A GIFT CERTIFICATE..
SCHULZ
12/19

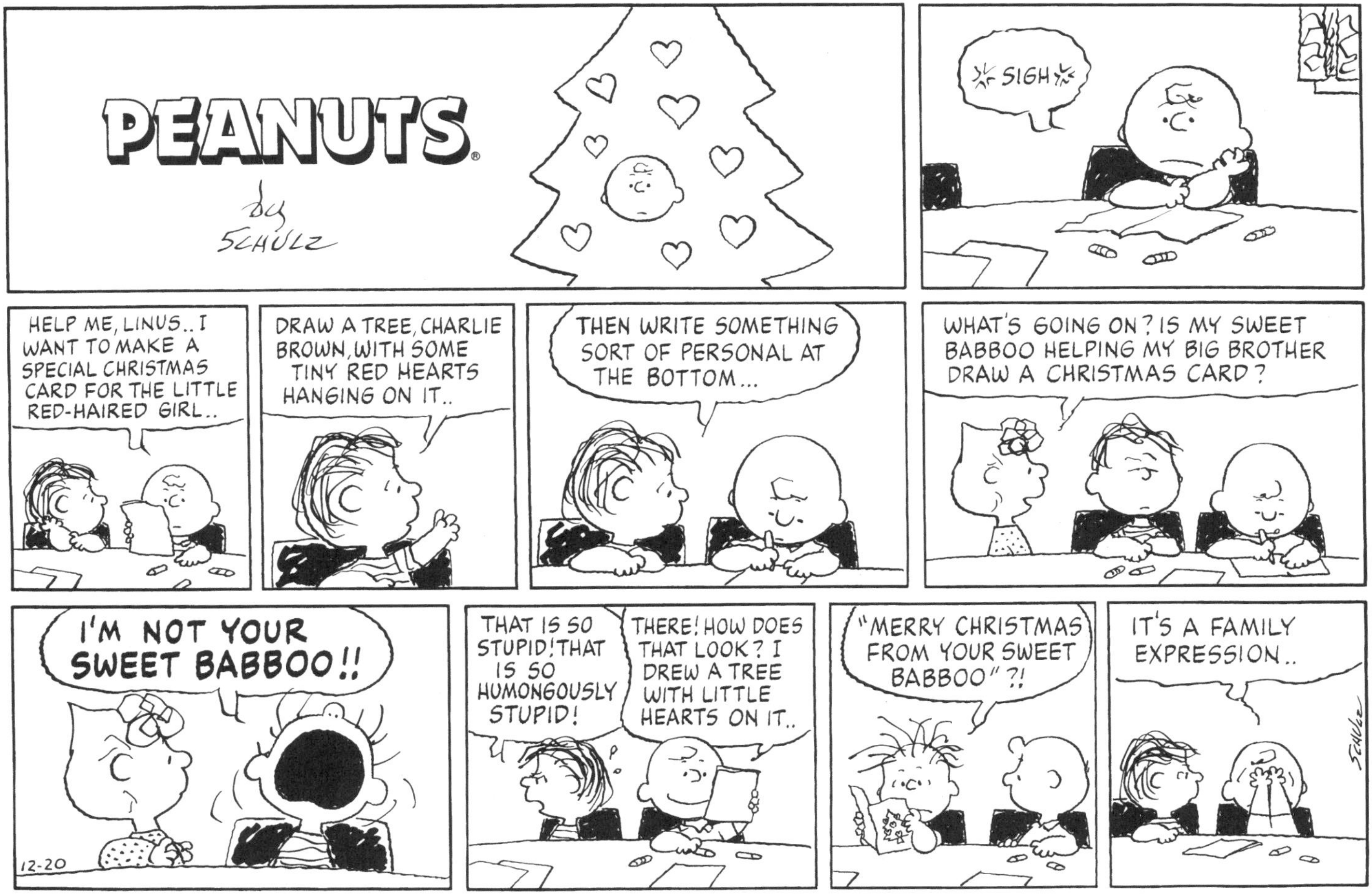
PEANUTS
SCHULZ
SIGH
HELP ME, LINUS.. I WANT TO MAKE A SPECIAL CHRISTMAS CARD FOR THE LITTLE RED-HAIRED GIRL..
DRAW A TREE, CHARLIE BROWN, WITH SOME TINY RED HEARTS HANGING ON IT..
THEN WRITE SOMETHING SORT OF PERSONAL AT THE BOTTOM...
WHAT'S GOING ON? IS MY SWEET BABBOO HELPING MY BIG BROTHER DRAW A CHRISTMAS CARD?
I'M NOT YOUR SWEET BABBOO!!
12-20
THAT IS SO STUPID! THAT IS SO HUMONGOUSLY STUPID!
THERE! HOW DOES THAT LOOK? I DREW A TREE WITH LITTLE HEARTS ON IT..
"MERRY CHRISTMAS FROM YOUR SWEET BABBOO"?!
IT'S A FAMILY EXPRESSION..
SCHULZ

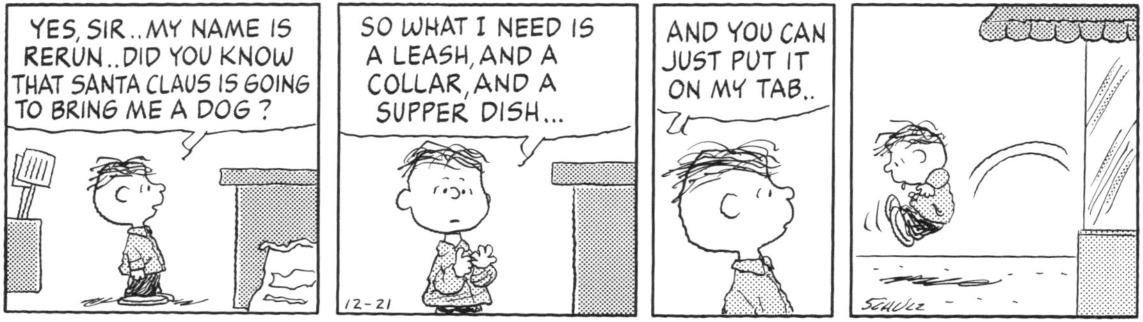
YES, SIR..MY NAME IS RERUN..DID YOU KNOW THAT SANTA CLAUS IS GOING TO BRING ME A DOG ?
SO WHAT I NEED IS A LEASH, AND A COLLAR, AND A SUPPER DISH...
AND YOU CAN JUST PUT IT ON MY TAB..
12-21
SCHULZ

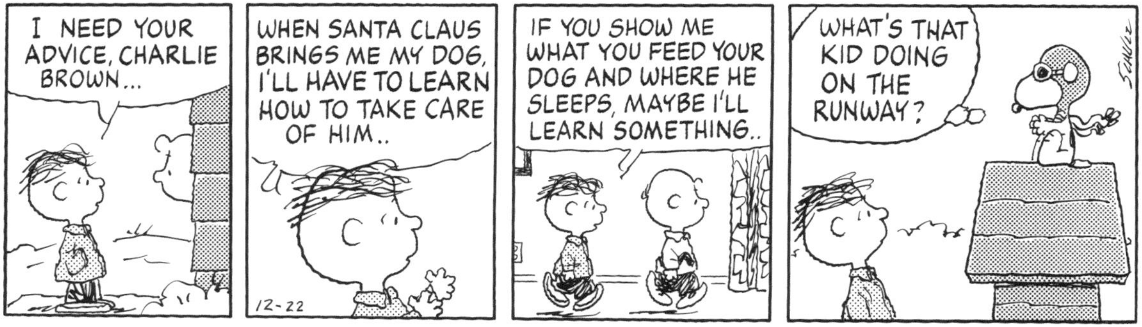
I NEED YOUR ADVICE, CHARLIE BROWN...
WHEN SANTA CLAUS BRINGS ME MY DOG, I'LL HAVE TO LEARN HOW TO TAKE CARE OF HIM..
IF YOU SHOW ME WHAT YOU FEED YOUR DOG AND WHERE HE SLEEPS, MAYBE I'LL LEARN SOMETHING..
WHAT'S THAT KID DOING ON THE RUNWAY?
12-22
SCHULZ

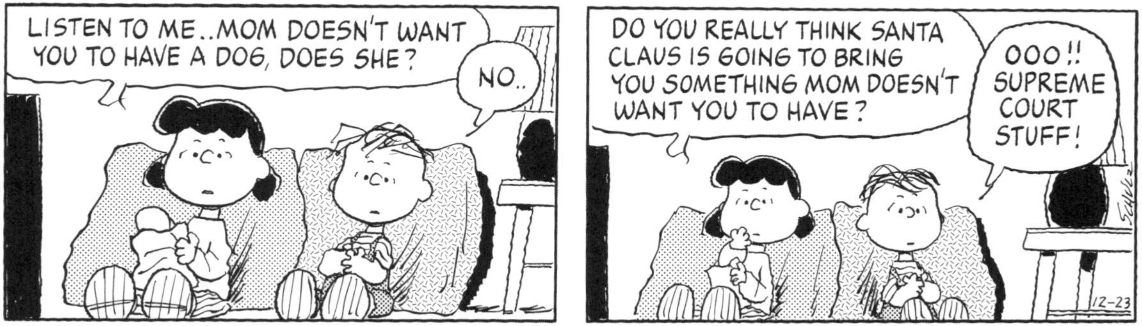
LISTEN TO ME..MOM DOESN'T WANT YOU TO HAVE A DOG, DOES SHE?
NO..
DO YOU REALLY THINK SANTA CLAUS IS GOING TO BRING YOU SOMETHING MOM DOESN'T WANT YOU TO HAVE?
OOO!! SUPREME COURT STUFF!
SCHULZ
12-23

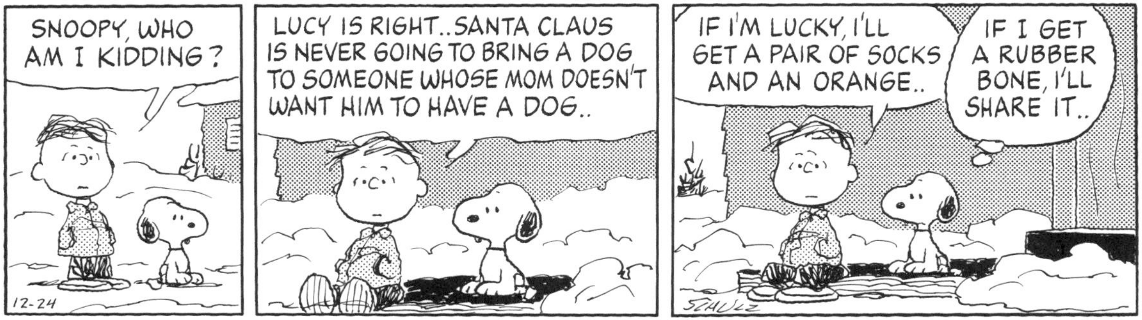
12-24
SNOOPY, WHO AM I KIDDING?
LUCY IS RIGHT..SANTA CLAUS IS NEVER GOING TO BRING A DOG TO SOMEONE WHOSE MOM DOESN'T WANT HIM TO HAVE A DOG..
IF I'M LUCKY, I'LL GET A PAIR OF SOCKS AND AN ORANGE..
IF I GET A RUBBER BONE, I'LL SHARE IT..

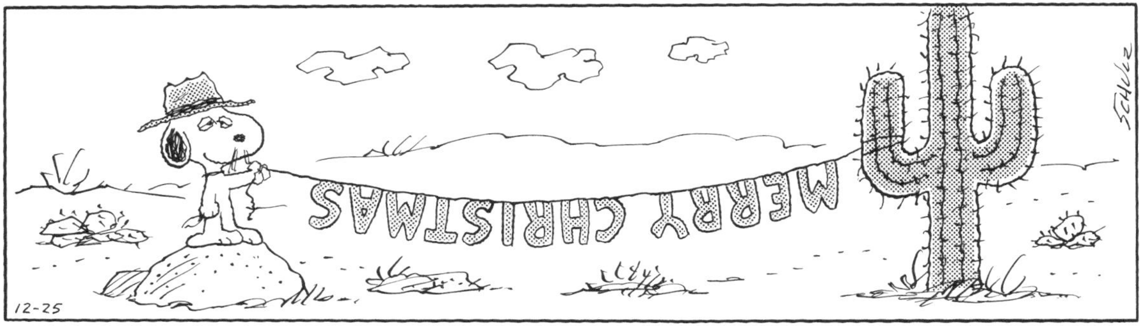
12-25
MERRY CHRISTMAS

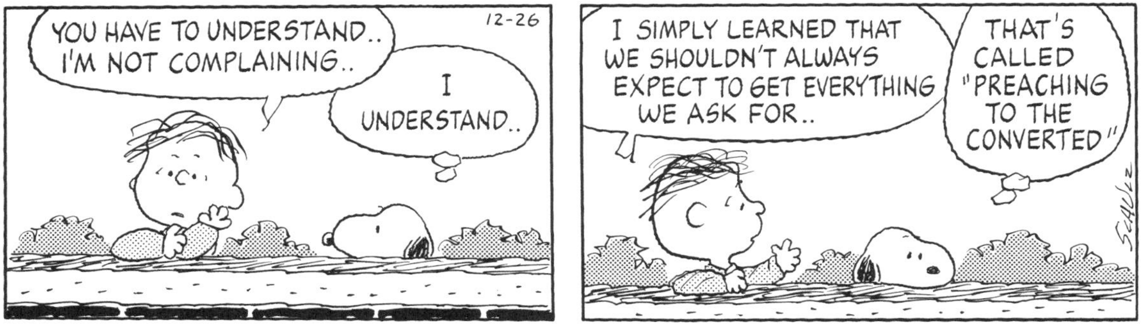
12-26
YOU HAVE TO UNDERSTAND.. I'M NOT COMPLAINING..
I UNDERSTAND..
I SIMPLY LEARNED THAT WE SHOULDN'T ALWAYS EXPECT TO GET EVERYTHING WE ASK FOR..
THAT'S CALLED "PREACHING TO THE CONVERTED"

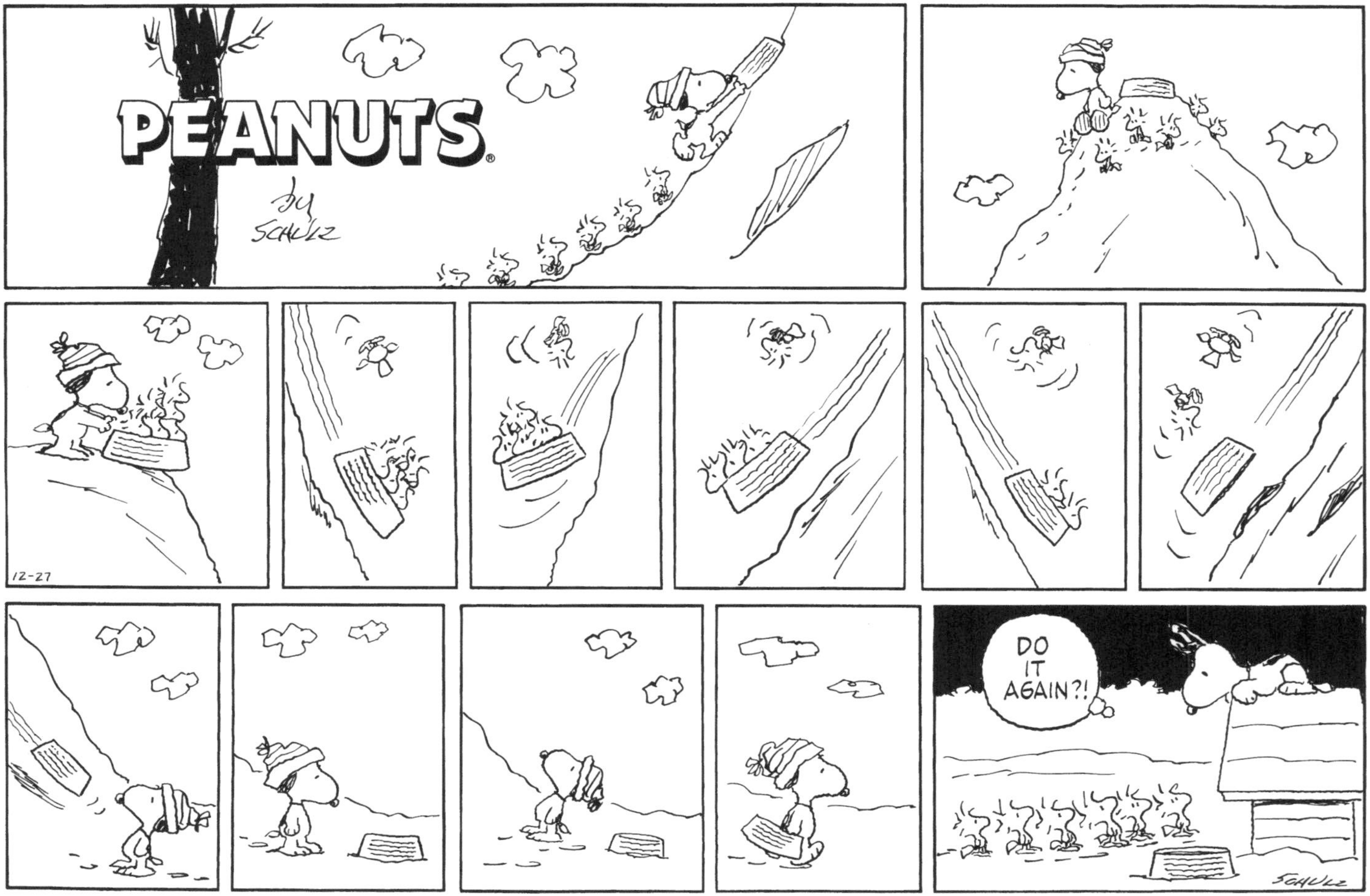
PEANUTS®
by SCHULZ
12-27
DO IT AGAIN?!
SCHULZ

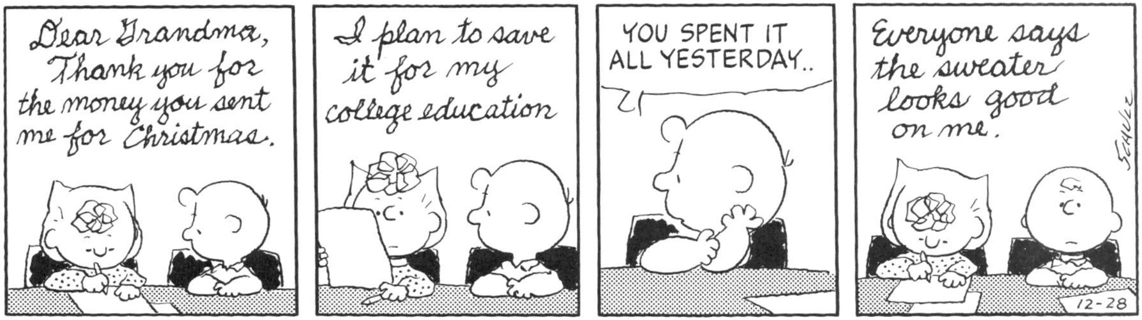
Dear Grandma, Thank you for the money you sent me for Christmas.
I plan to save it for my college education
YOU SPENT IT ALL YESTERDAY..
Everyone says the sweater looks good on me.
SCHULZ
12-28

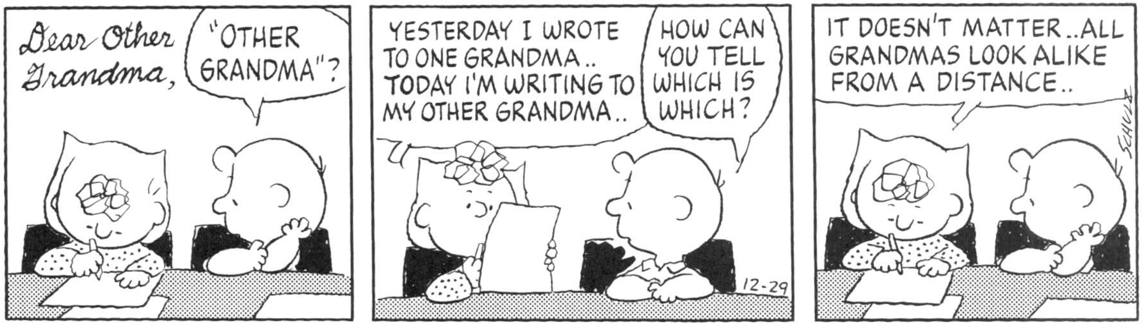
Dear Other Grandma,
"OTHER GRANDMA"?
YESTERDAY I WROTE TO ONE GRANDMA.. TODAY I'M WRITING TO MY OTHER GRANDMA..
HOW CAN YOU TELL WHICH IS WHICH?
12-29
IT DOESN'T MATTER..ALL GRANDMAS LOOK ALIKE FROM A DISTANCE..
SCHULZ

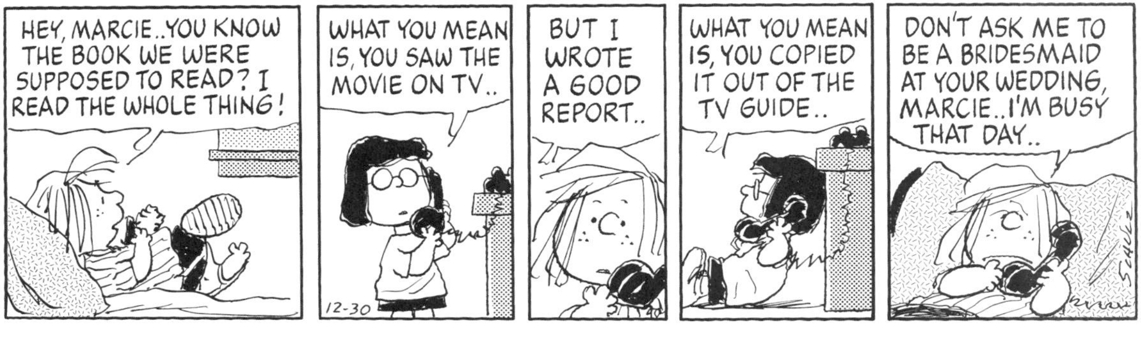
HEY, MARCIE..YOU KNOW THE BOOK WE WERE SUPPOSED TO READ? I READ THE WHOLE THING!
WHAT YOU MEAN IS, YOU SAW THE MOVIE ON TV..
12-30
BUT I WROTE A GOOD REPORT..
WHAT YOU MEAN IS, YOU COPIED IT OUT OF THE TV GUIDE..
DON'T ASK ME TO BE A BRIDESMAID AT YOUR WEDDING, MARCIE..I'M BUSY THAT DAY..
SCHULZ

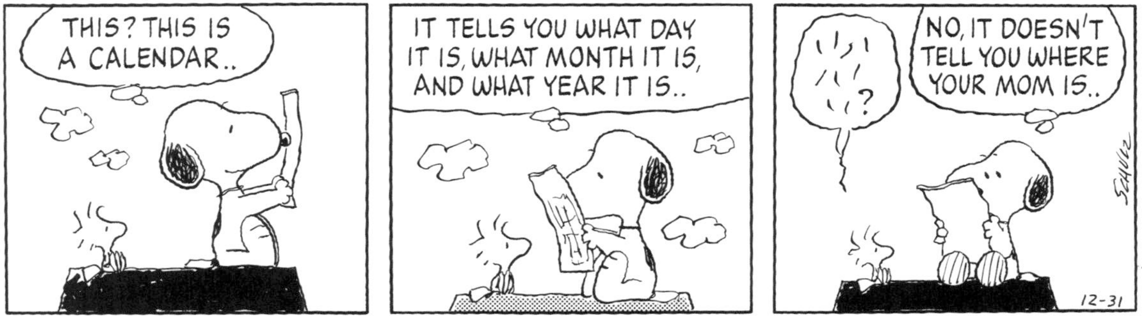
THIS? THIS IS A CALENDAR..
IT TELLS YOU WHAT DAY IT IS, WHAT MONTH IT IS, AND WHAT YEAR IT IS..
?
NO, IT DOESN'T TELL YOU WHERE YOUR MOM IS..
SCHULZ
12-31

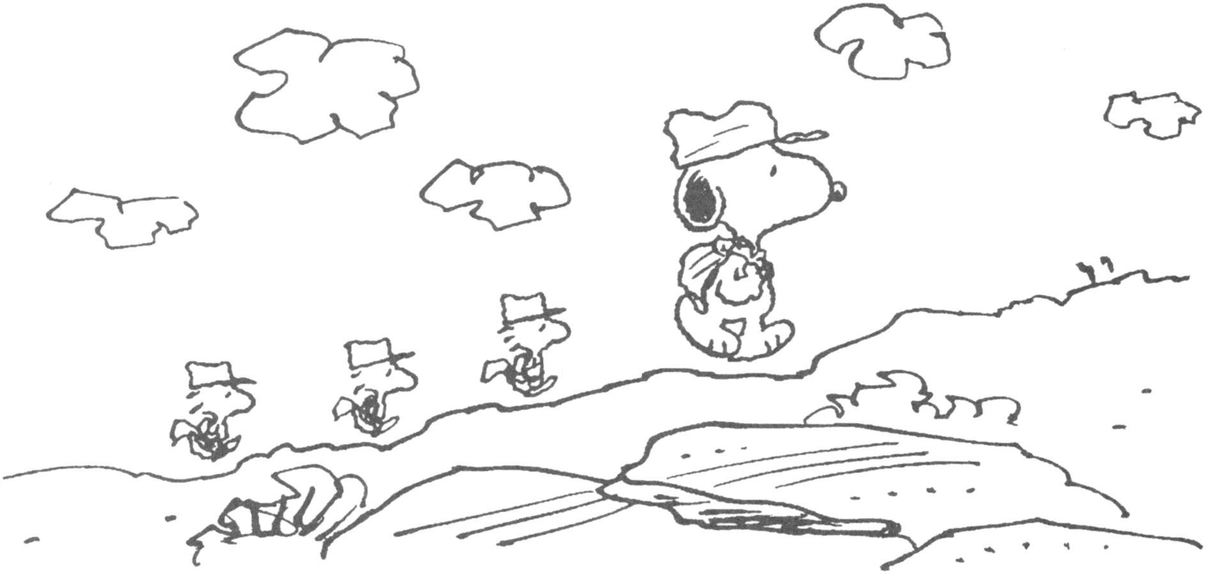

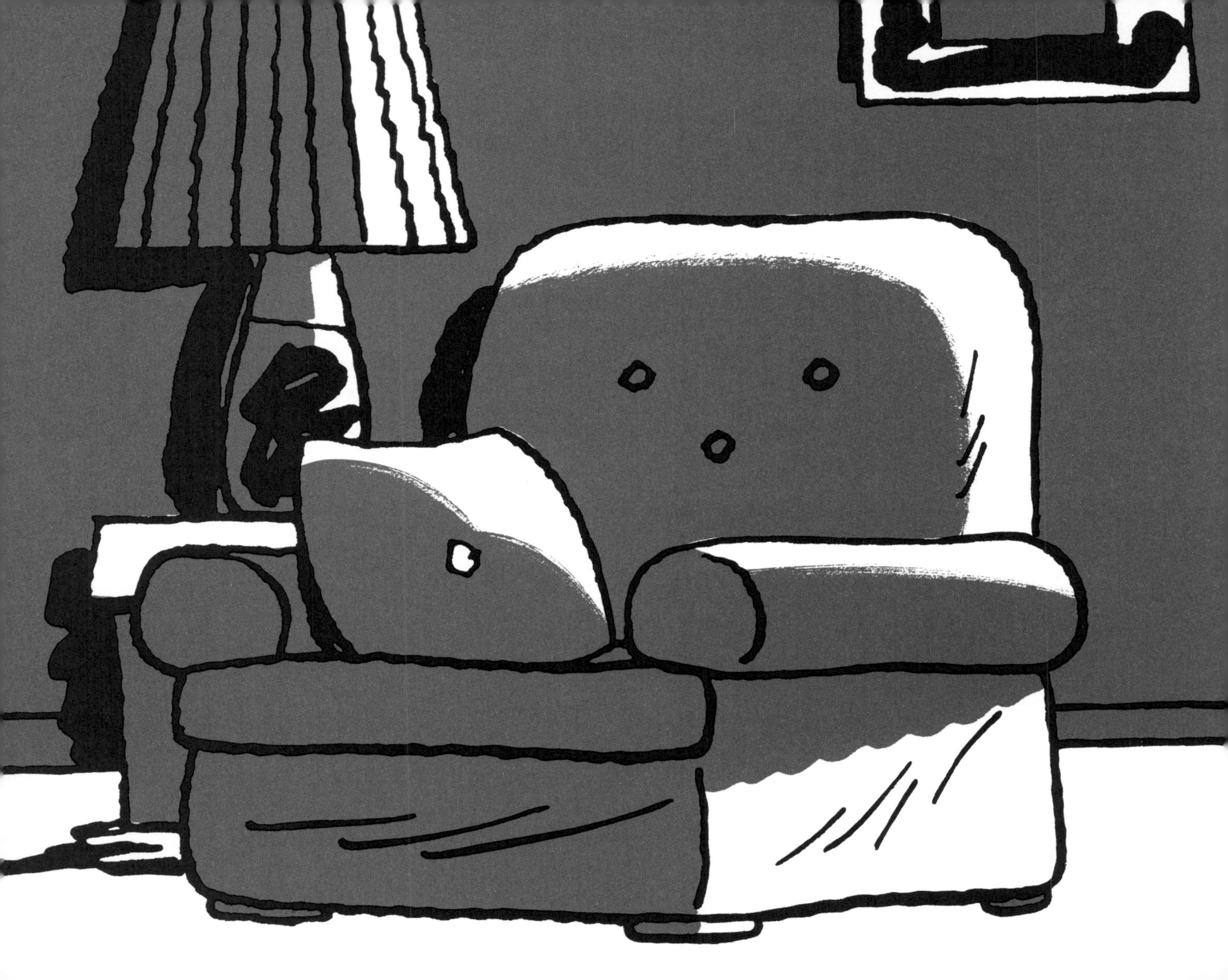

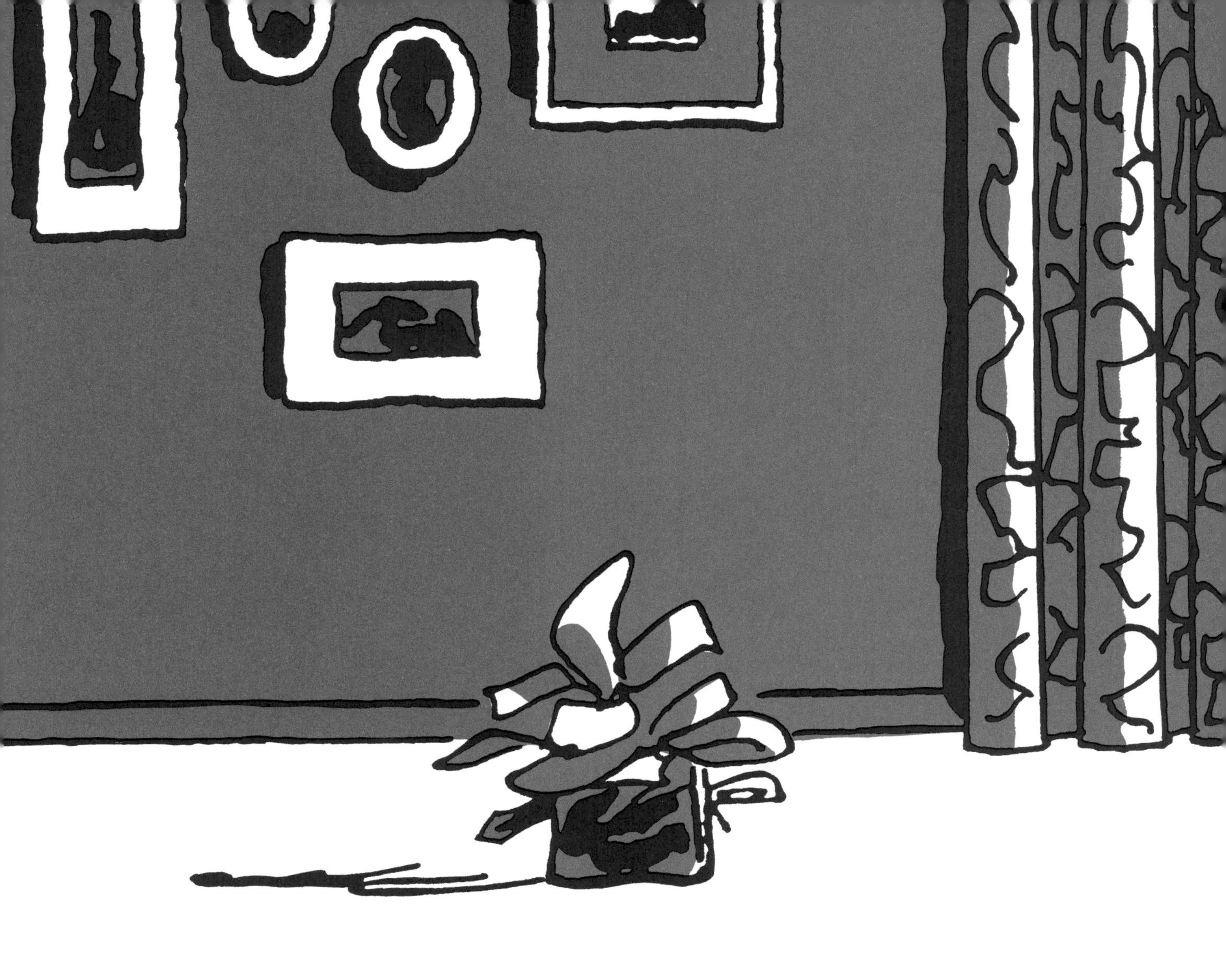

INDEX

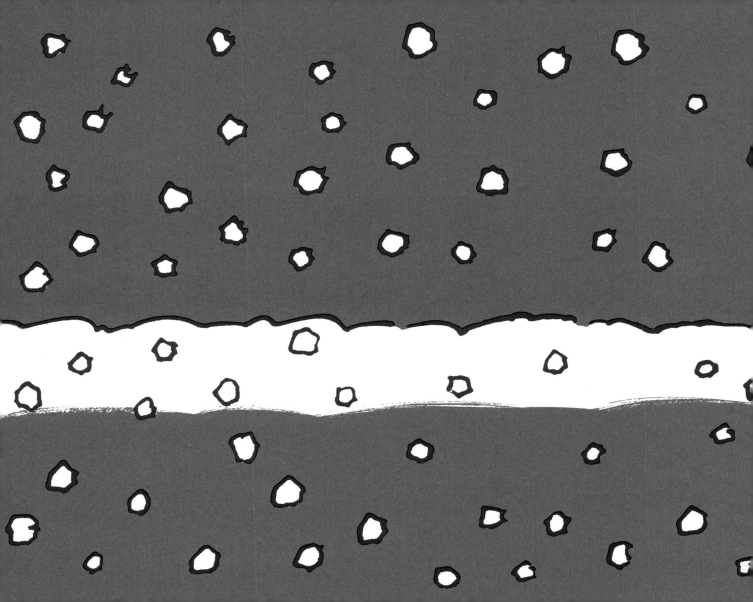

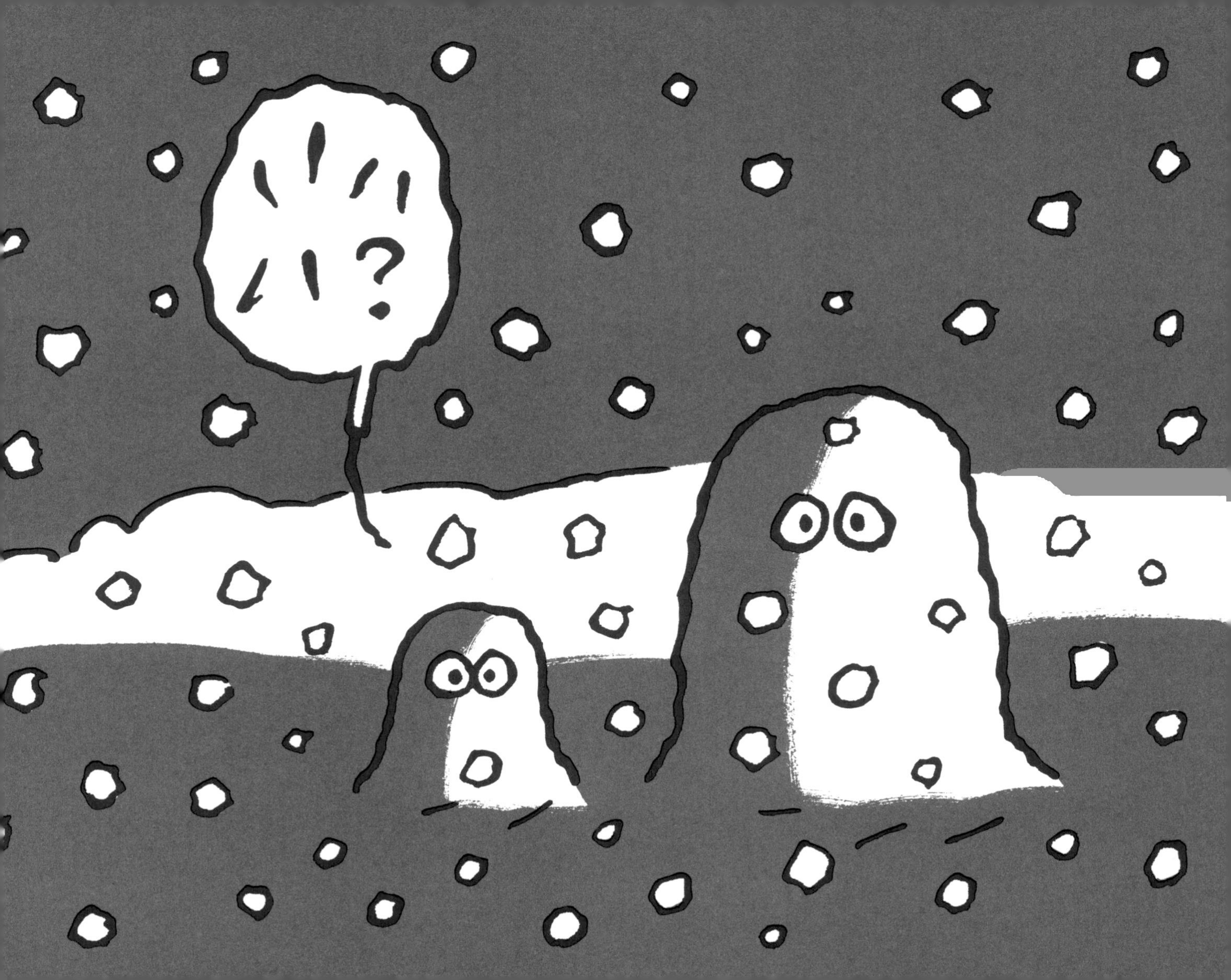

CHARLES M. SCHULZ · 1922 To 2000

Charles M. Schulz was born November 26, 1922, in Minneapolis. His destiny was foreshadowed when an uncle gave him, at the age of two days, the nickname "Sparky" (after the racehorse Spark Plug in the newspaper strip *Barney Google*).

Schulz grew up in St. Paul. By all accounts, he led an unremarkable, albeit sheltered, childhood. He was an only child, close to both parents. His eventual career path was nurtured by his father, who bought four Sunday papers every week — just for the comics.

An outstanding student, he skipped two grades early on, but began to flounder in high school — perhaps not so coincidentally at the same time kids are going through their cruelest, most status-conscious period of socialization. The pain, bitterness, insecurity, and failures chronicled in *Peanuts* appear to have originated from this period of Schulz's life.

Although Schulz enjoyed sports, he also found refuge in solitary activities: reading, drawing, and watching movies. He bought comic books and Big Little Books, pored over the newspaper strips, and copied his favorites — *Buck Rogers*, the Walt Disney characters, *Popeye, Tim Tyler's Luck*. He quickly became a connoisseur; his heroes were Milton Caniff, Roy Crane, Hal Foster, and Alex Raymond.

In his senior year in high school, his mother noticed an ad in a local newspaper for a correspondence school, Federal Schools (later called Art

Instruction Schools). Schulz passed the talent test, completed the course, and began trying, unsuccessfully, to sell gag cartoons to magazines. (His first published drawing was of his dog, Spike, and appeared in a 1937 *Ripley's Believe It or Not!* installment.)

After World War II had ended and Schulz was discharged from the army, he started submitting gag cartoons to the various magazines of the time; his first breakthrough, however, came when an editor at *Timeless Topix* hired him to letter adventure comics. Soon after that, he was hired by his alma mater, Art Instruction, to correct student lessons returned by mail.

Between 1948 and 1950, he succeeded in selling 17 cartoons to the *Saturday Evening Post* — as well as, to the local *St. Paul Pioneer Press*, a weekly comic feature called *Li'l Folks*. It ran in the women's section and paid $10 a week. After writing and drawing the feature for two years, Schulz asked for a better location in the paper or for daily exposure, as well as a raise. When he was turned down on all three counts, he quit.

He started submitting strips to the newspaper syndicates. In the spring of 1950, he received a letter from the United Feature Syndicate, announcing its interest in his submission, *Li'l Folks*. Schulz boarded a train in June for New York City; more interested in doing a strip than a panel, he also brought along the first installments of what would become *Peanuts* — and that was what sold. (The title, which Schulz loathed to his dying day, was imposed by the syndicate). The first *Peanuts* daily appeared October 2, 1950; the first Sunday, January 6, 1952.

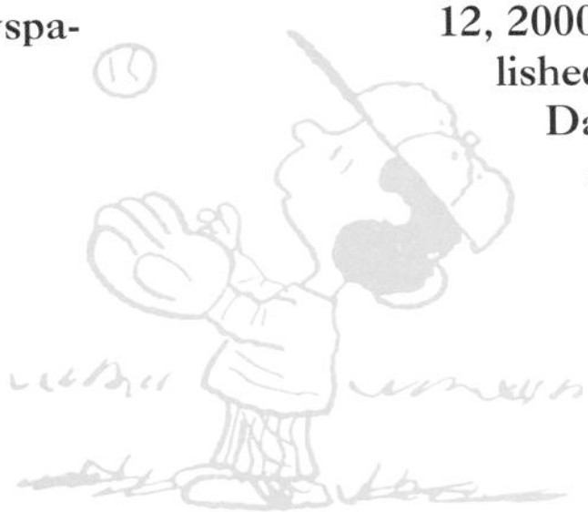

Prior to *Peanuts*, the province of the comics page had been that of gags, social and political observation, domestic comedy, soap opera, and various adventure genres. Although *Peanuts* changed, or evolved, during the 50 years Schulz wrote and drew it, it remained, as it began, an anomaly on the comics page — a comic strip about the interior crises of the cartoonist himself. After a painful divorce in 1973 from which he had not yet recovered, Schulz told a reporter, "Strangely, I've drawn better cartoons in the last six months — or as good as I've ever drawn. I don't know how the human mind works." Surely, it was this kind of humility in the face of profoundly irreducible human questions that makes *Peanuts* as universally moving as it is.

Diagnosed with cancer, Schulz retired from *Peanuts* at the end of 1999. He died on February 12, 2000, the day before his last strip was published (and two days before Valentine's Day) — having completed 17,897 daily and Sunday strips, each and every one fully written, drawn, and lettered entirely by his own hand — an unmatched achievement in comics.

—*Gary Groth*